Slavery *and the* Birth *of an* African City

Slavery *and the* Birth *of an* African City

Lagos, 1760–1900

Kristin Mann

Indiana University Press
Bloomington and Indianapolis

This book is a publication of

Indiana University Press
601 North Morton Street
Bloomington, Indiana 47404-3797 USA

www.iupress.indiana.edu

Telephone orders	800-842-6796
Fax orders	812-855-7931
Orders by e-mail	iuporder@indiana.edu

First paperback edition published 2010

∞ The paper used in this publication meets the minimum requirements of the American National Standard for Information Sciences—Permanence of Paper for Printed Library Materials, ANSI Z39.48-1992.

Manufactured in the United States of America

The Library of Congress has cataloged the hardcover edition as follows:

Mann, Kristin, [date]
Slavery and the birth of an African city : Lagos, 1760–1900 / Kristin Mann.
p. cm.
Includes bibliographical references and index.
ISBN-13: 978-0-253-34884-5 (cloth)
1. Slave trade—Nigeria—Lagos—History—18th century. 2. Slave trade—Nigeria—Lagos—History—19th century. 3. Lagos (Nigeria)—History—18th century. 4. Lagos (Nigeria)—History—19th century. 5. Lagos (Nigeria)—Commerce—History—18th century. 6. Lagos (Nigeria)—Commerce—History—19th century. 7. Slave trade—Great Britain—History—18th century. 8. Slave trade—Great Britain—History—19th century. 9. Great Britain—Commerce—History. 10. Great Britain—Colonies—Africa. I. Title.
HT1394.L34M36 2007
306.3'6209669109033—dc22
2006037963

ISBN 978-0-253-22235-0 (pbk.)

1 2 3 4 5 15 14 13 12 11 10

To Steve and Evan,
And from them, as well

Contents

Acknowledgments

This book draws on data collected over a long period of time, beginning with my dissertation research in Nigeria and England during the 1970s and continuing to the present. Financial support from a number of government agencies and private organizations has aided my work, and I am pleased to acknowledge and express thanks for several of the most salient grants. They include a Fulbright-Hays Dissertation Research Fellowship, a Fulbright Senior Research Award, a Social Science Research Council Research Planning Activity Award, a National Endowment for the Humanities Senior Research Fellowship, and two Emory University Research Committee Awards. A sabbatical from Emory University and a fellowship from the John Simon Guggenheim Memorial Foundation funded a leave from teaching in 2002, when I wrote or revised much of the manuscript.

The staffs at the many libraries, archives, and record offices cited in the endnotes and bibliography aided my research and deserve sincere thanks. A few, however, offered such sustained and generous support that I want to mention them individually. Elizabeth McBride, the African Studies Collection Development Specialist at Emory University's Woodruff Library, provided invaluable assistance at numerous stages of my research, as did the staff of Woodruff's Interlibrary Loan Department. The registrars and staffs at the Lagos Land Registry, Lagos Probate Registry, and Lagos State High Court granted me access to the public documents they oversee and week after week cheerfully welcomed me as I worked in their crowded quarters.

A number of scholars have generously shared data, documents, or ideas with me. Early in the project, when I had just begun research on the slave trade at Lagos, Paul Lovejoy and David Trotman folded me into the expansive embrace of the Nigerian Hinterland Project, based at York University in Toronto and funded largely by the Social Science and Humanities Research Council of Canada. There followed a moveable feast of workshops and conferences organized on four continents, which did much to stimulate my thinking and advance my research. Sandra Barnes,

Sara Berry, David Eltis, A. G. Hopkins, Robin Law, and Elisée Soumonni have all contributed essential data or sources. Sahid Adejumobi, A. O. Alaba, Stephen D. Berhendt, Toyin Falola, Margot Finn, Martin Lynn, Ann O'Hear, Afolabi Olabimtan, Ayodeji Olukoju, Oyekan Owomoleya, Ṣope Oyelaran, Kemi Rotimi, and Akin Tijani have also provided valuable information along the way.

Alberto da Costa e Silva, Martin Klein, Martin Lynn, Joe Miller, and David Richardson, as well as my Emory colleagues Eddy Bay, Clifton Crais, David Eltis, Sidney Kasfir, Randy Packard, and Pamela Scully, have carefully read and thoughtfully critiqued part or all of the manuscript at different stages. Innumerable conversations with Richard Roberts over the years enriched my thinking about colonial law and courts. Fred Cooper, Allen Isaacman, Martin Klein, and Joe Miller believed in me and lent key support at critical moments.

Many graduate students at Emory and elsewhere have assisted me with research and other tasks. They include Christopher Owen, Margaret Storey, Lara Smith, Carol Richards, Patrick Mbajekwe, Rebecca Shumway, Frank Proctor, Jeremy Pool, John Willis, Philip Misevich, Daniel Dominguez da Silva, Silke Strickrodt, Caroline Sorensen-Gilmour, and Beatriz Gollotti Manigonian Bessa. Many of these students have also read and insightfully critiqued parts of the manuscript. Ade Afonja, Kim Culbertson, Derek Spransy, and Laura Pokalsky of Emory University's Information Technology Division have repeatedly unlocked the mysteries of rapidly changing computer and cyber technology to me, while Patsy Stockbridge of Emory's History Department staff retyped portions of the manuscript lost electronically when a computer malfunctioned. Patsy has ever been ready to help me solve word processing problems. My sister Kathryn Herring painstakingly undertook the tedious task of checking the footnotes for accuracy and consistency. Sarah Zingarelli produced the maps and certain tables. My good friends Akanmu G. Adebayo, Marguerite Fletcher, and Jonathan Hillyer generously supplied the images for the book jacket. Dee Mortensen, my editor at Indiana University Press, has contributed many valuable suggestions that have improved the manuscript, and she has made the publication process a pleasure.

Work on this book has coincided with two major life events. Two days after commencing an NEH grant in 1990 to begin the project, I became the mother of a delightful baby boy. Since the beginning, the book and the boy have grown together, each making sacrifices in the interest of the other. The boy has certainly been worth it. I thank him for the many gifts, great and small, which he has given me. I treasure his goodness, intelligence, creativity, and athleticism, as well as his genius for relaxing and enjoying himself. I am also grateful to him for being willing to say things three times when necessary to get my attention. My husband, Steven M. Tipton, has loved me without falter for more than thirty years, even when, for long periods of time, I have not been very loveable. A gifted writer and fine scholar, he has always made time to help me turn a phrase or talk through an idea. Moreover, he completed a major book of his own the very week that I submitted mine. May we in future do a better job remembering Billy and Lester and "kiss when we want to kiss, laugh when we want to laugh," and get more fun out of life.

In the mid-1990s, I suffered a pelvic injury that plunged me into the abyss of severe chronic pain and carried me to the edge of genuine disability. My internist Sally West and her nurse Kelly Allred helped me navigate the health care system until I finally found a diagnosis and effective treatment. Walter Adamson was Chair of Emory's History Department during the worst of my plight, and I am grateful for his sensitivity, understanding, and support at that time. In 1999, Richard Nyberg, a gifted physical therapist at the Atlanta Back Clinic, diagnosed my ailment and with consummate skill and remarkable patience began working with me to heal my injury, restore my muscles, reeducate my nerves, and reverse the cycle of pain. Rich literally gave me my life back, and I am profoundly grateful to him and my other friends at the Atlanta Back Clinic. A semester's medical leave enabled me to turn a crucial corner, and I am thankful for the Family and Medical Leave Act of 1993, to Emory University's Human Resources Division, and to then Dean of Arts and Sciences Steven Sanderson for making it possible.

My greatest debt, of course, is to the many people in Lagos who welcomed me, offered me hospitality, and took time from their demanding lives to talk to me about their ancestors' past. The Department of History at the University of Lagos provided me affiliation and an intellectual home on successive visits to Lagos, and I am grateful to its faculty. An able young UniLag student, Olufemi Adebayo, worked as my research assistant during two extended field trips. Gladys Agbebiyi, Susan and David Aradeon, the late Alhaji Sanni Adewale, Ben and the late Nina Mba, Meghan and Gabriel Olusanya, and the late Irene Fatayi-Williams and her husband the late Honorable Atanda Fatayi-Williams regularly welcomed me in their homes and gave me their friendship, as did Thomas R.

Hutson, Delia Pitts, and John Vincent. Innumerable strangers–taxi drivers, market women, government clerks, and others–treated me kindly and helped me feel at home in their city. My personal experience in Lagos squares not at all with its terrible reputation among most expatriates. I hope that this book on the history of Lagos in a small way repays all that the residents of the city have given me over the course of my career. Finally, I thank my dear friend Diana Thorold, who has warmly welcomed and generously housed me during my many research trips to London.

Slavery *and the* Birth *of an* African City

Introduction

This book investigates the relationship between long-term changes in the economy and culture of the Atlantic world and the history of a small but globally significant portion of the West African coast. The slave trade, which in the roughly 350 years of its existence forcibly exported approximately 12.4 million Africans to the Americas to provide labor for the development of plantation societies there, first brought the West and the territory the world now knows as Lagos into steady and intimate contact with one another.[1] Yet soon after the commerce took root at Lagos in the late eighteenth century, a great shift in moral consciousness in the West led Britain, then the dominant power in the Atlantic world, to reconceptualize Europe's relationship with Africa and resolve to abolish the trade in human beings in the Bight of Benin, where Lagos is located, and elsewhere.[2]

By the time the slave trade finally ended at Lagos in the mid-nineteenth century, a new and, in the minds of many Europeans, revolutionary type of commerce had emerged to take its place. The commodity traded was now no longer human beings, but rather a mundane vegetable oil derived from palm fruit that grew wild in the interior of the West African coast, for which industrialization and urbanization were creating new uses in Europe. That many in Britain believed this new trade was necessary to abolition and, with its handmaiden Christianity, had the power to reform Africa and save her peoples at once from the sins of the slave trade and their own simple shortcomings reveals much about the early-Victorian worldview. Policymakers in Britain thought, moreover, that the trade played an important part in the vigorous expansion of their country's commerce overseas, which they saw as vital to its prosperity, stability, and continued march toward power and progress.[3] These two articles of faith combined in the mid-nineteenth century to lead Britain to conquer and colonize the area.

In the time between Lagos's rise to preeminence as a slave port, in the first quarter of the nineteenth century, and 1960, when it became the capital of black Africa's largest and most powerful new nation, Nigeria, the settlement on the West African coast was transformed from a crossroads of regional trade and the village capital of a small and comparatively insignificant kingdom into one of Africa's most important cities. The momentous birth of this now vast metropolis, which shaped the lives of its inhabitants for decades to come, can be traced to the time of slavery and abolition.

To start with a discussion of Atlantic influences is not to imply that the people who inhabited Lagos and, indeed, the wider region where it is located were passive subjects in history's unfolding. Nor is it to accept that external forces have been more important than internal ones in shaping their past. It is merely to acknowledge that global, as well as local and regional, processes of change affected their opportunities and helped create the conditions in which they acted.[4] More than a half century of scholarship has demonstrated that Africa had a history prior to European colonization and that even in the most unequal and oppressive environments after it, the continent's peoples have shaped the world in which they lived.[5] As a work of African history, this book is primarily concerned with the African side of the story. It seeks to understand how the inhabitants of Lagos and, to a lesser extent, the wider region shaped the Atlantic encounter in the eras of slavery and abolition, as well as how they were affected by it. The study probes the engagement of local peoples, and of the social structures, economic arrangements, political institutions, and cultural values that gave form and meaning to their lives, with shifting external opportunities and constraints. In the process, it uncovers how the world Lagosians inhabited changed as the settlement developed into a center of Atlantic commerce, first in slaves and then in palm produce, and finally into a British imperial capital.

Changes in the meaning and value of people lie at the heart of the story. It is by now well understood that in much of precolonial Africa wealth and power were rooted not in ownership of land but in control of people. As settlements grew and developed along the Bight of Benin and in its interior, like elsewhere in Africa, men built themselves up economically and politically and also acquired social prestige by enlarging the size of their households through polygynous marriages and reproduction, as well as by taking in wards, strangers, and kin.[6] So central to the process were marriage and reproduction that in some places prominent women could acquire "wives" and exercise rights of paternity in their offspring.[7]

Household size was critical because the heads of residential units could normally make demands on the labor and resources of all those who lived under their authority and also call on them for support in times of political, military, or ritual need. When small states developed in the region, the towns at their centers served as "magnets" that lured people because of the safety and opportunity they provided.[8] Successful households grew and prospered by absorbing these migrants. Alternatively, local leaders allocated strangers land on which to build residences and establish farms of their own, sometimes founding new quarters of the town. The large kingdoms that eventually emerged across the region competed for power in part by attracting and incorporating strangers.[9]

The Atlantic slave trade turned human beings, a scarce and valuable resource in Africa, into a commodity that had monetary value and could be bought and sold. Along the Bight of Benin, a type of local slavery probably antedated the foreign slave trade and had played a part in the accumulation of people.[10] The size of the market in slaves expanded dramatically, however, with the growth of the export trade from the end of the seventeenth century. After 1760, the gradual rise of the Atlantic slave trade at Lagos stimulated an expansion of local slavery and transformed the way those at the top of society acquired and held people. Then, in the second half of the nineteenth century, the development of the foreign palm produce trade created an even greater demand for slaves and also changed the way they were used in local society. The new export trade altered the cultural value of slaves, along with that of certain other kinds of dependents.

The ongoing relevance of control of people across the African continent is enshrined in the "wealth-in-people" paradigm, one of the most influential ideas in the past quarter century of African studies. This paradigm posits a close and necessary relationship between economic and political advancement in much of sub-Saharan Africa and the constitution of different kinds of social relationships—including marriage, parenthood, patronage, wardship, overlordship, and slavery—that conveyed rights in people. It further emphasizes the centrality of these relationships both in the organization of labor for production and other purposes and in the construction of allegiances for warfare, political competition, and social or ritual aggrandizement. The wealth-in-people paradigm has been fruitfully applied to such diverse cultures as precolonial central Africa, colonial Côte d'Ivoire, and twentieth-century Liberia.[11] At its best, this research has examined the agency of dependents themselves in defining reciprocal relationships of subordination, in which superiors have obligations, if usually unequal and sometimes unrealized ones, to people under their authority, as well as the reverse. Yet anthropologist Jane Guyer has cautioned against applying the idea in an "underspecified" way that ignores the "multiple dimensions of the value accorded to persons" or the changing ways different kinds of dependents were valued in relation to each other.[12] An investigation of the relationship between the shifting value and meaning of different kinds of dependents at Lagos and the rise and abolition of the slave trade followed by the quick transition to the palm produce trade opens these important issues to scrutiny.

The Argument

As the Atlantic slave trade entered its last, largely illegal phase in the mid-nineteenth century, the town of Lagos on West Africa's Bight of Benin became the leading slave port north of the equator. The reasons for its sudden rise to preeminence lie in the linked histories of Brazil and Cuba (markets for the slaves), the great African states inland from the Bight (suppliers of the slaves), and the small polities that dotted its shore (traders of the slaves). The slave trade forever altered the destiny of the tiny kingdom of Lagos and the town by the same name that formed its capital. In the short term, it increased the income of the local *ọba* (king) and certain chiefs, who invested their new resources in canoes, weapons, and critically people, which helped transform Lagos from a small and marginal state on a crossroads of regional trade into a major commercial and political power on the coast connecting the interior of Africa with the Atlantic world. The kinds of people that swelled the households and constituencies of the ruling oligarchy in this period included wives, children, other kin, wards, strangers, and clients as previously, if in expanded numbers thanks to the new money and material goods flowing into the kingdom. At the same time, the growth of the foreign slave trade in the town also greatly increased the local supply of slaves and gave certain *ọbas* and their supporters, who dominated the new commerce, income with which to buy them. This development introduced a major new means of acquiring and holding vitally important dependents, and it increased the importance of slavery in the local political economy relative to other methods of accumulating people.

The growth of the Atlantic slave trade did not, however, fundamentally change the nature of local slavery. In the era of the foreign slave trade, Lagosians continued to want slaves for the reasons they long had, both for the labor they performed in transportation, trade, production, and other economic activities and for the social, military, and political support they could provide in a culture where command of people was key. Owners preferred female slaves for certain kinds of activities, and as a consequence half or more of the town's slaves were probably women.

A distinctive ideology, with two main components, underpinned local slavery. The first tenet held that over time slaves or their descendants would be incorporated into the kin group of the slaveowner. The second maintained that owners should reward slaves for exceptional loyalty or service by helping them move up in society and out of slavery. The first part of this ideology may have appealed to owners because it could be expected ultimately to increase the size, and hence the wealth and power, of their kin groups. Both ideals helped slaveowners control bondwomen and -men whose work demanded great physical mobility and sometimes also access to arms and valuable commercial or other resources.

In the longer term, Lagos's growth as a slave port led to its conquest and colonization by Great Britain, which by the mid-nineteenth century had extended its anti-slavery crusade to West Africa in the name of spreading civilization and promoting trade in new commodities, such as palm oil and later palm kernels. The second half of the nineteenth century saw Lagos's rapid rise as an international port and gradual growth as a British colonial capital.

The production of and trade in palm produce were very labor-intensive, and tragically the development of the new foreign commerce led to a further expansion of local slaveowning. Unlike the growth of the slave trade, however, the development of the produce trade changed the nature of local slavery, by increasing the value of slaves as workers. To be sure, Lagosians continued to want slaves as a way of incorporating into their households and kin groups outsiders who could provide social and political support. But the balance between these *desiderata* shifted, as the labor slaves performed became more important.

Britain made no decision about what to do regarding slavery at Lagos prior to annexing the kingdom in 1861. Early British officials feared that undermining local slavery would create grave economic and social disorder and render the young colony more difficult and expensive to rule. The British Law Officers held in 1866, however, that slavery had ceased to exist in Lagos from the moment of the annexation, making policies that were being introduced to end it gradually both illegal and embarrassing. Soon after, the government fell back on the model adopted in India two decades before. It quietly abolished the legal status of slavery and maintained—but did little to publicize—that slaves could pursue difficulties with their owners in the new colonial courts that were being established. Subsequently, officials largely left it to time and the slaves themselves to redefine their relationships with their owners and their place in society.

Few slaves apparently ran away from Lagos following the annexation, because slavery and the slave trade were more entrenched elsewhere in the region than in the colony itself. In addition, economic, social, and legal changes within British territory were opening new opportunities to slaves there. The dictates of the work that slaves performed in transportation, trade, and palm produce production gave them some ability to engage in these activities for themselves and earn cash income. Moreover, the commercialization of urban real estate and development of private property rights in it after the annexation created new ways for a few fortunate slaves to obtain valuable landed property and commercial credit, even though most slaves still depended on their owners or other prominent Lagosians for access to the land, housing, patronage, and capital that they needed to live and work in the urban economy. Rapid economic growth simultaneously generated a huge demand for wives, workers, and dependents in the growing colonial city. Within the African community, most labor was not yet organized around work for wages in a free labor market, but rather around slavery and the other indigenous social relationships, such as marriage and overlordship, that households had long employed to incorporate outsiders. Moreover, Lagosians still sought dependents for reasons that were not strictly economic.

As colonialism checked the freedom of owners to use force and sale to control their slaves, bondwomen and -men without the resources to live on their own could nonetheless leave their owners by entering these other relationships of subordination. The gradual departure of slaves after the British intervention triggered a resurgence in the importance of these relationships as a means of acquiring workers and dependents. Moreover, the mobility that slaves and their descendants enjoyed pressured owners and others seeking their labor and allegiance to accommodate demands to reduce labor obligations, improve access to resources, and redefine social identities. Yet owners were not without recourse. For one thing, they began importing considerable numbers of children, who were easier to control and incorporate than adult slaves. For another, they often redefined the enslavement of women and girls as marriage and turned to local and colonial officials to uphold the authority of husbands over their wives. In addition, household heads began redefining the overlord-stranger relationship to make the labor obligations of strangers more explicit and exacting. This strategy helped meet the needs of Lagos's new palm produce traders for workers. Moreover, it narrowed the social distance between male strangers and slaves, making an important avenue of escape from slavery for men less attractive and affecting what it meant to be a stranger. Finally, prominent Lagosians discovered in their long-term control of land, housing, and credit new means of upholding their authority over slaves and other dependents.

Significance of the Project

This book advances knowledge about a number of central problems in African history, Atlantic history, and slave studies. It investigates the conduct of the Atlantic slave trade and its impact on the coastal societies that formed the points of closest contact between Africa, Europe, and the Americas, along with the subsequent abolition of the slave trade, transition to the palm produce trade, and their effects on the continent. The study takes slavery as a primary focus both because of its growing importance in Lagos during the first sixty years of the nineteenth century and because of its widespread comparative interest. The book also powerfully illuminates, however, the shifting balance among different kinds of relationships of dependency and their changing value as rich and powerful men and women in Lagos and their subordinates struggled over the course of the nineteenth century to adapt to new opportunities and constraints. Furthermore, the work provides one of the first detailed studies of the slow demise of slavery and reorganization of labor in a leading West African commercial and colonial capital during the closing decades of the nineteenth century.

Research on the Atlantic slave trade has advanced by leaps and bounds since the publication of Philip Curtin's seminal book, *The Atlantic Slave Trade: A Census*, in 1969.[13] We now know much more than before not only about the number of African men, women, and children violently torn from the continent and brutally transported to the Americas, but also about the regions of the coast from which they were exported, the places in the Americas to which they were shipped, and the age, gender, and ethnicity of the slave victims themselves.[14] Much still remains to be learned, however, about the largest forced migration in human history. This book addresses three of the major lingering questions. First, why did specific slave ports rise to preeminence at particular times in the history of the trade? More specifically, what combination of local, regional, and Atlantic factors pushed the commerce from Ouidah, which had dominated it in the Bight of Benin for more than two hundred years, and pulled it to Lagos in the first half of the nineteenth century?[15] Second, how was the trade linking African suppliers of slaves in the interior and foreign buyers on the coast organized? What role did African middlepeople based in the littoral play in it and why? Finally, and most significantly, how did the trade affect the parts of the continent touched by it, including the ports from which slaves departed for the Americas?

Perspectives differ on this third critical question, from those historians who think that the slave trade transformed Africa in a number of highly destructive ways—demographic, economic, or social—to others who believe that it did not necessarily do so or who, despite acknowledging the horror and brutality of the trade for the enslaved, evaluate certain of the transformations positively.[16] This study does not address the demographic effects of the trade. Previous research has by now established that during the eighteenth and early nineteenth centuries its scale and duration along the Bight of Benin were sufficient to cause serious population loss in the region as a whole, even if certain political and commercial centers increased in size.[17] The trade thus affected the distribution of people across the region and altered the balance of power among states competing for them.

So far as the economic effects of the trade are concerned, my research shows that, as in a number of other places, the growth of the commerce at Lagos stimulated a broader expansion of trade linking the town and markets in the interior or elsewhere on the coast. Moreover, the spread of new currencies associated with the slave trade promoted certain kinds of local and regional agricultural, craft, and other production. In Lagos, however, the benefits of this broader economic growth, as of participation in the slave trade itself, were distributed very unevenly.

Many studies have now documented far-reaching social and political changes among African peoples involved in the Atlantic slave trade. Among the most important of these changes were an increase in hierarchy and inequality within societies, sometimes accompanied by greater centralization of commercial, political, military, or religious power in the hands of ruling classes composed of some combination of monarchs, chiefs, merchants, and warriors. Centralization provided an effective response, although by no means the only one, to struggles to control trade routes, tolls, other taxes on trade, and often commerce itself, as well as to the need for better defense against kidnapping, raiding, banditry, and warfare.[18] The centralization of power within states was often related to territorial expansion facilitated by the acquisition of new military technology (especially horses, small arms, artillery, and war canoes in West Africa) that led to the conquest of surrounding peoples and sometimes to the establishment of empires. At least one historian has viewed these changes as progressive and a sign of precolonial Africa's capacity for development.[19] Many more, however, have seen them as ultimately producing one or more destructive effects, including an increase in kidnapping, banditry, warfare, and other forms of social violence; the militarization of ruling classes and deflection of their energies from more positive social purposes; and an escalation of competition and conflict within ruling classes so that the new states that developed during the era of the slave trade were often unstable. Finally, historians have argued that the commerce increased social oppression within African societies by altering local systems of slavery and marriage and making tributary relations more exacting.[20]

Despite considerable scholarship on Africa in the era of the slave trade, historians still have a very imperfect understanding of the relationship between political and social changes taking place on the continent at that time and participation in the commerce. Great ecological, social, and cultural diversity existed between and even within regions drawn into the slave trade. Moreover, the timing, extent, and duration of their involvement in the exchange differed. In general, coastal enclaves such as Lagos were more directly and profoundly affected than inland peoples. Among these important coastal intermediaries, however, many questions remain unanswered. Who were the local slave traders, and what was their relationship to established political and commercial elites? To what extent did the slave trade bring new income into coastal societies? How was this income distributed and used? What impact did the trade have on the structure of wealth and power within small kingdoms such as Lagos, including on vitally important methods of accumulating people? How did these changes affect the monarchy and the state? Robin Law has noted the "extreme factionalism" in many of the small kingdoms along the Bights of Benin and Biafra.[21] What was the relationship at Lagos between the slave trade and factionalism? Finally, how did the growth of the commerce at Lagos affect its place in the wider region? Answers to these questions will not only bring us much closer to understanding the impact of the slave trade on a major nineteenth-century slave port, but also illuminate the birth of the city that subsequently developed on the site.

Two leading historians of Africa have regarded the impact of the export trade in slaves on African slavery itself as such a vital subject that they have made it the central theme of books on the continent in the precolonial period.[22] African slavery, like African involvement in the Atlantic slave trade, is a sensitive subject, difficult to discuss objectively for fear that to portray it in the wrong light will somehow mitigate the evils of the international commerce in slaves. An early influential study of African slavery by Igor Kopytoff and Suzanne Miers treated it as but one of a broad range of servile relationships rooted, like kinship and marriage, in rights in people. The authors argued that African "slavery," which varied widely from society to society in any case, was so fundamentally different from American slavery that they used the word to refer to it only in quotation marks. Kopytoff and Miers maintained that in Africa slavery provided, first and foremost, a means of bringing outsiders into society and absorbing them into local kin groups.[23] Around the same time, French Marxist anthropologists published research that emphasized the role of African slavery in the organization of production and reproduction, and looked at class relations between owners, slaves, and other social groups. While Claude Meillassoux, the most influential among them, also saw slaves as outsiders and stressed processes of their incorporation, he regarded kinship and slavery as antithetical and argued that the origins of the latter lay not in a continuum of rights in people that began with kinship, but in markets and "merchant revolutions."[24]

The timelessness of both of these paradigms soon became apparent, sparking research by historians who sought, influenced by their Americanist colleagues, to make a number of contributions. The first was to view slavery as a dynamic relationship shaped by owners, slaves, and other actors as well. The second was to better understand African slavery in relationship to the organization of production and exchange and the control of labor in particular economic systems. Finally, these scholars wanted to comprehend slavery's role in the structure of economic and political power within African societies.[25] My study is informed by this important work.

In most of the ports of the slave trade, however, the basic questions that this book investigates remain unanswered. Who accumulated slaves in the era of the slave trade, and how did they use them? Why did owners value slaves both in their own right and relative to other kinds of dependents? How were owners able to control the growing number of alien slaves in their households? What was the relationship between the organization of the work and other activities that slaves performed and the system of discipline and control? What can be uncovered about the perspectives of the slaves themselves? And how did gender matter?

Answers to these questions cast important new light on African slavery. They illuminate both a range of slave experience and the artificiality of dichotomizing local slavery as a means of incorporating outsiders into households and kin groups, on the one hand, or of organizing labor and controlling people, on the other. Indeed, the data presented here reveal the role of the ideology and processes of incorporation foregrounded by Kopytoff and Miers and Meillassoux in the system of slave discipline and control at Lagos. The evidence indicates, moreover, that while slavery expanded dramatically in Lagos in the era of the slave trade, it did not change fundamentally in character. Meaningful transformation in the way slaves were used and in the cultural value attached to them awaited the era of palm produce trade and production.

At different moments in the nineteenth century, anti-slavery went to Africa. It arrived in the Bights of Benin and Biafra at mid-century, in the hearts and minds of government officials, naval officers, and Christian evangelists who believed they had at last found the true remedy for the slave trade and could deliver the continent from its miseries, while simultaneously advancing British interests.[26] The reform movement made its presence felt again later in the century, when officials and philanthropists convinced themselves that aggressive imperial expansion was necessary inland from the coast to end the scourge of indigenous slavery, which they believed mired the continent in barbarism and blocked its civilization. This second visitation gave the age of high imperialism a moral purpose, as Frederick Cooper has argued, and legitimized highly coercive colonial labor policies at odds with Britain's commitment to free labor.[27] My book analyzes the ideology and interests that underlay anti-slavery's first engagement with West Africa to construct a fresh interpretation of the causes of Britain's forcible intervention in the politics of the Kingdom of Lagos in 1851 and colonization of it a decade later. The work casts new light on why the thin edge of the imperial wedge pierced the coastline in the mid-nineteenth century, opening the way for it to be driven brutally into the Yoruba heartland little more than thirty years later. This portion of the book also presents a new interpretation of Lagos's early colonial state, enhancing understanding of long-term transformations in British colonial rule in Africa.[28]

If, in the minds of many contemporary Europeans, a new kind of commerce was to be a primary agent of Africa's liberation from the slave trade, exports of vegetable commodities did in fact expand rapidly from many regions beginning in the mid-nineteenth century, while those of slaves disappeared in the late 1860s.[29] The impact of this so-called "commercial transition" has been a seminal problem in the field of African history since its inception. Nigerianists have divided over whether the change unleashed a social revolution with far-reaching political consequences, as Europeans predicted, or was marked by essential continuity and occurred without rupture. Proponents of the first view argue that the transition undermined the ability of the old slave-trading ruling classes to dominate production or trade for foreign markets, opened new income-generating opportunities to other social groups (sometimes including slaves), and undercut the wealth and power of local rulers, giving rise to political instability and conflict that paved the way for British imperial expansion.[30] Advocates of the second view maintain that the new exports were produced and exchanged within existing agricultural systems and commercial networks, and that the shift from exporting slaves to palm oil did not open significant economic opportunities to new groups or disrupt older patterns of political authority.[31]

Members of both schools have long viewed the problem within a paradigm that foregrounds the relationship between the control of production or trade for export and the balance of political power, without always looking carefully at how those activities were organized. More recently, a few scholars have begun to examine the impact of the new trade on household and gender relations.[32] This book shifts the angle of vision to examine the critical question of the organization and control of labor necessary for palm produce trade and production. It shows that the new export trade initially further expanded slaveowning locally, affected the way slaves were used, and increased the value of their labor relative to that of their other contributions. The work looks secondarily at capital, heavily in the form of credit, and at landed property, which were closely bound up with one another and also had implications for the mobilization and control of workers.

Many of Lagos's big slave traders had no trouble switching over to the new commerce in palm oil. The two trades were complementary, and several important slave traders began dealing in palm oil while they were still selling slaves. Immigration of Europeans, Sierra Leoneans, Brazilians, and Africans from the interior and elsewhere on the coast starting in the 1850s, however, introduced new groups into the population, some with substantial commercial advantages, and created greater commercial competition. Then in 1861, British colonization ended the political autonomy of Lagos's rulers. Subsequently, members of the town's old ruling oligarchy found that they could not dominate foreign trade as they once had. The reasons lay not only in their loss of administrative control over external trade and of the political advantages they enjoyed in it, although these were important. They lay, as well, in the breakdown of the oligarchy's ability to control access to capital following an enormous expansion in the credit system, which became more open than before. The decline of this group's commercial dominance also stemmed from its weakening ability to control labor, especially that of its many slaves. The picture that emerges from this study is neither of a social revolution nor of a smooth, continuous transition, but rather of a slow, messy, and contested process of change, at the heart of which lay a struggle over labor.

The final chapters of this book provide one of the first detailed studies of the end of slavery in a West African commercial and colonial capital.[33] They simultaneously uncover how the African entrepreneurs who, until the building of the railroad at the end of the nineteenth century, organized the new export trade between the interior and the coast mobilized the very extensive labor necessary for its conduct.

A sizeable body of outstanding research by Africanists, Caribbeanists, and Americanists has demonstrated that in many parts of the world emancipation was a gradual process shaped by the complex interplay of the interests and ideologies of states, owners, and slaves themselves.[34] Where state policy in colonial Africa is concerned, studies of other regions in later periods have shown that tensions between the commitment of metropolitan philanthropists and statesmen to anti-slavery and the disinclination of local imperial representatives to jeopardize colonial exports or create social and political disorder led men on the ground to engage in "smoke and mirror" acts that presented an illusion of emancipation, while simultaneously doing much to uphold the control of owners over their slaves.[35] Similar tensions played out in Lagos decades before, where they were even more acute than in most colonies established later, because the kingdom became British soil at the moment of its annexation. British Law Officers soon ruled that Lagos Colony was bound by British anti-slavery legislation enacted in the first half of the century.[36] After a short debate with their superiors back home, local authorities resolved their dilemma by sweeping slavery within the colony under the rug and denying its existence through legal, linguistic, and epistemological sleights of hand. The profound embarrassment caused by having to deal with a thriving and entrenched system of local slavery in a substantial Crown colony bound by British law heightened imperial policymakers' consciousness regarding the difficulties posed by African slavery and helped reinforce their commitment, in territories acquired later, to a system of protectorate rule, under which British laws did not apply directly to colonial subjects. While previous studies have highlighted the role of developments on the Gold Coast in this process, equally important events at Lagos have been overlooked.[37]

Despite the conservative policies of the colonial state, economic, political, and legal changes began in Lagos from the 1850s that created new opportunities for slaves themselves to redefine their relationships with their owners and transform their status and identity in coastal society. Like studies of post-emancipation societies elsewhere, this book roots analysis of these opportunities in a discussion of the changing material, ideological, and social conditions that shaped slaves' lives. But unlike much of the previous research, my study looks not at a plantation society, where large landowners and merchants dominated the production and trade of exports and the state was committed to channeling former slaves into wage labor as a means of maintaining export production and of reforming freed men and women.[38] It focuses, instead, on an African urban setting where trade, which could be conducted on a small or large scale, was at the center of economic life, and opportunities also existed for slaves to engage in other income-generating activities. The book deals with a period, moreover, when colonial governments in West Africa were not yet much interested in the development of a free labor market, because they assumed a model of peasant production and small-scale trade for export that they believed would ultimately liberate slaves and help civilize free people, as well. Government officials largely left it to the Africans, who were already responding quite successfully to the new demand for palm produce, to organize the labor needed in the export sector.

Lagosians met the challenge in a number of ways. First, both members of the old slave-trading ruling oligarchy, who already owned large numbers of slaves, and rising new entrepreneurs, who were investing income from the palm produce trade in buying them, struggled to slow the decline of slavery and hold on to their bondwomen and -men. Second, members of both groups met their needs for workers by falling back on marriage, overlordship, patronage, and other indigenous relationships that brought outsiders into households, which led to a resurgence of their economic and social importance. In the case of overlordship, they also began redefining the relationship to make the obligations of strangers for labor more explicit and exacting. Polygyny and overlordship, in particular, enabled a number of Lagos's rising new palm produce traders to capture the labor and dependence of many of the female and male slaves who absconded from their owners in the early colonial period. Yet the emergence of these new ways of harnessing people was neither smooth nor unproblematic. For one thing, big men and women aggressively competed with one another for workers and dependents. For another, they had to contend with the slaves and other types of subordinates themselves, who had ideas and interests of their own. This work examines the conflict that unfolded between owners and slaves and between big men and women and other sorts of dependents over the terms of the relationship between them. It looks at how individuals on both sides of the divide between masters or mistresses and their dependents sought to acquire and use key resources—especially credit and urban housing—in this process. At key points, the work is able to uncover the discursive strategies that different sorts of actors employed in these conflicts, showing when they invoked new values and practices associated with money and contracts, commercial capitalism and British colonialism, or alternatively harkened back to older ones rooted in local tradition and patriarchy.

Evidence about women and children is often difficult for historians to find. Given a subject as hidden from view as slavery in colonial Lagos, it is no surprise that ferreting out data about the experiences of female and child slaves was particularly problematic. So far as possible, however, this study incorporates gender and age into the analysis. It examines the different opportunities that female and male slaves enjoyed in early colonial Lagos, as well as the contrasting strategies that owners and others pursued in an effort to capture and hold their labor and allegiance. Slave youths were the most vulnerable and probably also the most sought after in the final four decades of the nineteenth century. New quantitative data presented in this study illuminate the magnitude of the enslavement of children within the colony, but they can go only a limited way toward recovering these young peoples' experiences.

A further problem that complicates the analysis bears mention. For a number of reasons, including the ambiguity of state policies, the gradualism of the process through which many slaves redefined their relationships with their owners, and local ideology that emphasized the incorporation of slaves into kin groups but was unclear about precisely when and how it occurred, it is often impossible to tell when a slave stopped being a slave. For many bondwomen and -men in Lagos, there was no clear moment of emancipation, despite the British Law Officers' 1866 ruling. The precise timing of the redefinition of identity was not always apparent or uncontested even in the late nineteenth century, as both owners and slaves sometimes had reason to manipulate how they represented the relationship between them. The challenge for this study lies in the fact that it is often impossible to know just when individuals crossed the line between being slaves and former slaves, owners and former owners. I have used these labels as carefully and precisely as possible throughout the text, but ambiguity persists, and there is no way around it.

During the 1970s and 1980s, labor history captured the imagination of Africanists, as they came under the sometimes related influences of Marxism, economic anthropology, and radical British and United States history. Rich bodies of literature developed on the organization of rural labor in colonial and postcolonial West Africa and the growth of wage labor, tenancy arrangements, and sharecropping in the towns and on the farms of southern and eastern Africa.[39] To date, however, we know little about the organization of labor in nineteenth-century West Africa's burgeoning ports and commercial towns and cities. This work reveals how African entrepreneurs in one such place mobilized the very extensive labor they needed to respond to new opportunities in foreign trade during the lengthy interval between the gradual decline of slavery after mid-century and the slow development of wage labor from the 1890s. It demonstrates that while limited work for wages existed with the government, foreign firms, and missionary societies, as well as in other colonies and in the transportation sector of the local economy, wage labor held little appeal for most Lagosians, whether at the top or bottom of the social ladder. To begin with, most employers did not pay high enough wages to attract many Africans.[40] Beyond that, however, even those at the bottom of the social order, such as most slaves, did not much like the idea of selling their labor for wages. They preferred instead to set up as independent traders or producers, even if on a marginal scale and at the price of ongoing subordination to others. Most successful African traders, on the other hand, sought more from their workers than mere labor. They inhabited a world where, while the value of labor had increased, big men and women still sought dependents not only for the work they performed but also for the political support and social prestige they brought.

At the broadest level, *Slavery and the Birth of an African City* advances Atlantic history by furthering our understanding of the Atlantic basin as a single region with a shared past.[41] It illuminates the impact of the rise and fall of the Atlantic slave trade on an important slave port. Moreover, it probes the effects of the expansion of industrial production and mass consumption in northern Europe on the city that later developed on the site, fueled by trade in Africa's first major non-slave export. Finally, the book sheds new light on the changes wrought along the Bight of Benin by the long-term shift in the region's economic, political, and cultural orientation from the south to the north Atlantic.

Sources and Methods

Sources for the history of Lagos before 1800 are not abundant in comparison to those relating to a number of other places on the West African coast. The ones that exist fall, for the most part, into two categories. The first consists of accounts by a limited number of Europeans who visited the area to trade or explore. Few of these individuals had extensive experience at Lagos, because it was not yet an important center of overseas trade, unlike settlements to the west and east. What little they wrote, moreover, was colored by their own pronounced prejudices and preoccupations. The second category of sources consists of oral traditions, both those published in the nineteenth and early twentieth centuries, which emphasize the origins of the kingdom and conflicts within its ruling dynasty, and a corpus that I and others have collected from representatives of selected chieftaincy families. The traditions of these families illuminate their origins and the process of their incorporation into the community and polity, providing fresh perspectives on the history of the precolonial kingdom.[42]

There is significantly more documentation for the first half of the nineteenth century, owing to an increase in the number of literate foreigners who visited the area, still primarily for trade, and to the more detailed nature of the oral traditions for the period. British parliamentary papers produced by committees of inquiry into West Africa and Foreign Office Slave Trade Correspondence (FO 84) are extensive for the first half of the century. Although generally less concerned with Lagos than other parts of the West African coast, they too contain relevant data.[43] Narratives of two young slaves who were held at the town before being sold into the Atlantic trade and subsequently freed offer unique insights into the experiences of males exported from the port in the 1820s.[44] Finally, an exceptional African archive exists for the 1840s in the form of correspondence to Ọba Kosoko, mainly from commercial agents and slave traders in Bahia, that was seized at the palace when the British bombarded the town in 1851.[45]

Not until after the British intervention does the source material on Lagos expand exponentially. Regular British government documentation commences in 1852, when a resident consular official arrived, although the Foreign Office Slave Trade Correspondence remains more valuable for my purposes than the consular records (FO 2) throughout the 1850s. Then, after the annexation in 1861, new series of government documents commence, including original correspondence with the Colonial Office (CO 147), *Blue Books* of Annual Statistics, Annual Reports on the *Blue Books*, Departmental Reports, and Colonial Secretariat Office files (CSO). The arrival beginning in the 1850s of new inhabitants, including European merchants, Christian missionaries, and Brazilian and Sierra Leonean repatriated slaves (many of Yoruba descent and some literate) introduced a multiplicity of new perspectives into the written record. Members of these groups petitioned the government and testified before its committees and commissions of inquiry; wrote letters, reports, and other texts for audiences on the coast and abroad; and in some cases left personal papers. On occasion, they represented the views and experiences of locals, as well as themselves. Then, from the 1880s, an indigenous press developed, which provided regular commentary on public affairs. Relevant materials from these records are cited in footnotes throughout the text and in the bibliography.

Since beginning dissertation research on Lagos in the 1970s, I have supplemented data available in the written record by interviewing children and other descendants of a number of nineteenth-century Lagosians, including some of slave origin. Those who were economically and socially successful have generally been much easier to identify and trace than men and women lower down the social ladder. The majority of Lagos's slaves remain anonymous and thus impossible to track individually. Some of my informants were able to provide general information about slavery and its aftermath, and a number of them talked specifically about slaves who had belonged to their forebears, although often in circumspect ways. But perhaps not surprisingly, relatively few Lagosians with whom I spoke admitted to slave ancestry. When I conducted the bulk of my interviews, I had unfortunately not yet discovered a number of written records that identify particular individuals as slaves and might have helped me ask questions that would bring hidden information to light. Alas, the generation one remove from the second half of the nineteenth century, which was once so helpful to me, has now made the transition to join the ancestors and can no longer be interviewed. As Richard Roberts has noted, "the temporal boundary" for recovering good oral data about social and economic history moves forward with the passing of each generation.[46]

Archival sources for much of colonial Africa contain but veiled and shadowy references to slavery and emancipation, because of the kind of ambivalent European policies I have described. The problem is especially acute for Lagos after the mid-1860s, owing to the extremely awkward position in which government officials and many locals found themselves. There was, within little more than five years of the annexation, a conspiracy of silence in the official community on the subject of slavery within the colony. Nor were most Sierra Leoneans and missionaries more eager to discuss the subject than government representatives and indigenous slaveowners. Although the Sierra Leoneans or their parents had been direct victims of the slave trade, a number of them invested in slaves on their return to Yorubaland. Many of the missionaries, moreover, adopted a tolerant attitude toward local slavery for fear of offending powerful indigenous allies or turning fledgling converts against Jesus Christ.[47]

In an effort to overcome the limitations of more traditional sources, I have mined little-used land and court records for information about the changing relationship between owners and slaves. During the brief interval between colonization in 1861 and the British Law Officers' 1866 pronouncement that slavery could not exist in Lagos, local officials established a Slave Court to hear disputes between owners and slaves, as well as masters and apprentices. So far as I have been able to determine, the records of this court no longer exist. However, a few documents from it survive in the papers of Sir Samuel Rowe, a Slave Court commissioner, and I have used them to help illuminate the experiences of owners and slaves in the first years of colonial rule.[48]

A major judicial reform in 1876 eliminated Lagos's older colonial courts and created Police Magistrates' Courts, plus a Supreme Court with criminal and civil jurisdiction. Although African forums for settling disputes continued to exist in Lagos, the colonial state never officially recognized them and incorporated them into the colonial legal system, as happened elsewhere in British Africa later in the colonial period. These tribunals consequently left few records. I have been unable to locate the records of the early Police Magistrates' Courts, but those of the Supreme Court survive in the tower of the Lagos State High Court.[49] Records of civil cases heard by this court are among the few places where references to slaves and owners exist across the final decades of the nineteenth century.

The Supreme Court could not recognize and directly enforce obligations of slavery. However, former owners and former slaves, as well as their descendants, sometimes went to the court to pursue other sorts of conflicts with one another or third parties. Such cases often revolved around rights in landed property or obligations of credit, matters that the colonial courts defined as central to their jurisdiction. These disputes were at base, however, commonly also about struggles to renegotiate the terms of the relationship between owners and slaves or prominent people and the other sorts of dependents. Indeed, big men and women soon found in their control of housing and credit effective mechanisms for disciplining the labor and allegiance of men and women of slave origin. Thus the Supreme Court cases have much to teach us about the end of slavery and transformation of other relationships of dependency in early colonial Lagos.

Previous scholars have used court records to study slave emancipation in Africa, working, for the most part, with Native or lower European court records or alternatively with criminal cases. The documentation from the Native and lower courts has the great advantage that these tribunals were relatively accessible to Africans. Such courts heard hundreds, even thousands, of disputes in the years following the imposition of colonial rule. Their records, however, normally contain no more than brief summaries of each conflict.[50] Rarely do they yield evidence that illuminates the longer history of the dispute or the way litigants constructed their claims in court. Thus there are real limits to the ability of these documents to fulfill what Richard Roberts sees as one of their great promises: the recovery of African voices about the colonial experience that are growing fainter in the oral record with each decade that passes.[51] Pamela Scully has used sometimes more extensive criminal court records in creative ways to illuminate conflict among colonial actors (government officials, Christian missionaries, freed people, and former slaveowners) over the terms of post-emancipation societies.[52] But the Africans who were principals in these cases were rarely allowed to speak, particularly if they were women; white onlookers instead represented their experiences. Thus these criminal court records also fail to directly capture African perspectives.

The Lagos Supreme Court records contain only dozens, not hundreds, of cases that illuminate slavery and its aftermath. For one thing, they do not begin until after 1876. For another, the court was not as accessible to uneducated Africans as the lower courts other historians have studied, although there is ample evidence that a cross-section of Lagosians engaged in what Roberts has called "venue shopping" and brought cases before it to test what they could accomplish there.[53] The remarkable feature of the Supreme Court records, however, is that for many cases they consist of a number of extended narratives spoken by African litigants and witnesses themselves, although written down by

British judges. Chapter 8 evaluates the strengths and weaknesses of these documents as historical sources in greater detail. The point to be stressed here is that they sometimes contain data that illuminate the history of the relationship between parties who appeared in court and the development of the conflict between them. The narratives themselves, moreover, shed light not only on the actions of different kinds of Lagosians as they struggled to renegotiate their relationships, but also on the discursive strategies they employed inside and sometimes outside the court as they pursued particular ends. In all of these ways, the records throw African agency into sharper relief than can normally be found in other written records or in oral testimony. Moreover, the voices of different kinds of Lagosians occasionally leap from the page with startling clarity.

To gain insights into the changing uses and value of landed property in the urban economy, as well as to better understand credit arrangements, I traced a number of individuals from different social backgrounds, including some of slave origin, through Lagos land and probate records. The land records included not only government grants and private conveyances, but also mortgages pledging property to secure credit.

Chapter-by-Chapter Outline

Chapter 1 sets the historical stage by examining the origins and development of the precolonial Kingdom of Lagos. It analyzes the town's growth as a slave port and rehearses indigenous narratives of the history of the kingdom during the era of the slave trade. These oral traditions introduce important local actors and tell the story of what transpired as locals remember it. The second chapter probes the organization of the Atlantic slave trade at Lagos. It investigates the impact of the commerce on the local political economy, showing how it increased the wealth and power of certain members of the ruling oligarchy, improved their ability to acquire slaves and other dependents, and enhanced the importance of the kingdom in regional commerce and geopolitics. This chapter also asks how the growth of the foreign slave trade at Lagos contributed to chronic factionalism at the center of the state.

Chapter 3 analyzes the causes and consequences of British military and political intervention at Lagos in 1851 and then again a decade later, offering a new interpretation of British imperial expansion along the Bight of Benin. This chapter concludes by examining the creation and character of the early colonial state. The fourth chapter then deals with the rise of the palm oil and palm kernel trades at Lagos, looking briefly at the economic and social changes in Europe that created a new demand for the commodities, and then in greater detail at the expansion of palm produce production and trade locally. The analysis focuses on the organization of production and trade to better understand whether and how they created new economic opportunities for men and women outside the old ruling oligarchy that had dominated the slave trade. The discussion demonstrates the enormous demand for labor generated by the new commerce, which further expanded the local market for slaves and affected the nature of indigenous slavery. This chapter also investigates the central role of credit in the expansion of trade, as well as the meaning of credit and debt in the wider culture. Chapter 5 charts the evolution of British policy at Lagos regarding slaveholding, slave trading, and fugitive slaves from interior states. It shows what drove local officials to adopt the fiction that slavery posed no problem at Lagos and to turn their backs on it, leaving emancipation largely up to the slaves themselves.

The final three chapters examine the shifting relationship between owners and slaves during the final four decades of the nineteenth century. They show how slaves sought to reduce their labor obligations, improve their access to resources, and ultimately redefine their status and identity, while owners struggled to hold on to the labor and allegiance of their slaves and other dependents. Chapter 6 looks at what happened to slaves immediately following the annexation, to determine whether they fled the colony or stayed within it, absconded from their owners or remained attached in their households. It investigates three factors that, in the absence of official emancipation, helped open opportunities to slaves: 1) the dictates of the work they performed in palm produce trade and production, as well as certain other activities; 2) the local ideology regarding slavery; and 3) the enormous demand for people—wives, workers, and dependents—in Lagos, which ensured that bondwomen and -men had alternatives and gave them a degree of leverage with their owners. Chapter 7, which focuses on changes in land use, tenure, and value, and chapter 8, based on a close textual analysis of selected court records, identify mechanisms that owners developed in an effort to assert ongoing control over the labor and loyalty of women and men of slave origin, as well as certain other types of dependents.

1

The Rise of Lagos as an Atlantic Port, c. 1760–1851

In the second half of the seventeenth century, Europeans began arriving on the coast of West Africa's Bight of Benin in significant numbers to buy slaves for use on New World plantations. The rapid growth of this new international trade in human labor reoriented the external relations of a vast region of the interior, which had long had contact via the north with trans-Saharan commercial networks, to include the Atlantic basin as well. As new centers of foreign trade developed along the coast, the pace of economic growth and cultural change accelerated there and larger-scale polities emerged. The young and then regionally insignificant Kingdom of Lagos was eventually caught up in these processes of change, which between c. 1760 and 1850 transformed its capital into an international port linking West Africa's hinterland to the Atlantic world. The growth of the slave trade at Lagos in time also made it notorious in Britain and contributed to its colonization. The story of Lagos's transformation from a site of regional trade to a major international port, significant employer of slave labor, and eventual British colonial capital must begin with an account of the founding of the kingdom and its incorporation into the Atlantic slave trade.

The Origins of the Kingdom

The capital of the precolonial Kingdom of Lagos, as well as the pulsing, crowded, and constricted heart of the modern city that has grown from it, lies on a sandy, swampy island of only about two square miles in size, which is located in a large lagoon that opens onto West Africa's Bight of Benin. The island forms part of the southern border of a region that stretches from the Volta River in the west to the River Nun in the east and was inhabited historically by a number of peoples whose polities waxed and waned and who interacted with one another culturally. These inhabitants included Gbe-speakers (Aja, Fon, and Gun) in the west, Yoruba-speakers in the center, and Edo-speakers in the east. A vast network of lagoons, creeks, and estuaries, fed by sometimes navigable rivers flowing in from the north, runs parallel to the coast between the Volta and the Nun, constituting a four-hundred-mile inland waterway that facilitated movement and exchange. Near the center of this network, the island became a crossroads where peoples and cultures intermingled well before the arrival of Europeans on the West African coast.

At Lagos there occurs one of the few permanent breaks east of the Volta in the miles of beach and dunes that form the outer shore, opening the inland waterway to the Atlantic.[1] This natural phenomenon had limited significance until the mid-nineteenth century, because the indigenous peoples were not ocean-going and the entrance to the lagoon was sufficiently shallow and dangerous to discourage most ships from crossing it. An eighteenth-century European visitor to the coast referred to the "heavens-high breakers" that shut off the entrance to the lagoon and rendered the mainland unapproachable.[2] But the break in the outer coastline would prove fateful in the 1850s, when Great Britain resolved to abolish the Atlantic slave trade in the area and the new European commerce in palm produce developed to take its place.

Migrant fishing peoples first settled Lagos, and from the beginning water and canoes have played a prominent part in the lives of its inhabitants. Prior to the sixteenth century a number of Awori, the southernmost of the Yoruba-speaking peoples, dispersed from Isheri, a village twelve miles up the Ogun River, seeking refuge from a conflict remembered as the "war of the world."[3] A group of them settled at what is now Ebute Metta, on the mainland, until the need for greater security drove the community to a smaller island in the lagoon opposite Lagos island. There they established two settlements, Oto and Iddo, and soon attracted fresh migration. Over generations, the Awori immigrants intermarried with the earlier inhabitants, learning fishing, navigation, and other water-related skills from them and absorbing some of their population.[4]

In time, people from Iddo moved to the northwestern corner of the larger island opposite, which eventually became known as Lagos, looking for land to farm. The settlers recognized the paramountcy of a ruler

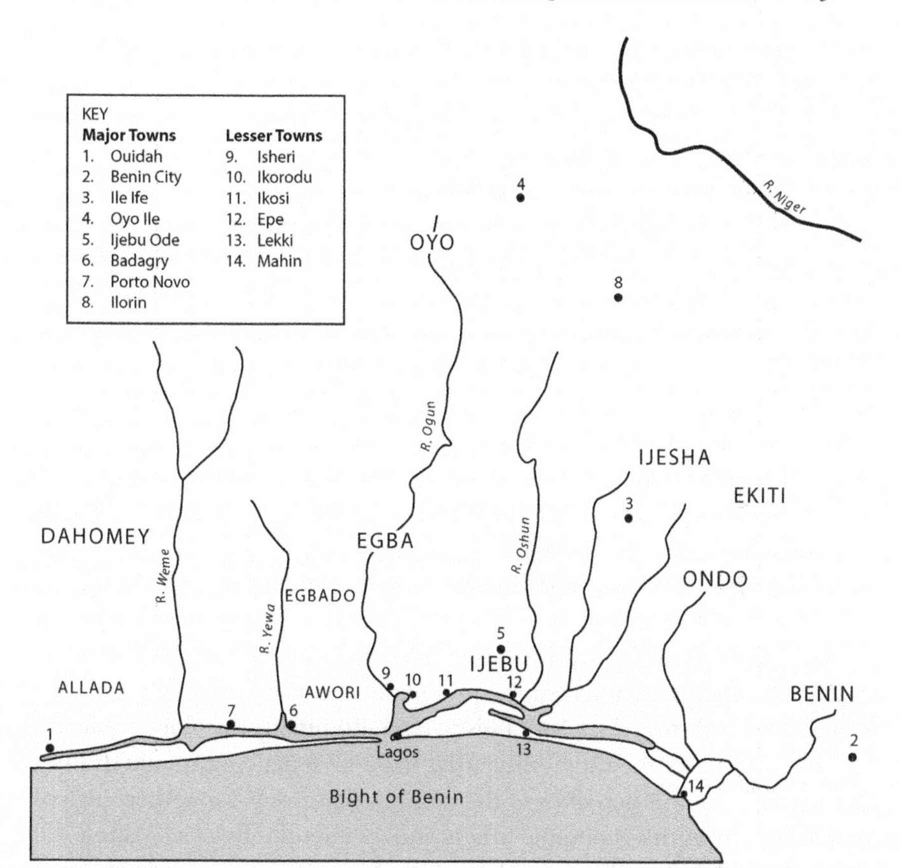

Map 1. The Slave Coast c. 1800.

called the *ọlọ́fin*, based at the more populous and powerful community of Iddo, but tracing mythical descent from Isheri and via the founder of that village to Ile-Ife, the cradle of Yoruba civilization. Elsewhere on Lagos island, Aja, Ijebu (also Yoruba-speaking), and other peoples founded autonomous settlements.[5]

Fishing dominated the island economy, but the local inhabitants also hunted and farmed a little, despite the fact that the sandy soil was not very good for agriculture. Iron working, salt making, and canoe building took place nearby, and perhaps even on Lagos island itself. Limited local trade occurred along the lagoon in these goods, as well as in smoked or dried fish and foodstuffs, although no permanent market seems to have existed at Lagos prior to the seventeenth century. Tradition recalls that from the time of the early *ọlọ́fin*, "Egbados and Aworis often met at Iddo wharf for the purpose of marketing."[6]

Little information exists about social organization prior to the nineteenth century, but it is likely that both production and trade were organized within families. A gendered division of labor probably existed between husbands and wives; however, spouses and children must also have cooperated to meet family needs. Children undoubtedly had obligations to work for their parents prior to marriage, as wives did to assist their husbands and senior members of the men's households. From early times, families incorporated outsiders—wards, immigrants, refugees, and slaves (*ẹrú*)—to increase their size. They valued these non-kin because a man's wealth and power rested heavily on the number of people—wives, children, and other dependents—whose labor and allegiance he controlled. Until the era of the Atlantic slave trade, however, slavery existed at Lagos only on a limited scale. It was not yet as important in the accumulation of dependents as marriage, reproduction, and the incorporation of strangers who migrated to the island.

Families related by kinship often lived together in a single vertically and horizontally extended compound, under the authority of a head, who came to be known as the *baálé*. This person, nominally the eldest male but in fact sometimes the most influential male or female, normally did not direct the economic activities of the families that resided together, each of which organized its economic affairs independently. But *baálé* often did receive regular contributions of fish, produce, labor, and support from those living under their authority, and these offerings increased the wealth and power of local compound heads. Family and household were usually the place where accumulation began. In return, *baálé* were expected to assist the members of their households in times of need, represent them in ritual, social, political, and legal affairs, and provide strangers with hospitality. The more powerful and influential the head of a household, the better off those who lived under his authority.[7]

During the fourteenth and fifteenth centuries, a maritime revolution in Europe enabled navigators to conquer the Atlantic Ocean, which had previously constituted a barrier separating the continents that ringed it. By the 1470s, European ships had sailed as far south along the West African coast as the Bight of Benin.[8] Within thirty more years, Portuguese sailors began trading across the lagoon behind Lagos island with the prosperous southeastern Yoruba state of Ijebu. There they bought slaves, cloth, and ivory, the first two of which they sold for gold on the Coast of Mina (later known as the Gold Coast) west of the Volta. Soon a few Dutch navigators joined them. The name Lagos, given by Europeans to the large island in the lagoon and, eventually, to the city that developed there, came originally from the designation "lago," or lake, on early Portuguese maps. No known sixteenth-century Portuguese or Dutch voyagers mentioned settlements on Lagos island, despite the fact that several traveled in the vicinity, an indication of the contemporary insignificance of the villages located there.[9]

Beginning about the thirteenth century, Edo-speaking peoples had forged a powerful kingdom at Benin City to the east. In the mid-fifteenth century, its *ọba*, or king, had introduced a series of political reforms, concentrated military power in his hands, and begun a process of imperial expansion west into Yorubaland. Throughout the sixteenth century, Benin was the largest and most powerful state between the Volta and the River Niger.[10] By the middle of the century, Portuguese traders had shifted the focus of their activity from Ijebu to the thriving Kingdom of Benin, so dominant in the area that contemporary European cartographers gave its name to the broad bight to the south. At Benin the Portuguese bought small quantities of pepper and slaves for export to Europe and the Americas and of slaves, beads, and cloth for sale on the coast of Mina and the Portuguese islands of São Tomé and Principé. The Portuguese offered in exchange manillas and cowries, which served as local currencies, and cloth, beads, and other luxuries for the personal adornment of the *ọba* and chiefs. Military expansion and economic growth occurred simultaneously in Benin. Both stimulated Edo canoe-borne warfare and trade along the creeks, lagoons, and rivers to the west. Much of the cloth exported from Benin came originally by canoe from Ijebu and other parts of Yorubaland. *Ọbas* themselves periodically led military expeditions west across the lagoon.[11]

In the second half of the sixteenth century, Ọba Orhogbua sent fleets of war canoes to attack Iddo, an eight-to-ten-day journey from Benin City. These expeditions may have represented an effort to retain control of European trade, which was beginning to shift west with the rise of a powerful Aja state at Allada. Repulsed on more than one occasion by a courageous and popular *ọlọ́fin*, Benin established a military camp on Lagos island, presided over by a number of generals, and used it as a base for pursuing the *ọba*'s political and commercial ambitions in the area. Andreas Josua Ulsheimer, a German in Dutch employ who left an eyewitness account of the settlement in 1603, referred to it as a frontier town, surrounded by a strong fence, belonging to the Kingdom of Benin and inhabited by none but soldiers and four military commanders. Subsequently, the island, lagoon, and channel connecting them to the sea were sometimes known as "Curamo," "Korame," "Ikurame," or other variants of a term that was probably Edo in origin. The modern city that originated on the island is still known to its indigenous inhabitants as *Èkó*, which most likely derives from the Edo word for war camp.[12]

Soon after encamping on Lagos island, Benin military commanders established a ceremonial meeting of the heads of local communities. This body developed into a governing council, reminiscent of early processes of state formation in both Benin and Yorubaland. The rulers of Iddo, Oto, and Eko were incorporated into the council, as were those of other local settlements that became important. Of disparate origins, the council members and their followers gradually took on through intermarriage and assimilation the Awori identity of the early settlers of Iddo and Oto.[13] Their successors became known as the *ìdéjọ* chiefs, and they are commonly remembered in local traditions as descending from the sons of the first *ọlófin*. Forging shared Awori identity built unity among the *ìdéjọ*. It also gave them first-settler status, which legitimized their claims to control fishing and, what has been more important in modern times, land rights in the area.[14]

Benin's dominance in the region did not last. Around the turn of the seventeenth century, Ọba Ehengbuda drowned while returning from an expedition on the lagoon east of Lagos. Subsequently, *ọbas* were forbidden to command troops in battle, and the responsibility devolved to war chiefs, ending the king's control of the military. Throughout the seventeenth century, conflict in Benin City between the *ọba* and chiefs and among different categories of chiefs themselves weakened the empire, which lost control of parts of eastern Yorubaland. During the seventeenth century, moreover, powerful empires emerged among the Yoruba at Oyo and Aja at Allada, rivaling Benin's influence west of Lagos. The borders of these three states shifted and overlapped in the second half of the century, as they fought for control of the region.[15]

Despite its decline, Benin continued to play a role in Lagos, however, perhaps because of the ease of commercial and military communication across the lagoon. Neither Oyo nor Allada extended its authority to the town, although Oyo's military might reached south to Allada, which it conquered at the very end of the century, and its political influence to Ifonyin, where it had a colony. Oyo's commercial hegemony extended all the way to the coastal ports of Jakin, Offra, and later Porto Novo. At its height, Allada's empire stretched as far east as Apa. From Yoruba- and Gbe-speaking communities to the west, involved in trade along the lagoon or displaced by warfare in the 1670s, the town of Lagos received fresh migration and new cultural influences.[16]

Sometime before 1682, the *ọba* of Benin appointed a viceroy to oversee the community and exact tribute from it. This emissary brought with him, in addition to his own retainers, at least two Edo advisors and their followers. Benin traditions remember the viceroy as the son or grandson of Ọba Orhogbua; Lagosian ones remember him as a member of the royal family of Isheri who was rewarded with the appointment when he escorted the body of one of the original Benin commanders home for burial. Whatever the origins of its founder, the office gave birth to a new royal dynasty that in time became identified with Lagos, as demonstrated by the local tradition of Awori ancestry. The new ruler took the name Ọba, and the title *ọlọ́fin* fell into disuse. In Robin Law's words, the Benin occupation "transformed Lagos from an unimportant dependency of Iddo into a state with its own king, deriving considerable importance from its role as the center of Benin power in the lagoon area."[17]

The offices of the Edo advisors who had accompanied the viceroy to Lagos became hereditary. Their holders bore the titles Eletu Odibo and Aṣogbon, and they came to be recognized as the heads, respectively, of classes of *àkárìgbèrè* administrative and *àbàgbọ́n* military chiefs into which men and a few women who became rich and powerful were incorporated as the kingdom developed. With a fourth class, the *ògáládé*, that had religious authority, these officials plus the *ọba* forged the institutions of the state and constituted its ruling oligarchy. Although the creation of the *àkárìgbèrè* and *àbàgbọ́n* grades, and indeed the appointment of particular *àbàgbọ́n* chiefs, may have been associated with the growth of royal power, the division of authority among the different types of chiefs, as well as between them and the *ọba*, was by no means fixed. It remained, instead, a matter of conflict and contestation into the twentieth century.[18] *Ọbas* of Lagos sent tribute to Benin and sought confirmation of their succession intermittently into the mid-nineteenth century, sometimes as a means of asserting their right to the crown in the face of local struggles over it.[19] In political, military, and commercial affairs, however, the emerging kingdom had become largely autonomous by the eighteenth century.

While these developments were taking place along the Bight of Benin and in its interior, across the Atlantic in the Americas a system of plantation agriculture introduced from the Mediterranean basin in the first half of the sixteenth century was expanding to supply growing European markets for sugar. By the second half of the century, plantation production had created a demand for slave labor in northeastern Brazil, which after the 1640s spread with the plantation system to the eastern Caribbean as well. During this period, Africa became firmly identified in the Western mind as the source of slave labor for New World plantations. Atlantic exports of slaves grew from about 276,000 between 1519 and 1600 to about 1,173,000 between 1651 and 1700.[20] As the volume of the Atlantic slave trade increased, its conduct spread from West-Central Africa, which had initially dominated supply, to the Bight of Benin and other regions.[21] Portuguese, English, Dutch, French, and other merchants all now participated in the commerce, and representatives of the first four nations opened establishments, known as factories, along the Bight of Benin at such places as Keta, Little Popo, Great Popo, Glehue, Jakin, Offra, and Apa.[22]

Ọbas of Benin had banned the sale of male slaves to Europeans since the early sixteenth century, but other rulers in the region did not share their concern about the foreign trade in humans. Both Allada and Oyo became heavily involved in the sale of slaves for export, which contributed to their rise to power. Once the slave trade clearly dominated European commercial interests in the region, the center of foreign trade there shifted from Benin to settlements between Keta and Apa. Europeans dubbed this short strip of shoreline "the Slave Coast," reflecting its growing importance in the supply of labor to the Americas.[23]

Both the expansion of European trade along the Bight of Benin and the growth of prosperity at Allada and Oyo, counterpoints to that of Benin in the east, increased commerce across the lagoon. From the Volta to the Nun, trade in locally produced and consumed goods such as salt, fish, cloth, beads, canoes, iron ware, and foodstuffs picked up in the seventeenth century, as did that in ivory, gum, cloth, pepper, and beads exported to Europe or by Europeans to other parts of the West African coast. Trade expanded as well in imports—cowries, manillas, textiles, and beads—although external commerce still remained limited in scale. The majority of slaves exported—now headed to the Americas, not other parts of West Africa or islands in the Atlantic—came from Allada and Oyo and traveled overland. But Edo, Ijebu, and Awori traders also transported a few slaves west across the lagoon for sale on the coast.[24]

During the seventeenth century, Lagos became an important center of the expanding local and regional trade, thanks to its central location on the water route linking Benin, Ijebu, and Allada, as well as Oyo's southern commercial termini. The town's emerging *ọbas* and chiefs furthered this development by providing security for trade. Ulsheimer observed at the beginning of the century that Lagos had "many people" coming to it, "by water and by land, with their wares."[25] Lagosians themselves traveled in their canoes west to Allada, north to Ijebu, and east to Benin, as well as to lesser places, buying and selling, although many of the town's several hundred inhabitants continued to live by fishing, hunting, and farming. In 1652, an English vessel, *Constant Ruth*, purchased 216 slaves in "the River [Curamo]" and sailed with them to Barbados, the first documented European shipment of slaves from the immediate vicinity of the town.[26] European traders would not visit Lagos regularly until after the 1760s, however, and it would not become as large or important as Offra, Apa, Glehue, Jakin, and other ports farther west on the Slave Coast until even later. Yet income from trade had begun to create social differentiation and support economic and political specialization. Inequality was not yet pronounced, but some Lagosians already enjoyed greater wealth and power than others. A small kingdom was taking shape, and it was strategically located to the south of a number of West Africa's most prosperous and powerful states, on the coast linking them to the Atlantic world. Geography and transportation, immigration and incorporation, trade and warfare—themes that would dominate its history for the next two hundred years—had already shaped its past. The very history of the young state's institutions briefly recounted here demonstrates the contributions of Yoruba, Edo, and less numerous coastal peoples to its culture. While the community's rulers gradually forged an Awori identity, the inhabitants of the town interacted continually with their neighbors and episodically with Westerners, borrowing from the lot as they saw fit.

The Rise of the External Slave Trade at Lagos: Atlantic and Regional Contexts

The foreign slave trade at Lagos developed as part of broader Atlantic and regional commercial networks. Indeed, the regular, direct export of slaves from the town began as a consequence of political and economic changes to the west along the Slave Coast and in the interior of the Bight of Benin. A discussion of the slave trade at Lagos must begin, therefore, with a consideration of broader Atlantic and regional contexts.

The external slave trade peaked during the eighteenth century, with the dramatic growth of sugar production on the western Caribbean islands of Jamaica and Saint Domingue, the explosion of gold mining in Mina Gerais in Brazil, and the production of staple crops such as tobacco, indigo, rice, coffee, and cotton in different parts of the Americas.[27]

African exports of slaves increased from about 28,000 per year between 1676 and 1700 to about 80,000 per year a century later. Of the roughly 12.4 million Africans exported during the 350-year history of the trade, more than half (about 6.4 million slaves) were shipped between 1701 and 1800. The Bight of Benin supplied between a sixth and a fifth of the total. Only West-Central Africa exported more slaves, and in the half century from 1676 to 1725 the Slave Coast lived up to its name by supplying more than one out of every three slaves shipped to the Americas.[28] The figures in table 1.1 show that slave exports from the Bight of Benin reached their highest levels in the first quarter of the eighteenth century and then declined for a hundred years before rising again slightly between 1826 and 1850.

Portuguese and Brazilians, many of them based in Bahia, dominated the export trade in slaves from the Bight of Benin over its long history, as shown by the figures in table 1.1. Eltis estimates that between 1601 and 1867 between five and six of every ten slaves leaving the Bight of Benin went to Bahia in Brazil, the majority in Bahian or Portuguese vessels.[29] The British trade in the Bight, however, took off before the Portuguese/Brazilian one, rivaled it between 1676 and 1700, and remained strong in the first quarter of the eighteenth century, after which both it and the much more substantial Portuguese/Brazilian trade declined. The French trade, on the other hand, grew dramatically between 1701 and 1750, and it remained strong through the 1780s. Dutch traders shipped almost 123,000 slaves from the region before 1751, but their traffic declined quickly thereafter, and it disappeared after 1776.[30]

When the French and British trades subsided around the time of their respective abolitions in 1794 and 1807, the Portuguese/Brazilian commerce expanded once more and a Spanish trade developed between the Bight of Benin and Cuba. Between 1800 and the end of the trade in the 1860s, about four out of every five slaves taken from the area between the Gold Coast and Benin were shipped to Bahia. After 1830 Cuba became a major market.[31] The high volume of slave exports from the Bight of Benin to northeastern Brazil over the long history of the trade and the continued heavy importation of slaves from the region into Bahia after the traffic had ended in most other places together laid the foundation for the close cultural connections that exist between the Bight of Benin and Brazil.

Until the 1720s, the external slave trade from the Bight of Benin centered first on the Kingdom of Allada and then on its rival the Kingdom of Ouidah, and on their ports of Offra, Apa, Glehue, and Jakin, although

Table 1.1 Slave Exports from the Bight of Benin by National Carrier

	Portuguese	*Spanish*	*Dutch*	*French*	*English*	*Danish*	*USA*	*total*
1601–1625	1920	1920	0	0	0	0	0	3840
1626–1650	290	482	6197	553	0	429	0	7951
1651–1675	361	5271	33789	2159	20003	571	0	62154
1676–1700	95199	0	34493	7189	93325	21587	0	251793
1701–1725	189036	0	34553	72361	99391	1904	0	397245
1726–1750	169730	0	13894	109587	35596	369	0	329176
1751–1775	157791	0	2048	85146	49553	152	1215	295905
1776–1800	138210	99	0	76774	46751	0	768	262602
1800–1825	211360	19481	0	5125	13791	195	1954	251906
1826–1850	167880	83676	0	6137	0	0	0	257693
1851–1867	2937	27916	0	255	0	0	0	31108
1601–1867	1134714	138845	124974	365286	358410	25207	3937	2151373

Source: David Eltis, personal communication, 24 December 2005, from David Eltis, David Richardson, Stephen D. Behrendt, and Manolo Florentino, *The Transatlantic Slave Trade Database*, 2nd ed., forthcoming.

Great Popo, Little Popo, and Keta further west exported smaller numbers of slaves. During these years, Allada, Ouidah, Oyo, smaller Yoruba states, and the emerging Fon kingdom of Dahomey supplied the majority of slaves exported from the western Slave Coast, but other polities in the interior and on the coast produced limited quantities. Most slaves exported were captives acquired in wars. Smaller numbers, however, were obtained as tribute, through kidnapping and trade, or in punishment for offenses such as theft, adultery, gambling, and indebtedness.[32]

Around the turn of the eighteenth century, the Fon had founded a new kingdom, Dahomey, in the interior of the Bight of Benin. In 1724 it conquered Allada, and in 1727 it defeated Ouidah. For the next century and a half, Dahomey's aspirations and ambitions shaped the history of the region, although Oyo invaded and defeated it intermittently until 1823 and the Fon kingdom never extended its hegemony as far east as Lagos.[33] After the defeat of Allada and Ouidah, refugees from these areas fled east and founded new polities, as well as a new Gun ethnic identity, at Badagry, Ekpe, and Porto Novo. A Dutch trader, Hendrik Hertogh, driven from Allada's port of Jakin when it was sacked by Dahomey in 1732, opened slave trading factories at Badagry and Ekpe in 1736 and 1737. João de Oliveira, a freed slave from Bahia, opened the slave trade at Porto Novo in 1758. Subsequently, other foreign slave traders anxious to escape the tight control that the king of Dahomey was attempting to impose on the commerce at Ouidah settled in the new Gun communities.[34] The slave trade soon expanded at these ports, although Ouidah still exported vastly more slaves than any other place on the Bight on Benin, with annual exports averaging between six and seven thousand slaves between 1726 and 1750.[35]

The Dahomian conquest of Allada and Ouidah disrupted trade routes and altered the flow of slaves from the interior to the coast, leaving Ouidah supplied less by trade with Oyo, Allada, and other neighboring peoples and more by Dahomey's own wars of expansion and raids for slaves. The rise of the Gun communities along the eastern bight, on the other hand, created outlets for slaves from Oyo and other eastern suppliers independent of Dahomey's control. From the 1730s, Oyo, for example, channeled its slaves first to Badagry and later to Porto Novo as well, contributing to the growth of these ports.[36] Differences in the organization of supply and in the freedom of outside traders to sell slaves in the coastal ports are reflected in the loading times of European vessels—always a variable crucial to the success of voyages. In the final quarter of the eighteenth century, slave ships obtained their human cargoes about 30 percent more quickly at Porto Novo and Badagry than at Dahomey-controlled Ouidah.[37] Because of these many advantages, Badagry and Porto Novo together replaced Ouidah as the primary outlets for slaves on the Bight of Benin between 1776 and 1780, while a decade later Porto Novo alone achieved the dubious distinction of being the leading slave port in the region.[38] Archibald Dalzel, a former resident of the coast, commented in his *History of Dahomy* that a "great number of ships" called at Ekpe, Porto Novo, and Badagry in the late 1770s and 1780s, while Ouidah "was almost totally abandoned."[39] In the final third of the eighteenth century, Oyo began obtaining an increasing proportion of its slaves through trade with the north. Subsequently, Muslim merchants from the north occasionally marched slaves directly to the coast, rather than selling them to traders from Oyo.[40]

The majority of slaves exported from the Bight of Benin were Gbe- or Yoruba-speakers and probably came from within two or three hundred kilometers of the coast. A small number of slaves may have been imported from elsewhere and assimilated into one or the other of these two dominant linguistic groups before being sold abroad. Slaves of other ethnicities—Chamba, Nupe, Hausa, and Eastern Akan, for example—were also sold on the Slave Coast, although their numbers varied with events in West Africa, as did the percentage of Gbe- and Yoruba-speakers shipped. In brief, Gbe-speakers predominated early in the history of the trade on the Slave Coast, but the percentage of Yoruba-speakers rose dramatically in the nineteenth century after the fall of the Oyo Empire and onset of the Yoruba wars. The percentage of Hausa, Nupe, and Bariba slaves exported increased from the final decades of the eighteenth century, when trade with the north became more important in the system of supply.[41]

Lagosians participated in the early eighteenth-century expansion of the slave trade from the Bight of Benin by transporting slaves across the lagoon for sale. A French trader reported in 1715 that slaves were being brought to Apa by merchants from "the kingdom of Benin," a comment that Law believes may refer to Lagos rather than metropolitan Benin. In the 1730s, the Dutchman Jan Bronssema established a staging post near Lagos to facilitate trade in slaves and other goods between Benin and the short-lived Dutch West India Company fort at Badagry. A 1743 document suggests that Lagosians were then selling slaves in the Portuguese fort at Ouidah.[42] No evidence survives that would permit even a crude calculation of the number of slaves Lagosians traded across the lagoon during the early and mid-eighteenth century, but it must have been small—probably no more than several hundred per decade. The major supplies of slaves from inland reached the coast to the west and east, at places where Lagos traders had to compete for them with Europeans and richer Africans. Throughout these years, Lagosians sold limited numbers of slaves acquired in local wars, purchased in northern and eastern lagoon-side markets, or brought to the town by Ijebu, Edo, and other eastern traders.

The lagoon trade in slaves continued, moreover, to form part of the diverse local and regional networks of exchange linking the peoples of the hinterland and the coast from the Volta to the Niger and beyond. Items traded included, as before, beads, cloth, salt, canoes, food, and iron ware, as well as slaves. Throughout the eighteenth and early nineteenth centuries, European visitors to the Slave Coast noted both extensive craft and agricultural production and markets where domestically produced commodities and imports were exchanged.[43] While trade with the Gold Coast in beads and cloth may have fallen off in the eighteenth century owing to the decline of the gold trade there, that in cloth and food with the western Slave Coast towns probably picked up. Town dwellers and trade slaves created a demand for locally produced food, and slave vessels carried ivory to Europe and Yoruba cloth to Bahia and elsewhere.[44]

The continuous direct export of slaves from Lagos to the Americas began in the 1760s, and it should be seen as part of the wider shift of Atlantic commerce east along the Slave Coast from Ouidah that began in the 1730s.[45] According to Lagos traditions, a dispute had arisen previously between the third *ọba* of the kingdom, Gabaro, and his brother Akinṣemoyin, possibly over the installation of descendants of *ọlófin* as chiefs and recognition of their authority over land. Akinṣemoyin was banished and fled west to Apa, home of his mother, or to Badagry. While in exile, he made the acquaintance of, and undoubtedly also began doing business with, European slave traders. In the early 1760s, Gabaro died and Akinṣemoyin was called home to wear the crown, bringing some of his new acquaintances with him.[46] Born on the western Slave Coast, taken to Pernambuco as a slave, and returned home to free himself by providing commercial assistance to Portuguese slave traders, João de Oliveira claimed to have opened the external slave trade at Lagos, as well as Porto Novo. He was almost certainly among those who accompanied Akinṣemoyin to the town in the early 1760s. In 1770, de Oliveira retired from trade on the West African coast after thirty-seven years and sailed for Bahia accompanied by four of Akinṣemoyin's "caboceers" (chiefs), lending credence to his claim. At least six French ships and two British ones joined Portuguese vessels in loading slaves at Lagos in the 1760s and 1770s.[47]

During these two decades, European traders on the Gold Coast also sent vessels to buy slaves at Lagos for export from their factories.[48] Richard Brew, the Irish founder of a prominent Gold Coast family, dominated this activity. Between 1767 and 1776, he employed several craft importing slaves and cloth from Lagos, and in the 1770s he maintained a factory in the town. Contemporaries estimated that Brew handled three-quarters of the roughly one thousand slaves exported from Lagos to the Gold Coast between 1770 and 1776.[49]

The direct export of slaves from Lagos began on a small scale, and after its onset commerce in slaves as well as other goods continued across the lagoon. Although it is impossible to determine how many slaves Lagosians sold in the lagoon trade before or after 1760, the number may have surpassed that of direct exports until the 1780s. Slave exports from Ouidah, Porto Novo, Badagry, and Benin exceeded or rivaled those from Lagos until after 1800.[50] When opportunities to sell slaves were not good locally, Lagosians could transport them across the lagoon for sale elsewhere.

The Volume of the External Slave Trade at Lagos

During the past thirty years, research by historians of national and local slave trades has made it possible, for the first time, to count slaves shipped from the coast of Africa. Previous work on the volume of the Atlantic slave trade rested primarily on estimates of imports into the Americas. David Eltis, Stephen D. Behrendt, David Richardson, and Herbert S. Klein combined and augmented data from these individual research projects in the comprehensive *Trans-Atlantic Slave Trade Database*, which the first three plus Manolo Florentino have updated through additional research.[51] Eltis believes that the second edition of the database contains documentary evidence on between eight and nine voyages out of every ten "that ever went out on a slaving expedition," and that for the period after 1700 the figure exceeds nine out of ten.[52] Point of embarkation is currently known for just under 40 percent of all slaves leaving the Bight between 1601 and 1867, although the proportion is higher for slaves carried on French and British vessels and for those that departed on Portuguese/Brazilian ships after 1815. The records documenting many of the Portuguese/Brazilian voyages before 1815 specify only the "Costa da Mina," and not particular ports of call. On the basis of known data, however, Eltis and his collaborators are able to estimate slave departures from the individual ports of the region. Table 1.2 contains figures for Lagos.

Table 1.2 Estimated Slave Departures from Lagos by Five-Year Periods, 1761–1851 (in thousands)

1761–65	269
1766–70	2,873
1771–75	1,848
1776–80	2,162
1781–85	3,870
1786–90	14,077
1791–95	4,186
1796–1800	3,282
1801–05	21,412
1806–10	28,418
1811–15	20,584
1816–20	22,683
1821–25	17,727
1826–30	31,776
1831–35	16,336
1836–40	27,582
1841–45	35,038
1846–50	37,715
1851–55	5,410
Total	297,248

Source: David Eltis, personal communication, 24 December 2005, from David Eltis, David Richardson, Stephen D. Behrendt, and Manolo Florentino, *The Transatlantic Slave Trade Database*, 2nd ed., forthcoming.

Although these numbers are provisional and in most cases probably represent minimum figures, the major trends they reveal are almost certainly accurate.

The data reveal that direct exports of slaves began slowly in the first half of the 1760s, but climbed to an average of about 575 slaves per year in the second half of the decade. They then declined by more than a third in the first half of the 1770s before picking up slightly in the later part of the decade. These figures for the first half of the 1770s are probably on the low side, however, because they do not include slaves shipped via Brew's coasting trade with the Gold Goast, which was then significant.

The foreign slave trade at Lagos expanded significantly in the 1780s, to almost 4,000 slaves in the first half of the decade and more than 14,000 slaves in the second half. A series of wars and shifting alliances among Porto Novo, Badagry, and lesser lagoonside communities, in which Dahomey, Oyo, and Lagos itself played an active part, fueled the expansion. These events produced war captives locally for export and also displaced populations, making them more vulnerable to raids and kidnapping. An attack by Lagos on Badagry in 1788 helps explain the dramatic increase between 1786 and 1790.[53]

Qualitative evidence corroborates the quantitative data for the 1780s. An employee of the Portuguese fort at Ouidah complained as early as 1781 that ships were not buying slaves there, because the growth of the trade at Ekpe, Porto Novo, Badagry, and Lagos meant that captains and supercargoes were "no longer obliged to suffer the despotism" of his fort's director, who was an official of the Dahomian king.[54] Four years later, the head of the French fort at Ouidah signaled to a passing ship that the slave trade was particularly good at Porto Novo and Lagos. In response, no doubt, to the dramatic expansion of the commerce at Lagos in the second half of the 1780s, the same man soon after advised the minister of the colonies in Paris to build a fort in the community. Although it was not pursued, the suggestion nonetheless provides evidence of Lagos's growing importance in the slave trade.[55] Then, at the end of the decade, the British Company of Merchants Trading to Africa sent an employee from Ouidah to open a factory on the island.[56] Robert Norris, a Liverpool slave trader who operated in the area for several years, told a select committee of the Privy Council in 1789 that 3,500 slaves per year were shipped from "Lagos and Benin."[57] As Lagos was then the more important of the two ports, it probably supplied the majority of these slaves.

Slave exports from Lagos then declined significantly in the 1790s, for reasons that are not altogether clear. The very significant French slave trade ended abruptly at Lagos in the early 1790s, as in the Bight of Benin more generally, owing to the slave revolution in Saint Domingue, warfare among European nations, and French abolition in 1794. British and Portuguese/Brazilian exports expanded over the decade, but they did not absorb what the French left.[58]

The slave trade changed dramatically at Lagos between 1800 and 1851. In the first quarter of the nineteenth century, the town became the leading slave port in the Bight of Benin, and then in the next twenty-five years it developed into the largest slave exporter north of the equator. Little in the community's eighteenth-century history predicts its preeminence later on. The data show a huge expansion in the external slave trade at Lagos in the first decade of the nineteenth century, to just under 50,000 slaves. Qualitative evidence from G. A. Robertson, who had first-hand experience on the coast and remarked that prior to British abolition "7,000 to 10,000 slaves" were sold annually in the town, corroborates these estimates from the updated *Transatlantic Slave Trade Database*.[59] Departures fell significantly in the early teens, as elsewhere in West Africa, during the period of uncertainty and reorganization in the commerce that followed abolition in Great Britain, the United States, and Holland, and legal banning north of the equator by Portugal after 1815.[60] Recovery began in the late teens, but rapid growth did not take place until between 1826 and 1830, when exports topped 30,000 slaves. A further downturn occurred in the first half of the 1830s, but it too was followed by recovery, and from the second half of the 1830s until the British intervention in 1851 exports continued at record levels, exceeding 100,000 slaves in all.

What accounts for Lagos's sudden and dramatic rise to preeminence as a slave port in the first half of the nineteenth century? Part of the explanation lies in developments outside the region. Brazil continued to be the largest market for slaves exported from Africa throughout the first half of the nineteenth century. Although prosperity ended in the Bahian sugar industry about 1820, slave prices remained high there because of the intra-Brazilian slave trade.[61] Not surprisingly, Bahian-based slave traders looked to the part of Africa with which they had historic ties and effective commercial relations to meet their continuing demand for slaves. The slave trade had already begun to decline, moreover, from many parts of West Africa, such as the Bight of Biafra and the Gold and Windward Coasts in the first quarter of the nineteenth century and the Senegambia in the second quarter. Only in West-Central Africa, South-East Africa, and the Bights of Benin and, to a lesser extent, Biafra did it remain robust.[62]

Against this background must be set regional factors that contributed to Lagos's new commercial importance. Circumstances both pushed the Atlantic slave trade away from ports further west and pulled it to Lagos. Warfare and internal instability drove foreign slave traders away from Badagry in the 1780s and 1790s, while Porto Novo's preeminence in the commerce was short-lived. Departures from there had already begun to decline in the 1790s, when Dahomian attacks on the kingdom at the beginning of the nineteenth century "severely disrupted the trade-routes between Oyo and Porto Novo" and drove Oyo traders to Lagos with their slaves. The governor of Bahia wrote in 1807, "Trade in the port of Onim," as the Portuguese then called Lagos, "is a result of the wars between Dagome (King of Dahomey) and the King of Porto-Novo. . . . This has driven trade towards the Port of Onim obliging our ships [to go there for slaves]."[63] The island capital of the Kingdom of Lagos lay beyond the reach of the land-based armies of Dahomey, Oyo, and the other major players in the early nineteenth-century competition for strategic locations along the eastern Slave Coast and in its interior. The town offered the most secure port in the area.

Developments inland from the coast also played a part in Lagos's rise as a slave port. In the first three decades of the nineteenth century, the balance of power that had maintained order among the Yoruba states and, for the most part, protected their peoples from becoming victims of the slave trade fell apart. A long series of wars commenced that yielded tens of thousands of Yoruba-speaking captives for sale first abroad and then, after the final suppression of the illegal trade, within Africa itself. The power of the Oyo Empire had been declining for some years. Resources newly made available by the Atlantic slave trade had "seriously destabilized relations within its capital" between the *aláàfin* (king) and powerful chiefs.[64] Moreover, an ambitious and disaffected provincial ruler named Afonja, at Ilorin, was fomenting rebellion and harassing Oyo towns. The rise of the slave trade at Lagos meanwhile created new economic and political opportunities for smaller southern kingdoms, most significantly Ijebu, and led to intensified slave raiding on their frontiers. When a number of Oyo traders were kidnapped at Apomu, an Ife market town on the Ijebu border, warfare broke out between Owu, Oyo's local client state, and Ife, which was joined in battle by Ijebu. The conflict culminated in Owu's defeat c. 1817 and sack five years later.[65]

Between 1817 and 1836, the Oyo Empire finally collapsed, following continued aggression by Afonja and his Muslim allies at Ilorin, a revolt by slaves of northern origin in Oyo itself, and the overthrow of Afonja by his Muslim supporters, who subsequently declared a holy war against Oyo. These calamities produced many war captives for sale, but, equally important, they sent thousands of refugees fleeing south. A number of the displaced men joined the allied armies of Ife and Ijebu and began attacking Egba towns. Soon after, groups of Oyo refugees and southern Yoruba-speaking peoples founded three new and quite different polities—Ibadan, Ijaye, and a new Oyo—in the forests of Egbaland, pushing several small

Egba kingdoms into a confederation at the new town of Abeokuta. In the 1830s and 1840s, Ibadan, Ijaye, and Abeokuta each pursued policies of expansion, in a rivalry to see which would replace Oyo's supremacy in the region. There ensued a succession of wars of different kinds, some short and sharp and others protracted and low-grade. During these years, Dahomey freed itself from Oyo overrule and commenced a period of military expansion into western Yorubaland.[66]

In the profound demographic, political, and cultural reordering that followed the breakup of the Oyo Empire, the center of political gravity in the Yoruba-speaking world shifted south and successful, self-made warriors whose position depended on the loyalty and obedience of large numbers of dependents—most refugees and slaves rather than freeborn wives and kin—became centrally important in Yoruba political culture. Guns, first used in Ijebu and Ife's attack on Owu in 1817, became necessary for military success, as the redistribution of imported goods did to retain the loyalty of dependents. Both changes underscored the centrality of trade with the coast to military and political success. The emergence of the new foreign trade in palm oil at the coast during the 1840s meant that when slaves were not available for sale, interior traders could nonetheless buy coveted imports. Slave labor was simultaneously growing more important in the local economy, to liberate free men and women from food and craft production, transport trade goods to the coast, and manufacture palm oil.[67] By the late 1850s, political tensions among the new Yoruba states drove Ijaye and Abeokuta into an alliance against Ibadan and its Remo supporters, which Ijebu joined in the early 1860s, when war broke out between the two sides.

The prolonged warfare and disruption north of Lagos in the first half of the nineteenth century created a vast supply of slaves for export. Proximity to this source contributed greatly to the town's growth as a slave port, particularly when coupled with its island security. Yet an additional set of factors also played a role. By the early nineteenth century, Lagos's rulers had established conditions conducive to trade at the port. On the one hand, the town's merchants were proving themselves effective middlepeople capable of buying large numbers of slaves in markets on the mainland, transporting them across the lagoon, and smoothly selling them to foreign exporters. On the other hand, despite periods of intense domestic political instability, its rulers maintained the order and provided the services necessary to attract both foreign buyers and interior sellers to the town.

The services performed by the ruling oligarchy changed with the nature of the trade in the first half of the century. They included, however, enforcement of credit, provision of housing and warehousing, and assistance in obtaining land and laborers once foreigners began building large baracoons on the coast following legal abolition. Foreign slave traders clearly preferred African markets that they perceived as safe and reliable, even when not most convenient geographically, and they returned again and again to do business with Africans whom they trusted.[68] During the first half of the nineteenth century, Lagos's *ọbas* and leading merchants succeeded in developing and maintaining a climate in the town that attracted foreign buyers. While the sources tell us little about Lagosians' relationships with traders from the interior, they reveal that members of the town's political and commercial elite sent diplomatic missions to Europe and Brazil and slaves or children to study in Bahia, in large part to encourage the development of trade.[69] By the 1840s, Ọba Kosoko was corresponding regularly with commission agents and slave traders in Bahia; the latter called on him for help collecting debts and securing landed property.[70] A large part of Lagos's development as a center of the slave trade must be attributed to the policies of its rulers and the acumen of its commercial community.

Was Lagos's commercial success during the first half of the nineteenth century partly due to the fact that trade there was freer from royal control, and hence more open, than at Ouidah? Robin Law's work on the important western Slave Coast port shows that the relationship between state and private enterprise changed there during the eighteenth and nineteenth centuries. The issue of royal control was complex even at Ouidah, and the question of whether it was weaker at Lagos in the nineteenth century must for now remain open. Certainly many of Lagos's *ọbas* and their leading supporters demanded and received privileges in the slave trade similar to those claimed by agents of the Dahomian king in Ouidah, as the next chapter will show. However, one clear difference existed between the two ports. The Kingdom of Dahomey was built on military expansion, which initially produced most of the slaves it exported, and a warrior ethos prevailed at the center of the state. Many Dahomian kings and their supporters viewed the buildup of wealth through commerce ambivalently, because it "posed a threat to the dominance of the martial values with which the monarchy was identified."[71] In Lagos, on the other hand, wealth acquired through trade is what enabled late eighteenth- and early nineteenth-century *ọbas* to increase their power, expand their kingdom militarily, and concentrate political authority in their hands. The buildup of wealth through commerce did not threaten the monarchy at Lagos, but instead dramatically enhanced its prestige. The kingdom's greatest precolonial *ọbas*—Akinṣemoyin, Ologun Kuture, Oṣinlokun, and Kosoko—wholeheartedly embraced entrepreneurial activities, because they made possible the growth of royal power and the development of the state.

Indigenous Narratives of the Kingdom's History in This Era

Oral traditions from Lagos provide indigenous narratives of the history of the kingdom during the era of the slave trade. As elsewhere in Africa, official traditions contain few explicit references to the commerce, although fragments of information about it can be teased out through close analysis and contemporary European documentation occasionally intersects with the oral traditions to yield additional insights.[72] In Lagos, moreover, stories collected from a number of the prominent chieftaincy families contain more explicit commentary on the slave trade.

The official dynastic traditions focus, as is so often the case in Africa, on politics, and in this instance particularly on deep-seated political conflicts that racked the kingdom from at least the mid-eighteenth century. Among the earliest of the documented disputes was the disagreement between Ọba Gabaro and his brother Akinṣemoyin, which culminated in the latter's banishment and subsequent contact with European slave traders at Apa or Badagry. The oral traditions portray the conflicts that divided Lagos as a product of recurring disagreements between *ọbas* and chiefs over the division of power and authority; repeated rivalries between members of the royal dynasty over succession to the crown; and a bitter personal feud between a powerful prince and an influential chief, which itself triggered succession disputes. The traditions bear recounting because they outline the political history of the kingdom during the era of the slave trade as locals remember it. They raise, in addition, fundamental questions about the relationship between domestic political transformations and external commercial developments.[73]

When Akinṣemoyin died c. 1775, he was succeeded by Gabaro's son Eletu Kekere, who ruled only a short time. Around 1780, Ologun Kuture became king. The new *ọba* was the son of Erelu Kuti, Gabaro and Akinṣemoyin's sister, by Alagba, Akinṣemoyin's *babaláwo* or medical herbalist and diviner. Traditions recall that Akinṣemoyin had dressed the infant Ologun Kuture in "royal robes, adorned him with all the paraphernalia of an

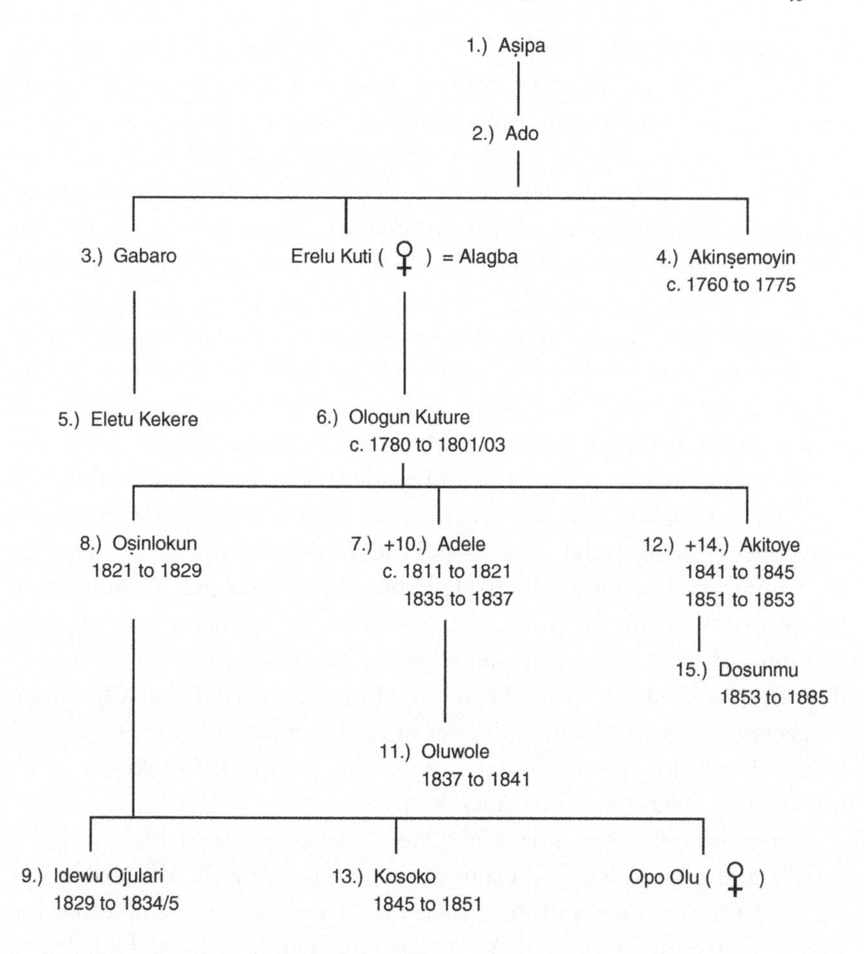

Figure 1. Genealogy of the *Ọbas* of Lagos.

Oba," and pronounced that he should reign after him in gratitude to Alagba for helping to deal with resistance from "chiefs," probably of the *ìdẹ́jọ* grade, and to his sister Erelu Kuti for marrying Alagba and keeping him at the palace.[74] Ologun Kuture, who occupied the throne during the expansion of the slave trade in the 1780s, is remembered as "a good king" who "reigned well over his people."[75]

When Ologun Kuture died soon after the turn of the nineteenth century, a protracted dispute broke out between two of his sons, Oṣinlokun and Adele. Both local traditions and contemporary European accounts identify Oṣinlokun, the elder, as the rightful heir, but Adele was crowned. Some oral and written sources indicate that Ologun Kuture wanted Adele to succeed because the boy had served him faithfully and become his favorite. Losi identifies Adele's service with care of his father's property, the Lander brothers with mechanical aptitude. These sources suggest in addition, however, that "the elders" or "a powerful party" also supported Adele's selection.[76] Another version of the oral traditions claims that initially Oṣinlokun did not want the *ọba*-ship. Wood states that the prince loved "money and held some position," undoubtedly in the expanding slave trade of the early nineteenth century, "which brought him good income." Wood maintains that Oṣinlokun feared that succession to the *ọba*-ship would increase his expenses and render his wealth "public money," a valid concern given that in many Yoruba kingdoms no distinction was drawn between the public coffers and the private income of the king.[77] A contemporary European, John Houtson, maintained that Oṣinlokun in fact placed Adele on the throne, because the former "had money enough, and did not wish to be troubled with the affairs of government further than in giving advice to his brother." Houtson asserted that Oṣinlokun "expected to have the sole direction of affairs, whilst his brother should have held all the responsibility."[78] At the very least, Oṣinlokun appears initially not to have opposed Adele's succession.

Later, however, the powerful older brother changed his mind and sought to depose Adele and claim the crown for himself. War broke out between the two men and their followers. Houtson maintained that the trouble started because after Adele was crowned, he "showed a spirit of independence" and "a capacity for both trade and government" that were incompatible with Oṣinlokun's interests.[79] Local traditions recall that around this time Adele "changed his mode of government" and the chiefs "grew tired" of his behavior toward them. They note, moreover, that his children introduced the *egúngún* masquerade, an Oyo ancestral cult that spread among western Yoruba-speakers at the time of Oyo colonization in the eighteenth century and was regarded in Lagos as "unbecoming to the dignity of a king." Adele is also said to have allowed Islam to spread unchecked, a development rendered more threatening perhaps by the 1817 slave revolt in Oyo.[80] These failings convinced the chiefs to invite Oṣinlokun, then in exile, home to become king. In the fighting that ensued, "the people" deserted Adele, and he and his immediate entourage fled to Badagry, where the local inhabitants made him the king they had never had. Between c. 1821 and 1835, while based at Badagry, Adele attacked Lagos intermittently in an effort to regain possession of the kingdom, but his troops ultimately suffered brutal defeat. When an explosion of gunpowder blew up his house, destroyed his property, and killed many of his dependents, the former *ọba* sank into despair.[81]

The conflict between Ọṣinlokun and Adele began between 1811 and 1820, years of recession in the external slave trade. Although there is no direct evidence to support the hypothesis, Ọṣinlokun's change of heart about the *ọba*-ship may have followed from the decline in the trade, which would have made commerce a less attractive calling and perhaps increased the appeal of serving as monarch. The recession may also have contributed to Adele's loss of popularity. Early in his reign, following years of relative prosperity in the slave trade, Adele is said to have been very generous, but he is remembered as having become harsh and arrogant by the time the conflict broke out with Ọṣinlokun.[82] The altered opinion of the king may reflect reductions in royal largess imposed by declining revenue, increases in taxes demanded from his subjects to offset lost income, or a combination of the two.

After Ọṣinlokun died in 1829, his son Idewu Ojulari became king. Idewu is said to have been unpopular because of his extreme avarice toward "his people" and "the elders," which may itself have been influenced by another sudden downturn in the slave trade following years of prosperity in the second half of Ọṣinlokun's reign. The chiefs communicated their displeasure with Idewu to the *ọba* of Benin, who sent him a skull, a sword, and a message that "the people of Lagos would no longer recognize him as their King." Seeing in the skull an invitation to take poison and in the sword a call to arms, the *ọba* chose the former and committed suicide soon after.[83]

Idewu died childless, but he had an able and ambitious brother, Kosoko, who might have succeeded had he not earlier offended a powerful chief, the Eletu Odibo. As head of the *àkárìgbèrè* class of officeholders, the Eletu Odibo was vested with authority to oversee the selection and installation of *ọbas*. Kosoko allegedly married a woman betrothed to the Eletu, and in consequence incurred his enmity.[84] A bitter and intractable feud developed between the two men and their supporters, which altered the succession on three occasions, divided the kingdom into opposing factions, and set the stage for the British occupation of the town in 1851.

With Kosoko unacceptable to the Eletu Odibo, the chiefs invited Adele home from Badagry to rule a second time. Adele reigned but two years and then died. Once again Kosoko might have succeeded; indeed some versions of the tradition identify him as the rightful heir. But once again the Eletu Odibo blocked his selection, and Oluwole, Adele's son, became *ọba* instead. The Eletu's vendetta then spread to Kosoko's wealthy sister Opo Olu, "owner of 1,400 slaves," whom the chief accused of witchcraft and causing the deaths of children.[85] Diviners found her innocent, but the king banished her nonetheless, leading Kosoko, Oṣinlokun's other children, and their followers, including Opo Olu's many slaves, to declare war on Oluwole and the Eletu Odibo. During the conflict, Kosoko resolved to remove Oluwole and seize the throne himself, but he was defeated and fled to Ouidah, home of his mother's father. While Kosoko was in exile, the Eletu "insulted him in the way most calculated to wound his feelings and bring him into contempt with the people." The chief had the remains of Kosoko's mother dug up and thrown into the lagoon. From that time on, according to tradition, "the . . . most undisguised hatred existed between the two men," and the feeling spread to their supporters.[86]

Soon afterward, Oluwole was killed when lightening triggered an explosion of gunpowder at the *ìgá*, or palace. The king's body was "blown to pieces" and could be identified only by "the royal beads" that adorned it.[87] This calamity serves as a fitting metaphor for the conflict between Kosoko and the Eletu, which had already begun to weaken the kingdom. For in Yoruba and Edo, as in many other African cultures, the body of the king symbolized the welfare of the polity.[88]

Tradition maintains that Kosoko might then have been called upon to reign, but his whereabouts were unknown. Instead, Akitoye, a younger son of Ologun Kuture and uncle of Kosoko, was crowned. In an effort at reconciliation, the new *ọba* located his nephew and announced that he intended to invite him home. The chiefs protested, none more forcefully than the Eletu Odibo, but Akitoye would not listen. Kosoko soon returned to Lagos in the ship of a famous West African slave trader, José Domingo Martinez.[89] Akitoye tried to appease his nephew, giving him gifts, granting him the title of *ọlọ́jà* of Ereko, or owner of Ereko market, and allowing him to establish a court at Lagos. Convinced that the town was not big enough for both of them, the Eletu Odibo departed for Badagry with many of his followers. When Akitoye insisted on the chief's return, Kosoko vowed to "make himself king" if his enemy reentered Lagos. He sent a crier around the town singing, "Tell that little child at court yonder to be careful; for if he is not careful he will be punished." Akitoye's crier replied, "I am like a pin firmly driven into the ground, which is always hard to root out but ever remain[s] firm." Kosoko's crier returned, "I am the digger who always root[s] out a pin."[90] Important chiefs and powerful warriors lined up on both sides—the Aṣogbon and lesser *àbàgbọ́n* or war chiefs behind Akitoye and the Oloto, other *ìdẹ́jọ* or landowning chiefs, and Oshodi Tapa, Ajenia, and Iposu—powerful warriors—behind Kosoko.[91]

War soon broke out between the two factions. Akitoye at last persuaded the Eletu Odibo to come home from Badagry, and he also appealed to the Egba for assistance. Kosoko sought help from Dahomey and Ijebu. These alliances drew Lagos into the broader regional conflagration. During the battle that ensued, Kosoko's forces burned the town and then surrounded the *ọba*'s troops, cutting off their supply of fresh water, which forced them to drink sea water and gave the encounter its name: *Ìjà Omiró*, or "the battle of salt water."[92] Kosoko's supporters subsequently captured the Eletu Odibo and, according to some versions of the tradition, took him to the middle of the lagoon and drowned him, in retaliation for his desecration of the remains of Kosoko's mother. Next Kosoko demanded Akitoye's head. As the *ọba*'s army was in disarray, his backers advised him to flee, and soon thereafter Akitoye embarked in a canoe for Abeokuta, home of his mother, leaving the kingdom to Kosoko.

From Abeokuta, Akitoye subsequently moved to Badagry, where he drew newly arrived Church Missionary Society (CMS) missionaries and eventually Britain's navy and its consul for the Bight of Benin into the conflict on his side.[93] In time, British forces defeated Kosoko, drove him and his war captains into exile at Epe on the northeastern shore of the lagoon, and reinstalled Akitoye, as we shall see in the third chapter, but at the high price of the permanent loss of the kingdom's autonomy.

The slave trade was not exclusively responsible for the deep-seated tensions among Lagos's rulers that local traditions encode so dramatically. The origins of these conflicts lay in the contested process of the growth of the state itself. This process began with the incorporation of the heads of local communities into the *ìdẹ́jọ* chieftaincy system. It continued through Benin's imposition of a new royal dynasty that stood in uneasy relationship to the *ìdẹ́jọ* chieftaincy families and the simultaneous introduction of classes of administrative and military chiefs identified with the development of royal authority. Founded only toward the end of the seventeenth century, the new dynasty was young, moreover, and rules of succession never became so firmly established that they could not be subverted by *ọbas* wanting to choose their successor, by powerful princes vying for the crown, or by an Eletu Odibo bent on preventing a personal enemy from becoming king.

Despite the ideological legitimation that myths tracing the ruling dynasty to Ile-Ife and installation and other rituals introduced from Benin provided the kingship, the structure of power in Lagos in certain ways paralleled that in Dahomey. Edna Bay has shown that there the monarchy should be thought of not as a single individual, but rather as a coalition of actors powerful enough to seize and hold the palace. She regards the Dahomian monarchy as a metaphor for a small and fluid group of individuals, and the king as one of a small number of royal sons who proved his worth and earned his office by forging decisive alliances with other prominent people. Much the same was true in Lagos, and this reality compounded the other sources of instability within the kingdom.[94]

Yet if the slave trade did not create the tensions that racked the young kingdom, local traditions contain powerful hints that it affected them. The commerce is identified explicitly with Akinṣemoyin's accession to the throne. It was also undoubtedly the source of the property valued so highly by Ologun Kuture that its good care led him to favor Adele over the rightful heir, Oṣinlokun. Then, too, it was slaves and their traders from the north who introduced Islam, the spread of which contributed to Adele's loss of popularity.[95] The slave trade figures further as a source of royal power in the crucial support that Opo Olu received from her many slaves and in Kosoko's triumphant return to Lagos in the ship of José Domingo Martinez. In addition, the story of Oṣinlokun shows vividly that wealth acquired through the slave trade had the power to turn men's heads from public duty to private gain, to their detriment and that of the kingdom. But most symbolically, gunpowder, a substance acquired through the slave trade, twice destroyed prominent royals, and in the second instance the victim was a reigning *ọba*, the embodiment of the kingdom itself.

What then was the relationship between the dramatic growth of the slave trade at Lagos and the history of the kingdom recorded in its traditions? To answer this question it is necessary to know how the slave trade was conducted, who profited from it, and what those who benefited did with their new income. Answers to these questions will further illuminate the growth and transformation of the precolonial state, as well as the changing place of slavery in the local political economy.

2

Trade, Oligarchy, and the Transformation of the Precolonial State

The rise of the slave trade at Lagos increased the income of its *ọbas* and a number of its leading chiefs. These individuals used their new wealth to expand their commercial activities and augment their military and political power, which strengthened their position within the kingdom and made the state a more significant player in regional affairs. During the era of the external slave trade, Lagos's rulers also invested in large numbers of slaves for their own use, and slavery acquired new importance in the local political economy as a means of organizing not only labor in trade and production, but also military and political support. Despite the growing power and prestige of the state, its ruling oligarchy was deeply divided internally, and tensions in the capital erupted intermittently into civil war.

This chapter examines the interrelationship of the rise of the slave trade at Lagos, the growth and development of the precolonial state, and the history of conflict within it that eventually contributed to colonization by Great Britain. The analysis also sheds new light on the changing place of slavery in coastal society relative to other means of accumulating dependents. The investigation begins with a discussion of the organization of the external slave trade and its impact on the distribution of wealth and power within the local community.

The Conduct of the External Slave Trade

Lagosians dominated the trade in slaves shipped from their town throughout the history of the commerce there. Unlike on certain other parts of the African coast, neither foreigners, nor Euro-Africans, nor powerful rulers in the interior succeeded in breaking the control of these coastal people over the sale of slaves at their port.[1]

The foreign slave trade was not a royal or state monopoly at Lagos. From the time of its origin until abolition, private individuals could engage in the commerce on their own behalf. However, *ọbas*, other members of the ruling oligarchy, and a few favored free and slave supporters of both enjoyed clear advantages in the trade and enriched themselves through it. Virtually all of the prominent slave traders who can be identified at Lagos throughout the history of the commerce there were close to the center of political and military power in the kingdom. If not *ọbas*, they were members of the royal lineage, prominent chiefs, or wives, clients, or slaves of royals and chiefs. Benjamin Campbell, a British consul at Lagos in the 1850s, observed that the slave trade in the town had been confined to "the king, his chiefs, and principal people."[2] Moreover, people outside the state hierarchy who became wealthy through the trade were normally incorporated into it by having titles—usually of the war grade—bestowed upon them.

Lagos warriors captured a number of the slaves shipped from the town, although the proportion of exports acquired in local wars declined as the commerce expanded after 1800. The small states along the Slave Coast fought intermittently throughout the late eighteenth and early nineteenth centuries, and Dahomey, Oyo, Ijebu, and other inland powers sometimes intervened in these wars as allies on one side or another. In addition, political conflicts within the kingdom itself exploded periodically into open warfare. Consul Campbell maintained that a "constant succession of civil wars" had resulted in the destruction of the kingdom and the enslavement "of a great portion of its inhabitants."[3] Detailed information about the distribution of war captives does not survive, but the available evidence suggests that they were shared among the *ọba*, war chiefs who led the campaign, and warriors who seized the slaves. The strong identification of *àbàgbọ̀n* (war) chiefs with the slave trade in popular memory underscores the relationship between warfare and the supply of slaves for sale.[4] The *ọba*'s and warrior elite's control over captives seized in battle gave them preferential access to slaves for export, which worked to their commercial advantage.

Ọbas, claimants to the crown, and certain chiefs also received slaves as gifts and tribute. The king of Dahomey, for example, sent Ologun Kuture "bribes," including a number of slaves, to persuade him to join an attack on Badagry in 1784, and the defeated town subsequently paid Lagos tribute in slaves and other commodities. The Lander brothers reported, moreover, that when Porto Novo and Badagry reached a peace agreement in 1830, the king of Porto Novo sent slaves to Adele at Badagry. *Ọbas* redistributed some of the slaves they received to their supporters, including important chiefs, as they did war captives.[5] Access to slaves received as gifts and tribute also gave kings and other members of the political elite advantages in the supply of slaves for sale.

Most slaves shipped from the port of Lagos were obtained, however, not through warfare, tribute, kidnapping, or other direct means, but through trade. Lagosians involved in the commerce traveled by canoe to slave markets on the northern shore of the lagoon, which were fed by the changing networks of supply in the interior. There they bought slaves and transported them to the island for sale. So long as Oyo sent the majority of its slaves to Badagry and Porto Novo, they remained the major sites of trade on the mainland. But when Oyo began selling slaves through Ijebu in the late eighteenth century and warfare broke out among the Yoruba states in the nineteenth century, the principal slave markets moved to Ikorodu, Ikosi, and Epe.[6]

Some Lagos traders also frequented slave markets up the rivers that flowed into the lagoon, proceeding as far as Abeokuta after the town's founding by the Egba in 1830.[7] Captain John Adams, who visited Lagos in the 1790s, provided a description of the organization of trade at the town that remained accurate throughout the era of the slave trade. He wrote, "It has always been the policy of the Lagos people . . . to be themselves the traders and not the brokers. They therefore go in their canoes to Ardah and Badagry, and to the towns situate at the N.E. extremity of the Crodoo lake, where they purchase slaves, Jaboo cloth, and such articles as are required for domestic consumption." Adams's distinction between traders and brokers refers to the fact that Lagosians conducted business on their own behalf, assuming risk, absorbing loss, and enjoying profits, not as agents of foreign buyers or interior sellers who received only a commission or share of the profits.[8]

The narratives of Samuel Ajayi Crowther and Joseph Wright, both shipped as slaves from Lagos before being freed by the British Antislavery Squadron and subsequently educated in Sierra Leone, provide slave perspectives that further illuminate the organization of commerce between the port and the interior. Crowther, later a renowned CMS missionary, remembered being bought by Lagos traders at Ikosi sometime around 1822, loaded into a canoe among "corn-bags," and shipped overnight to Lagos. He recorded that "the sight of the river terrified" him, and he barely moved during the nocturnal journey.[9] Wright, captured in Egbaland in the late 1820s, recounted being marched one day to a riverside slave market and lined up with hundreds of other slaves so that they "could be seen at one view by the buyers." In about five hours a Lagos trader purchased him, loaded him into a canoe, and then transported him overnight to the Ikorodu slave market. There Wright sat in the canoe all day, while the owner bought more slaves. When the vessel was "quite loaded" with human cargo it departed, also under cover of night, for Lagos.[10]

Lagos's island location at the mouth of a large lagoon and network of creeks and rivers connecting the coast and mainland markets dictated that water transportation was essential to the conduct of the slave trade at the town. The ability of Lagos's slave traders to organize and control water transportation between the port and the major slave markets on the mainland secured their role as middlepeople in the commerce. The foreign buyers, who until the abolition of the legal trade in the early nineteenth century anchored their ships offshore and subsequently began stationing resident agents in the town, did not frequent the mainland slave markets until the very end of the trade, and then only in limited numbers. Ijebu and certain other interior traders who themselves possessed canoes sometimes brought slaves to Lagos for sale, but the kingdom's rulers did not permit them direct access to foreign buyers.

From the inception of the external slave trade at Lagos, *ọbas* exercised a measure of administrative control over the commerce, which gave them advantages in its conduct. Akinṣemoyin first brought foreign slave traders to Lagos when he returned from exile to became king, and subsequently European and Brazilian buyers needed permission from the ruler to do business at the port. The captain of a French ship that anchored off the town in the reign of Ologun Kuture noted that "the king was absent" and trade could not commence until he returned.[11] A Portuguese observer wrote in 1807 that whereas Ologun Kuture had welcomed foreigners "with open arms," in the interregnum following his death Prince Oṣinlokun "turned out [shipments] on a thousand pretexts," indicating that he had the power to refuse trade.[12] Once greater numbers of foreign slave traders began living at Lagos following legal abolition, to accumulate slaves on shore for rapid loading in hopes of escaping detection by the British Anti-slavery Squadron, they remained in the town at the pleasure of the king.[13] Moreover, they depended on him for protection and many kinds of assistance. In short, most of the *ọbas* who reigned during the era of the slave trade exercised some control over the commerce in human beings.

On the western Slave Coast, the kings of Allada, Ouidah, and Dahomey had earlier enjoyed privileges in the slave trade and sometimes extended them to the officials who conducted business on their behalf. At Allada and Ouidah, kings had claimed the right to trade first, before Europeans bought slaves from anyone else, and they had commonly received a higher price for their slaves than other sellers. Moreover, Europeans had been compelled to take as many slaves as the kings wanted to sell, regardless of their quality. After kings, royal officials had enjoyed precedence in the commerce.[14] Because they traded first, these kings and officials had enjoyed the pick of imported goods offered in exchange for slaves, which gave them a competitive advantage in purchasing slaves. A European trader on the coast succinctly expressed the ongoing importance of attractive combinations of imports in buying slaves when he instructed a superior, "get me good assortments as you may depend by good assortments you'll get good slaves and more of them."[15]

The data for Lagos are not as extensive as those for the major ports to the west, because the town was a center of the slave trade for a shorter period, most of which fell during the era of the illegal trade when business was conducted covertly. The only hard evidence currently available that Lagos's *ọbas* enjoyed privileges in the slave trade comes from a French document written in the reign of Kosoko, which notes that 31 percent more had to be paid for slaves purchased from the king than for those bought from common citizens.[16] Yet it is likely, given their administrative control over the trade and growing if uneven power, that Lagos's kings sought and the strong among them could enforce commercial advantages similar to those enjoyed by their royal counterparts to the west. It is surely no accident that Akinṣemoyin, Ologun Kuture, Oṣinlokun, Akitoye, and Kosoko are remembered as among Lagos's biggest slave traders, although the commerce conducted by the last three greatly exceeded that of the first two.

At the same time, *ọbas* did not have, could not have had, and most of them probably did not even want an exclusive right to trade slaves. In the first place, commerce on the scale of that conducted throughout the first half of the nineteenth century required capital resources and presented logistical challenges that *ọbas* alone could not have met. The necessary resources included canoes to transport slaves, people and weapons to guard them, storage facilities to hold them, and food and water to keep them alive until they were sold to foreigners on the coast or shipped to commission agents in Bahia. The demands of water transportation alone underscore the logistical challenges. The canoe journey to Badagry, the closest major market, took six to eight hours, depending on the tides, winds, and currents, while that to Ikosi, an intermediate market, required up to seventeen hours. If traders ascended the rivers on the mainland, they needed even more time; Abeokuta was as much as four days away. Once the markets had been reached, buying and selling took additional time, and then the slaves had to be transported back to Lagos. The canoes that made the journeys varied in size, but some were as long as eighty feet, required a crew of thirteen, and carried up to a hundred slaves.[17]

Ọbas mobilized the resources and labor that they needed to trade on a large scale and surmounted the logistical and organizational problems that such commerce presented by using prominent chiefs, loyal clients, and trusted palace slaves (*ibigâ*) to conduct much of their business for them. These agents employed their own canoes, arms, storage facilities, and family and non-family labor, as well as resources and dependents of *ọbas* themselves, in the conduct of royal trade. They were also allowed to trade slaves and other goods on their own behalf, to reward them for their good service, maintain their loyalty, and further promote the kingdom's commercial development. The founders of the Suenu, Basua, Egbe Alaṣe, and Faji chieftaincy families came to Lagos with Akinṣemoyin when he returned from the west. They supported him in commercial, religious, and ritual activities, accumulated wealth through their own pursuits, and were soon given war titles and allowed to build palaces in Lagos.[18] Holders of the Aṣogbon chieftaincy title, who headed the war grade, are remembered by their descendants as having organized the slave trade of nineteenth-century kings. At the same time, they themselves traded heavily in slaves and other goods.[19]

Kosoko, on the other hand, apparently used palace slaves to handle most of his business. These slaves included Dada Antonio, Oshodi Tapa, and Ojo Akanbi, the first two of whom had traded for his father and all three of whom eventually traded on their own behalf as well, Oshodi Tapa on a large scale. Each of these slaves is remembered as having been an important war captain, and Oshodi Tapa was in time granted an hereditary *àbàgbọ̀n* title.[20] Kosoko's reliance on palace slaves to conduct his trade represented a shift away from using prominent chiefs, and it helped concentrate wealth and power in the hands of the *ọba* and those directly dependent on him. During Kosoko's reign, slaves sold by the king's "caboceers," which is normally translated as "chiefs" but may in this context mean simply "royally approved traders," commanded the same higher price as those bought from the *ọba* himself. This concession gave certain of the king's slaves a strong incentive to serve him faithfully.[21]

Princes, princesses, and royal wives also participated in the slave trade and were, in some cases, encouraged to do so by the king. Ọṣinlokun is said to have been schooled in the "arts of trade" as a boy, presumably with his father Ologun Kuture's approval, and he became one of the biggest slave traders during the early nineteenth century boom in the traffic before being crowned king.[22] Kosoko, Ọṣinlokun's son, also became a major trader in slaves and other goods while still a prince. Moreover, part of the income that paid for Kosoko's sister Opo Olu's many slaves was probably earned through the slave trade. Although information about royal wives is limited, the famous Madame Tinubu traded slaves and other goods and began her commercial ascent while she was Ọba Adele's wife, even though her greatest success occurred after his death.[23]

Why, beyond the practical reason that by the 1780s the volume of trade required it, did *ọbas* promote participation in the slave trade and indeed other types of commerce by other members of the political and military elite? They did so in part, certainly, to stimulate the commercial development of the kingdom and its capital, which through tolls on trade and other taxes enriched the monarchy and enhanced the power and prestige of the state. Trade, after all, is what was literally putting Lagos on the map regionally and internationally, and *ọbas* alone could not have realized the port's full commercial potential. But kings had a further reason to promote the economic success of promising princes and other members of the royal household, with which the monarchy was identified in the public imagination and on which its wealth and power rested in the first instance. Family and household were the place where accumulation and hierarchy began for Lagos's kings, just as they were for its common people. *Ọbas* generated significant revenue for the royal coffers both through their own economic activities and through transfers of resources from royal kin and wives, as well as from other dependents within the palace. The more successful these people were, the more that could be extracted from them. A rich and powerful king was unthinkable without a large and prosperous royal household.

An additional dynamic motivated kings and ambitious princes to encourage and facilitate participation in the slave trade by certain members of their retinues. In the century between 1750 and 1850, the royal family was often bitterly divided by succession disputes and policy questions, and periodically the conflicts wracked the palace itself. While rules of succession influenced the selection of *ọbas*, formal procedures existed for choosing them, and elaborate rituals were supposed to be performed to install them, these normative practices were not always followed.[24] In the first half of the nineteenth century, the power of particular princes to seize and hold the palace several times decided who would reign. In local political culture, the power of individual princes, and indeed of *ọbas* themselves, rested not only on the support of their own children, wives, slaves, and other dependents, but also on that of the coalition of people—other royals, prominent chiefs, and important commoners—allied with them. Princes who vied for the crown, and *ọbas* who wore it and wanted to keep it on their heads, recognized that they needed to build not only their own wealth and power but also that of their close backers. *Ọbas* and ambitious princes therefore saw it as in their best interest to open opportunities associated with the slave trade to certain members of their coalitions. A reciprocal relationship existed between the wealth and power of leading contenders for the crown and that of their key supporters.[25]

If opportunities existed in the slave trade for non-royals, particularly those close to the center of political power, a number of factors also restricted large-scale commerce to a relative few. For one thing, the labor and capital resources needed to handle large numbers of slaves were beyond the means of most common people. Private individuals could break into the trade by buying and selling a few slaves at a time and, if able and lucky, make money, carefully invest their profits, and become bigger traders; but such upward commercial mobility usually took time and was risky. Those who succeeded in establishing themselves as substantial traders were commonly recruited into the coalition of one member of the ruling oligarchy or another, and some ultimately had war chieftaincy titles conferred on them, so that they ceased to be private citizens. Beyond the labor and capital resources required to trade slaves in large numbers, however, capital was also needed in the form of imported goods and currencies to exchange for them. Many of the imported commodities—textiles, tobacco, spirits, hardware, and cowries—used to buy slaves were supplied on credit by foreign traders, who understandably preferred to grant it to well-known and reputable local merchants or to those who came with good introductions from royal officials or old established business partners.[26] *Ọbas*, princes, prominent chiefs, and other well-known merchants, or those sponsored by such people, enjoyed clear advantages in access to foreign credit, which in turn facilitated their predominance in the slave trade.

One further reality helped concentrate large-scale slave trading in the hands of a few. Some of the slaves shipped from the port were brought down to the coast by traders from the interior. *Ọbas* restricted the access of these people to foreign buyers in the interest of monopolizing the role of middleman for Lagosians, although official control may have diminished once greater numbers of foreigners began living in the town after legal abolition.[27] While in the port, interior traders, like their Atlantic counterparts, depended on locals for services, such as protection, housing, credit, brokerage, and warehousing. Visitors normally turned for such help to prominent men and women, if not *ọbas* themselves then state officials, influential chiefs, or other well-established merchants. The first Eletu Ijebu was appointed, for example, in the reign of Akinṣemoyin to deal with the growing number of Ijebu traders who were bringing slaves and other goods to the town.[28] In the 1840s, Madame Tinubu and her husband Obadina housed and otherwise assisted Egba who brought human and other wares to Lagos for sale.[29] These hosts did not necessarily buy their guests' commodities themselves, but they helped them make good commercial contacts and facilitated their business transactions. The superior ability of big men and women to perform the services expected of hosts for traders from the interior also helped funnel slaves through established commercial networks.

A number of factors, then, mitigated against the creation of a royal monopoly over the slave trade at Lagos. These included the logistical, financial, and labor requirements of the trade, the dictates of royal accumulation, and the dynamics of local political culture. Yet at the same time, the economic requirements of the trade, coupled with the administrative control that *ọbas* exercised over it, helped ensure that the commerce was dominated by a limited number of men and women near the center of political power who enjoyed substantial advantages in its conduct.

The Accumulation of Wealth by the Ruling Oligarchy

The growth of the external slave trade at Lagos brought substantial new income into the town. Data on slave prices on the African coast can be used with the figures on slave exports in table 1.2 to estimate income from the trade. Two sets of price data are available for the purpose. The first, calculated by David Eltis, provides the price in constant dollars (1821 through 1825 equals $100) of an "average" slave on the African coast for five-year periods from 1815 through 1865.[30] The second, calculated by Paul E. Lovejoy and David Richardson, gives the real price of slaves on the West African coast in pounds sterling between 1783 and 1850, also in five-year intervals, although unfortunately the dates of Lovejoy and Richardson's periods do not correspond with those of my figures on slave exports.[31]

Table 2.1 repeats estimates of slave exports from Lagos in column two, gives Eltis's price data converted into pounds sterling in column three, and gives Lovejoy and Richardson's price data in column four.[32] It then calculates two series of data on income from the slave trade between 1816 and 1855 by multiplying the export and price figures. The first series, derived from Eltis's converted data, appears in column five, while the second, based on Lovejoy and Richardson's data, can be found in column six. These two sets of income estimates are inexact, because of limitations in the price and export data on which they are based. The evidence in them nonetheless suffices to demonstrate major trends. Two reassuring facts emerge from the table. The first is that the trends in the two series run parallel, except for the years 1821 to 1825 and 1841 to 1845. The second is that if a king list is set alongside the income data, as in column seven, peaks and troughs in income from the foreign slave trade correspond with the reigns of *ọbas* who are remembered in the oral traditions as important slave traders, in the first case, or unsuccessful, parsimonious, or greedy rulers, in the second.

Income before 1816 cannot be estimated, because the dates of the export and price data do not correspond. Even so, the fact that both the volume of exports and the price of slaves rose from the mid-1780s through about 1790 indicates that income from the external slave trade grew significantly during those important years of Ologun Kuture's reign. This period of prosperity was followed, however, by a recession in the external slave trade in the later years of Ologun Kuture's rule. A huge increase in slave exports and a substantial jump in slave prices immediately followed, generating a big increase in income from the commerce between 1801 and at least 1807, a period that subsumes much of the interregnum between Ologun Kuture and Adele. Decline occurred once again between 1811 and 1820, in Adele's first reign, when the price of slaves declined by almost half and the volume also dipped in many years. Recovery did not commence once more until the second half of the 1820s, during Ọṣinlokun's final years, but at that time income from the external slave trade soared to unprecedented heights, reaching £343,400 to £547,000. There followed another sharp decline of about 60 percent between 1831 and 1835, the period of Idewu Ojulare's unsuccessful rule and subsequent suicide. Income from the external slave trade recovered again after 1836, during Adele's short second reign and Oluwole's ill-fated kingship. It may have held steady during Akitoye's first regime, before jumping dramatically in the final years of the commerce during Kosoko's rule. At that time, the volume of exports and price of slaves were both high and income

Table 2.1 Estimated Income from the External Slave Trade at Lagos, 1781–1855 (in thousands)

Date	*Slaves (in 1000's)*	*Eltis's Price Data (£ Sterling)*	*Lovejoy and Richardson's Price Data (£ Sterling)*	*Income I (£ Sterling)*	*Income II (£ Sterling)*	*King List*
1761–65	.3					
1766–70	2.9					
1771–75	1.8					
1776–80	2.2					
1781–85	3.9					
			15.6 ('83–87)			
1786–90	14.1					
			19.1 ('88–92)			
1791–95	4.2					Ologun Kuture (1780–1802)
			17.5 ('93–97)			
1796–1800	3.3					
			23.3 ('98–02)			
1801–05	21.4					
			25.3 ('03–07)			Interregnum between Kuture and Adele
1806–10	28.4					
			14.2 ('08–14)			
1811–15	20.6					
1816–20	22.7	5.5	7.7 ('15–20)	124.8	174.8	Adele (c. 1811–21)
1821–25	17.7	6.9	11.0	122.1	194.7	Oşinlokun (1821–29)
1826–30	31.8	10.8	17.2	343.4	547.0	Idewu Ojulari (1829–34/35)
1831–35	16.3	7.8	12.9	127.1	210.3	Adele (1835–37)
1836–40	27.6	10.6	18.5	292.6	510.6	Oluwole (1837–41)
1841–45	35.0	6.7	16.7	234.5	584.5	Akitoye (1841–45)
1846–50	37.7	13.9	23.1	524.0	870.9	Kosoko (1845–51)
1851–55	5.4	9.0	—	48.6	—	

Sources: The number of slaves comes from table 1.2

The price data can be found in Eltis, *Economic Growth*, 263; and Lovejoy and Richardson, "The Initial 'Crisis' of Adaptation," 35.

from the trade soared to £524,000 using Eltis's price data and £870,900 using Lovejoy and Richardson's.

No data are available on which to base even a crude estimate of what proportion of the income from the slave trade went to different types of traders. However, most of the profits were shared by *ọbas* and other members of the ruling oligarchy, who dominated the sale of slaves at Lagos. When the volume of exports and price of slaves were both high, these individuals made substantial money from the commerce.

Beyond what *ọbas* earned from their own traffic in slaves, they also derived revenue from taxes on the trade. These imposts, often referred to as "custom" in contemporary documents, took different forms. As elsewhere on the Slave Coast, fees were sometimes levied on ships that unloaded and loaded commodities at the port, and duties could also be charged on exports. Captain Adams complained that "duties," normally paid in imported goods and currencies, were "exorbitant" at Lagos.[33] A Brazilian who in 1807 supplied commercial intelligence to the governor of Bahia stated that during the interregnum between Ologun Kuture and Adele, Ọṣinlokun insisted on "contributions from the captains [of ships]," without which he did not "authorize them to negotiate."[34] Robertson observed that prior to British abolition "a tenth of the value of every article sold to Europeans was paid to the Cabocier," but that subsequently duties were more moderate and were "regulated by agreement."[35] If Robertson was correct, then the duty on slaves sold at Lagos may have been worth as much as £85,000 between 1801 and 1807.

Not until the reign of Kosoko does more precise information exist about the value of taxes levied on foreign traders. Table 2.2 includes the amounts that the French document from Kosoko's reign referred to above said each ship had to pay the king of Lagos. The figures in the two right-hand columns convert each tax into its equivalent value in slaves at the king's and common citizens' prices.

Assuming that Akitoye levied similar taxes on the thirty-two vessels that loaded slaves at Lagos between 1841 and 1845, he generated between £1,587 and £3,955 in revenue, converting the value in slaves at the king's prices into pounds sterling using the price data in table 2.1. Kosoko generated revenue of between £2,771 and £4,473 from the twenty-eight ships that loaded slaves at Lagos between 1846 and 1851, according to similar calculations.[36] The French document makes no mention of duties levied on slaves or other exports. It is clear, however, that during the 1850s the *ọbas* of Lagos charged foreign traders fixed fees for the privilege of living and trading in the town and also taxed palm oil, ivory, and other exports

Table 2.2 Taxes Imposed on Foreign Slave Traders by Kosoko

Tax in trade ounces	*Value in Slaves**	*Value in Slaves***
60 oz. for the "disembarkation" of the ship	3.5	4.6
36 oz. for the "house and domestics" of the king	2.1	2.8
20 oz. for the "hat and umbrella" of the king	1.2	1.5
10 oz. for the embarkation of the ship	.6	.75
Total	7.4	9.65

* at king's prices; ** at citizens' prices
Source: Castro de Araújo, "1846," 457.

leaving the port. Kosoko, like a number of his predecessors, probably imposed export duties as well, further increasing his income.[37]

Ọbas shared a portion of the taxes they levied on trade with the state officials who collected them. Early in the history of the kingdom such officials were drawn from the ranks of the *ìdẹ́jọ*, *àkárìgbèrè*, and *àbàgbọ́n* chiefs, but by Kosoko's reign, and perhaps even before it, some of them were palace slaves (*ibigá*). Oshodi Tapa is remembered as having become "a rich man" while collecting tolls on foreign trade, although the traditions erroneously date this service.[38] The disposition of the taxes for the "house and domestics" of the king is unclear. They may have helped defray the expenses of the king's palace and slaves, which provided hospitality and services to foreign traders. Alternatively, the sum may have been shared among free and slave retainers in the palace who conducted the king's business. Nineteenth-century *ọbas* may have sought to shift the collection of taxes on foreign trade to palace slaves as a way of increasing the king's control over revenue from the slave trade. The transfer of responsibility must have remained incomplete, however, because Consul Campbell reported to British authorities in 1854 that the gift of 134 pounds of cowries that they had sent a number of Lagos chiefs was unsuitable, owing to the fact that the men annually received "several tons of these shells for duty and customs."[39]

In addition to the taxes levied on foreign traders, *ọbas* and other officials also extracted gifts from them as part of the normal, if to Europeans often vexing, social etiquette of doing business on the coast. Portuguese slave traders are said to have given Akinṣemoyin tiles to roof the palace, objects of great value considering that the thatch previously used posed an enormous hazard in a town regularly laid waste by fires.[40] J. F. Landolphe mentioned that when British slave traders enlisted Ologun Kuture's help in attacking his factories at Benin, they gave the *ọba* "large presents." The hand organ, sedan chair, expensive sofas, and chairs of state that Captain Adams saw in the palace may have been gifts from slave traders as well. During Kosoko's reign, presents to the king of three casks of rum, worth 4.6 slaves at ordinary prices, were listed as a normal expense of trading at Lagos.[41]

The Lander brothers were not slave traders, but the gifts they were forced to give Adele and his chiefs while at Badagry nonetheless illustrate the worth of what Africans received from Europeans. Of Adele alone they wrote,

> [E]very thing he took a fancy to, was put into his hands at his own request; but as it would be grossly impolite to return it after it had been soiled by his fingers, with the utmost *non-chalance* the chief delivered it over to the care of his recumbent pages. . . . [I]t grieved us, to observe a large portion of almost every article . . . speedily passing through his hands into those of his juvenile minions. . . . [A]ltogether he has received guns, ammunition, and a variety of goods to the amount of nearly three hundred ounces of gold.

The Lander brothers also grumbled mightily about the frequent visits they had to endure from Adele's chiefs and their retainers, wanting alcohol and tobacco, if not more substantial gifts.[42] The presents that *ọbas*, important chiefs, and other state officials received from foreigners on the coast had great social and political as well as economic value, which subsequent analysis will illuminate. These gifts were given almost exclusively to members of the ruling oligarchy.

The growth of the slave trade at Lagos also stimulated the development of commerce in other goods and of certain kinds of production as well. Most land on the island was not very good for agriculture. Some Lagosians farmed on the mainland, and indeed the number of plots there increased as local households grew in size. However, investment in clearing and working the soil on the mainland was insecure and potentially dangerous so long as the area remained a site of conflict among coastal and inland states. The people of Lagos have depended on imported food throughout their history, for which they traded fish, salt, and a few locally produced craft items during the precolonial period.[43] Slow population growth in the era of the slave trade, combined with the presence in the town of foreign traders and trade slaves, both of whom had to be fed (if only minimally in the second case), enlarged the demand for imported food. These changes, along with increased prosperity, also expanded the Lagos market for textiles, canoes, and other items of local manufacture imported from the interior or elsewhere on the coast. Furthermore, slaves were not the only commodities for which foreign markets existed. Ivory was exported to Europe and cloth, beads, black soap, and other goods were shipped to Brazil throughout the era of the slave trade, even though they were less important than slaves. Then during the 1840s the British market for palm oil began to take off.[44] The years between 1760 and 1850 witnessed a substantial expansion of trade in Lagos. Robertson, familiar with the town in the early nineteenth century, praised its people for their "exemplary . . . mercantile energy and assiduity," while also noting that traders from elsewhere came constantly to Lagos to exchange their commodities.[45] In his *Merchant's and Mariner's Guide to Africa*, Edward Bold stressed that Lagos had "a very extensive trade with the interior."[46]

Ọbas and other members of the ruling oligarchy participated in this broader economic expansion during the era of the slave trade using the labor of dependent children, wives, slaves, and other subordinates, as did commoners in the town, who employed mainly family labor. Indeed, slave traders often bought more than one kind of commodity on their journeys to mainland markets, as Samuel Ajayi Crowther's reference to being carried back to Lagos among "corn-bags" suggests. The value of goods produced and traded in the local economy for domestic consumption may have exceeded that of exports in the eras of both the slave and palm produce trades.[47] *Ọbas*, chiefs, and other state officials further increased their incomes during the time of the slave trade and generated revenue for public and private purposes by engaging in trade and production for the domestic market. As the incomes of members of their households grew, moreover, big men and women also benefited by increasing their exactions from people living under their authority.[48]

Ọbas, chiefs, and state officials profited from the growth of trade and prosperity on the eastern Slave Coast in a further way: through increases in domestic taxation. When African traders entered the kingdom from the interior, they paid tolls, which were shared among the king, the chief of the district where they were collected, and the officials who levied them. The expansion of trade between the interior and the port, as well as along the lagoon, must have greatly increased revenue from this source. Citizens of the state also paid taxes to the *ọba* and chiefs—in the form of offerings at annual festivals, fees for appearing in court, labor to build defenses, palaces, and wharfs, and contributions in times of warfare or public calamity.[49] Beyond these levies, *ọbas* received tribute from conquered towns such as Badagry, and chiefs were given payments by residents of rural communities for whom they acted as *bàbá ìsàlẹ̀*, or representatives in the capital city.[50] Insofar as the expansion of trade and production during the era of the slave trade increased the prosperity of commoners on the eastern Slave Coast, *ọbas* and other members of the ruling oligarchy benefited indirectly through increases in taxation.

The above data show that the incomes of Lagos's rulers expanded dramatically during the era of the slave trade in the town, although the growth was uneven and unequal. Qualitative evidence reinforces the quantitative information, demonstrating that the wealth of leading members of the royal family grew significantly during the final decades of the eighteenth and the first half of the nineteenth centuries. John Houtson wrote that Ologun Kuture died "leaving great riches" and that his son Oṣinlokun amassed, while still a prince, "a larger fortune than . . . his father."[51] After becoming king, Oṣinlokun had sufficient money to import luxury goods and capital equipment directly from Brazil. Opo Olu, Oṣinlokun's daughter and Kosoko's sister, was so wealthy that she is remembered as having owned 1,400 slaves.[52] Kosoko himself made more than thirty-seven thousand *mil-réis* in the 1840s by shipping slaves directly to Brazil for sale, enough that he could commission the building of a ship there, pay for the foreign education of three "sons," and finance the importation of many luxuries.[53] Kosoko's income from the direct export of slaves was but the tip of the iceberg, moreover, because he sold the majority of his slaves to foreigners on the African coast.

Slavery and the Expansion of State Power

Lagos's rulers invested their new wealth from the slave trade in resources that expanded their commercial and productive capacity and increased their political and military power. As the might and prestige of *ọbas* and other members of the ruling oligarchy grew, so did the importance of the state in regional and Atlantic affairs.

Despite the fact that much foreign trade was conducted on credit, successful entrepreneurs no doubt reinvested part of their profits in trade goods to perpetuate and with luck expand their commercial enterprises. In addition, however, they bought canoes of different sizes to use in fishing, trade, and warfare. Inhabitants of an island town, the residents of the capital depended on water transportation for intercourse with the mainland and movement along the lagoon. Some canoe owners carried passengers and cargo for a fee, providing mobility to the poorer classes, but as soon as they could afford it, most Lagosians with commercial ambitions bought vessels of their own.[54]

Beyond their role in transportation and trade, canoes manned by armed warriors formed the backbone of Lagos's growing military. *Ọbas*, *àbàgbọ̀n* chiefs, and their war captains all bought large craft for naval use. Dalzel stated that Ologun Kuture, for example, deployed thirty-two large canoes in the campaign against Badagry in 1784; while T. Miles wrote with probable exaggeration nine years later that the same *ọba* had armed six hundred canoes for an attack on that town.[55] Throughout the 1820s, Ọṣinlokun's forces at Lagos and Adele's at Badagry traded naval attacks. Then, in the 1840s and 1850s, Kosoko launched a succession of large naval campaigns, some involving a hundred or more canoes each carrying as many as a hundred men.[56] Investment in such craft for commercial and military use must have been considerable, since the average life of a canoe on the lagoon was only two to three years.[57]

Members of Lagos's ruling oligarchy also spent their new income on arms needed to protect commercial voyages, guard slaves on the lagoon and at Lagos, and further develop the kingdom's military. These weapons included both swords, spears, knives, clubs, and bows and arrows produced locally and swords, muskets, and cannons imported from Brazil and Europe. *Ọbas*, war chiefs, and their war captains faced a large and growing demand for weapons, because they were responsible for equipping most of the soldiers who fought in their armies.[58] The Lander brothers documented the arms buildup among Lagos's rulers when they observed "a great quantity of muskets and swords" suspended from the sides of Adele's apartment at Badagry and remarked that loaded muskets, other firearms, and an "immense quantity of gunpowder" had previously exploded at his house. At the residence of Adele's deceased war chief "Posser," they also saw "muskets and other warlike instruments suspended from the sides."[59]

Many of the canoes used in lagoon warfare were armed with cannons mounted on swivels. *Ọbas* and perhaps a few of the richest war chiefs imported guns for this purpose and also for deployment on land. When discussing Lagos's decisive attack on Badagry in 1793, Robertson mentioned cannons mounted on canoes. In 1824, Ọṣinlokun ordered two batteries of artillery from Brazil, and in 1830, Adele pressured the Lander brothers to order him "two long brass guns to run on swivels," plus muskets, gunpowder, swords, and cutlasses, in return for protection. Europeans at

Badagry reported in 1851 that a hundred of Kosoko's canoes fired swivel guns on the town. When the British invaded Lagos later that year, they seized twenty-five cannons installed between the northern point of the island and the king's house.[60] The slave trade had clearly financed a major arms buildup among Lagos's rulers.

Given the importance of command of people in the local political economy, it is not surprising that in the era of the slave trade members of Lagos's ruling oligarchy also invested their new wealth heavily in social relationships that increased the number of their dependents. The kinds of people that enlarged the households of *ọbas* and chiefs in this period included wives, children, other kin, wards, and strangers as previously, if in increased numbers thanks to the growing wealth and power of the kingdom.

The accumulation of dependents normally began with marriage, which typically required a transfer of gifts and labor known as bridewealth from the family of the husband to that of the wife, and continued through biological reproduction. Marriage marked the moment when children began to define their identities as independent adults, and family relationships were deeply hierarchical. Parents exercised authority over their children, husbands over their wives, and both children and wives were ranked by age and seniority inside the household. People could make claims on the labor and resources of all those subject to their domestic authority.[61]

Polygyny was "integral to the social order," enabling men who could afford it and attract the women to take multiple wives.[62] If fortune smiled upon such individuals, they could also expect to have more children than their social inferiors. During the period of the external slave trade, ambitious men in Lagos used their incomes to marry large numbers of women, which over time dramatically expanded the scale of polygyny and size of families among the ruling elite, since *ọbas* and chiefs typically inherited their predecessors' widows, apart from their own mothers. By the mid-nineteenth century, *ọbas* had hundreds of wives and sometimes dozens of offspring, and prominent chiefs often had large numbers of both as well.[63]

The households of prominent individuals were commonly extended horizontally and vertically, so that they included more than one generation of adults and often siblings, spouses, and offspring within each generation. These compounds thus contained family members beyond wives and children, and such individuals too had obligations to those under whose authority they lived for certain kinds of labor and assistance. Resource flows within households played a vital role in accumulation and mobility.

There were limits, however, to how well marriage, kinship, and reproduction could meet the demands of ambitious men for dependents. Despite the fact that prominent Lagosians commonly drew some of their wives from neighboring towns and polities, in part to cement useful political and commercial alliances, the supply of freeborn women was finite. In their eagerness to snare eligible females, men sometimes robbed their peers and made powerful enemies, as Kosoko discovered. Then too, infertility and infant mortality made reproduction a risky strategy for increasing dependents. Even rich men with several wives sometimes faced the tragedy of remaining childless. Furthermore, social norms and emotional ties restricted what men could comfortably ask of wives, kin, and offspring. If bonds of affection did not ensure that these norms were observed, respected elders, influential affines, or public authorities might intervene and impose restraints. Marriage and reproduction certainly met the needs of ambitious women very imperfectly. On the one hand, wives profited from the assistance of their children after the first three or four years. But on the other, married women were constrained by obligations to their husbands, the men's kin, and senior wives within the same compound until they themselves were elders. Finally, adult kin could leave with their own dependents and move elsewhere, either because they had grown dissatisfied or because they had accumulated the resources to establish households of their own. Precisely because people had obligations to their domestic superiors that interfered with their own autonomy and accumulation, one of the first priorities of any ambitious man and of some ambitious women was to establish a household that they themselves headed.[64]

To enlarge their households beyond what marriage, kinship, and reproduction allowed, *ọbas*, chiefs, and wealthy commoners incorporated non-family of free birth into them. Young men sometimes left their natal families and attached themselves to the *ọba*, a chief, or a successful commoner as wards in hopes of bettering their opportunities.[65] Prominent Lagosians also swelled their households by offering hospitality and other forms of assistance to strangers migrating to the town. Refugees driven to Lagos by warfare and political instability and people attracted to the town by economic opportunity obtained temporary maintenance, a place to settle, and representation within the community by asking for help from a local big man or woman. A committee of educated Lagosians explained in the early twentieth century,

> [S]trangers, that is to say, members of other tribal states, if their communities are destroyed in war and they are deprived of their political independence and means

> of subsistence . . . look for protection in other states, and attach themselves to heads of families to whom they look for support and maintenance.[66]

Immigrants wanting assistance were typically introduced to leading chiefs, because such individuals were in a good position to act as patrons and protectors. However, strangers sometimes attached themselves to wealthy commoners, and if they had been powerful and influential in their hometowns, they were occasionally taken directly to the *ọba*.[67]

When immigrants arrived with large numbers of followers, as did the founders of the Ojora, Modile, Onisemo, and Kakawa chieftaincy families, they were allocated land on which to build compounds and establish farms, sometimes founding villages or new quarters of the town. When they came alone or in small groups, however, they typically entered the households of their hosts.[68]

Wards commonly worked closely with an adult in the compound to learn a skill, contributing vital labor during the period of their apprenticeship. The obligations of strangers to their benefactors varied, on the other hand, with the nature of the assistance and resources they received. Those who obtained land on which to build and farm were typically expected to give the head of the landowning family an annual gift known as *ịṣákọ̀lẹ̀*, often of agricultural produce, which did not have great economic value but symbolized the host family's continuing ownership of the land. In contrast, strangers who entered the household faced more substantial exactions. They were supposed to accompany their overlords when they went out, give them a part of the fruits of their labor, and work for them when asked to do so. Like wards, both types of strangers also had obligations to "serve" their overlords and "maintain [their] interests," which generally entailed contributing to family religious and life-cycle ceremonies, showing support in times of political conflict, and going to war if called upon to do so.[69] Non-kin who lived within the household were known generically as *aláàbagbé*, but at some point another term, *asáforígẹ*, also began to be used in Lagos to refer to strangers, who were regarded as "homeless" and like "dependent children."[70] The more prosperous and powerful Lagos became, the greater edge it enjoyed in the regional competition for wives, wards, and strangers.

Prominent men and women in Lagos further increased the size of their retinues by constructing patron-client relationships with other freeborn Lagosians of lesser status. Within the kingdom, access to opportunities and success in public life depended, as in many other precolonial and indeed modern African states, on effective representation by a well-connected member of the local political elite. Inhabitants of the town and surrounding villages who were not related by blood to a successful chief often entered a patron-client relationship with one in hopes of obtaining such assistance. A Yoruba term for client—*aláàgbàsọ*—captures the essence of the relationship. The word means, literally, one who has somebody to plead one's case.[71]

Unlike wards and strangers, clients did not normally live inside the households of their patrons. They were not "homeless" and therefore regarded as "dependent children," but rather resided with their own kin. In consequence, clients usually received more limited material assistance than wards and strangers, requiring neither daily sustenance nor access to land and housing. In return for representation and assistance, however, clients had obligations to help their patrons with certain kinds of labor, such as "building or repairing houses" and "gathering farm crops." Moreover, they were expected to swell their patrons' retinues on public occasions, while in times of political strife or warfare they were said to be "entirely" under their patrons' "command."[72]

Lagos chiefs did not all have equal power and influence, although in precolonial times no rigid system of ranking seems to have existed among them. Each of the four categories of officeholders had its own head, superior in rank to the other members of that grade. The *ìdẹ́jọ* and *àkárìgbèrè* both asserted primacy, the former on the basis of first-settler status and the latter on that of having come from Benin with Aṣipa and brought regalia and ritual knowledge. Members of the *àkárìgbèrè* and *àbàgbọ̀n* grades appear to have dominated during the era of the slave trade, however, because of their privileged relationship with the *ọba* and role in administration, warfare, and trade. That said, the power and influence of particular chiefs varied greatly with their individual achievements and personalities, and able men and women thrust themselves to the fore by dint of their own accomplishments more than because of the title they held.[73]

Lesser chiefs needed the patronage of greater ones, just as commoners needed theirs. In exchange, they deployed their own dependents in the service of their patrons on ceremonial occasions, in times of special economic need, and at moments of political or military crisis. As a result, the greatest chiefs in Lagos could mobilize not only their own wives, children, kin, wards, strangers, clients, and slaves, but also those of the chiefs who served them. *Ọbas* and powerful princes could call on the support of all the dependents of members of their coalitions, giving them command over thousands of men and women.[74]

While marriage, reproduction, kinship, overlordship, and patronage remained important in late eighteenth- and early nineteenth-century Lagos, the growth of the foreign slave trade at the port led to a dramatic expansion of local slavery as a means of acquiring people and increased its significance relative to these other types of dependency. This change occurred in part as a consequence of the sheer growth in the supply of slaves on the coast and of incomes with which to buy them. Put simply, the slave trade increased the availability of a particular kind of dependent in coastal society. But the change also reflected certain advantages to slavery, in comparison with other types of social relationships, as a way for ambitious men and women to organize labor and allegiance.

In the era of the slave trade, *ọbas*, war chiefs, and warriors retained a few captives and turned them into domestic slaves, but this strategy was risky because most such people came from nearby, and if they did not run away, then their kin might try to ransom them. Lagosians purchased the majority of their domestic slaves in the marketplace, and many of them came from distant parts of Yorubaland or non-Yoruba territories such as Mahi, Nupe, or Hausaland, which made flight much more difficult. In the first half of the nineteenth century, *ọbas* and powerful princes owned hundreds of slaves; while chiefs, especially of the war grade, also owned large numbers. Robertson saw numerous slaves employed around "the Cabocier," meaning probably Ologun Kuture or his son Oṣinlokun. The Lander brothers described Adele surrounded by slaves at Badagry, and they noted that his chiefs employed many slaves as well.[75] Adele's wife Tinubu got her start in trade by sending two slaves back and forth between Badagry and Abeokuta with goods. As her business expanded, she retained many of the strongest and healthiest slaves that she bought for use in her own household. The reference in local tradition to Opo Olu's 1,400 slaves should not be taken as fact, but it does provide evidence of large-scale slaveholding. At the height of his power, Kosoko went so far as to try to reverse the direction of the Atlantic slave trade by purchasing carpenters and coopers in Bahia for shipment back to Lagos.[76]

Beyond the ruling oligarchy, prosperous commoners also owned slaves, although probably only in the case of the wealthiest did the number reach ten or more. Slavery had existed in Lagos before the late eighteenth century, and it had long provided a means of incorporating outsiders into households to increase their size. However, the number of people owning slaves, the scale of slaveowning among the local political, military, and commercial elite, and the importance of slavery in the local political economy all increased dramatically in the era of the foreign slave trade. By the 1850s, Europeans who visited Lagos believed that the majority of its population were slaves.[77]

Most bondwomen and -men in Lagos spent part of their time working on behalf of their owners in transportation, trade, fishing, agricultural production, or craft manufacturing, whether owned by members of the ruling oligarchy or by commoners. A few had specialized religious, magical, or medical-herbal knowledge that they employed on behalf of their owners. Female slaves also performed much of the arduous premodern domestic labor needed to sustain their owners' households. Indeed, many of the tasks that slaves performed in trade, food processing, craft manufacturing, and domestic labor were considered women's work, and as a consequence female slaves were in especially great demand. The majority of slaves owned by Lagosians were most likely women.[78]

When slaves belonged to a big slaveholder, they normally lived in a separate section of the owner's compound or sometimes in a freestanding house that the slaves themselves built nearby. However, large-scale owners sometimes sent slaves to live with and work for a patron, client, or needy relative. Slaves of the wealthy who toiled in agriculture often spent part or all of the year in slave villages on the island or across the lagoon on the mainland, where the soil was better in some places. In that case, the slaves usually worked in groups under the supervision of a head slave. If owned by a small slaveholder, on the other hand, bondwomen and -men typically lived in their owner's compound and labored alongside family members. Both large- and small-scale slaveowners often allowed bondmen and, more rarely, bondwomen they had grown to trust to work on their own in canoeing, headloading, trading, farming, fishing, or some other activity, in return for a regular share of their earnings.[79]

Ọbas, chiefs, and other rich and powerful Lagosians used slaves, however, not only to perform unskilled and skilled labor, but also in supervisory positions. Both *ọbas* and holders of the Aṣogbon, Ojora, Oluwa, and other chieftaincy titles placed slaves in charge of farms in rural areas, a practice which increased as agriculture and palm produce production expanded on the mainland from the 1840s. Kings, chiefs, and other big men and women employed slaves, moreover, in supervising canoes on journeys to and from market and indeed, in some cases, in managing their trade. In addition, they put male slaves in charge not only of slave dwellings, but also of their own households, particularly when conflict divided the owner's wives and children.[80] Okediji and Okediji maintain, in their introduction to N. A. Fadipe's classic text *The Sociology of the Yoruba*, that slaves could become their owners' confidants, wielding more influence over them than wives and children. The close relationship that existed between certain male slaves in Lagos and their owners demonstrates that, while not representing the experience of most slaves, the Okedijis' assertion was not romanticized fiction.[81]

Members of the ruling oligarchy and their key supporters also called upon slaves to swell their retinues and serve as their warriors. Male slaves employed in these capacities sometimes performed so well and earned such trust that they were given responsibility for commanding troops in battle or helping to organize political coalitions. When this occurred, the slaves were often freed from more lowly sorts of labor. The Lander brothers observed, for instance, that at Badagry, Adele had a mulatto slave who was a political advisor and a number of Muslim slaves on whom he called only to go to war, otherwise allowing them to trade for themselves. Successive holders of the Aṣogbon chieftaincy title relied on slaves, moreover, to both man and command war canoes in battle, while Oshodi Tapa also used slaves to lead troops.[82] Slavery played an essential role in the buildup of the political and military, as well as the economic, power of big men and women in Lagos during the era of the slave trade, much as it did among the better-known warlords in the new states of the Yoruba interior after 1830.[83] The clear preference of Lagosians for male slaves not only as warriors but also in supervisory positions created a demand for them that counterbalanced that for female slaves.

But whereas Ibadan, Ijaye, and Abeokuta, the new states in the Yoruba interior, did not immediately recreate strong monarchies, in Lagos the *ọba* remained at the center of the expanding state. Powerful holders of that title employed a growing number of male and female palace slaves (*ibigá*) in ministering to their personal needs, administering the royal household, and developing the court as a social and political institution. When in Lagos around the turn of the nineteenth century, Robertson witnessed slaves "confidentially" employed about the person of the king, noting that they held the royal keys and fetched the royal water, a responsibility of vital importance in a society where poisoning was a favorite means of eliminating rivals and regicide an accepted practice.[84] *Ibigá* were also named keepers of the queens' apartment and burial grounds, enlisting them in the complex task of managing royal wives. Beyond the palace, *ọbas* had begun, by the 1820s, to use male *ibigá* to perform state functions such as collecting taxes, conducting diplomacy, carrying messages, and administering royal law courts, slowly withdrawing these responsibilities from chiefs of different kinds and preventing them from expanding their authority in the growing institutions of the state. Oshodi Tapa and Dada

Antonio both began their spectacular ascents within the palace when Ọṣinlokun sent them to Brazil to learn Portuguese and acquire cultural and commercial knowledge and then used them to collect duty from Portuguese slave traders.[85] By developing a cadre of royal slaves around them, strong *ọbas* were able to concentrate new authority in their hands and bolster the power of the king vis-à-vis the chiefs.

The reality of slaves' daily lives varied from what Peel has called the "extreme vulnerability" of the newly acquired to the incomplete incorporation of those born into their owners' households. The first had been torn violently from their home communities and turned into a commodity that was freely bought and sold. They usually arrived in Lagos without kin or friends and were the first picked for human sacrifice in the event of an important funeral or public calamity. The second had learned the local language growing up and formed social ties within their owners' households and community from birth. Such slaves often worshiped at an established shrine or, later, a mosque and, in addition, enjoyed some protection against sale thanks to strictures that discouraged owners from getting rid of slaves born into the family. The value of the work that slaves performed and the nature of their personal relationships with their owners also affected the conditions of their lives. Once slaves had settled into their owners' households sufficiently that the wariness with which most newly acquired slaves were greeted had worn off, bondwomen and -men were usually permitted some time to work for themselves. This arrangement had the advantage of lifting the burden of maintaining them from their owners or senior slaves within the household. It also enabled a number of slaves, however, over months and years of their own labor, to improve their consumption, accumulate some capital, and buy one or more slaves of their own, including a female to marry if they were men.[86]

That slaves along the Bight of Benin could and did themselves own slaves surprises many non-specialists. Yet in fact, one of the first investments that slaves in Lagos who accumulated some capital usually made was in the purchase of a slave for their own use.[87] Slaveowning had many of the same advantages for slaves as it did for persons of free birth. Slave/owners could employ their slaves in their own enterprises and also use them to fulfill obligations to others. In a culture where the acquisition of wealth and power normally began with control of people, the purchase of a slave gave the slave/owner authority over a dependent. If the slave acquired was female, that authority extended to the offspring she bore. Investment in a slave wife helped remove what Martin Klein has called the "essence of the male slave's subordination" within his owner's household—lack of control over paternity. It constituted, as Klein argues, a key step "in the slave's advancement through stages of integration" into the community.[88]

As the evidence presented here shows, slaves were neither necessarily the most powerless nor the poorest members of the community. Those who held positions of responsibility within the households of powerful chiefs, as well as *ibigá* who were close to the king or performed important state functions, wielded considerably more power and were often richer than many commoners. It was, indeed, sometimes in the best interest of owners to encourage slaves they trusted to accumulate slaves, canoes, and even weapons of their own, because owners enjoyed rights in their slaves' resources. They could make demands on these resources while the slaves lived and might inherit them after they died. Moreover, loyal slaves could usually be counted on to mobilize their resources on behalf of their owners when the need arose.[89]

What accounts for the dramatic expansion of slavery at Lagos in the era of the slave trade and for its growing significance as a way of acquiring dependents? Unlike elsewhere in the Atlantic world, no fundamental change had occurred in the organization of economic production. Lagosians used slaves in this period much as people throughout the region long had, if in increased numbers thanks to the economic, political, and military expansion that was taking place within the kingdom. The explanation of the growth of slavery lies elsewhere. As already suggested, supply had something to do with it. Trade slaves simply became more readily available and, despite fluctuating prices, more affordable to the political, military, and commercial elite than they had been prior to the 1780s. A number of other factors, however, also made slavery attractive to Lagosians.

First, slaves had fewer competing allegiances and loyalties than most other kinds of non-kin who could be incorporated into households and retinues. Wives, wards, strangers, and clients remained members of their own lineages and, if born outside Lagos, also of their natal communities. Many of them felt obligations to their own kin groups and hometowns that could conflict with those to the head of the household under whose authority they lived. Slaves, on the other hand, had normally been torn from their families and hometowns and sold afar. Once they began to settle into their owners' households, they had fewer competing loyalties than other dependents, which opened the possibility of a closer and more complete identification with their owners' interests.[90]

Second, owners could exercise tighter control over slaves than they could over other sorts of dependents. A number of scholars have viewed African slavery as but one of a range of relationships of subordination that existed in deeply patriarchal cultures and have stressed its continuity with other forms of social subordination.[91] This perspective misses the essential fact that the subordination of slaves was fundamentally different from that of many other kinds of dependents, because it was involuntary and, in the beginning, all-pervasive. The relationship between husbands and wives, overlords and strangers, and patrons and clients was voluntary and reciprocal, if hierarchical. Wives, clients, and even refugees could vote with their feet and leave their *bàbá* (fathers) if they became disaffected. Big men and women along the Bight of Benin and in its interior competed for followers, and this gave dependents of free birth ready alternatives. Although wives, wards, strangers, and clients might encounter resistance from other big men and women, as well as from the *bàbá* himself, if they left, they could normally count on the support of kin, friends, patrons, and local authorities if they had a good reason for wanting to go.[92] Slaves who fled, on the other hand, could expect public support only if they had been flagrantly abused.

Then too, owners had greater coercive power over slaves than over other dependents, both because they were freer to punish them physically and because slaves remained property that could be sold, even in the second generation or beyond. With slave ships arriving regularly at the port to buy cargoes for American markets, it was not hard to dispose of a troublesome slave and perhaps even turn a profit in the bargain. To be sure, freeborn dependents could also be sold, but in principle only for repeatedly violating fundamental social norms and after judicial proceedings. If problematic, they could not be gotten rid of with the ease or impunity of those who were already enslaved.[93]

Finally, the fact that bondwomen and -men depended on their owners for many of their most basic social needs reinforced their subordination. In precolonial Lagos, as elsewhere in West Africa, people relied on their identity as members of households, lineages, quarters of the town, or other communal groups for protection, access to resources, representation in political and legal affairs, and performance of crucial life-cycle ceremonies such as marriages and funerals. Dependents of free birth could often draw on a number of different relationships with others for these kinds of support, but most slaves had nowhere to go for them save to their owners or fellow slaves. In his work on the East African coast,

Frederick Cooper has shown how powerfully the combination of coercion and social dependence could discipline slaves. Dependence cut two ways. It both gave the slaves compelling reasons to identify with their owners and do their will and provided owners with an effective instrument of control. As Cooper has noted, owners who permitted slaves to work independently, entrusted them with costly trade goods and capital equipment, and allowed them to carry arms were "placing great faith in the bonds of loyalty between master and slave."[94] The reality of slaves' deep dependence on their owners helped make that faith possible.

A similar dynamic was at work in Lagos, but there it was reinforced by an explicit ideology that owners should reward slaves who served them faithfully. The putative rewards, which could take different forms across time, included obtaining wives for male slaves, marrying female ones or giving them in marriage to sons so that their children would be free, helping slaves develop their own economic enterprises, and ultimately enabling them to free themselves and move out of bondage. A locally recognized ritual of manumission during which slaves paid their owners money for redemption in the presence of witnesses, left town for several days, and were then readmitted as free members of the owners' families and sometimes also marked with appropriate facial scarification dramatically enacted the final reward.[95] Sandra T. Barnes has fittingly labeled this ideology of reward and mobility the "in-up-and-out" system and identified Oshodi Tapa as the paradigmatic example of it.[96] A further widely held idea allowed bondmen and -women who failed to move "up and out" in their own lifetimes to think that their descendants would nonetheless see a meaningful change in their status and enjoy many of the same privileges as persons of free birth. This second idea held that over generations slaves would be incorporated into their owners' kin groups.[97]

For ideologies to be believable, some people must benefit from them, and in Lagos a number of slaves, such as Oshodi Tapa and Dada Antonio, were in fact rewarded for their loyalty and helped by their owners to improve their circumstances and move out of slavery. Yet apart from the predominantly male slaves whom owners entrusted with supervisory, administrative, and military responsibilities, few first-generation bondmen and -women in the town accumulated wealth, shared power, and made the transition to freedom, much less experienced the meteoric rise of Tapa, Antonio, and a small number of others. Instead, they toiled at arduous tasks, lived in rudimentary shelters, ate poor food, and knew only limited personal autonomy. Even so, the promise of reward and upward mobility through loyal service proved a powerful instrument of control that helped discipline not only the slaves who tasted them, but also those who dreamed that one day they might. If reward for good service failed in the first generation, slaves could still imagine that the lot of their descendants would improve. In Lagos, as in most slave systems, owners and slaves struggled over the demands being made on the slaves and the rights and privileges that they enjoyed, as slaves sought to expand their autonomy and owners to maintain effective control. Although the sources are largely silent on the subject, some slaves surely resisted by running away or engaging in other overt acts of defiance. To many slaves in Lagos, however, faithful service came to make a kind of sense, and membership in an owner's household and retinue, even if in an inferior status, looked better than the other alternatives open to them.

The great advantage of slavery in Lagos, relative to other means of accumulating dependents, lay in the superior opportunities it afforded to promote identification with the owner and exercise discipline and control. Slavery gave members of Lagos's political, military, and commercial elite tighter command over their followers than did other relationships of subordination. It helped them turn fluid and sometimes mercurial retinues into more solid and dedicated bands of loyalists.

Members of Lagos's ruling oligarchy invested their new wealth from the slave trade in a further way that will come as no surprise to anyone familiar with the passion of the Yoruba-speaking people for spectacle and display. They used it to finance increased consumption of luxury goods, many of which were imported in exchange for slaves. The construction of new palaces and improvement of old ones during the period provide evidence of this trend, as do references in written documents to the tiles, candles, looking glasses, silver-handled knives, musical instruments, and Western furniture that were imported to appoint them.[98] Local tradition encodes this phenomenon in a reference to a "deep-jet-satin velvet" wall-hanging that Akinṣemoyin acquired for his receiving room that miraculously made it appear "dark in the day and bright at night."[99]

Consumption occurred most conspicuously, however, in dress. Richard Lander saw Adele at Badagry "gorgeously arrayed in a scarlet cloak, literally covered with gold lace, and [in] white kerseymere trowsers similarly embroidered." The deposed *ọba* wore a hat "turned up in front with rich bands of gold lace, and decorated with a splendid plume of white ostrich feathers."[100] So great was Adele's interest in clothing that he tried to import "four regimental coats" of the kind "worn by the King of England," yet rejected a little-worn but unfashionable naval surgeon's coat as "unworthy" of a monarch.[101] The passion for dress extended to chiefs and war captains, as well. Consul Campbell complained that foreign slave traders had bestowed on Lagos chiefs "expensive silks and gaudy" clothing, which they wore to make themselves appear grand in the eyes of their people.[102] The Lander brothers observed Adele's Muslim slave war captains and members of their families celebrating the end of Ramadan decked out in "[l]oose tobes, with caps and turbans" made of striped and plain red, blue, and black cloths and scarfs made "of green silk, ornamented with leaves and flowers of gold." Male members of the party completed their outfits by donning "[t]he Turkish scimitar, the French sabre, the Portuguese dagger, confined in a silver case, all gleam[ing] brightly; and heavy cutlasses," along with muskets and Arab pistols.[103] This lavish consumption of imported luxury goods by members of the ruling oligarchy was highly functional in that it enhanced their prestige and increased their ability to attract people.[104]

Evidence suggests that *ọbas* also incorporated goods they imported into the regalia of the state. A Brazilian document tantalizingly mentions "a case with rounded cover and the richest . . . decoration imaginable" that Oṣinlokun ordered in 1824. It was to hold damask cloth woven with golden boughs and as many of the "largest . . . coral beads" as possible.[105] *Ọbas* of Benin enjoyed a monopoly over coral beads, and they both wore large numbers themselves and distributed others to chiefs and courtiers, whose status could be deduced by "the relative lavishness of their beaded attire."[106] It is perhaps not too fanciful to imagine Oṣinlokun adding some coral to his costume on ritual occasions and giving other beads to chiefs in whom he was vesting royal authority.[107] The Brazilian document also refers to hats ordered by Oṣinlokun similar to those worn subsequently by *ọbas*. The Lander brothers in addition saw imported umbrellas, another popular West African symbol of royalty, unfurled over Adele's head and hanging in his apartment. Then, in the 1850s, Kosoko commissioned the manufacture of four bells in Brazil, which he may have intended for use by his crier or in his regalia.[108] Wealth from the slave trade made possible a greater elaboration of material and visual objects associated with state power, many of which were imported in exchange for slaves.

Beyond their own consumption, *ọbas*, chiefs, and other big men and women redistributed goods to signal their liberality and generosity and help them attract freeborn dependents and maintain the loyalty of both them and important slaves. Commodities flowed from *ọbas* to chiefs and other members of their coalitions and from chiefs and other big men and women to their followers. On ceremonial occasions, such as religious festivals honoring local gods, *ọbas* and chiefs had probably long feted their subjects with locally produced food and drink.[109] The introduction of scarce imported goods during the era of the slave trade, however, gave those involved in the commerce new opportunities to use the redistribution of commodities to create and bind followers. *Ọbas*, chiefs, and other big men and women made gifts of imported guns, ammunition, clothing, and textiles to those whose loyalty they sought. Adele's Muslim slave war captains may have purchased some of the fancy imports they wore, but tradition suggests that others were a gift from him.[110] Alcohol, tobacco, and cowries, however, were the most widely redistributed imports. Many European visitors to the coast commented on the great taste of locals for Brazilian tobacco and European and American spirits.[111] Kosoko himself told the British, when offered a stipend in return for ceding Epe in 1856, that he wanted it in articles of "ornament and utility" not in "cowries or specie," because if it came in the latter he would be "obliged to distribute the greater portion of it among his caboceers."[112] People could buy certain imports in local markets, but the goods were costly and beyond the means of most. Many Lagosians obtained access to coveted imports through a relationship with a superior.

In his work on the impact of the slave trade on the materially simpler and less hierarchical societies of West-Central Africa, Joe Miller has shown how aspiring big men there used the redistribution of imported goods to attract followers and help build political power bases. A similar phenomenon occurred in Lagos, despite the much greater availability of material possessions and fuller development of market exchange on the Slave Coast. In Lagos, however, unlike in West-Central Africa, what big men and women sought was not "abstract" claims to "future labor" and authority, but present and continuing control over the tangible labor and political and military support of dependents, in an environment of fierce competition for people.[113] Beyond financing the buildup of canoes, weapons, and subordinates of different kinds, the slave trade paid for the consumption and redistribution of imported goods, which helped create and maintain bonds of loyalty between members of the ruling oligarchy and their followers.

Against this backdrop, it is now possible to return to the question posed at the end of the first chapter about the relationship between the rise of the external slave trade at Lagos and the history of political conflict recorded so vividly in its traditions.

Conclusion

The shift of the slave trade along the Bight of Benin away from ports further west to Lagos increased the town's economic importance within the region and turned it into an Atlantic port of considerable significance. The related growth of foreign and domestic trade across the lagoon expanded the wealth of the kingdom's ruling oligarchy, many members of which participated directly in the commerce and also benefited from taxes on the trade and incomes of others. During the era of the slave trade, Lagos's *ọbas* and a number of its leading chiefs invested their rising incomes in canoes, arms, and critically important people—slaves above all—which greatly enhanced the commercial and military power as well as the geopolitical importance of the growing state. *Ọbas* undertook modest territorial expansion west and east along the coast and north onto the mainland in part to better control trade routes across the lagoon, along which goods flowed to the port. Meanwhile, strong kings began trying to concentrate greater domestic political authority in their hands. The Kingdom of Lagos remained small by the standards of the Bight of Benin's great inland states and empires, but it had nonetheless become a much more significant player in regional and Atlantic affairs. Its capital's island location in the lagoon helped protect the town from attack by the predominantly land-based armies of Oyo, Dahomey, Ijebu, and Abeokuta, the major powers in the area, while the state's growing navy enabled it to strike rival ports and major markets on the northern shore of the lagoon, in addition to trade canoes plying the waters.

If the rise of the slave trade at Lagos increased the power and importance of the state and thrust it onto the international stage, however, the expansion of foreign commerce also exacerbated conflicts within the kingdom that would contribute, in the long run, to its colonization by Great Britain and permanent loss of autonomy. The oligarchy that ruled the developing state was divided internally by a number of factors, including tensions between the ruling dynasty introduced from Benin and the *ìdẹ́jọ* chiefs who represented the older communities originally incorporated into the state, as well as groups of more recent immigrants. The sources of instability encompassed, as well, constitutional struggles between nineteenth-century *ọbas* such as Ọṣinlokun and Kosoko, who were seeking to concentrate new authority in their hands through the use of palace slaves, and administrative and military chiefs accustomed to exercising considerable power and authority in their own right. To compound matters, rules of succession to the kingship were not always followed, and rival princes organized the power they needed to claim the crown by forging coalitions of prominent supporters and their dependents, which quickly coalesced into hostile factions when succession disputes developed.

The limitations of the historical evidence make it impossible to know from this vantage point precisely how the many sources of political instability in Lagos interacted with one another, much less intersected more specific questions of domestic and foreign policy. Two conclusions, however, emerge from the data. The first is that economic expansion during the era of the slave trade enabled contestants for power in a highly charged political environment to amass armaments and warriors that they could deploy in domestic conflicts as well as interstate relations. Investment in canoes, weapons, and people turned a state riven with political tensions into a volatile mix of competing factions organized around local big men and women, which was capable of exploding into civil war. The second conclusion is that the growth of the slave trade at Lagos increased the stakes in succession disputes and made winning or losing more consequential. While *ọbas* could not monopolize the slave trade, they and their supporters enjoyed advantages in it that were worth fighting for.

Lagos reached its peak as a center of the slave trade at a time when the Bight of Benin supplied the bulk of West Africa's slaves, the vast trade from the Bight of Biafra having by then subsided. In the 1840s, the port thrived as one of the few remaining centers of supply north of the equator. Its commercial hegemony fatefully coincided with a resurgence of abolitionist sentiment in Great Britain. These two circumstances soon combined to fix the slave trade at Lagos in the British imagination as a last great scourge to be eliminated, with devastating consequences for the growing kingdom.

3

The Original Sin: Anti-slavery, Imperial Expansion, and Early Colonial Rule

In 1851, Britain bombarded Lagos, drove Kosoko into exile at Epe on the northeastern shore of the lagoon, and replaced him as *ọba* with Akitoye, whom the Foreign Office believed would make a more compliant local ally. A decade later, Britain annexed the kingdom, commencing a century of colonial rule that eventually engulfed all of what subsequently became Nigeria. Historians of these events have argued about why they occurred at a time when Britain was in general reluctant to acquire territory in Africa. Existing interpretations oppose motives deriving from a humanitarian desire to end the slave trade, on the one hand, and an economic interest in promoting the growth of the new palm oil trade, on the other, much as early interpretations of abolition juxtaposed morality and economic self-interest in their analyses.[1] This chapter argues that Britain's forcible intervention in the politics of Lagos in 1851 occurred as part of that country's lengthy campaign to end the slave trade, but that in the bombardment of Lagos, as in the anti-slavery movement more generally, activists and policymakers understood morality and self-interest not as opposing principles but as interconnected parts of a single great process of reform.

At the time of the annexation in 1861, the goal of eliminating the slave trade from the Bight of Benin remained important, largely because of the continuing menace that the Kingdom of Dahomey was believed to present. By then, however, many British officials on the coast and in London had become convinced that commerce in goods other than slaves would not continue to develop at Lagos without the introduction of new state structures capable of maintaining political stability locally and of promoting a new cultural and legal order. They saw the new, so-called "legitimate commerce" that Britain sought to develop as essential to the final eradication of the slave trade from West Africa. At the same time, many mid-Victorian policymakers regarded it as part of a further process of reform—the vigorous expansion of commerce abroad—that was vital to the stability and well-being of the British nation and improvement of peoples worldwide.[2]

A final section of this chapter examines the character of the early colonial state at Lagos. In the process, it illuminates the way a limited number of male slaves of northern origin managed to leave their owners. To uncover the relationship among anti-slavery, commercial expansion, and British intervention at Lagos, it is necessary to look briefly at the history of anti-slavery thought and action.

Anti-slavery and Commercial Expansion

During the very years that the external slave trade developed at Lagos, a movement emerged in Britain, the United States, and parts of Europe to abolish the abominable traffic in human beings. Abolition transformed British ideas about Africa and interests in it and eventually thrust the British into open conflict with the priorities of Lagos's rulers. A closely related set of religious and secular beliefs rooted in Protestant evangelical theology and Enlightenment social philosophy shaped the abolitionist worldview and informed British policy toward Lagos in the mid-nineteenth century.

Much simplified, these beliefs held that all men had a right to be free and that they shared a naturally benevolent human nature, which slavery had corrupted. The abolitionists' ideology also included a conviction that humans could improve themselves by overcoming sin through God's grace and that whole societies could be reformed by removing obstacles to liberty, benevolence, and happiness through the application of reason. Christians, in their view, had a personal moral duty to relieve the suffering of the innocent and root out obstacles to improvement at home and abroad. A belief in Providence as a transforming force and history as man's hope of salvation engendered a deep faith in the inevitability of moral and material progress. Influenced by the work of Adam Smith and other thinkers of the Scottish Enlightenment, moreover, many anti-slavery activists perceived a harmony between morality and utility, understood as the product of the "self-interested decisions" of economic men.[3]

To them "morality, self-interest, and human progress were mutually interdependent" and could be "achieved by the same means."[4] This constellation of ideas led abolitionists to regard slavery as the institution which, more than any other, prevented humans from realizing their true destiny, and it gave rise to sustained pressure for reform.[5]

The anti-slavery movement began in societies undergoing rapid economic growth, commercial expansion, and technological development, achieved largely through the use of free labor and loosening of external social controls. Experience as members of these societies caused most abolitionists to take as an article of faith that slave labor was less productive than free labor and to believe that in this way too it was antithetical to prosperity and human progress.[6] David Brion Davis has shown how "the needs and interests" of rising capitalists in Britain and North America affected receptivity to anti-slavery ideas and "thus the ideas' historical impact." He has explored the ideological functions of attacking slavery, a "symbol of the most extreme subordination, exploitation, and dehumanization, at a time when various enlightened elites were experimenting with internalized moral and cultural controls to establish or preserve their own hegemony."[7]

The history of the British anti-slavery movement is well known, and its details need not concern us here. Suffice it to say that reform was ultimately accomplished in a number of phases that spanned more than three-quarters of a century. During the opening attack on the British slave trade, which culminated in its abolition in 1807, leaders of the movement established national and grass-roots organizations, carried the movement to the people by developing techniques of popular agitation, and worked through parliamentary spokesmen to bring popular pressure to bear on national policy.[8] After 1807, attention shifted for a time to ending the foreign slave trade through diplomatic and naval pressure. In this context, Britain signed anti-slave trading treaties with such nations as Brazil, Portugal, and Spain and deployed a small naval squadron to patrol the West African coast and suppress illegal slave trading.[9] Although the anti-slavery squadron was always too small to have a decisive impact on the Slave Coast, it introduced an official British presence into the Bight of Benin and created opportunities for Akitoye, in exile at Badagry, to draw Britain into political conflicts in the Kingdom of Lagos in hopes of influencing the balance of power.

In the early 1820s, abolitionist leaders had begun directing their energy to ending slavery in Britain's colonial possessions. There was much continuity of leadership, organization, and tactics between the campaign for emancipation and that to abolish the slave trade thirty years before, although important changes also occurred in each of these areas that helped make anti-slavery even more popular than before. Large-scale slave resistance in the colonies fanned the flames of reform and kept anti-slavery in the public eye.[10] Thomas Fowell Buxton, the leader of the parliamentary campaign to end slavery since William Wilberforce's retirement in 1824, skillfully brought widespread popular pressure to bear on the government, culminating in the 1833 bill to abolish slavery in Britain's colonial possessions. The point to be stressed here is that in the course of the struggle to end slavery in the British colonies, the anti-slavery movement and many of the ideas underlying it became mainstream. Disparate elements of the British nation embraced them, albeit for different reasons, producing consensus. Henceforth, reformers and policymakers would debate tactics or the fate of owners and slaves following emancipation, but never again the need to eliminate forever both slavery and the slave trade.[11]

In the aftermath of the passage of the 1833 bill, Buxton turned his attention to the persistence of the African slave trade and its blighting effect on the continent. He set out to convince the British public and its government that the slave trade continued unabated, despite thirty years of diplomatic and naval pressure to eliminate it, because British policy had targeted slave traders and slaveowners rather than Africans themselves.[12] In keeping with the early nineteenth-century belief in the natural benevolence of the Negro and inner capacity of all humans for self-improvement, Buxton argued that the one true remedy of the slave trade lay in Africa. "It is not the partial aid, lent by a distant nation," he wrote, "but the natural and healthy exercise of her own energies, which will ensure success."[13] To deliver the continent from the slave trade once and for all, he preached, Britain must "elevate the minds" of Africa's people and "call forth the capabilities of her soil."[14] Through this program, Buxton fatefully shifted the focus of anti-slavery's reforming zeal to the continent of Africa itself.

The great mid-Victorian reformer argued that to elevate the minds of Africans missionaries should be sent to spread the Gospel and build schools. To call forth the capabilities of the continent's soils, its people would have to be taught to grow vegetable products for which there were markets in Europe, and "legitimate" commerce in these goods would need to be promoted. While Buxton and his supporters distinguished between the moral and the material, between the work of benevolent associations on the one hand and commercial companies on the other, they saw the two as necessarily interconnected parts of a single civilizing mission.[15] Buxton built upon and helped promote an early nineteenth-century view of Africa that was much more positive than the later high colonial image. He portrayed the continent as a place savaged by warfare and trapped in barbarism, where human life and suffering had very little value, but he did not think this was Africa's natural state. In his view, these atrocities were a product of the slave trade.[16] Most striking, from the high colonial perspective, Buxton saw Africans as energetic, responsive, and eminently teachable, although not yet themselves capable of innovation. European tutelage could be a gentle, voluntary process: no coercion would be necessary to erase "licentious custom."[17] All that need be done was to raise the morals of the people, teach them effective agricultural techniques, and show them that the sale of produce yielded a greater return than the sale of people. Africans would respond rationally; the slave trade would wither and die; and the continent would rapidly take off both morally and materially.

Buxton thought that Africans craved European products. Therein lay the root of the problem and also the hope of a solution. While they remained what they were, Africans could obtain these goods only via the slave trade; but transformed by the civilizing mission their craving would impel them to sustain hard work on their farms and in their markets. Although he failed to develop it in detail, Buxton assumed a model of African economic organization based on small-holder agricultural production employing free labor, in which internalized controls deriving from a desire for material goods would drive family members to disciplined work. Much as free labor regulated through internal moral and cultural controls would fuel the engine of progress in the industrializing societies of Europe and North America, so self-disciplining, small-scale producers and traders would propel it in Africa.[18]

A further important conviction underpinned Buxton's remedy for the Atlantic slave trade. It was that what would be good for Africa morally and economically would also be good for Britain. To him, one consideration alone sufficed to prompt the British nation to champion abolition: "a just appreciation of [Africa's] miseries."[19] But Buxton and his supporters also set out to demonstrate that Africa offered a vast field for European commerce and that Britain had an economic interest in remedying the slave trade inferior only to that of Africans themselves. In Britain as in Africa, he insisted, moral and material interests were congruent. The nation could confidently unite behind Africa's great cause, since abolition would simultaneously end the slave trade, open Africa to moral and material development, supply British factories with much-needed raw materials, increase foreign markets for British manufactures, and create good jobs at home for hungry workers.[20]

Buxton's views were not new. They grew out of the longer tradition of anti-slavery thought and action.[21] Interest in Africa had been expanding since the late eighteenth century, and by the 1830s a succession of travelers and explorers had visited it.[22] The Evangelical revival and abolition movement had both awakened philanthropic concern for the continent, and by the 1830s a few religious organizations had already founded mission stations there.[23] New information about the land and its peoples was flowing in, and scholars and other writers were interpreting it.[24] Buxton's ideas merit the attention they are given here not because of their originality, but because he synthesized contemporary currents of thought, developed the arguments about the relationship between abolition and African improvement more systematically than before, and then catapulted them to national prominence.[25]

Ideas about Africa were neither uniform nor politically neutral in the first half of the nineteenth century. There were those in the anti-slavery movement and the government who opposed part or all of Buxton's program.[26] Even so, his views prevailed. The belief that the only way to suppress the African slave trade was to promote "legitimate commerce" and that this new trade would launch Africa on the road to moral and material progress became the conventional wisdom in mid-nineteenth-century Britain.[27]

Earlier historians have shown the impact of Buxton's views on Lord Palmerston, foreign secretary from 1846 until late 1851 and prime minister at the time of Lagos's annexation in 1861, as well as on other ministers. Robert Gavin has demonstrated that Palmerston thought Africans had "a natural bent for commerce" and desired European goods, but believed "that . . . legitimate commerce could never thrive if the slave trade were not overthrown." In Palmerston's opinion, the primary obstacle "to a vast increase in Anglo-African trade was the power of those interested in the slave trade."[28] The consequences of Palmerston's views for the Kingdom of Lagos will soon become clear.

The campaign for the final eradication of the slave trade also stimulated new missionary activity in Africa. In 1842, an interdenominational competition offered a prize for the best essay on the duty of Christians to carry the Gospel to the heathens. The winning essay stressed the material as well as spiritual rewards that the enterprise would bring. It argued, in Philip Curtin's words, that "Christianity equals civilization, which equals production for the world market."[29] David Livingstone, then an unknown medical student, attended the 1840 meeting of the African Civilization Society where Buxton first announced his remedy for the slave trade. What Livingstone heard on that occasion helped inspire a lifetime of work and travel on the continent. Returning triumphantly from an expedition to Africa in 1857, he lectured on themes "indistinguishable" from those discussed by Buxton seventeen years before.[30] Livingstone's hold on the Victorian imagination helped keep alive the belief that "civilization and commerce," "the Bible and the plough" were the only way to free Africa from the slave trade and open a new era in her development. This ideology provided a manifesto for aggressive commercial and religious expansion abroad, much as the ideas of the Quaker abolitionists regarding slavery had for the rigors of free labor.

The campaign to end the British slave trade succeeded during a period of costly European warfare, which swelled to alarming proportions a national debt that had already been growing for many years. The financial burden that massive indebtedness imposed insured that questions of tax policy, fiscal responsibility, and budget reform would remain on the national agenda for years to come.[31] The anti-slavery movement continued, moreover, through a time of acute social and political unrest in Britain. Although the oligarchy that ruled the country remained firmly in control, it was being challenged from below by a growing middle class pressing for economic and political reforms and by robust working-class movements that were both democratic and anti-capitalist.[32] Anti-slavery was closely bound up with these broader reform movements—in its ideology, leadership, organization, and outcomes. The emancipation of slaves in Britain's colonial possessions won government support in 1833, in part because it did not alter the balance of domestic power and was the least threatening of the vigorous early nineteenth-century reform movements. By ending slavery and continuing the attack on the slave trade, the government reinforced its legitimacy and won popular support at a time of national political crisis.[33]

In the first half of the nineteenth century, Britain's ruling oligarchy strove to maintain stability and preserve "the monarchial, propertied, gentlemanly" social order by pursuing reforms that addressed problems associated with the contemporary crisis: national debt, population growth and food supply, excess capacity and low profitability in new industries, and political radicalism.[34] P. J. Cain and A. G. Hopkins have shown that, in this time of trial, the nation's leaders became convinced that Britain's renewed stability and strength depended, at home and abroad, on vigorous economic growth fueled by the expansion of foreign trade. British policymakers assumed such growth would work to the advantage of the poor, middle class, and rich alike. With European markets declining in importance and becoming more insecure, aggressive commercial expansion in more far-flung parts of the world was seen as the key to a secure social order. British leaders thought, moreover, that this development required from their nation's new trading partners specific cultural, legal, and political conditions, including free trade, private property rights, secure credit, and, perhaps most important, states capable of enforcing these arrangements. Cain and Hopkins have demonstrated how in the mid-nineteenth century Britain sought to create compliant satellites—" 'like-minded', co-operative" local elites—throughout the non-Western world in the interest of achieving these conditions, with Hopkins quoting Palmerston's dictum that the states where Britain had interests needed to be "well-kept" and "always accessible."[35]

In the drive for commercial expansion, as in the final campaign for abolition, trade, improvement, and the civilizing mission were closely entwined in the British imagination. Many mid-Victorian policymakers believed, few more strongly than Palmerston, that Britain could export a certain kind of development, that it had to do so to preserve the social order at home, and that the consequences of such a policy would be as good for Britain's trading partners overseas as they were for her citizens at home.[36] Foreign commerce, it was felt, would bring not only material progress but also moral uplift. In West Africa, the final campaign to end the slave trade and the drive for commercial expansion were intimately related and mutually compatible, as few episodes reveal more clearly than British intervention at Lagos in 1851 and again a decade later.

British Intervention at Lagos

Thanks to information provided by Britain's network of anti-slavery observers, officials in Whitehall knew that by the 1840s the Bight of Benin was the last major center of the slave trade in West Africa. They rightly identified Lagos as the leading slave port in the region and saw it and Dahomey as the primary obstacles to the final eradication of the slave trade from West Africa. Palmerston, then foreign secretary, making the case to the Admiralty for intervention at Lagos in September 1851, observed that Britain had "nearly rooted out the Slave Trade from the coast north of the

[Equator]" but that there remained "two persevering offenders, the King of Dahomey and the Chief of Lagos."[37]

Yet British officials saw signs of hope in this benighted region. The Royal Navy had taken slaves liberated by its cruisers patrolling the African coast to Freetown, Sierra Leone, founded in 1787 as a home for free blacks from England. There the "recaptives," as they became known, were registered and apprenticed to settlers from the Americas or allocated land in nearby villages. Many of the former slaves fell under the influence of missionaries, learned English, converted to Christianity, and began sending their children to school, although some retained their Islamic faith. While farming did not long prove a profitable or popular pursuit, members of the liberated slave communities soon showed themselves to be enterprising traders and contributed to the settlement's commercial development. Some of those who acquired Western education found jobs working for the government, missionaries, or British commercial establishments.[38]

In 1839, groups of liberated Yoruba slaves began returning to their homeland. After an early shipload was attacked and robbed attempting to land at Lagos, the Sierra Leonean repatriates settled at Badagry, and from there they began moving inland to Abeokuta. Substantial numbers of the repatriates were Christian, some had rudimentary Western education, and many made their living through trade. Political and religious leaders in Britain hoped they would become the advance agents of civilization.[39] On the Slave Coast and in its interior, the Saro, as the Sierra Leonean repatriates became known, met or were joined by freed slaves returning from Brazil in the aftermath of the 1835 Malê revolt.[40] Both migrations continued until several thousand Sierra Leonean and Brazilian former slaves lived on the Slave Coast.

As part of the broader, mid-nineteenth-century missionary expansion into Africa, the Wesleyan Missionary Society opened a station at Badagry in 1842, and the Church Missionary Society (CMS) followed suit in 1845. A year later the CMS sent two agents to Abeokuta to minister to the needs of Saro settling there, and soon after a Wesleyan missionary joined them. In both places, the missionaries began building churches, schools, and mission houses, and within a few months they attracted their first converts. Sodeke, the leader of the new Egba town at Abeokuta, welcomed the missionaries, as he had the Sierra Leonean and Brazilian repatriated slaves, and the evangelists soon began championing the cause of the Egba as a people among whom the sun of civilization was rising in the tropics against great odds. In time, Christianity would become an established part of the cultural landscape on the Slave Coast and in its interior, but in the 1840s the small Christian communities in Badagry and Abeokuta both saw themselves and were seen by many in Britain as highly vulnerable harbingers of progress.[41]

A further sign of hope, trade with Europe in palm oil, ivory, and other "legitimate" commodities was expanding in the Bight of Benin during the 1840s. Officials were aware of this, despite widespread belief in the incompatibility of the slave trade and legitimate commerce.[42] News trickled into Whitehall that a few British traders were doing business at Lagos, and by late 1851 some observers maintained that the town's legitimate commerce was considerable.[43] Palmerston and a number of other British policymakers came to believe that, because of the settlement's geographical location at the mouth of the lagoon and near the network of rivers connecting it with the hinterland, the community was poised to become the gateway to the interior for a vast trade in agricultural products, if only the slave trade could be eliminated. Palmerston wrote, "If Lagos, instead of being a nest for slave-traders were to become a port for lawful trade, it would, in connexion with the navigable river which there discharges itself into the sea, become an important outlet for the commerce of a large range of country in the interior, and instead of being a den of barbarism, would be a diffusing center of civilization."[44]

On the Slave Coast and in its interior, Britain's new plan for Africa soon collided with local and regional imperatives. After Akitoye fled Lagos in 1845, he settled in Badagry, a good position from which to continue his war against Kosoko. There the former *ọba* had ready access not only to the lagoon, along which he could attack his enemy, but also to foreign allies and the lucrative external trade necessary to finance his ambitions. Akitoye shrewdly grasped British priorities and manipulated them in pursuit of his feud with Kosoko and desire to reclaim the crown of Lagos. In Badagry, Akitoye carefully cultivated the newly arrived missionaries, with whom he enjoyed a natural advantage because of his close maternal connections with the Egba, convincing them that if reinstated as ruler of Lagos he would support abolition and encourage the spread of Christianity.[45]

Akitoye assiduously promoted an image of himself as the legitimate ruler of Lagos, "unanimously chosen" by its people and "confirmed by the King of Benin" according to tradition, who had been driven from office by Kosoko because, while *ọba*, he had decided to abolish the slave trade and invite the British to Lagos for lawful commerce.[46] With the help of the missionaries and certain Egba leaders, he propagated a view of

Kosoko, on the other hand, as a usurper who occupied a "blood-stained throne" and had never been confirmed by the king of Benin; as an inveterate slave trader and opponent of legitimate commerce; as an implacable enemy of the Egba and dedicated ally of Dahomey and the Brazilian slave traders; and, finally, as a hater of the Sierra Leonean repatriates, the Christian missionaries, and indeed the British nation.[47] Throughout 1851, Akitoye, the missionaries, the Sierra Leoneans, the Egba, and at critical junctures also the British merchants all portrayed themselves as surrounded by dangers and in need of protection, because of the hostility of Kosoko and his allies to them.[48] Directly and via the missionaries, Akitoye lobbied the British government and its naval and consular representatives on the coast to remove Kosoko from Lagos and reinstate him as *ọba.* Then in February 1851, he made John Beecroft, consul for the Bight of Benin, the following offer:

> My humble prayer to you, Sir, . . . is that you would take Lagos under your protection, that you would plant the English flag there, and that you would re-establish me on my rightful throne at Lagos, and protect me under my flag: and with your help I promise to enter into a Treaty with England to abolish the Slave Trade at Lagos, and to establish and carry on lawful trade, especially with the English merchants.[49]

At Badagry, Akitoye won the support of the Mewu, a powerful local chief, and strengthened allegiance to Kosoko among that man's opponents. In June, civil war broke out between the two groups of chiefs, with the Mewu emerging victorious and the others fleeing into exile.[50]

Throughout the previous decade, the Royal Navy squadron patrolling the West African coast had been pressuring African rulers to sign treaties by which they agreed to abolish the slave trade, expel slave traders, and permit Britain to use force against such traders if the commerce persisted.[51] By February 1851, even before he had received the full correspondence from the coast, Palmerston had decided that the time had come to conclude an anti-slave trade treaty with Kosoko. He instructed Beecroft to inform "the Chief of Lagos" that "lawful commerce is more advantageous to the nations of Africa than the Slave Trade," and that in putting down the slave trade and encouraging lawful commerce the British government "is conferring a benefit upon the people and chiefs of Africa." Beecroft was to offer British friendship if the treaty was signed and to threaten force if it was not, and also to remind Kosoko "that he does not hold his authority without a competitor, and that the chiefs of the African tribes do not always retain their authority to the end of their lives."[52] When the British consul and three naval officers visited Kosoko in November to present Palmerston's demands, he refused to sign the treaty, saying through Oshodi Tapa that he did not want British friendship.[53]

Rebuffed in this way, Beecroft and Commander T. G. Forbes, the senior officer in the Bights squadron, decided to use force against Kosoko. The story of the bombardment has been well told before, and its details need not be repeated here.[54] Suffice it to say that a first, unauthorized attack failed, with loss of life, and brought censure from Lord Granville, who had replaced Palmerston as foreign secretary.[55] Britain could not, however, allow defeat and humiliation to stand, for fear of the bad moral effect they would have on the natives. A second, authorized, and much larger and better coordinated attack in late December 1851 encountered well-planned resistance, but after two days of spirited fighting sent Kosoko, his chiefs, and many of their followers into flight across the lagoon and exile at the town of Epe. The foreign slave traders at Lagos also fled, most west to Ouidah, Porto Novo, or lesser coastal towns, but José Joaquim de Couto and José Joaquim de Britto Lima east to Epe with Kosoko. During the attack on the town or immediately after it, the houses and barracoons of important foreign and local slave traders were burned, and Kosoko's heavy guns were spiked or thrown into the lagoon. On December 29, Akitoye and his followers marched triumphantly into Lagos, reclaimed the *ìgá*, and began occupying land and houses vacated by those who had fled. Three days latter, Akitoye and two chiefs signed the treaty that the British wanted.[56]

Official discussions of the bombardment lay bare the motives underlying the first step in Britain's intervention in the politics of Lagos. They show that Palmerston, the Admiralty, and consular and naval representatives on the coast believed that Britain was pursuing a policy of reform that would simultaneously deal a fatal blow to the slave trade in West Africa, open the interior of the Bight of Benin to legitimate commerce for the good of Britain and West Africa, and make the region safe for other agents of civilization—the missionaries, the Sierra Leoneans, and the Egba. Consul Beecroft expressed this point of view succinctly when he wrote that military action was taken to "renovate and reform Africa and pull it out of the awful darkness that overshadows it."[57] The dual image of Lagos as one of the two last great holdouts in the West African slave trade—the other of which, Dahomey, could not be touched by sea—and as a town that because of its geographical location held the key to a potentially vast trade in vegetable products with a rich hinterland prompted the bombardment. Into the equation fed Britain's inability to understand local politics as anything more than a reflection of its own interests and its overly simplistic opposition of Kosoko as "a barbarous slave trader put up and supported by slave traders" and Akitoye as "a prudent man" anxious "to leave off the slave trade and support legitimate commerce."[58] Those responsible for the bombardment had convinced themselves that intervention represented "a grand opening" for the future of Britain and West Africa and that once Kosoko had been removed and Akitoye installed, "all [would] go right."[59]

Almost immediately after the bombardment more ships began coming to Lagos to buy palm oil and lesser exports. In February 1852, the new *ọba* and four chiefs signed an agreement with a group of European merchants and supercargoes that granted foreigners the right to trade at Lagos unmolested, to erect storage facilities on the southwest end of the island, and to choose their places of residence if they elected to settle in the town. The document also spelled out provisions for regulating trade, including that agreements to give or take goods at certain rates should be binding on all parties, that the *ọba* should be responsible for stoppages of trade, and that if they occurred he should compensate the injured parties in palm oil. The agreement made the king responsible for enforcing commercial credit, specifying that if a loan remained unpaid, he should sell the debtor's house or other property to liquidate it. So long as Africans had unpaid debts, moreover, they were to be prohibited from trading with anyone but their creditors, on penalty of a fine of a thousand gallons of palm oil. Breaches of these provisions were to be dealt with by a committee that had authority to impose fines and award their proceeds to injured parties. Misunderstandings among the *ọba*, chiefs, and foreign traders were to be settled before the king by two disinterested parties on both sides, with the *ọba* casting the deciding vote if a majority could not be obtained. In return for these protections, European merchants were to pay the *ọba* a duty of 3 percent on imports and 2 percent on exports.[60]

Commercial opportunities at Lagos looked sufficiently attractive that by the end of the year a Sardinian, a German, and three British merchants had opened commercial establishments on shore. Within two years, a French firm, Victor Régis, had joined them, and soon thereafter additional British and German merchants arrived as well. At mid-decade a British observer commented enthusiastically, "The palm oil trade is on the increase," as indeed it was.[61]

The British bombardment opened Lagos to Christian missionaries in addition to new European merchants. Within a fortnight of Akitoye's installation, the CMS sent Saro catechist James White to begin preaching the Gospel in the town. Mindful, undoubtedly, of the new *ọba*'s relationship with the missionaries as well as of his place at the center of local religious and political life, White conducted his first service in the courtyard of the king's palace.[62] In May 1852, he started a school attended by twelve boys. Before the end of the year, the CMS had moved its coastal headquarters from Badagry to Lagos, and soon after the Wesleyan missionaries did the same.[63]

With the merchants and missionaries came hundreds of former slaves from Sierra Leone and Brazil, as well as smaller numbers from Cuba, some from communities further west along the Slave Coast and others directly from Sierra Leone or the Americas. These immigrants swelled the congregations of the new churches and enrollments of the young schools, and they also established new mosques and Islamic brotherhoods. A disproportionate number of the Sierra Leoneans made their living by entering the town's expanding trade. While some of the Brazilians engaged in commerce, many were artisans, whose skills shaped the style of the settlement's ornate late nineteenth-century buildings.[64]

Toward the end of 1852, the Foreign Office appointed a vice-consul to Lagos, and half a year later it sent Benjamin Campbell there as consul. A man of some twenty years' experience on the Guinea coast, Campbell held office at Lagos until April 1859, and he played a major role in shaping the affairs of the town during the consular period.[65]

Despite these many positive developments, British officials soon concluded that all was not going to go right at Lagos simply because Kosoko had been removed and Akitoye installed. Conflict continued between the two men and their followers, who attacked each other on the lagoon, disrupting trade. Kosoko's supporters began drifting back to Lagos, moreover, and periodically hostilities broke out between them and followers of the puppet king, raising the specter of renewed civil war. Rumors circulated of an impending attack on Lagos, and on one occasion Kosoko's forces attempted a landing.[66] When Akitoye died suddenly in 1853, his successor and son Dosunmu, appointed quickly by the British, believed that his father had been poisoned by Ajenia, Ipossu, and Oshodi Tapa, chiefs loyal to Kosoko.[67]

Regional power struggles compounded these local conflicts. The Egba, many of whom remained loyal to Akitoye, regularly harassed Kosoko's people and were harassed by them. Dahomey, Ijebu, and Ibadan, on the other hand, maintained alliances with Kosoko and threatened the Egba. Moreover, several of Badagry's chiefs remained in exile, and the Mewu's meddling in affairs around the lagoon had provoked the king of Porto Novo to retaliate.[68] All this local and regional instability not only produced political unrest but also interrupted the supply of exports and other commodities to Lagos, such that foodstuffs doubled in price. Palm oil exports actually declined in 1859 and 1860.[69] To complicate matters, the entrepreneurial spirit and ongoing commercial success of Kosoko and his supporters at Epe were luring some of the new legitimate traders to Palma, a small port to the east, and away from Lagos.

Twice in 1853 the British mounted unsuccessful military expeditions against Kosoko. Unable to persuade the Navy and the Foreign Office to provide the support necessary to move decisively against the deposed *ọba*, Campbell suddenly shifted to a policy of trying to mediate a settlement in the local conflict. He opened discussions with Kosoko, offering to allow his people to use the port at Palma, to protect him against molestation by Dosunmu, and to treat him as a friendly chief, if he would renounce the slave trade and stop harassing Akitoye's supporters. Responding to a suggestion from Oshodi Tapa and some of Kosoko's other chiefs, Campbell then arranged a meeting between chiefs loyal to the two big men, and subsequently he signed a treaty with Kosoko. During the mid-1850s, the consul also began reforming British policy toward the Egba from unquestioning support to more critical engagement.[70] The long-standing feud dividing the two Lagos factions could not, however, be laid to rest so easily. Campbell's actions deeply threatened Dosunmu and his supporters, including the CMS missionaries, and relations between them and Campbell deteriorated. Dosunmu continued to refuse to permit Kosoko's people to come to Lagos to trade, and he troubled them in other ways as well. In time, Kosoko's supporters began attacking Lagos people on the lagoon once more, and rumors revived of an impending invasion.[71]

The small European population in Lagos was as badly divided as the African one continued to be. The merchants, the CMS missionaries, and Consul Campbell all fell to quarrelling over land along the waterfront, where the marina eventually developed. The CMS bitterly opposed the consul's rapprochement with Kosoko and his policy toward the Egba, and they intrigued against him locally and lobbied in Britain to have him removed. Campbell, for his part, greatly mistrusted them. The European merchants at Lagos initially supported Campbell, in part because they found Kosoko and his chiefs responsive trading partners. Later, however, several of them turned on the consul, and they also began fighting with one another over the collection of the *ọba's* custom duties and other matters.[72]

In this context, British consular and naval officials on the coast did what they could to suppress the foreign slave trade, reporting on the activities of suspected slavers, capturing the occasional slave ship, and signing additional anti-slave trade treaties with African rulers. But while slave exports ended from Lagos in 1851, they continued from Palma until the middle of the decade and from Ouidah and lesser ports on the western Slave Coast until after 1860.[73] British officials remained convinced that Dahomey was still committed to the abominable traffic, and although the market in Brazil had finally closed that in Cuba remained open. The French, moreover, appeared to be trying to revive the slave trade under another name by recruiting contract labor on the coast for shipment to the Antilles.[74] Marco Borges Ferras, Pedro Martins Jambo, Joaquim Pereira Machado, Louis Lemaignière, and other known slave traders periodically showed up in Lagos, and Campbell feared a revival of the commerce in the town. As the head of the local government, the *ọba* was responsible for expelling them, and under pressure from Campbell, Dosunmu generally fulfilled his duty.[75] But the consul believed that the king was less committed to ending the involvement of his own people in the slave trade than he was that of Europeans, and that he was also less able to control indigenous slave traders. The formidable Madame Tinubu, a major trader in slaves and other goods, who strongly opposed the British intervention at Lagos, was believed to be plotting to drive out the British and the Sierra Leonean repatriates and to revive the slave trade.[76]

Equally troubling, neither Akitoye nor Dosunmu appeared able to create the cultural and legal order thought necessary for the new legitimate commerce to flourish. Most of the provisions of the 1852 and subsequent commercial agreements with European merchants proved beyond the capacity of these two *ọbas* to fulfill. The palm oil trade rested heavily on credit, and both rulers had great difficulty enforcing payment of debts to the satisfaction of Europeans. When foreign merchants could not collect on loans, they sometimes resorted to violence to coerce payment. Locals, on the other hand, at times dealt with unpaid debts by seizing a relative or countryman of the debtor, too reminiscent of the slave trade for the liking of most British officers.[77]

The *ọbas* also proved incapable of handling disputes to the satisfaction of Europeans and the Sierra Leonean immigrants, who either took matters into their own hands or appealed to the British consuls, European missionaries, or an Italian merchant named G. B. Scala, consul to the king of Sardinia, for help in settling their differences. Consul Campbell complained, "my whole time was soon occupied in listening to complaints of wrong and oppression." To ease the burden, he encouraged the Sierra Leoneans, whom he regarded as a "better class of Africans . . . advanced in civilization . . . [with] correct notions of right and wrong," to establish a court for settling differences among themselves.[78] Yet it was unrealistic to think that their court could create the new cultural and legal order that the British desired. Moreover, when Akitoye or Dosunmu did act decisively in cases involving Europeans or Sierra Leonean repatriates, the consuls usually protested that an African ruler should not be allowed to exercise authority over more civilized beings.[79]

Within a decade of the bombardment, British officials on the coast and many of those in London as well had come to believe that the local state, Britain's compliant satellite on the Bight of Benin, was incapable of establishing the political, legal, and cultural order necessary for Lagos to realize its historic mission as the site from which innocent trade, disciplined work, Christian religion, and enlightened civilization would spread throughout the region. Writing to the foreign secretary, Lord Russell, in April 1860, the British consul G. Brand argued that since 1851 Lagos had changed from "a haunt of piratical slave dealers" to "the seat of a most important and increasing legal trade." He touted the kingdom as "the natural entrepôt of an immense country abounding in unlimited resources" and "the natural [base] of operations for extending the blessings of industry, commerce, and Christian civilization to this portion of . . . Africa." But he warned that Lagos would "never fully serve these great purposes under the Native Government," because the kings and chiefs were adverse to all progress and "the civilized portion of the community" was hopelessly divided. Brand complained that Lagos had no effective protection of property, no mode of enforcing credit, in short, "no government." The increase of trade, of civilized ideas, and of European interests and habits, he argued, demanded "civilized command." Brand told officials back home that, as a matter of necessity, British consuls were already exercising "a feeble, irregular, and irresponsible jurisdiction over a variety of judicial, police, and even administrative matters." He concluded, "To do justice to this place . . . and to put it in a position to become what it seems by nature intended to be," Britain should claim the town.[80]

The Colonial Office, whose responsibility the new possession would become, opposed annexation. Sir Frederick Rogers and T. F. Elliot, influential undersecretaries, foresaw administrative problems with the colony, and they had already come to doubt the power of British government action to reform Africa.[81] In June 1861, however, the colonial secretary, the Duke of Newcastle, finally acceded after continued pressure from the Foreign Office and the prime minister, Lord Palmerston. The foreign secretary communicated to H. G. Foote, by then the British consul, that Her Majesty's Government had decided to take possession of Lagos as a British dependency, changing "an anomalous protectorate into an avowed occupation." Annexation, he maintained, was indispensable to complete the suppression of the slave trade in the Bight of Benin, support the development of lawful commerce, and check the aggressive spirit of the king of Dahomey, whose "barbarous wars, and encouragement to slave-trading, are the chief cause of disorder in that part of Africa." In communicating the decision to Dosunmu, Foote was to reassure the *ọba* that it was not motivated by "any dissatisfaction with his conduct," but rather by a desire to exercise an influence in the town and the region that would be "permanently beneficial to the African race."[82]

In late July 1861, William McCoskry, a British merchant then serving as acting consul, and N. B. Bedingfield, commander of HMS *Prometheus* and the senior naval officer of the Bights Division, ordered Dosunmu to come to a meeting on board the *Prometheus*, unaccompanied by his chiefs. There, in view of the ship's guns and men, they told him that Britain had decided to annex Lagos. Dosunmu said he would have to lay the matter before his chiefs and promised a reply by the first of August. On that day, McCoskry and Bedingfield stationed the *Prometheus* in the river not far from the *ìgá* and then called on the king. Dosunmu told his visitors, in the presence of his chiefs, that he would not sign a treaty of cession, first offering excuses and then issuing threats. McCoskry and Bedingfield countered that they intended to take Lagos on the sixth of August and then departed.

Aware, undoubtedly, that he could withstand British military power no better than his far mightier predecessor Kosoko, Dosunmu called a meeting at the *ìgá* on the fifth, which he asked "all Europeans and immigrants" to attend. Accounts of what transpired on that day differ.[83] McCoskry and Bedingfield, who went accompanied by two gunboats and a number of well-armed marines, maintained that at the meeting Dosunmu and his chiefs extracted three concessions from them and then agreed to sign a treaty of cession at the consulate the next day. The concessions were that Dosunmu could continue to use the title of king, that he could settle disputes between natives of Lagos with their consent, subject to appeal to

British laws, and that in the transfer of land the *ọba's* stamp affixed to the document would constitute proof that there were no other native claims to the property. The *ọba* and chiefs claimed, on the other hand, that they had agreed only to sign a document allowing merchants and immigrants to handle their own affairs.

On August 6, Dosunmu and several of his chiefs went to the consulate. They later claimed that McCoskry and Bedingfield presented them with a treaty, the contents of which they had not agreed to sign, and that they put their marks to it under protest to prevent Bedingfield from firing on the town. McCoskry described the events that day as follows:

> Yesterday an immense crowd . . . collected about the Consulate . . . and at 1 P.M. the King landed under a salute of seven guns from the "Prometheus" anchored close by. After signing the Treaty, with four of his principal Chiefs, they were conducted to the flag-staff . . . ; the Proclamation [ceding Lagos to the Queen of Great Britain] was read, . . . the British flag unfurled, and saluted with twenty-guns; the National Anthem sung by a band of children from the Missionary Schools.[84]

The day concluded with a dinner on board the *Prometheus*, to which Dosunmu, his principal men, and nearly all of the Europeans in the town were invited. The first fateful step had been taken toward the creation of Nigeria, black Africa's most populous and powerful nation.

In London, the Colonial Office remained deeply ambivalent about the new colony. Undersecretaries there were convinced, on the basis of experience with Britain's other West African settlements, that places such as Lagos "were always likely to display an irresistible tendency to expand."[85] Not long after the annexation, the Duke of Newcastle worried with great prescience that "[t]he original sin of taking possession of Lagos" would lead inevitably to "intermeddling by force of arms" beyond the coast.[86]

Early Colonial Rule

The annexation opened a new era in the history of Lagos, but it did not immediately mark a radical break with the past. British consuls had for several years already been intervening in domestic political and legal affairs and working to influence the balance of regional power. Moreover, developing the new legitimate commerce and suppressing the external slave trade remained central preoccupations of the early colonial state, although after the Cuban market for slaves finally closed in 1867, anti-slavery arguments were invoked more to build support for other policies than because the foreign slave trade remained a real threat. While the annexation of Lagos ended the kingdom's autonomy and undermined the *ọba's* authority and prestige, it did not terminate his involvement in the affairs of his subjects or politics of the town.

No sooner had Britain annexed Lagos than the policies of the colonial government began to be dominated by another of the great mid-Victorian projects of reform: the quest for a cheap state and balanced budget. Britain acquired its new possession on the Slave Coast at a time when policies of strict economy and sound finance were as important to many British statesmen as free labor, free trade, and commercial expansion.[87] The foreign secretary, Lord Russell, had anticipated these concerns in his dispatch authorizing the annexation, when he asked Consul Foote for information about the expenditure that administration would entail and revenue that could be raised locally to meet it. Russell ordered Foote to keep costs "within the narrowest limits compatible with the safety of the place."[88]

Soon after the annexation, the colonial secretary instructed the first governor, H. S. Freeman, that civil government in Lagos should be formed "on the simplest and most economical scale."[89] Although Lagos received a small grant from Parliament to pay the salary of the governor and pension of the *ọba*, the British Treasury was rarely willing to further subsidize the cost of running the young colony. Administrators were expected to raise revenue locally and make the dependency self-supporting as quickly as possible, and most expenditures had to wait until there were funds in the local coffers to cover them. What Sara Berry has observed of a later colonial period in Africa was equally true of the 1860s and 1870s. Colonial administrators in Lagos "faced a continual struggle to make ends meet," and they established "hegemony on a shoestring."[90] From the moment of the annexation, concern about minimizing costs, raising revenue, and balancing the budget occupied a permanent place at the center of policymaking, which not only constrained the pace of development but also influenced the character of the early colonial state.[91]

Fiscal constraints ensured that the colonial state remained very small until the final decade and a half of the nineteenth century. From the annexation until 1866, Lagos was administered separately, but in that year it was joined with Britain's other West African settlements and brought under the authority of a governor-in-chief at Freetown, Sierra Leone, retaining only rudimentary local government. A further reorganization in

1874 led to administration from the Gold Coast until the two colonies were separated in 1886, and Lagos was once again granted its own government.[92] Separation from the Gold Coast brought slight growth, but significant expansion did not commence until the 1890s, with the extension of colonial rule into the Yoruba hinterland, construction of a railway linking the coast to points north, and establishment of technical departments in agriculture, forestry, and other fields. Throughout the 1860s and 1870s, the civil administration in Lagos normally employed only five or six Europeans—a chief administrative officer, a private or colonial secretary, a chief magistrate, a colonial surgeon, and a harbor master, although there were sometimes also a few British military officers in the colony involved in civil administration. In 1881 still only eleven Europeans held government posts at Lagos.[93]

The need to keep costs down, coupled with a desire to avoid the high mortality experienced by Europeans on the coast, dictated that the colonial government at Lagos be staffed mainly by Africans. Mulattos and liberated slaves educated in Sierra Leone, and later their descendants and other Africans educated locally, were used along with small numbers of blacks from North America, the West Indies, and the Gold Coast to fill jobs requiring literacy and numeracy.[94] In the 1860s and 1870s, educated mulattos and blacks held such high-ranking posts as acting colonial secretary, first clerk and treasurer, acting collector of customs and treasurer, acting colonial surveyor, and inspector of the civil police constabulary. Other groups of Africans whom Europeans identified with particular skills performed additional essential labor. Thus Kroomen and Gold Coast canoemen worked on government vessels and in the harbor, while slaves, most of northern origin, were recruited and trained to form an armed police force.[95] Slowly, the expansion of public works, construction of the railroad, and after 1907 construction of a deep-water port created additional demand for skilled and unskilled wage labor. The small size of the state is particularly noteworthy given that from the time of the annexation Britain sought to rule the town of Lagos, as well as Badagry and Palma (the western and eastern divisions of the colony), directly rather than through indigenous political authorities, the later high colonial response to the challenge of establishing "hegemony on a shoestring."

The branches of government that developed first reflected the priorities of the state. Within weeks of the annexation, a harbor master was appointed and a post office was created to facilitate the development of trade. Aware that direct taxation would arouse severe opposition from an already hostile local population, British administrators elected to raise revenue by continuing to levy duties on exports or imports, much as the *ọba* had done.[96] They soon set up a customs department to take over duty collection, and it quickly became one of the largest branches of the government. Britain compensated the *ọba* for his loss by granting him a pension of £1000, somewhat less than the taxes on foreign trade he had been accustomed to receiving.[97]

Commitment to enforcing debts and developing property rights had helped motivate the annexation.[98] In its wake, early administrators quickly organized a number of colonial courts to deal with disputes involving debt, property, and other civil as well as criminal matters, presided over by commissioners and magistrates who, with the exception of the chief magistrate, were drawn from European merchants or educated Africans in the town. While the composition and jurisdiction of the early tribunals changed periodically until the introduction of a Supreme Court and Police Magistrate's Court in 1876, they included a slave court, a commercial or "petty debt" court, a police court, which heard minor criminal cases, and a criminal court, which handled more serious criminal offenses. The Slave Court dealt with cases involving "run away slaves, apprentices, etc."[99]

With the courts came the introduction of a civil police constabulary, responsible for serving legal summonses, carrying out court orders, and enforcing colonial law in Lagos, Badagry, Palma, and subsequently other towns and villages within the colony. The largest branch of the civil government by far, this force comprised a Saro inspector, four sergeants, eight corporals, and a hundred constables as early as 1863. By the end of the decade it had grown to nineteen officers and 168 constables.[100] The jail, which Governor Freeman described as falling down, completed the institutions of the colonial legal system.[101]

Beyond these branches of the government, a rudimentary medical department dealt with sanitation and public health and ministered to the medical needs of ailing officials. The colonial secretary had instructed Freeman in December 1861 that one of the first steps of the government should be to enforce sanitary regulations.[102] Finally, a small secretariat handled routine government business and did the administrator's "dirtiest work."[103]

At the head of the local government sat the chief administrative officer, a governor until Lagos was joined with the West African Settlements and an administrator or lieutenant governor from then until its separation from the Gold Coast in 1886. Freeman, the first governor, wanted tight personal control of every department and argued that he needed it to keep expenses down and prevent "opposition from the natives." He maintained that the people of Lagos were accustomed to "a supreme and absolute authority" and would take from him what they would not from the courts.[104] But Freeman held office for only eighteen months, broken by a six-month home leave, not long enough to establish a political culture and entrench processes of rule. He was succeeded by John Hawley Glover, an ambitious, headstrong, and sometimes overbearing former naval officer, who had previous experience at Lagos as a member of Dr. William Baikie's 1857 Niger Expedition, the commander of a gunboat that patrolled the lagoon in 1861 and 1862, and the colonial secretary or acting governor in 1863 and 1864.[105] Glover served as Lagos's chief executive officer for eight years, with but two home leaves, and he more than Freeman molded the early colonial state. Between them, the two men, who shared many ideas and policies and worked closely together during the time they were both in Lagos, headed the government for all but nine months of the period between 1862 and 1872.

Freeman and Glover enjoyed considerable independence at Lagos, both because of the delays involved in communicating with their superiors and because higher-ups depended on them for knowledge of local affairs. Officials at the Colonial Office railed more than once about Glover's utter "disregard of all rules and orders."[106] For his part, Glover was determined to create a strong colonial state, and like Freeman he wanted tight personal control of it. He accomplished these goals in face of the very limited human and financial resources available to him in two ways. First, he constructed a dense network of patron-client relationships with a diverse group of influential Africans and Europeans from whom he could expect personal loyalty and support, and he incorporated them into the colonial power structure. Glover ruled the young colony as much through his personal relationships with his clients as through the formal institutions of the state. To construct relationships with Africans, he adopted patterns of behavior rooted in local political culture, setting himself up, in certain ways, as an African big man. Glover's second strategy was to develop, beginning during Freeman's tenure in office but continuing through his own, a locally recruited armed police force drawn from slaves of northern origin, which he alone controlled. He used this force to provide defense and security and, along with the civil constabulary, to pursue his interests inside the colony, on the frontier, and beyond.

Glover's clients included people working under him in the colonial service, from his European vice-consul on the western frontier, Thomas Tickel; the acting collector of customs and later district magistrate and superintendent of the Armed Hausa Police, Roger Goldsworthy; and the postmaster C. D. Turton; to his Saro inspector of the civil constabulary, I. H. Willoughby; his private messenger, A. C. Willoughby; and a clerk in the surveyor's office, J. T. Johnson. So tight was the relationship between Glover and I. H. Willoughby, who also translated for the administrator, that locals referred to the inspector of the civil constabulary as Lagos's "second or little Governor."[107] A contemporary remarked that Willoughby "was more a personal and political agent of Captain Glover than an officer of the British Government."[108]

Glover's clients also included Africans outside government employment, such as Kosoko, Oshodi Tapa, and the young but ambitious Taiwo Olowo.[109] Following the annexation, Ọba Dosunmu and his chiefs continued to oppose the kingdom's loss of autonomy. Moreover, they maintained support for the Egba, whom Freeman and Glover now held responsible for prolonging the Ijaye war that had broken out in the interior between Ijaye and Abeokuta on the one side and Ibadan and its supporters on the other. The two British administrators believed that this conflict was ruining the colony's trade, undermining its revenue, and hence threatening its very existence.[110] Relations between Dosunmu and first Freeman and then Glover grew ever more tense and hostile. By 1863, Glover was writing that the *ọba* was "both a rogue and a fool" and that he should be reminded that "he was not King of Lagos by his own right or might and that the same power that placed his father as King and who at his father's death took him out of a fishing canoe and made him King against the wishes of his chiefs had the full right to unking him."[111]

While this was going on, Freeman and Glover continued the policy of British consuls before them by pursuing an accommodation with Kosoko and Oshodi Tapa. These two big men, now out of power and ever responsive to changing opportunities, made peace with the British government, threw themselves into the new legitimate commerce, and began lobbying their new allies to be allowed to return to Lagos. When Freeman granted their request in 1862 over Dosunmu's protests, Kosoko and many of his chiefs performed a dramatic *volte-face* and became loyal supporters of the British administration.[112]

To build relationships with his African clients, Glover adopted strategies of attracting and holding followers that resembled those long employed by members of the local political elite. First, he used his position at the center of the state to help loyal members of his retinue obtain access to opportunities and resources that facilitated their social and economic advancement. For example, the administrator carefully promoted the careers of his educated African supporters, such as I. H. and A. C. Willoughby, in the colonial service, and he also found jobs in the government for junior members of their families.[113] After arranging Kosoko's and Oshodi Tapa's return to Lagos, Freeman had recommended them for pensions and granted them land on which they and their hundreds of followers could build compounds. Then Glover helped a number of Kosoko's and Tapa's key supporters establish contacts with European merchants in Lagos, obtain credit from them, and break into the new legitimate commerce on a large scale.[114]

Beyond assisting his clients materially, Glover acted as their protector and advocate, much as local patrons did for their *aláàgbàsọ*. When a junior member of the Willoughby family stole government money and I. H. Willoughby was investigated for handling the matter privately instead of charging the man with a criminal offense, for instance, Glover vigorously defended his inspector of police and eventually appointed the perpetrator to a new job in the colonial service.[115] Moreover, Glover consistently sought to protect Kosoko, Tapa, and their followers from harassment by Dosunmu and members of his faction. The administrator personally helped Kosoko's and Tapa's henchman and political successor Taiwo Olowo collect large debts owed him by Egba traders and establish himself as one of Lagos's wealthiest and most powerful men.[116]

No evidence has come to light of sexual liaisons between Glover and local women, but the administrator did cultivate the friendship of influential Saro females, including Mrs. Juliana Thompson and Mrs. Josiah Crowther, the Rev. Samuel Ajayi Crowther's daughter and daughter-in-law. C. D. Turton wrote to Glover in 1873, "your best friends outside our immediate circle are ladies."[117] In addition, the administrator accepted children of his African clients as wards and educated some of them, mimicking local practice.[118] To further consolidate his bond with Kosoko, Tapa, and other local chiefs who supported him, Glover introduced new state regalia—hats, staffs, and swords—and distributed them as a mark of the recipient's relationship to Lagos's new ruler and role at the center of the state, much as *ọbas* had done before him.[119] Finally, the administrator understood the meaning of hospitality in local culture and dispensed it shrewdly. In return for access to the center of the colonial power structure and the privileges it brought, Glover received loyal service and support from his many African clients.

J. H. Glover behaved like a local ruler in yet another way. He regularly heard disputes among Lagosians, bypassing the newly established colonial courts. Lady Glover wrote of her husband,

> After breakfast for two or three hours "Obba Globar" (as his people called him) was to be seen sitting on the verandah smoking a cigarette and listening to their grievances. He had always a native interpreter, and patiently listened to both sides of the question being explained to him amid the loud clamour of the aggrieved parties.[120]

Both in performing a judicial function and in hearing disputes the way he did, Glover acted very much like an *ọba*, as his local nickname attests.

Glover's African clients gave him a power base in the town and surrounding territory. Kosoko, Tapa, and their leading supporters had large followings, as, to a lesser extent, did I. H. Willoughby and a number of other Africans in the colonial service, which they mobilized to the administrator's advantage when necessary. Glover's many local clients and members of their retinues served as the eyes, ears, mouth, and occasionally strong arm of the early colonial state. Through them the administrator's reach stretched into Ereko, Epetedo, Olowogbowo, other quarters of Lagos, and beyond, keeping him informed about what was going on and giving him channels of communication with the African population. Glover relied heavily on his Saro inspector of police, I. H. Willoughby, to do his bidding, and of course Willoughby controlled his constables as well as his personal clients. Furthermore, the administrator in effect used Tapa and Taiwo Olowo as *bàbá ìsàlẹ̀* of Epe, Isheri, and elsewhere, big men in the capital who oversaw the affairs of these provincial towns and represented the interests of their inhabitants at the center of the state.[121] In addition, when Glover believed that Dosunmu threatened rebellion and the Egba invasion in 1865, he called on Kosoko's and Tapa's warriors for a show of mass support, helping to maintain the British in power. Seeking the support of Ibadan and Ijebu in an attack on the Egba that same year, Glover relied on Tapa and Kosoko to negotiate it for him.[122] All of these examples illustrate ways that Glover ruled through his local clients. Little shows their loyalty to him better than the letters they wrote after his policies were repudiated in 1872, and he returned to Britain to defend himself. This correspondence assured Glover that he had been grievously wronged, supplied him with detailed information about what his enemies were doing in his absence, and expressed great hope that he would one day return to Lagos.[123]

The locally recruited and trained civil police constabulary also contributed to the development of a cheap but strong colonial state over which Glover exercised tight personal control. Indeed, the colony was in many respects run as a police state. After Glover left Lagos, his nemesis

John Pope Hennessy, the acting governor-in-chief of the West African Settlements, accused I. H. Willoughby of using his position as inspector of police to "cow the natives down" and exercise "a widespread terror" in the town.[124] Glover himself credited Willoughby and his constables with shouldering heavy responsibility for the "entire revolution" in political, social, and domestic life needed at Lagos.[125]

Yet the civil constabulary was not trained to bear arms, and it did not meet the needs of local administrators for security. Lagos had been acquired by force, and force was necessary to maintain Britain's position there. Freeman and Glover feared rebellion in the town itself, and they rapidly became embroiled in unfriendly relations with communities on the frontier and states in the interior.[126] Force could be supplied when necessary by Royal Navy vessels that continued to patrol the West African coast and by troops of a West Indian Regiment stationed at Lagos. But Freeman and Glover neither deployed these forces nor commanded them. Moreover, the number of soldiers stationed at Lagos was never large enough, owing to cost considerations, to allow local officials to feel very confident.[127]

Early British administrators met their need for force partly through symbolic displays of military might that regularly reminded the local population what Britain could do, if pushed too far. Thus when Governor Freeman experienced "trifling opposition" from villages around Lagos and concluded that it was caused by fear of the British, he called a meeting of the surrounding chiefs to "establish more friendly relations." On this occasion he organized foot racing, horse racing, and games for the amusement of his guests, but he also ordered a display of rifle and heavy gun practice for their edification.[128] Glover turned a corridor at Government House into an armory so that when local rulers visited him they would be awed by a display of arms.[129]

Beyond manipulating symbolic displays of military power, however, Freeman and Glover met their need for force by creating the Armed Hausa Police. Glover recruited this militia from slaves, primarily of northern origin, who were either owned in Lagos or ran away to the colony from neighboring territories. Although it is doubtful that all were in fact Hausa, the force as a whole soon had that ethnicity inscribed upon it. Freeman and Glover intended the Armed Hausa to provide a cheap military unit, which they themselves could deploy and command.[130] Glover, however, used the troops not only as soldiers, but also as police, informers, and political agents, as subsequent data will show.

Glover and some other Europeans in Lagos believed that male Hausa slaves had a natural aptitude for military service, perhaps in part because of the role they had played as warriors in precolonial Lagos.[131] Glover was also convinced that as these men would owe Britain their freedom, had no ties to the local population "save those of slaves to their masters," and were too independent to be employed by other Europeans, they would be wholly dependent on the government.[132] In his view, all of these factors made them ideal candidates to become soldiers.

However, Glover also took pains to develop bonds of personal loyalty with the Armed Hausa, as he did with his clients. From the force's inception in 1862 until 1866, he trained and commanded it personally, and when he relinquished those responsibilities, he hand-picked a successor who would be good with the men and obedient to him.[133] Glover rewarded his troops by helping them obtain urban or rural land and build dwellings of their own, necessary for any real autonomy in the local community. He also raised their pay and provided them with smart uniforms that broadcast their status as free men and agents of the new colonial government.[134] It did not take long for Glover to develop the Armed Hausa into an effective fighting force, which served successfully in military engagements in and around Lagos and later in Britain's imperial conquest of other parts of West Africa.[135] As Glover had predicted, the Armed Hausa repaid his efforts with devotion not only to him, but also to Britain. When other former slaves of northern origin who had enlisted in the West Indian Regiment mutinied in 1865, the Armed Hausa Police subdued them, despite their common backgrounds.[136] Several years later when Glover left Lagos under a cloud, a number of the Armed Hausa resigned, stating that they would rejoin the force "when their father [came] back."[137]

Glover used the Armed Hausa to pursue policies in the region at odds with those of his superiors in London. Both Freeman and he placed a high priority on capturing for the colony trade flowing from the interior to the coast across the lagoon, so that Lagos could realize its promise as the natural entrepôt of the Bight of Benin's rich hinterland. They were motivated in this less by a desire to promote Britain's commercial interests than by a need to secure the young colony's tax base, render it self-supporting, and finance its development. To achieve the desired end, local administrators wanted the boundary of British territory around the lagoon defined widely enough so that most of the major trade routes from the interior would empty into it. Achieving this goal proved relatively unproblematic on the eastern frontier, where Kosoko willingly ceded his territory, including the ports of Palma and Lekki, to the British in 1863. But in the west, it generated sustained conflict with the French and the Kingdom of Porto Novo.[138]

Equally important, the two British administrators urgently wanted to maintain the free flow of trade goods between the interior and the colony, which they believed the war that had broken out in 1860 between Ibadan and Ijaye threatened. The conflict had escalated into the formation of two broad coalitions, after Ibadan had forged alliances with Oyo, Ijebu Remo, Dahomey, and Kosoko and Ijaye had appealed for support to Abeokuta, Ijebu Ode, Ilorin, and Dosunmu. Both sides also had influential friends and trading partners among the Saro in Lagos, as well as in Badagry and Porto Novo. First Freeman and then Glover held war chiefs in Abeokuta responsible for dragging out the conflict and interrupting the shipment of palm produce and other goods to the coast. Moreover, they believed that these chiefs were deeply hostile to the British government at Lagos. In response, the two men pursued a number of policies designed to pressure the Egba to end the war and punish them for their opposition, including an arms embargo, intermittent restrictions on the movement of goods and people between Lagos and Abeokuta, regular refusal to return runaway Egba slaves, and a toll imposed at the frontier on Egba goods entering the colony. In addition, Glover worked to open a new trade route from the interior independent of Egba control, especially for Ibadan. These policies led the British into prolonged conflict with the Egba, which had major repercussions for politics in Lagos itself.[139]

At the Colonial Office, on the other hand, officials opposed deeper British involvement on the Slave Coast and anything that smacked of the extension of British territory there. Opposition intensified following the report of the 1865 Select Committee on the State of British Settlements on the Western Coast of Africa, which recommended that any further expansion of British territory in the region would be inexpedient and that the government should, as quickly as possible, transfer to the natives the administration of all possessions except probably Sierra Leone.[140] The stance of officials in London led local administrators into prolonged struggle with their superiors back home over the definition of the boundary of the new colony, with the men on the spot favoring a greater Lagos to secure trade and revenue and those at home wanting a lesser one.

To skirt the Colonial Office's resistance to British interference beyond what it was willing to accept as the outer limits of the colony and to provide a means of implementing his Egba policy that he himself could finance and control, Glover used the Armed Hausa Police. He stationed them not only in Badagry and Palma, but also in Otta, Isheri, Ikorodu, Ejinrin, and other towns on the frontier and employed them at once as soldiers, police, and political agents. In 1863, he expanded the force beyond its then one hundred regular troops by recruiting an additional six hundred "irregulars," also from slaves of northern origin, whom he drilled in groups of a hundred for two months a year each. When not under drill, these "rural constables," as Glover called them, were expected to live on farms in outlying parts of the colony and serve as "guardians of the peace."[141] Then in 1865, Glover established two "cordons" of outposts, the first occupied by Hausa regulars eight miles from the base of the West Indian Regiment at Ebute Metta and the second occupied by irregulars eight miles further on. Glover regarded these troops as a defensive force, but he also employed them to implement blockades against the Egba, encourage their domestic slaves to run away, and collect tolls imposed on their goods. More broadly, the Armed Hausa provided intelligence and kept the administrator informed about what was happening on the frontier and beyond.[142]

Although organized hierarchically under the leadership of corporals and sergeants, the Armed Hausa on the frontier were supervised very lightly. They carried out Glover's will as they understood it and otherwise enjoyed great latitude to pursue their own interests. The irregulars, moreover, received no pay other than "the proceeds of such captures as they might be able to effect," except when on active duty.[143] It is not surprising that the Egba and Ijebu found the presence of these troops on their borders very offensive and complained bitterly about abuses of power.[144] One can easily imagine how galling it must have been for chiefs, warriors, and traders from the interior, many of whom were major slaveowners, to find former slaves harassing them on the frontier of the colony and encouraging further desertions, in the name of the new British government at Lagos.

The creation of the Armed Hausa Police opened one of the first breaches in the institution of slavery at Lagos, and the organization needs a separate study based on military records, provincial archives, and oral research with descendants. A shadowy picture emerges, however, of the opportunities that the Armed Hausa's farms and settlements on the frontier created for Lagos slaves from the frequent references in Supreme Court cases to former slaves who had left the town for periods of time to "go to farm."

Glover's method of ruling Lagos, coupled with the policies that Freeman and he pursued, had the unintended consequence of reproducing the intense factionalism that had divided Lagos in the precolonial period. This development led in the early 1870s to Glover's departure from the colony and to a number of abrupt policy changes. I. H. Willoughby, A. C. Willoughby, Kosoko, Oshodi Tapa, and others among the British administrators' leading African supporters were all identified with Ibadan or Oyo in one way or another. While Freeman and Glover had numerous reasons of their own for being anti-Egba, their African clients also influenced their views of interior affairs. Glover's Egba policies and his close identification with pro-Ibadan people quickly drove influential Saro of Egba and Ijebu descent, such as the merchants J. P. L. Davies and Henry Robbin and the sheriff J. A. O. Payne, into opposition with Ọba Dosunmu and his followers. When a commercial recession hit in 1872, Glover's anti-Egba stance also alienated a number of leading British merchants, some of whom had opened factories in Abeokuta.

A new acting governor-in-chief of Britain's West African Settlements, John Pope Hennessy, was appointed in the same year, and Glover summoned him to Lagos in hopes of winning his support and convincing him to annex Porto Novo to close off the Egba's last independent outlet to the sea. Glover's plan backfired, however, when Pope Hennessy concluded, after local investigation, that the administrator's own policies were responsible for many of the colony's problems and summarily reversed them.[145] The decline in trade, which had reduced colonial revenue, produced a deficit of almost £20,000, and would require a loan to cover the colony's obligations, made matters more urgent to money-minded officials in London.[146] Glover responded to Pope Hennessy's repudiation by immediately rushing home to defend his policies, never to resume authority in Lagos.

Soon after Henry Fowler, Glover's temporary replacement, began reversing his predecessor's policies, I. H. Willoughby, Roger Goldsworthy, and a number of Glover's other clients in the colonial service resigned or left Lagos, as did some of his beloved Armed Hausa.[147] Oshodi Tapa had died in 1868 and Kosoko followed him to join the ancestors in April 1872, the same month that Pope Hennessy came to Lagos, removing from the scene two powerful men who had dominated local affairs for more than three decades. Meanwhile, the new administration restored Dosunmu to favor and pressed him to implement a number of its most questionable policies, as well as to conduct diplomacy. J. P. L. Davies, J. A. O. Payne, and other Saro associated with the Egba and Ijebu quickly gained influence at Government House. The two local factions remained deeply entrenched and bitterly hostile, although the balance of power between them had shifted.[148]

Lagos's new executive officer pruned expenses and reorganized the administration in a number of ways.[149] The Armed Hausa Police were withdrawn from rural areas and small towns on the frontier, and Lagosians were warned against enticing Egba and Ijebu slaves to run away. For a short time, the government ordered Dosunmu to station canoes on the lagoon to turn back runaways, and a few who reached Lagos island were actually returned to their owners with the knowledge and complicity of government officials.[150] Over the course of the 1870s, the number of Armed Hausa declined and their command was combined with that of the Civil Police. Recruitment into the militia dwindled, such that by the end of the decade the force was no longer sufficient to meet the colony's needs for security.[151] Trade improved in the second half of the 1870s, generating a small surplus in the colonial revenue, which justified modest growth in expenditure on public works. However, the reorganization of the colonial legal system, creation of a Supreme Court presided over by a British judge, and more systematic extension of English law to Lagos in 1876 were surely the most significant reforms of the 1870s.[152]

Despite these signs of development, problems persisted on the western frontier, as Dahomey menaced the Egba, Porto Novo threatened Lagos trade and flirted with the French, and the towns of Appa and Katanu pleaded for British protection. Hostilities continued between Ibadan, the Egba, and Ijebu Ode, moreover, and war broke out again in the interior in 1879. The Lagos government also resumed efforts to open a new inland trade route via the eastern lagoon and Ondo, which would bypass the Egba and Ijebu, provoking the latter to harass Lagos traders on the lagoon.[153] To many interested in Lagos's future within the British Empire, the colony appeared to be stagnating. Critics blamed the town's failure to realize its great potential in part on the fact that the colony did not have its own government but was administered from the Gold Coast. A movement emerged locally and won support in influential quarters in Britain to separate the two colonies and allow Lagos an independent administration. The disappointments of the 1870s and 1880s were rooted, however, more in changes taking place in the palm produce trade than in a lack of administrative will. It is to the development and transformation of Lagos's new "legitimate" commerce that the analysis now turns. For the transition to trade in vegetable products not only shaped the young city's early colonial history, but also affected the experiences of its many owners and slaves.

Before leaving the subject of early colonial rule, however, it is telling to note that in subsequent years, after the administration of the colony was brought under tighter Colonial Office control and became more distant and bureaucratic, Lagosians looked back on their British *ọba* "Globar's" tenure in office as a golden age when the state was open to Africans and responsive to their needs. Nothing illustrates this better than the fact that when Glover died in 1885, his African friends and foes alike in Lagos raised money to build a public hall in his memory.[154]

4

Innocent Commerce: Boom and Bust in the Palm Produce Trade

Abolitionists and policymakers in mid-nineteenth-century Britain expected that the production and trade of cotton to supply Britain's burgeoning textile industry would rescue the peoples of the Bight of Benin from the slave trade. Yoruba farmers had in fact long grown cotton for use in domestic cloth weaving. In the 1850s, a number of organizations and individuals—from the Church Missionary Society, to Consul Campbell, to Thomas Clegg, a Manchester industrialist—supported schemes in the interior to promote the growth and trade of cotton for export. Quantities of the commodity shipped from Lagos expanded rapidly in the late 1850s, if from a very low level. Then for a brief moment during the 1860s, civil war in the United States interrupted supplies of the raw material, drove prices in Britain to unprecedented heights, and made cultivation of the staple for sale abroad profitable around Abeokuta and Ibadan.[1]

During the 1860s, Lagos exported an average of almost 600,000 pounds of cotton annually. With the revival of supplies from the United States following the Civil War and subsequent dramatic fall in prices, however, Yoruba farmers found that they could no longer make good money growing cotton for export to Britain. By the 1880s, quantities of the crop shipped from Lagos declined to about half what they had been twenty years before, worth a paltry £8,500 per year in Britain.[2] Despite the efforts of British missionaries, officials, and philanthropists, it was not cotton but palm produce—first palm oil and later also palm kernels—that dominated exports from Lagos, the Bight of Benin, and indeed West Africa as a whole throughout the second half of the nineteenth century.[3]

The Rise of the Palm Produce Trade

Oil palm trees (*Elaeis guineensis*) grew wild in the forest stretching 20 to 150 miles inland from the Slave Coast and providing a home to all or part of the Awori, Egbado, Egba, Ijebu, Ibadan, Ekiti, Ijesha, Gun, and Fon peoples. The trees required no cultivation, but they grew best near places of human habitation where the forest had been partially cleared for agriculture. As income from the export of palm produce rose, farmers increased the number of oil palms available for harvest by transplanting seedlings to newly farmed lands, and eventually they began to cultivate the trees. Local peoples had for centuries manufactured and traded palm oil (*epo*), which formed a mainstay of their diet and was used as a fuel in lamps.[4] Martin R. Delany, who traveled from Lagos to Abeokuta in 1859, wrote, "Palm oil is produced [here] in great abundance, as a staple commodity. . . . The oil of the nut is the most general in use among the natives, both for light and cooking."[5]

West Africans had exported small quantities of palm oil during the era of the slave trade, primarily to provision slave ships. In the second half of the eighteenth century, the commodity began to be imported into Britain and France on a limited scale to supply their markets for oils, but it was not until the early nineteenth century, following British abolition, that the foreign trade in palm oil took off. Liverpool and Bristol slave traders, worried about mounting pressure for abolition, searching for new exports from Africa, and aware of the changing needs of local industries, pioneered the commerce. In the final years of the slave trade, wrote B. K. Drake, "few slave ships returned to Liverpool without some African cargo on board," and as much as 20 to 30 percent of net profits from these voyages came from imports of produce.[6] All of Liverpool's seventeen African produce traders in 1809 "had earlier been slavers."[7]

Over the course of the nineteenth century, industrialization and urbanization created a vast new market for vegetable oils, first in Britain and later on the Continent. West African palm oil was one of the first imports to meet this demand, and that produced in the interior of Lagos was of the highest quality. Several industrial uses for palm oil existed, including as a lubricant for machinery and as flux in the expanding tin plate industry. From the 1840s, moreover, glycerine, a by-product of palm oil, began to be used extensively in medicines.[8]

But it was changing patterns of urban middle- and working-class consumption, coupled with technological innovations geared to satisfying them, that drove the demand for palm oil and later palm kernels. In the 1830s, as Martin Lynn has shown, "a new technique for bleaching palm oil enabled it to be used more extensively in the manufacture of soap," an industry whose rapid rise paralleled the growth of industrial towns and cities. After mid-century, consumption of palm oil by British and French soap makers exploded. Then in the 1840s, a British candle company adopted a method pioneered in France a decade earlier and started to substitute palm oil for more costly animal tallow in the manufacture of candles that burned with a brighter light. By mid-century, palm oil had become one of the principal raw materials in the candle industry.[9]

Palm oil production left as a by-product a nut at the center of the fruit, which contained an oil-bearing kernel. The Yoruba used the nuts to pave roads and the floors of houses, and they also burned them to produce charcoal employed by blacksmiths in building their fires. In addition, women roasted the nuts to make the "black" oil used in Yoruba soap making and cosmetics, as well as for fuel.[10] Until the 1870s, however, palm oil producers had discarded many of the nuts left from their work. In the 1850s, Marseilles firms commenced manufacturing a new and soon popular soap, *savon blanc cuit*, made in part from palm kernel oil. Then in the 1860s, a German named G. L. Gaiser began importing palm kernels as the sole raw material for his Harburg oil mill. Around the same time, German firms started pressing the residue left from palm kernel oil production into cakes, which had a high fat content, and selling them as feed to continental dairy farmers. These developments created a new demand in Europe for West African palm kernels, which further increased after 1884, when the British grocer William Lever pioneered the manufacture and marketing of his "Sunlight Self-Washer Soap." Aimed at working-class consumers in hard-water areas of northern England, Lever's new product was a huge popular success, and it was made from 41.9 percent palm kernel or copra oil.[11]

By the mid-nineteenth century, European agriculture could no longer meet the domestic demand for butter, lard, and animal fat. Supplies had to be imported from the United States and Australia, and the prices of butter and even lard were beyond the reach of many working people. Napoleon III encouraged research aimed at finding a cheap butter substitute for sale to the urban poorer classes, and in 1869 a French chemist developed a process for manufacturing margarine from animal fat and milk. Researchers soon began experimenting with substituting vegetable oils with a high melting point, such as palm kernel oil, for more expensive and sometimes scarce animal fat. Margarine manufacturers, however, did not convert widely to vegetable oils and begin using large quantities of palm kernel oil as a raw material until the discovery of hydrogenation in the early twentieth century. Only with the advent of that process could they transform liquid vegetable oils into solid forms imitating butter and lard and make them palatable to consumers. After the turn of the twentieth century, the rapid development of the European margarine industry to supply mass urban markets greatly expanded world demand for palm produce, at a time when a number of earlier uses had declined.[12]

Quantitative data throw light on the magnitude of the expansion of the new palm produce trade. In 1800 Britain, Europe's dominant consumer of palm oil throughout the nineteenth century, imported a scant 223 tons of the commodity. By 1854 the volume had grown to 36,583 tons, worth roughly £1,756,000. The rate of growth slowed thereafter, and during the remainder of the century imports ranged from about 38,000 to 49,000 tons per year. Because the price of the commodity declined sharply in the second half of the century, from a high of £42.83 per ton between 1855 and 1859 to a low of £21.66 per ton between 1885 and 1889, the value of the palm oil trade to Britain diminished over time. The decline occurred under pressure from new vegetable and mineral oils entering the market as well as from technological changes in a variety of production processes that made the demand for oils more specialized.[13] French imports of palm oil never reached the British level, totaling 3,403 metric tons in 1850 and 6,720 in 1870. Imports to Hamburg, Germany's leading port for the West African trade, stood at 2,566 metric tons in 1875 and expanded by almost 150 percent during the next fifteen years.[14]

Palm kernel imports into Britain grew even more dramatically in volume, from "some 592 tons" in 1855 to 43,372 tons by 1884, although because they fetched a much lower price per ton, the value of the kernel trade did not approach that of the oil trade. Figures for France's palm kernel imports are unavailable, but imports to Hamburg grew a whopping 700 percent, from about 6,500 metric tons in 1875 to about 52,440 metric tons in 1890.[15]

Throughout the first four decades of the nineteenth century, a handful of Liverpool traders doing business at the Niger Delta dominated Europe's palm oil trade, although London and Bristol each also had major palm oil traders. In the late 1830s and early 1840s, British merchants commonly made good returns on palm oil voyages, fostering a myth that the commerce could be hugely profitable and drawing new entrepreneurs into the business.[16] During these early years, a few of the big Brazilian slave traders on the Slave Coast, such as F. F. da Souza and José Domingo Martinez, bought palm oil as well as slaves and exported it to Britain and, in more limited quantities, Brazil. However, they could not compete effectively in the new commerce as it developed, given their more limited capital, weaker access to European markets, and social and cultural ties to the South rather than the North Atlantic. The big Lusophone merchants on the coast had risen to fill a niche in the illegal slave trade, and when it ended they and their less prosperous successors could do little more than struggle to maintain themselves in Brazil's shrinking legal commerce with West Africa.[17]

More significant than the Brazilians, several small new British firms located mainly in Liverpool, but also in Bristol and London, entered the commerce and began trading at the Gold Coast, the Slave Coast, and elsewhere, in addition to the Niger Delta. By the 1850s, they were importing about half of Britain's palm oil, and they continued to expand until they dominated the palm produce trade.[18] With the rise of markets for palm oil and palm kernels in France in the 1840s and 1850s and Germany in the 1860s and 1870s, moreover, merchants from these nations joined the scramble for palm produce. Colin Newbury has calculated that Britain's share of the total external trade from her settlements in West Africa declined from 64 percent for the period 1853 to 1862 to about 50 percent in each of the two subsequent decades, owing largely to competition from France and Germany.[19]

As the produce trade expanded on the Slave Coast in the 1830s and 1840s, a number of older London firms and newer Liverpool, French, and German ones opened factories at Ouidah and neighboring towns, where employees or partners received imports and bought palm oil and lesser exports such as ivory, cotton, shea butter, hides, and indigo for shipment home. While maintaining commercial establishments in these places, the agents also traveled via canoe, sailing vessel, and later steam launch among western Slave Coast communities, selling imports and buying exports.[20]

Until after the bombardment in late 1851, Lagosians participated in the new commerce on a small scale, primarily by transporting palm oil, ivory, and other commodities by canoe along the lagoon for sale at Ouidah, Porto Novo, or Badagry. Immediately following the bombardment, however, Europeans started arriving to open factories in Lagos, coming initially from towns to the west and then directly from Europe itself. In early 1852, the hot-tempered Scotsman William McCoskry, whom locals called Apọngbọn after his red beard, reached Lagos, having already represented the British firm W. B. Hutton in West Africa for seven years. Weeks later, J. G. Sandeman, agent of another British firm, Stuart and Douglas, joined his countryman in the town. In March, Lorenz Diederichsen, a German, arrived, and the following year he persuaded the Hamburg firm William O'Swald to open factories in Lagos and its environs. Then in 1853, A. Legresley came to Lagos to represent the London firm Banner Brothers, and by the mid-1850s, the Marseilles firm Victor Régis had commenced trading at Lagos. Régis and O'Swald also established close commercial relations with Kosoko and his chiefs at Epe.[21]

Belief that Lagos occupied a superior commercial position along the lagoon and that the newly appointed British consul would provide security and create conditions propitious to trade pulled the new merchants to Lagos. John Whitford, author of *Trading Life in Western and Central Africa*, expressed the first conviction when he wrote, "Lagos undoubtedly rejoices in the best situation for trade in the Bight of Benin."[22] Desire to escape the civil war at Badagry and machinations of the king of Dahomey, who was systematically attacking Ouidah's merchant community, pushed them from towns farther west.[23] Opportunities to export palm oil, ivory, and other "legitimate" commodities from Lagos quickly outstripped those to export slaves. Within only a few years, Lagos had supplanted Ouidah, Porto Novo, and Badagry as the center of European commerce along the Bight of Benin, as British officials had hoped it would, although the magnitude of its palm oil trade did not match that from the Niger Delta during this period.[24] By the 1880s, the port had earned the sobriquet "The Liverpool of West Africa" and was regarded as the "Queen" of Britain's settlements there.[25]

The transition from trade in slaves to that in palm produce coincided with a period of organizational and technological change in Europe's commerce with West Africa, and these transformations affected the conduct of foreign trade in Lagos. Commission houses that bought and shipped British exports to "correspondents" on the African coast and also received and sold palm produce in Europe, both in return for a percentage of their values, were proliferating in London, Liverpool, Bristol, and elsewhere, and they began handling an increasing volume of the palm oil trade.[26] In addition, steam gradually replaced sail in West African shipping between the 1850s and 1880s. In 1852, Macgregor Laird, a member of a Birkenhead shipbuilding family, received a contract to carry the British government's West African mail and founded the African Steam Ship Company, which began a monthly service between England and West African ports. A second service commenced in 1869, expanding opportunities for steam transport. While a number of the largest European firms doing business in West Africa continued to operate their own ships, the introduction of regular steamship service divorced trading from shipping and eliminated the need for participants in West Africa's export-import trade to own or charter vessels. This development removed a major capital barrier to entry and opened the commerce to anyone who could hire cargo space on a steamer. It also bolstered the palm oil trade by lowering transportation costs just as the price of the commodity began its long decline in Britain. The greater speed of steamers, moreover, cut the turnaround time on merchants' capital from a year or more to a few months, and it reduced the quantity of imports they needed to keep on hand to engage in business, further expanding opportunities for entrepreneurs with limited resources.[27]

The expansion of the commission house system and emergence of steamship services created new opportunities in West Africa's external trade for small-scale import-export merchants based on the coast.[28] Immediately following the bombardment, Europeans and Sierra Leonean liberated slaves rushed to take advantage of these opportunities. McCoskry, Sandeman, and other European agents traded on their own behalf, as well as for the firms they represented. To cite a further example, Giuseppe Carrena, a Genoese merchant resident in Bahia, arrived in Lagos in July 1856, possibly to settle some affairs with a former agent in the slave trade or perhaps to escape an outbreak of cholera in Bahia. Impressed by possibilities in the new palm oil trade, he settled in the town, went into business, and soon built a warehouse and grand residence that, according to the wife of the British consul, had floors "of inlaid marble" and pictures by "the best modern Italian masters" on the walls.[29]

Perhaps the most colorful of the new European merchants in Lagos was another Sardinian, Giambattista Scala, who had hired the brig *Felicita* in Bahia in November 1851, loaded her with rum, tobacco, foodstuffs, and manufactured goods, and set sail for Lagos, probably expecting to provide services to slave traders. When he arrived soon after the bombardment and found a Royal Navy vessel at the mouth of the river, Scala quickly realized that the British presence "made the slave trade impossible on these shores." He claimed in his memoirs already to have harbored hopes of ending the slave trade by promoting legitimate commerce. Whatever his true sentiments, Scala rapidly reinvented himself as a harbinger of lawful trade and enlightened civilization. He boarded the Navy ship and explained to its commander that he wanted to set up a business in Lagos "trading in the country's natural products as a substitute for the Slave Trade." Akitoye happened to be on board, and Scala used the occasion not only to obtain British protection but also to enlist the *ọba's* help spreading the word that "a European trader was going to settle on the island with a cargo of the goods which they liked most, and instead of demanding slaves would be content to exchange his merchandise for the natural products of the country." Scala reported that when the local people accepted that he wished to exchange foodstuffs, rum, and tobacco for palm oil, "their incredulity turned to astonishment and their astonishment into the greatest joy." "It was not long," he continued, "before men and women were rushing from all around to bring me their products and exchange them for my foodstuffs which they so badly needed." About a month after his arrival, Scala loaded the *Felicita* with "as many barrels of palm oil as [he] could" and sent them to a London commission house.[30]

The initial expansion of the palm oil trade at Lagos coincided with the arrival of the Sierra Leonean immigrants in the town. While many of them were men and women of modest means, some had engaged in the import-export trade with Britain at Sierra Leone. Ford Fenn, owner of a London commission house, wrote, "When the slave barracoons at Lagos were destroyed and Dosunmu was appointed King under British protection, several of my correspondents at Sierra Leone went down to Lagos." Of Walter Lewis, a Sierra Leonean merchant and colonial servant who lived for a time at Lagos, he remarked, "I have been in correspondence with him for many years, in fact before the suppression of the slave barracoons at Lagos. At that time Lewis went to Lagos, drawn by the wise policy of the English government."[31] In addition to valuable commercial experience, some of the Sierra Leoneans brought capital with them when they migrated to Lagos. A witness told the 1865 Select Committee Appointed to Consider the State of British Establishments on the Western Coast of Africa that, "having amassed fortunes," a number of the Yoruba in Sierra Leone returned to their homeland.[32] These immigrants moved quickly into the import-export trade at Lagos and played a major role in expanding it.

Other Sierra Leonean immigrants had previously been involved in commerce up and down the West African coast, as ship captains, traders, or both. Some got their start buying goods from condemned slaving vessels cheaply at auction in Freetown and then selling them at a handsome profit farther down the coast.[33] The most famous of these was J. P. L. Davies, educated at the CMS Grammar School in Freetown and, with his brother, trained in navigation on board a Royal Navy vessel. By 1852, Davies was captaining merchant vessels owned by liberated Africans from Sierra Leone and plying the coast between Freetown and the Niger Delta. He used the opportunity to trade on his own behalf, and within a matter of months he had purchased two condemned slavers at auction and was shipping palm oil directly to Britain from Lagos and the Niger Delta. In 1856, Davies settled in Lagos, where he became the agent of a "West Indian mercantile firm" based in London, and the following year opened a business of his own. Over the next few years, he became the most successful Sierra Leonean merchant in the town, shipping cotton and palm oil in his own boats, receiving consignments of imports from London, Liverpool, and Manchester, and employing dozens of workers in his substantial enterprises.[34]

In addition to capital and commercial experience, the Sierra Leonean merchants benefited from valuable personal connections with Europeans and one another. Walter Lewis, for example, was Consul Benjamin Campbell's son-in-law. J. P. L. Davies took as his second wife Sarah Forbes Bonetta, a protégée of Queen Victoria's, at a London ceremony presided over by the Reverend Henry Venn, honorary secretary of the Church Missionary Society.[35] These personal connections helped the Sierra Leoneans forge useful commercial contacts, obtain valuable information, secure essential credit, and enforce timely debt repayment, in addition to bringing other benefits. Sarah Davies and the Reverend Samuel Crowther were the only Africans whom the Royal Navy had orders to evacuate in the event of an uprising at Lagos.[36]

Consul Campbell recognized the significance of the Sierra Leonean merchants when he wrote, in 1857, that they enjoyed a large part of Lagos's trade and occupied "a considerable portion of the best part of the town."[37] Martin R. Delany observed two years later that the "merchants and business men of Lagos [are] principally native black gentlemen, there being but ten white houses in the place."[38] Several of the Sierra Leonean merchants also worked at the consulate or, after the annexation, in the colonial service, including Charles Foresythe, the colonial treasurer; Walter Lewis, the chief clerk; and I. H. Willoughby, the inspector of the Civil Police. An 1864 ordinance prohibited government officers from trading, but some skirted the law by conducting business through their wives.[39] From their salaries earned working for the government, these Sierra Leoneans accumulated capital for trade and supported their families, while establishing themselves in business. When Willoughby and Foresythe resigned from the colonial service in the early 1870s, they reentered commerce.

Brazilian *emancipados* did not occupy a position in Lagos's import-export trade equivalent to that enjoyed by Sierra Leonean liberated slaves. Most arrived with very little capital, and their commercial connections, so far as they existed, were to Bahia and the other Brazilian communities on the Slave Coast, not to Britain. A few, such as João da Rocha and Joaquim Francisco Devode Branco, who entered business in Lagos in the 1870s, traded directly with Brazil. Da Rocha had been born into slavery in Bahia, purchased his freedom, and made money in trade before emigrating to Lagos in 1871 with his wife and young son Candido.[40] Branco had been the slave of a Portuguese man, U. João Francisco Branco, from Figeira da Fos, who traded between Bahia and the Slave Coast. Both da Rocha and Branco consigned goods to ships sailing across the Atlantic and occasionally chartered vessels of their own. Both had agents in Brazil and traveled there periodically to maintain or improve their commercial connections.[41] Da Rocha remained in business in Lagos until his death in 1891, trading from his commercial establishment near Tinubu Square and living in his bungalow "Water House," immortalized as the setting of the Brazilian writer Antonio Olinto's romantic novel of the same name about an *emancipado* family on the Slave Coast.[42] In an act of extraordinary generosity, Branco bequeathed legacies of £500 to "Belmira da Conceicao Branco, daughter of my late master," £260 to each of two daughters of his master's elder brother, and £200 to "Amelia Francisco Branco, my . . . master's natural daughter now at Cotonu."[43]

In the 1850s and 1860s, few indigenous men or women of any origin imported directly from Britain or exported to it, although many traded locally. The commission houses were initially perhaps unwilling to deal directly with indigenous men, who as illiterates would in any case have had difficulty establishing connections with them. The early exclusion of *indigenes* from opportunities to import and export directly, in the way that Kosoko and some of his chiefs had previously traded with Brazil, undermined the commercial position of members of the old slave-trading oligarchy relative to the new Saro merchants. As indigenous men acquired Western education and commercial experience, commission houses began accepting them as correspondents, although until the end of the century, most of the biggest African merchants in Lagos were of Saro origin.[44]

The few women who imported and exported directly, such as Nelly Oyenkan, had in most cases entered liaisons with European, Euro-African, or prominent Sierra Leonean men and borne children to them. They probably secured their positions as correspondents through the recommendations of their mates or the men's European friends.[45] Sexually coded Victorian assumptions about who the agents of economic progress on the coast would be led commission houses to accept male Sierra Leonean correspondents, while eschewing their female counterparts. Indigenous women acquired Western education much more slowly than indigenous men and few, if any, became import-export merchants in the nineteenth century.

Quantitative data further illuminate the expansion of the palm produce trade at Lagos and chart the town's development as a port. The mean annual tonnage of palm oil exported increased moderately, from 3,984 between 1856 and 1860, to 5,697 between 1866 and 1870, and 7,202 between 1876 and 1880. Palm kernel exports rose much more dramatically, from an average of 14,524 tons per year between 1866 and 1870 to one of 29,350 tons per year between 1876 and 1880. Britain's share of the oil trade fluctuated but stood relatively constant at between 55 and 60 percent between 1870 and 1885, but her share of the kernel trade declined from 63 percent in 1870 to 48 percent in 1885. German firms enjoyed net gains, increasing their share of the oil trade from 8 percent in 1870 to 24 percent in 1885 and of the kernel trade from 13 percent in 1870 to 44 percent in 1885. The percentage of oil and kernels exported by French firms declined after the 1860s.[46]

In the second half of the nineteenth century, Lagos exported to Europe small quantities of ivory, shea butter, hides, and indigo, in addition to cotton and palm produce. Ivory exports, the most important of these in the early years of the commercial transition, peaked at around fourteen tons in a single year in the 1850s, but fell to about six tons per year by the late 1880s, owing to a decline in the elephant population.[47] The value of these lesser exports never approached those of palm oil or palm kernels, which together accounted for greater than 80 percent of Lagos's exports until the second half of the 1890s. The trade to Brazil in palm oil, locally woven cloth, kola nuts, black soap, pepper, and beads remained important economically and culturally to Lagos's Brazilian community, but its relative value declined with the reorientation of commerce from the South to the North Atlantic to only about 3 percent of Lagos's total external trade by the 1880s. The introduction of regular steamship service to England also linked West African ports, and in addition to expanding trade with Britain, it promoted commerce up and down the coast in locally woven cloth, kola nuts, black soap, potash, beads, and other commodities. This development diversified commercial opportunities and created niches for indigenous traders, but the value of intra-African coastal commerce did not approach that of the European palm produce trade.[48]

The aggregate value of Lagos's exports rose from an average of £166,763 per year between 1863 and 1865, to one of £499,214 per year between 1866 and 1870, and of £632,439 per year between 1876 and

1880. This represents an increase of almost 200 percent from the first to the second half of the 1860s, and a more modest growth of just over 25 percent from the second half of the 1860s to the end of the 1870s.[49]

Merchants on the coast bought exports with imported goods and, to a lesser extent, currency. Until the 1890s, most trade at Lagos was conducted by barter, with merchants using textiles, spirits, tobacco, salt, and other goods to pay Lagos middlepeople for produce, and the middlepeople doing the same with other traders from Lagos and the interior. Both import-export merchants and middlepeople—often called brokers or barracooners—derived a substantial part of their income from the profits they made exchanging imports for exports. As one European mercantile agent put it, he "tried to make a double profit on every barter transaction." If he gave twenty shillings for produce, he did not pay with goods that had cost him twenty shillings. African broker C. A. Oni likewise said that by using goods to pay for produce, he often made a double profit.[50]

The categories of goods imported remained much the same as during the era of the slave trade: textiles, alcohol, tobacco, guns, gunpowder, hardware, and miscellaneous items. Benjamin Campbell wrote,

> The European manufactures employed in . . . commerce under all flags are principally the cotton fabrics of Manchester and Glasgow; the hardware of Birmingham and other towns, gun powder, earthenware, [and] silks, [along] with velvet, silk, cotton, coral, and a small quantity of beads of Venetian and Bohemian manufacture. . . . From Bahia are imported large quantities of rolled tobacco and aqua diente, principally under the flags of Sardinia and Portugal.

Campbell and other commentators also stressed the significance of a growing trade in cowries, a local currency. "At Lagos, Palma, and [Ouidah]," Campbell observed, "it is necessary to import the cowrie shell, it being the currency of the country."[51]

Continuity in the categories of goods imported, however, masks significant changes taking place in the import trade. The origins of certain goods altered, as did their percentage of the whole. Cheap British cottons had by the 1820s all but driven out the East Indian textiles so popular in the eighteenth-century slave trade. After the middle of the nineteenth century, German spirits and French wine and brandy largely replaced Brazilian rum. Eventually, United States leaf tobacco supplanted the Brazilian rolled product.[52] The source of cowries shifted, moreover, from the Maldives to the East African coast, as the demand for them increased to pay for expanding exports. In the early 1850s, the Hamburg firm William O'Swald virtually monopolized the profitable cowrie trade between Zanzibar and West Africa, which Campbell believed gave it a substantial advantage in the competition for palm oil at Lagos and Palma, given that some local traders preferred to sell for currency rather than goods. But by 1855, Victor Régis had broken into the cowrie trade and during the next decade and a half these two houses imported a large quantity of shells into Lagos. The development of the East African cowrie trade increased the supply of money in the local economy at just the moment when the expansion of external trade was bringing new prosperity and a greater demand for currency.[53]

The proportion of different kinds of imports also changed following the commercial transition. The percentage of predominantly British cotton textiles increased, which given their falling price during this period meant an enormous growth in quantity. So important did British cottons become that without them "no Foreigners [could] carry on the trade in Palm Oil."[54] Scala observed, "The sale of cotton fabrics is vast . . . and it is in the hands of the Britons."[55] The percentage of spirits fluctuated but held steady, while that of tobacco and cowries decreased. With the exception of cowries, imports were made up almost entirely of consumer goods.[56] Merchants from different nations imported different combinations of goods, reflecting their competitive advantage in commerce. But all needed to be able to include in their offerings textiles, spirits, and European manufactured goods, and coastal merchants traded with one another to achieve desirable assortments of wares.

The aggregate value of imports, like that of exports, illuminates the growth of Lagos's trade and its development as a port. Import values rose from a mean of £135,406 annually between 1863 and 1865 to one of £502,007 annually between 1876 and 1880.[57]

Before 1852, Lagosians had sold limited quantities of local vegetable, animal, and manufactured products into the Atlantic economy. At the moment that the foreign slave trade from Lagos ended, however, a new trade with Europe in palm oil took off, cushioning the effects of abolition on the local economy. Lagos entered the new palm produce trade during its heyday. Demand was strong, prices were high, and the cost of most European imports, particularly textiles, had been falling since the beginning of the century. Key British trade goods cost in 1850 half to a quarter what they had in 1800. Until the 1870s, the barter terms of trade favored African participants in the commerce, who enjoyed the luxury of being able to buy a growing quantity of imports for a given quantity of exports. True, the expansion of West Africa's trade with Europe was not keeping pace with the growth of world trade. Relative to other parts of the globe,

West Africa was declining in economic importance to Britain.[58] But the people of Lagos and its interior did not know this. For them, economic conditions would not be so favorable again until the first decade of the twentieth century. A group of Lagos chiefs told the Rev. Samuel Crowther in 1857 that they had never before seen so much wealth flowing into their country.[59] In these heady conditions of prosperity, Lagosians threw themselves into the new foreign trade.

Palm Produce Production

When growing European demand for palm oil pushed prices up in local markets, indigenous peoples responded by increasing the supply of it for sale. Initially, they probably sold oil manufactured for local consumption, but soon they began producing explicitly for the European market. Moreover, individuals who had not previously manufactured palm oil moved into its production.

Manufacturing processes differed across Africa's oil palm belt, in ways that affected the amount of labor, fuel, and water required for producing palm oil. These differences, in turn, affected the oil's free fatty acid (FFA) content, which determined its quality, uses, and price. The lower the percentage of FFA, the softer the oil, the better its quality, and the higher its price, but the more labor, fuel, and water it took to manufacture it. "Fine Lagos" oil, produced by the Yoruba-speaking peoples, was the best in West Africa, but it was also the most labor- and resource-intensive to produce. Unlike elsewhere in the palm belt, the Yoruba did not alter their production process to reduce labor inputs as exports of the commodity increased.[60]

When clusters of palm fruit ripened between late December and early May, men and boys scaled the thirty- to sixty-foot-tall trees where they grew and harvested them. Women and girls helped carry the clusters to the production site and cover them with palm leaves, where they were left to ferment for a few days until the fruit could be separated from the stalk. On the day of production, batches of fruit weighing approximately fifty pounds were placed in large earthenware pots, the bottoms of which were plastered with a mixture of wood, ashes, and water. These were balanced on bricks above a hole in the ground with channels dug into it to ensure an even distribution of heat during a careful boiling process that lasted up to four hours.[61]

After boiling, the fruit was drained and put into a mortar or canoe for pounding or stomping by foot. If a canoe was used, cold water was added. If a mortar, then the pounded fruit was transferred into a large pit before adding the water. In either case, the fiber was regularly stirred and ladled until an oil-bearing scum rose to the surface, which was skimmed into a clean pot. Nuts wanted for their kernels were meanwhile separated by hand from the pressed fiber and set aside for drying. As the water in the canoe or pit grew dirty, it was replaced, and the washing process continued until all of the fiber had been thoroughly processed. In some households, slaves or young girls transferred the processed fiber into a second mortar, where they pounded and washed it again to remove remaining small amounts of oil, which they were allowed to keep.[62] When workers finished with the fiber, they pressed it into balls and put it aside to dry for use as an oil-rich fuel.

The scum that had been collected in pots separated as water sank to the bottom. The oil on the top was either skimmed into yet another pot for about thirty minutes of gentle boiling or boiled where it was. During the cooking, it was sieved to remove fragments of fiber. As oil rose once again to the top of small amounts of water, workers skimmed and boiled it a second time to evaporate the last traces of moisture. This lengthy manufacturing process was complete when a few drops of water sprinkled on the surface of the oil produced a crackling sound. Finally, the oil was transferred into clean containers for sale.

The quantity of fruit produced per tree and volume of oil that could be manufactured from a given amount of fruit varied with the level of rainfall, age of the tree, and other factors. By the 1890s, between 105,000 and 150,000 tons of fruit, harvested from as many as fifteen million trees, were required to manufacture the approximately 10,000 tons of palm oil exported annually from Lagos.[63]

An assistant colonial secretary observed in 1892 that the "whole process of palm oil making" took eight to fourteen hours, depending on the quantity of fruit handled and number of people employed. He remarked that workers commonly began manufacture about 4 o'clock in the afternoon and labored through the night, skimming the finished product in the cool of the early morning.[64] Botanist J. E. Gray calculated in 1922 that the extraction of 180 pounds of palm oil required 120 hours of labor, or fifteen eight-hour work days.[65] At that rate, the extraction of one ton of oil took 187 work days, but Gray's calculation did not include the very substantial labor involved in harvesting and transporting the palm fruit, removing it from the stalk, and hauling the necessary fuel and water. In nearby Dahomey, where the production process was much the same, Patrick Manning figured that the manufacture of one ton of palm oil required 315 days of labor.[66] O. T. Faulkner and C. J. Lewin, of the colonial Agricultural Department, calculated that it took 420 work days to produce one ton of soft oil.[67]

These numbers vary greatly, but they suffice to show the extensive labor required to manufacture the palm oil exported from Lagos. If we take Manning's figure of 315 work days per ton as an intermediate estimate, then at least 1.8 million work days went into producing the oil shipped annually in the late 1860s, while about 3.3 million work days were required to produce that exported annually in the 1890s. This labor had to be performed, moreover, during a season that lasted less than half the year.

How, then, was all this labor organized? Men sometimes called on their age mates, organized into communal work groups (*àáró, ọ̀wẹ̀*), for help with harvesting. By the end of the century, moreover, it was possible in some places to hire itinerant men and boys who specialized in reaping palm fruit.[68] Most of the actual manufacturing took place, however, within existing structures of domestic production, although these structures responded to increasing work demands in produce production by exploiting their labor more intensively, shifting it from other activities, and incorporating more laborers into them. Families, headed most commonly by married men and including their wives, children, slaves, and other dependents, continued to form the units of economic production, consumption, and trade throughout the era of the commercial transition. These units varied in size from two people in the case of newly married men to several hundred or more in that of rich and powerful chiefs who had many wives, children, slaves, strangers, and other dependents living under their authority.[69] Both the size of the group and identity of those composing it affected labor and other relationships within it, but ideologically the domestic groups of wealthy persons were regarded as extensions and elaborations of the family rather than as something different from it. Less affluent people saw enlarging their domestic groups as the rich and powerful were able to do as the cultural ideal. Although families were headed most commonly by men, wealthy women such as Fajimilola and Tinubu in Lagos, who owned many slaves and commanded the labor and support of other dependents as well, also sometimes established and headed large, independent units of production, consumption, and exchange.[70]

A gendered division of labor existed within families. In Lagos, as throughout mid-nineteenth-century Yorubaland, men hunted, fished, farmed, and specialized in certain crafts, while women dried fish, processed food crops, marketed both, and also performed other craft activities as well as most domestic labor. Although males harvested the palm fruit and helped transport it to the production site, palm oil manufacturing was regarded as women's work, and females performed much of the labor in it. William Clarke, an American Baptist missionary who traveled in Yorubaland during the 1850s, wrote that women were responsible for "the making and extracting of oil."[71] R. H. Stone, another American Baptist missionary, observed in the 1860s, "The women . . . make . . . palm-oil." Samuel Johnson, author of the famous nineteenth-century history of the Yoruba, referred to palm oil making as an "exclusively female" industry, while N. A. Fadipe wrote that the conversion of palm fruit into oil was "the work of the wife." Unlike elsewhere in West Africa, women in most parts of Yorubaland did not contribute much labor to farming, and the timing of palm oil production fit well with their role in harvesting, processing, and marketing major food crops such as yams and maize, which did not commence until the end of the oil season.[72] These facts help explain how women were able to mobilize the extensive labor required to expand palm oil production. Yet to do so, they must nonetheless have needed to shift time from other work as well as from leisure activities, and to increase the labor demands on their children and the other dependents subject to their authority.

Despite the fact that palm oil production was widely regarded as women's work, evidence exists of male involvement in it within the colony of Lagos and elsewhere. What the sources do not always reveal is whether these men were slaves or other dependents or family heads who, as elsewhere in West Africa, moved into manufacturing palm oil when it became a lucrative export commodity. Francine Shields has argued that the ideological association of work in palm oil production with women was so strong that men eschewed it, even when they entered more readily into palm produce trading, and that the males working in production were slaves. Her argument is attractive, but the evidence for it is not yet conclusive.[73]

Differences of opinion have long existed about the relative importance of small- and large-scale production in palm oil manufacturing. Although it may never be possible to know which provided the larger share of exports, it is now generally accepted that the two co-existed. Prior to the expansion of the export trade, much oil manufacturing was conducted on a small scale by wives, with the assistance of children and, in prosperous families, perhaps also a few slaves or other non-family laborers, producing for consumption by the family and sale in local markets. This type of production clearly expanded from the 1840s, as more women seized the opportunity to earn income by selling palm produce, although at different times and rates in different regions of the interior.[74]

Accounts from the 1850s and 1860s, however, also describe large-scale palm oil production. Clarke observed, "extracting . . . oil in the palm districts employs a large number of labourers and presents . . . the appearance of a manufactory. . . . I have seen establishments of this kind where perhaps fifty persons or more were engaged in labour." R. H. Stone discussed palm oil production in terms that imply, as Robin Law has noted, both large-scale enterprise and specialization of labor: "One set of women separates the nuts from their integuments, another boils them in large earthen pots and still another crushes off the fiber from the kernel nut in large mortars."[75] Across the Yoruba palm belt, much large-scale production was organized by senior wives of powerful chiefs or wealthy commoners, as well as by women who were rich and powerful in their own right, and it employed the labor of gangs of junior freeborn wives and children, in addition to female and male slaves and other dependents. While large-scale production no doubt existed prior to mid-century in the households of the rich and powerful, to provision their own needs and produce for the local market, it too expanded with the growth of the export trade.

Both small- and large-scale manufacturers increased their use of slave labor as palm oil production expanded. Warfare and regional insecurity were generating a continuing supply of slaves, while abolition was enlarging the number available for local acquisition. Kidnapping and military service provided a means for ordinary soldiers, as well as war captains and chiefs, to acquire male and female slaves on whose labor both they and their senior wives of free birth could draw. John Peel has observed, "Slaves were the soldier's reward, the anticipated outcome of going to war."[76] In addition, production and trade for growing foreign and domestic markets generated income with which some men and women were able to buy slaves, although as slave prices did not decline dramatically until the 1890s, it must have taken small producers and traders a long time to accumulate sufficient capital to purchase one. The rapidly growing need for labor in palm produce manufacturing and trade greatly enlarged the already strong demand for female slaves, helping to make them the most valuable. But it also led owners to use male slaves in these activities.[77]

If the use of slave labor expanded among small producers, it did so much more dramatically within the military, political, and commercial elite. The evidence indicates large-scale use of slaves in agriculture, palm produce and other manufacturing, and trade by rich and powerful men and women across the major Yoruba palm produce manufacturing regions throughout most of the second half of the nineteenth century. Tinubu, for example, is said to have had sixty people, many of them slaves, working for her after she was expelled from Lagos to Abeokuta in the 1850s.[78] Chief Abasi's father, at Badagry, later employed thirty female slaves and a number of male ones as well in making palm produce. J. P. L. Davies reported, moreover, that by the 1880s there were Egba men who owned as many as four hundred slaves and used them in large-scale palm produce production, while Bolanle Awe found that a number of wealthy chiefs in Ibadan had five or six farm villages colonized by women, children, and as many as six hundred slaves each. The *ìyálóòde*, or ranking female chief there, is remembered as having owned two thousand slaves, some of whom she employed in produce manufacturing and trade.[79] Powerful chiefs and wealthy traders found following abolition that they could replace income lost from the export of slaves and pay for imported arms and other goods, as well as for more domestic slaves and other sorts of dependents, by selling palm produce manufactured by slave labor.

Robin Law has cautioned, however, against equating large-scale and slave production, because slaves were sometimes allowed to produce small quantities of oil independently, in return for payments to their owners.[80] By the same token, economic specialization often existed within compounds, and wives who had limited access to non-family labor could achieve task specialization and larger-scale production by cooperating in oil manufacturing across domestic groups. This task specialization undoubtedly helped the Yoruba maintain production of high-quality soft oil, even while dramatically expanding output.

Freeborn Yoruba women enjoyed rights to retain and manage income from the fruits of their labor, including in oil manufacturing, although they also had obligations to their children, husbands, senior kin, affines, and co-wives that encroached on their time and drained their resources.[81] To limit these demands, wealthy women such as Tinubu often established domestic groups and sometimes founded compounds of their own.[82] Husbands could make much greater claims on the labor and income of slave wives and concubines than they could on spouses of free birth. Shields has shown that some Yoruba men increased their share of the income from the new foreign palm produce trade by acquiring slave wives and concubines and setting them to work in oil manufacturing and trade. She has also argued that compound heads (*baálé*) and other male political authorities extracted some of women's new wealth from palm produce production by levying tolls on their trade, as well as exactions on their incomes during public rituals and on other occasions. As the century wore on, local authorities in some places began asserting ownership of palm trees and granting rights to harvest them only in return for compensation.[83]

When freeborn women engaged in palm oil manufacturing, they claimed the nuts at the center of the fruit as a byproduct of their labor. As the demand for palm kernels increased on the coast from the 1870s, women, assisted by children and sometimes slaves, began retrieving more nuts from the fiber left after oil production, drying them, and extracting the kernels. This last process, identified especially with elderly women, involved cracking the nuts by hand and picking out the kernel at the center.[84] It too was highly labor-intensive: studies conducted elsewhere in West Africa found that about four hundred nuts had to be cracked to obtain a single pound of kernels.[85] The growth of the palm kernel trade further increased the already heavy demands on female and child labor, but it also introduced an additional source of income for women, and one that could be undertaken on a small or a large scale, as time and labor allowed.

Many factors, in addition to intermittently stronger prices, contributed to the greater volume of palm kernels than palm oil exported from Lagos. First, large quantities of palm oil continued to be consumed locally and never entered the export trade. Second, after the fruit was harvested, palm oil needed to be manufactured within a few days, before the fruit spoiled. The oil then had to be transported to market and sold quickly, before it turned rancid. Once dried, nuts had a much longer life, and they could be processed throughout the year as labor became available. Finally, kernels could be extracted from over-ripe fruit that fell from trees, was collected by women, children, or slaves, and could not be used for palm oil production.[86]

Trade in an Age of Prosperity

Some palm produce was manufactured in the rural areas immediately surrounding Lagos, creating opportunities for both small- and large-scale producers from the town, who commuted daily or seasonally to farm hamlets to pursue agrarian activities. Scala wrote that as the palm oil trade developed in the 1850s, Lagosians "gather[ed] the fruits of the trees" so as to extract oil from them, while Glover noted that palm oil production increased within the colony in the mid-1860s. Assistant Colonial Secretary Millson described palm oil production in "the neighbourhood of Lagos" in 1892, and an African employee of the Southern Nigerian Agricultural Station collected data on its manufacture at Agege, on the mainland north of the town, in 1907.[87]

Palm produce production remained comparatively limited, however, in the rural areas close to Lagos. Oil palm trees did not grow well in the sandy, swampy soil near the coast, and the city grew as a center of trade, not production. Most of the palm oil and palm kernels exported from the town came from farther inland, with the Egba, Egbado, and Ijebu first expanding output to meet foreign demand. Production took off around Ibadan in the 1860s and then in eastern Yorubaland in the 1870s, with the opening by the British of a new road linking Ijesha and Ekiti directly with the lagoon at Atijere via Ondo. In addition to these sources of supply, exports flowed into Lagos across the lagoon from Gun and Fon territories to the west.[88]

With a few exceptions, Europeans did not penetrate the palm produce manufacturing regions of the interior prior to the construction of the railroad, which began in 1896, reached Abeokuta in 1899, and arrived at Ibadan in 1901.[89] Throughout the second half of the nineteenth century, Africans continued to dominate trade between the interior and the coast, as they had in the era of slave exports. Farmers and produce manufacturers from rural areas near Lagos and from farther inland sometimes brought their goods directly to the town for sale to local traders or brokers. The majority of producers in the interior, however, transported their commodities to markets on the mainland, where they sold them for goods or currency to African traders, who either took them on to other markets for further exchange or transported them to the coast for sale.[90] By the closing decades of the century, some traders had also begun traveling to production sites and buying directly from manufacturers.[91]

Commodities flowed back and forth between the coast and interior along a number of trade routes, the importance of which changed with circumstances. When Lagos developed as the leading port, much Egba trade shifted away from the western route that in the era of the slave trade had linked Abeokuta and points north with Badagry and Porto Novo via the market at Okeodan. It moved to a more eastern one that flowed up and down the Ogun River via canoe during most of the year and across land by headload via Otta market if too much or too little water closed the river. The western route resumed some of its earlier importance when political unrest or conflict with the British blocked the eastern one. The missionary T. J. Bowen observed during a journey from Badagry to Abeokuta, "All along the road, we met numbers of men, women, and children going to the Badagry market, with palm-oil, corn, yams, fowls, firewood, etc., which they carried in heavy loads on their heads." On a trip up the Ogun in 1854, Clarke noted the "frequent passage of canoes laden with various articles of commerce . . . going down to town."[92]

Ijebu trade flowed south from Oru, Ijebu-Ode, and lesser towns and villages to the major lagoon-side markets of Ejinrin and Ikorodu.[93] People from Ibadan sold to Egba and Ijebu traders who frequented their Ojaba market, and they also transported goods for sale in Egba and Ijebu markets at Eruwa, Ipara, Iperu, Makun, and Oru. In the 1860s, Ibadan cooperated with the British in an effort to establish a road to Ikorodu independent of Ijebu or Egba control, but the attempt failed and, like the eastern Yoruba, Ibadan had to await the opening of the Ondo road in the 1870s for independent access to Lagos. Once that was achieved, Atijere, on the eastern lagoon, developed as a major site of trade. Then in the 1880s, Governor Moloney helped establish Obada market near the new Ijebu Remo town of Ṣagamu.[94]

Most Lagosians who entered the new "innocent" commerce did so not by importing and exporting directly to and from Europe, like the merchants described in the first section of this chapter. Rather, they worked as traders who traveled by canoe and on foot to markets on the mainland, where they bought produce, foodstuffs, and other items and transported them back to the town for sale. Alternatively, local brokers bought exports from Lagos or from interior traders who brought them down to the coast and then resold them to merchants for export. Individuals also sometimes combined these activities or moved between them as circumstances dictated. Scala observed that inhabitants of Lagos traveled across the lagoon in their canoes to trade in Ijebu, Egba, Badagry, and elsewhere, taking textiles, tobacco, and spirits with them to exchange for ivory, palm oil, and foodstuffs. Clarke noted that Lagos traders carried "all kinds of Manchester goods, . . . tobacco, gin, and almost endless numbers of articles to Abeokuta," while Campbell described Lagos canoes going and coming from the oil market at Ejinrin.[95] Akinpelu Possu, a broker, characterized his activities as follows: "Traders bring me oil which I buy and sell again to the merchants." Later James O'Connor Williams, another broker, said, "I buy from the natives and sell to the merchants. The natives from whom

KEY

1. Okeodan	6. Iperu	11. Addo	16. Palma	21. Okemesi
2. Otta	7. Makun	12. Ilaro	17. Ogbomosho	22. Akure
3. Oru	8. Atijere	13. Shaki	18. Oshogbo	23. Ado-Ekiti
4. Eruwa	9. Ketu	14. Iseyin	19. Ile-Ife	24. Owo
5. Ipara	10. Meko	15. New Oyo	20. Ilesha	

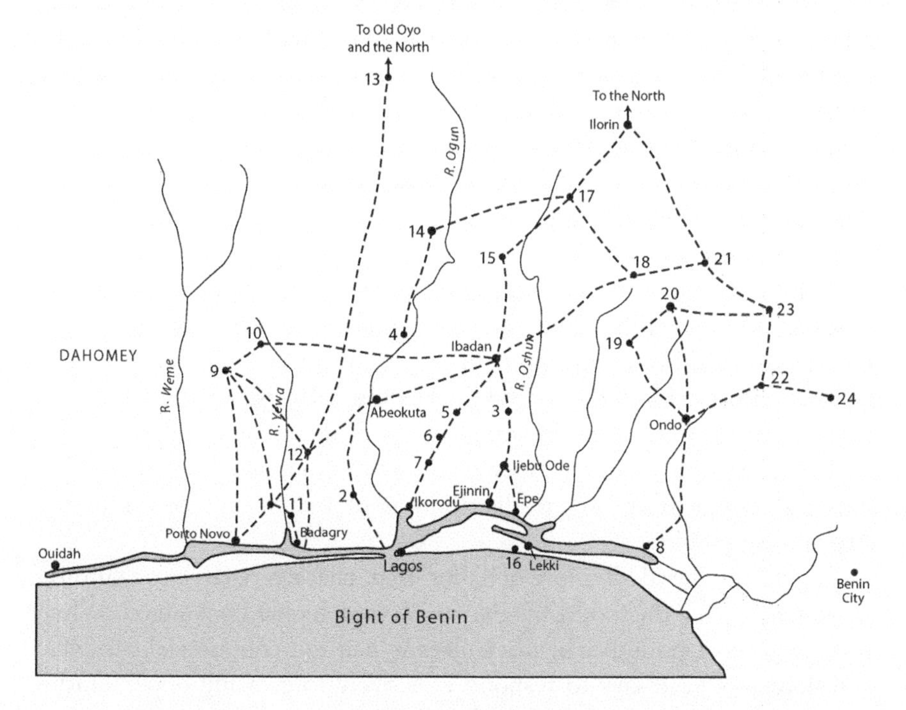

Sources: G. O. Ogunremi, *Counting the Camels: The Economics of Transportation in Pre-Industrial Nigeria* (New York: Nok Publishers, 1982), 53, 65, 244; C. W. Newbury, *British Policy towards West Africa: Selected Documents, 1786-1874* (Oxford: Clarendon Press, 1965), 526; Toyin Falola and G. O. Ogunremi, "Traditional, Non-mechanical Transport Systems," in *Transportation Systems in Nigeria,* ed. Toyin Falola and S. A. Olanrewaju (Syracuse: Foreign and Comparative Studies Program, 1986), 18-19; A. I. Asiwaju, *Western Yorubaland under European Rule, 1889-1945: A Comparative Analysis of French and British Colonialism* (Atlantic Highlands, NJ: Humanities Press, 1976), 24.

Map 2. Nineteenth-Century Yoruba Trade Routes.

I buy have already bought it from the natives of the interior."[96] Import-export merchants sometimes employed agents to trade on their behalf and paid them a commission or salary, but the vast majority of Lagosians who engaged in the new legitimate commerce did so as independent traders or brokers.

Some Lagosians also engaged in commerce farther afield. Like traders from other parts of Yorubaland, they organized caravans that transported goods by headload deep into the interior. On a journey from Lokoja, at the confluence of the Niger and Benue Rivers, to Lagos in 1872, Bishop Samuel Crowther met a caravan from Lagos bound for Ilorin, a major terminus of the northern trade more than two hundred miles from the coast.[97] In addition to pushing north over land, Lagosians took advantage of the steamship services along the coast to trade up the Niger River. Taiwo Olowo, William Shitta, Sunmonu Animaṣaun, Fanny Barber, Rebecca Phillips Johnson, and scores of lesser male and female traders conducted extensive business there until driven out by the Royal Niger Company in the late 1880s.[98]

Who were these local traders and brokers? Did the ruling oligarchy that had dominated the slave trade also control the new legitimate commerce? Or could new entrepreneurs break into the trade, make money from it, and establish themselves in business? British officials believed that the palm produce trade would be more democratic than the slave trade had been. Were their expectations borne out, and if so what effect did this change have on the distribution of wealth and power in the African community?

In the gendered division of labor that characterized local culture, women marketed the foodstuffs they processed, including palm oil. When the new export trade began, they already had the commercial expertise and networks necessary to respond effectively to growing opportunities to trade palm produce. It is, therefore, not surprising that they played an important role in pioneering the new legitimate commerce. In the 1850s, Bowen saw many women on the way to market with palm oil, while Benjamin Campbell observed in 1858, "it is the women that trade in the oil markets." John Whitford later witnessed "canoes bound for Lagos . . . crowded with passengers, chiefly women traders, . . . comfortably reposing on top of the cargo" of palm oil, palm kernels, and other goods.[99] Robin Law cites evidence to show that the perception of palm oil trade as women's work was sufficiently strong to discourage men in the interior from entering it as an alternative to the slave trade.[100] Yet enter the commerce Lagos men did—even those of high status—as soon as it became clear that they could make money by doing so.

A number of Lagos's big slave traders easily made the transition to exporting palm produce, cotton, ivory, and other "legitimate" commodities. The two trades overlapped and proved complementary, not mutually exclusive, as many abolitionists and policymakers had prophesied. From at least the 1840s, Kosoko, Akitoye, Oshodi Tapa, Madame Tinubu, Akinpelu Possu, Ajenia, and other big slave traders also dealt in other exports. Following abolition, many of them successfully turned their numerous canoes and slaves, as well as their extensive commercial networks, to large-scale palm produce trading.

Death in 1853 spared Akitoye the full impact of the commercial transition. Dosunmu, his successor, had not distinguished himself in trade prior to becoming *ọba*. Under the terms of an agreement with the European merchants in 1854, he relinquished his right to trade on his own account in exchange for customs duties, which he was forced to give up after the annexation in return for a pension of only about £1000 per year.[101] Dosunmu may subsequently have engaged in commerce surreptitiously, and he certainly benefited from the trade of his wives and slaves. The administrative ban on trade by the *ọba* nonetheless seriously undermined the monarchy's wealth, just as colonization by Britain was striking a blow to its power and prestige. During the era of the slave trade, the wealth of successful *ọbas* was unsurpassed within the community. In the second half of the nineteenth century, a number of African merchants and traders, most from outside the old ruling oligarchy, had incomes greater than the king's.

Kosoko, exiled at Epe, labored under no such restrictions on trade. He was a consummate businessman and entered the new legitimate commerce "with spirit," while continuing to export slaves and also to derive "a good revenue from duty on exports." Scala asserted that after being expelled from Lagos the former *ọba* "devoted all his energy to recovering his lost fortune by trading in slaves and palm oil." Campbell referred to Kosoko as "a great trader," whose primary commercial fault lay in trying to extend to the new commerce the same "monopolizing policy" he had pursued with the slave trade.[102]

Oshodi Tapa and Tinubu, the two most famous non-royal slave traders, made the transition to legitimate commerce no less successfully than Kosoko. The German firm O'Swald allegedly conducted all of its extensive business in the Lagos area through Tapa. At Epe, the great war chief and former slave continued his declining trade in slaves and expanding business in palm oil, cotton, and ivory via the port of Palma and by sending canoes to Porto Novo. He also invested in agriculture and palm produce production, using the labor of hundreds of slaves. After a visit to Epe in 1861, Lieutenant Bedingfield reported the town "much improved and extensively cultivated, the caboceer Tapa having one farm nearly three English miles in extent."[103] Tinubu began trading palm oil, cotton, and ivory while exiled in Badagry with Akitoye in the 1840s, and after her return to Lagos following the bombardment dealt in these commodities on a large scale. While she continued to be identified with the slave trade, the formidable woman was committed not so much to a particular kind of trade as to maintaining the power and autonomy of the political faction she had supported since the 1830s.[104]

The great warriors and slave traders Ajenia and Akinpelu Possu managed the commercial transition no less smoothly. Campbell described them as "two caboceers . . . , who being not only extensive traders but honest ones, were much courted and trusted by the merchants." When they decamped to Epe, European trade followed them, to the detriment of Lagos.[105]

Yet members of the old ruling oligarchy could not dominate the new export trade in palm produce as they had the older one in slaves. For one thing, the *ọba* no longer exercised the same administrative control over external trade. For another, he and his supporters no longer enjoyed the same prerogatives in it—privileged access to exporters, first choice of imports, preferential sale and sometimes price of slaves, and other political advantages. On the contrary, officials and merchants alike insisted on a policy of free trade in the era of legitimate commerce. Even at Epe, the merchants resisted Kosoko's desire for monopoly. The palm produce trade was indeed more open than the slave trade had been. Individuals could enter it on a small scale, with limited capital and labor, by buying oil, kernels, and other exports in mainland markets and bringing them back to Lagos for sale to the many local brokers and export merchants. A big expansion of external trade took place in the twenty years after the bombardment, and many sorts of Lagosians scrambled to participate in it: women and men, locals and Sierra Leoneans, Brazilians and other immigrants, even slaves and other subordinates. Consul Campbell commented on "the masses of the population" engaged in the palm oil trade, while Scala estimated that 20 percent of the town's inhabitants "drew their means of subsistence" from the new commerce. Almost a decade later, Governor Freeman remarked on the many small produce traders in Lagos who were affected when commerce with the Egba was interrupted.[106]

The growth of the new export trade also stimulated the development of the long-standing commerce with the interior and other parts of the coast in fish, salt, foodstuffs, livestock, and local manufactures. Although some Lagosians farmed on the mainland and food production in the territory increased when political instability disrupted trade, the town depended on imported food throughout the second half of the nineteenth century. Rising incomes from the production and trade of exports expanded the domestic market for many locally produced as well as imported commodities, moreover, further increasing commercial opportunities for Lagosians of modest means. The growing supply of cowries increased the availability of a currency that could be broken into very small units of exchange, and this too facilitated the expansion of small-scale trade. By 1881, half or more of the town's population of about 35,000 people made their living from commerce.[107]

Little information exists about profits in the palm produce trade during the early years of its prosperity, although some brokers claimed to have made 30 percent or more on capital invested in barter as late as the 1880s. Traders who in the 1890s realized 1.5 to 2.5 percent on produce insisted that earlier the commerce had been much more lucrative.[108] Small-scale traders could with luck make money from their commercial activities, reinvest part of their earnings, and expand the scope of their operations. Consular and colonial records from the 1850s on contain references to dozens of important traders from outside the old ruling oligarchy. Many new men and a smaller number of new women rose to economic prominence in the early decades of the palm produce trade.[109] While a number of Lagos's former slave traders themselves made the transition to large-scale palm produce trading without great difficulty, once death removed them from the scene, younger members of their families could not reproduce the commercial dominance of their forebears. Even when members of subsequent generations in these families succeeded in trade, as sometimes occurred, they had to compete with a large number of new entrepreneurs entering the commerce, some with superior connections and education. The declining commercial importance of the old ruling oligarchy compounded its loss of political power.

If thousands of Lagosians engaged in the town's expanding trade, many fewer were able to do so on a scale that enabled them to accumulate wealth and enjoy significant upward mobility, even in the early years of prosperity in the palm produce trade. Women, in particular, soon lost their early advantage and found that they faced significant disabilities in large-scale produce trading.[110] What, in addition to drive and ambition, did traders need to conduct business on a large scale? Why could some acquire these requisites and others not? Two resources that were particularly important will be discussed here: capital and labor. A third, land, which had major implications for the first two, will be taken up in chapter 7.

Credit and Labor in Trade

Both to commence trading and to expand their operations, Lagosians needed capital with which to buy goods for exchange, purchase canoes for transportation, or hire space in a craft belonging to another, as well as to support themselves while awaiting a return on their investments. Two local sayings, "Money is trade" (*Owó ni òwò*) and "It takes a rich person to know trade" (*Olówó ni o mọ òwò*), express the perceived relationship between capital and commerce.[111] Lagosians invested in trade money that they had saved, either on their own or through participation in local savings associations such as *ẹsúsú* or *ajọ*, to which members regularly contributed small sums in return for periodically receiving the pot.[112] In addition, husbands often gave new wives capital with which to begin trading.[113] But individuals could also borrow money, not only from kin, spouses, affines, and friends, who were regarded as having an obligation to lend to one another and regularly did so for many purposes, but also from patrons, overlords, and others with whom they did not necessarily have a close personal relationship. Credit and debt were common and well-accepted features of the local culture by the second half of the nineteenth century, and in Lagos moneylenders already existed, if banks had not yet made their appearance.[114]

Borrowers had long paid interest on loans by placing with their creditors a slave, child, or other dependent, known as an *ìwọ̀fà*, whose labor during the period of indebtedness served as interest on the loan. They could also pledge their own labor in lieu of interest.[115] As trade expanded and credit became even more widespread from the 1850s, Lagosians began backing loans by pledging as security clothing, jewelry, and livestock, or the right to collect palm fruit, palm wine, and kola nuts from trees that grew on their land.[116] For those who had it, however, privately owned landed property—and especially houses—quickly became the preferred form of collateral, as chapter 7 will show.

Slave traders along the Bight of Benin and elsewhere in Africa had conducted much of their business on trust, selling imports on credit to local traders who used them to buy slaves with the expectation that the exporters would be repaid in human cargo.[117] As the palm produce trade developed, its merchants also adopted the trust system, expanding the new commerce beyond what many of them or the local culture had the capital to finance by purchasing imports on credit in Europe and, in Scala's words, giving "their merchandise [on trust] to the natives, who will pay back . . . with the products of this land."[118] Lagos traders referred to what they called the "debit and credit" system, in which merchants sold them imported goods or cowries on credit at agreed-upon prices, and they repaid their debts in exports or, more rarely, currency, which most merchants preferred not to accept.[119] The amounts of credit involved were sometimes substantial. Rumor had it that Tinubu owed various European merchants palm oil worth £5000 when she was expelled from Lagos. In the late 1860s, the French firm Régis Ainé each year advanced Taiwo Olowo goods and currency sufficient to purchase forty thousand gallons of palm oil, worth approximately £3333.[120] Sierra Leonean merchants granted lesser but still substantial sums, with J. P. L. Davies's documented loans ranging from £50 to £1216.[121]

Lagos brokers and traders broke bulk and sold lesser quantities of imports or currency, often also on credit, to other traders from Lagos and the interior. Campbell noted in the 1850s that Saro traders from Lagos had given "considerable quantities of merchandise on credit" to Egba traders, while a decade later Glover also remarked on debts that the Egba owed Lagosians.[122] Mortgages on file at the Lagos Land Registry represent only the tip of the iceberg, because most commercial agreements between Africans went undocumented, but even so they demonstrate that big Lagos traders such as Taiwo Olowo, Fagbemi Dawodu, Fanny Barber, and Rebecca Phillips Johnson conducted much of their business on credit with other Lagos traders. Fagbemi's documented loans ranged from £18.16.6 to £1000, but only two were for more than £100; while Taiwo's ranged from £18.5.8 to £101, with only one worth more than £100.[123] This second tier of traders, whether from Lagos or the interior, likewise conducted much of its business on credit, thereby extending the network of indebtedness that linked participants in the new international commerce. The monetization of the economy through the importation of cowries, Spanish or South American dollars, and later British coins facilitated the expansion of credit, because these currencies could be easily divided for exchange and allowed wealth to circulate.[124]

The terms of credit varied within Lagos from lender to lender and, in the case of a given lender, from borrower to borrower. Merchants and traders typically intended loans to be short-term, lasting only three to six months during the peak oil season to enable customers to buy palm produce and bring it to the town. Such lenders commonly advanced credit in a series of installments as customers needed goods and currency, rather than in a lump sum. Yet creditors sometimes made loans for longer periods, if the amount of capital involved was substantial and the trust between lender and borrower was great.[125] During the life of the loan, debtors were supposed to make periodic payments in exports, either according to a fixed schedule or as they acquired them through trade. Big traders, however, occasionally negotiated more complex agreements with merchants. Taiwo Olowo, for example, had to repay Régis Ainé the full forty thousand gallons of palm oil he owed during the final eight weeks of his loan. Prior to that time, Taiwo could sell palm oil at the current market price to Régis or anyone else and with the proceeds presumably expand his trade.[126] Like other traders on the coast, Taiwo, whose full *oríkì*, or praise name, was *Olówó èlé* ("Owner of money lent at interest"), used the capital he borrowed not only to trade, but also for other purposes, such as buying slaves and houses and lending money at interest.[127]

If customers repaid a major portion of what they owed within the time specified, merchants and traders usually renewed their loans, establishing a revolving line of credit. Not uncommonly, however, the period specified for repayment ended with a major part of the debt outstanding. When this happened, debtors frequently pressed creditors for additional goods or money to engage in further trade in hopes of clearing their debts. Alternatively, they borrowed from someone else and used that capital to repay their earlier loans. Many merchants and traders allowed customers with a reasonable record of repayment a revolving deficit, and some Lagosians became locked in cycles of perpetual indebtedness, which robbed them of much of their commercial, social, and political independence.[128] The system of revolving deficits provided Lagosians who had capital to lend a means of tying customers to them and of building an elaborate network of distribution and collection. The ideal customer made regular, reliable payments, but remained indebted and thus dependent on his creditor. Debt provided an effective means of creating subordinates on whose support one could draw, as chapter 8 will illustrate. According to R. C. Abraham, the Yoruba word for creditor, *olówóòmi*, implies control or superiority over one's debtors.[129]

In the 1860s, many British merchants and commission houses charged African merchants interest of 10 to 12 percent on loans, although from the 1870s through the 1890s the typical rate fell to 5 percent. Some of the major British, German, and French firms, as well as some of the African merchants and traders, apparently did not charge interest on loans, but they must have figured the cost of capital into their prices. In addition, a number of Africans in Lagos, most of whom were or had at one time been merchants or traders, engaged in lending money at interest. In the 1860s and 1870s, Saro commonly charged 5 percent annually on loans. R. B. Blaize, B. C. Dawodu, and others made larger loans (£200–2500) at that rate in the 1880s, but by the 1890s Blaize and I. B. Williams were charging 10 to 15 percent interest on smaller loans. In the 1880s, local moneylenders such as Fạseke Olukolu made loans of £10 to £100 for periods of six to twelve months at much higher rates, which soared during the depression of the late 1880s to as much as 60 percent per year.[130]

Credit, firmly rooted in local culture prior to the expansion of the palm produce trade, fueled commerce at all levels of the economy. Without it the new external trade could not have grown as rapidly as it did or have penetrated as deeply into the regional economy. H. S. Freeman, Lagos's first governor, referred to credit as the great "genius of the African trade."[131] Through the credit system, Europe, and more particularly Britain's commission houses and palm produce trading firms, supplied much of the capital needed for the expansion of commerce. But African entrepreneurs also contributed a share, and it was African commercial and social relationships that enabled credit to diffuse so widely throughout the economy. The enormous expansion of credit in the era of the commercial transition played a vital role in opening the new palm produce trade to those outside the old ruling oligarchy, including some slaves and former slaves.

A vast interconnected network of debtor-creditor relationships bound Lagosians not only to one another, but also to inhabitants of other communities on the coast and in the interior. The fact that many individuals were simultaneously lenders and borrowers and that they had multiple creditors and debtors further elaborated the complex web of credit, which was rendered more complex still by the fact that credit flowed not only from Europeans to Africans, merchants to traders, and greater traders to lesser ones, but also horizontally within these groups and in reverse, if usually in smaller amounts. Perhaps nothing underscores the complex circulation of capital in Lagos so much as the fact that at times of budgetary deficit, the early colonial government demanded credit from African merchants, traders, and employees.[132] Africans, moreover, borrowed and lent funds not only or perhaps even primarily to finance trade and production, but also to pay for funerals and marriages, cover legal fees and fines, buy food in times of famine, ransom captured relatives, and finance religious rituals.[133]

All this borrowing and lending among many people and in multiple directions sometimes put individuals under great financial, social, and moral pressure. Peel recounts one story of a Lekki woman who was "so hard pressed by creditors that she tried to cut her throat." He includes another of a creditor who attempted several times to hang himself in his debtor's house, presumably to force repayment, until the debtor went to stay at *his* debtor's house "to pressure [that man] into paying."[134] Managing creditor-debtor relationships consumed great time and energy, as the local planter and produce broker J. K. Coker's correspondence from the early twentieth century shows so clearly. His papers contain copies of numerous anxious letters begging credit, pleading for repayment of debts, and explaining contritely why he could not possibly lend money to a given individual at a particular time.[135] The many pressures and anxieties Lagosians felt surrounding credit explain, perhaps, why the British-educated Saro doctor J. A. Caulcrick repeatedly cautioned his children to adhere to Polonius's injunction and "Neither a borrower nor a lender be!"[136] Despite these drawbacks, the pervasiveness of credit in small and large amounts and the moral obligation locals felt to lend helped make capital easily available to a wide spectrum of the population wanting to break into trade or needing money for other purposes. The easy availability of credit greatly contributed to the democratization of trade.

If Lagosians wanted to borrow from a European or an African outside their immediate social network, how did they obtain access to credit? Chapter 7 examines the changing role of land ownership in this process. Here it suffices to say that before they had established reputations as able, honest, and reliable traders, which spoke for themselves, they sought loans through social connections with kin, spouses, affines, friends, patrons, overlords, and, in the case of slaves, owners, who would introduce them to a potential creditor, vouch for their trustworthiness, and sometimes also pledge surety or otherwise back their loans. This pattern held true both for people at the bottom of the social hierarchy, particularly slaves and strangers, and for those who were better established. Tradition encodes this phenomenon by remembering that it was Taiwo Olowo's friend and patron J. H. Glover who helped him get his start in large-scale palm produce trading by introducing him to the agent of the German firm G. L. Gaiser, even if the story is anachronistic in certain respects.[137] At the lower end of the social spectrum, the "Report on the Yoruba" maintained that strangers in Lagos could buy and sell, "recover any debt and make any payment," only by submitting to the head of an established local family, who would transact the business for them.[138] Kin groups and, ultimately, communities were responsible for their members' debts, and to obtain credit from people outside their immediate social networks Lagosians needed to be able to show that they had relatives, friends, patrons, overlords, or owners who would fulfill that obligation for them. Many of Lagos's new palm produce traders acquired much of the capital they needed to engage in commerce through existing hierarchies of kinship, marriage, patronage, land ownership, and slavery. The quality of an individual's social connections, and the willingness of the person's friends and social superiors to facilitate and back loans, did much to determine access to credit and, thus, to the capital needed for trade.

African traders and Saro merchants willingly extended credit to both women and men. Most of the European firms, on the other hand (not surprisingly, given their nineteenth-century gender biases), lent much more commonly to men than to women. This basic fact made it significantly harder for women than men to obtain the large amounts of credit that the European houses could offer and greatly disadvantaged women in the import-export business. It helps explain why, over the long term, women had difficulty competing with men in that sector of the economy.

While Africans in Lagos commonly obtained access to credit through hierarchical social relationships, merchants and traders there also competed for customers, on whom they depended for the volume of their business. The number of individuals who regularly took goods and currency from them, the quantity of commodities these individuals could be relied upon to trade effectively, and the speed with which they repaid their debts all helped determine the size of a merchant's or trader's turnover, encouraging openhandedness. Chapter 8 will examine the relationship between credit and the mobilization and control of labor in the era of gradual emancipation. Patron-client calculations, however, also conditioned much lending. Gareth Austin has observed that in the nineteenth century the Yoruba "admired above all" other well-known people "the generous patron surrounded by many dependents."[139] One way that entrepreneurs created clients, demonstrated their social position, and enhanced their status was by generously making loans. Paradoxically, this process also helped establish their own credit-worthiness with Europeans by signaling that they were important businesspeople. All of these dynamics heightened the receptivity of African merchants, brokers, and traders to requests for credit and led them, in the view of many Europeans, often to make loans recklessly, on the basis of flimsy recommendations, to people who ought not have been trusted.[140] The prevailing commercial system, moral ethos, and social order in Lagos all encouraged freedom with credit, which in turn helped open economic opportunities to new entrepreneurs, including slaves and other subordinates. It did so unevenly, however, and also gave creditors powerful mechanisms of control over their debtors.

Trade required labor no less than capital. If the credit system was relatively open, helping to create opportunities for a broad spectrum of the population, labor was scarce and subject to acute competition. Exports, imports, and many local trade goods were bulky, with a single gallon of palm oil weighing about seven pounds. Unlike slaves, palm produce, ivory, and cotton could not walk to the point of embarkation, although until the gradual disappearance of the domestic slave trade around the turn of the century, slaves destined for sale in local markets sometimes carried exports part or all of the way to the coast. Except for steam launches employed by some merchants on the lagoon and Niger River, no mechanized transportation existed inland from the coast prior to the construction of the railroad. Goods had to be moved back and forth between the port and the interior via canoe and headload. Female and male porters typically carried loads weighing an average of fifty to eighty pounds as far as fifteen to twenty miles a day. Despite these impressive figures, the local population could not have transported by headload alone the many thousands of tons of exports and imports that needed to be moved between the interior and the coast every year. It was the proximity of the palm produce manufacturing areas to rivers and creeks navigable for part or all of the oil season and to the vast intracoastal waterway leading to the port that rendered the palm produce trade economically viable.[141] Even with waterborne transportation, hauling trade goods required the labor of tens of thousands of female and male porters and paddlers. Manning has estimated that in the era of the commercial transition transportation consumed 5 to 15 percent of all labor in the region.[142]

Producers occasionally brought their commodities directly to Lagos for sale. More commonly, however, they transported them to local or regional markets on the mainland for exchange. Until the construction of the railroad, and to an extent even after it, male and female traders from Lagos or the interior organized the land and water transportation between these markets and the port.[143] In Lagos itself, those engaged in commerce also required workers to bulk exports and divide imports, store commodities for shipment or sale, and transport them between their storehouses and the wharves that ringed the island. Swarms of people could be seen each day involved in these activities. In addition, the actual buying and selling of goods, whether on the mainland or in Lagos, also required labor. If Lagosians wanted to engage in commerce on anything more than a small scale, they needed to be able to mobilize substantial amounts of labor.

In the 1850s, some European businesses employed the labor of slaves. This practice soon died out, however, after Consul Campbell warned that for British citizens to do so violated imperial law.[144] By the 1860s, the European merchants hired most of the workers they needed, importing Kru from the Upper Guinea Coast and canoemen from the Gold Coast to load and unload ships, and also drawing limited numbers of Sierra Leoneans, Brazilians, and locals into wage labor or salaried employment. The European firms did not use large amounts of labor relative to Africans engaged in commerce or, by the end of the century, the colonial government, but they were among the first to create a market for wage labor.[145]

African entrepreneurs, whether locals or immigrants, used their own labor in transportation, handling, and exchange until they became so wealthy and important that manual work was beneath them. Many of them also drew on the labor of unmarried children and other dependent kin attached to their families. Wives, as already indicated, generally worked independently of their husbands and controlled their own income, but they could be called upon to assist their spouses in times of great commercial need. Among the Sierra Leoneans and Brazilians, moreover, husbands and wives sometimes traded jointly. Even when wives were not called upon to help their husbands in trade, the domestic labor the women performed freed the men from these time-consuming activities and gave them an economic advantage that few women enjoyed until they were past childbearing age.

Like generation and gender, seniority also continued to affect labor flows within families and compounds. Among polygynists, senior wives could make demands on junior co-wives, and within households all senior males and females could claim certain kinds of assistance from those junior to them. Because of the ongoing relevance of generation, gender, and seniority to the organization of labor, Lagosians responded to the growing demand for workers in trade in part by bringing more people into their families and households through marriage, reproduction, and kinship, as they had done in the precolonial period. Most of Lagos's important male traders and some of its African merchants, for instance, practiced polygyny in part because of the economic benefits it brought.[146]

Religion and status, however, sometimes affect men's and women's decisions regarding family labor. Soon after the arrival of the missionaries, Christian converts began sending some of their children to school, withdrawing them from labor during the hours they were in the classroom. Educated Christians, moreover, particularly those who aspired to high status within colonial society, not uncommonly embraced monogamy and middle-class, Victorian conjugal values, which taught that wives and mothers should retreat from the world of work and remain at home.[147] Many Muslim children, on the other hand, attended Qur'anic schools, which, although more flexible in their demands than their Christian counterparts, required the time of their students nonetheless. A few Muslim women in Lagos eventually entered purdah, secluding themselves within their homes.[148] For a variety of religious and social reasons, then, men and women in Lagos sometimes elected to withdraw family members from the pool of labor available to them.

The communal work groups that men in Lagos and elsewhere in the region could call upon for help with intermittent heavy male tasks, such as clearing farmland, reaping palm fruit, and building houses, were not well suited to the day-to-day labor requirements of commerce. Other means had to be found of mobilizing non-family labor in trade. Male and female porters and canoeists began selling their services in the era of the slave trade, long before wage labor developed in other sectors of the economy, enabling locals to hire some of the workers they needed in transportation.[149] While the supply of transport workers increased in the second half of the nineteenth century, however, it did not begin to keep pace with the explosion of demand. For one thing, the Yoruba generally regarded porterage as a low-status occupation. For another, they saw working for hire as an undesirable way of making a living, much preferring individual entrepreneurship, even if on a marginal scale. Oroge has written, "The Yoruba people hated the idea of working for wages."[150]

If Lagosians used family and small amounts of hired labor in the growing commerce of the second half of the nineteenth century, slaves performed much of the work in transportation and trade. As opportunities in warfare and the external slave trade declined after the British intervention, many slaveowners shifted the labor of their bondmen and -women to transportation and other types of exchange, as well as to palm produce, agricultural, and craft production. In addition, both members of the old ruling oligarchy who made the transition to legitimate commerce and rising new entrepreneurs, including some Brazilian and Sierra Leonean repatriated slaves, invested income from their new economic activities in purchasing female and male slaves. While the external slave trade ended in 1851, the domestic trade survived much longer. The development of new forms of trade and production after mid-century led initially to a further expansion of slavery in and around Lagos.[151] John Pope Hennessy wrote, after visiting the town in the early 1870s, that European products were "carried from the coast to the interior by slaves" and that thousands of them could be seen every day in Lagos "going and coming on their owners' business."[152] During this period, slaveowning diffused more widely through the population than before. In the era of the slave trade, a small number of men and women within Lagos's political and commercial elite had owned sizeable numbers of slaves. In that of the palm produce trade, on the other hand, a larger number of men and women owned smaller numbers of bondwomen and -men.

The *ìwọ̀fà* system, or pawning, as it was known in English, provided a further means of obtaining non-family labor. It too expanded in the second half of the nineteenth century with the proliferation of credit and growth in the demand for workers. Pawning was a contractual relationship, which ended when the debt was repaid. During the life of the loan, however, pawns worked a certain number of hours each week for the creditor—commonly a half day out of every four at mid-century, although that varied with the size of the loan and age of the pawn. The tasks that pawns performed generally followed the sexual division of labor, but males were often employed in palm produce manufacturing and trade. Pawns of free birth retained their rights in their own lineages and were not supposed to be sold. Those who were free adults commonly lived at home and regulated their own work regimens, but child and slave pawns often went to live in the creditor's household. When debtors pawned slaves, the creditors had no right to sell them, and if a slave died while in pawn, the death was said to cancel the debt. Locals sometimes regarded accepting a pawn as a humanitarian gesture, because it spared those who needed to borrow money from worse fates. This attitude may have helped turn some pawns into tractable workers.[153]

Finally, Lagosians obtained non-family labor by continuing to welcome wards and strangers into their households. Regional warfare and instability drove many thousands of people into flight during the second half of the nineteenth century, and some of them made their way as far as Lagos. British rule, moreover, soon began attracting to the colony fugitive slaves from surrounding territory and later from further afield. In addition, economic opportunity lured freeborn immigrants to the town. A steady stream of people flowed into Lagos and its vicinity, which, along with slavery, swelled the population of the metropolitan area to more than fifty thousand by 1881 and further enlarged it by the turn of the century.[154] Many of these strangers survived initially by attaching themselves to the households of established residents, augmenting the labor supply available to their hosts and performing vital work in transportation and trade.[155] The literal meaning of the term *asáforígẹ*, used locally to refer to strangers, is "one who hurries to tote loads with the head." This term graphically encodes an important type of work that strangers performed.[156]

Of the three types of non-family labor, slavery remained the most important into the 1870s, and it survived in gradually modified form until after the turn of the century. The heavy labor demands of palm produce trade and production in and around Lagos changed the character of local slavery, moreover, by increasing the value of slaves as workers. This process was compounded by the gradual decline in the need for warriors to serve in the armies of the *ọba* and chiefs, once the colonial government began to insist on a monopoly of military force. To be sure, ambitious Lagosians continued to want slaves for the social prestige and political support they could bring, the more so in the second case because the town remained deeply factionalized politically throughout the early colonial period. In addition, slavery continued to provide a means of integrating outsiders into the kin group over time and thus of increasing its size and importance. But with the rapid growth of the foreign trade in palm produce and enormous increase in labor it required, the work that slaves performed acquired new importance relative to the other contributions they made. During these years, the system of local slavery shifted in the direction of those in the Americas, where slavery was first and foremost a way of organizing labor.

As slaves became more difficult to obtain and the owner-slave relationship came under increasing pressure after the mid-1870s, creditors compensated in part by demanding more work from pawns. This adaptation occurred despite the fact that it was illegal to bring pawns into the colony after 1874, as the next chapter will show. Lagos chiefs claimed that by the end of the century pawns owed creditors half of their working hours.[157] Meanwhile, *asáforígẹ* also acquired greater importance in the urban labor force. Chapter 6 will show that as slavery slowly ended in Lagos, the overlord-stranger relationship offered locally owned slaves who wanted to remain in the town, but did not have the resources to establish households of their own, a way to leave their owners. It simultaneously gave Lagos's rising new entrepreneurs a means of obtaining labor and dependents at a time when slavery was ending but wage labor had not yet become widespread in the African community.

Success in mobilizing and managing labor played a critical role in building trade. Those with capital, either of their own or obtained on credit, which they could use to pay bridewealth, buy slaves, make loans, assist strangers, or hire labor, enjoyed clear advantages in the competition for workers. In all but the market-based transactions—purchasing slaves and hiring workers—however, other factors, such as reputation, influence, prestige, and power, also played a part in the ability of Lagosians not only to attract to their households people on whose labor and support they could draw, but also to keep them there. Women looked for husbands, debtors for creditors, and strangers for overlords, just as clients looked for patrons, who they believed would fulfill fundamental responsibilities to them and behave as good and generous patriarchs. When dependents were disappointed, they could vote with their feet by leaving and forging another relationship of dependency with someone else. That slaves did not enjoy the same latitude had long been one of their great advantages to their owners. As slavery itself unraveled in the closing decades of the nineteenth century, at once loosening the control of owners over bondmen and -women and putting more pressure on other relationships of dependency, the reputations of rising entrepreneurs took on heightened significance in the competition for people to perform labor in trade, as the final chapter will show.

The Collapse of the Palm Produce Trade

The new external trade had barely taken hold in Lagos when the prosperity associated with its opening years ended. Lynn has characterized the late nineteenth century as "a time of great stress" in West Africa's palm produce trade, and conditions in Lagos were no exception. British palm oil prices fell by 21 percent between 1855–59 and 1875–79, and they plunged a further 36 percent a decade later.[158] Oil prices on the coast also fell from the second half of the 1870s, if more slowly than in Britain thanks to local competition for exports. The growing volume of the oil trade and development of the kernel trade cushioned the effects of falling British oil prices in the 1860s, but kernel prices also soon began to decline. Three years of low prices and poor output of oil, kernels, or both beginning in 1872 reduced the value of Lagos's external palm produce trade by as much as 46 percent from its high of £542,676 in 1869, dealing the first alarming blow to commercial prosperity.[159]

The value of the oil trade and, more markedly, the kernel trade recovered in the second half of the 1870s, thanks to a revival of output, but then both tapered off in the early 1880s. The total value of the two trades plummeted once again between 1887 and 1889 to a low of £375,710, owing to shrinking output of oil and falling prices of both oil and kernels. To make matters worse for local people, the barter terms of trade turned against them from the 1870s, as the prices of British manufactured goods leveled off while those of palm produce fell. Whereas the purchasing power of West Africa's exports had strengthened for most of the first three-quarters of the nineteenth century, it weakened during the final quarter, cutting into consumption and adversely affecting the import trade.[160]

The more rapid decline of oil prices in Britain than on the coast squeezed the profits of Lagos merchants. A number of European exporters with greater capital reserves survived despite narrow profit margins by doing a large volume of business, but most of the African merchants either closed their doors or concentrated their activities on imports. Profits on imports also declined at this time, however, owing to keen—many said reckless—competition from new European firms and African traders, who in the 1890s began bypassing the merchants and ordering imports directly from Europe using the newly established Bank of British West Africa as intermediary. Emil Holtman, agent for G. L. Gaiser, observed that when he came to Lagos there were eight European firms in the import business, but that by 1898 there were eighteen, plus many "natives." In the past, European merchants had made 15 to 20 percent on imports alone, and the African R. B. Blaize claimed to have made 50 to 80 percent or more. By the end of the century, however, importers reported often selling at a loss. Uncertain demand forced them to dump excess stock at auction below cost, while cutthroat competition led them to try to eliminate one another through underselling.[161]

In a portent of still worse times to come, the great J. P. L. Davies arranged in 1872 to borrow £60,000 annually from Child Mills and Company of Manchester. Already indebted to twenty other British companies and banks for more than £20,000, he was caught in the downturn that followed and was forced to declare bankruptcy in a London court.[162] R. B. Blaize, who made a fortune in the 1870s and early 1880s, largely on imports, "was appalled" by the narrow profit margins that prevailed at the end of the century.[163] Nor were European firms immune from worsening conditions. In 1885, Banner Brothers, one of the pioneers of the produce trade, left Lagos, no longer able to earn a profit on exports. Its agent allegedly commented that the company had made its "money from the Africans and did not mean to give it back again."[164]

Increasing competition and falling profits took their toll on Lagos's brokers, traders, and producers, as well. While dumping imports below cost at auctions created windfall opportunities for some traders who took them to mainland markets for sale, both traders and brokers complained that they could no longer get produce at a price that enabled them to turn a good profit. At the same time, European firms began trying to cut costs by purchasing exports directly from traders and even producers, bypassing local brokers. An 1891 editorial in a local newspaper worried that the role of the "middleman" was close to elimination and that general commercial bankruptcy was possible.[165] Holtman observed that middlemen did not control as much of the produce as they once had, while C. A. Oni complained that brokers such as himself were gradually being driven out of business.[166]

Other factors compounded deteriorating commercial conditions and further squeezed the incomes of local merchants, brokers, and traders. The importation of cowries in the 1860s and 1870s, followed by speculation in South American dollars in the 1870s, rapidly increased the supply of money in the local economy so that barter trade gradually gave way to cash transactions. This change had a number of longer-term advantages, which included divorcing the import trade from the riskier and more capital- and labor-intensive export trade and opening the former to smaller-scale operators. But it also contributed to runaway competition in the import sector and eliminated the double profits that merchants, brokers, and traders had often made on barter transactions. The rapid growth in the supply of cowries and dollars, moreover, depressed their value, rendering shells too bulky for convenient use as money in all but very small transactions and culminating in the demonetization of dollars in 1880, with a mere ten days allowed for their redemption at face value. The government increased the supply of British coins to take the place of these older currencies, but the depreciation of cowries and dollars nonetheless decreased the wealth of locals caught holding large stores of them. Five African merchants probably lost £3175 on the demonetization of dollars alone.[167] The 90 percent decline in the value of cowries relative to sterling between 1851 and 1895 must have cut deeply into the wealth of the *ọba* and chiefs who had shells stockpiled in their treasuries.

The rising cost of money borrowed at interest in the 1880s and 1890s also adversely affected commerce, in part by checking the growth in consumption of imported and other goods. But it also stimulated the leakage of capital lent for trade to other purposes, because of the wide difference in interest rates charged on these two types of credit. In addition, the high interest that moneylenders could earn encouraged those with capital to lend it, rather than invest in trade or production. By the end of the century, moneylending was much more profitable than trade. A number of African merchants and traders who had been prominent into the 1880s, such as I. B. Williams and Ali Balogun, retired from commerce around 1890 and turned to moneylending instead. Others, such as R. B. Blaize and Taiwo Olowo, supplemented their income from trade with moneylending.[168]

From the second half of the 1880s, Lagos's merchants and traders also began to feel the effects of non-competitive business practices adopted by European firms looking for ways to increase their profits at a time of economic decline. No sooner had George Goldie amalgamated British businesses on the Niger in the mid-1880s to eliminate competition among them than the newly formed Royal Niger Company began imposing tariffs and licenses on Lagosians and other Africans operating there to drive them off the river. The RNC also diverted caravans from the north headed for Lagos to the Niger River instead.[169] Then in 1895 Elder Dempster and Woermanns, the leading British and German shipping lines, formed a conference and imposed a deferred rebate system that favored larger-scale exporters.[170] By the end of the 1890s, agents of a number of the European firms in Lagos had begun to advocate price fixing among themselves, anticipating later decisions by foreign companies on the coast to amalgamate, pool, buy out, and undersell in hopes of moderating competition, bolstering profits, and securing exports.[171] In the second half of the 1890s, moreover, the opening of the railroad gave European firms direct access to transportation and enabled them to establish branches in the interior, undermining the very need for African traders to link the coast with its hinterland. Lagos merchants and traders survived after the turn of the century, to be sure, and traders at least increased in number, but both faced harsher conditions and new challenges.

The value, although not the profitability, of the palm produce trades recovered briefly in the early 1890s, and a short-lived rubber boom between 1895 and 1899, followed by the development of a more modest timber trade, generated substantial new income for some local people.[172] Moreover, profits improved in the kernel trade for a time after 1906, when the new demand created by the growth of the margarine industry drove up prices in Europe. In addition, the barter terms of trade temporarily shifted once again in Africa's favor.[173] Of more lasting significance, J. P. L. Davies and a number of other Lagos entrepreneurs driven out of business by the earlier decline in the palm produce trade had begun experimenting with cocoa at farms on the mainland across from Lagos, and from their efforts the production and trade of the Yoruba's next great export commodity was born.[174] But the reprieve for palm kernels and success of cocoa lay in the future. When the century closed, Lagosians were still reeling from the effects of a trough in the cycles of boom and bust that have always characterized African production and trade of commodities for the fickle world market. Conditions had become so bad that three British firms declared bankruptcy or abandoned Lagos in 1900, a disturbing epitaph for the first half-century of legitimate commerce.[175]

In the context outlined here of a rapidly growing demand for labor in trade, production, and other activities and of initially favorable but then deteriorating economic conditions, British officials wrestled slowly with the question of what to do about African slavery at Lagos. These circumstances also affected the behavior of African entrepreneurs who struggled after 1861 to meet their needs for labor and dependents in the face of Britain's gradual assault on slavery and other forms of unfree labor. Perhaps most profoundly, however, they affected the experiences of Lagos's slaves, who sought after the annexation to redefine their relationships with their owners and place in society.

5

Britain and Domestic Slavery

The abolition of the external slave trade formed an essential part of the program of reform that drew Britain into Lagos. From the time of the bombardment in 1851, British officials and Christian missionaries in the town worked steadily to end the foreign commerce in slaves from the Bight of Benin. By the mid-nineteenth century, however, the anti-slavery movement was committed not only to suppressing the external slave trade but also to abolishing slavery worldwide.[1] Yet when Britain intervened at Lagos in 1851 and again a decade later, the issues of local slaveholding and the internal slave trade necessary to sustain it did not figure prominently in official discussions. These troublesome problems captured attention only subsequently, after Britain was entrenched in Lagos, and government representatives and missionary agents forged policies to deal with them gradually in the decades following the bombardment.

The missionaries' stance of condemning slavery in principle but soon widely accepting both slavery and pawning in practice, not only among heathens but also among converts and mission agents, is well known.[2] It is therefore subordinated in this analysis to an investigation of government (in)action. When formulating anti-slavery policies, government officials struggled with contradictory pressures to maintain stability and increase the revenue of the young colony, while at the same time avoiding censure by the abolitionist lobby at home and protecting the nation's international reputation as a leader in the crusade against slavery. Slaves themselves initially pushed the question of emancipation to the fore by taking advantage of the British presence to flee their owners.

By the mid-nineteenth century, most anti-slavery activists had long believed in the moral virtue of free labor and civilizing effect of disciplined hard work, and these beliefs had also taken root among the British public. Abolitionists had promoted the idea that, if they stimulated the produce trade with Europe and industrious agricultural production to supply it, legitimate commerce would help spread a new morality in Africa.[3] Yet few early Victorians knew enough about the continent to have fully developed ideas about how the production and trade of the new agricultural commodities needed to liberate the continent from the slave trade would be organized. Thomas Fowell Buxton wrote about "Africa"—her "population" and "people"— and "the African," and he occasionally referred to African "chiefs," "powers," and "nations," but while he generally assumed a model of small-holder production and individual entrepreneurship, he and others were very vague about how labor would be organized in these enterprises. Some commentators worried that in the course of the commercial transition Africans were simply putting slaves to work in agricultural production and trade rather than selling them. Most British humanitarians and the officials who advocated intervention at Lagos assumed, however, that the growth of the new legitimate commerce would stimulate the development of small-holder production employing mainly family labor and of free trade conducted largely by enterprising private entrepreneurs. Buxton's "people" were not members of local slaveholding ruling classes, but rather ordinary farmers and traders, and even slaves themselves. According to contemporary ideology, it was disciplined work by free peasants and regular industry by individual traders that, along with Christianity, would lift Africans out of barbarism.[4]

At that stage in the history of the relationship between Britain and West Africa, few Europeans imagined the development of a free labor market along the Bight of Benin. Large-scale production employing former slaves as wage laborers on white-owned plantations or farms, not peasant production, may have been the model for British colonies in other parts of the world, where ironically many of the former slaves keenly wanted to become peasant producers, but West Africa was not regarded as ready for it.[5] Nor had the government yet become a major employer of wage labor. Until Britain began to colonize the Yoruba interior in the 1890s, the colonial state largely left it to Africans themselves to organize the growing quantities of labor needed in trade, transportation, and production.

When Britain intervened at Lagos in 1851, its government had already had almost two decades of experience dealing with emancipation in the nation's overseas dominions. Developments in the West Indies, India, and the Gold Coast formed the backdrop against which officials eventually weighed the problem of what to do about slavery at Lagos. They shaped the formation of policy in the town, sometimes through explicit reference, but more commonly through the general sense that officials in London and Lagos had of what was being done elsewhere and how it had or had not worked.

At the time of the debate over the 1833 Abolition of Slavery Bill, the British government negotiated legislation that maintained the commitment to large-scale production in the West Indies and compensated owners for the loss of their slaves, while also giving them continuing rights in the slaves' labor through an apprentice system designed to last for six years. It was hoped that apprenticeship itself would help reeducate slaves to accept the idea of disciplined wage labor for their former owners and resocialize them to internalize the cultural values of the bourgeois social order. In the aftermath of the 1833 legislation, however, it soon became clear how difficult it was going to be to control the labor of the former slaves, much less reshape their values. Former slaves, it turned out, had interests of their own that were at odds with those of planters and the state.[6]

The 1833 bill had specifically omitted India and a number of Britain's other Far Eastern territories, but continuing humanitarian pressure forced the government to act there a decade later. Officials came up with an ingenious solution for ending slavery in name, while doing little to alter existing labor relations, which subsequently had a major impact on policy in Africa. The Indian law prohibited slave dealing and declared that slavery had no legal status in areas of British rule. Yet little was done to inform slaves of their freedom or encourage them to leave their owners, although if they did so they could not be recovered by legal action or through force. And no case arising out of any obligations of slavery could be brought to a British court. This set in motion a very gradual process of emancipation in which slaves became aware of their altered legal status only slowly and owners had many years to renegotiate labor relations.[7]

Britain had had forts on the Gold Coast administered by councils of merchants for many years, and it tolerated slaveholding and the rendition of fugitive slaves in them—even by British officials—until 1843, when the government acquired responsibility for these possessions. In part to minimize the problem of how to deal with domestic slavery and the internal slave trade, Britain subsequently restricted its sovereignty on the Gold Coast to the forts and their immediate surroundings. Official policy proscribed slavery and the slave trade in the limited area of British sovereignty, but other districts were defined as protected territory where British officers had no authority to interfere with local slavery or the internal slave trade. In general, officials in Britain and on the Gold Coast recognized that domestic slavery and other forms of involuntary servitude served British interests and chose not to interfere with them for fear of destabilizing the local social and political order. Under pressure from the abolition lobby, the government would in 1874 introduce a proclamation abolishing slave dealing and emancipating "persons holden as slaves" throughout the colony and protectorate. Influenced by slavery legislation in British India, however, these ordinances were designed to create the "illusion of legal abolition" and eradicate some of slavery's most oppressive features, while not interfering with the system of unfree labor on the Gold Coast.[8]

Although a high proportion—in fact probably the majority—of slaves in Lagos were women, the officials who gradually forged policies to deal with local slavery rarely paid explicit attention to gender. Indeed, the language they used in pronouncements on the subject normally assumed a male slave population. Yet Europe's civilizing mission was gendered to the core, with serious implications for female slaves. As elsewhere in the British Empire, implicit assumptions about the proper relationship between men and women in the home and wider society affected the experiences of male and female slaves in Lagos and the interior.[9]

Slaveholding in Lagos

Between the bombardment of Lagos in 1851 and its annexation a decade later, Britain regarded the kingdom as foreign soil under the political authority of the *ọba*. The treaty that Akitoye signed with Beecroft and Bruce in 1852 said nothing about domestic slavery or the internal slave trade, and in keeping with British policy that in the absence of specific agreements it had no right to interfere with slavery on foreign soil, neither consuls nor naval officers were supposed to intervene in relations between owners and slaves beyond "persuasion, negotiation and other peaceful means."[10] Instructions issued in 1844 and still in force told naval officers stationed on the West African coast to "clearly point out to [the natives] the distinction between the export of Slaves which Great Britain is determined to put an end to, and the system of Domestic Slavery with which she claims no right to interfere."[11]

Legislation passed in 1843 had finally made it an offense for British subjects to own slaves or deal in them anywhere in the world. When Consul Benjamin Campbell became aware that it was common practice at Lagos for British citizens, including a vice-consul, to receive young slaves as gifts and employ them in their households, he admonished the vice-consul and warned others about the risks involved in accepting slaves.[12]

The status of the Sierra Leoneans returning to Lagos and its interior was ambiguous—sometimes they were treated as British subjects and at other times not. Consuls knew that many of them bought, employed, and sometimes also sold slaves and that they accepted pawns in exchange for credit. Most British officers found this behavior very distasteful, because many of the Sierra Leoneans had experienced the horrors of slavery first-hand and owed their freedom to the anti-slavery campaign. Campbell and the CMS missionary Samuel Ajayi Crowther pressed the Sierra Leoneans at Lagos and Abeokuta to free their slaves, under threat of losing British protection, but with limited effect. Successive consuls informed repatriates at Lagos that if they sold slaves or pawns to slave traders, Ọba Dosunmu would be ordered to expel them from the town.[13]

Consuls and missionaries intervened in the relationship between indigenous Lagosians and their slaves much more selectively. The early CMS missionaries were closely allied with Akitoye and his successor Dosunmu, and while sometimes assisting individual slaves, they hesitated to openly attack an institution on which the wealth and power of the local political elite rested. When consuls interfered with slavery, they were often motivated more by political than humanitarian concerns. Thus Vice-Consul Fraser refused to let Britain's nemesis Madame Tinubu reclaim a slave girl she had sent to help Mrs. Sandeman, wife of the British trader.[14] Yet when a group of female slaves ran away from the *ìgá* and sought refuge at the consulate because they feared they would be sacrificed in the funeral ceremonies following Akitoye's death, Consul Campbell merely informed the new Ọba Dosunmu that he hoped there was no cause for alarm and sent the women back to the palace.[15] In doing so, he anticipated the practice of later officials on the west coast and elsewhere who justified upholding the control of male owners over their female slaves by equating it to that of husbands over their wives.

Campbell reported hearing complaints of kidnapping, seizure of third parties for debts, and selling free people into slavery, and he claimed to use his "utmost endeavours" to obtain redress for the victims.[16] However, he and the missionaries also helped promote a view of West African slavery that was gaining currency in Britain and subsequently dominated discourse about the institution in Lagos, its hinterland, and other parts of the region. According to this view, local slavery was a benign institution vastly different "in effect and influence" from the compulsory labor of slaves in foreign countries. Campbell wrote to the Earl of Clarendon, then foreign secretary, that in Africa the slave

> never loses the hope of being one day restored to his home and country, either through the instrumentality of his friends and family redeeming him, or . . . of trusting to his limbs and . . . ingenuity to again [regain] his liberty and home. Should his master be like himself a heathen, there is probably no intellectual difference between them . . . his master and himself work in the same field, frequently they eat out of the same bowl, and the slave is regarded as a member of the family; his state of subjection not being onerous he gets reconciled to it, particularly [if,] as is the common custom of the heathen slave proprietor, his master purchases for him a female slave as his wife and companion.[17]

Given widespread belief in the benign character of domestic slavery, neither consuls nor early missionaries thought that Britain labored under a great moral obligation to abolish it.

Campbell also promoted the idea that the growth of the palm oil trade would of its own accord improve the condition of local slaves and gradually end slavery. He wrote to his superiors, "this legitimate and peaceful trade is working its beneficial influence in gradually ameliorating the condition of that large proportion of the population held in a state of bondage, which is gradually becoming nominal."[18] The consul maintained that legitimate commerce was encouraging owners to allow slaves to work one, two, and even three days a week for themselves and that it seemed to be "the natural effect in this country of any commerce, based on the cultivation of the soil, to unshackle the bonds of the slave, not tighten them."[19] A year later he asserted that slaves were using the property they accumulated through their labors to purchase their freedom and that of their children.[20] Because many Europeans believed that legitimate commerce would inevitably undermine local slavery, which was in any case mild, they felt no great urgency about dismantling it. The duty of Christians, most missionaries counseled, was to heed the advice of St. Paul and be "kind, just, and liberal" in the treatment of their slaves.[21]

Toward the end of the decade, a few British officials in Lagos temporarily became more interventionist. Lieutenant Edward Lodder of the Royal Navy, who served as acting consul when Campbell was away in 1858 and again after his death the following year, evidently helped a number of female slaves redeem themselves and their children.[22] In 1859, W.

B. Baikie and Lieutenant John Hawley Glover, then of Britain's Niger Expedition, created a political crisis by enticing Nupe and Hausa slaves to flee their owners and join them as porters on an overland journey to the Niger River. As many as 450 slaves absconded at that time, provoking an attack aimed at upholding slavery when the party passed through Abeokuta, which poisoned Glover's relations with the Egba for years to come.[23] Missionaries in Lagos and the interior also used small sums to help slaves redeem themselves; however, they could ill afford to allow their stations to become havens for runaway slaves.

Flight from Lagos was difficult and very risky without the kind of protection Baikie and Glover offered, particularly if slaves came from places far from the coast. To begin with, escape required canoe transport across the lagoon to the mainland. Once there, many runaways had to traverse vast territories where the slave trade was still active and local peoples were at war with one another before reaching home. Fugitive slaves faced not only the challenge of surviving the journey, but also the likelihood of recapture, especially so long as facial scarification, language, dress, or other distinguishing features set them apart as strangers and probable slaves. In the 1850s and 1860s, moreover, recapture still carried the threat of sale into the Atlantic commerce. Finally, warfare had destroyed the towns and villages from which many of the slaves had come, sending their relatives into flight as refugees and leaving them no place to return. A slave named Yara, brought to Lagos in 1853, said in court as late as 1896 that he had never gone back to his country because "it was always disturbed."[24] Recognizing the dangers that freed slaves faced, Consul Brand, Campbell's successor, began issuing "passports" to those wanting to travel to the interior. He no doubt hoped that the documents would guarantee safe passage, but it is difficult to imagine that they had much effect.[25]

After the annexation, the question of how to deal with fugitive slaves from the interior who escaped to Lagos would absorb much official attention, but in the 1850s runaways did not present British representatives with a grave problem. Lagos was not yet a safe haven for fugitive slaves, and although some fled there, the number was not great. The *ọba* and chiefs were known to seize runaways and either return them to their owners or claim them as their own. In the aftermath of the exodus sparked by Baikie and Glover, moreover, British consuls conciliated local and interior opinion by restoring fugitive slaves when they thought that harboring them would arouse serious opposition.[26]

Consul Brand also began the practice of keeping a list of slaves emancipated at the consulate. Those enumerated by no means represent the totality of runaways in the town, because some slaves absconded without

Table 5.1 Slaves Liberated by Consul Foote, March through April 1861

	Apprenticed	*Liberated*
Women	90	91
Girls	75	—
Men	99	31
Boys	109	4
Total	373	126

Source: PP 1862.LXI.147, Class B. Correspondence with Foreign Powers Relating to the Slave Trade. McCoskry to Russell, 10 June 1861, 170.

seeking official protection. Indeed, Brand's figures—three in 1857, five in 1858, seventeen in 1859, and thirty-three in 1860—reveal the tiny number of slaves liberated by the British throughout most of the consular period. A dramatic increase occurred in the number of slaves registered in 1861, when H. G. Foote intervened to liberate or apprentice 499 in only seven weeks between March 12 and the end of April. The reasons for this expansion probably include renewed efforts by Foote to free slaves belonging to Sierra Leonean repatriates and growing awareness among slaves themselves that seeking British protection could lead to emancipation.[27] The sources do not reveal how long losses continued at that rate, which owners must have found alarming. However, William McCoskry, Lagos's first acting governor, hinted that there was substantial unrest among slaves immediately following the annexation.[28]

Redemption was paid for a number of the slaves liberated, more than 70 percent of whom were classified as women throughout both periods. Nearly three-quarters of those registered in March and April 1861 were apprenticed, moreover, rather than freed outright, and had to work off their redemption. The much higher percentage of females registered can probably be accounted for by the gender imbalance in the slave population, the more limited opportunities of females to rise out of bondage through military service, and their greater opportunities to escape by entering domestic and sexual relationships with men.

Despite the centrality of the abolition of the slave trade to contemporary discourse about the annexation of Lagos, officials at neither the Foreign Office nor the Colonial Office had given much thought to how to deal with slavery at Lagos when Britain seized the kingdom in 1861. The senior clerk of the Colonial Office's African Division had objected to the annexation on the grounds that domestic slavery at Lagos "could not be so easily winked at" as on the Gold Coast, and the Duke of Newcastle, secretary of state for the colonies, had expressed reservations about extending British territory in West Africa because of "the great difficulty of dealing with domestic slavery."[29] However, no decisions had been taken about local slavery. Newcastle minuted in July 1862 that the British government had yet to consider "the status of the domestic slaves of Lagos, . . . and the mode in which we are to deal with them."[30]

In the absence of clear directives from London, colonial policy regarding slavery at Lagos emerged slowly in the 1860s. It turned on the tensions between British law, which held after the 1833 Abolition of Slavery Bill that slavery was "forever abolished and declared unlawful throughout the British colonial plantations and possessions abroad," and fear that to end slavery immediately would create grave political and social problems in the new colony and render it more difficult and costly to rule.[31]

The British annexation clearly affected the relationship between owners and slaves in and around Lagos, although information regarding its immediate impact is limited. For one thing, suppression of the foreign slave trade diminished the usefulness of the threat of sale abroad as a means of disciplining slaves. Removal of this method of control widened the social space within which slaves could act and increased opportunities for redefining the owner-slave relationship. For another, the imposition of British rule seems to have led some slaves in Lagos, as later elsewhere in Africa, to think that they could leave their owners. For a brief moment immediately following the annexation, before it became clear that British officials would throw their weight behind upholding existing social relations, a number of slaves apparently acted in an effort to transform their identity. William McCoskry, the red-bearded merchant appointed acting governor shortly after the annexation, made the cryptic yet tantalizing remark that questions arising out of domestic slavery were giving him "more trouble than all the rest of the business together." He also referred to numerous slaves seeking protection at Lagos, suggesting that runaways from elsewhere were beginning to perceive the colony as a place where they might find freedom.[32]

Faced with slaves taking matters into their own hands, McCoskry quickly adopted a number of *ad hoc* measures to deal with the situation. He regarded Sierra Leonean and Brazilian repatriates as British subjects, now clearly under the authority of British law, and immediately apprenticed their slaves to them for up to seven years.[33] In addition, the acting governor established a court, presided over by two European merchants, to hear cases regarding slaves and apprentices in Lagos and runaways from the interior. He conceived of the tribunal as a place where slaves who were mistreated could bring their grievances and, if they received decisions in their favor, redeem themselves and obtain "letters of emancipation."[34] Few of the court's records apparently survive, making it impossible to draw firm conclusions about its workings. However, McCoskry's emphasis on both mistreatment and redemption as conditions of emancipation suggest that he intended it to recognize the rights of owners in their slaves, as did many missionaries when they facilitated redemption.

Many of the references in existing documents to cases heard by the Slave Court involve runaways from outside British territory. In such instances, owners had four months to apply for compensation, but in order to qualify for it they had to be able to provide evidence of right of possession, date and price of purchase, and time of flight. The compensation awarded depended on the price paid for the slave and the length of the slave's service, as well as on evidence of mistreatment.[35] To help meet the needs of slaves seeking protection, McCoskry created the Liberated African Yard, overseen by a Mr. Davis, who was to "take charge" of those freed and find work for them until they became known in the town and were capable of looking after themselves. McCoskry lamented that for want of such an arrangement many freed slaves at Lagos "had fallen into bad hands" and been sold again into slavery.[36]

McCoskry shared the contemporary view that African slavery was a mild institution, "not, properly speaking, slavery" at all. He argued that slaves in Lagos were treated more like servants than chattels, and that they stayed with their owners not through coercion but of their own free will. Moreover, McCoskry was convinced that it would be impractical to abolish slavery in Lagos, because it would lead to an insurrection of the owners, which the slaves themselves would support! The best course, he maintained, was to let slavery die out gradually under the improving influence of legitimate commerce and British rule.[37] Given these beliefs, it is unlikely that Lagos's first acting governor did much to encourage slaves to take advantage of the Slave Court or Liberated African Yard; and indeed, a year into the latter's existence H. S. Freeman, the first governor, reported that it had provided temporary support to only a small number of persons.[38]

Freeman continued the Slave Court and Liberated African Yard created by McCoskry.[39] When asked by the Colonial Office for a report on domestic slavery, he continued to press the case for gradual emancipation.

In his report, the governor differentiated between "slaves of the soil," presumably those born in Lagos, and "slaves bought from the interior." This distinction mirrors that of modern-day informants between *àrótà* (slaves born in their owners' households) and *ẹrú* (those bought in interior markets), and Freeman was probably following contemporary local usage in his analysis.[40] Slaves bought in the interior, the governor argued, were more frequently exported, "as they [hold] less to their masters, their principal aim being to redeem themselves and return to their country." Few succeeded in escaping, he noted, because on the slightest show of discontent they were sent to some distant market for sale. Freeman maintained that slaves of the soil were better off, and that their servitude was more like serfdom than slavery. He insisted that legislation would not immediately change the experience of these slaves, because they had grown up with fixed ideas which are not "easily eradicated from the black man's head."[41]

Freeman was about to present to the Colonial Office the plan that he and Glover had developed to recruit a locally trained, armed police force from among slaves of northern origin, and he framed further discussion of slaves bought in the interior to increase the likelihood of securing approval for this project. According to him, some of the slaves from the interior were Hausa Muslims, who "would work hard for their liberty as they scorn servitude especially under a pagan."[42] He claimed that many of these slaves were held by people who had no right to them other than that of kidnappers. Hundreds, Freeman asserted, had run away from Ouidah, Porto Novo, Abeokuta, or Epe and been seized again by Dosunmu and his chiefs. These Hausa slaves, Freeman implied, longed for freedom and deserved it. But the governor did not recommend interfering in the relationship between owners and other slaves bought in the interior. To justify his position, he invoked that widespread defense of slavery—the sanctity of private property rights. An immense number of slaves, the governor wrote, had been purchased in fair markets and were the legal property of their owners before Lagos was ceded to the British crown. To take them away without compensation would be unjust and impolitic.

If Freeman was to make a convincing case for moving slowly toward emancipation, he had to find a way around the 1833 Abolition of Slavery Bill. He tried to do so by arguing that no Act of Parliament could so overthrow international law as to give it retrospective authority in a newly ceded territory. If this view was adopted, he argued, owners in Lagos would retain a right to their slaves, and the colonial government could work toward gradual emancipation, "without prejudice to [the] masters' interests," by apprenticing slaves to their owners for periods determined by the slave's age and length of service.[43] As an alternative, Freeman suggested that the government could ignore the existence of slaves in Lagos, so that the law would not have to determine who was one and who was not. When any slave presented himself at the Slave Court, his case could be examined, however, and he might be freed, if there was good reason. The governor's use of the masculine pronoun in this and other general discussions of slavery is revealing. Like many of his contemporaries, he commonly equated female slavery and marriage and doubted that the government should interfere with the control of husbands over their wives.[44]

Freeman dismissed his second alternative in favor of the first, on the grounds that as soon as a critical mass of slaves had obtained emancipation "there would be a general rising of the rest." He concluded that if the Abolition of Slavery Bill was unequivocal and not subject to the interpretation he favored, then Lagos's slaves would have to be freed *en masse*, and their masters compensated for the loss of their property. Freeman warned that if this final course of action was taken he could not answer for the safety of the town without "a very much increased military force."[45] The governor knew that to contain costs the Colonial Office opposed sending more troops to Lagos and would not seriously consider compensating owners for the loss of their slaves. In presenting his proposal the way he did, Freeman identified emancipation with two consequences that he could be sure his superiors in London would find unacceptable. If approved, on the other hand, his recommendation would settle the question of domestic slavery in Lagos at once, and the natives would remain entitled to their slaves.

Officials at the Colonial Office accepted Freeman's assessment of slavery in Lagos. They agreed that a "state of transition" ought to be recognized and viewed a system of apprenticeship as a reasonable solution, which followed the example set by Great Britain in the West Indies. Yet they worried that British anti-slavery legislation was too unbending to permit a system of apprenticeship. The Duke of Newcastle summed up official concern by saying that it was not "a question of what appears to me or the government reasonable and just, but what is the law," and he instructed his subordinates to submit Governor Freeman's proposal for legal opinion.[46]

Asked for advice, Sir Frederic Rogers, the permanent undersecretary of state for the colonies, who had a legal background, made short work of Freeman's proposal. Retrospection and international law had nothing to do with the matter, he minuted. The first question was simply whether a British Act of Parliament would or would not prevail in a British territory. The second was not whether "the slaves have been hitherto free . . . but whether they are to be so hereafter." In Rogers's opinion, Freeman's legal reasoning was utterly misguided. In the eyes of the law, he concluded, "there is no such thing as a slave in Lagos."[47]

The legal opinion could not have been clearer. In light of it, the Colonial Office concluded that there were two possibilities. The first was an Act of Parliament suspending for a time the operation of British antislavery legislation so far as the indigenous inhabitants of Lagos were concerned. The second was a new treaty transforming Lagos, like much of the Gold Coast, from a colony into a protectorate, where British antislavery legislation would not apply. Officials failed even to consider options that would have helped make emancipation a reality for Lagos's slaves. Newcastle dismissed the first alternative on the grounds that it could not be accomplished without giving rise to the charge that Britain was reversing its position on slaveholding. He dismissed the second on the grounds that while it should have been done in the first place, it would be difficult now. In a fit of pique at the Foreign Office for having gotten the Colonial Office into such a mess, Newcastle instructed his subordinates to ask Lord Russell, the foreign secretary, how Britain was supposed to deal with domestic slavery at Lagos, which "can't be suddenly abolished without unfortunate consequences and can't be recognized given acts of Parliament regarding slavery throughout Her Majesty's dominions."[48] The Foreign Office apparently never replied, and in the short term Newcastle dealt with the matter simply by allowing it to drop. In effect, this gave local administrators a free hand to deal with slavery as they saw fit. Apprenticeship and his legal slight of hand rejected, Freeman fell back on his second alternative: to ignore the existence of slaves in Lagos so far as possible and to look into their grievances only when they presented themselves at the Slave Court.

In late 1863, J. H. Glover, acting as head of the government while Freeman was on leave, raised the question of apprenticeship once again by forwarding to the Colonial Office an ordinance that required the registration of all slaves in Lagos. Under the new law, those who were not registered would become free, and their owners would henceforth be unable to make claims against them in colonial courts. Slaves who were registered, on the other hand, would be apprenticed to their owners for periods determined by their age, health, and original cost. After completing their apprenticeship, they would become free. In addition, the law stipulated that the children of slaves could not be removed from British territory without the consent of a commissioner, a tacit acknowledgment of the greater vulnerability of children to the slave trade.[49]

In response to the proposed legislation, Sir Frederic Rogers stated Britain's dilemma regarding slavery at Lagos with new force. In the eyes of British law, he insisted, all slaves had been freed at the moment of the annexation, and slavery no longer existed in the colony. Yet authorities in Lagos and London feared that any step which called attention to the fact that slaves were no longer obliged to obey their owners would be "in the nature of a social revolution" and might expose the young colony to grave political dangers and make it more difficult to rule.[50] At this time, Rogers also introduced into the discussion an additional concern that he believed made settling the slavery question ever more urgent. He predicted, with great foresight, that contrary to conventional wisdom the expansion of legitimate commerce in the region would not promote emancipation but rather greatly increase the value of labor, transform the intermittent demands of local "serfdom" into a "grinding exaction of labor," and make owners less willing to part with their slaves. Despite the embarrassment it might cause, he and others at the Colonial Office favored dealing with slavery at Lagos by enacting a revised form of Glover's ordinance, if only the law officers would permit a colonial legislature to do such a thing.[51] Should they refuse, then the question arose whether a bill authorizing the registration and apprenticeship of slaves at Lagos should be introduced in the British Parliament. Proffering an opinion on the subject, C. S. Fortescue, an undersecretary for the colonies, displayed the linguistic guile that would be used increasingly in future to deal with slavery at Lagos, when he expressed frustration with the local authorities for having legislated in the first place "with such infantile simplicity, and call[ed] slavery 'slavery.'"[52] Officials were waking up to the fact that a slave by any other name need not be acknowledged to be a slave.

When consulted, the law officers replied that the Lagos ordinance was indeed at odds with British anti-slavery legislation and could not be approved. As apprenticeship had not been introduced when Lagos was first annexed and as every inhabitant was consequently free, the sanction of the imperial legislature would have to be obtained if the law was deemed essential for the welfare of the young colony. Put to the test, Edward Cardwell, who had replaced Newcastle as colonial secretary in April 1864, shrank from raising the question of apprenticeship at Lagos in the House of Commons, for fear that to do so would expose the government to the criticism of reestablishing a "modification of slavery in British dominions" at the same time that it was pressing anti-slavery "on other civilized countries." Cardwell concluded that the best course would be to rely "on the practical judgment and careful management of the local authorities [rather] than upon any legislation" to handle slavery at Lagos.[53]

With so few palatable options, officials at the Colonial Office now advocated a solution that directly conflicted with the interests of British authorities in Lagos. They pointed out that the government could minimize the problem of domestic slavery in its new colony by restricting British territory to the narrowest possible extent, as had been done on the Gold Coast. By the time he left office, even Newcastle had accepted that the island of Lagos could not be given up, but undersecretaries suggested that Badagry, Palma, and other territory acquired from Dosunmu might be proclaimed a protectorate, beyond the rule of British law.

In November 1864, Glover, by now lieutenant governor in charge of the local government, sent the Colonial Office a second ordinance, which created a new Slave Commission Court. The tribunal was designed to replace the older Slave Court and have responsibility for "matters relating to the amount of compensation to owners of liberated slaves and to their apprenticeship and to all disputes, etc., between slaves and owners."[54] Glover described the new court as both "a safety valve for the disaffection of the serf" and a place where masters could find "a certain amount of protection against the total or immediate loss of . . . [their] property."[55] He seems to have intended it to deal primarily with fugitive slaves entering the colony from the interior, and particularly from Egbaland, where he was embroiled in conflict, rather than with domestic slavery at Lagos. The lieutenant governor explained the need for the new court by saying that the older one was inadequate to deal with important political questions arising from interaction with Egba chiefs, because it was presided over by a commissioner drawn from the mercantile community, which had begun to oppose his policies, rather than the government. The new ordinance stipulated that owners of fugitive slaves would be compensated only if they inhabited places on friendly terms with the Lagos government. Glover apparently intended to use the new Slave Commission Court to pressure the Egba to conduct their foreign affairs as he wanted, by returning runaways belonging to chiefs who were conciliatory or compensating them for their losses while harboring those of hostile chiefs and denying them compensation.[56]

By the time this second ordinance reached London, officials at the Colonial Office believed that a select committee of the House of Commons would soon be sitting to investigate the state of British settlements on the West African coast. In anticipation, the colonial secretary had already sent Colonel Henry Ord to gather information locally, instructing him, among other things, to look into slavery at Lagos. Officials used these developments as an excuse to avoid taking any action on Glover's second slavery ordinance.[57]

When Colonel Ord arrived at Lagos, discussions with him apparently heightened Glover's awareness of the legal difficulties created by the two ordinances the lieutenant governor had submitted. Glover quickly advised London that he would tell the commissioner of the reconstituted Slave Court "to circumscribe its action, as applied to cases in the Colony within the narrowest possible limits," and eventually to act only on those arising "from the entrance into the settlement of persons from adjacent countries."[58] In future, the court was to stop hearing cases of Lagos slaves and restrict its attention to runaways from the interior—a neat solution since it was, in any case, the political leverage that the court gave Glover over the owners of fugitive slaves from the interior that was of greatest interest to him.

Two days later, Glover sent the Colonial Office a second dispatch, again prompted by discussions with Colonel Ord. Given the importance that local administrators attached to making the colony self-supporting and generating revenue for future development by defining its boundary widely enough to capture the lion's share of the trade crossing the lagoon for export, it seems likely that this communiqué was intended to forestall further discussion of the boundary question. In the dispatch, the lieutenant governor suggested what the Colonial Office was already considering: that slavery be dealt with by restricting the area over which Britain exercised sovereign rights and maintained British law. But he defined the territory that needed to be retained much more broadly than officials in London, to include not only the islands of Lagos and Iddo, but also the towns of Badagry, Palma, Lekki, and indeed the whole of the seaboard and lagoon from the River Addo in the west to a point east of Lekki.[59]

And so matters stood until early 1866. In the interim, the Select Committee Appointed to Consider the State of British Establishments on the Western Coast of Africa deliberated. A report by one of its commissioners, published in June 1865, concluded that domestic slavery still existed in Lagos, contrary to British law, and recommended terminating it as soon as possible.[60] The Colonial Office took advantage of the administrative reorganization that followed to try to settle the vexing question of slavery at Lagos once and for all. Mr. Cardwell dispatched Major Blackall, the new governor-in-chief of Britain's West African Settlements, to Lagos to deal with the now closely related questions of slavery and the boundary of the colony. The colonial secretary drew Blackall's attention to the embarrassing inconsistency, "published by the Select Committee for the world to see," that while "there can be no legal slavery" in Lagos, there was slavery *de facto.* The Colonial Office warned that this inconsistency might create scandal in foreign nations and that it placed the peace of the settlement itself "at the mercy of any adventurer or enthusiast who might choose to tell the slaves they are free."[61] Officials in London sympathized with the difficulties that local administrators faced in a territory where domestic slavery was part of the social fabric, but the fact remained that the ordinances passed at Lagos to deal with slavery were illegal because they recognized its existence. Blackall was instructed to announce their abrogation when he got to Lagos. His superiors also cautioned him, however, to avoid disturbances in the colony and conflict with neighboring chiefs whose slaves might seek refuge there. Cardwell suggested, moreover, that when disallowing the Lagos ordinances Blackall might at the same time strongly recommend that "labourers and servants" remain with their employers so long as they were well treated. Recognizing that the local authorities might want to introduce a new ordinance to regulate the relationship between "masters and servants," something that did not in fact occur until 1877, Cardwell told the governor-in-chief that such legislation should contain "no recognition of slavery in any shape."[62]

Officials in London believed that if domestic slavery was handled in this way, there would be little practical difficulty on the island. An undersecretary observed that matters would in fact remain much as they had been. On the one hand, the government would not attempt to enforce the payment of wages to people who preferred living in the families of their employers to working for hire; while, on the other, employers would have no legal power to detain workers against their will. There would be, as there had been, legal redress for every inhabitant of Lagos complaining of violence or compulsory detention.

Cardwell concluded his instructions by stating what Glover did not want to hear: that the "readiest and most effective way of escaping from all these embarrassments" was to confine British territory at Lagos to its smallest practical extent. If British law could not be established on the island and in the towns occupied by British forces, then it would be necessary to confine British territory to the land occupied by government buildings. The rest of the area acquired from Dosunmu would have to be made a protectorate, where British influence could be used to "soften and gradually destroy slavery," without being called upon to abolish it.[63]

What Blackall did in Lagos, what he and Glover said to one another about slavery and the boundary of the colony, the sources do not reveal. Soon after his arrival, however, the governor-in-chief sent the Colonial Office a brief dispatch articulating what became from then on the official British position on slavery in Lagos. Blackall told Cardwell that the country offered no difficulty with regard to slavery, because "it is sparsely inhabited and the people fully understand they are free."[64] He forestalled redefinition of the colonial boundary by arguing that all of the territory acquired from both Dosunmu and Kosoko would have to be retained, because any other course of action would create more problems than it solved.

Prior to the mid-1860s, shared concerns at home and on the coast had dictated an official policy of gradual emancipation, which would have tied most slaves to their owners for a period of time, as had been done in the West Indies, but would also have created institutions to help slaves who could prove ill treatment obtain immediate freedom. These concerns were expressed as fears about maintaining political stability and social order, not about meeting labor needs. However, a measure of commitment to helping Lagos's large slaveowners supply their ongoing demand for labor in a context of rapid commercial expansion was implicit in recommendations urging apprenticeship and encouraging "workers" to remain with their "employers." Belief that the patriarchal system of slavery in Lagos weighed lightly on the slaves and would die of its own accord as British civilization developed on the coast made accepting these practical accommodations with local unfree labor comparatively easy for British officials and Christian missionaries alike, despite their widespread commitment to the abolition of the international slave trade.

When gradual emancipation proved impossible because legislating against slavery required acknowledging its existence, contrary to British law, and risking a public relations problem for the British government, the Colonial Office favored minimizing the problem by fiddling with the boundary of the colony. Local administrators balked at this solution, however, because they feared that it would undermine the colony's trade and revenue, which in a context where African possessions were expected to pay for themselves would slow its development and perhaps jeopardize its very existence. Authorities could not resolve the dilemma by abolishing the legal status of slavery, as had been done in India and would be done again in many of Britain's future African possessions, because according to legal opinion that had been accomplished at the moment of the annexation.

Faced with this dilemma, local officials fell back on the fiction that Lagos's slaves were already free and that if they did not live as free people, it was a matter of their own choosing. Authorities then imposed the language of free labor, in the case of males, and often of marriage, in the case of females, on discussions of the owner-slave relationship. The state recognized the rights of slaves to bring court cases against their owners, but it encouraged neither the payment of wages nor the substantial redistribution of resources necessary to transform the position of slaves in society. Indeed, the colonial secretary counseled the governor-in-chief to use whatever influence he could bring to bear to maintain the status quo with respect to owner-slave relations. Henceforth, the colonial government turned its back on slavery in Lagos and dealt with the problem largely by denying that it existed. Officials would later debate slave dealing beyond the frontier, the fate of fugitive slaves from the interior, and slaveholding in the protectorate inland from Lagos, but never again slavery within Lagos Colony itself. The British presence made possible a redefinition of the owner-slave relationship but largely left it to Lagos's slaves themselves to accomplish the task.

Slave Dealing

Few things illustrate the persistence of slavery in Lagos after 1866 more clearly than the fact that Lagosians continued to buy slaves in markets on the mainland and import them into the colony. When it suited them, people living within British territory also sold slaves to one another and exported them to Porto Novo, Ouidah, and elsewhere. From the time of the annexation, British anti-slavery legislation made it illegal for anyone to engage in the slave trade on British soil and for British subjects to deal in slaves anywhere in the world.[65] Yet many local officials claimed to be ignorant of whether it was an offense for Lagosians, most of whom were not regarded as British subjects, to buy slaves or accept pawns beyond the frontier of the colony.[66] If it was not, then it would be impossible, all acknowledged, to prevent them from bringing some of these people into the colony.

After 1874, no uncertainty about the status of slave dealing beyond the frontier or the fate of newly imported slaves should have existed. In that year, the Gold Coast ordinance abolishing slave dealing, enacted in response to pressure to stop the practice in the Protectorate, was introduced simultaneously at Lagos. This legislation clearly made it an offense for a resident of the colony to "purchase, sell, barter, transfer, or take" a slave, no matter where, and it also prohibited accepting pawns. The law further proclaimed that every person brought into the Colony to "be a slave or be . . . transferred as a . . . security for debt" became "*ipso facto*" free.[67] Little was done initially to enforce the legislation, however, and despite its enactment the importation and sale of slaves and exchange of pawns continued in the colony. After the annexation, slave dealing within the town itself took place discreetly within houses, largely beyond the view of British authorities.[68] Officials could easily overlook it. Elsewhere in the colony, the state had few representatives and the boundary was ill-defined. In the opinion of several locals, the slave trade at Lagos actually increased in the mid-1870s, to the point that it was widespread.[69]

A letter to the *African Times* of London in 1876 from a Lagosian who adopted the pseudonym "Otitoro Koro," which he translated as "truth is stranger than fiction," brought the local slave trade to public attention in Britain and triggered stricter enforcement of the 1874 ordinance. Anti-slavery sentiment had begun to grow among a group of educated Africans in Lagos, inspired perhaps by the powerful preaching of the Rev. James Johnson, who had arrived from Sierra Leone in 1874 to become the rector of St. Paul's Breadfruit, Lagos's leading Anglican church.[70] The letter was probably written by a member of this group, and it led to one important change in policy—the introduction of a law requiring the registration of alien children in Lagos and prohibiting their removal from the colony without the permission of the governor. Otitoro Koro charged that slaves were regularly imported into Lagos by traders frequenting Ikorodu, Ejinrin, and other markets and that some of them were reexported to Porto Novo and Dahomey. The leader and correspondence that followed the publication of the letter sufficiently embarrassed the local administrator that he ordered the police to search canoes returning from markets on the northern shore of the lagoon, and within only a few hours constables found a number of slaves, many of them identified as children. Government dispatches discuss the fate of five girls said to be between the ages of eleven and fourteen, whose "appearance, condition and tribal marks, remove[d] every doubt . . . of their being slaves," but subsequent letters to the *African Times* put the number at twenty or more.[71]

The response of the colonial government to this incident further illuminates the weakness of its commitment to anti-slavery and willingness, in Otitoro Koro's words, to "wink" at the twin evils of local slaveholding and slave dealing.[72] The authorities did not immediately free the seized girls or initiate legal proceedings against their female owners, despite the fact that the women admitted—and the language used here is significant—having "redeemed" the girls in markets eighteen months before. Instead, the acting administrator, J. D. Dumaresq, ordered the owners and slaves brought to Government House, where he questioned the girls, who he later said told him that they had not been mistreated. He then instructed the owners to register their charges with the police and not to remove them from the colony. After telling the girls that they could report ill-treatment to the police, he allowed the owners to retain their slaves. Before the police searches further embarrassed the government, inconvenienced African traders, and annoyed the local population, the acting administrator ordered them stopped.[73]

For the next several months, letters to the *African Times* from anonymous correspondents at Lagos and articles by the editor of the paper kept pressure on the government by publicizing Dumaresq's failure to suppress the slave trade and calling for both the abolition of slave dealing and the emancipation of slaves at Lagos. Governor Sandford Freeling at the Gold Coast reviewed the situation and claimed to want to prosecute the owners of the five slave girls, but he decided against it on the grounds that the "adverse observation" caused by a trial would be "incommensurate with the advantage" it might bring. Freeling acknowledged that "a certain amount of slave dealing" was carried on at Lagos; yet he maintained that it was impossible to suppress the practice, because there was usually not sufficient evidence for officials to obtain a search warrant under English law.[74] When asked for legal advice about how to end "this infamous traffic," the queen's advocate presented three alternatives: 1) to issue a proclamation explaining the laws for the prevention of slave dealing and their penalties, 2) to pass an ordinance providing for methods of searching for slaves in Lagos, and 3) to pass an ordinance stipulating that it was an offense to bring into the colony persons "belonging to slave tribes or families or captured in interior wars," unless within a short period contracts hiring them were registered with the government or something else was done to show that they were free persons.[75]

Augustus W. L. Hemming, at the Colonial Office, insisted that the first of these options was "quite sufficient," as Britain would then "have made it clearly known that slave dealing was an offence against British law and morality, and would be punished if detected." He continued, "I cannot think there is any necessity for us to adopt such exceptional measures as the 2nd and 3rd alternatives . . . merely to vindicate our principles and uphold the truth of the assertion that everyone who sets foot on British soil is *ipso facto* free, and must be made so if he does not choose himself to throw aside his fetters—however light they may be."[76] The irony of making such a pronouncement following an incident when the colonial government had failed to check, much less punish, slave dealing and when the slaves in question were youths who had few if any means of throwing aside their fetters apparently escaped Hemming. He concluded by citing the precedent of Shebro, a British possession south of Freetown, where it had been decided that if there was a general awareness that slavery and slave dealing were illegal, then it was unnecessary for the government to take any further action against them.

When C. C. Lees, then lieutenant governor of Lagos, returned from leave, he evidently saw the limitations of Hemming's view so far as child slaves were concerned. Lees recommended the queen's advocate's first alternative for adults only and a greatly modified version of the third for people under twenty-one. To explain the laws for the prevention of slave dealing, Lees summoned "native merchants and traders" to a meeting at Government House and lectured them on the evils of slavery and the slave trade. He also announced a temporary dusk to dawn curfew on the movement of trade canoes to make the undetected import and export of slaves more difficult. Asked by those in the audience whether slaves already held were safe and their masters free from the law, the lieutenant governor replied that he was instructed "to punish offenders whether the slaves were bought ten years ago or yesterday."[77] Following the meeting, Lees assured officials at the Colonial Office that it was now "perfectly well known . . . that all persons coming into Lagos are free so long as they choose to remain there, and that they can claim the protection of the police if any coercion is attempted." Any adult slave who left the colony or performed an act of service at Lagos, he maintained, did so "entirely of his own free will, and his movements . . . do not . . . require, nor do they admit of interference."[78] The truth that this upheld, of course, was that while slaves brought into the colony from the interior might be considered free once they reached British soil, they could leave their owners and live as free people only if they had a better alternative. The principle that it vindicated was that the government would do very little to alter the relationship between owners and slaves in the colony, and that it was the responsibility of the slaves themselves to transform their identity.

In the aftermath of the meeting at Government House, officials temporarily became more vigilant in their efforts to suppress the slave trade, and arrests and prosecutions for slave dealing increased. Otitoro Koro wrote, with probable exaggeration, that following the lieutenant governor's meeting with the African traders, the hearing of slave cases at the Police Court became a daily occurrence. Six months later another correspondent reported that the criminal assizes sitting in the Eastern District had convicted five slave dealers and sentenced each to five years of penal servitude.[79]

There is no doubt that a lively market for child slaves existed in Lagos during the second half of the nineteenth century, although most Africans would have defined the category "child" differently than Europeans. In local culture, marriage, which females typically consummated soon after puberty and males only much later, at the end of their twenties or in their thirties, marked the transition to adulthood. Thus a fourteen-year-old girl, such as the one found on the lagoon in 1876, would have been perceived by locals as on the threshold of adulthood. A male of the same age would have been entering a long period of ten to twenty years when he was mature enough physically for heavy labor, but not yet old enough to demand a wife, greater economic autonomy, and more substantial opportunities for individual accumulation.

Many buyers on the coast evidently preferred immature slaves. They probably did so because, in a context of loosening controls, children were less able to resist enslavement than adults. Moreover, they offered the possibility of more complete assimilation into the kin group and community, because they were still developing cognitively and culturally. That said, young slaves whom Europeans would have identified as children were to most Africans just entering their prime years.

The trial of a Lagos man named Seidu for slave dealing, which occurred in 1877 on the heels of the scandal involving the five slave girls, heightened local officials' awareness of the plight of youths who were being bought in the interior, brought into the colony, and then sold again. Testimony in the case showed clearly that Seidu had purchased adult and child slaves at Ikorodu, brought them to his house in Lagos, and there sold them to traders who came to Lagos to sell palm produce. It revealed, moreover, that in this instance the buyer had expressed a clear preference for a young male slave.[80] In the case of children, it was more difficult for the government to maintain the fiction that all slaves who set foot on British soil were free, regardless of their subsequent experiences.

To deal with the problem of child slaves, Lieutenant Governor Lees recommended, the Legislative Council passed, and the colonial secretary quickly approved an ordinance requiring the registration of all African children within a defined territory whose births had not already been recorded at the government registry of births and deaths established in 1863. The law stipulated that children brought into the territory in future had to be registered within forty-eight hours of their arrival, and it prohibited receiving or housing unregistered children. Any change in a registered child's residence or custody had to be recorded, moreover, and the child could not be removed from the territory without the governor's written permission. Finally, children registered under the ordinance had to be produced on the request of proper authorities. To facilitate enforcement, the statute gave the colonial courts the power to grant search warrants, if reasonable suspicion existed that houses contained unregistered alien children.[81] Lees had recommended that the law require people bringing children into Lagos to provide them with education or industrial training, but his superiors in London decided that the settlement was not ready for such a measure.[82]

The new law aroused immediate opposition among the local population. From the crisis triggered by its introduction, a discourse about the importation of slaves into the colony emerged that enabled officials to see it as good for the enslaved and a step on the road to their civilization. This perspective helped justify the government's subsequent failure to stamp out the purchase, if not the sale, of slaves by Lagosians. When the Alien Children's Registration Ordinance was announced, a large delegation of chiefs, elders, and prominent African traders protested it in a meeting at Government House and subsequent petition to the government. The leaders of the protest did not complain about the law's impact on their own slaves, except to say, showing shrewd appreciation of anti-slavery rhetoric, that it would now be much harder for them to buy young victims of war and slavery in the interior and bring them to freedom in Lagos. Rather they stressed, also showing keen understanding of government priorities, that by requiring people visiting Lagos from the interior to register the children in their company, the ordinance would encourage the free and slave dependents of these people to run away, poison the government's relationship with its neighbors, and discourage traders from coming to Lagos. The net effect, they warned, would be to undermine the colony's commerce and, by implication, its revenue. The language used by the women and men apprehended during the brief period that canoes were searched for slaves in 1876 shows that by then Lagosians had already begun to represent the purchase of slaves beyond the frontier for use in the colony as a benevolent act of redemption.[83]

The public outcry over the Alien Children's Registration Ordinance greatly alarmed the government. Correspondence in its wake reveals much confusion about both the goals of the legislation and the meaning of its specific provisions. But ultimately, Governor Freeling at the Gold Coast advised, whether picking up on the language used by the local slaveowners or coming to it independently, and falling back once again on the linguistic guile and legal fiction that characterized British policy regarding local slavery, that the law was not intended to prevent Lagosians from "purchasing . . . slaves—or purchasing the freedom of slaves, to put it differently—in the interior." It was designed to prevent their reexport from the colony. For by bringing slaves bought in the interior into the colony, locals were opening to them the possibility of transforming their lot through disciplined labor in the expanding export sector and exposing them to the influence of civilization. Emancipation henceforth became a matter of the slaves' own free will, never mind that, as Freeling acknowledged, they might, in Lagos, "be treated [as] and consider themselves [to be] domestic slaves."[84]

Whether the protests of the local slaveowners suggested this resolution to Freeling or he arrived at it in some other way does not matter.[85] The important thing is that the Alien Children's Registration Ordinance in no way prohibited bringing children, even slave children, into Lagos and putting them to work there; it merely required that such children be registered and stipulated that they could not be removed from British territory without the governor's permission. Moreover, it engendered a way of thinking about local slave dealing that made the sale and reexport of slaves, not their purchase and import, the main problem. While this policy may have restricted the ability of local slaveowners to liquidate the capital they had tied up in their slaves, it did not threaten the flow of labor and dependents into the colony. This episode, and indeed Britain's entire handling of slavery at Lagos after 1865, calls to mind Martin Klein's pithy maxim, "The ability of Europeans in Africa to sustain an imperial agenda was based on their skill at deception."[86]

So far as visitors to Lagos from the interior were concerned, Governor Freeling seems to have wanted to say that they were unaffected by the Alien Children's Registration Ordinance, but he could not do so given the language of the law. Instead, he told the lieutenant governor to point out to the people of Lagos that children would not be separated from their parents, "actual or adoptive," and that visitors needed to register children only if they remained in the settlement for more than two days. Children in the company of visiting traders would not be able to run away, he insisted, unless Lagosians enticed and harbored them. Finally, Freeling bowed to local opinion by instructing that for a short time no action of any kind should be taken under the ordinance and that subsequently it should be enforced "temperately."[87] Local officials communicated these accommodations to the protesters, and evidently they quelled the unrest, because a report on the ordinance some months later commented, "all dissatisfaction has now disappeared and the measure is working well."[88]

After the Alien Children's Registration Ordinance was approved and all was said and done, Hemming minuted with regard to the discovery of the five slave girls, which had triggered its introduction, "I suppose it is all very wrong, but it seems to me to be 'much ado about nothing.' The children were apparently very well treated and contented."[89] So much for British commitment to ending the local slave trade.

In this context of increased foment over slavery, CMS agents from all parts of Yorubaland finally met in Lagos in 1879 to discuss the subject. The resolution adopted on the occasion shows the slow pace of change within the churches regarding slavery. While the resolution avowed that slavery was thoroughly alien to the spirit of the Gospel, it forbade only mission agents from holding slaves and pawns. Converts were merely prohibited from slave trading and called upon to allow slaves they already owned Christian instruction and time to work for their redemption. Even this temperate resolution was disseminated unevenly by missionaries.[90]

Criminal prosecutions for slave trading continued in the final decades of the century, although the offense to be curtailed was now regarded as the sale more than the purchase of slaves. Yet the slave traders who were caught, tried, and convicted represented but the tip of the iceberg, even granted this narrow definition of the problem. Between 1878 and 1887, only fourteen people were incarcerated at Lagos for "slave dealing," and another three for "slavery."[91] Lagosians, including Christians, continued to buy slaves at markets beyond the frontier, bring them back to the town, and sometimes sell them again until the end of the century, if in declining numbers. Government officials admitted that they could do very little to stop the practice.[92] As a contemporary remarked, a "floating population" was constantly arriving at Lagos and leaving it in pursuit of trade. During a six-month period in 1867, officials had counted almost 230,000 people arriving at or departing from a single wharf used by canoes traveling between Lagos island and Ebute Metta on the mainland.[93] This figure did not include the perhaps even larger number coming and going between Lagos island and the western, northern, and eastern lagoon. The itinerant population in the town can only have increased in subsequent decades. If government officials had had a will of iron, which clearly they did not, they would have had great difficulty ending the export, much less the import, of slaves, so long as a supply existed in the interior and slavery persisted as an important means of organizing labor and allegiance in the town and its environs. Slaves, especially young ones, could too easily be smuggled in and out of British territory along bush paths and concealed in canoes among pots of palm oil and sacks of other commodities. A number of highly publicized prosecutions occurred between 1890 and 1892, including one involving a man of "position and influence" at Ebute Metta who was convicted of selling three messengers from Ilesha to Egba buyers.[94] Indeed, the extension of British rule into the interior after the conquest of Ijebu Ode in 1892 initially created new opportunities for Lagosians to traffic in slaves. One of the earliest Hausa constables at Ibadan, for example, enticed a man, perhaps a runaway slave, to return with him to Lagos and then took him to Otta for sale.[95]

Youths began to be registered under the Alien Children's Registration Ordinance in February 1878. Although some of those brought into British territory slipped through the net of local officials, information collected under the new law yields insights into the gender and origins of the continuous stream of young slaves, pawns, and other dependents entering the colony. Table 5.2 provides a breakdown by gender of the young people registered at Lagos, Badagry, and Palma and Lekki between 1878 and 1887, and for the colony as a whole between 1893 and 1900.[96] The youths enumerated were not all slaves or pawns. For one thing, the ordinance required that freeborn children in the settlement whose births had not already been recorded should now be registered. Some of the young people entering the colony came, moreover, for education or to live with relatives or friends. Other freeborn young females and males arrived with a parent who came to trade or for some other reason. A few were brought to Lagos to work as domestic servants and were paid a wage, although their number remained small until the twentieth century. Nor did all of

Table 5.2 Children Registered by Date and Gender

	1878–1887			*1893–1900*		
	Male	*Female*	*Total*	*Male*	*Female*	*Total*
Lagos	1,067	1,628	2,695			
Badagry	385	328	713			
Palma and Lekki	88	60	148			
Total	1,540	2,016	3,556	755	1,033	1,788

Source: Annual Report, Lagos Colony, 1887, 28–30; *General Abstract of Registration*, Lagos Colony, 1893–1900.

Table 5.3 Origins of Children Registered at Lagos by Date and Gender, in Percentages (total numbers in parentheses)

	1878–1887			*1893–1900*		
	Male	*Female*	*Total*	*Male*	*Female*	*Total*
Central, eastern, and southeastern Yoruba	57	66	62 (2204)	44	46	45 (796)
Coastal/southern and western Yoruba	22	15	18 (645)	8	5	6 (113)
Northern	10	13	12 (415)	27	32	30 (526)
Igbo/Niger Delta	2	2	2 (73)	4	7	5 (94)
Other	7	2	4 (143)	11	3	6 (113)
Unidentifiable	1	1	1 (3)	1	1	1 (20)
Unknown	2	2	2 (65)	5	6	6 (103)
Total*	(1537)	(2011)	(3548)	(738)	(1027)	(1765)

*Percentages may not total 100 due to rounding.
Source: Annual Report, Lagos Colony, 1887, 28–30; *General Abstract of Registration*, 1893–1900.

the youths registered remain in the coastal towns. Five hundred and thirty-three removals were recorded between 1878 and 1887.[97] It is clear, however, from their places of origin, shown in table 5.3 and discussed below, that most of the young people registered were probably slaves or pawns. And the majority of them remained in the colony into adulthood, augmenting its supply of labor, wives, and other dependents.

The numbers submitted for Badagry, where 580 youths were registered in 1878 and only 133 during the remainder of the decade, and for Palma and Lekki, which are too small to be believable, suggest that people in these communities managed to avoid complying with the new ordinance. Differences in the gender of these youths are also noteworthy. The Lagos figures, which show more than 50 percent more females than males, conform to the pattern one would expect, given what we know about African preferences for female slaves.[98] The larger number of males than females registered at Badagry and Palma and Lekki indicate that in those towns the arrival of young females must have been especially likely to go unrecorded.

Table 5.3 shows that between 1878 and 1887, more than 60 percent of the youths registered came from central, eastern, or southeastern Yorubaland, areas affected by the expansion of Ibadan, the rise of Ekitiparapo, and wars between those two powers in the late 1870s and 1880s, which produced both a large supply of slaves and a need to sell them to help finance the purchase of firearms and other supplies for the wars. More youths (18 percent) came from Ijesha during these years than from any other single place, and most of them must have been slaves captured in war, although some may have been pawns sent to secure debts, and stories also circulated about the sale of freeborn Ijesha children to help pay for war matériel. Given the close ties of many Ijesha in Lagos to their homeland, it is also likely that some of these youths traveled to the coast to live with kin or countryfolk.[99] Many of the 567 Egba youths registered between 1878 and 1887 were undoubtedly war captives as well, but others may have been individuals of slave birth voluntarily sold to Lagos or pawns sent there in exchange for credit. In the Egba case, it is clear that a number of those registered were freeborn children who came to the colony with a parent or were sent there for education or to live with relatives. The third largest group of youths in this category was identified as "Yoruba," probably a reference to refugees from the old Oyo Empire who had resettled at Ibadan or elsewhere in central Yorubaland. Many of these young people, too, were war captives subsequently sold into slavery. The youths from central, eastern, and southeastern Yorubaland were disproportionately girls, reflecting the greater demand on the coast for female labor and perhaps also the greater reluctance of Yoruba from these areas to part with males who could be turned into "war boys."

Almost five hundred of the youths were identified as "Popo" and came from the western Slave Coast. Eighty-three percent of these were registered at Badagry, most in the first eight months of the Alien Children's Registration Ordinance's operation. This suggests that the majority of them were already living in the town in 1877, reflecting its close ties with coastal regions to the west. These "Popo" boys and girls constituted 57 percent of all youths registered at Badagry. Small numbers of youths registered in the colony between 1878 and 1887 came from elsewhere on the Slave Coast or from southern or western Yorubaland.

The third largest category of youths came from the north and were classified as Nupe, Hausa, "Gambari," and "Niger tribes." This large region had highly developed systems of slavery and had long traded slaves to the coast.[100] A few of these young people may have come south with a parent or other relative to trade. However, most were undoubtedly slaves, and the majority of them were females. Smaller numbers of youths came from other places—Benin, Igboland, the Niger Delta, the Gold Coast, and farther afield in Africa. Ninety-one "Kroo boys," who worked for wages loading and unloading ships, were registered between 1878 and 1887, while sixty-six children born in Lagos were registered. The origins of another sixty-eight youths either were unknown or cannot be identified.

Two significant changes occurred in the origins of youths registered between 1893 and 1900. First, the proportion from central, eastern, and southeastern Yorubaland, and especially from Efon, Egba, Ife, Ijesha, and "Yoruba," declined following the British occupation of the region and termination of the prolonged Yoruba wars. Second, the proportion of northern youths—"Gambari," Hausa, and Nupe—increased, a rise that would look even more dramatic if one included in this category those from Ilorin, the northernmost of the major Yoruba towns, which was then part of the Sokoto Caliphate. Both the central, eastern, and southeastern Yoruba and the northern youths registered continued to include more females than males. Many of the young people entering the colony from these regions were still slaves, although after the British penetration of the interior increased numbers of fugitive slaves began arriving in Lagos from as far north as the Caliphate, and some of them were undoubtedly children. The data indicate that in the final years of the century, an increase in the supply of young slaves, and particularly of young female ones, from the north partly compensated for the decline in the volume of slaves from the Yoruba interior.[101] The number of Lagos and "Popo" youths registered decreased, as did that of "Kroo boys" by about 40 percent, while the proportion of youths of unknown or unidentifiable origin increased.

A Master and Servant Ordinance, suggested in the 1860s, was finally introduced at Lagos only months before the Alien Children's Registration Ordinance of 1877, to regulate and help enforce labor contracts. It provided for the apprenticeship of young people in domestic service or any trade requiring skill and allowed apprenticed males to be flogged.[102] Some Lagosians found in the new law fresh means of exerting control over slaves and other dependents, at the same time that it looked toward the free labor market that would expand in the 1890s.

Fugitive Slaves

The question of what to do about fugitive slaves who escaped to Lagos from neighboring kingdoms had worried British officials from the moment of the annexation. After 1866, when little could be said or done openly about domestic slavery in Lagos, fugitive slaves absorbed most of the public attention that officials paid to local slavery. Until Britain began to colonize the interior in the 1890s, officials were much more comfortable dealing with fugitive slaves from elsewhere than domestic slaves in Lagos, because it allowed them to assume the role of liberator and attract workers and dependents to Lagos, without threatening the interests of their new subjects or boundary of their young colony. Attitudes toward fugitive slaves changed, however, in the final decade of the century as Britain moved inland. These changes are instructive, because they illuminate transformations in the colonial state and redefinition of its imperial project.

The number of runaways from surrounding territories who fled to Lagos increased in the 1860s, as slaves began to perceive the colony as a place where they might escape their owners and find new opportunities. A group of Sierra Leonean immigrants observed in the mid-1860s that hundreds of slaves had fled to Lagos since the cession, and Glover's papers contain dozens of letters pertaining to the problem of fugitive slaves.[103] Runaways escaped perhaps most commonly by attending lagoon- or riverside markets, sometimes on business for their owners, and there finding a trader or canoeist who would give them passage into British territory. Bondwomen and -men also fled on foot along the roads and bush paths that led through the forests and swamps into the colony, hiding when they met passersby who might recapture them. Those who made their way to the town of Lagos often broke their journeys into stages, finding refuge first in the household of someone who lived in a smaller community inside the frontier before coming on to the capital city.[104] Slaves also absconded when sent to Lagos to perform labor for their owners.

In the first half-decade of colonial rule, the number of runaways entering Lagos Colony was probably limited, however, to the hundreds rather than the thousands. William McCoskry testified in 1865 that he was "under the mark" in stating that five hundred fugitive slaves had arrived in British territory since 1861. Pope Hennessy commented, moreover, on how few of the domestic slaves who came to Lagos for their owners actually ran away.[105] Both men had reasons to downplay the problem of fugitive slaves, but even so flight to the colony does not appear to have been pervasive in the early years. For one thing, owners limited the mobility of slaves they did not trust and controlled them in other ways, as well. When bondmen and -women absconded, moreover, owners made every effort to recapture them, and the severe punishment meted out to those who were retaken was clearly intended to discourage further flight. The fact that runaways who arrived in Lagos without family or friends there were often worse off than trusted slaves also discouraged exodus and helps explain why those who absconded, in the interior of Lagos as elsewhere in Africa, were disproportionately newly acquired slaves.[106]

Despite their limited numbers, fugitive slaves were from the moment of the annexation a source of great tension between the British government and neighboring states, who regarded control of their slaves as vital to preserving both their social order and their political integrity. McCoskry stated that the fugitive slave question was "the whole cause of the dislike" that neighboring peoples felt for Britain.[107] He created and Freeman and Glover perpetuated the Slave Court in part to diffuse tension surrounding runaways by establishing a place where their owners could apply for compensation. The court did little, however, to solve the problem. Many owners were loath to appear in it, and those who did had to overcome serious obstacles to qualify for compensation, which when awarded was said often to be worth "not half the value of a slave."[108] What interior peoples wanted was to reassert control over their slaves, not to receive monetary compensation for those that ran away. Rather than seek redress in the Slave Court, owners often tried, sometimes with the support of their rulers, to recapture fugitive slaves on British soil. More worrisome still from the perspective of British administrators, they commonly retaliated by kidnapping Lagos people or seizing their goods and canoes on the way to market.[109]

The dissolution of the Slave Court in 1865 eliminated the possibility of compensation for runaways, unless owners could pressure the slaves themselves or a third party into paying redemption in return for relinquishing all claims to the slave. During his visit, Blackall reaffirmed that British soil was free soil and that fugitive slaves who reached it should not be returned, a policy that the government subsequently adhered to in name, if not always in practice, apart from a brief period in 1872. However, the Colonial Office also instructed Blackall to tell chiefs in surrounding territories that it was up to them to prevent their slaves from setting foot on British soil and to emphasize that no official inducements were to be held out to runaways. Moreover, freed slaves who subsequently left the colony did not carry British protection with them. Despite these precautions, the flow of fugitive slaves into Lagos picked up in the second half of the 1860s, as awareness of the opportunities that flight to British territory presented spread among slaves on and beyond the frontier.[110]

Interior peoples believed, with some justification, that Lagosians enticed slaves to run away when they met them at regional markets. Female slaves, who were in great demand in Lagos not only for the labor they performed but also as wives and concubines, were especially likely to receive offers of help and promises of a new and better life in the colony. G. W. Johnson, the Saro secretary of the Egba United Board of Management, complained hotly, if euphemistically, that Egba "domestic servants" regularly ran away through "the instigation of Lagos men," although women also sometimes assisted them in flight.[111] The role of the Armed Hausa Police on the frontier in encouraging slaves to flee and offering them asylum when they did aroused particular ire. Glover may privately have instructed the Armed Hausa to aid and abet runaways as a means of pressuring the Egba and Ijebu, and he certainly did little to check the practice. Oṣifilla, headman of the rural constables, was also the headman of runaway slaves in Lagos.[112] But the Armed Hausa probably needed little encouragement. Most of them were former slaves, and by enticing runaways they simultaneously struck a blow at slave owners and attracted followers to their own households and communities. E. A. Oroge has argued that the Armed Hausa Police were "the most powerful threat to slaveholding in Yoruba country."[113] So concerned were Egba chiefs about the flight of their slaves and wives to Lagos that they passed a law stipulating that anyone caught taking runaways to the colony would be killed and the house where the guilty party had lodged would be plundered.[114]

Following Pope Hennessy's reversal of Glover's policies in 1872, government officials sought to ease Egba opinion by withdrawing the Armed Hausa from the frontier. In addition, Henry Fowler, the acting administrator, ordered the *ọba* to send his bellman around the town warning Lagosians not to allow fugitive slaves to enter their canoes or otherwise assist them in flight on pain of severe punishment, and proclaiming that in future runaways would be sent back to their owners. Dosunmu was ordered to station canoes on the lagoon to stop fugitive slaves from entering the colony. Before Glover called these transgressions to the attention of officials in London, the *ọba*, with the assistance of Sheriff J. A. O. Payne, himself an Ijebu, and the knowledge of Acting Administrator Fowler, returned a number of fugitive slave women to their owners in Ijebu Ode.[115] Interior peoples for a time took advantage of the change in policy to retrieve runaway slaves from the colony with new boldness.[116] Although the Colonial Office subsequently repudiated the return of fugitive slaves, local administrators henceforth repeatedly urged the rulers of surrounding territories to adopt "every legitimate means . . . to prevent their slaves running away." They warned residents of the colony not to entice slaves from the interior to leave their owners, and informed government employees that if they did so they would be punished.[117] Even so, the flow of runaways into the colony picked up. The census commissioner observed in 1881 that much of the increase in the population of the town and surrounding territory, from 36,000 in 1871 to almost 53,500 a decade later, could be explained by the influx of runaway slaves and registration of alien children.[118]

The story of Ayeṣibi, one of the fugitive slave women returned by Dosunmu in 1872, sheds light on the experiences of runaways and strategies they used to escape to British territory. It also illuminates the means that owners employed to punish runaways and prevent further flight. Ayeṣibi was an Ijesha woman captured by Ibadan in war and sold to an Ijebu man, who claimed to have "made a wife of her." At Epe, where the woman was sent with another female slave to trade, she and her companion met a man from Lekki, inside British territory. The two women subsequently ran away from their owner and went to live with their new acquaintance, who was no doubt glad to add two females to his household. After some months, during which time the women traded for the man and may have accumulated a little capital, they left Lekki and made their way to Lagos. There they were taken—by whom it is unclear—to Glover, who told them they were free and could go where they liked and then gave each of them a shilling. The sources do not reveal where the women lived in the town, but they tell us that they made farina and sold it in a local market.

After seven months, the women's former owner came to Lagos to retrieve them, perhaps because news of the government's temporary change of policy regarding fugitive slaves had by then reached Ikorodu, where he lived. Dosunmu's staffman and Sheriff Payne then forcibly seized the women and returned them to their master, despite their vocal and persistent protests. Ayeṣibi, by now heavily pregnant, resisted reenslavement by plunging into the lagoon while being loaded into a canoe for the journey back to Ikorodu. Once there, she allegedly saw other former runaways killed or given to the *orò* secret society, which had authority over the shedding of blood. One man, she later said, had his head cut off and nailed to a tree and his hands and legs dismembered and placed before the *Ẹlẹ́gbára* shrine. When Ayeṣibi heard that she herself had been "sold to the town," which increased her likelihood of being sacrificed, she fled once again to Lagos and threw herself on the mercy of Glover's replacement.[119]

Sheriff Payne was later investigated for his role in the incident. He defended himself with an argument that was used widely not only in Lagos but also later across much of colonial Africa to uphold the control of male owners over female slaves. Payne maintained that Ayeṣibi and the other women were wives, not slaves, and that he had not been returning runaways, but merely enforcing the domestic authority of husbands. Although Payne's defense did not succeed in this particular case, the redefinition of the enslavement of women as marriage and the commitment of colonial regimes across Africa to upholding patriarchy after Europe expanded inland from the coast in the closing decades of the century rendered emancipation particularly elusive for female slaves.[120]

Until the early 1890s, Lagos's colonial administrators were concerned about fugitive slaves primarily because of the political and diplomatic difficulties they created with neighboring states. Desertions were not yet so numerous that they were thought to seriously threaten production or trade in the interior, and officials were not yet deeply concerned about protecting the authority of political elites inland from Lagos. Although fugitive slaves could be troublesome, flight to the colony was in the first three decades of colonial rule generally seen as good for the runaways, because it brought them freedom and exposed them to the influence of civilization. Moreover, the arrival of runaways in the colony was regarded as consistent with the needs of Lagosians for labor and dependents.

The attitude of Lagos officials toward fugitive slaves changed significantly, however, after Britain began to colonize the Yoruba interior. Many contemporary observers in Lagos and Britain blamed the uneven profitability that had plagued the colony's external trade since the 1870s not on falling palm produce prices in Europe and increasing competition on the coast, but rather on the wars that persisted among Yoruba states in the interior and were thought to have interrupted the supply of exports to the coast. Business interests in Britain and Lagos pressured the Colonial Office and the local government to restore peace in the interior, because they believed that trade would then recover.[121] In 1892, Governor Gilbert Carter responded by sending a military expedition to "pacify" Ijebu Ode. In the aftermath of what the Nigerian historian E. A. Ayandele has called its "bloody and spectacular" conquest, Carter swept through Oyo, Ilorin, and Ibadan armed with sufficient Maxim guns to increase his persuasive powers and signed treaties with frightened local rulers that made much of Yorubaland a British protectorate.[122] Britain's acquisition of the Lagos Protectorate profoundly altered the perspective of administrators on the coast and influenced the way they thought about fugitive slaves and other matters.

In the first place, the subjugation of the interior and its subsequent administration quickly increased the demand for labor in the colony and protectorate and heightened the interest of British officials in labor questions. Large numbers of porters were immediately needed to transport many tons of arms, equipment, and supplies inland. The construction of the railway between Lagos and Ibadan between 1896 and 1900, which employed more than ten thousand workers in 1899, further intensified demand. The onset of colonial rule in the protectorate, moreover, witnessed the beginning of rapid road building on the mainland and ambitious public works projects in Lagos itself that also required large quantities of labor.[123] In the 1890s, labor shortages became acute in both the colony and the protectorate, and the government's wage bill was rising to alarming proportions. Highly pejorative and racially coded ideas about Africans as workers, which gripped the imagination of public and private employers across Europe's expanding colonies on the continent at the end of the nineteenth century, took hold in Lagos as well. Capt. G. Denton, colonial secretary at Lagos for more than a decade, echoed prevailing sentiment when he wrote in 1898, "the people of [this] colony are lazy and idle to a degree unheard of in temperate climates and in the East."[124] So convinced was Sir H. E. McCallum, governor between 1897 and 1899, of the unfitness of wage laborers in Lagos that he resolved to lower the ninepence per day usually paid unskilled workers, despite the rapidly rising demand for labor. Indeed, McCallum saw cutting wages as a solution to the labor shortage. By the closing years of the century, the earlier Victorian view of Africans as driven by a desire for European imports that they would work hard to gratify had given way to a conviction that the inhabitants of the Dark Continent had but "specific and limited wants" and would work only as long as it took to meet them. By cutting wages, McCallum thought that he could lengthen the time that locals would need to remain in the paid labor force to satisfy their few material wants, and thereby increase the labor supply.[125]

Once the British government at Lagos presided over not just a small coastal colony, but also a much bigger inland estate that had to be ruled and developed, the outlook and interests of administrators in the capital changed in other ways as well. They were suddenly charged with helping to formulate policies for both the colony and the inland protectorate and had to weigh the needs of the former against imperatives in the latter. They did so, moreover, in a rapidly changing political and cultural context. The age of aggressive and confident European imperial expansion in Africa had dawned in the 1880s. Joseph Chamberlain's arrival at the Colonial Office in 1895 signaled the beginning of an era of much more rapid and forceful development of British interests in the African interior.[126] Most officials now assumed, moreover, consistent with the hardening racial attitudes of the last decade of the nineteenth century, that Africans would not, and indeed could not, respond positively to new opportunities as rational economic men, but rather would have to be remade through vigorous and, if need be, coercive European intervention. Local slavery was by then regarded as one of the benighted practices that mired African peoples in barbarism and blocked their development. The prospect of finally ending this savage and outmoded means of organizing labor in Africa itself provided a justification for colonial conquest in many parts of the continent. By conjoining colonialism and emancipation, Europeans gave the age of high imperialism a moral purpose, as Fred Cooper has argued, and linked it with a progressive project.[127]

Colonial governments across the continent faced ongoing economic constraints in their efforts to rule their growing African territories. For reasons of financial expediency and sometimes explicit philosophy, as well, most were forced to incorporate local authorities and indigenous systems of law and government and rule through them; never mind that when European officials could not find recognizable political and judicial institutions they invented them or that when local authorities would not cooperate they were deposed and replaced by others who would.[128] The administration of the Lagos Protectorate was no exception. While Britain continued to administer the older colony directly, indigenous authorities were integrated into the colonial state in the protectorate and charged with governing at the local level.[129]

Once Britain had resolved to rule the interior through indigenous elites, it became imperative for the colonial state to uphold their authority. This reality quickly complicated the problem of what to do about slavery in the newly acquired territories, although Britain stood by its earlier resolution in the colony itself. Administrators could ill afford to destabilize the indigenous political order in the interior by undermining the control of *ọbas* and chiefs over their subjects, including slaves. Officials began to worry, moreover, that if they disrupted the supply and drove up the cost of labor inland from the coast by immediately dismantling slavery, palm produce prices would rise to the point that Lagos oil and kernels would no longer be able to compete with exports from other parts of the globe. The fact that by the late 1890s Britain had begun to rely on local *baálẹ̀* (village heads) or other big men to recruit and supervise forced labor from their own communities for road building and other government projects compounded the problem and reinforced the need for social stability.[130]

The European penetration of the interior immediately loosened the control of owners over their slaves, as it did in other parts of colonial Africa. Slave flight increased dramatically in many Yoruba states from the mid-1890s. The *balógun* of Ikorodu, an Ijebu town, claimed that within a year of the sack of Ijebu Ode he had lost four hundred slaves valued at more than £4,000 and in consequence become "a poor man."[131] A chief from Ijebu Ode itself said not long after that "there was not a slave left in his town."[132] Around the same time, an observer commented that Egba slaves were running away "in great numbers," while a second wrote that the "burning question" at Abeokuta was "the constant escape of slaves."[133] Slaves fled in many directions, but large numbers moved south into the colony. In 1897, the governor claimed that runaways were pouring into Lagos "at a rate of more than 200 *per diem*."[134] A number of influential Lagosians held the exodus of slaves from the palm belt responsible for a decline in the quantity of oil and kernels reaching the port in the mid-1890s.[135]

This is not the place for an extended discussion of the end of slavery in the Yoruba interior. Suffice it to say that, as in other African territories acquired by Britain after 1885, the government tried to steer a course between helping local authorities reassert control of slaves and slow the pace of change and completely turning its back on anti-slavery. Administrators had a freer hand in the Yoruba interior than did their predecessors in the colony during the 1860s and 1870s, because the protectorate was deliberately defined as beyond the jurisdiction of British law. Explicit government policy was to end slave dealing, but to move cautiously against slavery itself. Agreements entered into in the 1890s assured a number of local rulers that Britain would not interfere with slavery, and British residents were instructed to leave relations between owners and slaves to local authorities, except in cases of inhumanity or when slaves could redeem themselves. Fugitive slaves who escaped to Lagos Colony were to be free so long as they remained there, but those who absconded to native states retained slave status. A proclamation issued in 1900 assumed the abolition of the legal status of slavery, which was no longer recognized in government courts, while an ordinance enacted the following year conferred free status on children born after 1901. To check the flight of slaves and other dependents to the town of Lagos and help restore social control, however, McCallum had earlier raised the price of canoe passage across the lagoon. Sir William MacGregor, his successor, ordered in 1902 that henceforth "laborers" could leave their districts only with the sanction of local chiefs. Not until 1916 was slavery formally abolished throughout Nigeria, and obligations of former slaves and their descendants to the families of their owners survived even afterward in many areas.[136]

One might think, given the labor shortages in Lagos and on government projects in the protectorate, that British officials would have welcomed the influx of fugitive slaves to the colony in the 1890s and afterward. They did not. The government's first priority was now to uphold the authority of the chiefs through whom it ruled the interior and prevent a mass exodus from their towns and villages. However, concern about maintaining order in the protectorate intersected changing ideas around the turn of the century about the developing colonial city itself, and it was reinforced by them. Lagos grew dramatically in size and changed significantly in character after the colonization of the interior. The town ceased to be primarily a port and commercial center and became a major British imperial capital as well, the importance of which increased further after the amalgamation of Lagos Colony and Protectorate and the Southern Nigerian Protectorate to form Southern Nigeria in 1906 and then the union of Southern and Northern Nigeria in 1914. The population of the municipal area swelled to about seventy-four thousand by 1911. Larger numbers of Europeans arrived at this time to work for the government, private firms, and missionary societies, and the composition of the white population changed to include wives and more working-class males.[137]

In the 1890s, British officials in Lagos began to imagine and work to develop a more orderly colonial city. This project led them to want to create and maintain a settled and stable urban environment. Changing British ideas about what a major colonial city should be like were reflected in municipal improvements undertaken at Lagos shortly before or after the turn of the century, which included improved sewage disposal, electric street lights, piped water, two bridges connecting Lagos island to the mainland, and a reserve where Europeans could live in tidy flats and bungalows away from the crowded African quarter.[138] They were also manifested, however, in a new preoccupation with the habits of the African urban population. British officials in Lagos began to worry that fugitive slaves and other migrants arriving in the city would be unable to find work or, worse yet, that once coercion was removed the former slaves would have no interest in civilizing labor and would turn into a "class of loafers."[139] Authorities feared that the men among them would turn to vagrancy and crime and the women to prostitution or polyandry, moving uncontrolled from man to man. Anxiety about the growth in Lagos of a population of urban "malcontents" reinforced official determination to uphold the control of local political elites in the interior over their dependents and check the exodus from inland towns and villages to the capital city.[140]

In the longer context of evolving British policy regarding slavery at Lagos, which this chapter has analyzed, owners and slaves in and around the town embarked after the annexation on a lengthy process of redefining the relationship between them. As they did so, other indigenous relationships of dependency revived in importance. To this story the narrative now turns.

6

Redefining the Owner-Slave Relationship: Work, Ideology, and the Demand for People

Although Britain did little to emancipate the many thousand slaves in Lagos, economic, political, and legal changes occurring in the colony created new opportunities for some of them to begin to redefine their relationships with their owners. The abolition of the foreign and, more slowly, the domestic slave trades meanwhile diminished the threat of sale and widened the social space within which slaves could act. The final chapters of this book examine the shifting relationship between owners and slaves in the early decades of colonial rule, as slaves sought to improve their access to resources and alter their obligations for labor and allegiance, at the same time that owners looked for ways to maintain control over their slaves and other dependents. A number of distinctive features of the local system of slavery operated to the advantage of slaves as they struggled to transform their place in society. These included the dictates of the work they performed, the content of indigenous ideology regarding slavery, and the great competition for workers, wives, and dependents that existed in the growing colonial city.

Yet powerful forces also constrained slaves, limiting their opportunities and autonomy and tying them to their owners or other superiors. While a minority of slaves quickly managed to accumulate wealth, redefine their identities, and acquire a measure of power and influence within the African community, the majority remained economically and politically marginal and many stayed trapped in relationships of subordination.

Gender and generation both affected the experiences of slaves as they struggled to renegotiate their relationships with their owners and position in society. Lagos's many female slaves enjoyed certain opportunities not open to their male counterparts, and they also faced a number of different constraints. Moreover, owners and others seeking labor and allegiance tried in different ways to attract, discipline, and control male and female dependents. Evidence in the previous chapter demonstrated, moreover, that a high proportion—perhaps the majority—of slaves imported into Lagos during the second half of the nineteenth century were youths. Age also shaped the experiences of slaves. Child slaves were more vulnerable and probably also easier to hide, control, and assimilate than those who had reached adulthood. The historical record contains all too little information about slavery in Lagos after 1866. The paucity of data about slave women and children is particularly glaring. The reconstruction that follows takes gender and generation into account where possible, but the analysis is unavoidably uneven and fragmentary.

Slaves had a range of experiences in Lagos during the second half of the nineteenth century. Following the British occupation, a few dramatically altered their relationships with their owners by running away from the town or the farms worked by its inhabitants. Some of these men and women fled beyond the slowly expanding frontier of British territory, bent on returning home or settling elsewhere in the interior. Others obtained access to land inside the colony and sought to support themselves by fishing, foraging, farming, manufacturing palm produce, or engaging in some other agrarian activity. Slave flight apparently occurred in spurts, concentrated at times of political or other turmoil and change.[1] Consul Beecroft reported that most of Oshodi Tapa's slaves ran away when the chief was driven into exile with Kosoko in 1851.[2] If Oshodi's slaves absconded at that time, those belonging to other chiefs and war captains in Kosoko's entourage probably did so as well. Later in the consular period, Sierra Leoneans complained about slaves who escaped to Abeokuta and elsewhere, while at the end of the decade an estimated 450 slaves of northern origin took advantage of Baikie and Glover's journey to the Niger to flee.[3]

The annexation of Lagos in 1861 and subsequent incorporation of Palma, Lekki, Badagry, and other territory also emboldened slaves to run away. A Badagry chief testified that many of his father's slaves had absconded by the early 1870s, although he gave no indication where they went.[4] A subsequent wave of former slaves from Lagos may have returned to their homelands at the time of the British penetration of Yorubaland in the 1890s.[5] There is no way to estimate the proportion of slaves that fled at the time of the bombardment and annexation or later, but the paucity of references to runaways from Lagos in the sources suggests that comparatively few chose that option.

Lagos's slaves shared certain characteristics that scholars believe predisposed bondmen and -women to flight in other parts of colonial Africa. Slaveholding had expanded rapidly in the kingdom from the 1820s, creating a large population of first-generation slaves with clear memories of their homes. While slaves in Lagos were of diverse origins, sizeable groups of them shared language, culture, nationality, or ethnicity, easing communication and cooperation in flight, as well as other activities. A certain number of slaves, moreover, worked on farms in rural areas attached to the town and were generally not supervised as closely as those in urban compounds. These rural slaves had more distant relationships with their owners and freer interaction with one another, both of which may have facilitated escape.[6]

Yet powerful countervailing forces constrained slaves in Lagos from running away. Owners, themselves, discouraged flight by selling slaves who showed signs of discontent, even though this form of discipline became more risky after the mid-1870s.[7] In addition, growing numbers of slaves were born in Lagos, leaving them without direct knowledge of another home and, in certain instances, giving them kin and life-long friends in the town, which bound them to it. Among first-generation slaves, great distance from their places of origin, coupled with ongoing warfare, disorder, and slave raiding in the interior of the colony, made flight from British territory very dangerous and trapped most slaves in it until the British penetration of the interior ended the prolonged Yoruba civil wars and curtailed the internal slave trade at the end of the century. A substantial number of Lagos's slaves, moreover, knew that their towns or villages had been destroyed, communities dispersed, and families divided at the time of enslavement or after, so that they no longer had homes to which they could return.

At the same time, economic, religious, and political changes taking place in Lagos and the rural areas surrounding it led some slaves to choose to remain in and around the town and try to make new lives for themselves within coastal society. The rise of European demand for palm produce and growth in the local market for foodstuffs, craft items, and other goods, coupled with the emergence of new ways of obtaining credit and owning land, had by the mid-1860s created more favorable economic opportunities for slaves within British territory than existed in most parts of the interior or elsewhere on the coast. Martin Klein found that whereas large numbers of slaves fled the Western Sudan following the French conquest, economic growth moderated the flight of slaves from the peanut basin of Senegal, because it created favorable opportunities for those who stayed. Much the same was true in and around Lagos. As in rural Senegambia, moreover, religious change also helped tie Lagos's slaves to the town.[8]

A significant number of slaves imported into Lagos during the first half of the nineteenth century and subsequently were Muslims. Many of them managed to continue to practice their religion, which helped them reforge worlds for themselves and endure slavery after arriving on the coast. Islam was not the religion of the slaveowning ruling class in the precolonial period, and practicing it may have helped slaves create a separate religious and social space for themselves inside the town. Judging both from changes in names and evidence in court cases, other slaves converted to Islam after reaching the coast, attracted perhaps by the vision it offered of a more just world as well as by the community of support it provided. Muslim slaves worked together to build early Lagos mosques and also founded a number of Islamic societies that sponsored regular festivals and engaged in self-help.[9]

Soon after the arrival of Christian missionaries, slaves also began converting to this second great religion of the book, despite the early missionaries' tolerant attitude toward slavery. James White stated that Taiwo Olowo, a man of slave origin, was his first male convert. Taiwo and a number of other former slaves contributed generously to the construction of the first native pastorate church at Lagos.[10] Another group of former Lagos slaves worshipped at Palm Church, Aroloya, and had sufficient corporate identity within the congregation that the Reverend Adolphus Mann distinguished them as one of its three main elements.[11] The growing Islamic and Christian religious communities in Lagos, with which slaves identified and to which they could turn for succor and support, helped tie them to the town.

Political changes also bore on the decision of slaves to remain in the colony. While Britain did little to emancipate Lagos's slaves, two factors combined to weaken the authority of owners over them. First, after 1866 the state rarely directly upheld the rights of owners to the labor of their slaves. Second, slaves themselves were beginning to discover new opportunities within colonial institutions such as the courts, militia, and police. If colonial rule did not immediately end slavery, it did dull some of its sharpest edges and give slaves new room to maneuver. Many of those who remained inside British territory after the annexation apparently did so because they believed it was their best alternative. The mass exoduses of slaves that have been documented in the French Sudan and Northern Nigeria around the turn of the twentieth century occurred as the colonial frontier pushed inland from the coast, leaving behind it previously conquered territory. Slaves there fled in an environment where slavery was beginning to crumble all round them. From the time of the bombardment through the mid-1890s, however, Lagos was in the vanguard of slave emancipation, surrounded by territory where slavery was more entrenched than in the colony itself. Some Lagos slaves braved flight beyond the colonial frontier despite these conditions, but the available evidence suggests that the majority did not, because they had no place better to go.[12]

More Lagos slaves probably escaped to undeveloped rural and coastal areas within British territory than fled beyond the colonial frontier. As new land was slowly incorporated into the colony during the final decades of the century, the territory available for settlement by runaways and recently liberated slaves expanded. In the narratives about their lives that former slaves told during court cases, recurring references to having left Lagos for periods of time to "go to farm" may, in fact, have been veiled allusions to flight within British territory.

Several factors facilitated movement into nearby rural areas. For one thing, many parts of the colony were sparsely populated, and in some places unoccupied or even unclaimed land could still be found. The details of land tenure in the outlying districts varied, but in most places arrangements existed for granting strangers use rights in land, trees, swamps, and other resources. Newcomers, moreover, could occasionally clear virgin forest and subsequently sustain rights of first settlers in the land. In addition to access to resources, the varied ecology of the coast opened a range of economic opportunities to runaway slaves. These included fishing in the lagoon, collecting sylvan produce in the swamps, and gathering firewood in the forests, all for sale in local markets, as well as transporting people and their wares along the lagoon and collecting palm fruit to manufacture oil and kernels. Because much of the land within the colony was so infertile that established populations did not want to farm it, runaways were sometimes also granted rights to grow annual crops near more valuable palm trees.[13]

With the exception of farming on the mainland due north of the island and harvesting palm produce and manufacturing oil and kernels, however, most of these rural activities enabled people to eke out only the barest existence and offered little hope of comfort or economic security.

Almost a century later, a British official remarked that rural areas within the colony district were still among the poorest places in southwestern Nigeria. When outsiders, including former slaves, were granted access to land for farming, moreover, they were often explicitly denied rights to harvest or plant lucrative palm trees, which were restricted to members of the earlier landowning family or community. There can be no doubt that from the 1850s, the town of Lagos itself offered the best economic opportunities along the Slave Coast.[14]

In addition to the harsh material conditions it usually imposed, fleeing to outlying parts of British territory—even to the settlements of the Armed Hausa—created substantial physical hazards, which also limited the number of slaves who chose that option. In the first place, distances within British territory were not great. Remote areas could be found in the swamps along the lagoon, rivers, and creeks, as well as on coastal sandbars, but few were beyond the reach of owners. Local authorities in a number of rural areas cemented patron-client relationships with prominent Lagos chiefs who acted as their *bàbá ìsàlẹ̀*, or representatives and advisors in the city, which gave Lagosians regular channels of communication with the countryside.[15] When their slaves absconded, owners in Lagos had means of broadcasting the news and discovering where they went. This reality made runaways who fled to outlying parts of British territory vulnerable to recapture and physical attack, as well as to witchcraft and magic. To compound matters, the frontier remained ill-defined and insecure until after the turn of the twentieth century, and fugitive slaves who settled too close to it sometimes fell prey to raids by marauders from Dahomey, Egba, Porto Novo, or Ijebu.

Even if runaways who stayed inside British territory managed to live in peace for a time, they could later suffer harassment. Possession of the land they occupied and access to the trees, swamps, or fishing grounds they worked remained insecure, because as these resources increased in value with the growth of the city and expansion of foreign and domestic trade, other inhabitants sometimes tried to run them off. Former slaves faced the risk of suddenly losing their livelihoods and perhaps also the dwellings they had built, or of being allowed to keep them but only in return for greater contributions in kind, labor, and eventually cash.[16]

These numerous disincentives to flight were compounded by the basic social fact that runaways, like all people, continued to be weak and vulnerable so long as they lived outside the protective structures of kinship, patronage, and political authority. In Lagos, as Joseph Miller has shown elsewhere in precolonial Africa, identities were primarily social; they were defined through connections with others. Security lay in belonging to communal groups constituted not only on the basis of kinship, but also through other relationships that incorporated people into the wider community.[17] For this reason, it was often much more difficult and dangerous for runaways from Lagos to live in isolation in remote rural areas of the colony than to remain subordinates—even slaves—of rich and powerful men and women in the capital. This fundamental cultural dynamic helps explain why, when slaves did abscond, they tended to do so in groups rather than alone. It also helps make sense of references in court records to former slaves who, after periods away, returned to the families of their former owners asking for help and support.[18] A Yoruba colleague repeated the proverb "Bí ewúrẹ́ bá jẹ lọ, a padà wá sí ilé," which can be translated as "Goats that are allowed to go fend for themselves will return to their owners at the end of the day," to illustrate the ongoing need of former slaves for a relationship with the families of their former owners.[19]

Many factors, then, discouraged flight and tied slaves to Lagos or the rural areas worked by its inhabitants. Future research is needed to learn more about the slaves who fled to the interior or outlying parts of the colony, but the evidence currently available indicates that more bondwomen and -men stayed in or around the town following the annexation than absconded from it. The growing colonial city absorbed many more runaway slaves than it lost in the second half of the nineteenth century.

If the majority of slaves in Lagos did not flee from the town or the rural areas attached to it during the early colonial period, what was the experience of these women, men, and children? How, in the absence of clear measures on the part of the new colonial government to emancipate the slaves, did those great forces of change—legitimate commerce, British rule, and Christian religion—which so many Victorians felt confident would naturally destroy the bonds of slavery, affect the lives of slaves? What more can be said about the impact of Islam on the relationship between owners and slaves?

In the short term, the *ad hoc* policies that British officials adopted in the late 1850s and early 1860s to deal with domestic slavery provided hope and relief to a few bondmen and -women, as did the assistance that mission agents sometimes granted individual slaves to prevent sale abroad or gross mistreatment. During the years of uncertainty and change that accompanied British intervention in Lagos, a small number of male and female slaves were able to turn to British officials, Christian missionaries, the Slave Court, or the Liberated African Yard for help in leaving their owners. For example, a runaway slave boy recaptured by a servant of the slave trader Senhor Marcos would probably have been exported had he not seized successfully upon a chance encounter with a Wesleyan catechist to beg for mercy.[20] To cite a case of government intervention, several slave women pleaded successfully with Consul Campbell in the late 1850s for help redeeming themselves and their children.[21] Registration by British officials, moreover, gave a small number of slaves emancipated in the consular period a measure of protection against reenslavement, just as it provided the slave youths imported after 1877 some safeguard against resale and export.

The few records I have found from the Slave Court suggest that owners who were looking for ways to control errant or rebellious slaves appealed to it more often than did slaves themselves. If accurate, this pattern can be explained in part by the fact that the court's commissioners normally insisted on payment of redemption before granting slaves freedom; and they commonly set the price at eighty to one hundred heads of cowries, above what most slaves or their friends and relatives could pay, if below what owners wanted. As an alternative, the court sometimes apprenticed slaves to an individual or the government in return for the price of redemption, which was then deducted from the former slave's wages.[22] The sources contain scant information about the apprenticeship system, but like similar arrangements introduced during emancipation elsewhere in the British empire, it apparently allowed only limited autonomy and brought few material rewards.[23] Apprenticeship was an option, moreover, only for male slaves, because it did not fit gendered European notions of how female labor in West Africa should be organized.

Despite the preponderance of cases initiated by owners, three surviving petitions to the Slave Court provide glimpses of slaves who took grievances to it or sought refuge at the Liberated African Yard. While the outcomes of these cases and the subsequent trajectory of the slaves' lives are unclear, the documents nonetheless demonstrate that some slaves tried to use the legal and other institutions of the early colonial state to leave their owners or obtain other benefits. In the process, they set an example for others who followed. The obstacles were always great, but some slaves, former slaves, and descendants of both managed to surmount them and initiate cases against their owners, former owners, or owners' heirs in later colonial courts, as subsequent data will show. The words of a slave woman who concluded a petition to the Slave Court in the early 1860s with the cry "I had no one to run to so I appeal before the Queen" convey a truth, however, that was widespread both when she uttered them and later.[24] Slaves usually turned to the colonial courts only as a last resort, when they had either exhausted alternatives within the indigenous community or felt they had none. Limited though the opportunity for immediate emancipation in the Slave Court was, even this narrow window closed after the mid-1860s.

A number of slaves in Lagos also fled their owners by enlisting in the civil constabulary, Armed Hausa Police, or West Indian Regiment. While joining these units brought certain advantages, most notably an inversion of the power relationship between owners and slaves, they were themselves deeply hierarchical and carried their own forms of subordination, discipline, and control within the new colonial state. Recruitment into them was limited, moreover, to several hundred men, and it privileged those of northern origin. Further research is needed to determine the extent to which police constables or Armed Hausa living in Lagos, towns on the mainland, or outposts on the frontier harbored runaway slaves from Lagos or elsewhere in the colony, which one can only imagine that they did. The frontier settlements clearly provided a home for and sometimes deliberately enticed fugitive slaves from Egba and Ijebu communities. Too little is known about them, however, to understand the role they played in creating a refuge for runaways from Lagos.

While a limited number of slaves in Lagos obtained their freedom in the 1850s and 1860s by appealing to British officials, Christian missionaries, or colonial institutions for help, the majority did not. Once it became clear that Britain would do little to interfere directly with the owner-slave relationship, the moment of opportunity for the slaves passed. Owners' worst fears subsided, and they settled down to the task of trying to control the labor and allegiance of their existing slaves, while also looking for ways to recruit new workers and dependents in a context of rapid economic, political, and social change. Periods of alarm recurred, as when the government announced the Alien Children's Registration Ordinance in 1877, but in general the British approach to emancipation at Lagos gave big traders and producers within the colony years to renegotiate labor relations. The slaves, on the other hand, soon realized that there would be no massive upheaval—no turning of the world on its head—and that it was going to fall primarily to them to renegotiate their relationships with their owners and place in society.

In the process that ensued, a number of factors operated in the slaves' favor, including the nature of the work many of them performed, the content of local ideology regarding slavery, and the large and growing demand for people in the young colonial city. Some slaves were able to take advantage of one or more of these factors to redefine their identities remarkably quickly and decisively after the annexation, acting alone or with the support of kin, friends, or countryfolk. For others the transformation took many years to accomplish and remained incomplete even then. The remainder of this chapter probes material, ideological, and other forces that shaped the opportunities and constraints of both owners and slaves as they struggled in the second half of the nineteenth century over the terms of the relationship between them.

Work

Historians of slavery in many parts of the world have shown that the labor requirements of specific systems of commodity production profoundly influenced the owner-slave relationship and, indeed, the characteristics of particular slave societies. Stuart Schwartz has argued that "the nature of labor demands varied considerably in different slave regimes according to the kind of economic activity and the level of technology available" and that work requirements were a "primary element" determining the nature of slave life.[25] Philip D. Morgan has stated even more categorically, "Work was the most important determinant of a slave society."[26]

The labor demands of staple crop production remained central as slave societies transformed during periods of emancipation. Studies of the end of slavery in different parts of the world have begun to show that as owners and states sought means to ensure that commodities would continue to be grown without slave labor, and as they began to adjust to the will of the former slaves, it soon became clear that the options available would be shaped in large part by the nature of the work that needed to be done.[27] Most of this important research has focused on societies where slaves were employed predominantly in agricultural production, but the fundamental point it makes holds true for urban economies such as Lagos's, as well. It is, therefore, to the work that slaves performed that this analysis of their shifting fortunes now turns.

In the second half of the nineteenth century, Lagosians employed slaves in many kinds of activities, including fishing, farming, palm produce manufacturing, craft production, and domestic work. The British annexation greatly reduced the scope of the *ọba* and war chiefs for independent military action, and thus their need for slave warriors. But rich and powerful Lagosians continued to use small numbers of slaves to supervise their households, maintain their shrines, oversee their farms, minister to their magical or medical-herbal needs, and organize their political supporters.[28] After 1850, however, transportation and trade absorbed more slave labor than any other activities. The town's hundreds of substantial traders needed slaves to handle the tens of thousands of tons of trade goods flowing in and out of it, to transport them between the port and the markets on the mainland and elsewhere along the coast where Lagosians bought and sold, and to transact commercial exchanges in these markets. Some big traders also used trusted slaves to manage their businesses.[29] As chapter 4 has shown, the growth of the palm produce trade at Lagos led initially not only to a further expansion of slavery at Lagos, but also to a diffusion of slaveholding within the population.

In the era of the commercial transition, Lagos traders who owned but a few bondwomen and -men sometimes toiled alongside their slaves handling goods, transporting them from place to place, and buying and selling in the town or regional markets. Once entrepreneurs became sufficiently wealthy that they owned numerous slaves, groups of their slaves commonly worked together bulking exports and dividing imports, headloading goods to and from the waterside, packing canoes and paddling them across the lagoon, and buying and selling commodities in markets or their owners' storehouses. Slave overseers or freeborn family members normally supervised such gangs of slaves. Bondwomen and -men also headloaded goods as part of the large caravans that some Lagos traders sent deep into the interior.[30]

In all of these cases, the work that slaves performed required mobility, both within the town itself and between Lagos and markets elsewhere. Moreover, it gave slaves access to the exchange sector. On their perambulations, slaves found opportunities to do things for themselves and particularly to trade, usually beginning on a small scale, sometimes no doubt with goods or cowries pilfered from their owners. The culture of credit and expansion of cowrie currency, the second of which could be broken into very small denominations for exchange, facilitated the movement of slaves into commerce. So did the fact that many trade goods could be easily divided and bought and sold in quite small quantities. This easy divisibility was less true of palm oil, which was transported in large pots, calabashes, or tins that contained several gallons, than of palm kernels, foodstuffs, and most imports, but even the oil trade allowed opportunity for slave initiative, if the landing places where canoes were loaded were close enough to the oil market to allow slaves to carry a container or two for themselves while working for their owners. Consul Campbell observed that the "bulk" of Lagos's population, "bond or free," participated in the palm oil trade.[31] A further reference to slave women who earned money from the palm oil trade and used it to redeem themselves and their children confirms that female as well as male slaves participated in the new commerce.[32] On their journeys to the oil markets, moreover, slaves sometimes bought other commodities, which they tied inside their loose clothing or added to their headloads and brought back to Lagos for sale.

The nature of the work that slaves were needed to perform in transportation and trade affected the conditions of their servitude in yet a further way. Much of it required not only manual labor, but also care, precision, honesty, reliability, and even ingenuity. Slaves employed in commerce could easily undermine the success of their owners' operations by allowing goods to be damaged, stealing commodities or cash, capsizing canoes, loitering on the job, misrepresenting information, or simply failing to promote the owners' interests. Although owners used trusted senior dependents to manage newer or less reliable ones, minute-by-minute supervision of all of the dispersed labor that slaves performed in trade was beyond the capacity of most of them, making tight control of their bondmen and -women next to impossible.[33] In order to prosper, owners had to find ways to elicit cooperation from their slaves, as well as mere work. This requirement put slaves in a strong position to negotiate the terms of their labor and other conditions of their lives. Senior slaves in supervisory positions and those responsible for conducting commercial exchanges probably had the most leverage, but even ordinary canoeists and porters had some.

Under the local system of slavery, most owners had long allowed many of their slaves a certain number of hours each day or days each week to work for themselves. In Lagos, as elsewhere in the world, slaves had met many of their own basic needs for housing, food, clothing, and other items through their own sweat and toil during the hours that they were not working for their owners.[34] At least since the era of the slave trade, moreover, owners had permitted some slaves they trusted—especially those employed in warfare and commerce—opportunities to work autonomously. In the era of the palm produce trade, a number of slaves were able to use the leverage they acquired by virtue of the kind of work they performed in transportation and trade to expand opportunities to work for themselves and also to organize the work they did for their owners more independently. Many owners apparently did not object when slaves, while working for them, also conducted some business of their own on the side, so long as the slaves did not slight the owners' affairs. Once slaves then became experienced produce traders and won their owners' trust, they were sometimes given goods to sell at a certain price and allowed to keep what they realized above that amount.[35] Still other experienced slaves were permitted to trade on their own full-time, in return for a payment from what they earned. Consul Campbell observed in the 1850s that many slaves were trading independently in palm oil and other articles.[36]

A number of contemporaries commented on the autonomy that Lagos owners often allowed their slaves in trade as well as other activities. John Davies wrote, for example, "Many who are slaves here after staying with their masters for some years are allowed to go anywhere they please, either to . . . visit their relations . . . or [to] trade about." He continued, "Nearly all slaves here are working for themselves and give only occasional help to their masters." Davies remarked that he himself had owned a slave for two years who "slept where he pleased in the town, and went about where he liked, but whenever his service was needed, he was sought for and after finishing what was required, he would then walk away."[37]

Allowing slaves to organize their labor in this way helped owners extract the kind of honest, attentive work they needed from them in commerce. Once the bonds of slavery began to loosen in the early colonial period, moreover, it also helped owners hold on to their slaves. Permitting slaves to organize their work autonomously offered a viable compromise between the demands of owners for high-quality work and the desires of slaves to maintain a valuable social connection with their owners, yet live and work more independently. Looked at from the perspective of owners, if letting slaves work for themselves on the side, giving them a bit more free time, or permitting those who were skilled and trustworthy to trade on their own elicited honest and careful labor, then the concessions could be well worth while. N. A. Fadipe concluded a discussion of similar opportunities that slaves in the Yoruba interior enjoyed to work for themselves with the telling remark, "The masters had no particular incentive other than . . . wanting to keep their slaves in bondage for their whole [lives]."[38] Slaves, on the other hand, used their autonomy both to improve their material conditions and to forge alternative social relationships among themselves and with others that might improve their prospects in the long term.

Lagosians employed slaves in growing crops and manufacturing palm produce in rural areas, as well as in trade, although not to the same extent as Yoruba-speakers farther inland. In these activities, as in commerce, slaves sometimes toiled alongside small-scale owners, their children, or their wives, if the owners were men, and moved with them between residences in town and farm huts in the countryside. Lagos trader Seidu Olowu testified in the late 1890s that slaves had formerly "worked the produce together with the children of the masters."[39] Francine Shields has shown, moreover, that women engaged in palm oil manufacturing employed female slaves of their own, as well as those belonging to their husbands.[40] Lagosians who owned large numbers of slaves, on the other hand, commonly settled some of them on rural estates not far from the town, where they worked in gangs supervised by slave or freeborn overseers. Oshodi Tapa and Odunran Aṣogbon, from the generation that rose in the late precolonial period, and Taiwo Olowo and Jacob Ogunbiyi, from the succeeding one, all employed sizeable numbers of slaves on farms on the mainland across from Lagos island.[41]

Whether Lagosians owned many slaves or a few, they commonly allowed those who worked in agriculture and oil manufacturing, and often those employed in trade as well, access to farm plots, where the slaves grew food and kept small livestock for their own consumption and sale in local markets.[42] The periodic movement of slaves back and forth between the town and countryside facilitated communication and helped foster and maintain community among them. It also expanded the economic opportunities of the slaves involved, who provided a link between rural and urban producers and consumers.[43]

The general argument about the dictates of the work requirements of slaves who labored in trade holds for those employed in oil manufacturing, as well. The process of producing high-quality soft oil demanded skill derived from experience and careful attention to timing and technique. It involved slaves, moreover, in work with costly equipment—pots, pits, mortars, canoes, ladles, and baskets—as well as with valuable water and fuel. Despite supervision, slaves could easily sabotage palm oil manufacturing through deliberate carelessness, as well as through more overt acts of destruction. Much as in other parts of the world where systems of commodity production required slaves to perform skilled tasks according to a strict time regimen or to work with expensive equipment, Lagosians who employed slaves in oil manufacturing needed not only ample labor, but also careful and disciplined work.[44] Owners tried to interest their slaves in oil production and elicit the quality of work they needed from them by allowing the slaves to share part of the fruits of their labor. In some cases, as noted in chapter 4, owners permitted slaves to pound and wash processed fiber a second time and retain the small amounts of oil extracted. In others, they rewarded slaves with part or all of the nuts left as a byproduct of oil production, from which the slaves could extract kernels or make other marketable products in their free time.[45]

Beyond employing agricultural slaves alongside family labor and in supervised gangs, however, owners also permitted some of them to farm or manufacture palm products independently, in return for a share of what they produced. The Saro doctor Oguntola Ṣapara, a keen student of Yoruba culture, told the West African Lands Committee that "according to old native custom" some slaves were given a portion of the family land to till in return for part of the crop at the time of harvest. When the external trade in palm produce took off, owners extended this arrangement to a number of slaves engaged in manufacturing oil and kernels, as well.[46] Permitting certain slaves to produce autonomously and retain part of what they manufactured provided an incentive that helped owners extract careful and diligent work not only from the slaves directly affected, but also from others. For the hope that they might one day benefit from such an arrangement apparently elicited good behavior from certain slaves even before they had tasted the rewards.

As slaves in rural areas became more aware, following the annexation, that the control of their owners was loosening and that they enjoyed new opportunities, many owners tried to retain their bondmen and -women by granting them access to land, tools, and equipment, letting them work more independently, and permitting them to keep a greater share of what they produced. Chief Abasi from Badagry testified, for example, that although a number of his father's approximately fifty male and thirty female slaves had run away by the 1870s, those who were given land had stayed. He stated that the females who remained "worked the oil" and were allowed to keep a third of what they produced. These women also got half of the nuts left as a byproduct of oil production, while the slave men took the other half.[47]

The dramatic growth in the market for palm kernels from the mid-1860s further expanded opportunities for independent enterprise among both slaves and former slaves. Palm kernel production required fewer skills than oil manufacturing. Moreover, it took no costly equipment or scarce resources and imposed no rigid time demands. For all of these reasons, kernel production was more open to slaves and other small producers than oil production or even farming. In addition to any nuts that workers were given following participation in oil manufacturing, they could scavenge production sites for discarded nuts, collect overripe fruit that fell from trees in the forest, and sometimes even harvest fruit from trees. No matter how slaves acquired nuts, they could extract kernels from them over the course of the year as time and the demands of other activities permitted. Furthermore, the small size and easy divisibility of kernels made it relatively easy for slaves to pilfer them from their owners or others.

From their work for themselves, whether in farming and palm produce processing or in craft manufacturing and other activities, slaves produced commodities that they consumed, improving the quality of their lives. They also marketed surpluses, which, like their activities in trade, generated income that they spent on consumption or invested as they saw fit.[48] After meeting their basic needs for food, housing, and other necessities and fulfilling their fundamental social and religious obligations, slaves often used any income they had left to expand their economic enterprises. They were, in addition, sometimes able to borrow capital from one another or others in the community to spend on economic, social, and religious activities. Female slaves channeled their economic resources into the purchase of more and better goods for trading and into inputs for food processing, food selling, palm produce manufacturing, and certain kinds of craft production. Male slaves funneled them into trade goods or supplies for fishing, farming, palm produce manufacturing, and other kinds of craft activities. Investment in a canoe often followed, when possible, to facilitate transportation and create additional income-generating opportunities. Slaves who could manage it, moreover, commonly bought slaves of their own, until the gradual elimination of the internal slave trade around the turn of the century.[49]

The acquisition of slaves by slaves had many of the same economic and social advantages after 1860 as it did earlier in the century. In an age when opportunities for emancipation were slowly expanding, however, the pressure among male slaves for wives, many of whom were purchased as slaves, was especially acute. This pressure existed in part because among male slaves marriage and paternity could help mark the redefinition of identity, movement out of bondage, and integration into the free population. When slaves wanted to redefine their identity, one of the most fundamental things they needed to do was begin exercising the rights and obligations of a free person. The children of even freeborn wives were normally regarded as belonging to the kin groups of their fathers when their parents divorced, and women of slave origin usually had only very weak rights in their offspring. However, an important step in the process of emancipation for male slaves was often to be able to claim paternity of their children. The surest way for them to accomplish this goal was to acquire a female slave and marry her, because any children the woman bore subsequently were widely regarded, in the colonial period, as belonging to her owner and husband. Many of the alien girls who entered Lagos after 1877 probably became the wives of men who had either recently become free or were still working their way out of slavery.[50]

Bondwomen and -men also used their resources to redeem themselves and their loved ones, countryfolk, and close friends. Scala observed that through their labor slaves could earn enough cowries to redeem themselves, while Benjamin Campbell wrote that in Africa "the slave never loses the hope of being restored to his country, . . . through the instrumentality of his friends and family redeeming him."[51] Redemption persisted well after it should have become unnecessary under British law for reasons that are not altogether clear, although it was by no means always practiced and it gradually disappeared. Perhaps some slaves did not fully comprehend how the nuances of British policy changed. Or perhaps they continued to see redemption and formal manumission as the surest way to unequivocally redefine their owners' rights in them and mark a change in their status and identity.[52] Either way, once the ownership of female slaves began to be redefined as marriage, their redemption by other men, particularly those who were suspected of having had sexual relations with them, became bound up with divorce, and the monetary transfer involved was often recast as the return of bridewealth.

Slaves in Lagos had long enjoyed some opportunity to improve their lives through working for themselves and to move out of slavery. At the moment that the decline of the military narrowed opportunities for slaves in warfare and the loss of the kingdom's political autonomy curtailed the privileges of *ibigá*, the expansion of foreign and domestic trade created new if generally more modest possibilities for the growing number of female and male slaves employed in transportation, commerce, palm produce production, and certain other activities. To the extent that this was true, there was some foundation for the belief of contemporary Europeans that the expansion of legitimate commerce was undermining local slavery and promoting emancipation. In the 1850s and 1860s, when conditions in the export trade were favorable, a limited number of slaves, some of whom are identified below, earned substantial incomes from it, became successful traders, and quickly redefined their relationships with their owners.

There were limits, however, to the new opportunities open to slaves. Most of those who engaged in the expanding produce and other trades on their own behalf did so on a small scale, owing to a lack of capital and labor. Much the same was true of the involvement of slaves in independent produce production. It has already been shown that slaves who obtained access to land in rural areas usually faced restrictions on their rights to reap and plant palm trees, which were claimed by earlier inhabitants.[53] When slaves exercised such rights for a time, they often found them challenged later as oil and kernel production expanded throughout the countryside.[54] The vast majority of slaves in Lagos earned only modest incomes following the annexation, and many of them remained economically marginal.

Gender and age affected the experiences of slaves. Palm oil and palm kernel production and trade had traditionally been women's work, and they were still widely perceived that way after the 1860s, even though men had moved heavily into the trade by then and there is evidence of their involvement in produce production, as well. Because female slaves already had experience in palm produce production and trade when the commercial transition began, they may initially have been able to respond more rapidly than male slaves to the new opportunities it created, giving them early economic advantages in the struggle for emancipation.[55] Women probably continued to dominate small-scale produce production, prolonging the superior access of female slaves to opportunities in that sector. Any advantages that they enjoyed in the produce trade, however, were short-lived.

A detailed study of women and trade in late nineteenth-century Lagos has shown that free women were generally at a distinct disadvantage relative to men in their access to credit and labor, resources essential to success in large-scale commerce. These disabilities made it difficult for women of free birth to compete with men in the new foreign trade and ultimately relegated many of them to the exchange of foodstuffs or other locally produced and consumed items or to small-scale, often petty, trade in imports and exports.[56] If the economic constraints that freeborn women faced pushed the majority of them to the margins of commerce relative to men, the situation was far worse for most female slaves.

Limited information exists about how the production and trade in which slaves engaged for themselves was organized or about how income from these activities was divided. Individual slaves apparently occasionally lived alone and had exclusive use of the commodities they produced and income they earned. The sources also contain references, however, to pairs, trios, or sometimes slightly larger combinations of slaves, often of the same sex, who lived and worked together as "partners" and presumably shared the proceeds roughly equally. But relationships among slaves in the process of emancipation were also hierarchical, and when groups of them banded together for support, they commonly reproduced among themselves the inequalities of gender and age that existed in the wider culture.[57]

That domestic relationships among the free population were hierarchical and led over time to a transfer of labor and resources inside households from women to men and juniors to elders has already been established in this study and elsewhere in the literature.[58] The same was true among many groups of slaves who lived or worked together. Male and female slaves not uncommonly established conjugal relations and cooperated in material and other pursuits. While preserving a measure of the economic autonomy characteristic of husbands and wives in most West African cultures, slave spouses also had obligations to one another for labor and assistance that generally favored husbands. When larger groups of slaves lived or worked together, they often recognized heads, whether or not they were related by kinship. These individuals, chosen on the basis of age, influence, wealth, ability, and gender, were more commonly males than females. They normally exercised authority over others within the group, which enabled them to make claims on their labor and support, and also had some responsibility for them.[59] When members of the group worked together, the head commonly took a larger share of what was produced or earned than the rest. If individual slaves or smaller combinations of them within the collectivity worked autonomously, the head was normally given something from what they produced. The transfers of resources within groups of slaves who lived or worked together, whether they were united by marriage, kinship, origin, or fictive social bonds, further disadvantaged most female slaves relative to a number of their more powerful and influential male counterparts.

Slave women participated in the new foreign commerce, to be sure, both as producers and traders of palm oil and palm kernels and as marketers of imports. They benefited, moreover, from the broader expansion of domestic trade that accompanied the growth of the export trade in palm produce. But the vast majority of them did so on a very small scale, which made it hard if not impossible for them to accumulate the resources necessary to dramatically transform their lives. While I have been able to identify a number of male slaves who rose from bondage to become big traders in the second half of the century, I have not been able to identify many such female slaves. In this instance, the difference can be explained only in part by the greater invisibility of women in the historical record.

Lagos's many first-generation child slaves probably enjoyed the fewest opportunities to work for themselves, and when they managed to do so it must have been on a very small scale. Freeborn youths had but limited control over their own time and labor, as children were expected to help not only their own parents, but also other elders within their compounds and families.[60] Child slaves were at a particular disadvantage, because they often faced demands not only from their owners but also from a senior slave or other dependent within the owner's household.[61]

Many newly imported slave youths had been forcibly removed from their families and communities as a consequence of warfare and political instability. They had in addition often endured long, difficult, and traumatic passages to the coast, so that they arrived in Lagos weakened and sometimes disoriented. Some of them did not yet speak Yoruba, the dominant language in the community, or have the skills necessary to support themselves in coastal society. Owners often placed such slave youths under the care and supervision of a more senior slave or other dependent, who commanded their labor. These supervisors often made demands of their own on their young charges, as well as organizing their work on behalf of the owner. In this way, the importation of large numbers of slave youths in the final decades of the nineteenth century benefited older and more settled slaves within the community, as well as the children's owners. Child slaves generally had very little control over their own time and labor beyond what they owed their owners.[62] Many Lagosians apparently hoped to incorporate them into their families over time, as wives or kin. They also gave slave girls as wives to male slaves they wanted to tie to their households.[63] These long-term goals may have led some owners to moderate demands on their child slaves, but even so the conditions in which they lived and worked must have been among the most oppressive in the colony.

The trade depression that struck Lagos in the 1870s and persisted with but short periods of relief until the 1890s also affected the opportunities of Lagos's slaves and former slaves. The high produce prices, good profits, and favorable terms of trade that benefited traders and producers and facilitated the upward mobility and rapid emancipation of a number of slaves in the 1850s and 1860s disappeared as the century wore on. Slaves seeking to make money by producing or trading palm produce and to use it for their own benefit or that of their loved ones had a more difficult time after the mid-1870s than before. Those who freed themselves around that time all too often found their hopes of a prosperous future disappointed.[64]

The growth of the palm kernel trade cushioned the effects of the depression for a time, but the reprieve did not last. Even during the recovery of the 1890s, two Lagosians with keen knowledge of rural affairs lamented that produce production no longer paid and that manufacturers were selling oil and kernels for only about half of what they had once received.[65] Local, regional, and intracoastal trade in food and other domestically produced commodities fared better, and some slaves and former slaves found niches in these types of commerce or fell back on fishing, farming, or craft manufacturing.[66] But economic conditions were not propitious for slaves or free people in the final quarter of the century, the very years when awareness that the colonial state would no longer uphold the rights of owners in their slaves was spreading in the population. The economic downturn at just this time further slowed the end of slavery by limiting the opportunities open to slaves.

Ideology

Ideas about the proper relationship between owners and slaves have existed in most slave regimes, and they have commonly been bound up with systems of discipline and control. Equally important, they have provided owners with moral justifications for highly exploitative ways of organizing labor and social relations. As Eugene Genovese has shown in the American South, however, slaves have often interpreted these ideas quite differently than their owners and either used them to expand the social space within which they acted or turned them into a "weapon of resistance."[67]

Reward for Good Service

At the heart of ideas about slavery in Lagos lay the notion that owners should reward slaves who served them faithfully and well either by toiling dutifully over a long period of time or by performing an act of extraordinary loyalty or significance. The rewards allegedly included such things as allowing slaves to work more autonomously, granting them more free time to work for themselves, helping male slaves marry and establish families, marrying females or giving them in marriage to a free or favored slave man within the family, and permitting slaves to accumulate property and improve their material conditions. Good owners, it was maintained, would over time help hardworking and trustworthy slaves improve their lives, with the ultimate reward being to let some of them move out of slavery.[68] By the second half of the nineteenth century, Muslim owners occasionally gave their own daughters in marriage to male slaves whom they prized.[69] During the commercial transition, moreover, it became common for owners to imply, if not outright promise, that they would one day give slaves capital to begin trading palm produce on their own or, once the slaves had acquired commercial experience, introduce them to a merchant so that they could get credit in their own names. Owners without descendants or close kin sometimes also left houses or other resources to their slaves, particularly ones who had cared for them during a serious illness or were entrusted with organizing their funerals.[70]

The ideology of reward for good service, as well as many of the specific benefits proffered, continued to have real advantages for owners in the second half of the nineteenth century. Allowing favored slaves to marry, have children, and acquire resources helped them acculturate and sink roots in the community. In addition, it enabled trustworthy slaves to accumulate dependents and other assets that could be mobilized on the owner's behalf in times of need.[71] Furthermore, the belief that owners would reward faithful slaves by helping them improve their lot and allowing them ultimately to move out of slavery encouraged slaves to identify with their owners and fostered ties of personal dependence on them. This ideological package as a whole gave slaves an incentive to work diligently and serve faithfully. In the era of the commercial transition, it helped owners elicit from slaves the high-quality work they needed in transportation, trade, palm oil production, and other activities. Moreover, as external controls over slaves weakened following the annexation and bondwomen and -men began to enjoy new opportunities to leave their owners, the ideology acquired new importance by sometimes enabling owners to hold on to slaves longer than would otherwise have been possible.[72]

By no means did all slaves receive rewards for good service; indeed, the majority probably did not. Owners and slaves struggled over and negotiated the terms of the relationship between them, and slaves not uncommonly found their hopes and expectations bitterly disappointed. Given the keen competition for women in Lagos, owners probably failed to provide wives for male slaves more often than they succeeded in doing so. Far from helping slaves become economically independent by enabling them to obtain credit from someone else, owners often tried to block access to such opportunity. For their part, female slaves regularly not only failed to welcome marriages to their owners or other men in the owners' households, but also vigorously resisted them. Moreover, manumission frequently proved elusive.[73]

Certain kinds of slaves were more likely to be rewarded for their labor and loyalty than others. These included the slave warriors, some already trading on their own behalf, who moved quickly and successfully into the palm oil trade in the 1850s and 1860s. They included as well the relatively privileged slaves who supervised trade, farms, fishing, or households for their owners or performed religious, magical, or medical-herbal services for them.[74] Such slaves were mostly male, and they were overwhelmingly adults.

At the other end of the spectrum stood newly acquired slaves whom owners did not yet trust or who had not yet acculturated by learning the local language and gaining experience with the kinds of work that slaves were needed to perform in the town. As the second half of the century progressed, these unfortunate slaves were increasingly young and female. Bondwomen and -men who, by virtue of the kind of work they did or the number of their owner's dependents, had little opportunity to develop face-to-face relationships with their owners probably also received relatively few rewards. Female slaves who were acquired by childless women or who became wives or concubines of male owners and bore offspring to them sometimes saw their conditions and opportunities improve. Yet in the 1850s, Consul Campbell believed that owners resisted bestowing the ultimate reward of manumission on female slaves more often and more forcefully than they did on male slaves. Robin Law has rightly attributed this difference to the greater value of females as workers, and it apparently persisted long after Campbell left Lagos.[75] In addition to these factors, deteriorating economic conditions during the final quarter of the century may also have discouraged owners from assisting slaves and other dependents. As prominent traders watched their own profits decline and grow more insecure, they may have felt that they could ill afford to invest resources in helping their slaves. Some traders may even have tried to compensate for declining profits by squeezing more work out of their slaves and other dependents.[76]

These data indicate that many slaves in Lagos never tasted the fruits of reward for their labor from their owners and comparatively few savored all of the benefits that the local ideology held out. For the idea of reward for good service to be believable and retain its power, however, owners needed to make good at least some of the time not only on its specific provisions but also on the ultimate prize of movement out of slavery. When owners fulfilled their end of the ideological bargain, it worked to the advantage of individual slaves and sometimes to that of others around them. Examples of slaves who moved up and out of slavery between 1851 and 1875 are not hard to find, although they are much more commonly male than female. They include some of the most remarkable figures of the second half of the nineteenth century: Jacob Ogunbiyi, Layeni, Taiwo Olowo, Sunmonu Animașaun, and Alli Balogun, to name but a few. All but one of this group joined twenty-five others in signing with their marks a letter to Colonel Ord in 1865 stating that they had been "born slaves" but "risen by [their] energies" to become slaveowners, canoe owners, planters, and important traders.[77]

The precise moment when these and other slaves redefined their identities and moved out of slavery can rarely be determined and may not always have been apparent even at the time. Details of the process of manumission have in most cases been lost to memory, not least because the descendants of slaves have in many instances rewritten the story of their ancestors' origins.[78] In some cases, the slaves clearly paid redemption or had it paid for them and may also have performed the rituals of manumission, while in others neither of these events occurred.[79] A number of slaves were probably freed at a specific moment in time, but others no doubt moved over months or years through a series of subtly shifting arrangements with their owners until obligations to them faded away. In addition, certain slaves were freed with the support of their owners, as the ideology of reward for good service promised. This usually occurred in recognition of outstanding personal achievement, as Sandra Barnes has shown for the precolonial period. It was, in her view, less dangerous to co-opt highly successful slaves by allowing them to become free and integrating them into the local power structure than to risk alienating them by thwarting their ambitions.[80] Other owners, however, let go of slaves grudgingly or after overt resistance, because they recognized that they could no longer hold the slaves against their will.

As gradually increasing numbers of slaves ceased after the annexation to depend so completely on their owners for protection, representation, and access to basic resources, and as external forms of control became more risky, owners began to find that they had few alternatives to letting some of their slaves go. These masters and mistresses apparently believed that it was better to accept the manumission of slaves in hopes of retaining them as kin or clients than to lose their allegiance entirely. This approach made sense given that many former slaves did not want to sever all relations with the families of their former owners.[81] When owners accepted manumission and redemption was paid, moreover, they stood to recoup part of the capital they had tied up in their slaves. If they had refused manumission, on the other hand, the slaves might well have left anyway without paying compensation. No matter in what spirit owners greeted the departure of their slaves, the ethical code inherent in the ideology of reward for good service may have made it easier for them to reconcile themselves to the loss of their bondmen and -women, while also giving the slaves a powerful moral argument to use against their owners.

The system of slavery in Lagos had always permitted a few fortunate and successful slaves who were useful and loyal to their owners to move up and out of slavery in their own lifetimes. A number of these individuals accumulated great wealth, established large compounds, founded well-known lineages, and became leading members of the community. In few societies outside Africa, and perhaps none where slavery was identified with race, could persons of slave origin, even though they remained comparatively few in number, rise so far in their own lifetimes and so fully overcome the disabilities of slavery.

Quantitative data of the kind needed to assess how the incidence of movement up and out of slavery in a single generation changed over the course of the nineteenth century will probably never be available, given the limitations of the sources on Lagos. The existing evidence suggests, however, that such mobility increased in the third quarter of the century, with the expansion of opportunities in palm produce trade and production, development of new ways of owning urban land that will be discussed in the next chapter, and decline in the freedom of owners to use force and the threat of sale abroad as mechanisms of controlling slaves. The conclusion to be drawn from this is neither that slavery was benign in Lagos nor that the integration of local peoples into Atlantic markets as producers and traders of vegetable commodities was antithetical to slavery, both of which contemporary Europeans believed. It is rather that the ideology of reward for good service and possibility of movement up and out of slavery for a few were integral to the system of discipline and control in Lagos, given the kinds of activities slaves were needed to perform and the way much of their work was organized. This form of discipline acquired new importance, moreover, as other means of control lapsed. Once slaves began to enjoy greater opportunities to leave their owners, the owners required new hooks to hold on to them as long as possible.

Incorporation

Slaves who succeeded economically and socially during the era of the commercial transition and moved quickly up and out of slavery to become influential members of the community are most visible in the historical record, but their experience was not the norm. Large numbers of slaves, perhaps the majority, stayed with their owners in the years following the annexation and saw little sudden change in their lives. William McCoskry, who knew Lagos as well as any European at the time, testified in 1865 that slaves had not left their owners *en masse* after British colonization, but rather remained with them of their own free will.[82]

Most slaves who stayed with their owners in the closing decades of the nineteenth century continued to have obligations to them for labor or payments in cash or kind, as well as for other forms of service. At the same time, they struggled to work for themselves and create alternative communities of support. Many of these slaves remained economically and socially marginal, however, and continued to depend on their owners or the owners' heirs for much of what they needed to live in or around the town. The essential forms of assistance included access to land, housing, credit, and other resources; protection from theft, kidnapping, assault, and other forms of harassment; help in the face of poverty, illness, fire, witchcraft, and other calamities; and representation in interpersonal conflicts and political affairs. In an unsettled and insecure world where, despite the introduction of new colonial institutions of law and order, chiefs and other prominent Lagosians continued to provide the first line of defense in times of need, these types of assistance counted for a great deal.[83] McCoskry may have accurately described the fate of many of Lagos's slaves following the annexation, but he was mistaken about what kept them in place. Most of those who stayed with their owners did so not of their free will, but because they depended on them for basic necessities and saw no better alternative.

A second influential idea about the owner-slave relationship affected the experiences of slaves who remained attached to their owners or the owners' heirs in the closing decades of the nineteenth century. It was that slaves who were well behaved would over time be incorporated into the family. The local system of slavery in theory allowed even first-generation slaves to pay redemption, perform the rituals of manumission, and return to their owners' compounds with most of the rights of freeborn family members, so long as their owners agreed. Scala maintained that slaves who freed themselves often chose "to belong to the family" of their owners, because they were "in a strange land" and had no one else to protect them.[84] Johnson observed that slaves who manumitted themselves and wished to stay with their masters simply "remove[d] to a friend's house for a short time and in that way publicly made known their freedom."[85]

If, as often occurred, redemption and manumission proved impossible in the first generation, then incorporation was supposed to take place in the second or a later one without the payment of redemption. Most contemporary references to slavery in Lagos, and indeed in other parts of Yorubaland, distinguished between the treatment of slaves bought in the marketplace and that of those born into their owners' households. By the second generation, according to local ideology, many of the differences between slaves and freeborn family members were already supposed to have disappeared. Second-generation slaves who behaved well, it was said, should not be sold, have obligations for work much different from those of freeborn offspring, or be at a great disadvantage in their rights to most family-owned resources. If incorporation remained incomplete in the second generation, then it was supposed to be realized in the third or a still later one, until virtually all of the distinctions between the descendants of slaves and those of freeborn ancestors were erased. Two Yoruba proverbs capture the spirit of the ideology of incorporation. The first, "Bí a se bí ẹrú la bí ọmọ," can be translated as "The slave and the child of the house have more in common than might be imagined." The second, "Ará òde ò mọ̀ni l'ẹ́rú, ará ilé ni ń nawọ́ ẹrú síni," proclaims that outsiders cannot tell which members of the household are slaves; family members must point them out.[86]

The ideal of incorporation over time was by no means always realized in Lagos, but it was widely enough practiced during the second half of the nineteenth century to enable a significant number of slaves to begin to redefine their identities from inside their owners' households. If slaves failed to erase the differences between themselves and freeborn family members during their own lifetimes, they could nonetheless believe that the lot of their children and grandchildren would improve.

Absorbing slaves into the family, like rewarding them for good service, had a number of advantages for owners and their kin. It too encouraged slaves to identify with their owners and perpetuated dependence on them for resources and assistance. Moreover, the expectation that, if not in the first generation then in the second or third, bondwomen and -men would see their conditions ameliorate and identity change helped owners hold on to slaves and their descendants as the bonds of slavery began to loosen following the annexation. Finally, the promise and practice of incorporation provided owners a means of disciplining slaves and their descendants, because rights conveyed could be withheld or withdrawn if such dependents proved troublesome or ill-behaved. Female slaves who became wives, for example, were sometimes treated as free, but they often lost that privilege if they displeased their husbands.[87] Good behavior could not under colonial law be overtly interpreted as including, by definition, regular labor on the owner's behalf, but as the final two chapters will show, it did come to embrace social and sexual conduct, as well as deference, allegiance, and appropriate use of family-owned resources such as land, housing, and trees.[88] Certain labor obligations continued, moreover, and they could be enforced by arguing that slaves had violated these other norms.

Incorporating slaves and their descendants into the family required relinquishing certain rights in them and accepting new responsibilities for them, and it thus involved sacrifice on the owner's part. The trade-off was apparently often seen as worthwhile, however, because it provided a means of enlarging families, households, and kin groups by integrating outsiders into them. In a culture where the size of these units directly influenced their wealth, power, and prestige, adding people to them was generally seen as highly advantageous. Resisting the incorporation of slaves too long in the decades after the annexation could threaten that goal, because it might lead the slaves to go elsewhere. By accommodating slaves' desires for incorporation, on the other hand, often through a series of gradual shifts in rights and duties, owners and their heirs were sometimes able to retain them and their descendants within the family. That many owners keenly wanted to do so, in an age when demands for labor were rising and new slaves were becoming harder to obtain, gave bondmen and -women a certain amount of bargaining power within their owners' families.

Slaves who remained with their owners following the annexation often played an active role in negotiating their incorporation. Females sometimes sought to accelerate or otherwise influence the process by entering a domestic and sexual relationship with their owner or another man in the owner's household or wider kin group. Women who bore children of such unions in many cases came to be regarded as wives, albeit usually ones of lower status than freeborn women for whom bridewealth had been paid. The offspring of these unions were commonly regarded as free, which in the long run normally benefited their mothers. If slave women sometimes exercised agency by forging relationships of marriage or concubinage with men in the slaveowning family, however, they also did so by resisting or abandoning such unions.[89]

Male and female slaves both sought to redefine their identity in the families of their owners by moderating the demands that were made upon them for labor and other kinds of support normally associated with slavery, until the rhythm and activities of their daily lives were as close as possible to those of freeborn family members of equivalent age and gender. Slaves also tried, however, to accelerate the process of their incorporation by voluntarily assuming the responsibilities of kin in family affairs, such as religious rituals or life-cycle ceremonies surrounding birth, marriage, and death, of which funerals were by far the most important. Care of an owner or prominent member of the owner's family during illness, especially a final illness, could also prove decisive. In addition, female slaves helped redefine their identities by mastering the *oríkì* (praise poems) of the lineage and reciting them on public occasions, much like young daughters of the family. Some slaves who acquired influence by virtue of their age, wisdom, achievements, or forceful personality further insinuated themselves into the family by exercising leadership in pressing internal or external affairs, such as a succession dispute or conflict with another prominent local lineage. In short, by behaving as kin, slaves were sometimes able to speed up the process through which they came to be regarded as such. When they succeeded, they often then tried to consolidate their new identity by exercising the same rights as kin in family-owned resources, such as land, housing, or eventually an inherited title.[90]

Despite the agency they exercised, slaves did not have a free hand in charting the course of their incorporation into the families of their owners or managing the redefinition of their identities. Following the annexation, owners and their kin retained certain older mechanisms of controlling slaves and their descendants, and they also forged new ones from changes occurring in the wider economy and culture, as the final two chapters will demonstrate. Even so, the ideology of incorporation lent considerable moral weight during these years to slaves' claims to rights within the families of their owners, especially when the slaves reinforced their claims by voluntarily assuming the responsibilities of kin. The ultimate prize for slaves was not only the transformation of their rights and duties within the slaveowning family, but also integration into a local kin group. This last transition held the promise of ending what Orlando Patterson has identified as the defining feature of slavery—natal alienation and its consequent isolation within the community.[91]

Anyone who is familiar with the history of Lagos in the late nineteenth and early twentieth centuries will be aware of the problem of the *àrótà*. The origins and literal meaning of the word, as well as the date when it entered the language in Lagos, are unclear. When asked about the difference between an *ẹrú*, the Yoruba word for slave commonly used in Lagos, and an *àrótà*, informants often stated that the former were slaves bought in the marketplace, while the latter were those born into the household. Other informants insisted, however, that there was no difference between the two. One elderly man commented wryly that after the British colonized Lagos, people could no longer call their slaves *ẹrú* so they began calling them *àrótà*.[92]

Whatever the origins of the word, it was used in late nineteenth- and early twentieth-century Lagos to refer to slaves and their descendants who remained attached to the slaveowning family in the decades following the annexation.[93] The prevalence of *àrótà* within old Lagos families demonstrates that large numbers of slaves did in fact stay with their owners in the decades after the British annexation. Subtle nods in the direction of particular individuals or sections of family compounds and whispered hints of their slave origin were a stock-in-trade of oral history interviews, although local etiquette discouraged informants from talking openly about such matters. The survival of descendants of *àrótà* as a distinct social category within Lagos families into the late twentieth century belies the notion that the incorporation of slaves was always complete. When questioned about the differences between descendants of *àrótà* and those of freeborn ancestors, two informants insisted that there were not any. Yet when pressed, they admitted that "you would not want your daughter to marry" the descendant of an *àrótà* because her offspring could not succeed to any titles belonging to the family.[94] In fact, a common way of trying to undermine the candidacy of claimants in disputes over succession to chieftaincy titles has been to allege that they descend from a slave rather than a freeborn family member.[95] To the extent that such disabilities persist in Lagos, the legacy of slavery remains alive even today.

In concluding this discussion of local ideologies of slavery, it is important to return briefly to the impact of Islam and Christianity. Prior to 1850, few slaveowners in Lagos belonged to these faiths, minority religions practiced primarily by outsiders to which indigenous Lagosians converted only slowly. As Muslim slaves became successful, acquired slaves of their own, and were integrated into the community and as Lagosians themselves converted to Islam, a cadre of Muslim owners began to emerge. The arrival of Muslim and Christian liberated slaves from Brazil and Sierra Leone, some of whom became slaveowners, and the gradual conversion of slaves who acquired slaves as well as other members of the community to Christianity added further religious diversity to the slaveowning population. This raises the question of how these new religions affected the treatment of slaves in Lagos and intersected the local ideologies of reward for good service and incorporation into the family. Did they open new space for slaves to redefine their relationships with their owners and reduce obligations to them for labor and support? The limited evidence available suggests that the answer to this question is a qualified yes. Where Christianity is concerned, a comment in a letter that the Reverend Samuel Crowther wrote to his supervisors indicates that as early as the mid-1850s some slaves seized on the idea that the Sabbath was a day of rest to demand that "their heathen masters" exempt them from working on it. The slaves in question had begun to attend church, although according to Crowther they had not yet "cast their lot decidedly among the followers of Jesus Christ."[96]

Both Muslim and Christian authorities in Lagos tolerated slavery, however, and usually taught at best that owners had a religious duty to treat their slaves humanely. The *shari'a*, or body of Islamic law, codified the specific obligations of the faithful to their slaves in a way that nineteenth-century Christian missionaries did not, and certain of these obligations paralleled local ideology, as did the Christian emphasis on humane treatment in a more general sense. Islam brought with it, moreover, an explicit tradition that the treatment of slaves was one measure of religious piety and could bring spiritual rewards. At the same time, Islam had a long history in West Africa of accommodating local practices in slavery and other areas of social life.[97] Lagos Muslims themselves commonly elected to follow local customs rather than be bound by Islamic law.[98] So far as the treatment of their slaves was concerned, the predilections and circumstances of individuals appear to have shaped receptivity to religious teaching. A few Muslim owners clearly took the precepts of their faith to heart. Sunmonu Animaṣaun, known (as his very name suggests) for his great generosity as well as his religious piety, provides one such example, at least with respect to his Muslim head slave Idrisu.[99] Other Muslims were less scrupulous, however, and how Animaṣaun himself thought about the female slave he sold at Pokra in 1890 we will probably never know.[100] Similar variation existed among Christian slaveowners. Religious faith and British anti-slavery propaganda led some to free their slaves, even without compensation, while others never acquired any. Yet Christians, even those related to catechists and clergymen, were also among the most brutal and exploitative owners in Lagos and other Yoruba towns.[101]

The Demand for People

A further dynamic shaped the experiences of slaves as they struggled to redefine their relationships with their owners. As this study has shown, the rapid growth of trade, transportation, and production in and around Lagos during the second half of the nineteenth century created a huge demand for labor that, in the African community, was only very slowly beginning to be organized around work for wages. Wives were also in great demand, not only for their labor, but also for their reproductive power and because of the symbolic importance of marriage in the movement of freeborn males from youth to adulthood and of male slaves out of bondage. Polygyny compounded the pressure for women. In addition to workers and wives, moreover, Lagosians continued to want followers on whose allegiance and support they could draw in times of political, religious, or social need. While labor in trade, transportation, and production had become crucial to economic success, political power and social prestige still rested heavily on the number of people under one's command. Without a large number of loyal followers, Lagosians could not rise to power and influence within the African community during the second half of the nineteenth century. As Sandra Barnes has written of a slightly earlier period, "The measure of one's power and prestige was taken in numbers."[102]

The size of a person's following was all the more important because political factions, which had so deeply divided the town in the precolonial period and first decade and a half of colonial rule, persisted as colonialism matured, although the actors and issues changed. The bitter conflict between Kosoko, Akitoye and his successor Dosunmu, and their supporters gave way in the 1880s to an equally divisive feud between Taiwo Olowo, a local political authority known as the *apènà*, and their partisans on both sides. Still later, conflicts over the government's attempts to introduce direct taxation and reform its land policies became entwined with schisms in Lagos's Muslim population and once again split the town into deeply hostile camps.[103] Unrest smoldered beneath the surface at each of these times and erupted intermittently into open violence. The power of local political actors in all of these conflicts depended on their ability to mobilize large numbers of loyal supporters and, when necessary, hostile crowds that would support them. As in the past, leaders expanded the number of their followers beyond those whose allegiance they personally could command by attracting influential clients, who themselves had a large number of loyal dependents that they could turn out on behalf of their patrons. The survival into the twentieth century of a political order that rested on bonds of personal allegiance further intensified the demand for people.[104]

In the precolonial period, Lagosians had met their need for people, beyond what kin, wives, wards, slaves, and clients could provide, by welcoming strangers into their households and offering them housing, food, protection, representation, and other forms of assistance in return for loyal support, periodic gifts, and occasional labor. As slavery slowly ended in Lagos, individuals looking for workers and dependents acquired them by taking three other kinds of people into their households. The first two were fugitive slaves and free immigrants arriving in the town from elsewhere.[105] The third was slaves from Lagos itself who wanted to leave their owners—but not the town or its surrounding territory—yet did not have the resources to establish residences of their own.

The fact that a social relationship already existed in the community that enabled prominent people to bring non-kin who were not slaves into their households through means other than marriage provided many of Lagos's male slaves and some of its female ones a way out of slavery. Moreover, it helped Lagosians meet their needs for workers and dependents at a time when slavery was slowly unraveling and wage labor had not yet taken hold. Male dependents of this type, often referred to as *asáfọ́rígẹ* in the local language, were commonly called "boys" in English, although that word was also sometimes used for male subordinates of other types, including *ẹrú* and *àrótà*.[106] The opportunity that becoming an *asáfọ́rígẹ* of a successful trader provided male slaves was especially important because, unlike females, they could rarely leave their owners by entering domestic and sexual relationships with others. As Lagosians adapted this older social relationship to their changing needs, however, they also transformed it by making obligations for labor more explicit and exacting, as subsequent data will show.

Two examples, both drawn from court records, further illuminate the experiences of male slaves who fled their owners by becoming the *asáfọ́rígẹ* of prominent Lagosians. These stories also cast light on the nature of the new relationship that the men entered in place of slavery. The first example involves two men, Seidu Ebite and Jinadu Akiola, who returned with Kosoko from Epe in 1862 and, although not explicitly identified as such, were almost certainly slaves belonging to him or a member of his retinue. On arriving in the colony, they left Kosoko, taking advantage no doubt of the weakening of owners' control over their slaves that immediately followed the British annexation. For about a year, Ebite and Akiola lived together, although the sources do not reveal where, and traded independently as "partners." By the end of that time, they apparently found living and working on their own problematic, because they divided their profits, approached a man named Jinadu Ṣomade, and asked to "serve" him. Ṣomade himself was a dependent of Jacob Ogunbiyi's, who was in turn a former slave and loyal supporter of Chief Aṣogbon's. Ṣomade lived in a house that Aṣogbon had granted Ogunbiyi for use by his "boys." Although there is no direct evidence on the point, Seidu Ebite and Jinadu Akiola may have chosen Jinadu Ṣomade as their overlord because he was a Muslim, as were they, judging from their names.[107]

Ebite, one of the *asáfọ́rígẹ*, described his sixteen-year relationship with Ṣomade as follows:

> The plaintiff sent me to market to trade for him as a boy. I received goods from the plaintiff who told me the price he got [them] for. . . . If I took eight tons of salt which the plaintiff bought for £5, and I sold it for £8 of produce, I brought him [all of] the produce.[108]

In addition to his own work, Ebite supervised eight more junior "boys."

By Ṣomade's account, in an echo of the system of reward for good service used with slaves, he remunerated Ebite with presents and promised to buy him land or a house, give him a share of the profits, and one day help him get started in business for himself. Jinadu Ṣomade said of the relationship,

> the . . . defendant was . . . my boy, and I cared for him and bought him anything he required. I fed and clothed him. I gave him no pay. It was not customary. I provided anything he wanted. I gave him a horse and a canoe. The horse died, and I gave him another. When the defendant married, I dashed him the expenses and bought a cloth for his wife and killed a bullock. I did not give him money, but I paid all the expenses. I never paid him wages, but if the defendant wanted money, if it was two bags I gave it to him. I gave him plenty of things I cannot name. . . . Wherever I sent him, he would go. The defendant could also send my children wherever he liked. He was in a place of confidence and trust.[109]

The second example involves three men from Ile-Ife—Oso, Opeluja, and Ogudula—who were enslaved, probably as a result of war, and sold to a Brazilian living in Lagos. Around 1874, the three slaves decided they wanted to leave their owner, and, acting in concert, they either ran away or redeemed themselves and were "told to go wherever [they] liked."[110] The men then approached a prominent Muslim trader named Brimah Apatira and "told him [they would] like to stay with him." Apatira settled the former slaves in a house of his. He subsequently characterized his relationship with them as follows:

> The defendants are my boys. I put them in [my] house. . . . In return the boys gave me their services when I required them. I promised to support them if they accepted my terms. By that I mean if any one of them got a wife I would share the expenses according to country custom. . . . The boys gave me their services as labourers when I required them, and in return I paid them no money but allowed them to live in my house rent free.[111]

The former slaves said of the relationship,

> We went to the plaintiff and told him we'd like to stay with him. . . . He put us in a house near his own. . . . We worked for him. He helped one of us take a wife. The plaintiff helped a brother of another to get goods to trade. . . . We went to the plaintiff because we [had] heard he was a good man.[112]

Oso, Opeluja, and Ogudula had not taken Muslim names, and there is no evidence that they practiced Islam. It is possible, however, that they were attracted to Apatira because he was a Muslim who, as their final comment hints, had a reputation for dealing justly with those living under his authority. The final chapter will return to the two cases introduced here for further analysis.

These examples nicely illustrate a number of phenomena. First, they show the dense web of interlocking relationships of subordination that connected people, in a regime where slaves could own slaves and acquire boys, and both slaves and boys could transfer their labor and allegiance from one Lagosian to another in hopes of improving their circumstances. They also enable us to glimpse the importance of what J. D. Y. Peel has called the "'horizontal' or egalitarian" bonds of companionship and friendship in helping individuals move out of slavery.[113] Most importantly, in this context, they expose to view a primary strategy that male slaves used to leave their owners, while also documenting a major means that Lagosians employed to recruit workers and dependents in the closing decades of the nineteenth century.

In time, the gradual development of a market for wage labor at Lagos further expanded the options available to slaves and *asáforíge̩* seeking to redefine their relationships with their owners or overlords. The government and private sector employed only a limited number of wage earners before the 1890s, but foreign labor recruitment introduced an outside demand from the 1880s. The brutal and rapacious Congo Free State absorbed more labor from Lagos than any other non-British territory; however, workers also left the town for Cameroons, Togo, and Fernando Po. At the end of the decade, other British possessions, including the Royal Niger Company, the Niger Coast Protectorate, and the Gold Coast, began looking to Lagos to meet their labor needs, as well. By 1890, Governor C. A. Moloney believed that Lagos was "generally viewed as the centre for the engagement of skilled and common labourers for service" in western Africa.[114] The government prohibited recruitment by non-British territories in 1897; yet men from Lagos and the interior, some of slave origin, continued to leave to work outside the British empire. Officials continued to permit recruitment by the Gold Coast and other British territories for several more years. Between July and December 1901 alone, 3,680 laborers left the colony to work in the mines and on the railroad in the Gold Coast.[115]

In the early 1890s, the demand for wage laborers in Lagos Colony and the Yoruba Protectorate themselves began to grow, opening additional employment opportunities. Judging from the serious problems that the government faced meeting its labor needs, however, it seems safe to conclude that work for the state at the wages it was prepared to pay and under the conditions it imposed did not appeal to most Lagosians, even those still living in relationships of subordination.[116] Although some men were pulled into wage labor, most preferred working for themselves, even on a marginal scale, in trading, farming, fishing, craft manufacturing, or some other activity, to working for wages. Men such as Seidu Ebite and Jinadu Akiola, who could not sustain independent enterprises, often chose to remain in or reenter relationships of dependency, rather than to sell their labor in the marketplace.[117]

The question of whether or not to work for wages hardly arose among female slaves, because few such opportunities existed for women until after World War II.[118] Despite its general lack of appeal, the gradual expansion of the wage labor market at Lagos from the 1880s contributed to the growing demand for men in the town and slowly helped create alternatives for them independent of indigenous structures of subordination.[119]

The robust demand for people at Lagos, whether as workers, wives, and dependents in the African community, or later as wage laborers, provided bondmen and -women alternatives to slavery, once colonialism began to weaken the coercive power of owners. These alternatives affected not only the slaves who took advantage of them to flee, but also those who stayed with their owners, because they gave slaves additional leverage in negotiating the terms of their relationships with their owners. Slaves exercised this leverage in their efforts both to redefine their identities within their owners' families and to move out of slavery by establishing residences of their own. For both owners and slaves came to understand that if owners pushed slaves too hard, if they continually refused to respond to the slaves' desires to control more fully their own time and labor, improve their economic conditions, and redefine their social identities, then the slaves might not only leave them, but also break with them completely and enter a relationship with someone else as a concubine, wife, *asáforígẹ*, or client.

Slaves and their descendants did not, however, have a free hand. The final chapters of this book examine a number of ways that owners and their heirs struggled to exert ongoing control over slaves and their descendants, as well as over other kinds of dependents. A number of the most important of these means grew out of fundamental changes occurring in land tenure, to which the analysis now turns. But surely one of the most potent mechanisms, at least where male slaves were concerned, was that by the 1870s overlords had begun defining the obligations of their new *asáforígẹ* to them in such a way that they differed little from those of male slaves to their owners. In addition, the rights of *asáforígẹ* in the families of their overlords were in certain respects more limited than those of slaves in the kin groups of their owners. When slaves left their owners to become "boys," they tragically often discovered that they had simply exchanged one relationship of subordination for another, as data in the final chapter will show. Wage labor, on the other hand, transformed the structural position of former slaves in the local economy, but it did not give them greater control over their time and the rhythm of their lives or necessarily improve their material conditions.

7

The Changing Meaning of Land in the Urban Economy and Culture

Commercial development and population growth in Lagos, fueled by the importation of gradually diminishing numbers of slaves as well as by the influx of runaway slaves and free immigrants, combined in the second half of the nineteenth century to increase the demand for dwellings, stores, and storehouses, or land on which to build them. At the same time, colonial rule and missionary activity created a need for houses, offices, churches, schools, and other structures, putting further pressure on urban real estate. The fact that the commercial and administrative center of the town lay on a small island, where much of the land was low-lying and swampy and needed to be improved before building, compounded the problem of land scarcity. In the decades following the annexation, good land in the town of Lagos became an ever more scarce and valuable commodity. Moreover, possession of real estate acquired new uses, value, and meaning in the growing urban economy. By the 1890s, similar changes had begun to occur in rural areas north of the city.

During these years, Lagos's slaves and former slaves sought and sometimes found new ways of obtaining access to landed property and of defining their rights in it, first in the town and later in the nearby countryside. When they succeeded, they gained important new opportunities that facilitated the redefinition of their relationships with their owners or overlords, as well as their status and identity within the community. Large slaveowners and rising new entrepreneurs seeking to mobilize labor and allegiance, on the other hand, strove, in the long run, to maintain control over land and houses as a means of disciplining the labor and support not only of the town's slaves and former slaves, but also of runaway slaves and free immigrants flocking to the colony from elsewhere. Although fundamental changes occurred in land tenure within the colony, opening significant new opportunities to *ẹrú*, *àrótà*, and *asáforíge̩*, the state ultimately upheld the rights of owners and overlords to property occupied by these subordinates. Struggle between owners and other people of wealth and power and their dependents for control of urban real estate lay at the heart of efforts to renegotiate the terms of the relationship between them. For this reason, an analysis of changes in land tenure, and in the uses, value, and meaning of land in the colony, lies at the heart of the story of emancipation in Lagos.

Land in the Precolonial Period

Just who owned the land in and around the town of Lagos and how they owned it have been questions of great political importance since the time of the annexation, if not before. Within months of the signing of the Treaty of Cession, by which Dosunmu did "give, transfer, and . . . grant . . . unto the Queen of Great Britain, her heirs and successors for ever, the port and Island of Lagos," a number of the *ìdéjọ* chiefs protested on the grounds that land in Lagos belonged to them and the *ọba* did not have the right to give it away.[1] In subsequent decades, as land became a scarce and more valuable resource, the issue took on major economic significance, as well.

Written records and oral traditions regarding land tenure in Lagos have been framed in the context of specific economic transformations and political struggles, by actors—European and African—who had clear interests and advocated particular policies. From the early decades of the twentieth century, for example, British administrators in Africa favored upholding local traditions regarding land and other matters, unless they were repugnant to "natural justice, equity, and good conscience," in the interest of preserving precolonial authority, managing change, and making the nation's vast new colonies there easier to rule. Aware that colonial governments were committed to preserving tradition, actors on all sides subsequently invoked and often invented "custom" to support their interests.[2] In Lagos, as in other parts of Africa, untangling precolonial norms and practices from the skein of conflicting evidence in colonial discussions of local land tenure presents a difficult task. Two general observations, however, bear remembering. First, norms and practices regarding land rights in Lagos have always been dynamic.[3] Second, customary land law as articulated in the colonial period emerged from a dialogue between the colonial state and its African subjects, which took place in a number of arenas—administrative, judicial, political, and academic.[4]

According to an important local myth, the *ọlọ́fin*, or first ruler of the settlement, divided the waters of the lagoon and the land on Iddo island, Lagos island, and parts of the nearby mainland among a number of men, represented as sons in some versions of the story and as prominent local lineage heads in others. These individuals are said to have received titles derived from the name of the territory where they had authority, been allowed to wear distinctive white caps as part of their insignia of office, and become the first *ìdẹ́jọ* chiefs. By the mid-nineteenth century and possibly before, an idea existed that the *ìdẹ́jọ* or the families they headed—for the specific rights of the chiefs and their families were contested—owned all of the land in the town of Lagos and its vicinity, as well as the fishing rights in the lagoon, by virtue of lineal succession from the first *ìdẹ́jọ* chiefs.[5] One of the earliest documented expressions of this belief occurs in the letter that Governor Freeman sent the British foreign secretary reporting the *ìdẹ́jọ*'s opposition to the Treaty of Cession, which stated, "[The White Capped chiefs] are the rightful possessors of the land. . . . the King and War-men hold no rights unless by grant from the White Capped chiefs."[6]

The origin of the idea that the *ìdẹ́jọ* or their families owned all Lagos land is uncertain. It may date from the time of colonization by Benin, when the occupying warlords and subsequently the new ruling dynasty accommodated the heads of local communities by recognizing their rights to land.[7] No matter what its origin, the belief gained new salience in the first two decades of the twentieth century for two reasons. First, the *ìdẹ́jọ* chiefs, who had been unable to uphold their claim to land in the opening decades of colonial rule, renewed their fight as its value increased with the rapid growth of the colonial and commercial capital from the mid-1890s.[8] Second, the conviction that the *ìdẹ́jọ* families owned all Lagos land provided an ideological basis for challenging claims by the colonial government that absolute ownership of land in Lagos, as well as sovereignty over it, had passed to the British Crown under the Treaty of Cession. For if the *ọba* had never enjoyed rights in Lagos land, then how could he have ceded ownership of it to the British Crown? The changing interests of the *ìdẹ́jọ* and their families coincided with growing alarm among educated Africans about Britain's land policies in West Africa. Influential members of these two groups made common cause, the struggle over land rights became a form of anti-colonial protest, and the idea that the *ìdéjọ* chieftaincy families owned the land in Lagos won widespread popular support.[9]

In practice, however, a larger number of extended families (*ìdílé*) had exercised communal rights in land at least as early as the mid-nineteenth century. This group included the families of the *ọ̀gáládé*, *àkárìgbèrè*, and war chiefs, as well as of the *ìdéjọ*, but it was not limited to them. Neither local traditions nor early colonial observers attempted to explain the discrepancy between the popularly held idea that the *ìdéjọ* families owned all Lagos land and the empirical fact that other families also exercised ownership rights in it, beyond the *ìdéjọ*'s assertion that all other owners had obtained their land from them. Chief Obanikoro, head of the *ọ̀gáládé* chiefs, expressed the conundrum succinctly when he said,

> It is not clear how [the *Ogalade* and *Akarigbere* chiefs] got their land. All we know is that both *Ogalade* and *Akarigbere* chiefs settled in Lagos, and that they actually own the land they have now got.[10]

The diffusion of rights of land ownership at Lagos can perhaps best be explained by reference to the process through which the settlement grew and incorporated new groups into itself. Early settlers and their descendants claimed land by virtue of being the first to occupy, clear, and develop it, as did the founders of many other towns in the Yoruba-speaking world. The heads of these families (*baálé*) exercised authority over land, which they retained as institutions of centralized government developed, and the most important of them were integrated into the changing political system as *ìdéjọ* chiefs.

Little evidence survives that illuminates land tenure during these early years. In the first decades of colonial rule, however, Lagosians reported that male and female kin enjoyed rights to use and participate in the management of town and rural family land, as well as rooms in town compounds. Females may sometimes have exercised their rights in landed property less actively than males, because women normally lived with their husbands after marriage. In addition, farming and gathering tree crops were men's work, in which female family members had limited direct participation. Women typically obtained the food crops and palm fruit they processed from their husbands, rather than their own male kin. Children commonly succeeded to farm plots, as well as rooms in town compounds, that had been occupied by their fathers and/or mothers. If they wanted additional property to use, they requested a further allocation from the head of the family. So long as land in the town and surrounding countryside was plentiful, male and female family members had little difficulty obtaining as much of it as they needed.[11]

The Beni viceroy and chiefs who had settled at Lagos by the mid-seventeenth century, founding the royal dynasty and *àkárìgbèrè* and *àbàgbọ̀n* classes of chiefs, apparently seized land for their own use and subsequently exercised ownership rights in it little different from those enjoyed by earlier inhabitants. They did not, however, immediately claim wider authority over land. As the young kingdom of Lagos grew and good, unclaimed land on Iddo island, Lagos island, and the nearby mainland ceased to exist, subsequent immigrants obtained both town and rural land to use by requesting it from a local chief or the head of a lesser landowning lineage. Alternatively, strangers sometimes asked, initially, to be allowed to live in the compound of a prominent Lagosian and only later requested land on which to build or farm. Migrants typically approached chiefs for land and housing, rather than other lineage heads, because rich and powerful titleholders were in the best position to act as effective patrons and protectors. Chiefs, on the other hand, usually welcomed strangers wanting access to landed property, because it gave them a means of increasing the number of their followers. Many early colonial observers insisted, however, that chiefs and the heads of lesser lineages could grant land to strangers only with the consent of their families as a whole.

Chief Obanikoro described the process through which strangers obtained access to town land as follows:

> When a man wanted land in a town he always went to the chief of the district, taking with him kola and rum.
>
> The chief then always consulted his family, and if they agreed he sent his land messenger . . . with the applicant, and the ground was pointed out.[12]

Grants of rural land were made in much the same way.[13]

Prior to the development of Lagos as an Atlantic port, the idea that land could be permanently alienated did not exist. Nor was there a market in land. The heads of landowning families did not grant land to strangers in perpetuity; rather they extended only certain usufruct rights in it. Chief Ojora, an *ìdéjọ*, observed, "[The chiefs] never gave absolute possession of the land."[14] Yet in Lagos, as in many other places in precolonial Africa, the value of followers generally exceeded that of land, so that landowning families normally allowed strangers to retain town and rural plots, so long as they fulfilled basic obligations. The responsibilities of strangers to their overlords differed depending on the location and type of property granted—whether town or rural, vacant plots or built structures, virgin forest or cleared farms. In addition, obligations were subject to conflict, negotiation, and change. Moreover, diverse peoples populated the frontier of the kingdom and later of the colony, so that the details of land tenure varied from place to place.

Despite this complexity, a number of general practices prevailed among strangers and their overlords in the town and its surrounding countryside. First and foremost, strangers were expected to be well behaved, which entailed showing deference and paying allegiance to the landowning family. Those who received grants of town land for building also had obligations to give gifts to the head of the landowning family on the occasion of its religious festivals and life-cycle ceremonies. Migrants who were granted rural land to farm were supposed, in addition, to make an annual payment of farm produce, known as *ìṣákọ́lẹ̀*, to the family head. This prestation did not constitute rent, as its monetary value was usually small and bore no relationship to the value of the land, but it served as a sign that the occupier acknowledged the ongoing claim of the landowning family to the property and owed allegiance to its head. Strangers who lived in the urban compounds of chiefs, on the other hand, normally made more substantial payments in kind from the fruits of their labor in fishing, trading, craft manufacturing, or other activities. They were also expected to accompany their overlords when they went out, swelling their retinues, chanting their praise, and demonstrating their wealth and power through gestures of homage and subordination. Failure to fulfill these obligations was regarded as grounds for ejection from land or housing, as was a propensity to cause trouble by committing crimes, sleeping with wives or daughters of the landowning family, plotting against its head, his patrons, or his clients, or claiming to own the land in question.[15] So long as strangers lived up to these expectations, however, they were usually permitted to retain the use of landed property they had been granted. As Faro—a former Chief Ojora deposed by J. H. Glover—testified, strangers could not be turned out if they "did not do anything wrong."[16]

Grantees often erected dwellings or other structures on the land they occupied, in both the town and countryside. This investment did not alter their rights in the land itself, but it did give them interests in the building different from those in the land on which it stood. The distinction recognized in local culture between rights in land that strangers were granted and those in structures that they erected on the land created social and legal complications as the town of Lagos grew and developed during the colonial period.[17]

When strangers who had been granted access to land died, their heirs were commonly allowed to continue using the property, although in theory only with the permission of the head of the landowning family. If there were no heirs or if the original grantee abandoned the land for a long period of time, it was said to revert to the family that had granted it, even if the grantee had built a house on the property or otherwise improved it. Strangers who were given access to land were not supposed to allocate portions of it to others without the consent of the head of the landowning family. Chief Obanikoro drove this point home with respect to town land by saying, "Even if [a man] wished to settle his father's brother in a house he had built himself, he had to introduce [the newcomer] to the chief," and by implication get his overlord's approval.[18] Restrictions also limited what strangers could do with farmland they were granted. In most rural areas, they were not supposed, as already indicated, to harvest palm or other tree crops on it, a valuable prerogative retained by the landowning family. Nor were they to plant crop-bearing trees, rights in which tended to be identified with ownership of rural land itself.[19]

Despite widespread acceptance of these normative ideas about the obligations that strangers who were granted land or space in urban compounds owed the head of the landowning family, performance of such duties sometimes fell into abeyance. Changes of this kind generally occurred either because the newcomers were in time absorbed into the landowning family as kin or because they successfully asserted their independence of it. Despite the restrictions commonly said to exist on what strangers could do with landed property they occupied, grantees or their descendants sometimes began exercising full rights in it, such as granting portions to others or planting crop-bearing trees on rural land. By negotiating such changes, strangers often came in time to regard themselves and to be regarded by others as the owners of the land they occupied. In this way, landownership gradually diffused from the lineages of the first settlers to others founded later. Redefining their rights in land was an integral part of the larger process through which immigrants transformed themselves from strangers into community members.

A brief example further illustrates the spread of land rights. In the 1860s, Fajimilola, a Mahi priestess who came to Lagos with Ọba Akinṣemoyin when he returned from exile, acquired land on which to establish a shrine and build a compound from Chief Aromire, an *ìdéjọ* who headed the family said to have first settled Lagos island.[20] Yet when Taiwo Olowo wanted land in the area for a compound a century later, his patron Chief Aṣogbon asked the head of the Faji family, not Chief Aromire, to give the rising trader what he needed, and the request was granted.[21] As late as the final decade of the nineteenth century, some local families did not jealously guard their rights in land, because it had always been an abundant resource whose value lay in its ability to attract dependents, rather than in a monetary equivalent.

In the precolonial period, slaves had normally obtained access to land for their own use through their owners. Once masters and mistresses trusted slaves sufficiently that fear of their flight subsided, owners often granted the slaves land in town on which to build dwellings where they lived and worked, as well as plots in the surrounding countryside where they grew food crops or pursued other agrarian activities. Groups of slaves commonly worked together to construct the buildings where they resided, although individual slaves sometimes inhabited preexisting space in their owners' town compounds or farm huts. Male slaves who were entrusted with supervising their owners' trade or households and females who were concubines or wives or who were owned by childless women most commonly lived in close proximity to their masters or mistresses. If owners did not have sufficient or appropriate land for their slaves to use, they asked a patron, client, friend, or spouse to supply what was needed. Moreover, owners sometimes sent male slaves to live with their patrons, clients, or friends, to meet the beneficiary's economic, political, or social needs, cement a relationship with the person, or provide the slave with discipline or training. In addition to these arrangements, slaves occasionally obtained access to land for their own use by clearing or filling and developing vacant plots of it without being driven off, although in theory there was not supposed to be any unowned land on Lagos island or the nearby mainland. Slaves who were lucky enough to acquire slaves or other dependents of their own and expand their households appear to have had little difficulty obtaining use of as much land as they needed.[22]

Elders and chiefs who advised the early colonial government about local customs claimed that neither *ẹrú* nor *àrótà* enjoyed ownership rights in the land and houses that they occupied, even if they had built the houses themselves. Faro testified that slaves who lived on family land had "no rights [in it] against their master or his family."[23] It was also commonly said, however, that, like strangers, slaves should not be driven off of land or out of housing they inhabited so long as they were well behaved. In a landmark case on the subject some years later, a local authority stated, "When an Arota was settled by his master in a compound, he acquired for himself and his descendants a right to live there in perpetuity subject to good behavior."[24] Much the same applied to land.

In the case of slaves, good behavior would normally have been defined in the precolonial period as including regular labor or, for bondwomen or -men who worked on their own, a share of the fruits of their independent enterprise. Such obligations remained in force until they were forgiven for good service or the slave was incorporated into the owner's family as kin. When slaves overtly and repeatedly resisted labor demands, they were punished and ultimately probably sold, either abroad or within West Africa. As with strangers, however, good behavior among slaves also included public displays of deference and allegiance, as well as conformity to the laws and mores of the community.

Individual slaves and, more commonly, groups of them who lived and worked together, however, sometimes retained use of land and housing that they occupied for long periods of time. When such slaves died, their fellow slaves, including in certain instances children or other kin of the deceased, often held on to the property. This practice occurred in principle with the consent of the landowning family, but it sometimes took place in fact without the family head's overt consideration. Prolonged use by slaves and their descendants of the same land or housing had certain advantages for owners, because it encouraged the slaves to develop attachments to the property and sink roots in the community. It also fostered ties to the landowning family and facilitated the process of controlling slaves and their offspring and eventually of incorporating them into the kin group.

Over time, slaves who succeeded economically and socially and accumulated dependents of their own were sometimes allowed to begin exercising ownership rights in land and houses they occupied, by granting portions to others without permission or planting and reaping crop-bearing trees, for instance. Some such slaves who moved up and out of slavery eventually came to be regarded as the owners of the land and houses they occupied. These individuals may for a time have ritually acknowledged the heads of the families from which they originally obtained their land, by presenting them with gifts on ceremonial occasions or token payments of fish, farm produce, or other goods. They did with the property what they wanted, however, and in time the prestations often lapsed. By the mid-nineteenth century, Oshodi Tapa, for example, was regarded as the owner of the land as well as the buildings that he occupied on the southern shore of Lagos island, near the baracoons of a number of Brazilian slave traders. When Oshodi fled into exile with Kosoko and Akitoye returned to Lagos as *ọba*, the new king ordered a number of his own slave warriors to occupy property vacated in the area. Mabinuori, father of the later successful palm produce trader Fagbemi Dawodu, seized and subsequently managed to sustain ownership rights in what had once been Oshodi's land.[25] Through means such as these, land ownership diffused further into the population. Even when slaves did not succeed in exercising ownership rights in land they occupied prior to the British annexation, prolonged possession of town plots put them in a strong position to claim title to the property after 1861.

Few questions about Lagos attracted greater interest in the colonial period than the rights of the *ọba* in land, because of the matter's relevance to Britain's claim to own all of the territory ceded by Dosunmu. Most local commentators, and even the king himself, albeit after transparent coaching, maintained that the *ọba* had no rights in land beyond that occupied by his family for its own use. Thus the *eléèkó*, as the *ọba* was then called, told government officials investigating land tenure in 1912, "The fundamental law . . . in and around Lagos was that all land was in the hands of the Idejo chiefs. The king had no control over land."[26] T. W. Johnson, who as court interpreter from 1876 to 1909 had heard most of the important litigation involving land, stated during the same inquiry, "The king had no control in land matters."[27] Buchanan Smith, the assistant commissioner of lands who was responsible for the investigation, concluded, "Most of the witnesses allege[d] that the king had no direct control over land, except that which belonged to him personally or to his family."[28] British officials, on the other hand, sought to construct and preserve, in the face of shifting judicial opinion on the subject, a legal argument that the *ọba* had nonetheless enjoyed some kind of authority over land. An often quoted dictum by Justice Smalman Smith tried to resolve the matter by acknowledging that the king had not enjoyed absolute ownership of land, but claiming for him and his council a "national proprietary right" in land, which entitled the *ọba* to alienate it.[29] This point of view continued to persuade many British representatives even after the Privy Council, in its famous 1921 decision in *Amodu Tijani v. The Secretary, Southern Nigeria*, upheld the Crown's ultimate title to land but ruled that it did not impair the rights of the *ìdéjọ* chiefs and other local landowners.[30]

There is no evidence that the *ọba*, as head of the community, received a share of the prestations that strangers gave landowning families in recognition of access to land.[31] Data do indicate, however, despite local representations of custom to the contrary, that by the first half of the nineteenth century *ọbas* were exercising authority over land and, in some instances, granting it independently to outsiders. In a revealing moment, the *eléèkó* told the 1912 land inquiry that the king had given certain chiefs their land, but he then reversed himself after protests from the chiefs present, exclaiming, "What I mean when I say that the king gave these chiefs their land is this: the king asked the Idejos to give them land."[32] Akinṣemoyin, Oṣinlokun, and Kosoko all enlarged their factions by urging powerful allies from neighboring towns and rural areas to move to Lagos with their followers and then ensuring that they received land on which to build compounds. Traditions of the origins of a number of chieftaincy families recount that when their founders migrated to Lagos, *ìdéjọ* granted them land at the behest of the *ọba*.[33] The chief of a leading *ìdéjọ* family indicated, moreover, that such grants were not necessarily made voluntarily. He stated,

> Before the Cession, if the King of Lagos wanted to give land to any person in [Oto], he would send to the chief and say that he wanted land in that place for the person, and the chief would give it to him and the chief could not say that he had no land to give to the King. The chief dare not refuse.[34]

Europeans and Brazilians who settled at Lagos in the era of the slave trade certainly looked to the *ọba* for help obtaining land and housing. J. B. Wood claimed that European slave traders had bought land at Lagos and that the king had received one-half of the proceeds, while the "White Capped chiefs" took the other half.[35] A letter from the slave trader José Lourenco Gomes pleaded with Kosoko to grant him "with ink and paper" a house that had formerly belonged to Marcos Borgas Ferras.[36]

Wood believed that the *ìdéjọ*'s authority over land diminished in the first half of the nineteenth century, while that of the *ọba* increased.[37] As the wealth and power of Lagos's kings grew in the era of the slave trade, they apparently sought to extend their authority over land as a means of further strengthening their position *vis-à-vis* the *ìdéjọ* and other chiefs. The fact that *ọbas* in Benin, unlike those in most Yoruba states, claimed ownership of all of the land within their kingdom may have helped inspire and legitimize the changing policy of Lagos's *ọbas* in land matters.[38]

Akitoye and Dosunmo, who reigned in the 1850s, took advantage of developments during that decade to consolidate their authority over land. Brazilian and Sierra Leonean repatriates and European merchants, missionaries, and consular officials who arrived in the town following the bombardment commonly turned to the *ọba*, not the *ìdéjọ* or other prominent chiefs, for grants of the land they needed, and the kings met their requests. The agreement that Akitoye signed with the European merchants in 1852 stated that the *ọba* would allow them to erect storehouses on the eastern point of the island and choose their places of residence. None of the four chiefs signing the agreement with Akitoye was an *ìdẹ́jọ*, and there is no evidence that he consulted them about its contents.[39] Moreover, the CMS missionary C. A. Gollmer obtained from his protégé Akitoye grants to five large plots in what Europeans and the Sierra Leonean repatriates soon came to regard as the best part of the town, although in this case the grants were made by the *ọba* "with his chiefs," and three *ìdẹ́jọ* and ten other chiefs put their marks to the document.[40] Subsequently, Benjamin Campbell asked the king for land on which to build the British consulate.[41] The merchant J. G. Sandeman described how he obtained land in Lagos:

> I called upon the King and told him I wished to make a factory and wanted a piece of ground. He told me to go and look for a place that I should like. I went first to that piece of ground fronting the river which belonged to Tappa late Vice Roi of Lagos, inquired if it was claimed by anyone and told, no, I went to the King and told him I wished that place, 103 feet of river frontage and 228 feet deep. He said I could have it and sent his stick with his own messenger and put my mark on the ground.[42]

At the end of the decade, the *ọba* confidently told Robert Campbell, an Afro-Caribbean exploring the region as a site for possible settlement by American blacks, that "so far as his dominions extended . . . emigrants might select land suitable to their purpose, and he would gladly give it" to them.[43] But the most decisive evidence of the *ọba*'s growing authority over land can be found in seventy-six written grants that Dosunmu, who succeeded Akitoye in 1853, made to Brazilians, Sierra Leoneans, and a few others. Only six of the earliest grants say that they were made "with the advice and consent" of the chiefs. The rest mention no authority but the *ọba*'s.[44]

More far-reaching changes, however, soon overtook the *ọbas* in their efforts to extend their control over land. As repatriated slaves and a few Europeans settled in the community, they introduced new ideas about how to own land and obtain access to it. Europeans regarded the slightly elevated ground along the waterfront on the south side of the island as the "airiest" building sites, freest from the "miasma and fever" they believed were so deadly to them. Land there also provided easy access to the harbor and was a safe distance from the "filthy" African quarter to the north-west, also prone to devastating fires because of the thatch used to roof local buildings.[45] The CMS missionaries encouraged their disciples among the Sierra Leonean repatriated slaves to obtain land and build houses nearby, on the southeastern corner of the island in a neighborhood that became known as Olowogbowo, while the Brazilian freed slaves settled in the interior of the island, developing Campos Square and Bamgbose Street.

As early as the 1850s, fierce competition existed for land in these areas.[46] Familiar with private property rights in land and houses through residence in Brazil and Sierra Leone, the liberated slaves, as well as the European missionaries and merchants, regarded their land grants from the *ọba* as giving them fee simple title, free of restrictions on alienation and of obligations under local tenure, although it is doubtful that this is what Dosunmu meant to confer.[47] Those who could not obtain grants from the *ọba* to property they wanted soon began buying it from locals or other immigrants who had earlier received land grants, and a market quickly developed for real estate in choice locations. When Sandeman, for example, ultimately failed to get the parcel he had hoped for from the *ọba* because the CMS already claimed it, he bought a different plot nearby.[48] To cite further examples of early land sales, a Brazilian bought a plot in 1854 from Dagra, one of the king's slaves, while the following year a Sierra Leonean woman who had been granted land died and her plot was sold at public auction.[49] Robert Campbell wrote after visiting Lagos that rural land could be obtained in the area, "as much as can be used, 'without money and without price,'" but that town plots already cost "from $2 to $50 and even $100."[50]

Dosunmu apparently grasped something of the increasing value and changing significance of land and wanted to retain control over its allocation. When forced by the British to sign the Treaty of Cession, one of the two concessions he negotiated was that "In the transfer of lands, the stamp of Docemo affixed to the document will be proof that there are no other native claims upon it."[51]

The Consolidation of Private Property Rights in Land

By the time Great Britain annexed Lagos, the alienation, commercialization, and privatization of land on the island were already well underway. These processes speeded up following the cession, and by the end of the century they had spread to parts of the mainland. The first governor, H. S. Freeman, observed that "in consequence of the rise in the value of

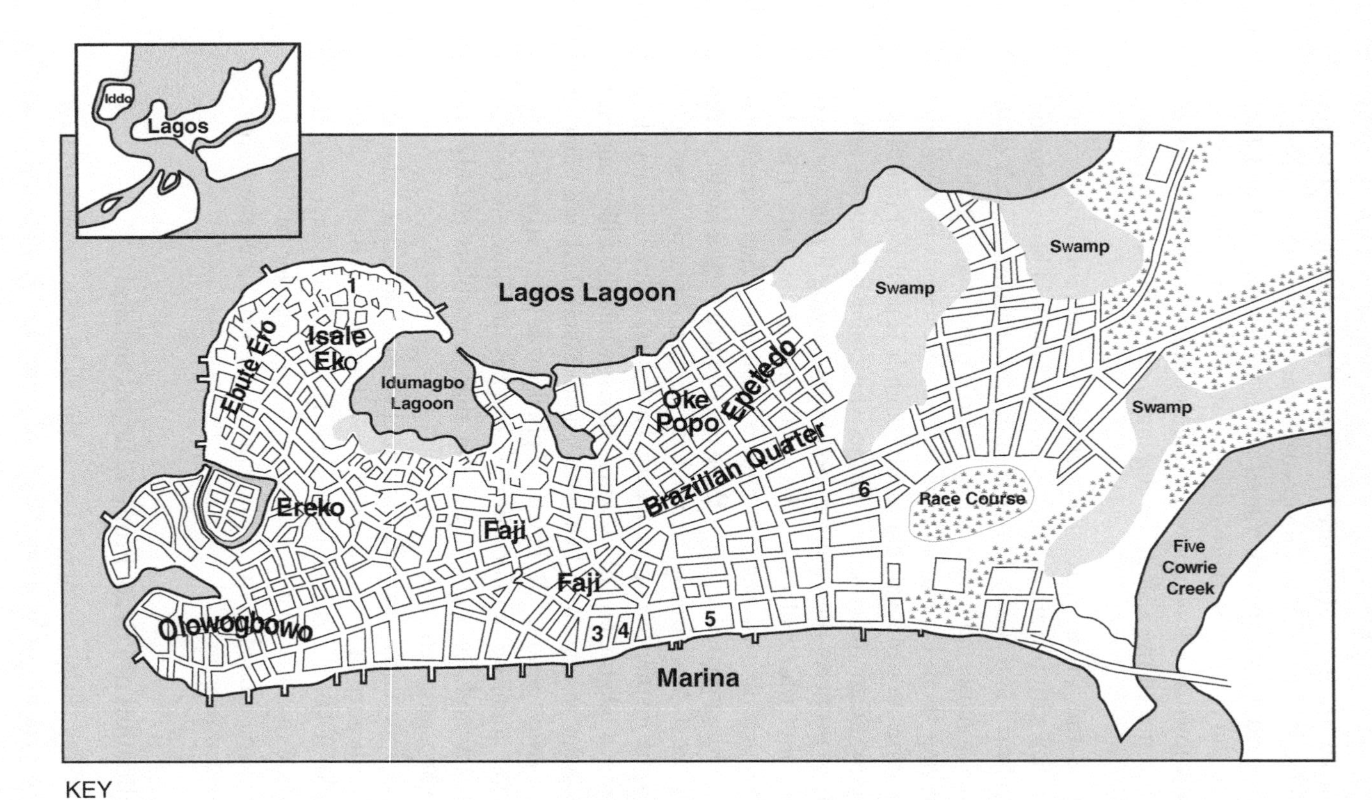

KEY

1. *Ọba's* Palace, 2. Tinubu Square, 3. Church Missionary Society, 4. Government House, 5. Wesleyan Mission, 6. Housa Barracks

Map 3. Town of Lagos, c. 1885.

land in Lagos, the settlers have not only claimed the land they were occupying . . . but have taken possession of other land, and in some cases have sold it."[52] The sale of land did not stop with Sierra Leoneans and Brazilians, moreover, but rapidly spread to chiefs, family heads, and occupants enjoying only usufruct rights in it, as well. Sir Mervyn Tew remarked in his *Report on Title to Land in Lagos* that after the annexation Africans began to sell land for monetary compensation, while Rayner and Healy commented in an earlier report that by the final decades of the nineteenth century land was "freely bought and sold in . . . Lagos."[53] The concept of private ownership of land simultaneously took hold, and rights acquired through purchase were widely regarded as absolute by educated and uneducated Africans alike. Justice Osborne observed that "A purchaser from a family acquire[d] an absolute interest," while Tew quoted Chief Aṣogbon as stating that since the cession a grant of land by natives for monetary consideration was intended to convey absolute ownership, the deciding factor being "the payment of money for land."[54]

British officials in London and Lagos assumed that the commercial growth and prosperity of the young colony depended on the continued development of private property rights in land. A. G. Hopkins has shown that Britain annexed Lagos in part to promote the establishment of new property rights believed to be necessary for the successful conduct of international trade.[55] Early colonial land policy was shaped, however, not by a clearly articulated vision from above, but piecemeal by efforts of local administrators to respond to what was happening on the ground.

Throughout the closing decades of the nineteenth century, the administration took the view that under the Treaty of Cession ultimate ownership of land in Lagos had passed to the British Crown. Governor Freeman's letters of commission empowered him to "make and execute in Our name and on Our behalf . . . grants and dispositions of any lands . . . within Our . . . Settlement."[56] Soon after his arrival, the governor began issuing land grants to some and refusing them to others, in an effort to disallow claims being made by Sierra Leoneans not yet resident in Lagos and uphold those of occupants who were improving land. Protests to the Colonial Office on behalf of a number of Sierra Leoneans whose claims were denied led officials in London to encourage the governor to ascertain what land in Lagos had been granted away and to whom and what remained at the disposal of the Crown.[57] In response perhaps to this instruction, officials in Lagos hastily enacted a fateful ordinance, No. 9 of 1863, which provided for the appointment of three commissioners to ascertain "the True and Rightful owners of the land within the settlement of Lagos."[58] The long-term consequences of this legislation far outweighed the care and consideration that went into its enactment.

The law called upon the three commissioners to sit once a week for about a year and inquire into "the titles by which . . . all the lands within the Settlement are held, occupied, or laid claim to." It opened to them the register that British consuls had created of Dosunmu's grants, along with other public records. Moreover, it empowered them to summon anyone "having or pretending to have any right or title to lands within [the] Settlement, either by Grant or otherwise," along with their witnesses and the "books, papers, or other documents . . . upon which . . . they found . . . their claim." In cases where the commissioners concluded that people had "good and valid" titles, they were to grant them certificates. In those where the commissioners believed that titles were invalid or without proof, they were to tell the claimants that they had no right to the property and make a note to that effect in a book kept for the purpose.

The first three commissioners were Henry Eales, the colonial surgeon, Thomas Mayne, the chief magistrate, and William McCoskry, formerly British consul and acting governor, but now a private merchant. Only Mayne had any legal background, and only McCoskry had much experience at Lagos. Whether these men summoned occupants of land or waited for them to come to the commission is unclear, but they soon began validating some claims to land and denying others.[59] Instead of issuing certificates of title as stipulated under the ordinance, however, the commissioners made recommendations to the governor, who in approved cases issued documents that came to be known as Crown grants. Once J. H. Glover became the chief administrator, he actively encouraged certain kinds of people, including his clients, prominent chiefs, and a number of their slaves, to apply for Crown grants to safeguard their title to land. Sir Mervyn Tew, who had access to the records of the Land Commissioners' Court, found that it systematically favored claims based on grants from Dosunmu, demise by will, purchase, gift, and long occupation, sometimes unsupported by any written documentation.[60]

The commissioners could not, of course, complete the work of inquiring into titles to land in Lagos within one year. The government reenacted the ordinance twice more, and it continued the practice of issuing Crown grants even after the legislation expired in August 1866. A subsequent ordinance, No. 9 of 1869, allowed anyone who had "been in possession by himself or by his tenant" of property within the settlement for a period of three years "without the payment of rent, or anything in the nature of rent, and without any acknowledgment of title to any person," to apply to the administrator for a grant of the land. This legislation also authorized the executive to declare reverted to the Crown the property of anyone who did not obtain a grant within six months of being ordered to do so. It further provided that disputes over land should be settled by the colonial Court of Civil and Criminal Justice, rather than an indigenous tribunal.[61] The language of the ordinance, which was gendered male, reveals implicit British assumptions about who landowners in the colony should be. To encourage draining swamps and improving land, the government introduced ordinances that required owners to fill swamp land and remove "rubbish, ordure or filth," under penalty of sale at public auction. It continued to issue Crown grants to people who filled swamp land until the end of the century.[62]

All of this early colonial land legislation gave Lagosians new ways of obtaining rights in land. It demonstrates, moreover, that by the 1860s land had acquired monetary value and its sale was well established on the island. These laws profoundly influenced the terms in which Lagosians subsequently articulated claims to land. By the time the government stopped issuing Crown grants, after the turn of the century, almost four thousand such documents had been executed, 75 percent of them to land on Lagos island.[63]

One further government action had long-term implications for land ownership in the town of Lagos. An anti-European uprising at Abeokuta in 1867 led many Egba Christians to flee south to the British colony.[64] Administrator Glover obtained for these refugees land at Ebute Metta, on the mainland across from Lagos island, from Chief Oloto, the *ìdéjọ* with authority over the area. Glover had the territory laid out in blocks, and he then entrusted the headman of the group with settling each refugee and "his family" on a plot and obtaining a ticket to the land for him. A few of the approximately seven hundred settlers who obtained land in this way subsequently applied for Crown grants to their parcels, but the majority did not. Much of the land in the government layout remained unoccupied following settlement by the Egba refugees, and as the population of the city subsequently grew, others acquired plots there through a variety of means—squatting, governmental allocation, and sale or grant by ticket holders or members of the Oloto family. In time, the question of who owned the land in this section of the city and how they owned it became very complicated and gave rise to "bitter conflict and much litigation," the more so because a land commissioner at some point burned the government's copies of the "Glover tickets" and many ticket holders lost or destroyed theirs.[65]

The *ọba* and some of the chiefs resisted the government's land policies, but with little effect. In the early 1860s, Dosunmu petitioned the British Parliament, admitting that under threat of force he had ceded sovereignty over Lagos, but saying nothing in this context about land. Later in the petition he urged, however, that "the course . . . adopted by the Executive, with regard to real property, should be changed" and that the *ọba* should be allowed to "use his seal according to the deed of cession."[66] Following the *ìdéjọ*'s failed protest against the Treaty of Cession and Glover's deposition of two of them, probably as a consequence, many of Lagos's chiefs apparently continued to protest the government's land policy silently by rejecting Crown grants. Tew maintained that some of them, such as Chief Aṣogbon, initially responded positively to Glover's encouragement to apply for grants, but then changed their minds when warned by "foreigners"—probably Sierra Leonean repatriates—that these documents meant that the government was claiming all Lagos land.[67]

The registers of Crown grants show that the Aṣogbon did indeed obtain a single such document in 1863, but then abruptly abandoned the practice until 1868, when he received two more.[68] Dosunmu took out a few grants, including to the land on which the *ìgá* stood, but many of the *ìdéjọ* and other chiefs did not obtain Crown grants to most of the land that they and their families occupied. There is no reason to think that the land commissioners rejected the applications of chiefs, who in most cases would have had no difficulty establishing their title to land. The failure of so many of the chiefs to obtain Crown grants can be explained only by assuming that they did not apply for them. The chiefs' rejection of Crown grants probably stemmed in certain cases from fear of what the documents meant or opposition to them. In others it may have been rooted in aversion to dealing with the new colonial government, disinclination to pay the fees necessary to obtain grants, or stubborn belief that for important chiefs and their families grants were unnecessary.

Beyond what Crown grants and Glover tickets communicated about the authority that the new colonial state was assuming over land, the meaning of these documents was ambiguous. None of the legislation that led the state to issue grants defined the rights they conferred. Government officials awarded them to validate title to land, but of what kind or on the basis of what rights was not specified. Administrators made the grants, however, in the name of individuals, not families or other groups.

Throughout the colonial period many British officials regarded African ideas about land ownership as antithetical to progress and development, and they assumed that colonial rule and economic development would eventually transform them. Until the administration of the Yoruba interior confronted the colonial state with new political and social imperatives from the 1890s, most British officers in Lagos believed that the demise of communal ownership by families was inevitable and would be a good thing. E. A. Speed, acting chief justice of the Lagos Supreme Court, expressed this view as late as 1909, when he wrote in an important legal decision,

> [F]amily ownership is gradually ceasing to exist [in Lagos]. In a progressive community it is of course inevitable that this should be so.

Speed went on to tell the litigants in the case that the ideas of their ancestors "as to ownership of property were utterly unsuited to modern requirements."[69]

Many British officials and African observers alike in Lagos maintained that Crown grants conferred a fee simple title. Yet some government officers and one influential African lawyer also acknowledged that the state had originally intended the grants to confirm a preexisting right of occupancy, which might rest on family as well as individual ownership. When disputes arose in the colonial courts between grantees and others claiming rights in property, judges—who under the 1876 Supreme Court ordinance were supposed to decide disputes among locals according to their own law and custom, unless doing so violated the repugnancy clause or was incompatible with local statute—sometimes upheld family or other collective ownership.[70]

It is harder to know how the recipients of Grown grants themselves understood the documents. Judging from the names of the people to whom they were issued, which indicate origins only imperfectly, about 70 percent of the Crown grants went to Sierra Leonean, Brazilian, or other Atlantic emigrés in the period 1863 to 1866. These recipients generally treated the documents as giving them fee simple title during their lives, and they sold, mortgaged, or otherwise disposed of the property as they saw fit. But in 1869, to cite a later year that was not atypical, about half of the grants issued went to local people, and this more democratic distribution continued as the century progressed. If the chiefs generally eschewed Crown grants, other members of the indigenous community did not.[71]

Some locals took out Crown grants as representatives of families or other groups that occupied the land and continued to regard it as collectively owned, even after obtaining the grant. In such cases, many or all of the adult members of the family or other collectivity continued to exercise rights in the land. None of them was supposed to sell or mortgage the property without the consent of the others, and all were supposed to enjoy rights to participate in its management and share in the benefits of its use. But other local people obtained grants to family-owned land, sometimes without the knowledge of their kin, and subsequently treated the property as though it were privately owned. At the end of the century, Lagosians complained that there was a growing tendency for people who had taken out Crown grants as representatives of families to claim private ownership of the land.[72] Thus the legal effects of Crown grants remained ambiguous. In a very real sense, the documents conveyed whatever rights in landed property the recipients could use them to exercise.[73] Despite this ambiguity, however, Crown grants offered an important new means of asserting rights in land, and they were widely identified with private rather than communal ownership. The acquisition of a Crown grant commonly became the first step in exercising rights of private property in land or a house.

The government defined the rights conferred by Glover tickets no more clearly than it did those vested in Crown grants. Over time, however, judges and officials treated the tickets much the way they did Crown grants—as conveying fee simple title subject, in certain cases, to family rights. The recipients of the tickets themselves sometimes sold or mortgaged their plots as though they were privately owned and, if these transactions were not challenged by family members, the state and the public commonly accepted their legitimacy.[74]

If the land commissioners had accepted purchase, gift, long occupation, and demise by will as evidence of title to land and justification for issuing Crown grants to it, so the colonial courts and the public sometimes interpreted these practices as conferring rights of private property in land, whether or not a Crown grant had been obtained. Purchase, gift, inheritance, and long occupation without acknowledging the rights of a grantor all became additional means by which Lagosians could obtain fee simple title to landed property. I have found few records from the colonial courts that existed prior to 1876. Documents from the Lagos Supreme Court established in that year, however, show that while judges sometimes refused to uphold the sale of family land without the consent of kin, they treated sales as conferring absolute ownership if consent had been obtained or if the property was privately owned. A justice of the court acknowledged this fact many years later when he wrote, "since the arrival of Europeans in Lagos . . . a custom has grown up of permitting the alienation of family lands with the general consent of the family."[75]

Following the annexation, Lagosians could also be given privately owned landed property. When the donors executed deeds of gift or otherwise made their intentions very clear, as commonly occurred among Sierra Leonean and Brazilian immigrants, these transfers proved relatively unproblematic.[76] Locals and immigrants from the interior and elsewhere on the coast, however, much more commonly obtained access to land through the grants of usufruct that indigenous peoples had long made. Both the colonial courts and many local authorities eventually took the position that absolute ownership of family land could not be given away without the consent of the family.[77] Yet in the nineteenth century, the Lagos Supreme Court sometimes treated long occupation of land without the performance of ritual or economic obligations to an overlord as evidence of absolute ownership, and Lagosians themselves occasionally adopted this perspective. If those who occupied landed property could hold on to it and over time cease paying the grantor the homage, prestations, and service associated with usufruct, then they could often redefine their rights in the property and assert fee simple title to it. Judicial decisions upholding claims to absolute ownership in certain instances confirmed and lent the authority of the state to the process of redefinition.

Inheritance offered another means of obtaining privately owned land in Lagos, if one that was less common than Crown grants, purchase, and the gradual redefinition of rights during long occupation. In a development that deviated from the evolutionary expectations of British officials and led them to grumble about the "peculiar" state of land law at Lagos, land and houses in which people had exercised fee simple title during their lives usually devolved to their heirs as family property.[78] In time, this type of succession, which transformed privately owned landed property into family-owned property on the death of the person who had obtained it, came to be accepted as local custom. Buchanan Smith noted that in Lagos Colony "a Crown grant often becomes after the first generation . . . a piece of inalienable family land" and that the "native who purchases [land] at a sale can sell it again if he so chooses, but that, if he fails to do so, at his death it becomes vested in his descendants as a whole." He observed, moreover, that in Lagos people often bought real estate "with the view that on their death it should pass in bulk to their descendants and be considered family land, and as such be inalienable."[79]

After the introduction of English law and establishment of the colonial legal system, individuals could have wills drawn up that provided for the disposition of their landed property. Although Lagosians commonly used wills to ensure that self-acquired land and houses devolved as family property, they also sometimes employed them to leave real estate to individuals or groups in fee simple or according to other specifications.[80] The courts finally held in the twentieth century that only self-acquired property and not family land could be affected by wills, because individuals did not enjoy alienable rights in the latter.[81] Most of the inhabitants of the town did not leave wills, of course, and their landed property devolved according to local practices. The majority of those who did make testamentary dispositions were Sierra Leonean or Brazilian immigrants, their descendants, or other educated Africans. But locals who were neither literate nor Christian sometimes also had wills drawn up and used them to bequeath absolute ownership of self-acquired land and houses to children or others.

As this brief discussion of inheritance makes clear, family ownership did not die out in Lagos following the introduction of new forms of land tenure. Indeed, it remained dominant in the sense that more people continued to exercise rights in land that way than any other. Buchanan Smith called the "tenacity" of "ownership by the family, under the control . . . of its head," even in cases where the proprietor had an undoubted freehold title vested in himself personally, one "of the most curious features" of Lagos's modern system of land tenure.[82] Sir Melvyn Tew concluded in 1939, "I do not believe . . . that even in Lagos today family ownership can be said to be a dying institution."[83] Despite the persistence of family tenure, however, the introduction and spread of new ways of obtaining access to land and houses and of defining rights in them co-existed with older practices and gave Lagosians, including some fortunate slaves and former slaves, new means of acquiring and owning what was rapidly becoming one of the most valuable resources in the growing colonial city.

Slaves, Former Slaves, and the Acquisition of Privately Owned Land

In the decades after the annexation, most owners allowed the slaves who remained attached to their households to retain use of the land and housing they occupied, so long as the slaves were well behaved. Many overlords did the same with the strangers who lived under their authority. Big men and women in Lagos had to permit their dependents ongoing access to landed property in order to retain their labor and allegiance, as well as to enjoy the possibility of eventually absorbing them or their descendants into the family as kin. If slaves or strangers had been turned out, they would undoubtedly have transferred their labor and allegiance elsewhere, and few Lagosians wanted to take such a risk, given the keen competition for workers and dependents that existed within the community. Help with the provision of land and housing continued to be regarded as a type of assistance that big men and women owed their dependents. Even when slaves redeemed themselves, many continued to use land or housing they had obtained through their owners.[84] Land had not in the past been a scarce resource, and in the third quarter of the nineteenth century there was still limited reason to worry about who occupied it and how. Managing relationships with dependents was a much more pressing concern. As the value of land increased and competition for it grew, landowners in fact sometimes deliberately placed slaves or strangers on property they could not occupy themselves to prevent others from encroaching on it.[85]

The changes in land tenure taking place during the early colonial period gave people of slave origin, like other Lagosians, opportunities to redefine their rights in land and dwellings they occupied, whether they had been granted the property by their owners or overlords or had squatted on it without anyone's permission. Soon after the colonial government began issuing Crown grants, slaves started applying for them in their own names, sometimes with the knowledge of their owners and other times not. A slave of Chief Aṣogbon's, for example, testified in the case *Ajose v. Efunde*, "I told Asogbon Odunran that I wanted a grant and he told me to go and get one. . . . All of us [slaves] at Faji took grants in Governor Glover's time, and in our own names."[86] Other slaves managed to obtain tickets or grants to plots in the new government layout at Ebute Metta.[87] It is well known, moreover, that after Oshodi Tapa's death Glover encouraged the heads of compounds the chief and his followers had founded at Epetedo, including a number of slaves, to obtain Crown grants to the properties in their own names. This policy created much bitter conflict between the family and its *àrótà* in the twentieth century. Why certain chiefs allowed a number of their slaves to obtain Crown grants, when they themselves failed to do so, remains unclear. Perhaps they feared that if they protested, these dependents would leave them and transfer their labor and allegiance elsewhere. It is clear, however, that some of the chiefs did not think that the grants should alter their slaves' rights in the land in question or their relationship with them.[88]

Once slaves and former slaves obtained Crown grants in their own names, however, they began using the documents as evidence that they enjoyed private property rights in the land, much like other members of the community. Slaves soon began selling and mortgaging land for which they held grants without the permission of the original landowners, for example, and they also used the documents to resist ejection—even for bad behavior. So strong was the association between possession of a Crown grant to land and rights of private property in it that individuals, including slaves and strangers, commonly competed for control of the documents, even when they were not in their own names. Court records contain numerous references, moreover, to people who stole Crown grants, presumably in hopes of using them to exercise private property rights in land. It did not take long for the grants, conveyances, and deeds of gift associated with private ownership of land to acquire value in their own right.[89]

Other means also existed for slaves and former slaves to acquire privately owned land. Both individuals and groups of such people were sometimes able to redefine their rights in land or houses through long occupation, even when they did not have Crown grants to the property, particularly if they could show that they did not perform for anyone the duties normally associated with usufruct. In such cases, however, titles to landed property often remained vulnerable to challenge by others. Sometimes people of slave origin eventually succeeded in upholding ownership rights in the property they acquired through litigation in the colonial courts, in which case the judicial decision in their favor validated their claims, much as a Crown grant would have done. Two examples illustrate this phenomenon.

A number of male slaves who belonged to the war chief Saṣore obtained land before 1845 from "the owners" of a quarter of Lagos known as Oke Popo. In the early 1850s, they built a dwelling on it with six separate rooms, and they or their wives lived there until about 1890, although one of the men, Fatosha, spent much of his time outside the town. When the last of the wives left the house because she was ill, Fajimi, a son of Saṣore, who was by then deceased, repaired and rented it. This man's sudden intervention in the management of the property prompted Fatosha to have the land surveyed, install new locks on the doors, and bar his former owner's son from the house, whereupon Fajimi initiated a suit in the Supreme Court to obtain possession of the property. The judge was not satisfied that either man had proved his claim to the land, but he ruled that the former slave had possessed the house for a long time and should therefore retain it.[90]

In a second case, Layeni, a successful trader of slave origin, himself owned a number of slaves who with their descendants inhabited a house at

Agbowodo Street, although it is not clear how they had obtained it. When Layeni died in the early 1890s, his two sons sought repeatedly, but without success, to eject their father's slaves from the house and claim it for his heirs, perhaps because they feared that if they did not, the family would lose the property forever. The sons eventually wearied of trying to drive out their father's slaves and sold the house to an unsuspecting woman, realizing its cash value and leaving the problem of obtaining possession to her. The woman brought suit against the occupants in the Supreme Court to eject them, but the judge eventually concluded that, while he could not untangle the conflicting evidence in the complex case, the slaves had possessed the property for many years and should be allowed to keep it. Henceforth, the victors in both of these cases could point to the judges' decisions as proof that they owned the land and houses in question, consolidating their ownership of valuable assets.[91]

In some instances, slaves, former slaves, or their descendants themselves decided to sell land or houses that they occupied, whether because they wanted the money they could obtain by doing so or because they believed that they might not, in the long run, be able to uphold ownership rights in the property and elected, in the short run, to convert possession of it into its cash equivalent. Either way, the occupants were attempting to exercise new rights in the land, and while their owners or overlords sometimes heard about the sales and thwarted them, this strategy often succeeded.

Slaves and former slaves, like others in Lagos, also obtained privately owned town and later rural land by purchasing it with income from their work for themselves or with the proceeds from the sale of other land they had inhabited. Most slaves who were fortunate enough to buy land acquired only modest holdings. Some began by investing in a small unfilled or uncleared plot and then improved and built on it over time, while others bought only a portion of a rudimentary dwelling along with a few square feet of yard. So finely divisible had urban land become, and so powerfully did even the poor want to own it, that one man reported buying a corner of a room.[92] A number of slaves who became successful produce traders, however, eventually invested in large amounts of real estate, some of it quite valuable. By 1867, Taiwo Olowo already owned seventeen properties, many of them in prime locations.[93] Two other slaves in Kosoko's retinue, who traded together after returning with the former *ọba* to Lagos, were in time able to buy eight plots in the town.[94] Over the course of his life, Sunmonu Animaṣaun, also once a slave, obtained through purchase or trade twenty-six properties near his residence in central Lagos and used them to house his family and other dependents. Animaṣaun owned, in addition, four plots along Broad Street, one at Itolo facing the lagoon, and four at Ebute Metta, as well as farmland near Abeokuta and Ilorin.[95]

Finally, slaves sometimes obtained privately owned land through gifts or inheritance from their kin, spouses, friends, fellow slaves, or occasionally owners. A slave, for example, who had been captured in warfare and sold to Lagos bought a house in the town for which he had a conveyance. When he died without heirs some years later, it was inherited by the fellow slaves who had cared for him during his final illness and performed his funeral ceremonies.[96] Another man of slave origin, who by the mid-1880s had redeemed himself and bought a house at Victoria Road, later also died leaving no children or kin, only three widows. The son of the man's former owner went to court and insisted that he was entitled to inherit the house, but the assessors called to advise the judge in the case held that the property should pass to the former slave's widows.[97] A few loyal and lucky slaves were given privately owned real estate by their owners. Sunmonu Animaṣaun, for instance, deeded a house near his own to his head slave Idrisu and also bequeathed the property to the man in his will, so that the gift could not be challenged by Animaṣaun's children.[98] A group of female slaves, on the other hand, inherited a house from the woman who owned them when she died childless.[99]

The Changing Uses, Value, and Meaning of Land

If changes in land tenure and other legal practices during the early colonial period created new ways for Lagosians, including some slaves and former slaves, to obtain access to landed property or redefine their rights in it, then economic and social transformations taking place also gave land and houses new uses and altered their value and meaning in the community. Land and dwellings remained important for the reasons they always had been—as sites of economic enterprise, places of domestic shelter, and centers of individual and family religious, social, and political activity. So long as Lagosians lived in households headed by others, they had obligations to their heads and other senior members for labor and support that drained their own time and resources. Slaves and strangers faced the heaviest obligations, but wards, junior wives, and kin felt them as well. Adults could markedly reduce their obligations to others and simultaneously improve their own ability to attract dependents, both of which facilitated individual accumulation, by establishing their own residences. For this reason, men and, less commonly, women who could manage it—both free and slave—often elected to leave the households of others and build residences of their own. A number of scholars have remarked on the strong desire of nineteenth-century Yoruba big men to found their own compounds in an effort to advance their competitive struggles for self-aggrandizement and also immortalize their names.[100] Free people, of course, succeeded in acquiring land and establishing residences much more easily and commonly than most slaves, but no group had more to gain from doing so than slaves. The pressure that Lagosians of different kinds felt to establish separate residences intensified the already strong demand for urban real estate created by population growth and commercial and administrative development, and it helped drive up real estate prices. Palm produce production, food farming, and later cocoa farming had similar effects, though more slowly, in rural areas on the mainland north of the city.[101]

In addition to the age-old uses of land and housing, however, real estate acquired important new functions during the early colonial period—as collateral for commercial and other credit, a source of rental income, and the object of speculative investment. These new uses, which emerged first within the town but (after the development of cocoa farming and construction of the railroad) also spread north to rural areas, further stimulated the scramble for landed property and also increased its value.

The credit system, on which the expansion of both foreign and much domestic trade rested in the second half of the nineteenth century, created substantial problems from the beginning. One of the most serious of them was that debtors routinely failed to repay their loans. Mechanisms for enforcing debt repayment existed in local culture, and they were practiced in Lagos into the colonial period. These techniques included sending a representative to harass the debtor, seizing a relative, townsperson, or slave of the debtor and holding the hostage until the loan was repaid, seizing property belonging to the debtor and holding it to apply pressure for repayment, and calling upon public authorities to seize and sell property or people from the debtor's family to cover the loan.[102] A number of these customs, however, were too reminiscent of the slave trade for the liking of British officials, who tried to suppress them.[103]

During the 1850s, European merchants had looked to the *ọba* to bring defaulters to terms, and agreements signed with Akitoye in 1852 and Dosunmu in 1854 called on them to sell houses and other property of delinquent debtors for the benefit of their creditors.[104] Despite Dosunmu's efforts to fulfill this obligation, the volume of credit, problems with trade, and opportunities for non-payment were sufficient that he could satisfy neither the demands of European merchants nor the expectations of British consuls. The consuls themselves were soon devoting much of their time to adjudicating disputes over debt, as was the short-lived court founded by Sierra Leonean immigrants. These new authorities had little more success than the *ọbas*, however, when it came to policing repayment of debts.[105]

To provide themselves a modicum of protection against default, European and Sierra Leonean merchants began requiring that many of the Africans to whom they extended commercial credit pledge land or houses in Lagos as security for their loans.[106] At first the merchants demanded mortgages, as the pledges were called, from traders who had loans outstanding that they could not repay. Thus in the 1850s, Madame Tinubu secured a prior debt to J. P. L. Davies by pledging part of her landed property in central Lagos to him.[107] But subsequently, merchants began insisting on mortgages before giving credit, and soon many African traders adopted the practice, as well.[108] By the end of the 1860s, the custom of mortgaging urban land and houses to obtain credit had become widespread, not only among people borrowing large amounts from European and Sierra Leonean merchants, but also among those wanting smaller sums from locals, including for non-commercial purposes.

Two examples illustrate how far down the social ladder the practice of pledging land to secure credit quickly spread and what small loans it could be used to secure. In 1872 a sick, blind man mortgaged land to a trader named Idowu to secure a loan of twelve bags of cowries worth approximately £10.5.[109] Not long after, T. W. Johnson, the court interpreter, required Ajayi Oloworira, one of Kosoko's former slaves, to mortgage a house before lending him 120 heads of cowries valued at £6.[110]

Contemporaries described a local and, presumably, older practice that they called "pawning" land. Under this arrangement, creditors obtained the use of land pledged in exchange for credit during the life of the loan, but the property could not be alienated and was forever redeemable by any member of the debtor's family.[111] The new mortgages, on the other hand, usually specified that debtors retained the use of land pledged as security unless and until they defaulted on the loan, but that if default occurred the property could be sold and the proceeds used to repay the debt. Foreclosures on mortgaged land and sales of it occurred so commonly that some observers feared that control of landed property in Lagos was passing into the hands of moneylenders.[112]

The 1864 legislation establishing a Petty Debt Court had provided that when property was seized and sold to cover a debt, the court could summon interested parties and adjudicate the claim. This practice gave family-owned land some protection against sale to cover the debts of individuals.[113] Although Lagosians mortgaged both land in which they enjoyed rights as family members and that to which they had been granted access by their owners or overlords, a presumption existed among merchants and officials, as well as among many Lagosians themselves, that only privately owned property should be pledged to cover debts. Most of the mortgages recorded at the Land Registry carefully documented the transmission of title to the land being pledged from the current owner back to the original Crown grant or sale that established private property rights in it.[114] Then from the early 1880s, landmark judicial decisions began to rule that Lagosians did not have the right to alienate landed property on which they had been placed by others and that family land could be alienated only with the consent of the family as a whole.[115] The widespread need of Lagosians for property they could mortgage without consulting kin helped fuel the demand for privately owned land and houses in Lagos. The mere knowledge that individuals asking for credit owned such property often helped dispose lenders to advance them goods or currency, even when mortgages were not executed. So great was the pressure to demonstrate private ownership of land when asking for credit that Lagosians sometimes fraudulently appropriated Crown grants and presented them for the purpose without the knowledge of the landowner.[116]

By no means was all credit in Lagos secured through mortgages of landed property. Much borrowing and lending took place among locals without the pledge of any kind of security, and enforcement of these debts rested on the social ties that bound parties to them, on underlying cultural values, and, in some instances, on indigenous mechanisms of debt collection. Lagosians, moreover, occasionally pledged personal property as security for loans.[117] Even so, a relationship soon developed between access to credit for commercial and other purposes and private ownership of urban real estate. Thus when a woman Asatu asked the Saro merchant Charles Foresythe to sell her goods on credit, he flatly refused unless she could secure the loan by mortgaging landed property.[118]

Possession of privately owned land was especially important when Lagosians wanted large amounts of credit. In 1867, Taiwo Olowo received goods and currency on credit from Régis Ainé sufficient to purchase forty thousand gallons of palm oil, but he had to secure the loan by mortgaging his seventeen properties.[119] Five years later J. P. L. Davies mortgaged fourteen parcels of prime real estate in exchange for £60,000 of credit annually, while in 1919 P. J. C. Thomas mortgaged the bulk of his substantial landed property for £150,000 of credit.[120] However, private ownership of only a single parcel of urban real estate was often sufficient to open new sources of credit to Lagosians, create wider opportunities for them, and lessen the dependence of slaves and former slaves on their owners or overlords. These realities rapidly created a strong demand in the town for privately owned land.

By the early 1910s, the practice of mortgaging land to obtain credit had spread from the city to rural areas on the mainland near the railroad and cocoa-producing regions. Many observers believed that as a consequence much rural land was passing from its original owners to educated African moneylenders from the capital. Others complained that educated Lagosians were lending money to small farmers at interest rates of 50 percent and then forcing them to supply cocoa in return for "a sort of wage," when they were unable to repay their loans.[121]

As Lagos grew and developed in the second half of the nineteenth century, a market for rental property emerged. In addition to providing collateral for credit, real estate acquired new use and value as a source of rental income during these years. Many of the Europeans, Sierra Leoneans, and Brazilians then arriving in the town did not immediately buy land and build dwellings, factories, and storehouses, but instead rented structures from local landowners. Between 1865 and 1869, the government paid an average of £420 per year in rent, and the commercial community probably paid more.[122] People who owned desirable property along the waterfront and in Olowogbowo, Faji, or the Brazilian quarter found that they could earn cash income by renting it. In 1868, Taiwo Olowo leased land on the Marina to Robert Campbell for £18 per year, while three years later Walter Lewis leased a European merchant land, storehouses, and a dwelling for £80 per year.[123] Although Europeans, Sierra Leoneans, and Brazilians normally rented land and buildings, they sometimes rented land alone with the provision that they could erect structures on it that would belong to the landowner when the lease expired.[124]

Government expenditure on rents declined from the early 1870s, as the state built the offices and houses it needed on vacant land that it claimed or purchased properties from local landowners, but the rental market more generally picked up in the closing decades of the century. The continuing influx of Europeans increased the demand for high-end properties. Concerned about the alienation of land to foreigners, the government proposed legislation in 1897 that prohibited land sales to them and provided for long-term leases instead. Local protest blocked the legislation, but long-term leases, rather than sales, to Europeans subsequently became the norm nonetheless.[125] As rents in the heart of the town escalated, these arrangements became a source of steady and substantial income. In 1895, for example, the merchant J. S. Leigh leased the British firm Holt and Welsh a dwelling, shop, storehouses, and wharf on the Marina for ten years at an annual rent of £280.[126] Fourteen years later, the trader Disu Ige leased the Compagnie Bordelaise des Comptoirs Africans two properties in the commercial district for fifty years, at £500 per year for the first half of the period and £600 per year thereafter.[127] As in earlier decades, European firms sometimes erected structures on land they rented, which subsequently passed to the landowner on very favorable terms.[128]

The growth of the rental market for land and housing touched poorer Lagosians as well. By the end of the century, a demand existed for rental housing among local people themselves. Moreover, the thousands of men, women, and children migrating to the town from elsewhere needed places to live. Many of them found accommodation by asking to be taken into the compounds of chiefs, wealthy traders, or other prominent people, and some did not pay monetary rent but instead, as in precolonial times, gave their overlords service, labor, and periodic gifts in kind. Still other migrants found places to live in the houses of kin or acquaintances from their hometowns.[129] Yet by the closing decades of the century, a demand existed for rental housing to accommodate African immigrants to the city. Individuals who owned but a single modest house in the town could make small sums by renting out all or part of it. In the mid-1880s, for example, a woman named Mayeni rented a portion of a dwelling for four shillings a month, while a few years later a "fetishman" rented a small house at Oke Popo for two shillings and sixpence a month.[130] Renting accommodation in return for a cash payment was attractive to some poorer Lagosians precisely because it enabled them to avoid the demands associated with living in the household of an overlord.

The rental market in land spread to rural areas north of the city, as cocoa farming expanded there in the 1890s. When African entrepreneurs from Lagos began experimenting with cocoa at Agege, some of them initially obtained farmland to use by asking for it from local landowners. F. E. Williams, treasurer of the Agege Planters' Union, testified, for example, "I came to Agege in 1891 from Lagos. . . . I asked the original owner to let me have the piece of land which I hold there. That was according to local custom."[131] As cocoa and later kola farming expanded in the area, however, some landowners began demanding "right of entry" fees payable in spirits or cash and also charging monetary rent. Around Agege and Ikeja, cocoa farmers soon preferred to buy land outright in which they subsequently claimed fee simple title. But in other areas, where rural owners held on to their land, the heads of prominent families subsequently increased their incomes by demanding substantial cash payments in return for rights to use land.[132] As the railroad opened the interior to new kinds of European and African enterprise, the practice of leasing, like selling and mortgaging, land traveled with it.[133]

The fact that landed property could be rented to generate cash income increased its attractiveness as an economic asset and contributed to the scramble for privately owned land in the town of Lagos and, later, in parts of the surrounding countryside. Both individuals and groups of kin could and did rent family property; however, many members of the family might then demand a share of the income.[134] To profit exclusively from rents, derive significant income from them, and enjoy undisputed management of the real estate, Lagosians needed land and houses that they themselves owned.

The steadily growing demand for land and houses in Lagos pushed up the price of real estate throughout the second half of the nineteenth century, making it an excellent speculative investment. The price of good property in prime locations rose particularly fast, but eventually even swamp land in outlying areas appreciated in value.[135] Time series data on the price of land and buildings unfortunately do not exist for the early colonial period. Changes in property values are difficult to reconstruct from conveyances, because owners sometimes subdivided or improved properties between sales, and real estate could also deteriorate over time. Conveyances rarely mention the condition of land or buildings, and they often refer to the division of plots only in ambiguous terms. Despite these limitations, sufficient evidence exists to show that real estate prices appreciated significantly on Lagos island and the nearby mainland during the early colonial period.

In 1863, the Legislative Council decreed that vacant land behind Broad Street, in the heart of the commercial and administrative district, should be sold for £100 per acre, although the government sold land in Lagos as a whole for a mean price of £82 per acre between 1865 and 1869. A decade later the average price of vacant land sold by the government on Lagos island had quadrupled to £328 per acre.[136] In 1886, the governor valued land along Broad Street at £968 per acre. Two years later, the colonial surveyor priced good land facing the Marina at £1,456 per acre, and reclaimed swamp land between the Marina and Broad Street at £490 per acre.[137]

Land with buildings on it fetched more, of course, particularly if they were solidly constructed. In 1879, a plot at Tinubu Square of only about one-twentieth of an acre, but with a substantial building on it, sold for £614. Later that year, an acre and one-tenth occupying "a commanding position" on the Marina and having two dwelling houses on it, one of them quite grand by local standards, sold for £3000. In 1882, three-quarters of an acre on the Marina with a dilapidated house on it fetched £1,650.[138]

In addition to long-term gains, buyers sometimes realized substantial profits on quick purchases and sales. Between 1887 and 1890, a small piece of vacant land bordering Tinubu Square rose in value from £539 to £600. A man who bought a property in Bamgbose Street for £50 in 1899, moreover, nearly doubled his money when he sold it for £90 fifteen months later. Another who bought land at Broad Street for £105 in August 1899 sold it again for £240 twenty-eight months later. In addition to having use value, real estate had become a good speculative investment.[139]

The development of cocoa farming and construction of the railroad stimulated the market for rural land north of the city and also increased its value. The attorney general remarked in 1912, "Up the rail line from Ebute Metta there has been a huge amount of alienation going on," while the court interpreter observed that the practice of selling land had spread "right up to the Egba boundary."[140] The price of land at places like Agege and Ikeja shot up, with that at Ikeja bringing four times as much in 1915 as it had ten to fifteen years earlier.[141] While some Lagosians bought land in rural areas for agricultural or commercial development, others purchased it as a speculative investment. The commissioner of lands told a story about a Lagos man who purported to buy land in Ibadan and then tried to sell it to Europeans at "a very considerable profit."[142] A later colonial official reported the purchase of three plots at Ejinrin, a produce buying and shipping point on the lagoon, for £380 in 1920 and their partition and sale within a few months to Europeans for £14,000.[143]

The changes in land use, tenure, and value that have been discussed in this section altered the meaning of landed property as a resource in Lagos. In the second half of the nineteenth century, land ceased to be purely an abundant, family-owned resource in which outsiders could obtain certain kinds of use rights relatively easily in return for loyalty, labor, and prestations of great worth for what they communicated about control over the people who gave them, but of limited monetary value. It became, in addition, almost overnight, a scarce resource with great commercial and, hence, monetary value in which individuals could exercise rights of private property. Land and especially buildings continued to have important use value for dwelling, working, storing, and socializing, as well as for sheltering dependents and conducting political affairs. They also became, however, in and of themselves, a major form of wealth and path to it, because of their role in securing credit, generating income, and ensuring long-term capital gain. These transformations did not occur at the same rate in all parts of the city, much less in its surrounding countryside, and they gained momentum in the twentieth century. Even so, the trajectory of change became clear to many Lagosians, including some slaves and former slaves, within the first two decades of colonial rule.

During the second half of the nineteenth century, many prosperous Lagosians—particularly merchants, traders, colonial servants, lawyers, doctors, moneylenders, and landlords—invested in substantial amounts of privately owned real estate and used it to secure their economic, social, and in some cases political positions in the town.[144] As a mark of the enduring power of certain Yoruba cultural values, however, these individuals often turned some or all of their privately owned land into family property when they died, creating lasting monuments to themselves and legacies for their descendants. All one need do to be reminded of this fact is walk the streets of Lagos island and look at the surviving family houses established by prominent nineteenth-century Lagosians. A descendant of Taiwo Olowo's remarked in the 1980s that the family founded by her illustrious ancestor was still deriving wealth from property he had acquired more than a century ago.[145] As the data presented here have shown, women were sometimes able to acquire privately owned real estate in their own names. For reasons analyzed elsewhere, however, they did so much less commonly than men. Women's disabilities regarding access to privately owned landed property compounded their weaker access to commercial credit, as well as to rental income and good speculative investments, and put them at an economic disadvantage *vis-à-vis* men.[146]

The acquisition of privately owned land had the same advantages for slaves and former slaves that it did for freeborn members of the community. These benefits were sufficient that obtaining a privately owned plot often marked a major step forward in the struggle of slaves and former slaves to work on their own, retain more of what they earned, and redefine their identities in the community. It was normally the acquisition of a privately owned dwelling, however, more than of undeveloped land itself that marked the critical turning point in the relationship between slaves or former slaves and their superiors, because of the close association between residence in the household of an owner or overlord and obligations for homage, labor, and support. So long as slaves and former slaves depended on their owners or overlords for a place to live in the growing city, the landowners had mechanisms of control over them and could continue to make demands on them, as cases analyzed in the final chapter will demonstrate. This dynamic changed significantly only if and when such subordinates were fully incorporated into the landowning family as kin.

The power that landowners exercised over those who depended on them for housing found legal expression in the concept of service land tenure. Although the sources do not permit me to date the development of this phenomenon precisely, within little more than twenty years of the annexation, chiefs, elders, and other household heads in Lagos had succeeded in establishing and often upholding the principle that non-kin who occupied their dwellings could be ejected for failing to show proper deference and support or to perform "service" demanded of them. Under service tenure, people outside the family were allowed to occupy family- or privately owned land and housing without paying rent in return for periodic displays of respect, loyalty, and support and for certain kinds of assistance. Data in the next chapter, where the court cases that succeeded in defining service tenure as customary law are analyzed, will show that the assistance demanded often had clear labor content. The disputes in which the doctrine of service tenure was articulated involved male former slaves in Lagos who had left their owner and attached themselves to the household of another prominent man, or they involved male non-kin resident in a household whose origins were left ambiguous. The judicial formulation of service tenure was gender-neutral, but the law appears to have been invoked primarily to control male dependents. Discourses surrounding marriage and patriarchy were generally used in efforts to exert ongoing control over female dependents, as chapter 8 will show.

Lagosians apparently did not initiate cases that explicitly tested whether the Supreme Court would uphold service tenure where *ẹrú* and *àrótà* were concerned. By the late 1870s, following the controversy over the Alien Children's Registration Ordinance, it was well understood that individuals could not ask the court to overtly sanction the labor obligations of slavery. In a case that revolved around the land rights of slaves, however, Justice Smalman Smith stated in 1892 that he had repeatedly affirmed in judicial decisions the rights of landowners to "recover possession . . . where there is a tenure by service or rent or tribute and . . . [these obligations are] refused by tenants, and when such a tenant deliberately applied himself to injure or annoy his chief or [the chief's] family."[147] Smith's judgment may have signaled to some that service tenure did apply to slaves and *àrótà*, even if the principle was not tested in court when resistance was encountered.

Inside their households, Lagosians clearly sometimes used the threat of ejection to discipline people of slave origin who did not behave to their satisfaction.[148] Informants indicated, moreover, that owners continued to expect labor and support from the "domestics" who lived in their dwellings.[149] Nor have I found cases in which slaves defended their access to housing by arguing that they were being ejected for refusing to work adequately. Slaves were normally at a disadvantage where access to the Supreme Court was concerned, because of the financial, social, and cultural obstacles to mounting litigation, and this fact may in part explain their failure to initiate such cases. But other factors probably also played a role. For one thing, individuals would have needed to publicly avow their slave origin to defend themselves against ejection for failing to serve satisfactorily, something that those in the process of incorporation into the families of their owners or the wider community would normally have been loath to do. For another, the court was already starting to make clear by the 1890s, as subsequent data will show, that it would recognize only limited rights of *ẹrú* and *àrótà* in landed property to which they had acquired access through their owners. The service that slaves and their descendants owed in return for access to urban land and housing remained shadowy territory around which property owners and people of slave origin danced in their ongoing efforts to negotiate the terms of the relationship between them.

In one way, however, the emergence of the doctrine of service tenure clearly affected the experience of male slaves and *àrótà*. As the cases analyzed in the final chapter will make clear, service tenure subjected male *asáforígẹ* to obligations for labor and support that were not so different from those of slaves, and it gave overlords the legal power to enforce these obligations. By narrowing the social distance between the experiences of men who were first- or second-generation slaves and remained with their owners after the annexation and of those who fled by attaching themselves to the households of overlords, service tenure constrained the opportunities of male slaves. It limited the possibility that they could transform their lot by leaving their owners and entering a less exacting relationship of subordination with someone else. In this way, service tenure helped slaveowning families hold on to their male slaves.[150] The fact that *ẹrú* and *àrótà* were widely regarded as having more rights in the households of their owners than *asáforígẹ* did in those of their overlords reinforced owners' control. The surest route up and out of slavery may consequently have appeared to many bondmen to lie not in flight, but rather in continued loyalty to the families of their owners, in the expectation that they or their descendants would one day redefine their identity from within the family.

If the development of the concept of service tenure helped prominent Lagosians turn ownership of urban housing into an instrument for disciplining and controlling slaves and former slaves, as well as others who depended on them for a place to live in the growing city, then property owners also manipulated charges of misbehavior as an instrument of subordination. It was widely acknowledged that non-kin who resided in the dwellings of others could be turned out for refusing to show respect for the head of the household or its other senior members, repeatedly failing to support family religious or lifecycle ceremonies, causing trouble inside the household, or violating basic social norms. When a household head wanted to eject a slave, *àrótà*, or *asáforígẹ*, one of the most common ways of doing so was to argue that the individual had disregarded a fundamental standard of good behavior. Thus when Brimah Akilogun went to court to eject Faliyi, one of his deceased father's male slaves, from a family compound, he argued that the man had ravished girls and entertained thieves there.[151]

Slaves and former slaves might slowly redefine obligations associated with residence in the household of another through gradual incorporation into the family. However, they could quickly and decisively turn their backs on such obligations and redefine their identities as subordinate members of the household only by leaving it and establishing a residence of their own. People of slave origin therefore struggled to obtain privately owned housing not only because of the material benefits it brought, but also because of the reordering of symbolic behaviors of dependence and subordination that it made possible. When slaves or former slaves became successful, amassed sizeable landholdings, and built up compounds of their own that rivaled those of chiefs or other prominent Lagosians in size, wealth, and influence, it signaled their incorporation into the community as social and cultural equals and over time helped erase from public discourse references to their slave past. Female slaves achieved the economic success necessary to establish large landholdings and substantial compounds of their own much less often than male slaves. For them, the path to the redefinition of identity and incorporation into the community as equals of freeborn women was normally more constrained and passed through the thicket of concubinage, marriage, and motherhood.

So significant was the acquisition of privately owned land and, particularly, of a privately owned dwelling in the redefinition of the relationship between owners and slaves and overlords and their "boys" that it commonly triggered major conflict between them. The same soon came to be true of events typically associated with the assertion of private property rights in land, such as applying for a Crown grant or calling a surveyor to measure a plot. These acts often provoked reprisals, including physical assault, magical retribution, or ejection from the property in question, not only because the original landowners wanted to protect their rights in a valuable resource but also because they wanted to prevent their dependents from acquiring them. Once dependents did so, they could take advantage of the new opportunities and greater autonomy that private ownership of a house in Lagos usually brought with it. In time, applying for a Crown grant, having land surveyed, or attempting to alienate it came to be defined by the chiefs and elders who advised the colonial courts, and thus by the courts themselves, as types of bad behavior that constituted legitimate grounds for ejection from landed property.[152] The bitter struggle between Lagosians and their *àrótà*, boys, and strangers over rights in land sparked endless costly litigation that played out in court into the second half of the twentieth century.[153]

The Final Assault on the Land Rights of *Àrótà*

As Britain began to administer the new territory it acquired inland from Lagos in the 1890s and the imperatives facing the colonial state changed, officials rethought land policies and quickly retreated from encouraging the development of private property rights in land. Once it became clear that Britain would rule its vast inland empire through local authorities, officials began to fear that changes in land tenure that undermined the control of chiefs and elders over such a vital resource would threaten their power and consequently jeopardize the stability of the colonial state. During these same years, officials also began thinking more explicitly about the organization of production for export and, in Nigeria, committed themselves clearly to the path of peasant agriculture rather than large-scale foreign plantations. By the 1910s, some officials had begun to worry that a market for land and private property rights in it were spreading from Lagos Colony into the Yoruba Protectorate and would dispossess local farmers from the means of rural production. Policymakers feared that this process would drive landless peasants into the capital city, where they would become a "burden on the nation," descending into vagrancy and crime if males and prostitution and polyandry if females.[154]

The details of the evolution of land policy in this period are beyond the scope of this study and have, in any case, been analyzed elsewhere. Suffice it to say that the colonial government soon resolved to uphold communal ownership of land as a means of preserving the authority of local rulers and protecting the access of African farmers to land.[155] Places such as Lagos, where a market in land was already well developed and rights of private property had long made their mark, soon became sources of irritation and inconvenience. The realities of land tenure in Lagos and certain other towns and cities on or near the West African coast did not fit well with Britain's revised development plan for its now larger and much more important empire inland from the Atlantic.

By the turn of the twentieth century, the market for land in Lagos was too deeply entrenched to be eliminated, but even there Britain slowly and unevenly shored up communal tenure and the rights of certain chieftaincy families to land in and around the town. The shift occurred in fits and starts, largely through judicial decisions, which were sometimes inconsistent or contradictory, but occasional legislation reinforced what was taking place in the courts.[156] Around the same time, groups of *àrótà* also began turning to the colonial courts in efforts to uphold their rights in landed property to which one of them, or of their forebears, had obtained a Crown grant in his own name.[157]

The reinvigoration of communal tenure did not forestall further conflict and litigation over land rights, as Lagosians continued to invoke history and custom in support of competing claims and to contest social identities and relationships. When coupled with accelerating land shortages and land prices, it did, however, lay the foundation for attempts by some Lagos families to restrict more tightly what their *àrótà* could do with the land and housing they occupied. From the 1920s through the 1940s, representatives of these families went to court with increasing frequency to uphold the principle that *àrótà* could not sell, mortgage, or use independently in other sorts of ways landed property that their forebears had been granted by their owners. It did not take long for justices to begin ruling, in effect, that even when slaves or former slaves had obtained Crown grants to land in their own names, their descendants did not enjoy rights of private property in it. They instead occupied it only in trust, subject to the restrictions of customary law.[158]

This rolling back of rights that slaves, former slaves, and their descendants had often been able to exercise in land for which they held Crown grants, and sometimes had managed to assert even in property for which they did not, outraged many *àrótà* in Lagos. In Epetedo, the quarter occupied by Oshodi Tapa and his many slaves and other dependents when they returned from Epe in 1862, it spawned an explosive political conflict.[159] The judicial decisions did not, however, stop the sale and mortgage of land by *àrótà*.

The gathering storm over Lagos land led the government to conduct a major inquiry into the subject during World War II, when only the most pressing local problems received attention, and eventually to seek to settle matters through legislation. A series of ordinances enacted in the late 1940s affirmed the following principles: that land covered by Crown grants would henceforth be treated as communally owned family property, unless it had been sold or partitioned, and that even then the land became family property on the death of the purchaser except in special circumstances; that *àrótà* held land allotted to them in trust for their families and that if the family became extinct or forfeited the property for attempting to alienate it or other reasons, it reverted to the chief of the family that had granted it; and finally that dependents of Chief Oshodi in Epetedo were subject to similar restrictions, except that they could elect to terminate the rights of the Oshodi family in the land they occupied in return for monetary compensation.[160] This constriction of the rights of the descendants of slaves in land they had long occupied marked Britain's final abnegation of responsibility for emancipation. It ensured that *àrótà*, who continued to depend on the families of their ancestors' owners for the land and housing they needed to live in the city, would remain a distinct social group of inferior status.

8

Strategies of Struggle and Mechanisms of Control: Quotidian Conflicts and Court Cases

Slavery was such a sensitive subject in Lagos during most of the second half of the nineteenth century that Europeans and Africans were both normally disinclined to discuss it. Their reticence has left historians with a dearth of records that illuminate the institution's gradual demise. Silences on the subject of slavery pervade the records for most parts of colonial Africa, but in few places are they more deafening than in British Crown colonies such as Lagos, where the continued existence of slave labor on British soil was acutely embarrassing because it violated the statutory law of the nation that was holding itself up as the leader in the global crusade against slavery.

Oral data of the kind used by historians of the end of slavery in certain other parts of the continent later in the colonial period are more problematic in Lagos, where slavery's slow death began thirty to forty years earlier than in most other places. By the time I began conducting research on slavery in Lagos in the 1980s, few individuals survived who had been bought as slaves or been born of slave parents in the nineteenth century. Memories of slavery were more distant in Lagos than in parts of the continent where the institution started to unravel only in the 1890s.[1] Although descendants of former slaveowners would sometimes talk discreetly about their families' *àrótà*, few descendants of slaves would acknowledge their unfree ancestry and some appear to have erased it from memory.

Court records provide the only place in the documentation on Lagos where references to owners, slaves, and their descendants exist across the second half of the nineteenth century. Although anthropologists and historians have as yet only begun to explore what research using such sources can teach us about the African past, the extraordinary potential of these documents to illuminate long-term social and cultural change is by now well recognized.[2] This study of emancipation in Lagos concludes by analyzing a number of court records that offer a rare opportunity to look inside shifting relationships of labor and dependency during the late nineteenth century and see how the lives of different kinds of people—owners, slaves, and their descendants, as well as other sorts of subordinates—played out on the ground. A number of the records analyzed foreground the experiences of female and male slaves who left their owners, yet remained in Lagos, by entering other relationships of dependency. Thus they provide a valuable complement to the discussion of land law in the previous chapter, which illuminated the fate of slaves who stayed with their owners. The records examined here have been chosen not at random, but rather for the specific processes of struggle and change that they uncover and help explain. The approach in this chapter adds a human face to the end of slavery in Lagos. It yields additional insights, moreover, into the agency of different kinds of men and women in shaping the profound transformations that were altering their lives and in forging a new urban colonial social order.

The records examined in this chapter come from the few petitions I have been able to locate that were submitted to the early Slave Court and from the much more numerous judges' notes on civil cases heard by the Lagos Supreme Court, established in 1876. Unlike the Slave Court, the Supreme Court could not recognize and enforce the rights of owners in their slaves, but masters, mistresses, and their descendants soon found ways to shape cases against slaves and former slaves that fit the kinds of obligations the courts would enforce. Despite great asymmetries of power, moreover, slaves in the process of emancipation occasionally managed to haul their owners into court. In addition, owners, slaves, and their descendants sometimes appeared in court during cases that had nothing directly to do with slavery, yet when they did so gave testimony that sheds light on the shifting relationship between owners and slaves or prominent people and other sorts of dependents.

Court records were created for use in particular legal institutions, and the conventions of these bodies shaped what comes down to us in the sources. For this reason, it is essential to know something about the nature of the courts for which the documents analyzed in this chapter were produced—as well as about the process of the records' production—in order to evaluate the evidence they contain.

The Slave Court was an *ad hoc* tribunal presided over by members of the mercantile community and later the government, none of whom had formal legal training. Although we know little about its operation, the procedures of the court were probably comparatively informal. The tribunal's stated mission was to provide a place where slaves who were mistreated by their owners could find redress and perhaps redeem themselves, but, with a few exceptions, the records of the court that survive were submitted by slaveowners or their representatives seeking to enforce obligations of slavery.[3] These records take the form of petitions of under five hundred words written by the petitioner or another African—probably a friend or professional letter-writer, judging from their rudimentary English usage. The documents state the owners' concerns regarding their slaves and implicitly or explicitly beg the court for help in dealing with them. While the outcome of the petitions is never revealed, the documents themselves often communicate strong sentiment on the part of owners and slaves and show something of the feelings of both.[4]

The Supreme Court was created in 1876 as part of an effort to systematize the colony's judicial administration. It had most of the jurisdiction, power, and authority of the High Court of Justice in England, and the laws in force in it included Common Law, Equity, and English Statutes of General Application. In contrast to policy in many other parts of Africa later in the colonial period, the Lagos government did not officially recognize African courts and incorporate them into its legal system. Even so, African forums for dispute settlement continued to function, and the state tolerated their intervention in civil matters, although it claimed exclusive jurisdiction in criminal affairs. The Supreme Court, however, was the official court of first instance for all civil cases involving claims valued at more than £25, and suits involving lesser amounts could be appealed to it from Magistrates' Courts.[5]

The ordinance that established the Supreme Court explicitly stated that nothing in the legislation should deprive "natives" of the benefit of their own "law and custom," unless specific practices were "repugnant to natural justice, equity, and good conscience" or incompatible with local statute.[6] In fact, Supreme Court judges commonly sought to decide cases between locals according to what they understood to be native law and custom. The early colonial state did not attempt, however, to codify local law for the guidance of the judiciary. When judges had questions about native custom, they called senior males from the community, designated assessors, to advise them. Over time, a body of precedent developed in case law that shaped legal opinion regarding native law and custom, as the discussion of land tenure in the last chapter demonstrated.

When an individual initiated a case in the Supreme Court, its registrar framed the conflict to fit specific categories of rights and wrongs over which the court recognized jurisdiction before issuing a writ of summons. If the plaintiff had engaged legal counsel, which became increasingly common as the century wore on, even among illiterates, that individual's lawyer had presumably already formulated the subject of the claim before approaching the registrar.[7] A number of scholars have remarked on the narrowing effect of colonial courts' treatment of litigation as cases involving clear-cut rights and wrongs, in which what were, from the point of view of the participants, highly personal and idiosyncratic situations had to be pigeonholed to fit the reach of some specific concept of legal wrong.[8] Far and away the majority of civil cases heard by the Lagos Supreme Court centered on land rights or contractual obligations involving debt. Whether or not the African litigants would have formulated their grievances as the court did is usually impossible to know. In general, however, Africans involved in dispute settlement construed "appropriate, relevant, and correct facts and arguments" much more broadly than did British colonial courts.[9]

The Supreme Court followed, albeit sometimes loosely, formal procedures that shaped processes of litigation both before cases came to trial and during courtroom encounters themselves. Those that structured courtroom conduct are of greatest interest here because of their impact on the way contestants expressed conflicts. Rules of evidence that affected what judges could take into account when deciding cases also bound the court, and these too probably influenced the verbal strategies of litigants and witnesses.[10]

When a civil case came to trial, the plaintiff was normally given time, after the opening formalities, to state his or her grievances directly to the judge, which was usually done in narrative form. If the plaintiff was represented by counsel, it seems fair to assume that the lawyer helped shape the content of the opening statement. After the plaintiff had spoken, he or she could be cross-examined by the defendant or the defendant's counsel and also by the judge. Although the questions asked on cross-examination are never included in the records, the replies are distinguished from other testimony and often read like answers to very specific questions. When the plaintiff had finished, his or her witnesses spoke, sometimes at length, and generally also in narrative form.

Once the case for the plaintiff was concluded, the defendant normally had an opportunity to speak, and when that person was advised by counsel, it must be assumed, as with the plaintiff, that the lawyer influenced what was said. After the defendant had spoken, he or she could also be cross-examined, and then the witnesses for the defense told their stories. In cases involving multiple plaintiffs, a representative of the group, usually the one with greatest influence or most seniority, normally spoke on behalf of the rest. If there were multiple defendants, it was not uncommon for more than one of them to testify. After the participants and their witnesses had spoken and the assessors, if called, had advised the judge, he rendered a decision in the case.[11]

The Supreme Court Ordinance charged the presiding judge with taking down in writing, at "every stage" in "every case," all oral evidence given before the court.[12] The Judges' Notebooks of Civil Cases, which I used in my research, appear to have served this purpose. The notes on individual cases typically take the form of multiple short and overlapping narratives written by the judge from what the litigants and witnesses said. These short narrative passages are punctuated by responses to questions asked on cross-examination. At the end of their notes, judges recorded their decisions in most cases.[13]

The Lagos Supreme Court records are quite detailed, sometimes to the point of including direct quotations, but they are not verbatim transcripts. What survives from the courtroom testimony was filtered through the mind of the judge making the notes, who, although instructed to write down "all oral evidence," no doubt listened for facts and arguments that he deemed relevant to the case and shaped what he wrote accordingly. That the judges' notes were written in English also presents challenges, because much of the testimony was given in Yoruba or another African language and had to be translated for the judge by the court interpreter, usually a Saro officer whose control of language gave him considerable unacknowledged power in the courtroom. While the judges occasionally included Yoruba terms such as *ẹrú* and *àrótà* in their notes, they more commonly employed English translations, losing much specificity in the process. Information in the court records is, therefore, often two removes from what was said in court. It is well recognized, moreover, that even verbatim transcripts in the original language fail to capture much telling non-verbal courtroom communication.[14]

In sum, the Judges' Notebooks of Civil Cases contain uniquely valuable records of conflict among Africans in Lagos, including some owners, slaves, and their descendants. It is important to bear in mind, however, that the conflict was framed to fit specific categories of dispute that the Supreme Court recognized and over which it would exercise jurisdiction. While African litigants and witnesses occasionally broke out of these categories and found ways to express concerns in their own terms, much court talk was shaped by British legal presumptions, practices, and procedures. The cases were reported on, moreover, by British judges listening for specific sorts of evidence and concerned with creating a record to satisfy specific legal and institutional requirements.

For all of their limitations, court records provide virtually the only sources that allow us to look inside the changing relationship between owners and slaves and prominent people and other sorts of dependents during the second half of the nineteenth century. The quotidian conflicts documented in them enable us to glimpse in sharp relief, if intermittent occurrence, some of the strategies that slaves and former slaves used to try to reduce obligations to others for labor and support and improve their access to housing, land, capital, patronage, and other vital resources in hopes, ultimately, of redefining their identity in the community and position in society. The records illuminate, at the same time, mechanisms that owners developed to discipline slaves and their descendants in an effort to maintain control over them. Beyond this, they show how rising entrepreneurs harnessed the labor and allegiance of the freed and runaway slaves from Lagos and elsewhere who were entering their households as dependents. The close analysis of selected court cases undertaken in this chapter demonstrates that owners, slaves, and their descendants both drew on indigenous customs and values and engaged new possibilities created by colonial rule and European commercial expansion in their efforts to reshape the relationship between them. Changes in land tenure, credit arrangements, and commercial practices spawned the most important of the new possibilities.

Lloyd Fallers argued in his work on law among the Busoga in late colonial Uganda that disputes arise from the "matrix" of wider social systems. He maintained that most societies have their own particular troubled areas of life—or "trouble spots," as he called them—from which disputes "sprout like weeds." Fallers believed that for this reason conflict and litigation within societies tends to fall into ordered and distinctive patterns.[15] Richard Roberts has used the concept of "trouble spots" in a quantitative study of cases from the provincial tribunals in the French

Sudan (1895–1912) to uncover strains in social relations during a period of rapid change and determine how they interacted with transformations in legal institutions to produce discernable patterns of litigation.[16]

The cases analyzed in this chapter grew out of and illuminate a "trouble spot"—shifting relationships of labor and dependency in early colonial Lagos. They have been selected for discussion, however, not on the basis of the kind of quantitative research that Roberts has undertaken with the brief and summary French records, but rather after careful qualitative study. The often long and verbally complex judges' notes from the Lagos Supreme Court are not best approached through quantitative investigation, because distilling and coding quantifiable variables from them would sacrifice too much rich textual information. On the other hand, the more extensive data in the Lagos court records allow me to move beyond simply identifying trouble spots. The stories of conflict in the Lagos documents often also illuminate turning points in strained social relations—in this instance between owners, slaves, and their descendants, as well as between prominent people and other kinds of dependents. The owner-slave relationship was sometimes redefined definitively at a particular moment in time, if for example a slave redeemed himself and performed the rituals of manumission, or if she ran away and severed all contact with her owner. Very commonly, however, slavery and indeed other relationships of dependency were renegotiated over time through a series of gradually shifting accommodations. The conflicts reported in the Supreme Court enable us to see critical junctures in the process of redefinition. They reveal events and behaviors that were regarded as so threatening to the status quo by one party or another that he or she initiated litigation in the Supreme Court to block it. This type of inquiry sheds light on developments that actors themselves perceived as decisive in the transformation of relationships. It shows, moreover, some of the ways that individuals responded to these developments. In aggregate, the cases analyzed in this chapter illuminate where pressure built up and ruptures occurred in relationships between Lagosians and their dependents.

Wider social systems provide not only the matrix from which disputes arise, but also the moral environment in which legal processes are embedded. Legal precepts, as Fallers reminded us, are not coextensive with the everyday morality of communities, but rather involve simplifications and rationalizations of it. When litigants went to the Supreme Court, they needed to persuade the judge not only that they had been treated wrongly by the standards of commonly accepted norms, but also that the treatment they had received was illegal.[17] At the same time, essentially moral claims underlay much legal argument. In the Lagos courts, litigants regularly invoked normative visions of the way social relations were supposed to be when presenting their claims. Most of the surviving petitions to the Slave Court were written by Africans and directly communicate how they represented wrongs committed against them, as well as what they hoped for from the court. British judges, on the other hand, turned talk in the Supreme Court into the texts that come down to us from that tribunal. Fortunately for our purposes, the judges' notes of what Africans said in the courtroom are sometimes sufficiently extensive to capture speakers' discursive strategies. Careful analysis of the Supreme Court records can illuminate how Africans constructed their claims in court, showing when they harkened back to the past and drew on a repertoire of moral meaning rooted in precolonial practices and when they appealed to new values associated with the increasingly commercialized, monetized, and contractual culture of the early colonial period.

Courtroom encounters usually reflect but a moment in an ongoing relationship.[18] They too often enable us to glimpse only a short interlude in the lives of parties who had a past prior to coming to court and would have some kind of a future together, even if one permanently changed by the experience of the legal proceeding itself. The fact that petitioners to the Slave Court and, to an even greater degree, litigants and witnesses in the Supreme Court commonly constructed narratives to frame what they had to say, however, often adds a diachronic dimension to the information in the court records. Indeed, as Sara Berry has observed of land cases in Ghana, parties in court regularly referred explicitly to history when presenting their claims.[19] The time perspective in a given case can occasionally be extended and the story fleshed out, moreover, by locating multiple cases that grew out of the same or related conflicts and analyzing them together to inform one another, as in the final two sections of this chapter. In addition, it is sometimes possible to link information in court records with that from other sources to piece together a richer and fuller picture than emerges from the court records alone.[20]

Because the colonial state in Lagos did not recognize African tribunals, the Supreme Court did not hear appeals from courts presided over by local elders and chiefs. When litigants came to court, however, they nonetheless sometimes told stories about having previously taken their disputes to an African authority and communicated the outcome of that process. For this reason, it is occasionally possible to glean from the court records information about prior stages in the conflict. By closely analyzing the multiple and overlapping stories in court records and, when possible, by linking data in these texts with that from other sources, it is often possible to gain insights into the actions and experiences of different kinds of individuals across time. That these methods can be applied to a number of cases involving slaves and former slaves, owners and former owners, as well as descendants of both, makes court records uniquely valuable for the study of the end of slavery in Lagos.

The three sections that follow analyze cases selected because they throw into sharp relief basic behavioral strategies employed by slaves who left their owners in an effort to redefine their place in the community. Equally significant, the cases expose to view important mechanisms that older slaveowners and rising new entrepreneurs developed as they struggled to hold on to slaves of their own or capture the labor and support of runaways who fled to their households. The sections are organized around three of the most fundamental institutional arrangements—marriage, service land tenure, and debt—in which late nineteenth-century mechanisms for controlling people were rooted and from which relationships of dependence developed to replace slavery.

Gender figures centrally in the story. Male and female slaves and former slaves enjoyed different opportunities in Lagos, and they also faced different constraints. Moreover, some of the new institutional mechanisms of subordination, as well as the cultural values and legal rights associated with them, affected men and women differently. Thus the cases analyzed in the final three sections of this chapter shed additional light on the role of gender in shaping the experiences of slaves, former slaves, and their descendants in early colonial Lagos. Because a number of the litigants were Muslims, Islam also enters the analysis, but in a more shadowy way, since it does not appear to have influenced behavior or discourse decisively.

Slaves, Wives, and Wayward Women

One of the most common ways for Lagos slaves of either sex to leave their owners was by constructing a new relationship of dependency with someone else, who would take the former slave into his or her household and provide protection, representation, and other types of social support in return for deference, allegiance, and labor of different kinds. Given the enormous demand for women's work and reproductive power, female slaves could readily abscond by entering the household of a man as his concubine or wife. Occasionally, however, female slaves left by going to live with another woman. Two of the surviving Slave Court petitions illustrate this phenomenon.

The first petition, written by a man named Oddunimi in July 1863, stated that a woman named Famuyiwas

> has now been with me for about fifteen years; being taken as a wife, and as such, she has been well taken care of fed and clothed. But some years back she walked away from me, wishing me to take the money paid for her; but I refused to do so, considering that it was improper to take money or sell one that has been a wife. In her roving about she had a child for another man. At the close of three years . . . , she voluntarily returned . . . to me with her child. But the child died afterwards.
>
> Some two years ago she ha[d] a child for me, and now she wishes to leave the child to me and go away; assuring me that she would redeem herself. I told her that she is a free woman that I would not take a cowrie or a farthing from her; but she . . . has . . . gone away, leaving the child to me.[21]

Oddunimi begged the court to detain the woman out of pity for his child, which was too young to be separated from its mother, as it was still nursing. He promised that once the infant was "strong," he would bring Famuyiwas to the Slave Court and set her free, concluding that he had done her no wrong, "as she would testify."

In the second petition, a man called Obashua complained to the Slave Court about Asatoo, a "maid" of his brother Adeogun's. According to the petition, Adeogun had "redeemed" Asatoo for 102 heads of cowries about ten years before and "trained" her within the family so humanely that nobody "who is not their neighbor knows she is a slave, but thought that she must be one of the family." Obashua stated further that "in order to make known to . . . Asatoo that [Adeogun did] not wish her for a slave, he gave her to his own son for wife." The young woman apparently did not want the union, however, because as soon as it was proposed, she "changed her conduct," according to Obashua, and began "going from house to house in search of men," sometimes remaining away for two or three days. The document claimed that no one chastised her when she returned home, but that they beseeched her only to avoid such conduct in future. Even so, the woman continued to "sleep out." Soon after, Asatoo stole some of her "husband's and mother-in-law's" clothes, and then she left altogether "to one her sister who wishes to redeem her." Obashua stated that his brother so loved the woman, despite her conduct, that he did not want to sell her, but that if she refused to return home he would "not be sorry" for the 102 heads of cowries he had paid for her "redemption." Obashua then pleaded with the Slave Court for help and counsel in the matter.[22]

These two Slave Court cases have a number of things in common. First, each involved a female slave who absconded from her owner. Famuyiwas's departure happened prior to the annexation, according to the petitioner, showing that even in the precolonial period slaves sometimes ran away. Asatoo's departure, on the other hand, occurred immediately after the annexation, during the moment of uncertainty about slavery in the early 1860s. The two cases cast light on strategies that women employed to leave their owners, although what we learn is limited by the fact that the events are communicated exclusively from the perspective of the male petitioners.

The first document indicates that a liaison with another man facilitated initial flight, but that subsequently the woman returned to her owner and then left him once more, to go we know not where. In the second case, the petitioner accused the female slave of staying away from home and seeking out relationships with other men, but ultimately she departed to live with a woman who offered to redeem her. The benefactor was defined as a "sister," which implies a hierarchical relationship, but not necessarily a biological one.[23] In both of these cases, a female slave managed to leave her owner by negotiating a relationship with someone else who could offer her help and protection, but who would undoubtedly also make ongoing demands on her. In neither case did the woman run to the Slave Court for support. In the second case, the female slave was accused of committing a further act of rebellion by stealing her "husband's and mother-in-law's" clothes before she left. If the accusation was true, the gesture struck a parting blow at the owner's family and also gave the woman material resources that would help her in her new life.[24]

The actions and arguments of the petitioners themselves also illuminate ways that male owners sought to retain control of female slaves after the annexation. These two men, like a number of others, quickly enlisted the short-lived colonial Slave Court in their struggles.[25] Perhaps most significantly, however, the first man identified the slave woman as his wife, while the second portrayed the conflict that provoked the case as developing when the owner sought to give the slave woman to his son as a wife. No matter what the past relationship between the male owners and female slaves, we see in these cases clear evidence of a fundamental way that men sought to achieve ongoing control over female slaves and legitimize it in the eyes of the early colonial state. They redefined the owner-slave relationship as marriage, which both African and European authorities openly accepted as giving men rights in women's labor and bodies, and called upon the institutions of the new colonial state to uphold the power of husbands over their wives.[26]

The petitioners further grounded their claims to the slave women in assertions of benign treatment of them, which is not surprising given that the Slave Court was supposed to free slaves who could prove abuse. One of the owners argued that he fed and clothed his wife, responsibilities that even freeborn women were normally expected to assume for themselves. Both of the men emphasized that the women had been dealt with kindly, saying such things as that the owners did not fight with them, call them slaves, or chastise them for misbehavior. The second petitioner stated that the slave woman was treated so well that only immediate neighbors knew she was a slave, while the first pointed out that he had taken his runaway slave wife and her child by another man back in after three years of "roving." The petitioner in a third case explicitly invoked the paternalistic ideology that overlay slavery, saying that he took a runaway slave woman, whom he had earlier identified as his wife, to be his daughter and sister. Only in this third case did the petitioner say anything about the labor the slave woman was expected to perform, acknowledging that he depended on her to cook for him, otherwise attend him, and "help do business" in the house.[27]

Redemption figured in all three of the cases referred to here. In the first, the petitioner made a point of stating that he had consistently refused it, both because he considered it improper to take money from someone who was his wife and because the woman was already free. This argument no doubt strengthened the man's moral appeal to the Slave Court for help in temporarily detaining the runaway woman out of pity for their suckling child. In the second case, payment of redemption figured as a clear second-best alternative. The petitioner stressed that his brother, the slave owner, so "loved" the errant slave girl that, despite her conduct, he did not want to sell her, implying that he would much prefer to have her return to his household. In the final case, redemption had already been awarded by the Slave Court, and the fact that the slave woman had failed to pay it opened the way for the owner to plead for her return.

The actions of the slave women who left their owners in these cases speak louder than the words of the men who professed kind treatment, paternalistic feelings, and even the freedom of their slaves to the commissioners of the Slave Court. That the women chose to leave their owners reveals something of their hatred of slavery. Indeed, the third petitioner recognized his female slave's feelings toward him, even if he was apparently unable to understand them, inveighing, "she hate me for nothing."[28]

While some female slaves elected to remain in the households of their owners, the behavior of the women in these cases shows clearly that they believed they would be better off apart from men who might claim the affection of fathers or husbands for them, but had also been their owners. In the second and third cases, the petitioners still recognized ownership rights in the women sufficiently that they felt entitled to the price of their redemption.

Supreme Court records and other sources on Lagos from the late nineteenth century are replete with references to women who exercised autonomy in their domestic and sexual arrangements. They contain numerous stories of women who refused men to whom they had been betrothed or deserted their husbands, as well as of women who stood up to pressure from kin in conjugal affairs. A girl named Oshunbunmi, for instance, was betrothed by her parents in 1882 to a man who paid bridewealth for her and performed other obligations of a prospective son-in-law. But when the girl was old enough to wed and the man went to claim her several years later, she told him saucily, "I do not want you any more. I've got a husband."[29] By the turn of the twentieth century, Lagosians were complaining bitterly about girls who ran away to live with men without the consent of kin. They lamented the breakdown of patriarchal control over marriage and the loss of "regulation, restriction, and safeguard" in domestic and sexual life.[30] "It costs a woman nothing," one writer moaned, "to exchange her husband for another man."[31] Someone else worried that "[t]he sanctity [of] domestic relations . . . of parents and children, of husband and wife, of master and servant, and the chastity of the female sex . . . so strictly and jealously guarded under patriarchal rule, have been sacrificed."[32] While women often resisted or ended a relationship with one man by entering a different one with another, they also sometimes did so by remaining with their own kin or going to live with a woman, like the subject of the second Slave Court case. Life alone was rarely an attractive option for women or men, because most individuals needed and wanted the security that attachment to a larger domestic group provided.

Men clearly believed that the economic, political, legal, and cultural changes that had taken place during the early decades of colonial rule had given women new autonomy and made them more difficult to control. Although impossible to prove quantitatively, this interpretation is historically plausible, and the qualitative evidence supports it. The growth of the palm produce trade, as well as the expansion of domestic exchange that accompanied it, created new economic opportunities for many kinds of people, including some near the bottom of the social order. These developments, some of which initially favored women, apparently increased the economic independence of certain females *vis-à-vis* their menfolk.[33] The spread of Islam and arrival of Christian missionaries and British officials, moreover, gave women new authorities to whom they could turn in conflicts with both their kin and men to whom they had been betrothed or married. The more gradual creation of colonial courts and consolidation of the colonial legal system reinforced this trend, to a certain extent. One man stated baldly, "We live under a law that gives women too much freedom"; while the "Report on the Yoruba" by educated Africans in Lagos concluded that the establishment of the colonial legal system had suppressed "paternal power."[34]

A number of contemporary observers also believed that new ideas about the self and the importance of the individual over and against collective kin and other groups, which they blamed on Christianity and colonialism, also encouraged women to act independently.[35] Again and again in newspaper articles and pamphlet literature, men worried about women who moved in and out of relationships with impunity. While these commentaries were written by literate men, there is no reason to think that their illiterate brethren held different views on the subject. After the turn of the century, observers began expressing outrage about the incidence of polyandry, suggesting that some women were entering multiple domestic and sexual relationships simultaneously.[36] It is not surprising that women seized new openings to exercise autonomy in conjugal affairs. Domestic and sexual relationships impinged directly and powerfully on the opportunities of women, who needed to think about them strategically, regardless of the other considerations that affected their behavior.[37]

Few women in most of these sources are referred to as slaves or the descendants of slaves. This silence is not surprising given the sensitivity of the subject of slavery within the colony and the fact that most of the written records were created by Europeans or educated Africans. In the Supreme Court records, however, we can glimpse Ramatu, the daughter of a slave, who after being promised by her father to the grandson of his owner in gratitude for permission to live in a house in the owner's compound, resisted by marrying another man.[38] In addition, we can recover the story of Lanlatu, a slave near the Niger, whose mistress hired her out as a carrier. On successive journeys to the river, Lanlatu met Q. F. Gomez, a Brazilian trader from Lagos, whom she eventually persuaded to help her escape to the city. There the woman soon moved into Gomez's household, and before long she bore a child to him, which died. Within six months, however, Lanlatu quarreled with Gomez and left him, despite his efforts to persuade her to stay. Of greatest interest here is the way that Lanlatu managed to leave. Witnesses reported that she had "got married" to another man and that she was wearing, probably quite self-consciously, the clothing and jewelry of "newly married women."[39]

There is no reason to think that women of slave descent who had kin and friends on the coast, or even many first-generation female slaves who had lived in the town long enough to form communities of support for themselves, exercised less domestic and sexual autonomy than freeborn women in Lagos. To be sure, some slave women worked under close supervision on rural farmsteads manufacturing palm produce, processing foodstuffs, or engaged in other activities. Others were confined for periods of time inside urban compounds dyeing or weaving cloth, making other craft items, or performing domestic labor. For owners to realize the worth of their slaves fully, however, and for the slaves to be able to maintain themselves, these dependents needed to be allowed to move about the town, as well as to travel between it and locations elsewhere. This mobility gave slaves opportunities to meet others and form relationships with them. When coupled with the strong and competitive demand for wives and concubines in and around Lagos, it meant that many women of slave origin enjoyed wide latitude to leave their owners.

The alien girls brought into Lagos after 1877 may initially have been more vulnerable because of their youth and the fact that most of them lacked relatives and friends to whom they could turn for help and support in conjugal and other matters. The sources tell us little about the experiences of these youths, but it is not hard to imagine them, like the five slave girls whom Administrator Dumaresq returned to their owners in 1876, being absorbed into the households of Lagosians through slavery and domestic service. It was, indeed, the age and isolation of these girls, as well as their gender, that made them especially attractive to Lagosians as a source of labor and support. With luck, these girls might one day be integrated into the families of their owners through marriage to a son or trusted male dependent, as Adeogun tried to do with Asatoo in the 1860s or Abuduramanu with Ramatu thirty years later. Ultimately, however, they grew up and made acquaintances in Lagos, gaining access to the kinds of alternatives exercised by Asatoo and Ramatu.[40]

If women of slave origin in Lagos began to enjoy new latitude to leave their masters and mistresses during the second half of the nineteenth century, slaveowning families also struggled to hold on to the female slaves and *àrótà* who remained attached to their households. Men and women employed a number of age-old methods in their efforts to discipline their female dependents and restrict their autonomy, including physical force, magic, and witchcraft. Francine Shields has documented that Yoruba authorities accepted the use of sometimes severe physical coercion as a legitimate way for husbands and fathers to rule troublesome wives and daughters. If the patriarchal culture tolerated beating and restraining freeborn women within the family as a sometimes necessary practice, then female slaves and *àrótà* must have been even more vulnerable to corporal punishment.[41]

The wellspring of fear as an agent of social control was not fed, however, by the exercise of physical violence alone. Karin Barber has argued that a "view of the world as pervaded by 'enemies,' declared and undeclared, whose intentions are unknown but who can be assumed to be full of malice and envy" is deeply rooted in Yoruba culture and was clearly present in the nineteenth century.[42] J. D. Y. Peel has observed that people "at all levels feared what their rivals or 'enemies' (*ọta*) might do to them—if not openly, then by witchcraft, evil charms, or poison." Social or economic success of one kind or another commonly excited envy that could lead to harm perpetrated by witches (*àjẹ́*), who were normally female. Anger, if provoked, could "rebound in some form of hurt or harm."[43] Magic and witchcraft were turned against slaves, *àrótà*, and former slaves, as well as other members of society. Female dependents, including those of slave origin, needed to exercise caution in their relationships with both their superiors and peers lest their behavior provoke witches to destroy their fertility, injure their lovers, kill their children, ruin their economic enterprises, or undermine their activities in myriad other ways. Magic and witchcraft were deadly serious and few could ignore them, despite efforts by the colonial state to suppress such practices and by the missionaries to convince converts that "fetish" had no power against the followers of Jesus Christ.[44]

Witchcraft cut two ways. In addition to being attacked by witches, female slaves and *àrótà* could also be accused of being witches, which exposed them to severe punishment or even death. In modern times, witchcraft accusations have been directed most commonly against successful older women.[45] If the same was true in the second half of the nineteenth century, then women of slave origin may have been less likely than freeborn women to have been regarded as witches. Even so, some female slaves and *àrótà* fell victim to the charge of being witches. Consul Campbell told the story, for example, of two female slaves in Lagos who expressed support for Kosoko following his exile and were soon after accused of witchcraft by a chief, seized, and put to death.[46] Shields argues that male authorities leveled witchcraft accusations against women with increasing frequency in the second half of the nineteenth century, in an effort to maintain control over them, and some of the victims were undoubtedly women of slave origin.[47]

Law, Shields, and others have also found evidence that men used male-dominated masquerade societies—especially *orò* and *egúngún*—to counter the growing independence of women. In certain instances, disgruntled husbands, acting as individuals, called upon *egúngún*, which represented the ancestors, to rein in or punish obstreperous wives by humiliating, frightening, or physically abusing them. In others, male political authorities acting in an official capacity and implementing public policy called out *orò* to impose curfews, confine women to their homes, and limit their physical mobility. For when *orò* was about, women were not allowed out of doors under penalty of death. Law has also suggested that through the masquerade societies men found ways to get their hands on some of women's new income from palm produce production and trade, both by assessing contributions that the men then consumed during masquerade festivals and by pilfering women's wares in local markets during performances themselves. In the second half of the nineteenth century, moreover, male-dominated masquerades appear to have taken over much of the authority to police and punish witches from female cults that had exercised it previously, further evidence perhaps of efforts by men to counter the growing autonomy of women.[48] While much of this evidence refers to actions taken by the masquerades against women in general, rather than female slaves in particular, what the associations could do to women of free birth, they could also perpetrate against those of slave origin.

The widespread strategy of redefining the relationship between female slaves and their owners or other males in the owners' households as marriage, visible already in the Slave Court cases, also gave men mechanisms of ongoing control over women of slave origin. This smoke-and-mirrors act often enabled owners to enlist the support of indigenous and colonial authorities in their efforts, because both groups of men were concerned about women's growing independence and commonly sought to uphold the authority of husbands over their wives. The support on which owners could draw took a number of forms, from social pressure and not-so-friendly persuasion to physical coercion. After Sheriff Payne's indiscretion in 1872, colonial officials dared not openly sanction the use of force to pressure slave women to remain with their owners, but clerks, constables, and other Africans who worked for the government or had influence with it sometimes took matters into their own hands and used their positions to intervene privately in local affairs.[49] As the colonial state matured, much went on in the African community that reached the attention of British authorities only if a criminal complaint was lodged or a civil case was initiated. Although people at the bottom of the social order sometimes instigated legal proceedings, the obstacles to their doing so were great. Few Africans liked becoming entangled in the colonial legal system, but its procedures and practices—to say nothing of its fees—must have been particularly off-putting to the poor and powerless, such as most Lagosians of slave origin.

Redefining the owner-slave relationship as marriage had a further tangible benefit that worked to the advantage of owners. In local culture, husbands whose wives deserted them were entitled, except in special circumstances, to demand that the bridewealth they and their kin had paid prior to marriage be returned. Both indigenous and colonial authorities recognized this obligation and normally attempted to enforce it. Aware that they could be called upon to repay bridewealth, kin often pressured women within the family to remain in marriages they no longer wanted.[50] In point of fact, men rarely paid bridewealth for slave wives, but not having made such prestations did not stop some Lagosians from claiming that they had when female slaves and *àrótà* absconded from their households. Men could always argue that gifts they had given or payments they had made for other purposes constituted bridewealth, ascribe a monetary value to them, and demand its return.[51] This practice provided owners a modicum of protection by giving them grounds to demand monetary compensation when women of slave origin left their households. It continued, moreover, long after the colonial government had stopped requiring runaway slaves to pay redemption. The threat that owners could demand and potentially enforce the return of bridewealth sometimes deterred female slaves and *àrótà* from running away, because the value of what a prosperous man could plausibly claim to have given in marriage prestations far exceeded the monetary resources of most poor Lagosians.[52]

All of these data on the exercise of physical force, use of magic, witchcraft, and masquerades, and role of bridewealth repayment indicate that owners, household heads, and male religious and political authorities found methods rooted in local culture of resisting the new freedom that women of slave origin enjoyed after 1861 to leave the families of their owners and commence new lives elsewhere. Force and magic were certainly used against male slaves and *àrótà* as well, who also sometimes fell victim to witchcraft and the disciplinary authority of secret societies, if in different ways than their female counterparts.[53] Alongside the positive inducements that the ideology of reward for good service and possibility of incorporation into the family held out to slaves and their descendants to remain where they were hovered always the threat of severe retribution if they did not. In addition to the indigenous mechanisms of control open to them, however, Lagosians also soon forged new methods of disciplining people of slave origin out of the changes occurring in land law and commercial culture.

Ownership of Urban Housing as a Mechanism of Control

Data in chapter 7 have shown that landowners in the town of Lagos were often able to turn the dependence of slaves, *àrótà*, former slaves, and strangers on them for access to land and, more particularly, housing into an instrument of control. So long as men and women in Lagos depended on owners or overlords for a place to live in the town, the property owners had a means of disciplining their behavior. This mechanism of control was used against both male and female dependents, as subsequent data will show. It was especially significant, however, where males were concerned, because unlike their female counterparts, they could not normally leave the families of their masters or mistresses by entering domestic and sexual relationships with others. Slave men commonly absconded by asking to be taken into the household of a prominent male trader in Lagos as his *asáforígẹ*, or "boy." This arrangement usually left the former slave highly dependent on his new overlord not only for housing but also for the material and social assistance associated with residence in the household of a local big man. Such dependence rendered former slaves vulnerable to ejection, the threat of which became an effective means of disciplining and controlling them. A number of court cases expose this phenomenon to view and show how it was used against both males and females.

The first case, introduced in the final section of chapter 6, was initiated in 1879 by a Muslim trader, Brimah Apatira, against Oso, Opeluja, and Ogudula, the three former slaves who had entered his household as "boys" when they left their Brazilian owner.[54] The three men had lived for five years in a house which belonged to Apatira, giving him their "services as labourers" and "repairing" the dwelling in return for help of various kinds. Evidence internal to the case indicates that open conflict erupted between Apatira and the three men when they tried to redefine their obligations to him for labor. Apatira stated, "About three years ago [Oso, Opeluja, and Ogudula] ceased to work for me." Oso testified, "The plaintiff got annoyed and told us to leave when we did not spend all of our time working for him."[55] The trouble began, significantly, soon after two of the men managed to buy houses of their own, when they must have felt freer than before to resist their overlord's demands because they no longer depended on him for housing. Apatira evidently feared that home-ownership would weaken his control over his dependents, because he testified that soon after the two men bought their houses, he told them to leave his house or pay rent. The third man, who had acquired land but not a house, was allowed to remain in Apatira's dwelling.

Ordered to quit, the former slaves got "people," including a Muslim "priest," to beg Apatira to allow them to stay, rent free. Apatira testified that he had relented for six months but then insisted that the men vacate. When they refused, he initiated a suit against them in the Supreme Court. In this instance, the acquisition of privately owned housing marked the turning point in the relationship between Apatira and his two male dependents, who were newly freed slaves, because both sides recognized that it gave the men new autonomy to resist their overlord's demands for labor and probably also other types of support.

The court treated the conflict between Apatira and Oso, Opeluja, and Ogudula as a dispute over landed property. The registrar entered Apatira's claim as a request to recover possession of the house, establish title to it, and recover back rent. Perhaps Apatira, who like the defendants had not retained legal counsel, formulated his grievances this way; or perhaps the registrar imposed this formulation on his more open-ended complaints. The three ex-slaves, wittingly or not, played into this definition of the conflict when they defended themselves by arguing that they were, in fact, buying the house in question from Apatira. Oso maintained that they had given Apatira cowries when they entered the house and that these were partial payment for it. Apatira countered that the men had given him the cowries for safekeeping, a common practice between overlords and strangers, and that he had spent the money on the marriage of one of them and the brother of another. The former slaves asserted that Apatira had contributed to these causes in his capacity as their overlord and patron.

While the court narrowed the focus of the dispute to landed property, the conflict was in fact not only over that but also over the terms of the relationship between overlords and their "boys," and particularly over the labor obligations of the latter. The discursive strategies of both sides in court illustrate this point very clearly. Apatira drew on changes occurring in the wider culture to present his relationship with the three men as a straight exchange of labor for housing and assistance. In an effort to retain control over the labor of men who no longer depended on him for accommodation, he commodified the relationship by calling them tenants and demanded a cash equivalent, rent, when they stopped working to his satisfaction. Although two of the men had succeeded in acquiring houses of their own and the third could doubtless have lived with one of them, they may not have had the capital to pay back rent. Even if they had had it, they surely would not have wanted to spend their money in that way. Apatira culminated his argument by asserting that the relationship between him and his "boys" was rooted in a written contract, a modern legal arrangement associated with the penetration of commercial capitalism and advent of British colonialism. He produced a document, which the men acknowledged signing, purporting to be such a contract.

Oso, the headman of the defendants, presented their case quite differently, using the language of kinship rather than of exchange, money, and contract. Despite his ineffective attempt to prove that the three men were buying Apatira's house, he stressed their overlord's promise to "be as a father to us and to help us in any difficulty," stating, "We were to be his sons and do what he wished us to." By implication, fathers could not turn sons out "at any time." The relationship between them was certainly not based on an exchange of labor for housing and assistance, which could be converted into a monetary equivalent. Oso also introduced morality into the argument. Before the dispute came to trial, the three men had enlisted public opinion and Islamic authority on their side. In court, Oso concluded his testimony by stating that he and his companions had approached Apatira in the first place because they had heard he was "a good man." By this remark Oso signaled that social norms governing the relationship between overlords and their *asáforígẹ* existed in local culture, to which a good man should conform. Likened to the relationship between fathers and sons, these norms were rooted in custom, not contract. If Oso could accomplish nothing else, he could throw Apatira's virtue into question by pointing out his failure to abide by accepted social norms. In a community where upwardly mobile traders depended on the labor of dependents and where great competition existed for workers, Oso's argument was not without force.

The judge ruled in favor of Apatira, who recovered possession of the house, while Oso, Opeluja, and Ogudula were ordered to pay ten shillings in back rent. The prosperous Muslim trader had successfully used the colonial court to uphold his rights in landed property, but that was not all he had accomplished. He had also disciplined three subordinates and upheld the rights of overlords to the labor of their *asáforígẹ*. The judicial decision established the precedent that if such people failed to work to the satisfaction of their overlords, they could be ejected from housing they occupied and ordered to pay back rent. Ejection, moreover, would surely also mean the loss of protection, representation, and other types of social and material assistance that overlords were supposed to provide their "boys."

A second brief case involving Apatira and Oso came before the court about three weeks after the first. Ordered to vacate and pay rent, Oso, perhaps with the help of the other two men, tore doors, ceilings, and other improvements out of Apatira's house.[56] This behavior may have constituted an act of rebellion. On the other hand, Oso may have thought that he was within his rights to remove such things, because in some West African cultures strangers who improved their hosts' houses were entitled to take what they had added when they left.[57] Regardless of Oso's motivation, Apatira turned to the Supreme Court once again not only to enforce his rights in property, but also to uphold his authority over the three men. Threatened with damages, Oso pleaded in court that he had removed the doors through ignorance, expressed regret for what he had done, and promised to repair all of the damage. He then "begged" Apatira to drop the proceedings against him. Apatira's second case, in effect, compelled Oso, the leader of the men and clearly the strongest among them, to submit to his authority.

Having succeeded in using his rights in an urban house to discipline the labor of three dependents who were recently freed slaves, Apatira articulated the arrangement as "native law and custom" when he was called to the Supreme Court as an assessor in another case two years later. The judge recorded Apatira's pronouncement at the beginning of his notes on the case and clearly treated it as an authoritative statement of customary law regarding the relationship between Lagosians and their "boys." The judge paraphrased what Apatira said as follows:

> The native law and custom with our boys in relation to us is for them to live with us in the house or compound and we feed them, clothe them, treat them as if they were our own family, but pay them no wages, as should they require money we dash them some. If they conduct themselves well we get them wives and give them money to start for themselves. If they behave badly we send them away without anything. In return for this, they do our work and go to market or where we wish them to go.[58]

The legal precedent established in these cases made the labor obligations of *asáforíge̩*, many of them recently freed slaves, to their overlords explicit, exacting, and enforceable under colonial law.

A judicial decision in two similar cases, which the court ruled on together three years later, solidified the doctrine of service tenure and extended it to include obligations for deference, loyalty, and social and political support, as well as labor. These two cases further illuminate the use of ownership of urban housing to discipline male dependents. Chief Aṣogbon was the plaintiff in both cases. The identities of the defendants, Jinadu Ṣomade and Yesufu Okin, were left ambiguous, although both were referred to as "boys" of the Aṣogbon and his powerful client Jacob Ogunbiyi. Ṣomade and Okin both lived in a house that the chief's predecessor had granted Ogunbiyi for use by his male dependents, and they said they had been there since childhood. Ogunbiyi had once had some kind of a relationship with Ṣomade's mother, for whom he claimed to have bought a house, although he denied being married to her. The woman may been a slave belonging to Ogunbiyi or someone else, as neither she, Ṣomade, nor Okin appear to have had kinship ties to an established Lagos lineage. Ṣomade had clearly worked for Ogunbiyi, who said to him, "You superintended the building of my house. You were my groom and did other services."[59]

The Aṣogbon, who was not represented by legal counsel, went to the Supreme Court to have Ṣomade and Okin ejected from the house where they were living, for which he held a Crown grant in his predecessor's name. The chief had earlier sent Ṣomade letters demanding that he pay rent. In court, the Aṣogbon stated his grievance against Ṣomade as follows: "I was dissatisfied with the defendant's conduct and wished him to go. . . . You go about abusing me and Ogunbiyi, and you refuse to obey Ogunbiyi." Ogunbiyi himself seized the opportunity to shape native custom regarding the obligations of "boys" to their overlords by saying, "It is the law among natives that boys living in a compound should give service to their chiefs as they pay no rent. If a boy gives no service, he must pay rent. Six months ago [Jinadu Ṣomade] refused service." The Aṣogbon said of Yesufu Okin in court, "The defendant . . . has given up the service of his master [Ogunbiyi]. . . . When I went to go out the defendant never came with me as was his duty. [He] does no service for me . . . so I want his house."

These two disputes occurred in the wider context of a long and bitter feud then raging between Taiwo Olowo and a local chief known as the *apènà*, in which Dosunmu, the Aṣogbon, and Ogunbiyi initially sided with the latter.[60] Evidence in the court records indicates that Jinadu Ṣomade had recently sided with Taiwo against the Aṣogbon and Ogunbiyi, deserting them to become one of Taiwo's "boys," in the Aṣogbon's view. This treacherous shift of allegiance marked a serious rupture in the relationship between Ṣomade and his overlords and constituted the turning point in the conflict between them. Ṣomade's action provoked the Aṣogbon to discipline him by demanding first that he pay cash rent and then that he leave the house. Okin, on the other hand, had deserted Ogunbiyi and the Aṣogbon twelve years earlier by going to serve Taiwo at Eggan and Isheri. He had recently returned to Lagos, however, and resumed residence in the Aṣogbon's house, possibly to escape his new overlord, but perhaps to engage in foul play there on Taiwo's behalf. Ogunbiyi testified that the chief wanted to eject Okin because his presence was disturbing other "boys" in the house; however, the Aṣogbon was at the same time punishing the man for his disloyalty. The chief's two court cases sent a broader message to his dependents: he and Ogunbiyi would brook no disloyalty, and certainly not at a time of political crisis. One further aspect of these cases is revealing. Apparently, both Ṣomade and Okin expressed contrition when defending themselves in court. According to the judge's notes, Ṣomade pleaded, "I swear I am not one of Taiwo's boys now. I am willing to do what Aṣogbon says now." Okin repented, "I've done wrong. I've been led astray. I ask Aṣogbon . . ."

Like Apatira, the Aṣogbon and Ogunbiyi had gone to court and used rights in urban housing, which they defined as customary law, to uphold their authority over male dependents who were not kin but lived in their households. All three of these big men took advantage of the commercialization of land in Lagos to give the provision of housing a market value and then required that their "boys" pay it with labor, and in the latter two cases also with deference, loyalty, and support. If such dependents failed to satisfy their overlords, cash rent could be charged, which if it remained unpaid provided legitimate grounds for ejection under British law. These cases show how prominent Lagosians were able to use changes occurring in land tenure and economic culture to forge new means of enforcing a widespread relationship of labor and dependency that was emerging to take the place of slavery, and, indeed, had helped many male slaves to leave their owners. Justice Smalman Smith declared seven years later that he had repeatedly upheld the obligations of "tenure by service or rent or tribute," suggesting that in the aftermath of Apatira's and the Aṣogbon's court cases, inhabitants of the town quickly caught on to the legal power that ownership of urban housing gave them over the male dependents who lived under their authority and did not fail to use it.

No cases have come to light that show Lagosians going to the Supreme Court to discipline people explicitly identified as *ẹrú* or *àrótà* in precisely the same way. Although slaveowning families sometimes privately threatened ejection from land and housing in their continuing efforts to control slaves and their descendants, as further discussion of the woman Ramatu's experience will show, they apparently stopped short of asking the Supreme Court to back them in these efforts. Lagosians must have understood, after the events of the mid-1870s, that the institutions of the colonial state could no longer intervene directly in support of slavery. If slaveowning families wanted the backing of the Supreme Court in forcing slaves or their descendants off of land or out of housing, they had to argue that the individuals had violated fundamental social mores, not obligations for labor and allegiance, and were therefore guilty of "bad behavior."

From another perspective, however, the very process of defining the relationship between dependent males resident in the household, many of whom were former slaves, and their overlords as involving legally enforceable obligations for labor, deference, loyalty, and support tightened the hold of Lagosians over male *ẹrú* and *àrótà*, by limiting their options elsewhere. Subsequently, men who were slaves or *àrótà* found that they might simply be jumping from the frying pan into the fire if they left the families of their owners by asking to serve someone else, never mind that they had heard their new overlord was "a good man." This reality put a special premium on the acquisition by people of slave origin of privately owned dwellings, in which they could establish households of their own—the surest way to redefine the demands that superiors could make on them. However, it also increased the appeal of incorporation into the slaveowning family as kin, which would gradually erode many of the disabilities of slavery.

The treatment of Ramatu, the daughter of a slave referred to in the second section of this chapter, and her family after she refused to marry the grandson of her father's owner shows that rights in urban housing could be used to discipline obstreperous women, as well as men, of slave origin. The grandfather and his son were both dead by then, but the grandson Abuduramanu's uncle responded by ordering Ramatu's father, his wives, and his children out of the house they occupied in a family compound. Whether because Ramatu's father, Awodu, realized that his accommodation and thus perhaps his livelihood were threatened or for some other reason, he soon after left Lagos for Ijesha, where he died three years later. His wives and children, however, remained behind in the Lagos house. Under pressure from a Muslim *imam*, who argued that it was wrong for the children of a slave to be turned out unless they had done something wrong, the uncle relented. But when the disappointed grandson came of age, he renewed the vendetta by informing Ramatu that he had obtained his family's permission to sell the house she and her kin inhabited. Abuduramanu was evidently quite serious, because he hired a surveyor to measure the land.[61]

The case between Apatira and the three former slaves from Ile-Ife and that between Ramatu and Abuduramanu yield tentative insights into the role of Islam in shaping the changing relationship between Lagosians and their dependents. In both cases, before the conflict landed in colonial court, the dependents had appealed to Muslim religious authorities to intervene on their behalf and help persuade the landowners not to eject them or, in the first case, to demand that they pay rent. There was nothing uniquely Islamic about the values the *imams* advocated on behalf of Ramatu, the daughter of a slave, or Oso, Opeluja, and Ogudula, Apatira's boys. The principle that slaves and their descendants and boys who had faithfully served their overlords should be allowed to retain access to housing they occupied, unless they breached fundamental social norms, was subscribed to by Lagosians who practiced Islam, Christianity, and indigenous religions alike. Nor was there anything specifically Islamic about the way Apatira, on the one hand, or Abuduramanu and his uncle, on the other, sought to discipline unruly dependents by ejecting them or charging rent. Apatira, a Muslim, Ogunbiyi, a Christian, and the Aṣogbon, a practitioner of Yoruba religion, all articulated the doctrine of service land tenure in much the same way. Ramatu, as well as Oso and his companions, had probably appealed to the Muslim *imams* not because they could be expected to advocate and uphold distinctive norms, but rather because of the religious influence and authority they might be able to exercise over fellow Muslims. In both cases, the strategy worked only temporarily. Apatira relented for six months, but he then invoked the authority of the secular colonial Supreme Court to enforce his demand for ejection and back rent. Abuduramanu's uncle was evidently swayed by the *imam*'s intervention, but when the young man himself came of age, he moved ahead with efforts to sell the house out from under Ramatu and her family.

All of the cases discussed in this section show the way that Lagosians were able to use their control of urban housing to discipline the behavior of dependents, most of them of clear slave origin.

Credit and Debt as Mechanisms of Control

Lagosians also found new mechanisms of domination and control in credit and debt, which were so pervasive in local culture, as well as in the market-based trading relations that had been expanding in the town since the mid-nineteenth century. In some instances, they employed actual indebtedness to discipline behavior that threatened their interests. Creditors, for example, not uncommonly tolerated debts for long periods of time, as seen in chapter 4, but then called them in, foreclosing on landed property if necessary, when their debtors behaved in ways that they did not like.[62] In other instances, however, traders fabricated claims of indebtedness in an effort to hold on to dependents against their will or punish those who challenged them. A number of court cases expose these processes to view.

Three interrelated cases grew out of conflict between Jinadu Ṣomade and Seidu Ebite, the slave introduced at the end of chapter 6 who left his owner by asking to serve Ṣomade as his "boy."[63] Ṣomade himself, it will be remembered, was a dependent of Jacob Ogunbiyi's, who figured in the case initiated by Chief Aṣogbon that was discussed in the previous section of this chapter. By 1879, Ebite had lived under Ṣomade's authority for sixteen years, trading on his overlord's behalf, supervising his more junior "boys," and showing him deference, in return for material assistance, social support, and promises that Ṣomade would one day buy Ebite land, give him a share of the profits from their trade, and help him set up in business on his own. At some point, Ebite began to press Ṣomade to fulfill these long-standing promises, and when Ṣomade failed, Ebite both refused to go to market for him any more and threatened to summon him to colonial court for services rendered for so many years.

Seidu Ebite did not follow through on this second threat, perhaps because he realized that he was unlikely to get what he wanted by doing so. Instead, a trader named Jose, whose prior relationship with Ebite is unclear but who was acting as his *aláàgbàsọ* or spokesperson in this situation, sued Ṣomade in the Supreme Court to recover possession of a house and land occupied by Ṣomade's mother. Both men were represented by legal counsel, Jose by the European Allan McIver and Ṣomade by the locally trained lawyer Charles Foresythe. Ebite claimed in court to have built the house, with some help from Ṣomade, on land that he had been granted by Chief Wajoba, Jose's now deceased brother. He also said that he had granted Ṣomade's mother permission to live in the dwelling. Ebite explained that he did not live there himself because he was Ṣomade's boy, and if he had lived in the house alone Ṣomade would have considered him "proud."[64] Jose and Ebite may have had a number of motives when they initiated the suit.[65] Most obviously, they sought to eject Ṣomade's mother from the house and, by inconveniencing her, to strike a blow at Ṣomade. Jose and Ebite's initial attempt to use control of landed property to attack

Ṣomade failed, however, when the court dismissed the case on the grounds that the children of Chief Wajoba, not Jose, were the proper plaintiffs.

The conflict between Ebite and Ṣomade did not end there. Ṣomade retaliated by hauling Ebite into court two months later and arguing that he was indebted to him for £106.13.6. Invoking the model of the new market-based commercial transactions that were becoming increasingly common in the town, Ṣomade, still represented by Charles Foresythe, argued that he had given Ebite goods on credit so that he could trade for himself, not to conduct business for Ṣomade. The overlord produced a passbook, moreover, of the sort that merchants and traders used to record debts in kind, as well as payments in produce deducted from them, which presumably showed a balance in his favor. Ṣomade further represented himself as having in fact introduced Ebite to a German merchant, Escherick, his own supplier, and stood surety for him so that he could obtain goods on credit directly. Ṣomade stated clearly that he and Ebite had been together for sixteen years, but that the day he took his "boy" to Escherick's was "the last day he did business with me."[66] Ṣomade undoubtedly told the story about taking Ebite to Escherick's to show that he had indeed fulfilled his responsibility as an overlord by helping his dependent establish an independent commercial relationship with a European merchant. Ṣomade signaled, by way of conclusion, that he had pressed Ebite to repay his debt only after the man had stopped working for him.

When it was Ebite's turn to speak, he denied any knowledge of the passbook. He portrayed his commercial relationship with Ṣomade in terms characteristic of those between Lagosians and their "boys," stating that he had traded as a representative of Ṣomade, not on his own behalf. He stated that when Ṣomade had given him goods to take to market, he had neither kept any of the profits nor been liable for any losses, but rather had turned all of the income over to Ṣomade. Ebite continued, "The plaintiff used to remunerate me by presents for my service. I never got into his debt."[67] Ebite went on to argue that when he began pressing Ṣomade to live up to his promises and fulfill his obligations as an overlord, Ṣomade endeavored to placate him, including by taking him to Escherick's, in an effort to retain Ebite's services as a dependent. Ebite also stated that at about the same time, he had begun getting goods "to go to market" for Fagbemi Dawodu, another successful local trader. It was then, Ebite claimed, when by implication he was on the point of transferring his labor and allegiance elsewhere, that Ṣomade had first threatened to charge him the value of prior trade goods. Ebite suggested by his remark that his overlord had acted in an effort to dissuade him from switching his service to Fagbemi and retain authority over him. Indeed, the turning point in the relationship between Ebite and Ṣomade appears to have been reached when Ebite made it clear to his overlord that if he did not keep his long-standing promises, Ebite would transfer his labor and allegiance to someone else. Ebite concluded his testimony by saying that after Ṣomade gave him Escherick's "paper," the two men had no more transactions.

Both men called witnesses whose testimony corroborated their own. The court subsequently called Ṣomade's clerk, who allegedly had made the entries in Ebite's passbook, from Little Popo, a town to the west. When the clerk never appeared, the case was apparently allowed to drop.

Ṣomade's and Ebite's representations of the commercial relationship between them were fundamentally different. On the face of it, the evidence favors Ebite. His portrayal of the way the men worked together was more consistent with the overlord-boy relationship admitted by both men than was the monetized exchange posited by Jinadu Ṣomade. In addition, a number of the statements made by Ṣomade's witnesses are implausible, such as a remark that there was never any profit to enter in Ebite's passbook, that he lost money every single time he went to market.[68] Finally, the facts that the clerk, a key witness for the plaintiff, never appeared and that the case was apparently allowed to drop prior to judgment suggest that Ṣomade ultimately realized that he was not going to be able to sustain a claim that Ebite was indebted to him in the British court.

But more important than who was telling the truth is what each side wanted to accomplish in this series of conflicts. After long service, Ebite was attempting to redefine his relationship with Ṣomade by pressing him to fulfill what Ebite represented as the customary obligations of good overlords. Had Ṣomade lived up to these expectations, Ebite would have been able to begin trading for himself, and, if Ṣomade had bought him land, perhaps eventually to have built a dwelling on it and established an independent household. The first change would have increased Ebite's autonomy and presumably also his income, while the second would have significantly reduced the demands that Ṣomade or others could make on him for labor and support.[69] When Ṣomade refused his dependent's requests, Ebite evidently enlisted Jose's help, and the two men commenced the first court case against Ṣomade for the reasons already explained. Around the same time, Ebite also began to diversify his options by initiating the relationship with Fagbemi Dawodu. He did so in part by going to market for the prominent trader.

Ṣomade responded to Ebite's actions by arguing that a market-based commercial relationship existed between them, drawing on the model of developments that had been taking place in the community for more than two decades. Ṣomade ascribed a cash value to the goods and equipment that he had given Ebite for the purpose of trade, as well as to the produce that his dependent had brought him, and he attempted to show that Ebite came up short and was indebted to him. Ṣomade had apparently first tried this line of argument outside the colonial courts. When that failed, he hauled Ebite before British legal authorities, who saw enforcing commercial debts as one of their primary responsibilities. Ṣomade may have hoped by doing so to frighten Ebite off leaving his service and thereby retain the man's labor and allegiance. If that failed and Ṣomade won his case, he would at least receive a cash award that compensated him for the loss of his "boy" and exacted a price from Ebite for challenging him. The charge of indebtedness had two further advantages. It implied that far from benefiting Ṣomade, the overall exchange between the two men had in reality benefited Ebite. This strategy underscored Ṣomade's generosity as an overlord, as well as Ebite's dependence on him. Finally, like Apatira's and the Aṣogbon's cases discussed earlier, Ṣomade's suit sent a wider message that "boys" could not challenge their overlords with impunity. But whereas Apatira, the Aṣogbon, and Ogunbiyi had used their rights in urban housing to discipline and control their dependents, Ṣomade attempted to employ the new system of commercial credit as the mechanism of domination. It is significant that he did not attempt to recover the value of the food, clothes, horse, money, and bridewealth that he said he had given Ebite, because these were widely regarded as forms of support that good overlords owed their most trusted "boys." And despite his effort to commercialize and monetize his trading relationship with Ebite as a way of punishing the man, Ṣomade was also attempting, throughout the case, to demonstrate that he was a good overlord and to protect his ability to attract other male dependents to his household and hold them there.

If wider purposes underlay what Ṣomade said in court, the same was true for Ebite. The dependent sought to show that Ṣomade had not been a reliable overlord; after extracting sixteen years of loyal labor and support, Ṣomade had failed to keep his promises. Ebite had been one of Ṣomade's senior "boys," in charge of eight more junior ones. As Ṣomade said, he had occupied a position "of confidence and trust" within his overlord's household.[70] Ṣomade had recently lost the service of at least one other "boy," Jinadu Akiola, for failing to assist him satisfactorily. The trader must have been worried about the loyalty of his other *asáforíge*, as well as about his ability to attract and hold new dependents. Disappointed in his aspirations and betrayed by the man who should have been "like a father to him," Ebite struck a blow at Ṣomade and perhaps also stirred up more junior "boys" in his service to rebel by broadcasting just what kind of overlord he had been. While Ṣomade, like Apatira, used the language of exchange, money, and contract to pursue his conflict with his "boys," the dependents themselves, in both cases, employed the language of kinship. Ebite and Apatira's dependent Oso likened overlords to fathers and "boys" to sons. They implied that the father-son relationship rested on an unbreakable moral bond, which could never be commodified and converted into a cash equivalent.

Jinadu Ṣomade and Seidu Ebite found themselves in court again in May 1879, about a month after the second case began, when Oruoloye, Abuduranami, and Amore, the children of Chief Wajoba, sued Ṣomade to recover possession of the land at issue in the first case. The plaintiffs argued, much as Jose had before them, that their father had allowed Ebite to build a house on the property, but that the land belonged to them. The house, they said, was a matter between the defendant and Ebite. Ṣomade countered that the land had belonged to him for fourteen years. He asserted that he had bought one portion of it, asked Chief Wajoba for another, and obtained a third from a man named Adesina. Ṣomade claimed that he alone had built the house which stood on the land, and that his "boys," excluding Ebite, had lived there until five years ago, when he sent his mother to inhabit the dwelling. Ṣomade argued that when he had asked Ebite to pay his trade debt, the man had "set up a claim to the ground."[71] The plaintiffs, he concluded, were "friends" of Ebite's. The court then called Ebite, who repeated in shortened form the argument he had made in the first case: Wajoba had given him the land to build on; he and Jinadu Ṣomade were trading together and built the house jointly; Ṣomade's mother went to live in the property with Ebite's permission. A number of assessors carried over from the first case, themselves overlords, advised the judge that as Ebite had allowed Jinadu Ṣomade to build on the land and as his mother had been in possession of the property for many years, Ṣomade was justified in claiming the land. The judge followed the assessors' advice and ruled in Jinadu Ṣomade's favor. Ebite and his friends had failed in their second attempt to drive Ṣomade's mother out of the house and strike a blow at her son.

Ṣomade may have been unable to hold on to the loyalty, labor, and support of one of his senior "boys," who succeeded ultimately in obtaining an introduction from him to the German merchant Escherick. He also failed to punish his rebellious underling by sustaining a charge of indebtedness against him. But Ṣomade did succeed in protecting his claim to the property inhabited by his mother and keeping it out of Ebite's hands. We have no way of knowing what subsequently became of the former slave, but he did not yet own the housing necessary to establish a residence of his own. He may have been forced to fall back for accommodation and, indeed, other forms of assistance on the relationship he had forged with Fagbemi Dawodu, or he may have gone to live with Jose. Either way, he remained a dependent in another man's household and thus was subject to his demands and authority.

A further case, *Taiwo v. Ekorwu, Ayiekoroju, and Okilu*, illustrates the way big men in Lagos used the system of commercial credit and allegations of indebtedness in an effort to control female dependents. There is no evidence that the defendants in this case were former slaves, although one of them almost certainly owned a female slave. But if employed against women of free birth, this strategy was surely also turned against those who were still or recently had been slaves, as the case between Jinadu Ṣomade and Seidu Ebite shows it was against men of slave origin. The plaintiff and defendants in *Taiwo v. Ekorwu, Ayiekoroju, and Okilu* told quite different stories in court.

The plaintiff, Taiwo Olowo, then near the end of his life and at the height of his power and prestige, represented himself and spoke first. The gist of Taiwo's claim, which his witnesses supported, was that some years before the three defendants had gotten into trouble at Ikorodu, a town on the northern shore of the lagoon, where they lived and Taiwo exercised considerable influence. They had approached him through an intermediary, Bakare Majolagbe, asked for help, and subsequently come to live in his Lagos household for a period of time. Taiwo asserted that the defendants were indebted to him for £35, the price of textiles that he had obtained from a European merchant for them to send to Ikorodu to placate their foes there. He acknowledged that the defendants had paid him £10 in installments, which his "boy" Odunsi was holding, because he, Taiwo, only accepted payments in full. Taiwo maintained that he had been very patient about the debt, because the defendants had little money, but that he now needed to be repaid. Like Jinadu Ṣomade, he introduced a book in which he claimed to have recorded the debt. Finally, Taiwo denied that the third defendant Okilu had ever been his wife, stating, "She did not cook for me."[72]

The defendants were represented by the English-trained barrister J. E. Shyngle, and he may have influenced their discursive strategies. When it was their turn to speak, Okilu tried to establish that she had once been Taiwo's wife. She said that she had run away from Ikorodu some years before, because "people" there would not let her have the man she wanted. She claimed that on reaching Lagos an intermediary, Bakare Majolagbe, had taken her to Taiwo, who had asked her to become his wife. Okilu asserted that she had lived with Taiwo as his wife for a number of years, and that her mother and brother had joined her in his household. The woman insisted that the cloth Taiwo had sent to Ikorodu was intended to repay bridewealth her kin had previously received for her. Okilu emphatically denied being indebted to Taiwo.

The defendants and their witnesses claimed that while living in Taiwo's compound, Okilu's mother, Ekorwu, had given Odunsi, one of Taiwo's "boys," £10 for safekeeping, which the old woman later repeatedly asked him to return, but to no avail. The defendants and their witnesses maintained that at some point Okilu and Taiwo had quarreled, and Okilu had left Taiwo to live with another man. Witnesses on both sides revealed that about two months before the trial Okilu had gone to Taiwo's house, accompanied by one or two other people. While there, she and Taiwo had fought bitterly, about the money in Odunsi's keeping according to some evidence. What particularly interests me is that soon thereafter, Taiwo began pressing Okilu and her kin to repay a debt. When they failed to do so, he brought suit against them in the Supreme Court for £35.[73]

How are we to make sense of these stories? They agree on certain fundamental points. The first is that Okilu had run away from Ikorodu against the will of people there, and that in Lagos she and her kin had lived for a time in Taiwo's compound. The second is that Okilu's mother had given one of Taiwo's male dependents £10, although the accounts differ about why. The evidence indicates that later Okilu left Taiwo's compound and went to live with another man, taking her relatives with her. Their departure must have displeased Taiwo, even if Okilu was not his wife. Few big men in Lagos would have wanted to see a group of their dependents transfer their allegiance elsewhere. If Okilu had, indeed, been regarded as Taiwo's wife, her departure would have been an affront to his masculinity, as well as his authority. Finally, witnesses on both sides concurred that soon before the case came to court, Okilu had, in front of witnesses, stood up to Taiwo and opposed his will.

It is possible that Taiwo had genuinely understood his arrangement with Okilu regarding the cloth differently than she did. Even if Taiwo's representation of the transaction was sincere, however, he had tolerated her debt for many years. Then, after she and her kin had left to live with another man and Okilu had challenged Taiwo publicly, he took steps to force repayment of the money. It seems to me equally plausible that Taiwo had, in fact, initially sent the cloth to Ikorodu on Okilu's behalf, probably to repay her bridewealth, but certainly to placate aggrieved people there, so that she could enter his household legitimately. In that case, Okilu ought not to have been indebted to him, although Taiwo might reasonably have sued her new mate for the value of the cloth had he been willing to identify it as bridewealth. The judge must have found the defendants' claims more plausible than Taiwo's, because he ruled in their favor. The evidence in this case suggests to me that Taiwo invoked the new commercial practices that had taken hold in Lagos during the early colonial period, and in particular the widespread custom of lending goods on credit, to fabricate a claim that Okilu was indebted to him. It appears that he was demanding repayment of a fictitious loan as a way of punishing a female dependent who had both deserted him by going to live with another man and stood up to his authority. By denying that Okilu had ever been his wife, moreover, and representing the pieces of cloth as a loan rather than bridewealth repayment, Taiwo Olowo saved face and protected his reputation as a powerful man who could control his wives, even if not always the ungrateful strangers who sought refuge in his household.

The court cases analyzed in this chapter have further illuminated basic strategies that male and female slaves employed in Lagos during the early years of colonial rule to leave their owners, yet remain in the town. In them, we encounter female slaves who seized upon the strong demand for women's labor and reproductive power to desert their owners by going to live with other men as their wives or concubines. We see male slaves, on the other hand, finding a way out of slavery by asking to enter the households and live under the authority of prominent Lagosians looking for workers and dependents, in much the same way that strangers had long done when arriving in the community.

If the records reveal strategies that many slaves used in an effort to leave their owners, they also uncover powerful mechanisms that owners and other big men and women in Lagos employed to retain control of their dependents. In these cases, we see male owners and their kin redefining female slaves as wives and appealing to local and British authorities to help husbands maintain control over them, a ploy that often won support in Lagos as it did later elsewhere in colonial Africa. If this strategy failed, owners were sometimes still able to insist on their customary right to the return of bridewealth, generating a monetary compensation for their loss. These mechanisms supplemented physical violence, magic, witchcraft, and masquerades as means of disciplining female dependents. Redefining slave women as wives enabled owners to root their claims to ongoing control over them in patriarchal values indigenous to local culture, which British officials often sought to support.

The court records show that owners also found mechanisms of control in changes occurring in land law and commercial culture. So long as slaves, *àrótà*, and former slaves depended on prominent Lagosians for housing and other forms of assistance associated with living in the household of another, their owners and overlords had means of disciplining them. Where slaves and *àrótà* were concerned, ongoing access to housing was defined by the final quarter of the century as requiring "good behavior," an amorphous standard interpreted as conformity to basic social mores, which gave owners wide latitude to turn out people of slave origin with whom they became dissatisfied. In the case of dependent males living under the authority of overlords—commonly called "boys" in English—influential Lagosians had by the mid-1880s used the British courts to define the standard of behavior required more narrowly to include obligations for deference, social support, and periodic labor. This more explicit definition of the obligations of "boys" to their overlords narrowed the distance between them and the male slaves and *àrótà* who stayed with their owners or members of the owners' families, rendering an important alternative to slavery for men less attractive. Evidence in the court records further enables us to see how, when some "boys" sought to redefine their obligations for labor, deference, and support, their overlords responded by converting the value of the housing the "boys" occupied into a monetary equivalent (rent) and using failure to pay it as grounds for ejection. In these instances, overlords rooted their claims to the obligations of their male dependents in a new discourse of exchange, money, and contract associated with the spread of commercial capitalism and imposition of colonial rule. The dependents themselves, on the other hand, harkened back to the older cultural ideals of kinship and patriarchy in an effort to defend their interests.

Finally, the court records analyzed in this chapter have exposed to view the way owners, overlords, and sometimes husbands used credit and debt as instruments of domination and control. The pervasiveness of borrowing and lending in Lagos for commercial and other purposes created dense networks of indebtedness, which made it comparatively easy for superiors to find real financial obligations that could be called in to put pressure on dependents. The cases analyzed in the final section of this chapter show, however, that the spread of the credit and debit system of exchange in the second half of the nineteenth century also enabled prominent Lagosians to invent plausible claims of indebtedness, when looking for ways to constrain their subordinates. Although these ruses did not always succeed, the mere fact of being hauled into a British court and charged with indebtedness was sufficient to inconvenience and intimidate many dependents. Credit and debt provided powerful instruments of subordination in the young colonial city.

Conclusion

The slave trade and abolition, slavery and emancipation were closely related themes in the history of nineteenth-century Lagos. In the second quarter of the eighteenth century, the Atlantic slave trade on the Slave Coast of West Africa began shifting east from Ouidah, which had long dominated it, and by the final quarter of the century eastern ports had supplanted their western rival. Then in the first half of the nineteenth century, the eastern town of Lagos rose to preeminence in the commerce, thanks to its island security and proximity to new sources of supply in the interior, as well as to the policies and acumen of its political and commercial elite.

The rise of the external slave trade at Lagos turned what had previously been a crossroads of regional trade along the lagoon and the island capital of a minor coastal kingdom into an Atlantic port. Moreover, it increased the incomes of local *ọbas*, other members of the ruling dynasty, and certain chiefs, who dominated the role of commercial middleman at the town between foreign buyers on the coast and slave suppliers in the interior. These individuals also profited from taxes on the trade and resources of others. Lagos's ruling oligarchy invested its new income in trade goods, canoes, arms, consumption, and other resources that expanded its economic, political, and military power both within the kingdom and in relation to other states in the region. The growth in the wealth and power of prominent members of this group, however, also exacerbated factionalism inherent in the local political system, both by providing new resources with which to pursue rivalries and by raising the stakes in them. Factional conflict undermined the stability of the state and, in the long term, laid the foundation for British conquest and colonization.

In local culture, wealth and power were rooted in control of people—wives, children, wards, strangers, slaves, and clients—on whose labor, resources, and allegiance prominent men and women could draw. The growth of the slave trade at Lagos improved the ability of its political and commercial elite to compete for dependents of free birth both within the kingdom and across the region. It also led, however, to a dramatic expansion of slaveowning among the ruling oligarchy, owing to an increase in the supply of bondwomen and -men on the coast and of income with which to buy them, as well as to the advantages of slavery relative to other relationships of dependency. These advantages included tighter discipline and control and the possibility of more complete identification with the owner's interests. In the era of the foreign slave trade, slavery took on major new importance within the kingdom as a means of obtaining and holding vitally important dependents. At that time, the wealth and power of Lagos's ruling oligarchy came to rest on large-scale slaveowning.

Previous research on African slavery has debated its fundamental nature. Some scholars have viewed it as but one of a continuum of unequal relationships rooted in rights-in-people that existed in most precolonial African societies. These studies have emphasized that African slavery provided, first and foremost, a means of incorporating outsiders into kin groups and communities to increase their size and, ultimately, the power of their leaders relative to local and regional competitors. Other scholars have treated slavery as a dynamic relationship central to the organization and control of labor and to class relations in specific economic systems. As Martin Klein has recently observed, these different interpretations have been shaped in part by whether scholars studied more exchange-oriented and hierarchical societies in West Africa or on the East African coast or materially simpler and comparatively egalitarian ones elsewhere on the continent.[1]

The data presented in this study of Lagos show the fallacy of dichotomizing African slavery in these ways. In a culture where, on the one hand, production and trade were organized and accumulation and hierarchy began within domestic groups and, on the other, political and military power depended heavily on the number of people whose allegiance big men and women could command, Lagosians valued slaves *both* for the labor they performed and as a means of acquiring dependents on whom they could call for different kinds of support. While Lagosians rewarded a minority of comparatively visible slaves who performed important command, supervisory, or administrative functions by releasing them from manual labor or allowing them to work independently in return for a share of their earnings, most slaves were expected both to work for their owners in production, transportation, and/or trade *and* to serve them socially, politically, militarily, and ritually when the need arose. This study has argued that ideologies and processes relating to the transformation of slaves from outsiders to insiders—whether through reward for good service and upward social mobility or incorporation into the owner's kin group, which are central to the rights-in-people paradigm, were closely bound up at Lagos with the system of slave discipline and control. These practices made good sense in a context where much of the work that slaves performed required mobility, access to valuable resources, and even the use of arms, and where loyalty and allegiance were paramount.

Beyond its internal effects, the growth of the Atlantic slave trade at Lagos also led in 1851 to the kingdom's conquest and, a decade later, colonization by Great Britain, which was then shifting the focus of its antislavery campaign to Africa, source of the slaves. Abolition was bound up at Lagos with the development of a new export trade in palm oil, for which industrialization and urbanization were creating new markets in Europe. Many in Britain understood the growth of this and other new kinds of commerce as at once necessary for abolition and progress in West Africa and vital to the continued prosperity and stability of their own nation. By the time Britain annexed Lagos in 1861, key British officials had come to believe, however, that new types of trade capable of reforming Africa could not develop at Lagos under indigenous rule. Instead they required civilized, British command.

With an official British presence at Lagos after 1851 came Christian missionaries and European merchants, as well as repatriated former slaves from Brazil, Sierra Leone, and Cuba. The missionaries and repatriated slaves introduced new Christian religious beliefs and practices, as well as Western education, and the latter also contributed to the spread of Islam. Christianity and Western education affected the gender roles and domestic ideology of some converts, but in many respects they also reinforced local patriarchy.

The missionaries, merchants, and repatriated slaves all helped create a market for landed property in Lagos, where none had previously existed. In addition, they spawned the development of private property rights in land and houses, which rapidly became scarce and valuable resources on the island. Many of the Sierra Leoneans and some of the Brazilians worked in the new import-export trade and played an important role in expanding it. Along with the European merchants, they adopted commercial practices, such as the "credit and debit" system of exchange, that helped open the new Atlantic commerce to a much broader spectrum of the population than had been able to engage in the slave trade on a sizeable scale.

British colonization in 1861 resulted in Lagos's permanent loss of autonomy and slow development as an imperial capital. Within only a few years, colonial officials had established a strong executive, supported by a handful of essential departments and a civil police and armed militia recruited locally, largely from former slaves, as well as a system of courts that remained rudimentary until 1876. This lean colonial state ruled the colony directly and meddled endlessly in the affairs of interior peoples, despite only modest growth until the 1890s. It did so in the first dozen years of the state's existence primarily through a network of patron-client relationships that J. H. Glover, an early administrator, established with certain local big men, influential repatriates, and loyal Europeans. The new state threw its weight behind enforcing credit and other commercial relations that underpinned the expanding trade. While its courts recognized and often upheld local family ownership of land, they also favored the development of private property rights in land and housing until expansion into the Yoruba interior changed imperial priorities at the end of the century.

The early colonial state sought sole authority over criminal matters, but it allowed the *ọba* and local chiefs and elders to continue to hear many other kinds of disputes involving Africans, subject to appeal to English law. With the Christian missionaries, Muslim leaders, and British officials themselves, the colonial courts, however, introduced new authorities to whom Africans could turn in conflicts with one another. Although the British courts were supposed, after 1876, to decide disputes among locals according to "native law and custom" unless their dictates were repugnant to "natural justice, equity, and good conscience" or incompatible with local statute, the repugnancy clause itself opened the way for British judges to interject nineteenth-century British cultural values into the public and private affairs of local peoples. The emphasis on native law and custom, moreover, created opportunities and incentives for local peoples to contest the substance of local traditions, in an effort to shape them to their own interests.[2]

Studies of the transition from the slave trade to the palm produce trade along the Bights of Benin and Biafra have disagreed about whether it occurred smoothly or confronted local elites with a "crisis of adaptation" that undermined their wealth and power, created political instability, and set the stage for the European partition of Africa.[3] The transition occurred in a different context at Lagos than in many other places. For one thing, the produce trade was more important in the economy of the town than produce manufacturing, although some of the latter occurred in nearby rural areas. For another, the transition coincided at Lagos with a number of other far-reaching changes, including British colonial rule, substantial immigration from Sierra Leone, Brazil, and surrounding African territories, and Christian and Islamic religious conversion. Each of these developments also affected the power and prestige of the *ọba* and chiefs and introduced competing sources of influence and authority. By the early 1860s, Lagos had become much more heterogenous demographically and culturally than most parts of its interior and many other towns on the coast. Moreover, overt control of the local state had shifted from Africans to Europeans.

Yet even within this new context, several of Lagos's big slave traders clearly made the initial transition to the palm produce trade smoothly and successfully. Some of them, in addition, engaged in limited production for export. At the same time, however, the new Atlantic commerce also created opportunities for other elements in the population. These groups included not only repatriates and immigrants from elsewhere, some of whom enjoyed clear commercial advantages, but also locals and a number of slaves. Most notable among the slaves were males who had served as warriors or performed administrative or supervisory functions for their owners and, in reward, were allowed to trade on their own behalf, following a pattern established in the era of the slave trade. Less privileged slaves, however, sometimes also broke into trade or production for export. Among this group, females probably benefited first, because they had earliest exposure to the new opportunities in the export sector, given that palm oil manufacturing and trading were initially considered women's work. During the early years of prosperity in the new Atlantic commerce, it was possible for people outside the old ruling oligarchy—including some slaves—to commence trading or producing on a small scale, make money from these activities, and expand their operations.

Many of Lagos's new palm produce traders and manufacturers, however, and certainly most of the female slaves referred to by early European observers, remained confined to small-scale enterprise. Large-scale produce trade and production required heavy labor inputs, and large-scale trade also demanded substantial capital, both of which created barriers to entry. Of the two resources, capital was the easier to come by, thanks to the rapid expansion of the credit system of trade, infusion of new currencies, and existence of indigenous cultural values that encouraged borrowing and lending. Once merchants, traders, and moneylenders began accepting title to privately owned land as security for loans, access to credit widened further and became more divorced from hierarchical social relationships. This last development benefited males more than females, however, because men enjoyed superior access to privately owned land.[4] Labor, on the other hand, remained scarce and subject to acute competition.

The heavy labor requirements of palm produce trade, transportation, and production led to a further expansion of slaveowning in and around Lagos during the third quarter of the nineteenth century. A simultaneous increase in other types of agricultural and craft production, as well as of trade in these commodities, to supply the growing urban market further intensified the demand for labor. Although Lagosians continued to use family and other types of non-family labor in their enterprises, slaves initially performed much of the work in the growing export and domestic sectors of the economy. During these years, slaveowning diffused more widely through the population than in the era of the slave trade, if it rarely reached the same large scale. Because the tasks that slaves performed often followed the gendered division of labor in local society, the expansion of palm produce trade and manufacturing created an especially strong demand for female slaves. However, Lagosians also began to use male slaves in these activities. A market for wage labor developed much more slowly at Lagos than those for land and capital, because the free exchange of labor for a monetary equivalent met the needs and interests neither of Lagos's successful new entrepreneurs nor of those at the bottom of the social order.

In addition to stimulating a further expansion of slaveowning, the rapidly growing demand for labor also affected the character of local slavery. It did so by increasing the value of the work that slaves performed in transportation, trade, and production relative to their other contributions. Colonialism soon curtailed the demand for slave warriors at Lagos. Thereafter, Lagosians continued to want slaves as a source of social and political support and as a means of bringing outsiders into their households and kin groups to increase their size. In the case of females, they also still valued the reproductive power of slaves. However, the importance of the work that slaves performed in transportation, trade, and production increased in the era of the commercial transition relative to other types of service.

After annexing Lagos, Britain did not respond to the expanding system of local slavery, or to the domestic slave trade necessary to sustain it, with the same moral purpose that it had to the external slave trade. British policy regarding slaveholding and slave dealing at Lagos evolved gradually between the 1850s and mid-1870s. *Ad hoc* measures adopted by officials and missionaries immediately before and after the annexation opened opportunities for a limited number of slaves to leave their owners. The males of northern origin recruited into the Armed Hausa Police were among the most important of these. From the late 1850s until the mid-1860s, however, officials in Lagos and London generally favored a system of apprenticeship for most slaves, following the model adopted in the West Indies in 1833. As in other parts of Africa later in the colonial period, officials feared that to end slavery in the colony immediately would create grave disorder and make it more difficult and costly to rule. Moreover, they regarded West African slavery as a mild institution that would die out naturally under the influence of legitimate commerce and British civilization.

When legal authorities in Britain disallowed the measures that were being introduced at Lagos to end slavery gradually, the colonial office advocated minimizing the problem by restricting British territory there to the narrowest possible extent, as had been done on the Gold Coast. This proposal conflicted directly, however, with the interests of local administrators, who were committed to defining the boundary of Britain's new colony widely enough to capture the lion's share of trade flowing to the coast from the interior. Faced with this contradiction, officials in West Africa fell back on the fiction that Lagos's slaves were already free and dealt with local slavery largely by denying its existence. British policy thus opened the possibility of redefining the owner-slave relationship, but largely left it to the slaves themselves to accomplish the task.

An 1874 ordinance prohibited residents of the colony from trading slaves and accepting pawns, but little was done to enforce it and subsequently British officials continued to wink at slave dealing as well as slaveholding on British soil. Then in 1876 and 1877 two scandals brought the ongoing trade in slave youths to public attention in Britain, embarrassed the local government, and led to the passage of an ordinance requiring the registration of alien children brought into the colony. In the course of popular resistance to this legislation and official discussion of it, a new discourse emerged that defined the purchase of slaves in the interior for use in the colony as a benevolent act of redemption and made the sale and export of slaves from Lagos, rather than their purchase and import, the primary problem. Data collected under the 1877 ordinance indicate that young slaves continued to be imported into Lagos to the end of the century.

In this environment of a growing demand for workers and dependents, ambivalent and sometimes ambiguous British policy regarding emancipation, and rapidly changing economic, legal, and social opportunities, owners and slaves began the process of redefining the relationship between them. Lagos slaves had a range of experiences during the first half century of imperial penetration. A minority left the colony in an effort to return home or migrate elsewhere, but the number remained small until Britain moved inland from the coast at the end of the century. Of those who stayed within British territory, some took advantage of the presence of British officials, the Slave Courts, or the Liberated African Yard to leave their owners and soon found themselves apprenticed to repatriates, Europeans, or locals. A few hundred males, primarily of northern origin, transformed their status through recruitment into the Armed Hausa Police, Civil Constabulary, or West Indian Regiment stationed in Lagos. Although the proportion of slaves who seized these opportunities can only be guessed at, it probably reached no more than 5 to 10 percent of the slave population in the first decade of colonial rule. Even so, the number was sufficient to alarm local and interior slaveowners. By the end of the 1860s, however, the Slave Courts and Liberated African Yard had disappeared and recruitment into the constabulary, military, and local militia had slowed.

Other fortunate slaves managed over time to obtain access to land and dwellings and establish independent residences, which—if not necessarily severing all relations with their owners—nonetheless increased their ability to manage their own time and resources. Some of these slaves were able, through Crown grants, judicial decisions, or long occupation, to assert private property rights in valuable land and housing. Doing so widened their access to credit, improved their ability to attract dependents of their own, and helped them engage in new income-generating activities. The male slaves who had served as warriors or performed supervisory or administrative functions and became successful produce traders provide the most visible evidence of this phenomenon, but their experience was not the norm.

Most slaves who left their owners in the years following the annexation did so not by establishing independent households, but rather by going to live under the authority of another man or woman in a new relationship of dependence. Females commonly turned to marriage or concubinage as a way out of slavery; males to a modified form of the overlord-stranger relationship. Evidence in the court records analyzed in the final chapter suggests that slaves chose these options not only when they lacked the material resources necessary to establish residences of their own, but also when they had them yet wanted the social, economic, and political advantages that could come from living under the protection of a prominent member of the community. In a highly contingent world, most Lagosians, but particularly those on the margins of society, still needed the representation and assistance of people more powerful and influential than they. Entering the household of a local big man or woman as a wife, concubine, or *asáforígẹ* offered the hope of such help.

This behavior on the part of slaves led to a resurgence in the importance of marriage, concubinage, and overlordship as ways of acquiring workers and dependents during the final four decades of the nineteenth century. These means became especially important once the decline of slavery speeded up after the mid-1870s. A number of Lagos's rising new entrepreneurs used marriage, concubinage, and overlordship to capture the labor and allegiance of slaves fleeing their owners and meet their own needs for workers and dependents, in an era when slavery was slowly ending and wage labor had not yet taken hold in the African population. The data on this subject presented here show, for the first time, how much of the very extensive labor needed for the development of the new palm produce trade was organized in West Africa's leading commercial and colonial capital in the aftermath of abolition.

A large number of Lagos's slaves, on the other hand, did not leave their owners in the years following the annexation, but instead remained attached to their households and families. These men and women often sought over time to redefine their opportunities and identities from inside their owners' families, by making incorporation into the kin group a reality. The presence of sizeable numbers of *àrótà*, or slave descendants, within Lagos families into the twentieth century provides the clearest evidence of this phenomenon.

This study has shown that as slaves and their owners jockeyed to redefine the terms of the relationship between them, a number of factors worked to the slaves' advantage. Owners had long allowed most of their slaves some time to work for themselves, and many had permitted those they trusted to work independently in return for a share of what they produced or earned. However, the work that slaves performed in the expanding fields of palm produce transportation and trade gave them new mobility both within the town and between it and markets elsewhere. These activities and produce manufacturing, moreover, allowed slaves access to the growing exchange sector. In the early years of prosperity in produce manufacturing and trade, and to a lesser degree thereafter, slaves could enter these occupations on a small scale, make money, and expand the scope of their operations. Finally, much of the work that slaves performed in transportation, trade, and produce manufacturing required skill, precision, honesty, and reliability, which, as studies of slavery in other parts of the world have shown, often gave bondmen and -women some leverage in negotiating the conditions of their lives and terms of their subordination. If making concessions to slaves' interests helped elicit high-quality work from them, then the tradeoff was often well worth their owners' while.

Indigenous ideas about the proper relationship between owners and slaves also sometimes worked to the benefit of bondwomen and -men in the process of emancipation. This study has argued that the ideologies of reward for good service, movement up and out of slavery, or, alternatively, incorporation into the owner's kin group were bound up in nineteenth-century Lagos with the system of slave discipline and control. Indeed, each of these ideals acquired new importance in the system of domination as force and sale declined as ways of punishing slaves in the early colonial period. Yet these local ideologies also gave slaves a measure of moral suasion in their dealings with their owners, as the testimony of elders in the court cases analyzed in the last chapter revealed. When owners lived up to their end of the ideological bargain, it worked to the advantage of the individuals in question, and sometimes to that of their kin, countryfolk, and friends as well.

Finally, the large and rapidly growing demand for people in and around Lagos as workers, wives, and dependents and, much more slowly, as wage laborers gave slaves alternatives. Once the presence of the colonial state undermined force and sale as means of control, owners soon learned that if they steadfastly ignored the interests of their slaves, then the slaves could go elsewhere. To retain slaves and their descendants within the family, many owners made gradual concessions to their desires for greater autonomy, better access to family-owned or other resources, and swifter redefinition of identity. This strategy sometimes led to absorbing the slaves or their offspring into the kin group, although memories of slave origin or ancestry often survived and could be invoked in later struggles within the family. However, the concessions could also entail permitting successful slaves to establish households and found lineages of their own with the consent of the slaveowning family, in hopes of retaining them as loyal clients. Male slaves benefited from this last option much more commonly than female ones. Slave women who left the families of their owners usually did so through marriage or concubinage.

If slaves enjoyed new opportunities and even certain advantages in the early colonial period, owners also discovered fresh mechanisms of domination and control. For one thing, Lagosians began importing considerable numbers of youths, initially many of them slaves and, into the twentieth century, a disproportionate share of them females. These young people were more vulnerable than adults would have been, and they were often easier to control. They also offered the possibility of more complete incorporation into the family and community than adult slaves did, because they were young and still developing cognitively and culturally.

In addition, many owners began to equate the enslavement of women and girls with marriage and betrothal. This strategy had two potential advantages. On the one hand, it sometimes increased the identification of female slaves with their owners' families and gave the women stakes in them, particularly when they bore offspring to a family member or a favored male slave. On the other hand, representing enslaved women as wives enabled owners to appeal to local and colonial officials for help in controlling those who became obstreperous or ran away to live with someone else. Both sorts of men were deeply concerned about maintaining the authority of husbands and fathers over their wives and daughters and commonly threw their weight behind upholding it. Patriarchy was one place where Victorian and West African cultural values overlapped and largely reinforced each other.

Furthermore, many of the household heads who took in male slaves leaving their owners, much as Lagosians had long taken in strangers, began redefining the overlord-stranger relationship to make the obligations of the latter for labor, support, and deference more explicit and, in the case of labor, exacting than they had been in the past. This strategy helped meet the demands of produce and other traders for workers as well as dependents. It also narrowed the social distance between slaves and the large number of male non-kin living under the authority of prominent Lagosians. In the long run, it helped tie many male slaves to the families of their owners, by making an important avenue of escape from slavery for men less attractive.

Finally, this study has shown that rich and powerful Lagosians found new ways of disciplining and controlling both slaves and other kinds of dependents in changes that were occurring in law, credit, and land tenure. Credit, already widespread in local culture, proliferated with the growth of the palm produce trade during the early colonial period. When coupled with the firm commitment of the colonial state to upholding credit obligations, this development enabled big men and women to ensnare slaves and other dependents in webs of debt that they could not repay and then use the threat of foreclosure on these loans to constrain their autonomy. The pervasiveness of credit also made it possible for Lagosians to fabricate plausible claims of indebtedness in an effort to punish and control dependents, as court cases analyzed in the last chapter showed. As profits from produce trade and production declined and interest rates rose in the final two decades of the century, the effectiveness of indebtedness as an instrument of subordination increased.

Developments in colonial land law, actively pursued by chiefs, members of their families, and prominent traders, also helped maintain the authority of Lagosians over their slaves and other dependents. While some slaves and former slaves managed to take advantage of changes in land tenure to obtain privately owned landed property during the early decades of colonial rule, many continued to depend on their owners or overlords for a place to live in the colonial city. In this context, a prominent Muslim trader with a reputation as a "good man" went to the Supreme Court in the late 1870s to uphold the principle that three recently manumitted slave men who lived under his authority needed to work to his satisfaction or pay monetary rent. Within only a few more years, chiefs and local big men had used the court to define and uphold the concept of "service [land] tenure," which they applied to an amorphous category of dependent males living under their authority. Those affected almost certainly included slaves and *àrótà*, as well as former slaves who had sought refuge in their households.

Service tenure was explicitly defined as including not only labor, but also deference and social support. Soon thereafter, the heads of certain slaveowning families turned to the Supreme Court to establish as local custom the principle that the use rights of slaves and *àrótà* in land and housing to which they had obtained access through the slaveowning family depended on "good behavior." In this instance, local authorities defined good behavior as conformity to fundamental social mores, not fulfillment of obligations for labor and allegiance. The principle nonetheless gave property owners wide latitude to eject slaves and *àrótà* with whom they became dissatisfied. It was also used to prevent these dependents from engaging in activities identified with the assertion of private property rights in the land and housing they occupied and thus to limit their control of valuable resources, which would give them new opportunities and autonomy.

Lagosians employed the emerging body of customary land law that they helped forge in the late nineteenth century to enforce the ongoing obligations of the many non-kin living within their households for labor, support, and deference. So long as people of slave origin in Lagos depended on others for a place to live in the growing colonial city, the property owner had mechanisms of control over them. Then, in the early decades of the twentieth century, a number of prominent landowning and former slaveowning families consolidated these gains through court cases and eventual colonial legislation that rolled back the rights of *àrótà* even in the land to which their ancestors had obtained Crown grants in the 1860s and in which they and their forebears had long exercised rights of private property.

In Lagos, the "queen" of Britain's nineteenth-century West African settlements, begotten of the slave trade but born of abolition, local slavery itself grew, transformed, and ended only very slowly in the colonial period. Its gradual, contested demise was shaped as much by the needs and interests of the owners and slaves who struggled to renegotiate the terms of their relationship as it was by colonial policy. The growth of the palm produce trade and imposition of British colonial rule created new opportunities for some bondwomen and -men to move out of slavery. Many did so, however, not by establishing residences of their own, but by entering the household of a different big man or woman in another indigenous relationship of dependency. This development enabled Lagos's rising new palm produce traders to meet their very considerable needs for labor long before work for wages took hold in the African community. Prominent household heads then found ways to tighten their control over these dependents and reproduce their subordination in the colonial state's long-term support for patriarchy and their own superior access to capital and landed property. Through their actions, slaves, owners, and descendants of both forged a new urban colonial social order.

Notes

List of Abbreviations

AEH	*African Economic History*
AHR	*American Historical Review*
APB	Arquivo Público do Estado da Bahia, Brazil
ASR	*African Studies Review*
AST, MPE	Archivio di Stato Sezione Prima, Turin, Materie Politiche Relative al Estero
BL	British Library
CEA	*Cahiers d'études africaines*
CJAS	*Canadian Journal of African Studies*
CMS YM	Church Missionary Society, Yoruba Mission Papers, Birmingham University Library
CO	Colonial Office Papers
COL	Colonial Office Library
CSO	Records of the Nigerian Secretariat, Lagos
FO	Foreign Office Papers
GP	Papers of John Hawley Glover, Royal Commonwealth Society Collections, Cambridge University Library
IJAHS	*International Journal of African Historical Studies*
JAH	*Journal of African History*
JHSN	*Journal of the Historical Society of Nigeria*
JNCC	Judges' Notebooks, Civil Cases, High Court, Lagos State
LLR	Lagos Land Registry
LPR	Lagos Probate Registry
LS	*Lagos Standard*
LWR	*Lagos Weekly Record*
NLR	*Nigerian Law Reports*
NNA	Nigerian National Archives, Ibadan
OR	Report of Col. Ord, Commissioner to Inquire into the Condition of British Settlements on the West Coast of Africa, Parliamentary Papers 1865.XXXVII.287
PP	Parliamentary Papers (House of Commons Sessional Papers)
P&P	*Past and Present*
PROL	Papers Relating to the Occupation of Lagos, 1861, Parliamentary Papers 1862.LXI.339
PRRL	Papers Relative to the Reduction of Lagos, 1851, Parliamentary Papers 1852.LIV.221

RHL	Rhodes House Library
RP	Papers of Sir Samuel Rowe, Record Office for Leicestershire, Leicester, and Rutland
RWCA	Report from the Select Committee Appointed to Consider the State of British Establishments on the Western Coast of Africa, Parliamentary Papers 1865.V.1
S&A	*Slavery and Abolition*
T	Treasury Office Papers
UIL	University of Ibadan Library
WALC	West African Lands Committee
WMQ	*William and Mary Quarterly*

Introduction

1. David Eltis, "The Transatlantic Slave Trade: A Reassessment Based on the Second Edition of the Transatlantic Slave Trade Database" (paper presented at the annual meeting of the American Historical Association, Philadelphia, Pa., January 2006).

2. David Brion Davis, *The Problem of Slavery in the Age of Revolution, 1770–1823* (Ithaca, N.Y.: Cornell University Press, 1975), 39–49; Howard Temperley, *British Antislavery, 1833–1870* (London: Longman, 1972), chap. 9; Philip D. Curtin, *The Image of Africa: British Ideas and Action, 1780–1850* (Madison: University of Wisconsin Press, 1964), chaps. 9–12.

3. P. J. Cain and A. G. Hopkins, *Innovation and Expansion, 1688–1914*, vol. 1 of *British Imperialism* (London: Longman, 1993).

4. A long debate has played out in the literature over the relative importance of external and internal forces of change in Africa during the era of the slave trade, which Patrick Manning usefully reviews in "Contours of Slavery and Social Change in Africa," *AHR* 88 (1983): 835–57. More recent contributions include John Thornton, *Africa and Africans in the Making of the Atlantic World, 1400–1680* (Cambridge: Cambridge University Press, 1992); and David Eltis, *The Rise of African Slavery in the Americas* (Cambridge: Cambridge University Press, 2000), chaps. 6–7. The goal, surely, ought to be not to show that one was more important than the other, but to better understand the relationship between them in specific times and places.

5. The former was, of course, a major goal of the nationalist historiography of the independence period. Classic texts include J. F. A. Ajayi and Robert Smith, *Yoruba Warfare in the Nineteenth Century* (Cambridge: Cambridge University Press, 1964); Bolanle Awe, "The Ajele System (A Study of Ibadan Imperialism in the Nineteenth Century)," *JHSN* 3 (1964): 47–60; Bolanle Awe, "The End of an Experiment: The Collapse of the Ibadan Empire, 1877–1893," *JHSN* 3 (1965): 221–30; J. D. Omer-Cooper, *The Zulu Aftermath: A Nineteenth-Century Revolution in Bantu Africa* (London: Longmans, 1966); and Ivor Wilks, *Asante in the Nineteenth Century: The Structure and Evolution of a Political Order* (Cambridge: Cambridge University Press, 1975).

Nothing demonstrates the second point better than the history of blacks in modern South Africa. Suggestive titles include Charles van Onselen, *Studies in the Social and Economic History of the Witwatersrand, 1886–1914*, 2 vols. (Harlow, U.K.: Longman, 1982); William Beinart and Colin Bundy, *Hidden Struggles in Rural South Africa: Politics and Popular Movements in the Transkei and Eastern Cape, 1890–1930* (Berkeley: University of California Press, 1987); Belinda Bozzoli, with Mmantho Nkotsoe, *Women of Phokeng: Consciousness, Life Strategy, and Migrancy in South Africa, 1900–1983* (Portsmouth, N.H.: Heinemann, 1991); Clifton Crais, *White Supremacy and Black Resistance in Pre-industrial South Africa: The Making of the Colonial Order in the Eastern Cape, 1770–1865* (Cambridge: Cambridge University Press, 1992); and Keletso E. Atkins, *The Moon Is Dead! Give Us Our Money! The Cultural Origins of an African Work Ethic, Natal, South Africa, 1843–1900* (Portsmouth, N.H.: Heinemann, 1993).

6. Robin Law, *The Slave Coast of West Africa, 1550–1750: The Impact of the Atlantic Slave Trade on an African Society* (Oxford: Clarendon Press, 1991), 64–66; Sandra E. Greene, *Gender, Ethnicity, and Social Change on the Upper Slave Coast: A History of the Anlo-Ewe* (Portsmouth, N.H.: Heinemann, 1996), 41; J. D. Y. Peel, *Ijeshas and Nigerians: The Incorporation of a Yoruba Kingdom, 1890s–1970s* (Cambridge: Cambridge University Press, 1983), 44–45; R. E. Bradbury, *Benin Studies* (London: Oxford University Press, 1973), 133–56.

For Africa more generally, see Jack Goody, *Production and Reproduction: A Comparative Study of the Domestic Domain* (Cambridge: Cambridge University Press, 1976), 108–109; A. G. Hopkins, *An Economic History of West Africa* (London: Longman, 1973), 21–23, 35; Igor Kopytoff and Suzanne Miers, introduction to *Slavery in Africa: Historical and Anthropological Perspectives*, ed. Suzanne Miers and Igor Kopytoff (Madison: University of Wisconsin Press, 1977), 7–11; John Iliffe, *Africans: The History of a Continent* (Cambridge: Cambridge University Press, 1995), 76–96.

7. Kopytoff and Miers, introduction to *Slavery in Africa*, 9; Percy Amaury Talbot, *The Peoples of Southern Nigeria: A Sketch of Their History, Ethnology, and Languages with an Abstract of the 1921 Census* (London: Frank Cass, 1969), 2:431.

8. Ade M. Obayemi, "The Yoruba and Edo-Speaking Peoples and Their Neighbours before 1600," in *History of West Africa*, ed. J. F. A. Ajayi and Michael Crowder, 3rd ed. (Harlow, U.K.: Longman, 1985), 1:260.

9. Peel, *Ijeshas and Nigerians*, 30; J. D. Y. Peel, *Religious Encounter and the Making of the Yoruba* (Bloomington: Indiana University Press, 2000), 32.

10. Law, *Slave Coast*, 66; A. F. C. Ryder, *Benin and the Europeans, 1485–1897* (London: Longmans, 1969), 26, 35, 43–44; Ray A. Kea, *Settlements, Trade, and Polities in the Seventeenth-Century Gold Coast* (Baltimore: Johns Hopkins University Press, 1982), 20, 56; Ivor Wilks, *Forests of Gold: Essays on the Akan and the Kingdom of Asante* (Athens: Ohio University Press, 1993), 14, 41–90.

11. David Birmingham, *Central Africa to 1870: Zambezia, Zaire, and the South Atlantic* (Cambridge: Cambridge University Press, 1981), 31; Joseph C. Miller, *Way of Death: Merchant Capitalism and the Angolan Slave Trade, 1730–1830* (Madison: University of Wisconsin Press, 1988), 43, 47, 50; Claude Meillassoux, *Anthropologie économique des Gouro de Côte d'Ivoire: De l'économie de subsistance à l'agriculture commerciale* (Paris: Mouton, 1964); and Caroline H. Bledsoe, *Women and Marriage in Kpelle Society* (Stanford: Stanford University Press, 1980), 46–80.

12. Jane I. Guyer, "Wealth in People and Self-Realization in Equatorial Africa," *Man*, n.s., 28 (1993): 244, 259.

13. Philip D. Curtin, *The Atlantic Slave Trade: A Census* (Madison: University of Wisconsin Press, 1969).

14. Chapters 1 and 2 cite much of the new work on the Atlantic slave trade. David Eltis et al., *The Trans-Atlantic Slave Trade: A Database on CD-ROM* (Cambridge: Cambridge University Press, 1999), combined the new quantitative information into a single database, which the authors and Manolo Florentino have continued to update through new research. For a preliminary analysis of the new data, see Eltis, "The Transatlantic Slave Trade: A Reassessment."

15. David Eltis and David Richardson, "West Africa and the Transatlantic Slave Trade: New Evidence of Long-Run Trends," in *Routes to Slavery: Direction, Ethnicity, and Mortality in the Transatlantic Slave Trade*, ed. David Eltis and David Richardson (London: Frank Cass, 1997), 16–35; Robin Law, *Ouidah: The Social History of a West African Slaving Port* (London: James Currey, 2004), 1; Eltis, *African Slavery*, 182.

16. Walter Rodney, "African Slavery and Other Forms of Social Oppression on the Upper Guinea Coast in the Context of the Atlantic Slave Trade," *JAH* 7 (1966): 431–43; Walter Rodney, *How Europe Underdeveloped Africa* (Washington, D.C.: Howard University Press, 1982), 95–113; Joseph E. Inikori, "Africa in World History: The Export Slave Trade from Africa and the Emergence of the Atlantic Economic Order," in *Africa from the Sixteenth to the Eighteenth Century*, vol. 5 of *UNESCO General History of Africa*, ed. B. A. Ogot (Berkeley: University of California Press, 1992), 74–111; and Patrick Manning, "Contours," 835–57, and *Slavery and African Life: Occidental, Oriental, and African Slave Trades* (Cambridge: Cambridge University Press, 1990), chap. 7, provide examples of the first view, while John Fage, "Slaves and Society in Western Africa," *JAH* 21 (1980): 289–310; John Fage, "African Societies and the Atlantic Slave Trade," *P&P* 125 (1989): 97–115; Philip D. Curtin et al., *African History: From Earliest Times to Independence* (New York: Longman, 1995), 211–12; David Eltis and Lawrence C. Jennings, "Trade between Western Africa and the Atlantic World in the Pre-colonial Era," *AHR* 93 (1988): 936–59; David Eltis, "Precolonial Western Africa and the Atlantic Economy," in *Slavery and the Rise of the Atlantic System*, ed. Barbara L. Solow (Cambridge: Cambridge University Press, 1991), 97–119; and Eltis, *African Slavery*, 179–84, are associated with the second.

17. Law, *Slave Coast*, 38, 58–63, 221–24, 349–50; Manning, *Slavery*, 66–68; and Ralph A. Austen and Jonathan Derrick, *Middlemen of the Cameroons Rivers: The Duala and Their Hinterland, c. 1600–c. 1960* (Cambridge: Cambridge University Press, 1999), 25.

18. For other types of responses, see David Northrup, *Trade without Rulers: Pre-colonial Economic Development in South-Eastern Nigeria* (Oxford: Clarendon Press, 1978), chaps. 4–5; Austen and Derrick, *Middlemen*, chap. 2; Walter Hawthorne, *Planting Rice and Harvesting Slaves: Transformations along the Guinea-Bissau Coast, 1400–1900* (Portsmouth, N.H.: Heinemann, 2003); Caroline Sorensen-Gilmour, "Slave-Trading along the Lagoons of South-West Nigeria: The Case of Badagry," in *Ports of the Slave Trade (Bights of Benin and Biafra)*, ed. Robin Law and Silke Strickrodt (Stirling, U.K.: University of Stirling, Centre of

Commonwealth Studies, 1999), 84–95; and Rebecca Shumway, "Between the Castle and the Golden Stool: Transformations in Fante Society in the Eighteenth Century" (Ph.D. diss., Emory University, 2004).

19. Fage, "African Societies."

20. Philip D. Curtin, *Economic Change in Precolonial Africa: Senegambia in the Era of the Slave Trade* (Madison: University of Wisconsin Press, 1975), 177–87; Boubacar Barry, *Senegambia and the Atlantic Slave Trade* (Cambridge: Cambridge University Press, 1998); Martin A. Klein, "The Impact of the Atlantic Slave Trade on the Societies of the Western Sudan," in *The Atlantic Slave Trade: Effects on Economies, Societies, and Peoples in Africa, the Americas, and Europe*, ed. Joseph E. Inikori and Stanley L. Engerman (Durham, N.C.: Duke University Press, 1992), 25–48; James F. Searing, *West African Slavery and Atlantic Commerce: The Senegal River Valley, 1700–1860* (Cambridge: Cambridge University Press, 1993); Robin Law, *The Oyo Empire, c. 1600–1836: A West African Imperialism in the Era of the Atlantic Slave Trade* (Oxford: Clarendon Press, 1977); Robin Law, "The Atlantic Slave Trade in Yoruba Historiography," in *Yoruba Historiography*, ed. Toyin Falola (Madison: African Studies Program, University of Wisconsin–Madison, 1991), 123–34; Law, *Slave Coast;* Manning, *Slavery;* Edna G. Bay, *Wives of the Leopard: Gender, Politics, and Culture in the Kingdom of Dahomey* (Charlottesville: University of Virginia Press, 1998); A. J. H. Latham, *Old Calabar, 1600–1891: The Impact of the International Economy upon a Traditional Society* (Oxford: Clarendon Press, 1973), chaps. 2–4; Miller, *Way of Death*, pts. 1 and 2.

21. Robin Law and Silke Strickrodt, introduction to Law and Strickrodt, eds., *Ports*, 5.

22. Paul E. Lovejoy, *Transformations in Slavery: A History of Slavery in Africa* (Cambridge: Cambridge University Press, 1983); Manning, *Slavery.*

23. Kopytoff and Miers, introduction to *Slavery in Africa*, 3–81.

24. See, especially, Claude Meillassoux, *Anthropology of Slavery: The Womb of Iron and Gold*, trans. Alide Dasnois (Chicago: University of Chicago Press, 1991), 9–40; and Claude Meillassoux, ed., *L'esclavage en Afrique précoloniale* (Paris: Maspero, 1975). Martin Klein, *Slavery and Colonial Rule in French West Africa* (Cambridge: Cambridge University Press, 1998), 9–11, perceptively compares Kopytoff and Miers's approach with Meillassoux's.

25. Pivotal studies include Frederick Cooper, *Plantation Slavery on the East Coast of Africa* (New Haven: Yale University Press, 1977); Martin Klein, "The Study of Slavery in Africa," *JAH* 19 (1978): 599–609; Frederick Cooper, "The Problem of Slavery in African History," *JAH* 20 (1979): 103–25; Martin A. Klein and Paul E. Lovejoy, "Slavery in West Africa," in *The Uncommon Market: Essays in the Economic History of the Atlantic Slave Trade*, ed. Henry A. Gemery and Jan S. Hogendorn (New York: Academic Press, 1979), 181–212; Lovejoy, *Transformations;* and Richard Roberts, *Warriors, Merchants, and Slaves: The State and the Economy in the Middle Niger Valley, 1700–1914* (Stanford: Stanford University Press, 1987). Cooper's work, in particular, shows the influence of scholarship on American slavery.

26. J. F. A. Ajayi, *Christian Missions in Nigeria, 1841–1891: The Making of a New Elite* (London: Longmans, 1965), chaps. 1, 3; J. F. A. Ajayi, "West Africa in the Anti–Slave Trade Era," in *The Cambridge History of Africa: From c. 1790–c. 1870*, vol.

5, ed. John E. Flint (Cambridge: Cambridge University Press), 207–10; Christopher Lloyd, *The Navy and the Slave Trade: The Suppression of the African Slave Trade in the Nineteenth Century* (London: Longmans, Green, 1949); Howard Temperley, *White Dreams, Black Africa: The Antislavery Expedition to the River Niger, 1841–1842* (New Haven: Yale University Press, 1991). For anti-slavery's earlier impact at Cape Colony, in southern Africa, see Nigel Worden and Clifton Crais, eds., *Breaking the Chains: Slavery and Its Legacy in the Nineteenth-Century Cape Colony* (Johannesburg: Witwatersrand University Press, 1994); and Pamela Scully, *Liberating the Family? Gender and British Slave Emancipation in the Rural Western Cape, South Africa, 1823–1853* (Portsmouth, N.H.: Heinemann, 1997).

27. Frederick Cooper, "Conditions Analogous to Slavery: Imperialism and Free Labor Ideology in Africa," in *Beyond Slavery: Explorations of Race, Labor, and Citizenship in Postemancipation Societies*, by Frederick Cooper, Thomas C. Holt, and Rebecca J. Scott (Chapel Hill: University of North Carolina Press, 2000), 107–49.

28. Colonial states have too often been treated as static entities. For a compelling analysis of the transformations in an East African colonial state, see Bruce Berman and John Lonsdale, *Unhappy Valley: Conflict in Kenya and Africa* (London: James Currey, 1992).

29. Hopkins, *Economic History*, 128; George Brooks, "Peanuts and Colonialism: Consequences of the Commercialization of Peanuts in West Africa, 1830–1870," *JAH* 16 (1976): 29–54; Curtin, *Economic Change*, 230; Eltis and Jennings, "Trade," 945–47; Martin Lynn, *Commerce and Economic Change in West Africa: The Palm Oil Trade in the Nineteenth Century* (Cambridge: Cambridge University Press, 1997), 13–14, 113; Eltis, "The Transatlantic Slave Trade: A Reassessment," 17.

30. K. Onwuka Dike, *Trade and Politics in the Niger Delta, 1830–1885* (Oxford: Clarendon Press, 1956), chaps. 1–2; J. B. Webster and A. A. Boahen, *The Revolutionary Years: West Africa since 1800* (London: Longman, 1967), 193–207; A. G. Hopkins, "Economic Imperialism in West Africa: Lagos, 1880–92," *Economic History Review* 21 (1968): 586–92; Hopkins, *Economic History*, 125–26, 142–46.

31. Ajayi, "West Africa," 210–14; Ralph A. Austen, "The Abolition of the Overseas Slave Trade: A Distorted Theme in West African History," *JHSN* 5 (1970): 257–74; Patrick Manning, "Slave Trade, 'Legitimate' Trade, and Imperialism Revisited: The Control of Wealth in the Bights of Benin and Biafra," in *Africans in Bondage: Studies in Slavery and the Slave Trade*, ed. Paul E. Lovejoy (Madison: African Studies Program, University of Wisconsin–Madison, 1986), 203–33; Latham, *Old Calabar*, 111–12. Robin Law, "The Historiography of the Commercial Transition in Nineteenth-Century West Africa," in *African Historiography: Essays in Honour of Jacob Ade Ajayi*, ed. Toyin Falola (Harlow, U.K.: Longman, 1993), 97–115, perceptively reviews the literature on the commercial transition. For Law's interpretation of its impact on politics at the center of the Dahomian state, see "The Politics of Commercial Transition: Factional Conflict in Dahomey in the Context of the Ending of the Atlantic Slave Trade," *JAH* 38 (1997): 213–33. My book was largely completed before the publication of Law's new monograph, *Ouidah*.

32. Susan M. Martin, *Palm Oil and Protest: An Economic History of the Ngwa Region, South-Eastern Nigeria, 1800–1980* (Cambridge: Cambridge University Press, 1988), chap. 4; Susan Martin, "Slaves, Igbo Women and Palm Oil in the Nineteenth Century," and Robin Law, "'Legitimate' Trade and Gender Relations in

Yorubaland and Dahomey," in *From Slave Trade to "Legitimate" Commerce: The Commercial Transition in Nineteenth-Century West Africa*, ed. Robin Law (Cambridge: Cambridge University Press, 1995), 172–94 and 195–214; Francine Shields, "Palm Oil and Power: Women in an Era of Economic and Social Transition in Nineteenth Century Yorubaland (South-Western Nigeria) (Ph.D. diss., University of Stirling, 1997).

33. My book was completed before the publication of Trevor R. Getz's useful *Slavery and Reform in West Africa: Toward Emancipation in Nineteenth-Century Senegal and the Gold Coast* (Athens: Ohio University Press, 2004).

34. Frederick Cooper, *From Slaves to Squatters: Plantation Labor and Agriculture in Zanzibar and Coastal Kenya, 1890–1925* (New Haven: Yale University Press, 1980); Gerald M. McSheffrey, "Slavery, Indentured Servitude, Legitimate Trade, and the Impact of Abolition on the Gold Coast, 1874–1901: A Reappraisal," *JAH* 24 (1983): 349–68; Rebecca J. Scott, *Slave Emancipation in Cuba: The Transition to Free Labor, 1860–1899* (Princeton: Princeton University Press, 1985); Richard Roberts and Suzanne Miers, introduction to *The End of Slavery in Africa*, ed. Suzanne Miers and Richard Roberts (Madison: University of Wisconsin Press, 1988), 3–68; Thomas C. Holt, *The Problem of Freedom: Race, Labor, and Politics in Jamaica and Britain, 1832–1938* (Baltimore: Johns Hopkins University Press, 1992); Paul E. Lovejoy and Jan S. Hogendorn, *Slow Death for Slavery: The Course of Abolition in Northern Nigeria, 1897–1936* (Cambridge: Cambridge University Press, 1993); Worden and Crais, eds., *Breaking the Chains;* Toyin Falola, "The End of Slavery among the Yoruba," in *Slavery and Colonial Rule in Africa*, ed. Suzanne Miers and Martin A. Klein (London: Frank Cass, 1999), 234–42; Klein, *Slavery;* Scully, *Liberating;* Cooper, Holt, and Scott, *Beyond Slavery.*

In the United States, emancipation occurred more abruptly, but even so labor and other relations between former owners and former slaves took years to work out. See, for example, Jonathan M. Wiener, *Social Origins of the New South: Alabama, 1860–1885* (Baton Rouge: Louisiana State University Press, 1979); Eric Foner, *Nothing but Freedom: Emancipation and Its Legacy* (Baton Rouge: Louisiana State University Press, 1983); Ira Berlin et al., eds., *The Wartime Genesis of Free Labor: The Upper South*, vol. 2 of *Freedom: A Documentary History of Emancipation, 1861–1867* (Cambridge: Cambridge University Press, 1993), 1–82; and Julie Saville, *The Work of Reconstruction: From Slave to Wage Laborer in South Carolina, 1860–1870* (Cambridge: Cambridge University Press, 1994).

35. The phrase comes from Klein, *Slavery*, 141. See also Cooper, *Slaves to Squatters*, chaps. 2–3; Roberts and Miers, introduction to Miers and Roberts, eds., *End of Slavery*, 21–24; Lovejoy and Hogendorn, *Slow Death;* and Richard Roberts, "The End of Slavery in the French Soudan, 1905–1914," in Miers and Roberts, eds., *End of Slavery*, 284–87.

36. For brief discussions of this legislation, see David Eltis, *Economic Growth and the Ending of the Transatlantic Slave Trade* (New York: Oxford University Press, 1987), 21, 83–84; and Howard Temperley, "Abolition and Anti-slavery: Britain," in *A Historical Guide to World Slavery*, ed. Seymour Drescher and Stanley L. Engerman (New York: Oxford University Press, 1998), 12–13.

37. John Grace, *Domestic Slavery in West Africa* (New York: Barnes and Noble, 1975), 25–34; Raymond E. Dumett and Marion Johnson, "Britain and the Suppres-

sion of Slavery in the Gold Coast Colony, Ashanti, and the Northern Territories," in Miers and Roberts, eds., *End of Slavery*, 73–75.

38. Cooper, *Slaves to Squatters*, chap. 2; Holt, *Problem of Freedom*, chaps. 4–5; Foner, *Nothing but Freedom;* Saville, *Work of Reconstruction;* Lovejoy and Hogendorn, *Slow Death*, 199–203.

Although it was not a plantation society, officials and reformers at the Cape of Good Hope were also strongly committed to fostering the development of wage labor to supply white-owned farms and businesses. See Scully, *Liberating;* Worden and Crais, eds., *Breaking the Chains;* and Elizabeth Elbourne, "Freedom at Issue: Vagrancy Legislation and the Meaning of Freedom in Britain and the Cape Colony, 1799–1842," *S&A* 15 (1994): 114–50.

39. On the former, see, for example, Sara S. Berry, *Cocoa, Custom, and Socio-economic Change in Rural Western Nigeria* (Oxford: Clarendon Press, 1975); Claude Meillassoux, *Maidens, Meal, and Money: Capitalism and the Domestic Community* (Cambridge: Cambridge University Press, 1981); Frederick Cooper, "Africa in the World Economy," *ASR* 24 (1981): 1–88; Keith Hart, *The Political Economy of West African Agriculture* (Cambridge: Cambridge University Press, 1982); Jane I. Guyer, "Women's Work and Production Systems: A Review of Two Reports on the Agricultural Crisis," *Review of African Political Economy* 27–28 (1983): 186–92; Inez Sutton, "Labour and Commercial Agriculture in Ghana in the Late Nineteenth and Early Twentieth Centuries," *JAH* 24 (1983): 461–83; Gareth Austin, "The Emergence of Capitalist Relations in South Asante Cocoa-Farming, c. 1916–1933," *JAH* 28 (1987): 259–79; and Judith Carney and Michael Watts, "Disciplining Women? Rice, Mechanization, and the Evolution of Mandinka Gender Relations in Senegambia," *Signs* 16 (1991): 651–81.

Works that illustrate the latter point include Charles van Onselen, *Chibaro: African Mine Labour in Southern Rhodesia, 1900–1933* (London: Pluto, 1976); Shula Marks and Richard Rathbone, eds., *Industrialisation and Social Change in South Africa: African Class Formation, Culture, and Consciousness, 1870–1930* (Harlow, U.K.: Longman, 1982); Frederick Cooper, *On the African Waterfront: Urban Disorder and the Transformation of Work in Colonial Mombasa* (New Haven: Yale University Press, 1987); Bill Freund, *The African Worker* (Cambridge: Cambridge University Press, 1988); Patrick Harries, *Work, Culture, and Identity: Migrant Laborers in Mozambique and South Africa, c. 1860–1910* (Portsmouth, N.H.: Heinemann, 1994); and Charles van Onselen, *The Seed Is Mine: The Life of Kas Maine, A South African Sharecropper, 1894–1985* (New York: Hill and Wang, 1996).

40. A. G. Hopkins, "The Lagos Strike of 1897: An Exploration in Nigerian Labour History," *P&P* 35 (1966): 133–55. There is a dearth of literature on the origins of wage labor in southern Nigeria prior to World War I. In addition to Hopkins's article, Anne Phillips, *The Enigma of Colonialism: British Policy in West Africa* (London: James Currey, 1989), chap. 3, is another rare exception. Bill Freund, *Capital and Labour in the Nigerian Tin Mines* (Atlantic Highlands, N.J.: Humanities Press, 1981); Lisa A. Lindsay, *Working with Gender: Wage Labor and Social Change in Southwestern Nigeria* (Portsmouth, N.H.: Heinemann, 2003); and Carolyn A. Brown, *"We Were All Slaves": African Miners, Culture, and Resistance at the Enugu Government Colliery* (Portsmouth, N.H.: Heinemann, 2003), deal with wage earners in later periods.

41. For earlier examples of this approach and discussions of its recent popularity, see Pierre Verger, *Flux et reflux de la traite des nègres entre le Golfe de Bénin et Bahia de Todos os Santos, du XVIIe au XIXe siècle* (Paris: Mouton, 1968); Miller, *Way of Death;* Thornton, *Africa and Africans;* Eltis, "Precolonial Western Africa"; Bernard Bailyn, "The Idea of Atlantic History," *Itinerario* 20 (1996): 19–44; and Robin Law and Kristin Mann, "West Africa in the Atlantic Community: The Case of the Slave Coast," *WMQ*, 3rd ser., 56 (1999): 307–34. Verger's pathbreaking study was translated by Evelyn Crawford and republished as *Trade Relations between the Bight of Benin and Bahia from the 17th to 19th Century* (Ibadan: Ibadan University Press, 1976).

42. Published versions of Lagos traditions are cited in chapter 1. Sandra T. Barnes has worked extensively on traditions of Lagos chieftaincy families, including in such essays as "Lagos before 1603," cowritten with B. A. Agiri, in *History of the Peoples of Lagos State*, ed. Ade Adefuye, Babatunde Agiri, and Jide Osuntokun (Ikeja: Lantern Books, 1987), 18–32, and "The Organization of Social and Cultural Diversity: An Historical Inquiry," in *Culture and Contradiction: Dialectics of Wealth, Power, and Symbol*, ed. Hermine G. De Soto (San Francisco: EmText, 1992), 243–57. Takiu Folami, *A History of Lagos, Nigeria* (Smithtown, N.Y.: Exposition Press, 1982), also contains limited data relevant to a number of chieftaincy titles. My own interviews with representatives of Lagos chieftaincy families are cited throughout the text and included in the bibliography.

43. The bibliography cites the Parliamentary Papers that have been most important for my purposes. Large sections of the Foreign Office Slave Trade Correspondence (FO 84) were printed in the House of Commons Sessional Papers. I would like to thank Christopher Owen, then a graduate student in Emory's Department of History, for reading through the House of Commons Slave Trade Correspondence for me and locating material relevant to Lagos, often referred to before the 1850s as Omin, Kuramo, or variants thereof. For the decade of the 1850s, I read the Foreign Office Slave Trade Correspondence for the Bight of Benin in the original.

44. "Letter of Mr. Samuel Crowther to the Rev. William Jowett . . . Detailing the Circumstances Connected with His Being Sold as a Slave, Fourah Bay, 22 February 1837," *Church Missionary Record* 8 (October 1837): 217–23; "The Life of Joseph Wright: A Native of Ackoo," Methodist Missionary Society Archives, Sierra Leone, 1835–40. These narratives have been edited and annotated by J. F. A. Ajayi and Philip D. Curtin, respectively, and are published in *Africa Remembered: Narratives by West Africans from the Era of the Slave Trade*, ed. Philip D. Curtin (Madison: University of Wisconsin Press, 1967), 289–316 and 317–33. A third remarkably useful text, M. d'Avezac-Macaya, "Notice sur le pays et le peuple des Yébous, en Afrique," *Mémoires de la Société ethnologique* 2 (1845): 1–105, relevant to the area around Lagos in the 1810s, has been translated by Philip D. Curtin, annotated by P. C. Lloyd, and also published in *Africa Remembered*, 224–88.

45. Most of the letters seized were translated and reprinted in the House of Lords Sessional Papers, 1852–53, 22:327–66. I have been unable to locate the originals of these documents, which were sent by the British Foreign Office to Brazil in the nineteenth century. A few additional letters can be found enclosed in FO 84/886, Beecroft to Palmerston, 19 February 1852. I am grateful to David Eltis for

helping me locate the letters in the Lords Sessional Papers and to Carol Richards for translating the letters in the Slave Trade Correspondence.

46. Richard Roberts, *Litigants and Households: African Disputes and Colonial Courts in the French Soudan, 1895–1912* (Portsmouth, N.H.: Heinemann, 2005), 22.

47. Ajayi, "West Africa," 214.

48. RP, 18D33/1–18. I would like to thank Margaret Bonney, Assistant Keeper of Archives, for supplying me with photocopies of these documents.

49. When I began to work on these records in 1980, they were in terrible shape, covered with years of harmattan dust and piled on the floor of a room open to the elements at the top of the tower. The spines of many of the bound volumes had been broken, and some of the books had been torn apart. Whole sections of certain volumes were missing. I cleaned, sorted, reassembled, and shelved the Chief Registrar's Minutebooks of Civil and Criminal Cases and the Judges' Notebooks of Civil and Criminal Cases from the Lagos Supreme Court. When I returned three years later to continue my research, the volumes were once again strewn on the floor. A more professional staff was subsequently appointed, and the records are now in much better order. Where volumes were incomplete, and it was impossible to tell where one ended and another began, I have designated the volume number with a question mark. In such instances, cases can be traced by date and page number.

Omoniyi Adewoye, *The Judicial System in Southern Nigeria, 1854–1954* (Atlantic Highlands, N.J.: Humanities Press, 1977), 102 n. 18, cites a "Minute Book" of the Chief Magistrate's Court from the early 1870s and a "Criminal Record Book" covering the years 1871–75, giving their location as the High Court Archives. I did not find these records when I worked there.

50. Marcia Wright, "Justice, Women, and the Social Order in Abercorn, Northern Rhodesia, 1897–1903," in *African Women and the Law: Historical Perspectives*, ed. Margaret Jean Hay and Marcia Wright (Boston: Boston University, African Studies Center, 1982), 33–50; Martin Chanock, *Law, Custom, and Social Order: The Colonial Experience in Malawi and Zambia* (Cambridge: Cambridge University Press, 1985), chaps. 9–11; Allen Christelow, "Slavery in Kano, 1913–1914: Evidence from the Judicial Record," *AEH* 14 (1985): 57–74; Allen Christelow, ed., *Thus Ruled Emir Abbas: Selected Cases from the Records of the Emir of Kano's Judicial Council* (East Lansing: Michigan State University Press, 1994), 8–20, chaps. 8–9; Roberts, *Litigants*, 20–30, chap. 4.

51. Roberts, *Litigants*, 22.

52. Scully, *Liberating*, 135–43.

53. Roberts, *Litigants*, 13–20.

1. The Rise of Lagos as an Atlantic Port, c. 1760–1851

1. M. A. A. Abegunde, "Aspects of the Physical Environment of Lagos State," and B. A. Agiri and Sandra Barnes, "Lagos before 1603," in *History of the Peoples of Lagos State*, ed. Ade Adefuye, Babatunde Agiri, and Jide Osuntokun (Ikeja: Lantern Books, 1987), 6–9, 18–32; A. I. Asiwaju and Robin Law, "From the Volta to the Niger, c. 1600–1800," in *History of West Africa*, ed. J. F. A. Ajayi and Michael Crow-

der, 3rd ed. (Harlow, U.K.: Longman, 1985), 1:412–16; Robert S. Smith, *Kingdoms of the Yoruba* (Madison: University of Wisconsin Press, 1988), 72; Robin Law, "Trade and Politics behind the Slave Coast: The Lagoon Traffic and the Rise of Lagos, 1500–1800," *JAH* 24 (1983): 321. For contemporary descriptions of the lagoon, see Duarte Pacheco Pereira, *Esmeraldo de situ orbis: Côte occidentale d'Afrique du Sud Marocain au Gabon*, ed. and French trans. R. Mauny (Bissau: Centro de Estudos da Guiné Portuguesa, 1956), 130–47; P. E. H. Hair, Adam Jones, and Robin Law, eds., *Barbot on Guinea: The Writings of Jean Barbot on West Africa, 1678–1712* (London: Hakluyt Society, 1992), 2:664–69.

2. Algemeen Rijksarchief, The Hague, *Archief van de Nederlandische, Bezittingen ter kuste van Guinea*, vol. 83, Heyman to Roberts, 4 September 1716, quoted in A. F. C. Ryder, *Benin and the Europeans, 1485–1897* (London: Longmans, 1969), 157.

3. Robert S. Smith, *The Lagos Consulate, 1851–1861* (Berkeley: University of California Press, 1979), 4; J. Buckley Wood, *Historical Notices of Lagos, West Africa* (Exeter: James Townsend, n.d.), 9–16; John B. Losi, *History of Lagos* (Lagos: Tika Tore Press, 1914), 1–4; and Percy Amaury Talbot, *The Peoples of Southern Nigeria: A Sketch of Their History, Ethnology, and Languages with an Abstract of the 1921 Census* (London: Frank Cass, 1969), 1:79–90, record traditions of Lagos's origin.

4. Agiri and Barnes, "Lagos," 18–32; Ade Adefuye, "Oba Akinsemoyin and the Emergence of Modern Lagos," and B. A. Agiri, "Architecture as a Source of Nigerian History: The Lagos Example," in Adefuye, Agiri, and Osuntokun, eds., *History of the Peoples of Lagos State*, 34, 342–43.

5. Sir Alan Burns, *History of Nigeria* (London: Allen and Unwin, 1969), 38–40; A. B. Aderibigbe, "Early History of Lagos to about 1850," in *Lagos: The Development of an African City*, ed. A. B. Aderibigbe (Ikeja: Longman Nigeria, 1975), 1–5, 9; Smith, *Kingdoms*, 73–74; Law, "Trade and Politics," 327–28; Agiri and Barnes, "Lagos," 20–29.

6. Losi, *History*, 5. On the economic and political relationships among peoples along the lagoon, see Robin Law, "The Gun Communities in the Eighteenth Century" (paper presented at the annual meeting of the African Studies Association, St. Louis, Mo., November 1991), 6.

7. For discussions of domestic production and social hierarchy among Yoruba-speakers in the nineteenth century, see Samuel Johnson, *The History of the Yorubas* (London: Routledge and Kegan Paul, 1969), 113–18, 123–25; J. D. Y. Peel, *Ijeshas and Nigerians: The Incorporation of a Yoruba Kingdom, 1890s–1970s* (Cambridge: Cambridge University Press, 1983), 44–54; Toyin Falola, *The Political Economy of a Pre-colonial African State: Ibadan, 1830–1900* (Ile-Ife: University of Ife Press, 1984), 42–87; Kristin Mann, *Marrying Well: Marriage, Status, and Social Change among the Educated Elite in Colonial Lagos* (Cambridge: Cambridge University Press, 1985), 39–40; Kristin Mann, "Women, Landed Property, and the Accumulation of Wealth in Early Colonial Lagos," *Signs* 16 (1991): 699–701; Francine Shields, "Palm Oil and Power: Women in an Era of Economic and Social Transition in Nineteenth Century Yorubaland (South-Western Nigeria)" (Ph.D. diss., University of Stirling, 1997), 114–88; J. D. Y. Peel, *Religious Encounter and the Making of the Yoruba* (Bloomington: Indiana University Press, 2000), 47–87. N. A. Fadipe, *The Sociology of the Yoruba* (Ibadan: Ibadan University Press, 1970), 99, 105,

111, 147–57, and A. G. Hopkins, "A Report on the Yoruba, 1910," *JHSN* 5 (1969): 77, 81–82, contain data about these subjects in the early twentieth century.

8. John Thornton, *Africa and Africans in the Making of the Atlantic World, 1400–1680* (Cambridge: Cambridge University Press, 1992), 21–29; Pierre Chaunu, *L'expansion européenne du XIIIe au XVe siècles* (Paris: Presses Universitaires de France, 1969), 152.

9. Akin L. Mabogunje, *Urbanization in Nigeria* (London: University of London Press, 1968), 79; Law, "Trade and Politics," 324–27; Smith, *Lagos Consulate*, 2.

10. Ryder, *Benin*, 1–12; Ade M. Obayemi, "The Yoruba and Edo-Speaking Peoples and Their Neighbours before 1600," in Ajayi and Crowder, eds., *History of West Africa*, 1:300–306; Asiwaju and Law, "From the Volta to the Niger," 416; R. E. Bradbury, *Benin Studies* (London: Oxford University Press, 1973), 17–24, 44–75; Paula Girshick Ben-Amos, *Art, Innovation, and Politics in Eighteenth-Century Benin* (Bloomington: Indiana University Press, 1999), 12–20.

11. Ryder, *Benin*, 24–75; Law, "Trade and Politics," 331–33; P. J. Darling, "The Ancient Canoe Port of Benin," *Nigerian Field* 46 (1981): 40–51.

12. Andreas Josua Ulsheimer, "The First Voyage to Africa," in *German Sources for West African History, 1599–1669*, ed. Adam Jones (Wiesbaden: Franz Steiner Verlag, 1983), 40; FO 84/1031, Campbell to Clarendon, 4 April 1857; Law, "Trade and Politics," 330–31; Robin Law, *The Slave Coast of West Africa, 1550–1750: The Impact of the Atlantic Slave Trade on an African Society* (Oxford: Clarendon Press, 1991), 26–32, 118–27.

13. Obayemi, "The Yoruba," 268–312; Agiri and Barnes, "Lagos," 22–25. Ulsheimer, "First Voyage," 404, contains an early description of the governing council.

14. Wood, *Historical Notices*, 13–14; Losi, *History*, 3–4.

15. Ryder, *Benin*, 15–17; Asiwaju and Law, "From the Volta to the Niger," 419–28; Robin Law, *The Oyo Empire, c. 1600–1836: A West African Imperialism in the Era of the Atlantic Slave Trade* (Oxford: Clarendon Press, 1977), 47–242; Law, *Slave Coast*, 33–115.

16. Law, *Oyo Empire*, 150–57, 207–28; Law, "Gun Communities," 5; Law, *Slave Coast*, 30, 232–38.

17. Law, "Trade and Politics," 328. Also see Burns, *History of Nigeria*, 34; Aderibigbe, "Early History," 7; Robin Law, "Jean Barbot as a Source for the Slave Coast of West Africa," *History in Africa* 9 (1982): 163; Adefuye, "Oba Akinsemoyin," 35; and interviews with Chief Ishola Bajulaiye and Alhaji A. W. A. Akibayo. For the Benin and Lagos traditions, see Joseph Egharevba, *A Short History of Benin* (Ibadan: Ibadan University Press, 1968), 29; Losi, *History*, 4–7; and WALC, "Correspondence," Statement of the Prince Eleko, 179, and Statement of Obanikoro, 228–29. I am grateful to Sara Berry for a copy of the WALC materials.

18. Adefuye, "Oba Akinsemoyin," 35; Wood, *Historical Notices*, 23; Takiu Folami, *A History of Lagos, Nigeria* (Smithtown, N.Y.: Exposition Press, 1982), 108; interviews with Alhaji A. W. A. Akibayo and Chief Ishola Bajulaiye.

19. Agiri and Barnes, "Lagos," 21; Folami, *History*, 108, 125; Aderibigbe, "Early History," 8; Wood, *Historical Notices*, 24.

20. David Brion Davis, *Slavery and Human Progress* (New York: Oxford University Press, 1984), 51–82; Sidney W. Mintz, *Sweetness and Power: The Place of*

Sugar in Modern History (New York: Viking, 1985), 19–150; Philip D. Curtin, *The Rise and Fall of the Plantation Complex: Essays in Atlantic History* (Cambridge: Cambridge University Press, 1990), 3–110; David Eltis, *The Rise of African Slavery in the Americas* (Cambridge: Cambridge University Press, 2000), 9, 57, 85, 139. The figures on slave exports come from David Eltis, "The Transatlantic Slave Trade: A Reassessment Based on the Second Edition of the Transatlantic Slave Trade Database" (paper presented at the annual meeting of the American Historical Association, Philadelphia, Pa., January 2006), table 2.

21. Philip D. Curtin, *The Atlantic Slave Trade: A Census* (Madison: University of Wisconsin Press, 1969), 95–126; Paul E. Lovejoy, *Transformations in Slavery: A History of Slavery in Africa* (Cambridge: Cambridge University Press, 1983), 44–59; Curtin, *Plantation Complex*, 42–45; Eltis, *African Slavery*, 166; David Eltis, "The Volume and Structure of the Transatlantic Slave Trade: A Reassessment," *WMQ*, 3rd ser., 58 (2001): 44; Herbert S. Klein, *The Atlantic Slave Trade* (Cambridge: Cambridge University Press, 1999), 208–209.

22. Eltis, *African Slavery*, 9; Patrick Manning, "The Slave Trade in the Bight of Benin, 1640–1890," in *The Uncommon Market: Essays in the Economic History of the Atlantic Slave Trade*, ed. Henry A. Gemery and Jan S. Hogendorn (New York: Academic Press, 1979), 107–41; Patrick Manning, *Slavery, Colonialism, and Economic Growth in Dahomey, 1640–1960* (Cambridge: Cambridge University Press, 1982), 27–36; Law, *Slave Coast*, 116–55.

23. Ryder, *Benin*, 45; Law, *Oyo Empire*, 228–36; Asiwaju and Law, "From the Volta to the Niger," 421–36; Law, *Slave Coast*, 156–224.

24. Law, "Trade and Politics," 333–39; Law, *Slave Coast*, 116–27, 148–50, 192–99, 219–24; Ryder, *Benin*, 195–204.

25. Ulsheimer, "First Voyage," 41. See also Smith, *Kingdoms*, 74.

26. British National Archives, Kew: HCA 13/69, evidence of Thomas Morley, 3 July 1654. I am grateful to Robin Law for this reference.

27. Klein, *Atlantic Slave Trade*, 32–46; Curtin, *Plantation Complex*, 129–43; David Eltis, *Economic Growth and the Ending of the Transatlantic Slave Trade* (New York: Oxford University Press, 1987), 31–46; Joseph C. Miller, *Way of Death: Merchant Capitalism and the Angolan Slave Trade, 1730–1830* (Madison: University of Wisconsin Press, 1988), 447–52; David Richardson, *The Years of Decline, 1746–1769*, vol. 3 of *Bristol, Africa, and the Eighteenth-Century Slave Trade to America*, ed. David Richardson (Bristol: Bristol Record Society, 1991), xxiii–xxiv.

28. These figures on slave exports are derived from data in Eltis, "The Transatlantic Slave Trade: A Reassessment," tables 2 and 5. Eltis's paper provides a preliminary analysis of the second edition of David Eltis et al., *The Trans-Atlantic Slave Trade: A Database on CD-ROM* (Cambridge: Cambridge University Press, 1999), updated by David Eltis, David Richardson, Stephen D. Behrendt, and Manolo Florentino after much new research. Eltis's 2001 paper, "The Transatlantic Slave Trade," discusses major advances in the long debate over the volume of the Atlantic slave trade that followed the publication of Curtin, *Atlantic Slave Trade*.

29. David Eltis, personal communication, 24 December 2005. See also David Eltis and David Richardson, "West Africa and the Transatlantic Slave Trade: New Evidence of Long-Run Trends," in *Routes to Slavery: Direction, Ethnicity, and Mortality in the Transatlantic Slave Trade*, ed. David Eltis and David Richardson (London:

Frank Cass, 1997), 20; Pierre Verger, *Trade Relations between the Bight of Benin and Bahia from the 17th to 19th Century*, trans. Evelyn Crawford (Ibadan: Ibadan University Press, 1976); Manning, *Slavery, Colonialism, and Economic Growth*, 27–31; and Law, *Slave Coast*, 116–55. The Portuguese conducted two largely independent trades in slaves, one between the Bight of Benin and Bahia and the other between Angola and Rio de Janeiro. On the second of these, see Miller's monumental *Way of Death*.

30. On the Dutch trade, see Johannes Menne Postma, *The Dutch in the Atlantic Slave Trade, 1600–1815* (Cambridge: Cambridge University Press, 1990), 201–26, 284–303.

31. David Eltis, personal communication, 24 December 2005. See also Manning, *Slavery, Colonialism, and Economic Growth*, 27–31; Herbert S. Klein, *The Middle Passage: Comparative Studies in the Atlantic Slave Trade* (Princeton: Princeton University Press, 1978), 209–27; and Eltis and Richardson, "West Africa," 211.

32. Law, *Slave Coast*, 118–48, 182–87; Manning, *Slavery, Colonialism, and Economic Growth*, 37–38; Lovejoy, *Transformations*, 54–55, 78–80, 83–84; Patrick Manning, *Slavery and African Life: Occidental, Oriental, and African Slave Trades* (Cambridge: Cambridge University Press, 1990), 88–92; Robin Law, "The Slave Trade in Seventeenth-Century Allada: A Revision," *AEH* 22 (1994): 59–92.

33. I. A. Akinjogbin, *Dahomey and Its Neighbours, 1708–1818* (Cambridge: Cambridge University Press, 1967), 69–71; Law, *Slave Coast*, 278–323; Edna G. Bay, *Wives of the Leopard: Gender, Politics, and Culture in the Kingdom of Dahomey* (Charlottesville: University of Virginia Press, 1998), 40–51, 56–63.

34. Law, *Slave Coast*, 309–14; Law, "Gun Communities," 8–9; Verger, *Trade Relations*, 179, 181; Adefuye, "Oba Akinsemoyin," 38.

35. David Eltis, personal communication, 24 December 2005.

36. Law, *Slave Coast*, 190; Manning, "Slave Trade," 122; Law, *Oyo Empire*, 220–23; Verger, *Trade Relations*, 180–89; Bay, *Wives*, 42–51. On the rise of Badagry, see Robin Law, "A Lagoonside Port on the Eighteenth-Century Slave Coast: The Early History of Badagri," *CJAS* 28 (1994): 32–59; and Caroline Sorensen-Gilmour, "Slave-Trading along the Lagoons of South-West Nigeria: The Case of Badagry," in *Ports of the Slave Trade (Bights of Benin and Biafra)*, ed. Robin Law and Silke Strickrodt (Stirling, U.K.: University of Stirling, Centre of Commonwealth Studies, 1999), 84–95.

37. Calculated by David Eltis from the second edition of the *Transatlantic Slave Trade Database*.

38. David Eltis, "The Diaspora of Yoruba Speakers, 1650–1865: Dimensions and Implications," in *The Yoruba Diaspora in the Atlantic World*, ed. Toyin Falola and Matt D. Childs (Bloomington: Indiana University Press, 2004), 25; Eltis and Richardson, "West Africa," 27.

39. Archibald Dalzel, *The History of Dahomy, an Inland Kingdom of Africa* (London: Frank Cass, 1967), 166, 194.

40. Law, *Slave Coast*, 188–91; Law, *Oyo Empire*, 225–26; Mahdi Adamu, "The Delivery of Slaves from the Central Sudan to the Bight of Benin in the Eighteenth and Nineteenth Centuries," in Gemery and Hogendorn, eds., *The Uncommon Market*, 171–80; Paul E. Lovejoy and David Richardson, "The Initial 'Crisis of Adaptation': The Impact of British Abolition on the Atlantic Slave Trade in West Africa,

1808–1820," in *From Slave Trade to "Legitimate" Commerce: The Commercial Transition in Nineteenth-Century West Africa*, ed. Robin Law (Cambridge: Cambridge University Press, 1995), 39.

41. Manning, *Slavery, Colonialism, and Economic Growth*, 30–32; Paul E. Lovejoy, "The Impact of the Atlantic Slave Trade on Africa: A Review of the Literature," *JAH* 30 (1989): 376, 379; Law, *Slave Coast*, 187–91; Paul E. Lovejoy and David Richardson, "Demographic Patterns in the Trans-Atlantic Slave Trade: The Yoruba Factor" (paper presented at the annual meeting of the African Studies Association, San Francisco, Calif., November 1996); Robin Law, "Ethnicity and the Slave Trade: 'Lucumi' and 'Nago' as Ethnonyms in West Africa," *History in Africa* 24 (1997): 205–19; Eltis, "The Diaspora of Yoruba Speakers," 21–22.

Data on the ethnicity of slaves imported into Bahia confirm these patterns. See, for example, Stuart B. Schwartz, *Sugar Plantations in the Formation of Brazilian Society: Bahia, 1550–1835* (Cambridge: Cambridge University Press, 1985), 341, 437; and João José Reis, *Slave Rebellion in Brazil: The Muslim Uprising of 1835 in Bahia*, trans. Arthur Brakel (Baltimore: Johns Hopkins University Press, 1993), 139.

42. Archives Nationales (Paris): c.6/25, Du Colombier, Whydah, 17 April 1715, quoted in Law, *Slave Coast*, 185; Law, "Trade and Politics," 342–43.

43. See, for example, William Smith, *A New Voyage to Guinea* (London: Frank Cass, 1967), 193–95; Robert Norris, *Memoirs of the Reign of Bossa Ahadee, King of Dahomy* (London: Frank Cass, 1968), 142–46; Dalzel, *History*, 183, 186; Captain John Adams, *Remarks on the Country Extending from Cape Palmas to the River Congo* (London: Frank Cass, 1966), 74, 79–81, 88–90, 97, 107–108; G. A. Robertson, *Notes on Africa; Particularly Those Parts Which Are Situated between Cape Verd and the River Congo* (London: Sherwood, Neely, and Jones, 1819), 266, 274, 279, 281, 287, 301; and Richard Lander, *Records of Captain Clapperton's Last Expedition to Africa* (London: Henry Colburn and Richard Bentley, 1830), 1:36, 50.

44. For accounts of the rise and decline of the external gold trade from the Gold Coast, see Ivor Wilks, *Forests of Gold: Essays on the Akan and the Kingdom of Asante* (Athens: Ohio University Press, 1993), 2–4, 72–78; Ray A. Kea, *Settlements, Trade, and Polities in the Seventeenth-Century Gold Coast* (Baltimore: Johns Hopkins University Press, 1982), 11, 103–104, 187–201; Larry W. Yarak, *Asante and the Dutch, 1744–1873* (Oxford: Clarendon Press, 1990), 95–96, 112; and Law, *Slave Coast*, 194–97. For references to trade among Slave Coast towns, see Robertson, *Notes*, 302; Adams, *Remarks*, 97; T. E. Bowdich, *Mission from Cape Coast Castle to Ashantee* (London: Frank Cass, 1966), 226; and Lieutenant Edward Bold, *The Merchant's and Mariner's African Guide; Containing an Accurate Description of the Coasts, Bays, Harbours, and Adjacent Islands of West Africa* (London: J. D. and T. C. Cushing, 1819), 66.

45. Manning, "Slave Trade," 122–23; Law, "Trade and Politics," 343–44; Adefuye, "Oba Akinsemoyin," 36–38; Verger, *Trade Relations*, 179–84.

46. Losi, *History*, 12–13; John Augustus Otonba Payne, *Table of Principal Events in Yoruba History* (Lagos: Andrew M. Thomas, 1893), 2, 10; Adefuye, "Oba Akinsemoyin," 36–37; Law, "Trade and Politics," 344; Kunle Lawal, "The 'Ogu-Awori' Peoples of Badagry before 1950: A General Historical Survey," in *Badagry: A Study in History, Culture, and Traditions of an Ancient City*, ed. G. O. Ogunremi, M. O. Opeloye, and Siyan Oyeweso (Ibadan: Rex Charles, 1994), 19.

47. Verger, *Trade Relations*, 167, 179, 224, 477.

48. A Collection of Board of Trade Papers, "Report on the Trade to Africa and the Settlements There [1776]," BL Add.Mss. 14034, part II, 182; T 70/1534, Clemison to Miles, 27 January 1777, reprinted in Thomas Hodgkin, *Nigerian Perspectives: An Historical Anthology*, 2nd ed. (London: Oxford University Press, 1975), 225–26.

49. T 70/1535, "The Council's Answer to the Return of the Lords of Trade, submitted for the consideration of the Committee by their faithful servants, R. Miles, T. Westgate, R. Collins, M. Watts," 25 June 1778. See also T 70/31, Dalzel to the Africa Committee, 27 September 1768; T 70/1534, Brew to Miles, 28 May 1776; T 70/1532, Brew to Miles, 26 July 1774; T 70/1534, letter, Annamaboe Fort, 28 September 1776. I am grateful to Robin Law and Stephen D. Behrendt for these references. For a history of the Brew family, see Margaret Priestley, *West African Trade and Coast Society: A Family Study* (London: Oxford University Press, 1969). On William Collow's trade between the Gold Coast and the Slave Coast at the end of the century, see Stephen D. Behrendt, "The Journal of an African Slaver, 1789–1792, and the Gold Coast Slave Trade of William Collow," *History in Africa* 22 (1995): 61–67.

50. Eltis, "The Diaspora of Yoruba Speakers," 25.

51. Curtin, *Atlantic Slave Trade*. Studies of the national and local trades included Jean Mettas, *Répertoire des expéditions négrières françaises au XVIIIe siècle*, ed. Serge Daget and Michèle Daget, 2 vols. (Paris: Société Française d'Histoire d'Outre-Mer, 1978, 1984); Serge Daget, *Répertoire des expéditions négrières françaises à la traite illégale (1814–1850)* (Nantes: Centre de Recherche sur l'Histoire du Monde Atlantique, 1988); Richardson, ed., *Bristol, Africa, and the Eighteenth-Century Slave Trade;* Eltis, *Economic Growth;* Postma, *The Dutch in the Atlantic Slave Trade;* Stephen D. Behrendt, "The Annual Volume and Regional Distribution of the British Slave Trade, 1780–1807," *JAH* 38 (1997): 187–211; Jay Coughtry, *The Notorious Triangle: Rhode Island and the African Slave Trade, 1700–1807* (Philadelphia: Temple University Press, 1981); Svend E. Green-Pedersen, "The Scope and Structure of the Danish Negro Slave Trade," *Scandinavian Economic History Review* 19 (1971): 149–97; and unpublished or smaller datasets by Herbert S. Klein; David Richardson, Kathy Beedham, Maurice M. Schofield; and others, cited in full in Eltis et al., *Trans-Atlantic Slave Trade Database*. Eltis, "The Transatlantic Slave Trade: A Reassessment," summarizes and evaluates additions to the 1999 database.

52. Eltis, "The Transatlantic Slave Trade: A Reassessment," 2.

53. Mettas, *Répertoire*, 2:767; Dalzel, *History*, 179–98; Law, "A Lagoonside Port," 47–51; L. C. Dioka and Siyan Oyeweso, "Intergroup Relations in a Frontier State: The Case of Badagry," in Ogunremi, Opeloye, and Oyeweso, eds., *Badagry*, 140–44.

54. Arquivo Histórico Ultramarino, Lisboa, S. Tomé, caixa 10, quoted in Verger, *Trade Relations*, 181. See also Robin Law, "The Rise and Fall of the Merchant Class in Whydah in the Nineteenth Century" (paper presented at the annual meeting of the Canadian Association of African Studies, Montreal, May 1996), 3. Adams, *Remarks* (97), observed that the Portuguese had long carried on "an extremely active trade in slaves" at Porto Novo and Lagos, as well as Ouidah.

55. Mettas, *Répertoire*, 2:355; Verger, *Trade Relations*, 186.

56. Law, "Trade and Politics," 347. See also J. F. Landolphe, *Mémoires du Capitaine Landolphe* (Paris: A. Bertrand, 1823), 2:98–103.

57. "Report on the Committee of the Privy Council, 1789," in *Documents Illustrative of the History of the Slave Trade to America*, ed. Elizabeth Donnan (Washington, D. C.: Carnegie Institution, 1931), 2:598 n. 6.

58. In the 1780s, the French exported about 47,000 slaves from the Bight of Benin, while their commerce declined to just over 5,000 slaves in the first half of the 1790s and then virtually disappeared. British trade in the Bight grew from about 17,000 slaves in the 1780s to around 21,500 in the 1790s, while the Portuguese/Brazilian trade expanded from about 53,500 slaves in the 1780s to around 63,000 in the next decade. David Eltis, personal communication, 24 December 2005.

59. Robertson, *Notes*, 290, 296.

60. Eltis, *Economic Growth*, 62–64.

61. Eltis, "The Transatlantic Slave Trade: A Reassessment," table 3; Schwartz, *Sugar Plantations*, 422–31; Reis, *Slave Rebellion*, 13–15.

62. Eltis, "The Transatlantic Slave Trade: A Reassessment," table 5.

63. APB, G. C. to S. M., vol. 11, f. 109, quoted in Pierre Verger, "Notes on Some Documents in Which Lagos Is Referred To by the Name 'Onim' and Which Mention Relations between Onim and Brazil," *JHSN* 1 (1959): 346. See also Law, *Oyo Empire*, 274; Law, "A Lagoonside Port," 47–52; and Eltis, "The Diaspora of Yoruba Speakers," 25.

64. Peel, *Religious Encounter*, 33–34. The best works on the causes and consequences of the fall of the Oyo Empire remain Johnson, *History;* J. F. A. Ajayi, "The Aftermath of the Fall of Old Oyo," in *History of West Africa*, ed. J. F. A. Ajayi and Michael Crowder (New York: Columbia University Press, 1973), 2:129–66; Law, *Oyo Empire;* and Robin Law, "Making Sense of a Traditional Narrative: Political Disintegration in the Kingdom of Oyo," *CEA* 22 (1982): 387–401.

65. A. L. Mabogunje and J. Omer-Cooper, *Owu in Yoruba History* (Ibadan: Ibadan University Press, 1971), 45–70; R. C. C. Law, "The Chronology of the Yoruba Wars of the Early Nineteenth Century: A Reconsideration," *JHSN* 5 (1970): 219–22; Law, *Oyo Empire*, 273–76; and Dare Oguntomisin, "Warfare and Military Alliances in Yorubaland in the Nineteenth Century," in *Warfare and Diplomacy in Precolonial Nigeria*, ed. Toyin Falola and Robin Law (Madison: African Studies Program, University of Wisconsin–Madison, 1992), 31–32.

66. Smith, *Kingdoms*, 125–40. See also, in addition to the works cited in notes 64 and 65, S. O. Biobaku, *The Egba and Their Neighbours, 1842–1872* (Oxford: Clarendon Press, 1957), 1–52; J. F. A. Ajayi and Robert Smith, *Yoruba Warfare in the Nineteenth Century* (Cambridge: Cambridge University Press, 1964), 9–55, 63–75; Falola, *Political Economy*, 15–41; Bolanle Awe, "The Rise of Ibadan as a Yoruba Power, 1851–1893" (D.Phil thesis, Oxford University, 1964); G. O. Oguntomisin, "New Forms of Political Organization in Yorubaland in the Mid-Nineteenth Century: A Comparative Study of Kurunmi's Ijaye and Kosoko's Epe" (Ph.D. diss., University of Ibadan, 1979); S. A. Akintoye, *Revolution and Power Politics in Yorubaland, 1840–1893* (New York: Humanities Press, 1971), 33–101; Toyin Falola, "The Yoruba Wars of the Nineteenth Century," in *Yoruba Historiography*, ed. Toyin Falola (Madison: African Studies Program, University of Wisconsin–Madison, 1991),

137; and Toyin Falola and G. O. Oguntomisin, *Yoruba Warlords of the Nineteenth Century* (Trenton, N.J.: Africa World Press, 2001), 229–75.

67. Peel, *Religious Encounter*; Karin Barber, *I Could Speak until Tomorrow: Oriki, Women, and the Past in a Yoruba Town* (Washington: Smithsonian Institution Press, 1991), 183–212; and Margaret Thompson Drewal, *Yoruba Ritual: Performances, Play, Agency* (Bloomington: Indiana University Press, 1992), 135–53, are particularly good on cultural changes in the nineteenth century.

68. Stephen D. Behrendt and David Eltis, "Competition, Market Power, and the Impact of Abolition on the Transatlantic Slave Trade: Connections between Africa and the Americas" (paper presented at the annual meeting of the American Historical Association, New York, N.Y., January 1997).

69. Mettas, *Répertoire*, 2:376; Verger, "Notes," 344–49; Verger, *Trade Relations*, 24, 224–25, 235–36; Losi, *History*, 81.

70. See the correspondence to Kosoko seized by the British at the palace in 1851. House of Lords Sessional Papers, 1852–53, 22:327–66.

71. Robin Law, "The Origins and Evolution of the Merchant Community in Ouidah," in Law and Strickrodt, eds., *Ports*, 59. See also Law's earlier articles "Royal Monopoly and Private Enterprise in the Atlantic Trade: The Case of Dahomey," *JAH* 18 (1977): 555–77, and "Slave-Raiders and Middlemen, Monopolists and Free-Traders: The Supply of Slaves for the Atlantic Trade in Dahomey, c. 1715–1850," *JAH* 30 (1989): 45–68; along with Bay, *Wives*, 16, 40.

72. For an interesting discussion of the role of oral traditions and European documentation in the study of the impact of the slave trade on Africa, see Ralph A. Austen, "The Slave Trade as History and Memory: Confrontations of Slaving Voyage Documents and Communal Traditions," *WMQ*, 3rd ser., 58 (2001): 229–44.

73. Wood, *Historical Notices;* Payne, *Table*, 1–21; and Losi, *History* collected and published the dynastic traditions. Folami, *History*, repeats Losi when discussing *ọbas*, but he includes new information about chieftaincy families. My own interviews also yielded new data about a number of prominent Lagos chiefs.

74. Folami, *History*, 115. Also Wood, *Historical Notices*, 23; and Talbot, *Peoples*, 1:84.

75. Losi, *History*, 14.

76. Losi, *History*, 16–17; Payne, *Table*, 2; Folami, *History*, 25–28; Abiola Dosumu Elegbede-Fernandez, *Lagos: A Legacy of Honour* (Ibadan: Spectrum Books, 1992), 11–12; Richard Lander and John Lander, *Journal of an Expedition to Explore the Course and Termination of the Niger* (New York: Harper and Brothers, 1842), 1:78. For a biography of Adele, see Robin Law, "The Career of Adele at Lagos and Badagry, c. 1807–c. 1837," *JHSN* 9 (1978): 35–59.

77. Wood, *Historical Notices*, 34; Fadipe, *Sociology*, 217.

78. John Houtson, "An Account of Adeely Ex-Caboceer of Lagos," November 1825. BL Add.Mss. 55/11, fols. 15, 16, 23–24. I am grateful to Robin Law for a copy of this document.

79. Ibid.

80. Losi, *History*, 17, 19. On the history of the *egúngún* masquerade, see Henry John Drewal and Margaret Thompson Drewal, *Gelede: Art and Female Power among the Yoruba* (Bloomington: Indiana University Press, 1983), 221; and Babatunde

Lawal, *The Gelede Spectacle: Art, Gender, and Social Harmony in an African Culture* (Seattle: University of Washington Press, 1996), 16.

81. Lander and Lander, *Journal*, 1:49–51, 80; Houtson, "An Account of Adeely"; Law, "The Career of Adele," 43; Smith, *Lagos Consulate*, 14–16; Lawal, "The 'Ogu-Awori' Peoples," 20–21.

82. Losi, *History*, 17, 19.

83. Ibid., 23–24.

84. Wood, *Historical Notices*, 36; Losi, *History*, 30.

85. Losi, *History*, 24–25; Wood, *Historical Notices*, 37.

86. Wood, *Historical Notices*, 38.

87. Losi, *History*, 29.

88. Smith, *Kingdoms*, 6.

89. Losi, *History*, 30; Wood, *Historical Notices*, 41. On José Domingo Martinez, see David A. Ross, "The Career of Domingo Martinez in the Bight of Benin, 1833–1864," *JAH* 6 (1965): 79–90; Jerry Michael Turner, "Les Bresiliens—The Impact of Former Brazilian Slaves upon Dahomey" (Ph.D. diss., Boston University, 1975), 100–102; and Robin Law and Kristin Mann, "West Africa in the Atlantic Community: The Case of the Slave Coast," *WMQ*, 3rd ser., 56 (1999): 324.

90. Losi, *History*, 30–32; Wood, *Historical Notices*, 41.

91. Losi, *History*, 29–44; Wood, *Historical Notices*, 50; interviews with Chief Ishola Bajulaiye, Alhaji A. W. A. Akibayo, and Chief Mobolaji Oshodi.

92. Payne, *Table*, 9. Losi, *History*, 33, gives the name as *Ogun Olomiró*, or "the war of those who have sea-water." Also see Smith, *Lagos Consulate*, 16–17.

93. Losi, *History*, 33; Talbot, *Peoples*, 1:89; Smith, *Lagos Consulate*, 18–26.

94. Interview with Chief Ishola Bajulaiye; RWCA, Minutes of Evidence, W. McCoskry, 6 April 1865, 66; "Notes on the Obanikoro Chieftaincy," Herbert Macaulay Papers, UIL, 10/2. Bay's discussion of the Dahomian monarchy can be found in *Wives*, 6–9.

95. Lander and Lander, *Journal*, 1:45–82, documents the importance of Muslim slaves in Adele's entourage. See also T. G. O. Gbadamosi, *The Growth of Islam among the Yoruba, 1841–1908* (London: Longman, 1978), 7, 26, 69–70.

2. Trade, Oligarchy, and the Transformation of the Precolonial State

1. Philip D. Curtin, *Economic Change in Precolonial Africa: Senegambia in the Era of the Slave Trade* (Madison: University of Wisconsin Press, 1975), 105–12, 173–76; Joseph C. Miller, *Way of Death: Merchant Capitalism and the Angolan Slave Trade, 1730–1830* (Madison: University of Wisconsin Press, 1988), 245–62, 273–83; Robin Law, *The Slave Coast of West Africa, 1550–1750: The Impact of the Atlantic Slave Trade on an African Society* (Oxford: Clarendon Press, 1991), 301, 342–43.

2. FO 84/950, Campbell to Clarendon, 1 June 1854.

3. FO 84/950, Campbell to Clarendon, 1 May 1854. See also Archibald Dalzel, *The History of Dahomy, an Inland Kingdom of Africa* (London: Frank Cass, 1967), 183; J. F. Landolphe, *Mémoires du Capitaine Landolphe* (Paris: A. Bertrand, 1823), 2:98–103; Richard Lander and John Lander, *Journal of an Expedition to Explore the Course and Termination of the Niger* (New York: Harper and Brothers, 1842),

1:50–51; and John B. Losi, *History of Lagos* (Lagos: Tika Tore Press, 1914), 17–18, 29–43. Robin Law, "The Career of Adele at Lagos and Badagry, c. 1807–c. 1837," *JHSN* 9 (1978): 44–46; and Robin Law, "The Gun Communities in the Eighteenth Century" (paper presented at the annual meeting of the African Studies Association, St. Louis, Mo., November 1991), 19–28, discuss the wars among the Gun states and between them and Dahomey, Oyo, and Lagos.

4. Andreas Josua Ulsheimer, "The First Voyage to Africa," in *German Sources for West African History, 1599–1669*, ed. Adam Jones (Wiesbaden: Franz Steiner Verlag, 1983), 24; A. G. Hopkins, "A Report on the Yoruba, 1910," *JHSN* 5 (1969): 76; A. K. Ajisafe, *The Laws and Customs of the Yoruba People* (Lagos: CMS Bookshop, 1924), 21. Also interview with Alhaji A. W. A. Akibayo.

5. Dalzel, *History*, 183; Lander and Lander, *Journal*, 1:78; "A Brief History of Badagry," encl. in FO 84/920, Fraser to Clarendon, 13 January 1853; Losi, *History*, 15–16, 23.

6. Losi, *History*, 15; Robin Law, *The Oyo Empire, c. 1600–c. 1836: A West African Imperialism in the Era of the Slave Trade* (Oxford: Clarendon Press, 1977), 176–77, 222–28; Patrick Manning, "The Slave Trade in the Bight of Benin, 1640–1890," in *The Uncommon Market: Essays in the Economic History of the Atlantic Slave Trade*, ed. Henry A. Gemery and Jan S. Hogendorn (New York: Academic Press, 1979), 127; and Robin Law, "Trade and Politics behind the Slave Coast: The Lagoon Traffic and the Rise of Lagos, 1500–1800," *JAH* 24 (1983): 343–48, discuss the shifting networks of slave supply to the coast. On the procurement of slaves, see E. A. Oroge, "The Institution of Slavery in Yorubaland, with Particular Reference to the Nineteenth Century" (Ph.D. diss., University of Birmingham, 1971), 114; Toyin Falola, *The Political Economy of a Pre-colonial African State: Ibadan, 1830–1900* (Ile-Ife: University of Ife Press, 1984), 63–64; and J. D. Y. Peel, *Religious Encounter and the Making of the Yoruba* (Bloomington: Indiana University Press, 2000), 63.

7. "The Narrative of Joseph Wright," in *Africa Remembered: Narratives by West Africans from the Era of the Slave Trade*, ed. Philip D. Curtin (Madison: University of Wisconsin Press, 1967), 329; PRRL, Gollmer to Venn, 3 January 1851, 313.

8. Captain John Adams, *Remarks on the Country Extending from Cape Palmas to the River Congo* (London: Frank Cass, 1966), 96. See also 107–108, 219–20 of that work and T. E. Bowdich, *Mission from Cape Coast Castle to Ashantee* (London: Frank Cass, 1966), 225. Ray A. Kea, *Settlements, Trade, and Polities in the Seventeenth-Century Gold Coast* (Baltimore: Johns Hopkins University Press, 1982), 46, 57, 212, passim, documents the role of brokers who bought and sold for others in the external trade of the Gold Coast.

9. "The Narrative of Samuel Ajayi Crowther," in Curtin, ed., *Africa Remembered*, 309.

10. "Narrative of Joseph Wright," 329.

11. Jean Mettas, *Répertoire des expéditions négrières françaises au XVIIIe siècle*, ed. Serge Daget and Michèle Daget (Paris: Société Française d'Histoire d'Outre-Mer, 1984), 2:376. On the administrative supervision of the kings of Allada, Ouidah, and Dahomey of trade at western Slave Coast ports, see the following works by Robin Law: *Slave Coast*, 208–15; *The Kingdom of Allada* (Leiden: School of Asian, African, and Amerindian Studies, 1997), 94–101; "Royal Monopoly and Private Enterprise in the Atlantic Trade: The Case of Dahomey," *JAH* 18 (1977): 555–77; "Slave-

Raiders and Middlemen, Monopolists and FreeTraders: The Supply of Slaves for the Atlantic Trade in Dahomey, c. 1715–1850," *JAH* 30 (1989): 45–68; and "The Origins and Evolution of the Merchant Community in Ouidah," in *Ports of the Slave Trade (Bights of Benin and Biafra)*, ed. Robin Law and Silke Strickrodt (Stirling, U.K.: University of Stirling, Centre of Commonwealth Studies, 1999), 55–70.

12. APB, 143, f. 109, quoted in Pierre Verger, *Trade Relations between the Bight of Benin and Bahia from the 17th to 19th Century*, trans. Evelyn Crawford (Ibadan: Ibadan University Press, 1976), 236.

13. On the movement from ship to shore to gather slaves together and on other changes in the organization of the trade following legal abolition, see David Eltis, *Economic Growth and the Ending of the Transatlantic Slave Trade* (New York: Oxford University Press, 1987), 153, 180–81; Kristin Mann, "Las redes comerciales: De la Bahía de Benín al sur del Atlántico, 1750–1850," in *Rutas de la esclavitud en África y América Latina*, ed. Rina Cáceres (San Jose: Editorial de la Universidad de Costa Rica, 2001), 45–82; and Ubiratan Castro de Araújo, "1846, um ano na rota Bahia-Lagos: Negócios, negociantes e outros parceiros," in *Identifying Enslaved Africans: The "Nigerian" Hinterland and the African Diaspora*, ed. Paul E. Lovejoy (Proceedings of the UNESCO/SSHRCC Summer Institute, York University, Toronto, 1997), 446–72.

14. Law, *Slave Coast*, 206–12; Law, *Allada*, 94–101. For the evolution of Law's views on the involvement of Dahomian kings in the slave trade at Ouidah, see the articles cited in note 11.

15. T 70/1534, Clemison to Miles, 27 January 1777.

16. Correspondance consulaire et commerciale du Ministère des affaires étrangères, Consulat de Bahia, vol. 5, f. 25, quoted in Araújo, "1846," 457.

17. For more information on the design of canoes and the time required to reach various markets, see Kristin Mann, "The World the Slave Traders Made: Lagos, c. 1760–1850," in Lovejoy, ed., *Identifying Enslaved Africans*, 209.

18. Losi, *History*, 14; Takiu Folami, *A History of Lagos, Nigeria* (Smithtown, N.Y.: Exposition Press, 1982), 128, 131; interview with Prince A. L. A. Ojora; N. Mba, "Women in Lagos Political History," and B. A. Agiri, "Architecture as a Source of Nigerian History: The Lagos Example," in *History of the Peoples of Lagos State*, ed. Ade Adefuye, Babatunde Agiri, and Jide Osuntokun (Ikeja: Lantern Books, 1987), 244, 341.

19. Interview with Alhaji A. W. A. Akibayo.

20. John Augustus Otonba Payne, *Table of Principal Events in Yoruba History* (Lagos: Andrew M. Thomas, 1893), 3, 9; J. Buckley Wood, *Historical Notices of Lagos, West Africa* (Exeter: James Townsend, n.d.), 51, 55–57; Losi, *History*, 26, 32–39, passim; Verger, *Trade Relations*, 236, 240; *Oshodi Chieftaincy Family: Records and Achievements* (Lagos: A.E.P., n.d.); interview with Chief Mobolaji Oshodi. Oshodi Tapa and Akanbi are both listed among people who loaded slaves on the ship *Santa Anna* in 1844, which was seized by the British Anti-slavery Squadron. PP 1845.XLIXI.1, Class A, Correspondence with British Commissioners . . . Relating to the Slave Trade, 1844, encl. 1 in Melville and Hook to Aberdeen, Sierra Leone, 27 April 1844, 37–38. Tapa is also mentioned in the correspondence of Bahian consignment agents to Kosoko reprinted in the House of Lords Sessional Papers, 1852–53, 22:327–66. Sandra T. Barnes, "Ritual, Power, and Outside Knowledge,"

Journal of Religion in Africa 20 (1990): 248–68, discusses Tapa's early experiences in Lagos and his incorporation into the political elite.

21. Araújo, "1846," 457. See also FO 84/1002, Campbell to Clarendon, 30 August, 1 October 1856.

22. John Houtson, "An Account of Adeely Ex-Caboceer of Lagos," November 1825. BL Add.Mss. 55/11, fols. 15–16, 23–24; Verger, *Trade Relations*, 235–36.

23. Oladipo Yemitan, *Madame Tinubu: Merchant and King-Maker* (Ibadan: University Press, 1987), 11–14. Also see S. O. Biobaku, "Madame Tinubu," in *Eminent Nigerians of the Nineteenth Century* (Cambridge: Cambridge University Press, 1960), 33–41; and Cheryl Jeffries Johnson, "Nigerian Women and British Colonialism: The Yoruba Example with Selected Biographies" (Ph.D. diss., Northwestern University, 1978), 74–96.

24. Interview with Chief Ishola Bajulaiye.

25. Edna G. Bay, *Wives of the Leopard: Gender, Politics, and Culture in the Kingdom of Dahomey* (Charlottesville: University of Virginia Press, 1998), 6–9, 81–91, has influenced my thinking about these issues.

26. On the role of credit in the African slave trade, see Curtin, *Economic Change*, 139, 302–308; Kea, *Settlements*, 239; A. J. H. Latham, *Old Calabar, 1600–1891: The Impact of the International Economy upon a Traditional Society* (Oxford: Clarendon Press, 1973), 28; Paul E. Lovejoy and David Richardson, "Trust, Pawnship, and Atlantic History: The Institutional Foundations of the Old Calabar Slave Trade," *AHR* 104 (1999): 332–55; and Miller, *Way of Death*, 131–32, 152, 168, 175–89, 284–313, 515–16, 537–41. For information about credit on the Slave Coast, see Law, *Slave Coast*, 217–19; Yemitan, *Madame Tinubu*, 16; and letters from Archibald Dalzel to his brother dated May 1768, 28 March 1771, and 13 April 1771, in the Dalzel Correspondence at Edinburgh University Library.

27. Bowdich, *Mission*, 226; G. A. Robertson, *Notes on Africa; Particularly Those Parts Which Are Situated between Cape Verd and the River Congo* (London: Sherwood, Neely, and Jones, 1819), 287–89; *The Narrative of Robert Adams, an American Sailor, Who Was Wrecked on the Western Coast of Africa, in the Year 1810* (Boston: Wells and Lilly, 1817), xxvi.

28. Folami, *History*, 124. For further evidence relevant to Ijebu traders in Lagos, see M. d'Avezac-Macaya, "The Land and People of Ijebu," in Curtin, ed., *Africa Remembered*, 236, 243, 251, 269–70.

29. Losi, *History*, 28; Yemitan, *Madame Tinubu*, 7, 12–13.

30. Eltis, *Economic Growth*, 263.

31. Paul E. Lovejoy and David Richardson, "The Initial 'Crisis of Adaptation': The Impact of British Abolition on the Atlantic Slave Trade in West Africa, 1808–1820," in *From Slave Trade to "Legitimate" Commerce: The Commercial Transition in Nineteenth-Century West Africa*, ed. Robin Law (Cambridge: Cambridge University Press, 1995), 35. In reality, of course, the price of slaves varied at Lagos and elsewhere on the coast, depending primarily on gender, age, and condition. Eltis's and Lovejoy and Richardson's price data are derived from cargoes that included mixtures of slaves and thus, to some degree, take these price differences into account.

32. I have converted Eltis's price data in constant dollars into pounds sterling using the exchange rate of £1=$4.80, which was relatively stable throughout the period. For exchange rates, see Eltis, *Economic Growth*, 290.

33. Adams, *Remarks*, 95. For information about taxes levied by state officials on the western Slave Coast, see Patrick Manning, *Slavery, Colonialism, and Economic Growth in Dahomey, 1640–1960* (Cambridge: Cambridge University Press, 1982), 82; and Law, *Slave Coast*, 208–10, and *Allada*, 95–97.

34. APB, 143, f. 109, quoted in Verger, *Trade Relations*, 236.

35. Robertson, *Notes*, 290.

36. The number of ships loading slaves at Lagos in these years comes from David Eltis, David Richardson, Stephen D. Behrendt, and Manolo Florentino, *The Transatlantic Slave Trade Database*, 2nd ed., forthcoming. I am grateful to David Eltis for these figures.

37. FO 84/950, Campbell to Clarendon, 1 June 1854; FO 84/1002, Campbell to Clarendon, 14 May 1856. During the 1850s, Akitoye and Dosunmu also charged freed slaves from Brazil and Cuba who wanted to settle in the town a tax of ten bags of cowries per family. FO 84/1031, Campbell to Clarendon, 5 June 1857. When driven into exile at Epe, Kosoko imposed duties on goods at the eastern ports of Palma and Lekki. RWCA, Minutes of Evidence, W. McCoskry, 6 April 1865, 75, and D. Chinery, 15 May 1865, 208.

38. Losi, *History*, 81; interview with Chief Mobolaji Oshodi.

39. FO 84/950, Campbell to Clarendon, 2 May 1854.

40. Losi, *History*, 14; Kunle Akinsemoyin and Alan Vaughan-Richards, *Building Lagos* (Lagos: F and A Services, 1976), 12.

41. Landolphe, *Mémoires*, 2:100; Adams, *Remarks*, 102; Araújo, "1846," 457.

42. Lander and Lander, *Journal*, 1:56, 63–65. See also Richard Lander, *Records of Captain Clapperton's Last Expedition to Africa* (London: Henry Colburn and Richard Bentley, 1830), 1:236.

43. FO 84/976, Campbell to Clarendon, 30 August 1855; FO 84/1002, Campbell to Clarendon, 26 May 1856; CO 147/3, Freeman to Newcastle, 3 January 1863; CO 147/8, Glover to Cardwell, 14 March 1865; CO 147/11, Blackall to Cardwell, 6 March 1866; RWCA, Minutes of Evidence, Dr. H. Eales, 29 March 1865, 279–80. Interviews with Mrs. Kofo Pratt, Chief Mobolaji Oshodi, and G. B. Animaṣaun, Saif Akanni Animaṣaun, and Rufai Arufai Animaṣaun.

44. For references to trade between the interior and the coast in commodities other than slaves see, in addition to the works by Adams and Robertson already cited, d'Avezac-Macaya, "The Land and People of Ijebu," 236, 243, 251, 269–70; and Lieutenant Edward Bold, *The Merchant's and Mariner's African Guide; Containing an Accurate Description of the Coast, Bays, Harbours, and Adjacent Islands of West Africa* (London: J. D. and T. C. Cushing, 1819), 64–74. Law, *Slave Coast*, 116–21, 143, 147; C. W. Newbury, *The Western Slave Coast and Its Rulers* (Oxford: Clarendon Press, 1961), 57–58, 86; and Marion Johnson, "Ivory and the Nineteenth Century Transformation in West Africa," in *Figuring African Trade: Proceedings of the Symposium on the Quantification and Structure of the Import and Export and Long Distance Trade in Africa, 1800–1913*, ed. G. Liesegang, H. Pasch, and A. Jones (Berlin: D. Reimer, 1986), 103–104, 107, discuss the history of the ivory trade, while Pierre Verger, "Influence du Brésil au Golfe du Bénin," in *Les Afro-Américans*, ed. Theodore Monod (Dakar: Mémoires de l'Institut français d'Afrique noire, 1953), 11–101; Robin Law and Kristin Mann, "West Africa in the Atlantic Community: The Case of the Slave Coast," *WMQ*, 3rd ser., 56 (1999): 307–34; and Jerry

Michael Turner, "Les Bresiliens—The Impact of Former Brazilian Slaves upon Dahomey" (Ph.D. diss., Boston University, 1975), 60–64, document trade in goods other than slaves between Brazil and the Slave Coast. On the origins of the palm oil trade, see chapter 4.

45. Robertson, *Notes*, 287.

46. Bold, *Merchant's and Mariner's Guide*, 67.

47. David Eltis and Lawrence C. Jennings, "Trade between Western Africa and the Atlantic World in the Pre-colonial Era," *AHR* 93 (1988): 936.

48. Interviews with Prince A. L. A. Ojora and Chief Mobolaji Oshodi.

49. "Observations on a Letter from Banner Brothers," encl. in CO 147/8, Glover to Cardwell, 9 January 1865; RWCA, Minutes of Evidence, W. McCoskry, 6 April 1865, 80; Ajisafe, *Laws*, 25–27; N. A. Fadipe, *The Sociology of the Yoruba* (Ibadan: Ibadan University Press, 1970), 109, 111–13, 141, 165, 217–23, 231. Toyin Falola, "The Yoruba Toll System: Its Operation and Abolition," *JAH* 30 (1989): 69–78, discusses toll collection by Yoruba states in the interior.

50. T 70, Miles to Dalzel, 10 October 1793, reprinted in Thomas Hodgkin, *Nigerian Perspectives: An Historical Anthology*, 2nd ed. (London: Oxford University Press, 1975), 226; Lander and Lander, *Journal*, 1:78. Adams, *Remarks*, 100, refers to two or three populous villages on the north side of the lagoon over which the king of Lagos had jurisdiction. He does not mention tribute, but it was probably paid. Patrick D. Cole, *Modern and Traditional Elites in the Politics of Lagos* (Cambridge: Cambridge University Press, 1975), 24–29, discusses the *bàbá ìsàlẹ̀* system.

For useful discussions of the material basis of political power in other precolonial West African kingdoms, see Robin Law, "Slaves, Trade, and Taxes: The Material Basis of Political Power in Pre-colonial West Africa," *Research in Economic Anthropology* 1 (1978): 37–52; Ivor Wilks, *Forests of Gold: Essays on the Akan and the Kingdom of Asante* (Athens: Ohio University Press, 1993), 127–67; T. C. McCaskie, *State and Society in Pre-colonial Asante* (Cambridge: Cambridge University Press, 1995), 25–73; and Bay, *Wives*, 96–110.

51. Houtson, "An Account of Adeely."

52. Verger, *Trade Relations*, 242; Losi, *History*, 25.

53. These data come from Kosoko's correspondence, cited in note 20.

54. Interview with Chief Mobolaji Oshodi; GP f5, Statement by Kuṣegbe, 25 January 1872; Robert S. Smith, "The Canoe in West African History," *JAH* 11 (1970): 521, 525; Gabriel Ogundeji Ogunremi, *Counting the Camels: The Economics of Transportation in Pre-industrial Nigeria* (New York: Nok, 1982), 155–59.

55. Dalzel, *History*, 183; T 70, Miles to Dalzel, 10 October 1793, in Hodgkin, *Nigerian Perspectives*, 226. On the 1793 attack, see also Adams, *Remarks*, 95; Robertson, *Notes*, 283; and Robin Law, "A Lagoonside Port on the Eighteenth-Century Slave Coast: The Early History of Badagri," *CJAS* 28 (1994): 32–59. Smith, "The Canoe," 526–31, discusses the growth and significance of naval power at Lagos.

56. Law, "The Career of Adele," 44–46; Wood, *Historical Notices*, 42; PRRL, The Residents at Badagry to Capt. Jones, 11 July 1851, 349; Toyin Falola and G. O. Oguntomisin, *Yoruba Warlords of the Nineteenth Century* (Trenton, N.J.: Africa World Press, 2001), 151.

57. Smith, "The Canoe," 520. John Clemison begged his superior at Cape Coast Castle to send him a copper-bottomed boat for use on the lagoon, because no

other would "stand this river a month on account of worms." T 70/1534, Clemison to Miles, 27 January 1777.

58. Ajisafe, *Laws*, 20–21; Fadipe, *Sociology*, 202. Robert Smith, "Yoruba Armament," *JAH* 8 (1967): 87–106, discusses locally manufactured weapons.

59. Lander and Lander, *Journal*, 1:49, 51, 60.

60. Robertson, *Notes*, 283; Verger, *Trade Relations*, 242; Lander and Lander, *Journal*, 1:71–72; PRRL, Residents at Badagry to Capt. Jones, 11 July 1851, 349, and Coote to Capt. Jones, 29 December 1851, 431.

61. Kristin Mann, *Marrying Well: Marriage, Status, and Social Change among the Educated Elite in Colonial Lagos* (Cambridge: Cambridge University Press, 1985), 39–42; Kristin Mann, "Women, Landed Property, and the Accumulation of Wealth in Early Colonial Lagos," *Signs* 16 (1991): 699–701.

62. Peel, *Religious Encounter*, 74–75. See also Mann, *Marrying Well*, 40.

63. Interviews with Prince A. L. A. Ojora, Chief Ishola Bajulaiye, Chief Mobolaji Oshodi, and Alhaji A. W. A. Akibayo.

64. In addition to my own research on marriage, kinship, and household in Lagos cited in note 61, this analysis draws on Fadipe, *Sociology*, 71, 87–89, 115, 147–55; William R. Bascom, "The Principle of Seniority in the Social Structure of the Yoruba," *American Anthropologist* 44 (1942): 37–46; Gloria Marshall, "Women, Trade, and the Yoruba Family" (Ph.D. diss., Columbia University, 1964), 184–248; Simi A. Afonja, "Current Explanations of Sex Roles and Inequality: A Reconsideration," *Nigerian Journal of Economic and Social Studies* 21 (1981): 96–99; Sandra T. Barnes, "Women, Property, and Power," in *Beyond the Second Sex: New Directions in the Anthropology of Gender*, ed. Peggy Reeves Sanday and Ruth Gallagher Goodenough (Philadelphia: University of Pennsylvania Press, 1990), 255–80; Falola, *Political Economy*, 46, 51–58; J. D. Y. Peel, *Ijeshas and Nigerians: The Incorporation of a Yoruba Kingdom, 1890s–1970s* (Cambridge: Cambridge University Press, 1983), 36–54; Karin Barber, *I Could Speak until Tomorrow: Oriki, Women, and the Past in a Yoruba Town* (Washington, D.C.: Smithsonian Institution Press, 1991), 191–203, 215–20; and Peel, *Religious Encounter*, 71–80.

65. Interviews with Prince A. L. A. Ojora and C. B. Thomas.

66. Hopkins, "Report on the Yoruba," 77; *Fanojoria v. Kadiri*, 22 June 1881, JNCC, 3, 265. See also Fadipe, *Sociology*, 117, 174; Falola, *Political Economy*, 32–33, 44–53; Peel, *Ijeshas and Nigerians*, 28; and G. O. Oguntomisin and Toyin Falola, "Refugees in Yorubaland in the Nineteenth Century," *Asian and African Studies* 21 (1987): 165–85.

67. Interviews with Prince A. L. A. Ojora and Chief S. B. A. Oluwa. Also FO 84/1031, Campbell to Clarendon, 14 March 1857; and WALC, "Correspondence," Statement of Obanikoro, 229, and Statement of Ṣapara Williams, 244.

68. Interview with Prince A. L. A. Ojora; Folami, *History*, 107, 118–19.

69. T. C. Rayner, "Land Tenure in West Africa," in *Reports on Land Tenure in West Africa (1898)*, COL, West Africa Pamphlet, No. 19, 1; Hopkins, "Report on the Yoruba," 78, 85; WALC, "Draft Report," Memorandum by Sir W. Napier, 140–42, and "Correspondence," Statement of Z. S. Taylor, 230; C. K. Meek, *Land Tenure and Land Administration in Nigeria and the Cameroons* (London: Her Majesty's Stationary Office, 1957), 115, 189–91; interviews with Prince A. L. A. Ojora and Chief S. B. A. Oluwa.

On the payment of *iṣákọ̀lẹ̀* in other parts of Yorubaland, see Fadipe, *Sociology*, 178; P. C. Lloyd, *Yoruba Land Law* (London: Oxford University Press, 1962), 64, 181–82, 209–21; Sara S. Berry, *Cocoa, Custom, and Socio-economic Change in Rural Western Nigeria* (Oxford: Clarendon Press, 1975), 90–125; Peel, *Ijeshas and Nigerians*, 70, 124–29, 209; and Falola, *Political Economy*, 49.

70. Interview with Prince A. L. A. Ojora; Sandra T. Barnes, personal communication, 7 May 1991.

71. R. C. Abraham, *Dictionary of Modern Yoruba* (London: University of London Press, 1958), 236. On the importance of patron-client relationships in nineteenth-century Yorubaland, see Peel, *Ijeshas and Nigerians*, 40–43, 81; Falola, *Political Economy*, 28–32; and Barber, *I Could Speak*, 241–44. For discussions of their relevance in twentieth-century Nigeria, see Sara Berry, *Fathers Work for Their Sons: Accumulation, Mobility, and Class Formation in an Extended Yoruba Community* (Berkeley: University of California Press, 1985), 10–13, 28, 145–55; Sandra T. Barnes, *Patrons and Power: Creating a Political Community in Metropolitan Lagos* (Bloomington: Indiana University Press, 1986); and Richard A. Joseph, *Democracy and Prebendal Politics in Nigeria: The Rise and Fall of the Second Republic* (Cambridge: Cambridge University Press, 1987), 55–68, 189–92.

72. Hopkins, "Report on the Yoruba," 78. Also interview with Prince A. L. A. Ojora; and Sandra T. Barnes, personal communication, 7 May 1991.

73. Payne, *Table*, 6; Losi, *History*, 3–10; A. B. Aderibigbe, "Early History of Lagos to about 1850," in *Lagos: The Development of an African City*, ed. A. B. Aderibigbe (Ikeja: Longman Nigeria, 1975), 8; and Folami, *History*, 101–102. Also interviews with Chief Ishola Bajulaiye, Prince A. L. A. Ojora, Alhaji A. W. A. Akibayo, and Chief S. B. A. Oluwa.

74. Interviews with Alhaji A. W. A. Akibayo and Chief Mobolaji Oshodi.

75. Robertson, *Notes*, 295; Lander and Lander, *Journal*, 1:57, 70, 78.

76. Yemitan, *Madame Tinubu*, 14; Losi, *History*, 25; House of Lords Sessional Papers, 1852–53, 22, Bello to Kosoko, 8 November 1849, 338. Members of important chieftaincy families can today still name numerous slaves who belonged to their ancestors more than 130 years ago. Interviews with Alhaji A. W. A. Akibayo and Chief Mobolaji Oshodi.

77. FO 84/950, Campbell to Clarendon, 1 May 1854; FO 84/976, Campbell to Clarendon, 4 October 1855; FO 84/1002, Campbell to Clarendon, 18 February 1856; FO 84/1031, Campbell to Clarendon, 14 March, 2 July 1857; FO 84/1061, Campbell to Clarendon, 28 March 1858.

78. The preference of Africans for female slaves is well known. See Claire C. Robertson and Martin A. Klein, "Women's Importance in African Slave Systems," in *Women and Slavery in Africa*, ed. Claire C. Robertson and Martin A. Klein (Madison: University of Wisconsin Press, 1983), 3–25; Paul E. Lovejoy, *Transformations in Slavery: A History of Slavery in Africa* (Cambridge: Cambridge University Press, 1983), 6–8, 16, 109, 118–19; Miller, *Way of Death*, 130–36, 149, 159–69; and Patrick Manning, *Slavery and African Life: Occidental, Oriental, and African Slave Trades* (Cambridge: Cambridge University Press, 1990), 22. Barnes, "Ritual, Power, and Outside Knowledge" stresses the importance of new forms of knowledge brought by slaves.

79. Sir Mervyn Tew, *Report on Title to Land in Lagos* (Lagos: The Government

Printer, 1947), 36–38; WALC, "Correspondence," *Ajose v. Efunde and others*, 14 July 1892, 246–48; *Lewis v. Bankole*, 12 November 1908, 1 *NLR* 88–90; Fadipe, *Sociology*, 117, 184; interviews with Chief Mobolaji Oshodi, Alhaji A. W. A. Akibayo, Prince A. L. A. Ojora, Alhaji Atanda Balogun, and S. B. Affini.

80. Lander and Lander, *Journal*, 1:59; Yemitan, *Madame Tinubu*, 14; M. R. Delany, "Official Report of the Niger Valley Exploring Party," in *Search for a Place: Black Separatism and Africa, 1860*, by M. R. Delany and Robert Campbell (Ann Arbor: University of Michigan Press, 1969), 79; Meek, *Land Tenure*, 171. *Ajose v. Efunde*, 246–48, documents a chief's use of a redeemed slave to oversee the affairs of other slaves. Toyin Falola, "Power Relations and Social Interactions among Ibadan Slaves, 1850–1900," *AEH* 16 (1987): 95–114, argues that slaves who served as supervisors were often hated as cruel and oppressive.

81. Francis Olu Okediji and Oladejo O. Okediji, introduction to Fadipe, *Sociology*, 12; interviews with G. B. Animaṣaun, Saif Akanni Animaṣaun, and Rufai Arufai Animaṣaun.

82. Lander and Lander, *Journal*, 1:56, 70, 78; interviews with Alhaji A. W. A. Akibayo and Chief Mobolaji Oshodi; FO 84/950, Campbell to Clarendon, 1 May, 1 December 1854.

83. Oroge, "The Institution of Slavery," 83–90, 101, 153–57, 181–83, 198–99; Falola, *Political Economy*, 142–50; Toyin Falola, "Slavery and Pawnship in the Yoruba Economy of the Nineteenth Century," *S&A* 15 (1994): 221–45; Peel, *Religious Encounter*, 63–71.

84. Robertson, *Notes*, 295. The use of royal slaves developed independently at Lagos, but it was consistent with and may have been inspired in part by traditions in Benin discussed by P. A. Agbafe, *Benin under British Administration: The Impact of Colonial Rule on an African Kingdom, 1897–1938* (Atlantic Highlands, N.J.: Humanities Press, 1979), 23–27. Law, *Oyo Empire*, 67–70, 110–18, 186–90; and Oroge, "The Institution of Slavery," 2–81, discuss the use of palace slaves to consolidate royal power in Oyo and other Yoruba kingdoms north of Lagos.

85. Losi, *History*, 80–82; Tew, *Report*, 26; FO 84/950, Campbell to Clarendon, 29 January 1854.

86. Peel, *Religious Encounter*, 63, 69–70. Also interviews with Prince A. L. A. Ojora, Alhaji A. W. A. Akibayo, and C. B. Thomas. FO 84/950, Campbell to Clarendon, 20 December 1854; and CO 147/1, Freeman to Newcastle, 9 October 1862, refer to the sacrifice of slaves at Lagos.

For discussions of the lot of slaves in other parts of Yorubaland see, in addition to the works already cited, Ann O'Hear, *Power Relations in Nigeria: Ilorin Slaves and Their Successors* (Rochester, N.Y.: University of Rochester Press, 1997), 21–61; and H. C. Danmole, "Islam, Slavery and Society in Nineteenth Century Ilorin, Nigeria," *Journal of the Pakistan Historical Society* 42 (1994): 341–53.

87. Thomas J. Hutchinson, "The Social and Domestic Slavery of Western Africa, and Its Evil Influence on Commercial Progress," *Journal of the Society of Arts* 21 (26 February 1875): 315, wrote that in Lagos there existed "a sort of democratic sliding-scale" of slavery, by which "a boy, who is my property, may be owner of another boy, or several boys, each of whom may be [the] owner of boys in his turn." Hutchinson's gender bias obscures the fact that a few of the slaves who owned slaves were women and that many of the slaves owned by other slaves were female.

88. Martin A. Klein, *Slavery and Colonial Rule in French West Africa* (Cambridge: Cambridge University Press, 1998), 10.

89. *Alaka v. Alaka*, 23 January 1904, 1 *NLR* 55–56, contains information about the rights of owners in slaves belonging to their slaves.

90. Frederick Cooper, *Plantation Slavery on the East Coast of Africa* (New Haven: Yale University Press, 1977), 17–18; Lovejoy, *Transformations*, 17; Klein, *Slavery*, 7–8; and Peel, *Religious Encounter*, 67, all emphasize the importance of slaves' status as outsiders when discussing their value as henchmen.

91. Igor Kopytoff and Suzanne Miers, introduction to *Slavery in Africa: Historical and Anthropological Perspectives*, ed. Suzanne Miers and Igor Kopytoff (Madison: University of Wisconsin Press, 1977), 3–81; Peel, *Religious Encounter*, 64.

92. Much work on nineteenth-century Yorubaland emphasizes the voluntary and reciprocal, if unequal, character of most relationships of dependence and the fact that clients, strangers, and wives could leave big men who failed to fulfill their expectations. See, for example, Peel, *Ijeshas and Nigerians*, 40–45; Barber, *I Could Speak*, 183; Mann, *Marrying Well*; and Kristin Mann, "The Historical Roots and Cultural Logic of Outside Marriage," in *Nuptiality in Sub-Saharan Africa: Contemporary Anthropological and Demographic Perspectives*, ed. Caroline Bledsoe and Gilles Pison (Oxford: Clarendon Press, 1994), 167–93.

93. Interviews with Prince A. L. A. Ojora and C. B. Thomas.

94. Cooper, *Plantation Slavery*, 188, and 4–6, 16–18, 189–95, 213–52.

95. Hopkins, "Report on the Yoruba," 76–77, 90. Samuel Johnson, *The History of the Yorubas* (London: Routledge and Kegan Paul, 1969), 325, includes a description of this ritual that differs only in detail. See also Fadipe, *Sociology*, 12–13, 182–87; Ajisafe, *Laws*, 54–55; and Oroge, "The Institution of Slavery," 133–45.

96. Barnes used this phrase when presenting a paper, "Decentering Lagos: A City and Its Precolonial Region" (Conference on Africa's Urban Past, School of Oriental and African Studies, University of London, June 1996), which drew in part on her essay "Ritual, Power, and Outside Knowledge." Hopkins's "Report on the Yoruba" (90) clearly articulates this ideology.

For an interesting discussion of how female slaves were used to incorporate male slaves and ensure their continued loyalty in another region of West Africa, see Martin A. Klein, "Women in Slavery in the Western Sudan," in Robertson and Klein, eds., *Women and Slavery*, 82–84.

97. Interviews with Prince A. L. A. Ojora and C. B. Thomas.

98. Losi, *History*, 14; Agiri, "Architecture," 345; Adams, *Remarks*, 101–102; T 70/1534, Clemison to Miles, 27 January 1777; and House of Lords Sessional Papers, 1852–53, 22, Lire to Kosoko, 1 February 1850; Godinho to Kosoko, 30 April 1850; and Godinho to Kosoko, 13 July 1850, 346, 353, 358. Z. R. Dmochowski, *South-West and Central Nigeria*, vol. 2 of *An Introduction to Nigerian Traditional Architecture* (London: Ethnographica, 1990), 52, documents Portuguese stucco work in courtyards of the *ìgá*, but it is unclear when this was added.

99. Losi, *History*, 13.

100. Lander, *Records*, 1:46–48.

101. Lander and Lander, *Journal*, 1:55, 72.

102. FO 84/950, Campbell to Clarendon, 2 May 1854. Also FO 84/1002, Campbell to Clarendon, 1 May 1856.

103. Lander and Lander, *Journal*, 1:66–67.

104. Barber, *I Could Speak*, 199–203, perceptively analyzes images in the *oríkì* of nineteenth-century big men to show the relationship between consumption and the attraction of followers. Margaret Thompson Drewal, *Yoruba Ritual: Performers, Play, Agency* (Bloomington: Indiana University Press, 1992), 135–59, hints at the role of consumption in both the rise of a nineteenth-century Ijebu warrior/trader and the performance of contemporary rituals commemorating him.

105. Quoted in Verger, *Trade Relations*, 242, from "an official order," recorded in Rio de Janeiro on 31 July 1824.

106. Kate Ezra, *The Royal Art of Benin: The Perls Collection in the Metropolitan Museum of Art* (New York: The Metropolitan Museum of Art, 1992), 24–25, 277. The eastern Yoruba kingdom of Owo, which came under Benin's influence in the fifteenth century, also incorporated coral beads into the regalia of its king and chiefs. Ekpo Eyo and Frank Willett, *Treasures of Ancient Nigeria* (New York: Knopf, 1980), 15–16.

107. Photographs of Lagos chiefs taken during the twentieth century show them wearing both rich damask *agbádá* (gowns) and coral necklaces as part of their regalia. Folami, *History*, 103–20; interview with Chief Ishola Bajulaiye.

108. Lander, *Records*, 1:45; Lander and Lander, *Journal*, 1:49; House of Lords Sessional Papers, 1852–53, 22, Pereira to Kosoko, 5 November 1850, 365.

109. Adams, *Remarks*, 100, and Lander and Lander, *Journal*, 1:61, both document *ọbas* sharing meat and agricultural produce with their courtiers. Edna Bay (*Wives*, 65–67) notes the relationship, elsewhere in the region, between the redistribution of goods during the ceremonial cycle in Abomey, capital of the Kingdom of Dahomey, and the creation and maintenance of ties of mutual dependence between its rulers and their subjects. T. C. McCaskie (*State and Society*, 144–242) offers a more extended analysis of the cultural meaning of the famous *odiwira* festival in Asante, during which the state-sponsored collection and redistribution of new-season yams and other goods played a vital role.

110. Losi, *History*, 17.

111. Lander, *Records*, 1:48–49, 51; Lander and Lander, *Journal*, 1:60, 72; Richard Francis Burton, *Abeokuta and the Camaroons Mountains: An Exploration* (London: Tinsley Brothers, 1863), 1:139; FO 84/950, Campbell to Clarendon, 2 May 1854; FO 84/1002, Campbell to Clarendon, 1 May, July 1856.

112. FO 84/1002, Campbell to Clarendon, 1 May 1856.

113. For Miller's argument, see *Way of Death*, 46–53.

3. The Original Sin

1. For opposing interpretations of the annexation of Lagos, see Sir Alan Burns, *History of Nigeria* (London: Allen and Unwin, 1969), chap. 10; and J. F. A. Ajayi, "The British Occupation of Lagos, 1851–1861: A Critical Review," *Nigeria Magazine* 69 (1961): 96–105. Robert S. Smith, *The Lagos Consulate, 1851–1861* (Berkeley: University of California Press, 1979), develops a multi-causal explanation, but concludes that "the struggle of the British against the slave trade . . . was the foremost, though certainly not the single, cause of their violent irruption into

the affairs of Lagos" (33). Frederick Cooper, *From Slaves to Squatters: Plantation Labor and Agriculture in Zanzibar and Coastal Kenya, 1890–1925* (New Haven: Yale University Press, 1980), 24–33; and Howard Temperley, "Capitalism, Slavery and Ideology," *P&P* 75 (1977): 94–118, usefully critique the idealist-materialist debate over the causes of abolition and cite the relevant literature.

2. Anthony G. Hopkins, "Property Rights and Empire Building: Britain's Annexation of Lagos, 1861," *Journal of Economic History* 40 (1980): 777–98; and P. J. Cain and A. G. Hopkins, *Innovation and Expansion, 1688–1914*, vol. 1 of *British Imperialism* (London: Longman, 1993), 42–46, 71–101, 351–96, have shaped my thinking about these issues.

3. David Brion Davis, *The Problem of Slavery in Western Culture* (Harmondsworth, Middlesex: Penguin Books, 1970), 467–68; Roger Anstey, "The Pattern of British Abolition in the Eighteenth and Nineteenth Centuries," in *Anti-slavery, Religion, and Reform: Essays in Memory of Roger Anstey*, ed. Christine Bolt and Seymour Drescher (Folkestone, Kent: Wm. Dawson and Sons, 1980), 20–24.

4. David Brion Davis, "Slavery and 'Progress,'" in Bolt and Drescher, eds., *Anti-slavery, Religion, and Reform*, 353.

5. For additional works on anti-slavery thought, see Roger Anstey, *The Atlantic Slave Trade and British Abolition, 1760–1810* (Atlantic Highlands, N.J.: Humanities Press, 1975); Seymour Drescher, "Capitalism and Abolition: Values and Forces in Britain, 1783–1814," in *Liverpool, the African Slave Trade, and Abolition*, ed. Roger Anstey and P. E. H. Hair (Liverpool: Historic Society of Lancashire and Cheshire, 1976), 167–95; essays by Drescher and Temperley in Bolt and Drescher, eds., *Anti-slavery, Religion, and Reform;* and essays by Temperley and Anstey in *The Abolition of the Atlantic Slave Trade*, ed. David Eltis and James Walvin (Madison: University of Wisconsin Press, 1981).

6. Howard Temperley, "Anti-slavery as a Form of Cultural Imperialism," in Bolt and Drescher, eds., *Anti-slavery, Religion, and Reform*, 341–46. Seymour Drescher, *The Mighty Experiment: Free Labor versus Slavery in British Emancipation* (New York: Oxford University Press, 2002), chaps. 2–4, analyzes in more detail the complex relationship between abolition and changing labor ideology in Britain.

7. David Brion Davis, *The Problem of Slavery in the Age of Revolution, 1770–1823* (Ithaca, N.Y.: Cornell University Press, 1975), 49.

8. In addition to works already cited, see James Walvin, "The Public Campaign in England against Slavery, 1787–1834," in Eltis and Walvin, eds., *The Abolition of the Atlantic Slave Trade*, 63–79; Seymour Drescher, *Capitalism and Antislavery: British Mobilization in Comparative Perspective* (New York: Oxford University Press, 1987); Clare Midgley, *Women against Slavery: The British Campaigns, 1780–1870* (London: Routledge, 1992); and J. R. Oldfield, *Popular Politics and British Anti-slavery: The Mobilisation of Public Opinion against the Slave Trade, 1787–1807* (Manchester: Manchester University Press, 1995).

9. Christopher Lloyd, *The Navy and the Slave Trade: The Suppression of the African Slave Trade in the Nineteenth Century* (London: Longmans, Green, 1949); W. E. F. Ward, *The Royal Navy and the Slavers: The Suppression of the Atlantic Slave Trade* (London: George Allen and Unwin, 1969); Leslie Bethell, *The Abolition of the Brazilian Slave Trade: Britain, Brazil, and the Slave Trade Question, 1807–1869* (Cambridge: Cambridge University Press, 1970); David Eltis, *Economic Growth and the*

Ending of the Transatlantic Slave Trade (New York: Oxford University Press, 1987), 81–101.

10. Michael Craton, "Slave Revolts and the End of Slavery," in *The Atlantic Slave Trade*, ed. David Northrup (Lexington, Mass.: D. C. Heath and Co., 1994), 203–17; Robin Blackburn, *The Overthrow of Colonial Slavery, 1776–1848* (London: Verso, 1988), 419–72.

11. Howard Temperley, *British Antislavery, 1833–1870* (London: Longman, 1972); Anstey, "The Pattern of British Abolition," 24–30; Walvin, "Public Campaign," 71–77; Drescher, *Capitalism and Antislavery*, 111–34; Midgley, *Women against Slavery*, 43–118. Thomas C. Holt masterfully deconstructs the relationship between Anglo-American liberal economic and political ideology and British thought and action regarding slave emancipation in *The Problem of Freedom: Race, Labor, and Politics in Jamaica and Britain, 1832–1938* (Baltimore: Johns Hopkins University Press, 1992), 3–53, and "The Essence of the Contract: The Articulation of Race, Gender, and Political Economy in British Emancipation Policy, 1838–1866," in *Beyond Slavery: Explorations of Race, Labor, and Citizenship in Postemancipation Societies*, by Frederick Cooper, Thomas G. Holt, and Rebecca J. Scott (Chapel Hill: University of North Carolina Press, 2000), 33–59.

12. Temperley, *British Antislavery*, 42–61.

13. Sir Thomas Fowell Buxton, *The African Slave Trade and Its Remedy* (London: John Murray, 1840), 264.

14. Ibid., 247.

15. Ibid., 297, 463.

16. Ibid., 190–93. Also see Philip D. Curtin, *The Image of Africa: British Ideas and Action, 1780–1850* (Madison: University of Wisconsin Press, 1964), 235–43, 364–65, 415–31; and Howard Temperley, *White Dreams, Black Africa: The Antislavery Expedition to the River Niger, 1841–1842* (New Haven: Yale University Press, 1991), 12.

17. Buxton, *African Slave Trade*, 272, 297.

18. Buxton, *African Slave Trade*, 244; J. F. A. Ajayi, *Christian Missions in Nigeria, 1841–1891: The Making of a New Elite* (London: Longmans, 1965), 11; Eltis, *Economic Growth*, 119–20, 223–24. Jean Comaroff and John Comaroff, *Christianity, Colonialism, and Consciousness in South Africa*, vol. 1 of *Of Revelation and Revolution* (Chicago: University of Chicago Press, 1991), 80, note that the Nonconformist missionaries who went to South Africa in the early nineteenth century dreamed of creating a "society of independent peasants."

19. Buxton, *African Slave Trade*, 241–42.

20. Ibid., 268, 295. Curtin, *Image*, 434–35, and Comaroff and Comaroff, *Christianity, Colonialism, and Consciousness*, 79–80, provide further evidence of the interconnectedness of Christian and commercial, moral and material concerns in mid-nineteenth-century British thought.

21. Curtin, *Image*, 253, 284–85, 300–302; Davis, *Slavery in Western Culture*, 466; Eltis, *Economic Growth*, 21–27, 119–20, 223–24.

22. Curtin, *Image*, 140–76; Robin Hallett, *The Penetration of Africa: European Enterprise and Exploration Principally in Northern and Western Africa up to 1830* (London: Routledge and Kegan Paul, 1965); F. J. McLynn, *Hearts of Darkness: The European Exploration of Africa* (London: Hutchinson, 1992), 13–38.

23. Eugene Stock, *The History of the Church Missionary Society*, vol. 1 (London: The Church Missionary Society, 1899), chaps. 8, 9, 24; Christopher Fyfe, *A History of Sierra Leone* (London: Oxford University Press, 1962), 94–95, 103–104, 127–31, 153–54; John Peterson, *Province of Freedom: A History of Sierra Leone, 1787–1870* (London: Faber and Faber, 1969); Comaroff and Comaroff, *Christianity, Colonialism, and Consciousness*, chaps. 5, 6; essays by Elbourne and Ross, Hodgson, and Beck in *Christianity in Southern Africa: A Political, Social, and Cultural History*, ed. Richard Elphick and Rodney Davenport (Berkeley: University of California Press, 1997).

24. Buxton's views were shaped by reading the contemporary literature on Africa. Buxton, *African Slave Trade*, 190–247; Temperley, *White Dreams*, 9–12.

25. This occurred most notably in the government support he won for an expedition up the Niger River in 1841 to found an agricultural and philanthropic colony. J. Gallagher, "Fowell Buxton and the New African Policy, 1838–1842," *Cambridge Historical Journal* 10 (1950): 36–58; Temperley, *White Dreams*, 15–39.

26. Curtin, *Image*, 316–17, 443; Temperley, *British Antislavery*, 62–92.

27. For evidence of the influence of these ideas on a broad range of people involved with Africa, see the testimony of Broadhead, Hutton, Denman, Clegg, Seward, and Levinge in PP 1842.XI.1, Report from the Select Committee on the West Coast of Africa, Minutes of Evidence; and that of Keogh, Birch, Carr, Denman, Duncan, and Hutton in PP 1847–8.XXII.1, First–Fourth Reports from the Select Committee on the Slave Trade.

28. Robert Gavin, "Nigeria and Lord Palmerston," *Ibadan* 12 (1961): 24–27. Also Gallagher, "Fowell Buxton," 47; and PRRL, Palmerston to Beecroft, 30 June 1849, 227.

29. Curtin, *Image*, 421.

30. Temperley, *White Dreams*, 168. See, for example, David Livingstone, *Dr. Livingstone's Cambridge Lectures* (Cambridge: Deighton, Bell, 1858).

31. H. G. C. Matthew, "Disraeli, Gladstone, and the Policy of Mid-Victorian Budgets," *Historical Journal* 22 (1979): 616; Gareth Stedman Jones, *Languages of Class: Studies in English Working Class History, 1832–1982* (Cambridge: Cambridge University Press, 1983), 177–78; Eugenio F. Biagini, "Popular Liberals, Gladstonian Finance, and the Debate on Taxation, 1860–1874," in *Currents of Radicalism: Popular Radicalism, Organised Labour, and Party Politics in Britain, 1850–1914*, ed. Eugenio F. Biagini and Alastair J. Reid (Cambridge: Cambridge University Press, 1991), 134–62; Cain and Hopkins, *Innovation and Expansion*, 71–104; Philip Harling, "Rethinking 'Old Corruption'," *P&P* 147 (1995): 127–58.

32. E. P. Thompson, *The Poverty of Theory and Other Essays* (New York: Monthly Review Press, 1978), 258–60; Jones, *Languages of Class*, introduction, 21–22; Eugenio F. Biagini and Alastair J. Reid, "Currents of Radicalism, 1850–1914," in Biagini and Reid, eds., *Currents of Radicalism*, 1–7.

33. The middle class found anti-slavery compelling in its own right and congruent with its political and economic objectives: free trade as well as free labor; parliamentary and religious reform; and state intervention to correct the worst abuses of pure market forces. To some working-class radicals, anti-slavery seemed to extend traditional concepts of English liberty and open the way for an examination of the evils of capitalism, as well as of slavery. Blackburn, *Colonial Slavery*, 436–72. See also the essays by Drescher, Harrison, and Walvin in Bolt and Drescher,

eds., *Anti-slavery, Religion, and Reform;* Drescher, *Capitalism and Antislavery;* and Midgley, *Women against Slavery.*

34. Boyd Hilton, *Corn, Cash, Commerce: The Economic Policies of the Tory Governments, 1815–1830* (London: Oxford University Press, 1977); W. D. Rubinstein, "The End of 'Old Corruption' in Britain, 1780–1860," *P&P* 101 (1983): 55–86; Harling, "Rethinking 'Old Corruption,'" 127–58; Miles Taylor, *The Decline of British Radicalism, 1847–1860* (Oxford: Clarendon Press, 1995); Philip Harling, *The Waning of "Old Corruption": The Politics of Economical Reform in Britain, 1779–1846* (Oxford: Clarendon Press, 1996).

35. Cain and Hopkins, *Innovation and Expansion*, 53–104; A. G. Hopkins, "The 'New International Economic Order' in the Nineteenth Century: Britain's First Development Plan for Africa," in *From Slave Trade to "Legitimate" Commerce: The Commercial Transition in Nineteenth-Century West Africa*, ed. Robin Law (Cambridge: Cambridge University Press, 1995), 250.

36. R. J. Gavin, "Palmerston and Africa," *JHSN* 6 (1971): 93–99.

37. PRRL, Palmerston to Lords Commissioners of the Admiralty, 27 September 1851, 361. Also PRRL, Bruce to Secretary of the Admiralty, 1 November 1851, 385.

38. Fyfe, *History of Sierra Leone*, 114–51; Peterson, *Province of Freedom*, 17–117.

39. Jean Herskovits Kopytoff, *A Preface to Modern Nigeria: The "Sierra Leonians" in Yoruba, 1830–1890* (Madison: University of Wisconsin Press, 1965), 36–60; Ajayi, *Christian Missions*, 29–34.

40. Pierre Verger, *Trade Relations between the Bight of Benin and Bahia from the 17th to 19th Century*, trans. Evelyn Crawford (Ibadan: Ibadan University Press, 1976), 314–22, 469–70, 532–66; Jerry Michael Turner, "Les Bresiliens—The Impact of Former Brazilian Slaves upon Dahomey" (Ph.D. diss., Boston University, 1975), 51–84. On the 1835 slave revolt and its consequences, see João José Reis, *Slave Rebellion in Brazil: The Muslim Uprising of 1835 in Bahia*, trans. Arthur Brakel (Baltimore: Johns Hopkins University Press, 1993).

41. S. O. Biobaku, *The Egba and Their Neighbours, 1842–1872* (Oxford: Clarendon Press, 1957), 27–37; C. W. Newbury, *The Western Slave Coast and Its Rulers* (Oxford: Clarendon Press, 1961), 42–56; Ajayi, *Christian Missions*, 31–42; J. D. Y. Peel, *Religious Encounter and the Making of the Yoruba* (Bloomington: Indiana University Press, 2000), 123–51. For missionary representations of their position, see PRRL, Gollmer and Van Cooten to Fanshawe, 22 October 1850, encl. in Secretary of the Admiralty to Stanley, 3 January 1851, 308–309; Gollmer to Venn, 2 January 1851, 313; Townsend to Trotter, 10 December 1850, 314; Gollmer to Trotter, 13 January 1851, 316, all forwarded to Palmerston in 1851.

42. Bernard Schnapper, *La politique et le commerce français dans le Golfe de Guinée de 1838 à 1871* (Paris: Mouton, 1961), 118–28; Martin Lynn, *Commerce and Economic Change in West Africa: The Palm Oil Trade in the Nineteenth Century* (Cambridge: Cambridge University Press, 1997), 34–44; Marion Johnson, "Ivory and the Nineteenth Century Transformation in West Africa," in *Figuring African Trade: Proceedings of the Symposium on the Quantification and Structure of the Import and Export and Long Distance Trade in Africa, 1800–1913*, ed. G. Liesegang, H. Pasch, and A. Jones (Berlin: D. Reimer, 1986), 103–107; Eltis, *Economic Growth*, 83. Also PP

1842.XI.1, Report from the Select Committee on the West Coast of Africa, especially testimony by Swanzy, Clegg, Dring, and Broadhead.

43. PRRL, Bruce to Secretary of the Admiralty, 1 November 1851, encl. in Secretary of the Admiralty to Stanley, 10 January 1852, 385.

44. PRRL, Palmerston to Lords Commissioners of the Admiralty, 27 September 1851, 362.

45. Smith, *Lagos Consulate*, 1–26, provides a good discussion of local and regional politics during the 1840s and 1850s.

46. PRRL, Akitoye to Beecroft, no date, but 15 February 1851, encl. in Beecroft to Palmerston, 24 February 1851, 323–24.

47. PRRL, Gollmer to Fanshawe, 26 March 1851, encl. in Secretary of the Admiralty to Stanley, 30 March 1851, 331–32; Townsend to Beecroft, 20 March 1851, and Gollmer to Beecroft, 18 March 1851, encl. in Beecroft to Palmerston, 2 June 1851, 337–40; Obba Shoron to Jones, 3 July 1851, encl. in Secretary of the Admiralty to Stanley, 10 September 1851, 356–57; Secretary of the Church Missionary Society to Palmerston, 20 August 1851, 359–60; Chiefs of Abeokuta to Palmerston, 15 August 1851, 365. For a fuller analysis of these events, see E. H. Phillips, "The Church Missionary Society, the Imperial Factor, and Yoruba Politics, 1842–1873" (Ph.D. diss., University of Southern California, 1966).

48. In addition to the documents cited in the previous two notes, see Letters from the Residents of Badagry to Captain Jones, 11 July 1851, Captain Foote, 16 June 1851, and Commander Heath, 17 June and 18 June 1851, all encl. in Secretary of the Admiralty to Stanley, 10 September 1851, 346–55.

49. PRRL, Akitoye to Beecroft, no date, but 15 February 1851, encl. in Beecroft to Palmerston, 24 February 1851, 323–24.

50. Phillips, "The Church Missionary Society," 285; Smith, *Lagos Consulate*, 23–25; L. C. Dioka and Siyan Oyeweso, "Intergroup Relations in a Frontier State: The Case of Badagry," in *Badagry: A Study in History, Culture, and Traditions of an Ancient City*, ed. G. O. Ogunremi, M. O. Opeloye, and Siyan Oyeweso (Ibadan: Rex Charles, 1994), 144–48.

51. Lloyd, *The Navy and the Slave Trade*, 150; Ward, *The Royal Navy and the Slavers*, 182; Curtin, *Image*, 468; Eltis, *Economic Growth*, 88–89.

52. PRRL, Palmerston to Beecroft, 21 February 1851, 311–12.

53. PRRL, Beecroft to Palmerston, 26 November 1851, and "Minutes of a Conference with Kosoko, Chief of Lagos," encl. in Beecroft's letter, 371–74.

54. Burns, *History of Nigeria*, 115–26; Lloyd, *The Navy and the Slave Trade*, 149–62; Ward, *The Royal Navy and the Slavers*, 205–15; Smith, *Lagos Consulate*, 26–31; Obaro Ikime, *The Fall of Nigeria: The British Conquest* (London: Heinemann, 1977), 93–101.

55. PRRL, Granville to Beecroft, 24 January 1852, 393.

56. Accounts of the two engagements can be found in PRRL, Beecroft to Palmerston, 26 November 1851, and Beecroft to Palmerston, 3 January 1852, 371–438.

The exodus of the foreign slave traders, who were never permitted to return, had a lasting effect on the composition of the Brazilian community at Lagos, which descends, more exclusively than elsewhere on the Slave Coast, from freed Brazilian slaves who emigrated in the mid-nineteenth century rather than from slave traders.

57. FO 84/856, Beecroft to Palmerston, 21 February 1851.

58. PRRL, Beecroft to Palmerston, 21, 24 February 1851, 317–22. Also PRRL, Bruce to Secretary of the Admiralty, 17 January 1852, encl. in Secretary of the Admiralty to Mr. Layard, 24 February 1852, 438.

59. PRRL, Beecroft to Palmerston, 21 February 1852, 317–22.

60. PROL, "Agreement with the King and Chiefs of Lagos," 28 February 1852, 342–44.

61. FO 84/976, Campbell to Clarendon, 2 June 1855.

62. For a description of this event, see the *Church Missionary Intelligencer* 3 (1852): 124–26.

63. Ajayi, *Christian Missions*, 77.

64. Kopytoff, *Preface*, 44–137; Verger, *Trade Relations*, 532–66; Turner, "Les Bresiliens," 85–213; Manuela Carneiro da Cunha, *Negros, estrangeiros: Os escravos libertos e sua volta à África* (São Paulo: Editora Brasiliense, 1985); Kunle Akinsemoyin and Alan Vaughan-Richards, *Building Lagos* (Lagos: F and A Services, 1976), 3–29; Marianno Carneiro da Cunha, *From Slave Quarters to Town Houses: Brazilian Architecture in Nigeria and the People's Republic of Benin* (São Paulo: Nobel/Edusp, 1985); Lisa A. Lindsay, "'To Return to the Bosom of Their Fatherland': Brazilian Immigrants in Nineteenth-Century Lagos," *S&A* 15 (1994): 22–50; Rodolfo Sarracino, *Los que volvieron a Africa* (Havana: Editorial de Ciencias Sociales, 1988), 47–64.

65. Smith, *Lagos Consulate*, 48–50.

66. Reports to the Foreign Office throughout 1853 document these problems. See, for example, FO 84/920, Fraser to Malmesbury, 28 January 1853, Fraser to Clarendon, 30 May 1853, plus encls., and Campbell to Clarendon, 28 July, 1, 10 September, 31 October, 30 November, 20 December 1853. For Akitoye's perspective on the conflicts, see a letter from him to Campbell dated 29 July 1853, encl. in FO 84/920, Campbell to Clarendon, 19 September 1853. Smith, *Lagos Consulate*, 52–58, provides a fuller discussion of these events.

67. See a report by the missionary E. G. Irving, *Church Missionary Intelligencer* 5 (1854): 106–109. Accounts also circulated that Akitoye died by his own hand. FO 84/920, Campbell to Clarendon, 3 September 1853; John B. Losi, *History of Lagos* (Lagos: Tika Tore Press, 1914), 39.

68. Biobaku, *The Egba*, 38–52; J. F. A. Ajayi and Robert Smith, *Yoruba Warfare in the Nineteenth Century* (Cambridge: Cambridge University Press, 1964), 76–128; J. F. A. Ajayi, "The Aftermath of the Fall of Old Oyo," in *History of West Africa*, ed. J. F. A. Ajayi and Michael Crowder (New York: Columbia University Press, 1973), 2:145–66; Smith, *Lagos Consulate*, 84–85; Robert S. Smith, *Kingdoms of the Yoruba* (Madison: University of Wisconsin Press, 1988), 125–51.

69. Smith, *Lagos Consulate*, 54; Sara S. Berry, *Cocoa, Custom, and Socio-economic Change in Rural Western Nigeria* (Oxford: Clarendon Press, 1975), 23.

70. Biobaku, *The Egba*, 38–63; Smith, *Lagos Consulate*, 58–65, 87–88.

71. FO 84/950, Campbell to Clarendon, 1, 4, 18 May 1854; FO 84/976, Campbell to Clarendon, 30 July 1855; FO 84/1002, Clarendon to Campbell, 17 May 1856, Campbell to Clarendon, 26 March, 1 October 1856, and Williams to Campbell, 10 August 1857.

72. Correspondence documenting these developments is too voluminous to

cite individually but runs through FO 84/886, 920, 950, 976, 1002, 1031, 1061, 1088, and 1114–15. Newbury, *Western Slave Coast*, 55–62; Ajayi, *Christian Missions*, 76–83; Phillips, "The Church Missionary Society"; and Smith, *Lagos Consulate*, provide further discussion of these events.

73. David Eltis and David Richardson, "West Africa and the Transatlantic Slave Trade: New Evidence of Long-Run Trends," in *Routes to Slavery: Direction, Ethnicity, and Mortality in the Transatlantic Slave Trade*, ed. David Eltis and David Richardson (London: Frank Cass, 1997), 26. Also FO 84/950, Campbell to Clarendon, 27 March 1854; FO 84/1002, Campbell to Clarendon, 18 August 1856; FO 84/1031, Campbell to Clarendon, 27 July, 5, 31 August, 5 September, 3 October, 3 November 1857.

74. FO 84/1031, Campbell to Clarendon, 5, 10, 31 August 1857, and Clarendon to Campbell, 31 August 1857. Newbury, *Western Slave Coast*, 62–64; Smith, *Lagos Consulate*, 68–70; Schnapper, *La politique et le commerce français*, 159–60; Elisée Soumonni, "The Compatibility of the Slave and Palm Oil Trades in Dahomey, 1818–1858," in Law, ed., *From Slave Trade to "Legitimate" Commerce*, 84–88.

75. See dispatches from Fraser to Clarendon dated 30 May 1853 in FO 84/920. Also FO 84/920, Campbell to Clarendon, 7 October 1853; FO 84/950, Campbell to Clarendon, 5, 21 December 1854; FO 84/968, Ward to Macedo, 26 April 1855; FO 84/976, Campbell to Clarendon, 2 February 1855; FO 84/1002, Campbell to Clarendon, 16 August 1856.

76. FO 84/920, Fraser to Clarendon, 30 May 1853, and encls.; FO 84/1002, Campbell to Clarendon, 19 August 1856.

77. FO 84/976, Campbell to Clarendon, 2 August 1855; FO 84/1002, Campbell to Clarendon, 6 May, 25 September 1856; Hopes to Adams, 10 October 1856, encl. in McCoskry to Campbell, 7 November 1856.

78. Fo 84/976, Campbell to Clarendon, 2 August 1855; PROL, McCoskry to Russell, 7 August 1861, 347. Also Kopytoff, *Preface*, 100–101; Omoniyi Adewoye, *The Judicial System in Southern Nigeria, 1854–1954* (Atlantic Highlands, N.J.: Humanities Press, 1977), 46.

79. See, for example, FO 84/1002, Campbell to Clarendon, 25 September 1856.

80. PROL, Brand to Russell, 9 April 1860, 344–45.

81. John D. Hargreaves, *Prelude to the Partition of West Africa* (London: Macmillan, 1963), 38–41.

82. PROL, Russell to Foote, 22 June 1861, 345–46.

83. For the conflicting accounts of the events leading up to the cession, see McCoskry to Russell, 7 August 1861; Chiefs of Lagos to Queen Victoria, 8 August 1861, and King Dosunmu to Queen Victoria, 8 August 1861, encl. in Venn to Russell, 20 September 1861; and Chiefs of Lagos to Queen Victoria, 10 September 1861. These are reprinted in PROL, 347–56. The original of McCoskry's letter can be found in CO 147/2.

84. CO 147/2, McCoskry to Russell, 7 August 1861.

85. Hargreaves, *Prelude*, 40.

86. CO 147/6, Freeman to Newcastle, 9 January 1864.

87. Matthew, "Disraeli," 615–17; Biagini, "Popular Liberals," 134–62; Harling, "Rethinking 'Old Corruption,'" 127–58.

88. PROL, Russell to Foote, 22 June 1861, 345–46.

89. CO 147/1, Newcastle to Freeman, 16 December 1861.

90. Sara Berry, *No Condition Is Permanent: The Social Dynamics of Agrarian Change in Sub-Saharan Africa* (Madison: University of Wisconsin Press, 1993), 24. For evidence of policies regarding budgets in Lagos see, for example, CO 147/4, Glover to Newcastle, 10 August 1863; and CO 147/6, Freeman to Newcastle, 9 May 1864.

91. P. J. Cain and A. G. Hopkins, in *Crisis and Deconstruction, 1914–1990*, vol. 2 of *British Imperialism* (London: Longman, 1993), 232–34, make a similar argument about a later period in the history of British imperialism.

92. Burns, *History of Nigeria*, 138–39.

93. Estimates of Revenue and Expenditure submitted annually to the Colonial Office and found in the CO 147 series, along with *Blue Books* for the colony, contain information about administrative and other workers employed by the government.

94. In addition to higher salaries, Europeans received passage, accommodation or housing allowances, and lengthy paid home leaves, which made them much more expensive to employ than educated Africans.

95. CO 147/6, Freeman to Newcastle, 8 February 1864. Also RWCA, Minutes of Evidence, W. McCoskry, 6 April 1865, 72; and OR, Appendix D, 46, 57.

96. CO 147/1, Newcastle to Freeman, 16 December 1861; CO 147/3, Freeman to Newcastle, 8 January 1863, and "Extract of the Minutes of the Council," 24 June 1862–30 June 1863; CO 147/6, Freeman to Cardwell, 4 July 1864. Information about the growth and development of the local administration comes from analysis of the annual Estimates of Revenue and Expenditure.

97. FO 84/1002, Campbell to Clarendon, 14 May 1856; CO 147/2, McCoskry to Russell, 5 August 1861; RWCA, Minutes of Evidence, W. McCoskry, 6 April 1865, 71.

98. Hopkins, "Property Rights and Empire Building," 777–79.

99. CO 147/1, Freeman to Newcastle, 8 March 1862; CO 147/3, Freeman to Newcastle, 10 April 1863, Freeman to Queen's Advocate, 17 July 1863. On the history of the colonial legal system, see Adewoye, *Judicial System*, 45–50; and T. Olawale Elias, *The Nigerian Legal System* (London: Routledge and Kegan Paul, 1963), 44–57.

100. CO 147/1, Freeman to Newcastle, 10 June 1862; RWCA, Minutes of Evidence, Col. Ord, 3 April 1865, 57; CO 147/17, Glover to Kennedy, 1 January 1870. On the history of the Nigerian police, see Tekena N. Tamuno, *The Police in Modern Nigeria* (Ibadan: Ibadan University Press, 1970), 10–17.

101. CO 147/7, Freeman to Cardwell, 4 July 1864.

102. CO 147/1, Newcastle to Freeman, 16 December 1861.

103. CO 147/31, Strahan to Carnarvon, 28 June 1875.

104. CO 147/1, Freeman to Newcastle, 8 March 1862.

105. *Dictionary of National Biography*, 1967 ed., s.v. "Sir John Hawley Glover"; W. D. McIntyre, "Commander Glover and the Colony of Lagos, 1861–73," *JAH* 4 (1963): 57–79. See also CO 147/4, Glover to Newcastle, 10 September 1863; CO 147/6, Freeman to Newcastle, 10 February 1864; and Colonial Office minutes on these dispatches.

106. See the minutes attached to CO 147/4, Glover to Newcastle, 10 September 1863; CO 147/4, Glover to Newcastle, 8 August 1863; and CO 147/6, Freeman to Newcastle, 9 January 1864.

107. CO 147/24, Pope Hennessy to Kimberley, 14 October 1872, and encls., quoted in Tamuno, *The Police*, 22.

108. CO 147/24, Pope Hennessy to Kimberley, 4 November 1872, quoted in Tamuno, *The Police*, 22.

109. On the relationship between Glover and Taiwo, see Kristin Mann, "The Rise of Taiwo Olowo: Law, Accumulation, and Mobility in Early Colonial Lagos," in *Law in Colonial Africa*, ed. Kristin Mann and Richard Roberts (Portsmouth, N.H.: Heinemann, 1991), 93–102.

110. See letters and a petition from Dosunmu and Chiefs of Lagos to Queen Victoria, 8 August, 10 September, 1861, PROL, 349–52, 355–59. Also CO 147/1, Freeman to Newcastle, 10 February, 8 March, 4 June 1862; and CO 147/4, Glover to Newcastle, 10 October 1863. Criticism of the Egba runs through government dispatches written during the 1860s and early 1870s. On the Ijaye war and response of the Lagos government to it, see Biobaku, *The Egba*, 64–95; Ajayi and Smith, *Yoruba Warfare*, 40–43, 59–128 passim; Toyin Falola, "The Yoruba Wars of the Nineteenth Century," in *Yoruba Historiography*, ed. Toyin Falola (Madison: African Studies Program, University of Wisconsin–Madison, 1991), 135; and Dare Oguntomisin, "Warfare and Military Alliances in Yorubaland in the Nineteenth Century," in *Warfare and Diplomacy in Precolonial Nigeria*, ed. Toyin Falola and Robin Law (Madison: African Studies Program, University of Wisconsin–Madison, 1992), 31–39.

111. CO 147/4, Glover to Newcastle, 10 August 1863. Also GP f1, Glover to ex-king Dosunmu, 24 May, 12 September 1863.

112. Smith, *Lagos Consulate*, 58–65, 127; FO 84/950, Campbell to Clarendon, 18 May 1854; FO 84/976, Campbell to Clarendon, 2 June, 3 October 1855; FO 84/1002, Campbell to Clarendon, 2 May, 1 October 1856; CO 147/1, Freeman to Newcastle, 7 June, 1 July, 8 December 1862; CO 147/2, McCoskry to Russell, 4 October, 5 December 1861, 10 January 1862; CO 147/3, Freeman to Newcastle, 5 January, 7 February 1863.

113. Interview with Emmanuel Molade Willoughby.

114. CO 147/1, Freeman to Newcastle, 1 July, 6 October 1862; CO 147/2, McCoskry to Russell, 7 January 1862; CO 147/4, Freeman to Newcastle, 10 December 1863. Also Mann, "Taiwo Olowo," 93–94; and Sir Mervyn L. Tew, *Report on Title to Land in Lagos* (Lagos: The Government Printer, 1947), 36.

115. GP f6, Glover to My Lord, n.d. (but 1873). For correspondence relevant to this affair, along with a copy of the report of the inquiry into it, see GP f2; and CO 147/29, Glover to Kimberley, 19 June 1873.

116. GP f2, Glover to Kennedy, 4 April 1870, encl. in a note from Pope Hennessy, 4 January 1873, and Memorandum of Agreement . . . between the elders of . . . Igbehin . . . and Taiwo of Lagos, January 1871; GP f5, Petition of merchants and traders of Lagos to Pope Hennessy, 29 April 1872; GP f6, Pope Hennessy to Kimberley, 5 October 1873; and CO 147/27, Pope-Hennessy to Kimberley, 5 February 1873.

117. GP f6, Turton to Glover, 18 January 1873.

118. CO 147/11, Glover to Cardwell, 6 January 1866; interview with Chief Durojaiye Olajuwon Oshodi; Lady Glover, *Life of Sir John Hawley Glover* (London: Smith, Elder and Co., 1897), 111.

119. CO 147/1, Freeman to Newcastle, 9 July 1862; CO 147/11, Blackall to Cardwell, 21 March 1866.

120. Glover, *Life*, 106.

121. CO 147/2, McCoskry to Russell, 7 January 1862; GP f5, Williams to Glover, January 1872, and Taiwo's supporters to Pope Hennessy, 28 May 1872. Also Patrick D. Cole, *Modern and Traditional Elites in the Politics of Lagos* (Cambridge: Cambridge University Press, 1975), 31–35, 170; and Mann, "Taiwo Olowo," 102.

122. CO 147/8, Glover to Cardwell, 5, 9 April, 8 May 1865; CO 147/9, Glover to Cardwell, 7 July 1865.

123. See, for example, GP f4, Johnson to "Pa," 19 October 1872; GP f5, Foresythe to Glover, 7 August 1872, Porter to Glover, 6 August 1872, Turton to Glover, 16, 19 June, 1, 5, 6 July 1872, and Willoughby to Glover, 29 August 1872; GP f6, Turton to Glover, 18, 31 January, 29 June 1873, and Willoughby to Glover, 23 January, 24 June 1873.

124. GP f2, Report of the Commission of Inquiry Regarding Emmanuel Willoughby, 1870, and Memorandum by Sheriff J. A. O. Payne, July 1872.

125. GP f6 Glover to My Lord, n.d. (but 1873).

126. Expressions of concern about unrest in Lagos run through dispatches from the colony into the mid-1860s. See, for example, CO 147/2, McCoskry to Russell, 5 December 1861, 6 January 1862; CO 147/4, Glover to Newcastle, 10 October 1863; CO 147/8, Glover to Cardwell, 9 April 1865; and CO 147/11, Glover to Cardwell, 3 February 1866. On relations with frontier communities and interior states, see CO 147/3, Freeman to Newcastle, 26 February, 2, 30 March 1863; CO 147/4, Freeman to Newcastle, 31 December 1863; CO 147/5, Freeman to Newcastle, 3 June 1863; CO 147/6, Freeman to Newcastle, 9 May 1864; CO 147/8, Glover to Cardwell, 14 March, 5 April 1865; CO 147/9, Glover to Cardwell, 9 June, 4 September 1865. Relevant secondary literature includes Biobaku, *The Egba;* Newbury, *Western Slave Coast*, 89–95; Kopytoff, *Preface*, 141–53; Ajayi and Smith, *Yoruba Warfare*, 97–128; and Smith, *Kingdoms*, 135–38.

127. CO 147/2, McCoskry to Russell, 5 August 1861; CO 147/3, Freeman to Newcastle, 6 January 1863; CO 147/4, Freeman to Newcastle, 10, 31 December 1863; CO 147/6, Freeman to Newcastle, 9 January, 6, 9 May, 4 July 1864; CO 147/8, Glover to Cardwell, 2 February 1865; CO 147/9, Glover to Cardwell, 9 June 1865.

128. CO 147/3, Freeman to Newcastle, 7 February 1863.

129. Glover, *Life*, 105.

130. RWCA, Minutes of Evidence, Col. Ord, 3 April 1865, 57, and W. McCoskry, 6 April 1865, 72. Also PROL, McCoskry to Russell, 7 June 1861; CO 147/1, Freeman to Newcastle, 3, 4 July, 9 October 1862; CO 147/3, Glover to Newcastle, 10 June 1863; CO 147/4, Freeman to Newcastle, 31 December 1863; CO 147/6, Freeman to Newcastle, 6 May 1864; Tamuno, *The Police*, 15–19; E. A. Oroge, "The Fugitive Slave Question in Anglo-Egba Relations, 1861–1886," *JHSN* 8 (1975): 61–80. On the British use of the term "Hausa" to embrace Africans

from different ethnic backgrounds who were identified as good soldiers, see David Killingray and David Omissi, eds. *Guardians of Empire: The Armed Forces of the Colonial Powers, c. 1700–1964* (Manchester: Manchester University Press, 1999), 15.

131. Glover, *Life*, 83; Oroge, "Fugitive Slave Question," 65; Richard Francis Burton, *Abeokuta and the Camaroons Mountains: An Exploration* (London: Tinsley Brothers, 1863), 1:297. Also Tiffany Gleason, "Entrenching Identity: The Creation of the Hausa Armed Force in Nineteenth-Century Lagos" (Department of History, Emory University, first-year research paper, 2005).

132. CO 147/1, Freeman to Newcastle, 3 July 1862. Also FO 84/1175, Freeman to Russell, 1 July 1862, quoted in Oroge, "Fugitive Slave Question," 65; CO 147/4, Freeman to Newcastle, 31 December 1863; CO 147/6, Freeman to Newcastle, 6 May 1864.

133. RWCA, Minutes of Evidence, Col. Ord, 3 April 1865, 63; CO 147/6, Freeman to Newcastle, 6 May 1864; CO 147/9, Glover to Cardwell, 7 July, 14 August 1866; CO 147/11, Glover to Cardwell, 8 January, 3 February, 21 June 1866.

134. Glover, *Life*, 83–84; Oroge, "Fugitive Slave Question," 74; CO 147/7, Glover to Cardwell, 2 May 1865, and Grey to Elliot, 20 August 1864; CO 147/11, Glover to Cardwell, 3 February 1866. The Annual Estimates of Revenue and Expenditure record wages paid to the Armed Hausa Police.

135. On the role of the Armed Hausa in the sack of Epe in 1863, see Lethbridge to Admiralty, 23 March 1863, encl. in CO. 147/5, Admiralty to Rogers, 13 May 1863. On their involvement in the rout of the Egba at Ikorodu in 1865, see CO 147/8, Glover to Cardwell, 5 April 1865, plus enclosures. For discussions of their later involvement in campaigns against the Asante and the Ijebu, see CO 147/28, Berkeley to Administrator-in-Chief, 17 June 1873; CO 147/116, McCallum to Bronston, 13 July 1897; and Robert B. Edgerton, *The Fall of the Asante Empire: The Hundred-Year War for Africa's Gold* (New York: The Free Press, 1995), 103. Murray Last discussed the role of colonial soldiers of Hausa origin in Britain's conquest of Northern Nigeria during a seminar at Emory University's Institute of African Studies, 12 September 2002.

136. CO 147/9, Glover to Cardwell, 9 June 1865.

137. GP f6, Willoughby to Glover, 24 June 1873.

138. Throughout the second half of the century, the colony of Lagos in fact shared palm oil exports roughly equally with ports further west on the Slave Coast, but it dominated the palm kernel trade from the region. Newbury, *Western Slave Coast*, 58, 66–72, 75, 147; Patrick Manning, *Slavery, Colonialism, and Economic Growth in Dahomey, 1640–1960* (Cambridge: Cambridge University Press, 1982), 52; Hargreaves, *Prelude*, 59–61, 110–20. Correspondence in GP f1, as well as in colonial dispatches, documents the Lagos government's preoccupation with events on the western frontier of the colony.

139. Biobaku, *The Egba*, 64–89; Newbury, *Western Slave Coast*, 89–95; Ajayi and Smith, *Yoruba Warfare*, 76–128; S. A. Akintoye, *Revolution and Power Politics in Yorubaland, 1840–1893: Ibadan Expansion and the Rise of Ekitiparapo* (New York: Humanities Press, 1971), 78–80; Ajayi, "Aftermath of the Fall of Old Oyo," 159–63; Smith, *Kingdoms*, 132–40; Falola, "The Yoruba Wars," 135–45; Oguntomisin, "Warfare and Military Alliances," 31–39; Peel, *Religious Encounter*, 35–44. Note 126 cites some of the abundant original correspondence relevant to the Lagos govern-

ment's interior policy. Other pertinent documentation can be found in CO 147/10–25 and GP f1, 2, 4.

140. Hargreaves, *Prelude*, 64–78.

141. CO 147/4, Glover to Newcastle, 10 October 1863. Also GP f5, Petition of merchants and traders of Lagos to Pope Hennessy, 29 April 1872.

142. CO 147/8, Glover to Cardwell, 10 April 1865; CO 147/28, Lees to Governor-in-Chief, 26 September 1873. Also CO 147/8, Glover to Cardwell, 14 March, 5 April 1865; CO 147/9, Glover to Cardwell, 7 August, 5 September, 4 October, 9 December 1865, 14 August 1866; CO 147/11, Blackall to Cardwell, 5 April 1866; GP f5, Petition from merchants and traders of Lagos to Pope Hennessy, 29 April 1872; and Report from Abeokuta, 11 May 1872.

143. CO 147/9, Glover to Cardwell, 4 October 1865; CO 147/28, Berkeley to Harley, 17 June 1873.

144. Biobaku, *The Egba*, 81–93; Oroge, "Fugitive Slave Question."

145. Biobaku, *The Egba*, 79–91; Kopytoff, *Preface*, 155–59, 190. Also correspondence in GP f5, such as Arabic letters from . . . Ibadan to Willoughby, n.d. (but 1872); Petition from merchants and traders of Lagos to Pope Hennessy, 29 April 1872; and Willoughby to Glover, 29 August 1872; along with correspondence running through the CO 147 series for the late 1860s and early 1870s, especially CO 147/27, Pope Hennessy to Kimberley, 31 January 1873, plus encls.; Berkeley to Administrator-in-Chief, 16 May 1873; and CO 147/28, Berkeley to Administrator-in-Chief, 2 August 1873; Berkeley to Kimberley, 22 November 1873.

146. CO 147/27, Pope Hennessy to Kimberley, 8 February 1873; CO 147/29, Reply to a Question in the House of Commons, 31 December 1872.

147. Kopytoff, *Preface*, 205–206. Also GP f5, Willoughby to Glover, 12 July 1872; Turton to Glover, 20 August 1872; and information in the *Colonial Office List*, 1871–75.

148. Kopytoff, *Preface*, 177, 190; Oroge, "Fugitive Slave Question," 78; "Lagos in 1872," *Royal Commonwealth Society Library Notes*, n.s., 94 (1964); GP f5, Aboriginal Inhabitants of Lagos to Pope Hennessy, 10 May 1872; Members of the Yoruba National Association of Lagos to Pope Hennessy, 26 May 1872; Turton to Glover, 1 July 1872; Willoughby to Glover, 29 August 1872, 24 June 1873; CO 147/27, Fowler to Pope Hennessy, 21 September 1872; Berkeley to Keate, 29 March 1873; Berkeley to Administrator-in-Chief, 2, 24 April, 16 May 1873; CO 147/28, Berkeley to Kimberley, 3 September 1873; Lees to Governor-in-Chief, 26 September 1873; and CO 147/31, Strahan to Carnarvon, 6 May 1875.

149. CO 147/27, Pope Hennessy to Kimberley, 6 February 1873; CO 147/28, Berkeley to Kimberley, 22 November 1873. Also annual Estimates of Revenue and Expenditure from the early 1870s.

150. CO 147/27, Pope Hennessy to Kimberley, 6, 8, 19 February 1873, plus encls.; CO 147/28, Berkeley to Administrator-in-Chief, 17 June 1873; Lees to Governor-in-Chief, 26 September 1873, plus encls.; CO 147/29, Evidence taken at four sittings of the Slave Court, 12 February 1873; GP f5, Willoughby to Glover, 29 August 1872.

151. Annual Estimates of Revenue and Expenditure for the 1870s; CO 147/28, Berkeley to Administrator-in-Chief, 6 June 1873; CO 147/38, Ussher to Hicks-Beach, 25 October 1879.

152. Elias, *Nigerian Legal System*, 17–18, 67–69; Adewoye, *Judicial System*, 50.

153. Newbury, *Western Slave Coast*, 77–95; Akintoye, *Revolution*, 102–31, Falola, "The Yoruba Wars," 139; CO 147/32, Strahan to Carnarvon, 28 January, 19 February, 14 March, 16 August 1876; Lees to Carnarvon, 30 September 1876; CO 147/33, Freeling to Carnarvon, 8 January, 23 July 1877; CO 147/36, Lees to Hicks-Beach, 14, 18 October, 15, 17, 20, 23 November 1878; CO 147/37, Lees to Hicks-Beach, 30 January, 17 February 1879; CO 147/38, Ussher to Hicks-Beach, 29, 30 August, 29 September 1879; CO 147/39, Foreign Office to Hicks-Beach, 29 May, 22 November 1879.

154. *Eagle and Lagos Critic*, 9 January 1886; *Lagos Observer*, 21 January 1886; CO 147/61, 12 July 1887.

4. Innocent Commerce

1. John Robert Hose, "Britain and the Development of West African Cotton" (Ph.D. diss., Columbia University, 1970), 17–20, 34–44, 49–53; Brian B. Vincent, "Cotton Growing in Southern Nigeria: Missionary, Mercantile, Imperial, and Colonial Governmental Involvement versus African Realities, c. 1845 to 1939" (Ph.D. diss., Simon Fraser University, 1977), 5–79; J. F. A. Ajayi, *Christian Missions in Nigeria, 1841–1891: The Making of a New Elite* (London: Longmans, 1965), 84–85, 145, 156, 167; Barrie M. Ratcliffe, "Cotton Imperialism: Manchester Merchants and Cotton Cultivation in West Africa in the Mid-Nineteenth Century," *AEH* 11 (1982): 87–113; Judith A. Byfield, *The Bluest Hands: A Social and Economic History of Women Dyers in Abeokuta (Nigeria), 1890–1940* (Portsmouth, N.H.: Heinemann, 2002), 16–22.

2. Figures on cotton exports are derived from Sara S. Berry, *Cocoa, Custom, and Socio-economic Change in Rural Western Nigeria* (Oxford: Clarendon Press, 1975), 23.

3. C. W. Newbury, *The Western Slave Coast and Its Rulers* (Oxford: Clarendon Press, 1961), 49–77; A. G. Hopkins, *An Economic History of West Africa* (London: Longman, 1973), 125–28; Patrick Manning, *Slavery, Colonialism, and Economic Growth in Dahomey, 1640–1960* (Cambridge: Cambridge University Press, 1982), 12–14, 50–52; Martin Lynn, *Commerce and Economic Change in West Africa: The Palm Oil Trade in the Nineteenth Century* (Cambridge: Cambridge University Press, 1997), 11–33.

4. H. C. Billows and H. Beckwith, *Palm Oil and Palm Kernels, the Consuls of West Africa* (Liverpool: Charles Birchall, 1913), 14; C. W. S. Hartley, *The Oil Palm* (London: Longman, 1977), 4; Lynn, *Commerce and Economic Change*, 2, 43; "Notes on the Oil Palm (*Elaeis Guineensis*) of Southern Nigeria," Supplement, *Government Gazette* 10 (5 February 1908): ii–iv.

5. M. R. Delany, "Official Report of the Niger Valley Exploring Party," in *Search for a Place: Black Separatism and Africa, 1860*, by M. R. Delany and Robert Campbell (Ann Arbor: University of Michigan Press, 1969), 72. For other contemporary references to the production and consumption of palm oil, see Captain John Adams, *Remarks on the Country Extending from Cape Palmas to the River Congo* (London: Frank Cass, 1966), 171–72; W. H. Clarke, *Travels and Explorations in Yoruba-*

land (1854–1858) (Ibadan: Ibadan University Press, 1972), 100, 201, 274; and Richard Francis Burton, *Abeokuta and the Camaroons Mountains: An Exploration* (London: Tinsley Brothers, 1863), 1:60.

6. B. K. Drake, "Liverpool's African Commerce before and after Abolition of the Slave Trade" (master's thesis, University of Liverpool, 1974), 61–62, quoted in Martin Lynn, "The West African Palm Oil Trade in the Nineteenth Century and the 'Crisis of Adaptation,'" in *From Slave Trade to "Legitimate" Commerce: The Commercial Transition in Nineteenth-Century West Africa*, ed. Robin Law (Cambridge: Cambridge University Press, 1995), 62. See also H. N. Stilliard, "The Rise and Development of Legitimate Trade in Palm Oil with West Africa" (master's thesis, University of Birmingham, 1938), 24–25; Newbury, *Western Slave Coast*, 91–94; A. J. H. Latham, *Old Calabar, 1600–1891: The Impact of the International Economy upon a Traditional Society* (Oxford: Clarendon Press, 1973), 55–56; and Joseph E. Inikori, "West Africa's Seaborne Trade, 1750–1850: Volume, Structure, and Implications," in *Figuring African Trade: Proceedings of the Symposium on the Quantification and Structure of the Import and Export and Long Distance Trade in Africa, 1800–1913*, ed. G. Liesegang, H. Pasch, and A. Jones (Berlin: D. Reimer, 1986), 69.

7. Lynn, *Commerce and Economic Change*, 26, 82–84.

8. Allan McPhee, *The Economic Revolution in British West Africa* (New York: Negro Universities Press, 1970), 31–35; J. H. Jones, *The Tinplate Industry: A Study in Economic Organisation* (London: P. S. King, 1914), 17–18; W. E. Minchinton, *The British Tinplate Industry: A History* (Oxford: Clarendon Press, 1957), 27–30, 55, 58, 84, 102; Lynn, *Commerce and Economic Change*, 28–30.

9. Lynn, *Commerce and Economic Change*, 29–30; Bernard Schnapper, *La politique et le commerce français dans le Golfe de Guinée de 1838 à 1871* (Paris: Mouton, 1961), 121–27; L. Gittins, "Soapmaking in Britain, 1824–1851: A Study in Industrial Location," *Journal of Historical Geography* 8 (1982): 30–31.

10. Robert Campbell, "A Pilgrimage to My Motherland," in Delany and Campbell, *Search for a Place*, 72, 187; Burton, *Abeokuta*, 1:111, 129, 161; N. A. Fadipe, *The Sociology of the Yoruba* (Ibadan: Ibadan University Press, 1970), 152.

11. Schnapper, *La politique et le commerce français*, 127; Ernst Hieke, *G. L. Gaiser, Hamburg-Westafrika: 100 Jahre Handel mit Nigeria* (Hamburg: Hoffmann und Campe Verlag, 1949), 21–25; "Germany and the Palm Kernel Trade," *Journal of the African Society* 14 (1914–15): 194–95; A. H. Milbourne, "Palm Kernels from West Africa: Movement to Establish the Industry in Great Britain," *Journal of the African Society* 15 (1915–16): 134–35; Charles Wilson, *The History of Unilever: A Study in Economic Growth and Social Change* (London: Cassell, 1954), 1:10–11.

12. J. H. van Stuyvenberg, ed., *Margarine: An Economic, Social, and Scientific History, 1869–1969* (Liverpool: Liverpool University Press, 1969), 7, 13–16, 38–39, 74–76, 84, 91, 165–70; Frederick A. Talbot, *The Oil Conquest of the World* (London: Heinemann, 1914), 208–22; M. K. Schwitzer, *Margarine and Other Food Fats: Their History, Production, and Use* (New York: Interscience Publications, 1956), 59–62, 65–66, 79, 113–14; T. P. Hughes, "Technological Momentum in History: Hydrogenation in Germany, 1898–1933," *P&P* 44 (1969): 106–32.

13. Lynn, *Commerce and Economic Change*, 13, 29, 112–13, 142. See also C. W. Newbury, "On the Margins of Empire: The Trade of Western Africa, 1875–1890," in *Bismarck, Europe, and Africa*, ed. Stig Förster, Wolfgang Mommsen, and Ronald

Robinson (Oxford: German Historical Institute, 1988), 40; and C. W. Newbury, "Trade and Authority in West Africa from 1850 to 1880," in *The History and Politics of Colonialism, 1870–1914*, vol. 1 of *Colonialism in Africa, 1870–1960*, ed. L. H. Gann and Peter Duignan (Cambridge: Cambridge University Press, 1969), 76.

14. Schnapper, *La politique et le commerce français*, 140; Newbury, "Margins of Empire," 45; L. Harding, "Hamburg's West Africa Trade in the Nineteenth Century," in Liesegang, Pasch, and Jones, eds., *Figuring African Trade*, 363–91.

15. Lynn, *Commerce and Economic Change*, 14, 121; Newbury, "Margins of Empire," 45.

16. Lynn, *Commerce and Economic Change*, 27–30, 96–97, 112. See also Newbury, *Western Slave Coast*, 60; Hopkins, *Economic History*, 131–32; Latham, *Old Calabar*, 69; and David Eltis and Lawrence C. Jennings, "Trade between Western Africa and the Atlantic World in the Pre-colonial Era," *AHR* 93 (1988): 946.

17. PP 1842.XI.1, Report from the Select Committee on the West Coast of Africa, Minutes of Evidence, H. Seward, 10 May 1842; FO 84/816, Palmerston to Beecroft, 25 February 1850, Beecroft to Palmerston, 4 May 1850; FO 84/950, Campbell to Clarendon, 7 December 1854. On the history of the Brazilian traders in the nineteenth century, see Pierre Verger, *Trade Relations between the Bight of Benin and Bahia from the 17th to 19th Century*, trans. Evelyn Crawford (Ibadan: Ibadan University Press, 1976), 427, 501, 541–43; A. G. Hopkins, "An Economic History of Lagos, 1880–1914" (Ph.D. diss., University of London, 1964), 33–34; David A. Ross, "The Career of Domingo Martinez in the Bight of Benin, 1833–1864," *JAH* 6 (1965): 79–90; Jerry Michael Turner, "Les Bresiliens—The Impact of Former Brazilian Slaves upon Dahomey" (Ph.D. diss., Boston University, 1975), 61–62, 223–69; Manning, *Slavery, Colonialism, and Economic Growth*, 12–13, 46–47, 67; Manuela Carneiro da Cunha, *Negros, estrangeiros: Os escravos libertos e sua volta à África* (São Paulo: Editora Brasiliense, 1985), 108–20; and Robin Law and Kristin Mann, "West Africa in the Atlantic Community: The Case of the Slave Coast," *WMQ*, 3rd ser., 56 (1999): 307–34.

18. Lynn, *Commerce and Economic Change*, 98–100; Martin Lynn, "Change and Continuity in the British Palm Oil Trade with West Africa, 1830–55," *JAH* 22 (1981): 347.

19. Newbury, "Trade and Authority," 79. See also Newbury, *Western Slave Coast*, 57–62; Schnapper, *La politique et le commerce français*, 121–28; Hopkins, *Economic History*, 129–30; Manning, *Slavery, Colonialism, and Economic Growth*, 77.

20. Lynn, *Commerce and Economic Change*, 86–94; Lynn, "Change and Continuity," 333; Lynn, "The West African Palm Oil Trade," 66; Hopkins, "Economic History of Lagos," 16–19; Verger, *Trade Relations*, 498; Schnapper, *La politique et le commerce français*, 22–23, 147; Frederick Pedler, *The Lion and the Unicorn in Africa: A History of the Origins of the United Africa Company, 1787–1931* (London: Heinemann, 1974), 8–151, passim. See also FO 84/816, Beecroft to Palmerston, 13 August 1850; FO 84/920, Fraser to Malmesbury, 3 March 1853; FO 85/976, Campbell to Clarendon, 1 September 1855.

21. FO 84/976, Campbell to Clarendon, 1 September, 3 October 1855; Régis to Campbell, 11 September 1856, encl. in FO 84/1002, Campbell to Clarendon, November 1856; Hieke, *G. L. Gaiser*, 16.

22. John Whitford, *Trading Life in Western and Central Africa* (Liverpool: The Porcupine Office, 1877), 86.

23. Robin Law, "The Origins and Evolution of the Merchant Community in Ouidah," in *Ports of the Slave Trade (Bights of Benin and Biafra)*, ed. Robin Law and Silke Strickrodt (Stirling, U.K.: University of Stirling, Centre of Commonwealth Studies, 1999), 65–66; Robert S. Smith, *The Lagos Consulate, 1851–1861* (Berkeley: University of California Press, 1979), 84; Kehinde Faluyi, "The Fluctuating Economic Fortunes of a Nigerian Sea Port: Economy and Trade in Badagry to 1900," in *Badagry: A Study in History, Culture, and Traditions of an Ancient City*, ed. G. O. Ogunremi, M. O. Opeloye, and Siyan Oyeweso (Ibadan: Rex Charles, 1994), 65.

24. FO 84/1031, Campbell to Clarendon, 11 May 1857; Manning, *Slavery, Colonialism and Economic Growth*, 52–53; Lynn, "Change and Continuity," 339–40.

25. Lady Glover, *Life of Sir John Hawley Glover* (London: Smith, Elder and Co., 1897), 91; CO 147/40, Ussher to Kimberley, 5 March 1880; CO 147/42, Griffith to Ussher, 25 October 1880.

26. Lynn, *Commerce and Economic Change*, 87, 138, 157–58.

27. Martin Lynn, "From Sail to Steam: The Impact of the Steamship Services on the British Palm Oil Trade with West Africa, 1850–1890," *JAH* 30 (1989): 227–30; Martin Lynn, "Technology, Trade, and 'A Race of Native Capitalists': The Krio Diaspora of West Africa and the Steamship, 1852–95," *JAH* 33 (1992): 424–25; Martin Lynn, "The Profitability of the Early Nineteenth Century Palm Oil Trade," *AEH* 20 (1992): 81; Lynn, *Commerce and Economic Change*, 105–16; Charlotte Leubuscher, *The West African Shipping Trade* (Leyden: A. W. Sythoff, 1963), 14; P. N. Davies, "The Impact of the Expatriate Shipping Lines on the Economic Development of British West Africa," *Business History* 19 (1977): 6–9; Latham, *Old Calabar*, 59–64.

28. McPhee, *Economic Revolution*, 72–73; Lynn, "Technology, Trade, and 'A Race of Native Capitalists,'" 421–40.

29. FO 84/1002, Campbell to Clarendon, 16 August, 25 September 1856; AST MPE: Consolati Nazionali, Lagos, 1856–1857, Scala to Minister of Foreign Affairs, 20 June 1856; Mrs. Henry Grant Foote, *Recollections of Central America and the West Coast of Africa* (London: T. Cautley Newby, 1869), 190–91. I am grateful to Sandra T. Barnes for copies and translations of documents cited from the Archivio de Stato, Turin.

30. *Memoirs of Giambattista Scala: Consul of His Italian Majesty in Lagos in Guinea (1862)*, trans. Brenda Packman and ed. Robert Smith (Oxford: Oxford University Press, 2000), 12, 22–24.

31. Memorial from Ford Fenn, 16 April 1863, encl. in CO 147/5, Charles Buxton to Newcastle, 18 April 1863; CO 147/7, Ford Fenn to Cardwell, 20 June 1864. On the history of the Sierra Leoneans who returned to Lagos, see Christopher Fyfe, *A History of Sierra Leone* (London: Oxford University Press, 1962), 317–18; and Jean Herskovits Kopytoff, *A Preface to Modern Nigeria: The "Sierra Leonians" in Yoruba, 1830–1890* (Madison: University of Wisconsin Press, 1965).

32. RWCA, Minutes of Evidence, quoted in Verger, *Trade Relations*, 492.

33. Lynn, "Technology, Trade, and 'A Race of Native Capitalists,'" 426–27; Verger, *Trade Relations*, 490; Fyfe, *History of Sierra Leone*, 317.

34. Kopytoff, *Preface*, 96–97, 286–87; Fyfe, *History of Sierra Leone*, 318, 459; Obituary, J. P. L. Davies, *LWR*, 5 May 1906, p. 3, col. 1; FO 84/950, Campbell to Clarendon, 14 August, 30 May 1854.

35. CO 147/11, Glover to Cardwell, 8 January 1866. See also Fyfe, *History of Sierra Leone*, 318; and Kristin Mann, *Marrying Well: Marriage, Status, and Social Change among the Educated Elite in Colonial Lagos* (Cambridge: Cambridge University Press, 1985), 88.

36. CO 147/8, Glover to Cardwell, 2 February 1865.

37. FO 84/1031, Campbell to Clarendon, 7 April 1857.

38. Delany, "Official Report," 113–14.

39. CO 147/6, Freeman to Newcastle, 9 March, 9 May 1864.

40. Interviews with Dr. da Rocha-Afodu and Mrs. Angelica Thomas.

41. Hopkins, "Economic History of Lagos," 30–40; Turner, "Les Bresiliens," 133, 147; da Cunha, *Negros, estrangeiros*, 12, 108–36.

42. Antonio Olinto, *The Water House* (Walton-on-Thames: Nelson, 1982); N. Mba, "Literature as a Source of History: Case Study of *The Water House*," in *History of the Peoples of Lagos State*, ed. Ade Adefuye, Babatunde Agiri, and Jide Osuntokun (Ikeja: Lantern Books, 1987), 351–63.

43. Will, J. F. D. Branco, 14 June 1919, LPR 6, 325.

44. RWCA, Minutes of Evidence, W. McCoskry, 6 April 1865, 70; Kristin Mann, "Women, Landed Property, and the Accumulation of Wealth in Early Colonial Lagos," *Signs* 16 (1991): 682–706; interview with S. A. Oni; testimony of C. A. Oni, "Evidence to the Commission on Trade," encl. in CO 147/133, Denton to Chamberlain, 4 June 1898.

45. Mortgage, Nelly Oyenkan to J. H. Weatherdon, 15 July 1870, LLR, 7, 210; Deed of Gift, C. C. Banfield for T. Mayne to Nelly Oyenkan, 8 January 1875, LLR, 22, 115; Deed of Gift, Nelly Oyenkan to J. R. Leaver, C. C. Banfield, and J. J. Winser, 12 May 1876, LLR, 23, 320.

46. These percentages are calculated from data in Berry, *Cocoa*, 23; and Newbury, *Western Slave Coast*, 87–88.

47. Newbury, *Western Slave Coast*, 57–58, 86; Marion Johnson, "Ivory and the Nineteenth Century Transformation in West Africa," in *Figuring African Trade*, 103–104, 107. Consul Campbell's 1856 report on trade (FO 84/1031, Campbell to Clarendon, 5 February 1857) observed that ivory and cotton trailed palm oil in exports.

48. Hopkins, "Economic History of Lagos," 32–42; Lynn, "Technology, Trade, and 'A Race of Native Capitalists,'" 427–33. For information about trade with Brazil see, in addition to the sources cited in note 17, Pierre Verger, "Influence du Brésil au Golfe du Bénin," in *Les Afro-Américans*, ed. Theodore Monod (Dakar: Mémoires de l'Institut français d'Afrique noire, 1953), 88–95. Clarke, *Travels*, 264; Burton, *Abeokuta*, 1:316; and *Barber v. Benjamin*, 17 February 1879, JNCC, 2, 60, illuminate the intra-African coastal trade.

49. These figures are derived from data in C. W. Newbury, *British Policy towards West Africa: Selected Documents, 1875–1914; with Statistical Appendices, 1800–1914* (Oxford: Clarendon Press, 1971), 614–15.

50. "Evidence to the Commission on Trade." See also FO 84/976, Campbell to Clarendon, 1 September 1855.

51. FO 84/1031, Campbell to Clarendon, 5 January 1857. For additional discussions of the import trade, see Burton, *Abeokuta*, 1:316; AST MPE: Consolati Nazionali, Lagos, 1856–1857, Scala to Minister of Foreign Affairs, 10 March 1856.

52. Hopkins, *Economic History*, 110, 126; Manning, *Slavery, Colonialism, and Economic Growth*, 9, 13, 51; Eltis and Jennings, "Trade," 946.

53. FO 84/1002, Campbell to Clarendon, 14 May 1856; FO 2/20, Clarendon to Campbell, 21 May 1857, Campbell to Clarendon, 29 June, 30 July 1857, plus encls.; AST MPE: Consolati Nazionali, Lagos, 1856–1857, Scala to Minister of Foreign Affairs, 10 March 1856, 15 February 1857.

East African cowries were cheaper and more numerous than those from the Maldives that had provided currency for the slave trade. Moreover, the distance to the West African coast was shorter from East Africa than from the Maldives, lowering transportation costs. These attractions outweighed the disadvantages of the East African shell's distinctive appearance and greater size, the latter of which made them bulkier, heavier, and thus more cumbersome as currency. On the history of the cowrie trade, see A. G. Hopkins, "The Currency Revolution in South-West Nigeria in the Late Nineteenth Century," *JHSN* 3 (1966): 471–83; Jan Hogendorn and Marion Johnson, *The Shell Money of the Slave Trade* (Cambridge: Cambridge University Press, 1986), 64–79; and Ernst Hieke, *Zur Geschichte des deutschen Handels mit Ostafrika: Das hamburgische Handelshaus Wm. O'Swald and Co.* (Hamburg: Verlag Hans Christians, 1939), 1:101–48, passim.

54. FO 84/1031, Campbell to Clarendon, 5 January 1857.

55. AST MPE: Consolati Nazionali, Lagos, 1856–1857, Scala to Most Illustrious Minister, 10 March 1856.

56. On the changing composition of imports, see Newbury, *Western Slave Coast*, 88; and also Hopkins, *Economic History*, 110, 126; Manning, *Slavery, Colonialism, and Economic Growth*, 9, 13, 51; Inikori, "West Africa's Seaborne Trade," 60–65; and Eltis and Jennings, "Trade," 948.

57. These figures are calculated from data in Newbury, *British Policy towards West Africa, 1875–1914*, 614–15.

58. Hopkins, *Economic History*, 132; Eltis and Jennings, "Trade," 940–41; Newbury, "Margins of Empire," 48; Lynn, "Technology, Trade, and 'A Race of Native Capitalists,'" 79.

59. CMS YM, CA2/O32, Journal of the Rev. Samuel Crowther, quarter ending 31 March 1857.

60. Lynn, *Commerce and Economic Change*, 44–49; Susan M. Martin, *Palm Oil and Protest: An Economic History of the Ngwa Region, South-Eastern Nigeria, 1800–1980* (Cambridge: Cambridge University Press, 1988), 32–35.

61. For nineteenth- and early twentieth-century descriptions of palm oil production in Yorubaland see, in addition to the works cited in notes 4 and 5 above, *Memoirs of Scala*, 25–26; "Lagos Palm Oil," *Kew Bulletin* 262 (1892): 200–208; Fadipe, *Sociology*, 149; and J. E. Gray, "Native Methods of Preparing Palm Oil in Nigeria," *First Annual Bulletin of the Agricultural Department, Nigeria* (1922): 29–51.

62. Gray, "Native Methods," 32.

63. "Lagos Palm Oil," 208.

64. Ibid., 206, 208.

65. Gray, "Native Methods," 48.

66. Manning, *Slavery, Colonialism, and Economic Growth*, 99.

67. O. T. Faulkner and C. J. Lewin, "Native Methods of Preparing Palm Oil, II," *Second Annual Bulletin of the Agricultural Department, Nigeria* (1923): 22.

68. Fadipe, *Sociology*, 150, 256; Toyin Falola, *The Political Economy of a Precolonial African State: Ibadan, 1830–1900* (Ile-Ife: University of Ife Press, 1984), 60–61; NNA, Epediv, 5/1, Pinkett to Colonial Secretary, 8 November 1898; RHL, Oxford (Colonial Records Project), Mss.Afr.L15, W. Fowler, "A Report on the Lands of the Colony District," 46. I am indebted to Sandra T. Barnes for a copy of the Fowler manuscript.

69. Fadipe, *Sociology*, 147; Falola, *Political Economy*, 88–95; interviews with Alhaji A. W. A. Akibayo and Chief D. A. Ogunbiyi.

70. Oladipo Yemitan, *Madame Tinubu: Merchant and King-Maker* (Ibadan: University Press, 1987), 11–54; N. Mba, "Women in Lagos Political History," in Adefuye, Agiri, and Osuntokun, eds., *History of the Peoples of Lagos State*, 243–44; LaRay Denzer, "Yoruba Women: A Historiographical Study," *IJAHS* 27 (1994): 1–39; Karin Barber, *I Could Speak until Tomorrow: Oriki, Women, and the Past in a Yoruba Town* (Washington, D.C.: Smithsonian Institution Press, 1991), 231–34.

71. Clarke, *Travels*, 245, quoted in Robin Law, "'Legitimate' Trade and Gender Relations in Yorubaland and Dahomey," in Law, ed., *From Slave Trade to "Legitimate" Commerce*, 204. For discussions of the gendered division of labor in Yoruba society see, in addition to Law's essay, Mann, *Marrying Well*, 39–40; and Simi A. Afonja, "Changing Modes of Production and the Sexual Division of Labor among the Yoruba," in *Women's Work, Development, and the Division of Labor by Gender*, ed. H. Safa and E. Leacock (South Hadley, Mass.: Bergin and Garvey, 1986), 122–35.

72. R. H. Stone, *In Afric's Forest or Jungle, or Six Years among the Yorubans* (Edinburgh: Oliphant, Anderson, and Ferrier, 1900), 23–24, quoted in Law, "Trade and Gender," 204; Samuel Johnson, *The History of the Yorubas* (London: Routledge and Kegan Paul, 1969), 124; Fadipe, *Sociology*, 147–49; Percy Amaury Talbot, *The Peoples of Southern Nigeria: A Sketch of Their History, Ethnology, and Languages with an Abstract of the 1921 Census* (London: Frank Cass, 1969), 2:909.

73. *Legbishi v. Alason and Kukunduku*, 6 May 1880, JNCC, 2, 366; *Dorishawa v. Obalorisha of Gbogbele and Singbokurunu*, 14 November 1887, JNCC, 7, 280. A. Millson's photographs of the boiling and washing processes ("Lagos Palm Oil") show men performing tasks, as well as looking on. See also Francine Shields, "Palm Oil and Power: Women in an Era of Economic and Social Transition in Nineteenth Century Yorubaland (South-Western Nigeria)" (Ph.D. diss., University of Stirling, 1997), 87–103.

74. For the debate over the importance of small- versus large-scale production in Yorubaland, see A. G. Hopkins, "Economic Imperialism in West Africa: Lagos, 1880–92," *Economic History Review* 21 (1968): 580–606; Hopkins, *Economic History*, 104–106, 125–26; Ralph A. Austen, "The Abolition of the Overseas Slave Trade: A Distorted Theme in West African History," *JHSN* 5 (1970): 257–74; Julian Clarke, "Households and the Political Economy of Small-Scale Cash Crop Production in South-Western Nigeria," *Africa* 51 (1981): 807–23; and Law, "Trade and Gender," 195–214. Robin Law, "The Historiography of the Commercial Transition in Nineteenth-Century West Africa," in *African Historiography: Essays in Honor of Jacob Ade Ajayi*, ed. Toyin Falola (Harlow, U.K.: Longman, 1993), 91–115; and Lynn, *Commerce and Economic Change*, 34–81, 151–70, discuss the wider West African context.

75. Clarke, *Travels*, 274, and Stone, *In Afric's Forest*, 24, both quoted in Law, "Trade and Gender," 197.

76. J. D. Y. Peel, *Religious Encounter and the Making of the Yoruba* (Bloomington: Indiana University Press, 2000), 64.

77. "Evidence to the Commission on Trade"; FO 84/1002, Campbell to Clarendon, 18 February 1856; FO 84/1031, Campbell to Clarendon, 14 March 1857; RWCA, Minutes of Evidence, W. McCoskry, 6 April 1865, 76; CO 147/13, Blackall to Buckingham, 6 May 1867. See also B. A. Agiri, "Aspects of Socio-economic Changes among the Awori Egba and Ijebu Remo Communities during the Nineteenth Century," *JHSN* 7 (1974): 465–83; S. A. Akintoye, *Revolution and Power Politics in Yorubaland, 1840–1893: Ibadan Expansion and the Rise of Ekitiparapo* (New York: Humanities Press, 1971), 150; Falola, *Political Economy*, 88–95; Barber, *I Could Speak*, 203–12; and Shields, "Palm Oil and Power," 47, 90–96.

78. Delany, "Official Report," 79.

79. "Evidence to the Commission on Trade"; Bolanle Awe, "Militarism and Economic Development in Nineteenth Century Yoruba Country: The Ibadan Example," *JAH* 14 (1973): 69–71. See also Agiri, "Aspects of Socio-economic Changes," 468; Akintoye, *Revolution*, 213; and Falola, *Political Economy*, 138–45.

80. Law, "Trade and Gender," 200.

81. Mann, *Marrying Well*, 40–41; Mann, "Women, Landed Property," 699–701; Shields, "Palm Oil and Power," 127–63.

82. Yemitan, *Madame Tinubu;* Bolanle Awe, "Iyalode Efunsetan Aniwura (Owner of Gold)," in *Nigerian Women in Historical Perspective*, ed. Bolanle Awe (Lagos: Sankore, 1992), 55–71; Barber, *I Could Speak*, 231–34; interview with Alhaji A. W. A. Akibayo. After Tinubu's husband Ọba Adele died, she married a powerful slave warrior, Yesufu Bada, also known as Obadina. Marriage to a slave, even a powerful one, inverted the usual subordination of wife to husband and minimized obligations to affines. Had Tinubu borne children, she would have had primary authority over them.

83. Shields, "Palm Oil and Power," 131–34, 163–68.

84. Burton, *Abeokuta*, 1:29; Fadipe, *Sociology*, 149; "Palm Kernels from West Africa," 134; A. C. Barnes, "The Recovery of Palm Kernels," *Fifth Annual Bulletin of the Department of Agriculture, Nigeria* (1926): 24, 29; Billows and Beckwith, *Palm Oil and Kernels*, 41–42.

85. Lynn, *Commerce and Economic Change*, 124.

86. Patrick Manning, "Slave Trade, 'Legitimate' Trade, and Imperialism Revisited: The Control of Wealth in the Bights of Benin and Biafra," in *Africans in Bondage: Studies in Slavery and the Slave Trade*, ed. Paul E. Lovejoy (Madison: African Studies Program, University of Wisconsin–Madison, 1986), 211–12; Hartley, *The Oil Palm*, 8.

87. *Memoirs of Scala*, 25; CO 147/3, Glover to Newcastle, 8 June 1863; CO 147/8, Glover to Cardwell, 9 January 1865; CO 147/11, Glover to Cardwell, 8 January 1866; "Lagos Palm Oil," 203; "Notes on the Oil Palm," i.

88. Clarke, *Travels*, 263; Thomas Jefferson Bowen, *Adventures and Missionary Labours in Several Countries in the Interior of Africa from 1849 to 1856* (London: Frank Cass, 1968), 103; FO 84/976, Campbell to Clarendon, 30 August 1855; FO 84/1002, Campbell to Clarendon, 26 February, 14, 26 May 1856; FO 84/1031, Campbell to Clarendon, 6 August 1857; CO 147/6, Glover to Cardwell, 10 October 1864; CO 147/7, Watts to Cardwell, 12 May 1864; CO 147/8, Glover to Card-

well, 14 March, 8 May 1865; CO 147/9, Glover to Cardwell, 9 June, 5 August 1865. Also Lynn, *Commerce and Economic Change*, 2, 41; Awe, "Militarism and Economic Development," 68–73; Falola, *Political Economy*, 15–41, 88–91; Akintoye, *Revolution*, 78–82, 150–51; and Manning, *Slavery, Colonialism, and Economic Growth*, 65–68.

89. Scala, who opened a factory at Abeokuta in 1856 "to take the civilizing element of legitimate trade into the very center of slavery," was perhaps the earliest of these exceptions. *Memoirs of Scala*, 53. For references to others, see Delany, "Official Report," 75; Burton, *Abeokuta*, 1:72, 78, 128, 224; CO 147/2, Foreign Office to Colonial Office, 20 October 1862; CO 147/4, Glover to Newcastle, 6 November 1863; CO 147/7, Banner Brothers to Cardwell, 8 November 1864; and CO 147/11, Glover to Cardwell, 7 February 1866.

90. Clarke, *Travels*, 262, 265.

91. "Evidence to the Commission on Trade."

92. Bowen, *Adventures*, 103, 112; Clarke, *Travels*, 5. See also Delany, "Official Report," 112–13; FO 84/976, Campbell to Clarendon, 2 October 1855; FO 84/1002, Campbell to Clarendon, 26 February, 26 May 1856; CO 147/3, Freeman to Newcastle, 2 March 1863; CO 147/8, Glover to Cardwell, 10 April 1865.

93. FO 84/1002, Campbell to Clarendon, 1 October 1856; CO 147/1, Freeman to Newcastle, 10 September 1862; CO 147/2, McCoskry to Russell, 4 October, 5 December 1861; CO 147/3, Freeman to Newcastle, 6 January 1863, and Glover to Russell, 9 June 1863; CO 147/5, Freeman to Newcastle, 3 June 1863; CO 147/8, Glover to Cardwell, 14 March 1865; CO 147/8, Glover to Cardwell, 10 April, 8 May 1865.

94. Falola, *Political Economy*, 30; Akin L. Mabogunje, *Urbanization in Nigeria* (London: University of London Press, 1968), 86; J. F. A. Ajayi and Robert Smith, *Yoruba Warfare in the Nineteenth Century* (Cambridge: Cambridge University Press, 1964), 71, 120–21; S. O. Biobaku, *The Egba and Their Neighbours, 1842–1872* (Oxford: Clarendon Press, 1957), 74; Agiri, "Aspects of Socio-economic Changes," 475; Gabriel Ogundeji Ogunremi, *Counting the Camels: The Economics of Transportation in Pre-industrial Nigeria* (New York: Nok, 1982), 49–54; Toyin Falola, "The Yoruba Caravan System of the Nineteenth Century," *IJAHS* 24 (1991): 120, 129–30.

95. AST MPE: Consolati Nazionali, Lagos, 1856–1857, Scala to Minister of Foreign Affairs, 10 March 1856; Clarke, *Travels*, 264; FO 84/1031, Campbell to Clarendon, 6 August 1857. See also Whitford, *Trading Life*, 105.

96. Possu to Fraser, encl. in FO 84/920, Fraser to Clarendon, 14 March 1853; "Evidence to the Commission on Trade." Also interview with I. L. Apatira.

97. CO 147/131, McCallum to Chamberlain, 22 April 1898; CO 147/142, Denton to Chamberlain, 5 April 1899; interviews with A. W. Animaṣaun, G. B. Animaṣaun, Rufai Arufai Animaṣaun, and Saif Akanni Animaṣaun; Falola, "The Yoruba Caravan System," 120; Mabogunje, *Urbanization*, 88–89.

98. CO 147/64, Moloney to Knutsford, 16 June 1888. See also Lynn, "Technology, Trade, and 'A Race of Native Capitalists,'" 430.

99. PP 1858–9.XXXIV.281, Class B, Correspondence with Foreign Powers Relating to the Slave Trade, II, no. 11, Consul Campbell, Lagos, 28 March 1858, quoted in Law, "Trade and Gender," 205; Whitford, *Trading Life*, 105.

100. Law, "Trade and Gender," 204–207. Also Shields, "Palm Oil and Power," 35–40, 73–74.

101. FO 84/1031, Campbell to Clarendon, 1 September 1857; AST MPE: Consolati Nazionali, Lagos, 1856–1857, Agreement between Dosunmu and the European merchants, 27 March 1854; CO 147/1, Freeman to Newcastle, 8 March 1862.

102. FO 84/976, Campbell to Clarendon, 2 June 1855; FO 84/1002, Campbell to Clarendon, 1, 10 October 1856; *Memoirs of Scala*, 43. Also FO 84/950, Campbell to Clarendon, 27 March, 18 May 1854; and Abiola Dosunmu Elegbede-Fernandez, *Lagos: A Legacy of Honour* (Ibadan: Spectrum Books, 1992), 19.

103. Report of Bedingfield's visit to Epe, 2 October 1861, encl. in CO 147/2, Foreign Office to Rogers, 4 October 1861. FO 84/976, Campbell to Clarendon, 3 October 1855; Merchants of Lagos to Adams, 2 October 1856, encl. in FO 84/1002, Campbell to Clarendon, 7 November 1856; FO 84/1002, Campbell to Clarendon, 16 August 1856; Report of Burton's journey to Abeokuta, 20 November 1861, encl. in CO 147/2, Foreign Office to Colonial Office, 15 January 1862.

104. Yemitan, *Madame Tinubu*, 14–17, 22–23, 26; *Memoirs of Scala*, 29–38.

105. FO 84/920, Campbell to Clarendon, 19 September 1853; FO 84/950, Campbell to Clarendon, 1 May 1854.

106. FO 84/1002, Campbell to Clarendon, 14 June 1856; *Memoirs of Scala*, 43.

107. COL, Lagos Colony, Census, 1881; Hopkins, "Economic History of Lagos," 24–25.

108. "Evidence to the Commission on Trade."

109. See, for example, FO 84/976, Campbell to Clarendon, 2 June, 30 August 1855; OR, Taiwo and others to Ord, 27 December 1864, Appendix E, 335; CO 147/11, Blackall to Cardwell, 21 March 1866; "Evidence to the Commission on Trade."

110. Mann, "Women, Landed Property."

111. Mr. A. O. Alaba, Department of African Languages and Literatures, University of Lagos, personal communication, December 1984.

112. Gareth Austin, "Indigenous Credit Institutions in West Africa, c. 1750–c. 1960," in *Local Suppliers of Credit in the Third World, 1750–1960*, ed. Gareth Austin and Kaoru Sugihara (New York: St. Martin's, 1993), 102–103; Toyin Falola, "Money and Informal Credit Institutions in Colonial Western Nigeria," in *Money Matters: Instability, Values, and Social Payments in the Modern History of West African Communities*, ed. Jane I. Guyer (Portsmouth, N.H.: Heinemann, 1995), 170–71; William Bascom, "The Esusu: A Credit Institution of the Yoruba," *Journal of the Royal Anthropological Institute* 82 (1952): 63–69; Fadipe, *Sociology*, 256.

113. Mann, *Marrying Well*, 40; Kristin Mann, "The Historical Roots and Cultural Logic of Outside Marriage in Colonial Lagos," in *Nuptiality in Sub-Saharan Africa: Contemporary Anthropological and Demographic Perspectives*, ed. Caroline Bledsoe and Gilles Pison (Oxford: Clarendon Press, 1994), 178.

114. In 1909, a man wrote to A. E. Carrena ending their friendship because Carrena refused to lend him money. Papers of A. E. Carrena, in the possession of the Carrena family, Lagos. I am grateful to E. E. I. Carrena for allowing me to consult these documents. Also E. A. Oroge, "Iwofa: An Historical Survey of the Yoruba Institution of Indenture," *AEH* 14 (1985): 86; Peel, *Religious Encounter*, 60–61; J.

Mars, "The Monetary and Banking System and the Loan Market of Nigeria," in *Mining, Commerce, and Finance in Nigeria*, vol. 2 of *The Economics of a Tropical Dependency*, ed. Margery Perham (London: Faber and Faber, 1948), 177–224; and Richard Fry, *Bankers in West Africa: The Story of the Bank of British West Africa, Limited* (London: Hutchinson, 1976).

115. Bowen, *Adventures*, 103; Thomas J. Hutchinson, "The Social and Domestic Slavery of Western Africa, and Its Evil Influence on Commercial Progress," *Journal of the Society of Arts* 21 (26 February 1875): 317; Johnson, *History*, 126–30; A. K. Ajisafe, *The Laws and Customs of the Yoruba People* (Lagos: CMS Bookshop, 1924), 63–66; Adebesin Folarin, *The Laws and Customs of Egbaland* (Abeokuta: E. N. A. Press, 1939), 8–10, 57–59, 80–81; Fadipe, *Sociology*, 163–65, 189–93. See also Oroge, "Iwofa," 75–104; Robin Law, "On Pawning and Enslavement for Debt in the Precolonial Slave Coast," Judith Byfield, "Pawns and Politics: The Pawnship Debate in Western Nigeria," and Toyin Falola, "Pawnship in Colonial Southwestern Nigeria," in *Pawnship in Africa: Debt Bondage in Historical Perspective*, ed. Toyin Falola and Paul E. Lovejoy (Boulder: Westview Press, 1994), 55–69, 187–216, and 245–66.

116. UIL, Africana Collection, Minutes of the Central Native Council, 17 April 1902. See also A. G. Hopkins, "A Report on the Yoruba, 1910," *JHSN* 5 (1969): 91; and *Dorishawa v. Obalorisha and Singbokurunu*, 280.

117. K. Y. Daaku, *Trade and Politics on the Gold Coast, 1600–1720: A Study of the African Reaction to European Trade* (Oxford: Clarendon Press, 1970), 41–44; Robin Law, *The Slave Coast of West Africa, 1550–1750: The Impact of the African Slave Trade on an African Society* (Oxford: Clarendon Press, 1991), 217–19; Paul E. Lovejoy and David Richardson, "Trust, Pawnship, and Atlantic History: The Institutional Foundations of the Old Calabar Slave Trade," *AHR* 104 (1999): 332–55; Robin Law, "Finance and Credit in Pre-colonial Dahomey," in *Credit, Currencies and Culture: African Financial Institutions in Historical Perspective*, ed. Endre Stiansen and Jane I. Guyer (Uppsala: Nordiska Afrikainstitutet, 1999), 15–37; Herbert S. Klein, *The Atlantic Slave Trade* (Cambridge: Cambridge University Press, 1999), 123.

118. AST MPE: Consolati Nazionali, Lagos, 1856–1857, Scala to Minister of Foreign Affairs, March 1857.

119. *Blaize v. Francisco*, 13 July 1881, JNCC, 3, 299, 323; *Blaize v. Johnson*, September 1881, JNCC, 3, 359; C. W. Newbury, "Credit in Early Nineteenth Century West African Trade," *JAH* 13 (1972): 81–95; Lynn, *Commerce and Economic Change*, 74–81.

120. FO 84/1002, Campbell to Clarendon, 26 May, 1 October 1856; Taiwo to J. B. Bounard, 20 February 1867, LLR, 4, 247; Taiwo to H. Rowland, 29 October 1867, LLR, 5, 139; Taiwo to A. Barry, 16 October 1868, LLR, 7, 5; Taiwo to A. Barry, 24 January 1870, LLR, 7, 120.

121. These data come from mortgages on file at the LLR.

122. FO 84/976, Campbell to Clarendon, 30 August 1855; CO 147/9, Glover to Cardwell, 7 October 1865.

123. In addition to mortgages at the LLR naming these traders as vendees, see *Barber v. Benjamin*, 17 February 1879, JNCC, 2, 62; and *Barber v. Ojigobi*, 5 January 1883, JNCC, 5, 156.

124. Law, "Finance and Credit," 16.

125. These data come from an examination of mortgages on file at the LLR.

See also *Labinjoh v. Williams*, 21 February 1889, JNCC, 9, 66; and "Evidence to the Commission on Trade."

126. See Taiwo's mortgages cited in note 120.

127. Austin, "Indigenous Credit Institutions," 132–33; Professor A. I. Asiwaju, Department of History, University of Lagos, personal communication, April 1988.

128. *Fagbemi v. Amobiojo*, 8 September 1879, JNCC, 2, 156; *Blaize v. Johnson*, 175; *Escherick v. Bioku*, 22 November 1880, JNCC, 3, 80–82; *Blaize v. Francisco*, 299, 323.

129. R. C. Abraham, *Dictionary of Modern Yoruba* (London: University of London Press, 1958), s.v. *owó*, 7(b).

130. These data come from an analysis of mortgages at the LLR naming selected African merchants and traders as vendees or vendors. Also "Evidence to the Commission on Trade."

131. CO 147/6, Freeman to Newcastle, 9 March 1864.

132. FO 84/976, Campbell to Clarendon, 3 October 1855; CO 147/27, Pope Hennessy to Kimberley, 8, 22 February, 10 April 1873, plus encls.; *Balogun v. Pearse*, 13 July 1896, JNCC, ?, 394. For a discussion of credit that Africans at Ouidah extended to Europeans, see Law, "Finance and Credit," 15–37.

133. Austin, "Indigenous Credit Institutions," 100, 117–18; Peel, *Religious Encounter*, 60–61; Oroge, "Iwofa," 76–86; Byfield, "Pawns and Politics," 192–93.

134. Peel, *Religious Encounter*, 332 n. 55.

135. NNA, J. K. Coker Papers, especially letters in files 1/2/1–4, 1/4/1,3, and 2/1/1–2.

136. Interview with Mrs. Michael Abiodun. The quotation is, of course, from *Hamlet*, I.iii. Caulcrick, in fact, lent money to the early Nigerian nationalist Herbert Macaulay, with whom he was associated, and as far as I can tell both men avoided what Polonius considered the primary dangers of debt: "For loan oft loses both itself and friend, And borrowing dulls the edge of husbandry."

137. John B. Losi, *History of Lagos* (Lagos: Tika Tore Press, 1914), 83; Kristin Mann, "The Rise of Taiwo Olowo: Law, Accumulation, and Mobility in Early Colonial Lagos," in *Law in Colonial Africa*, ed. Kristin Mann and Richard Roberts (Portsmouth, N.H.: Heinemann, 1991), 93–94.

138. Hopkins, "Report on the Yoruba," 89.

139. John Iliffe, "Poverty in Nineteenth-Century Yorubaland," *JAH* 25 (1984): 57, quoted in Austin, "Indigenous Credit Institutions," 113.

140. CO 147/28, Berkeley to Administrator-in-Chief, 14 July 1873; "Evidence to the Commission on Trade."

141. Ogunremi, *Counting the Camels*, 72–91, 127–32, 152–71; Robin Law, introduction and "Trade and Gender," in *From Slave Trade to "Legitimate" Commerce*, ed. Law, 10–11, 204; Lynn, *Commerce and Economic Change*, 43, 52, 65–66; Shields, "Palm Oil and Power," 69–72, 98–99.

142. Patrick Manning, "Merchants, Porters, and Canoemen in the Bight of Benin: Links in the West African Trade Network," in *Workers of African Trade*, ed. Catherine Coquery-Vidrovitch and Paul E. Lovejoy (Beverly Hills: Sage, 1985), 71. For a few of the many contemporary references to carriers and canoeists, see Clarke, *Travels*, 265; Campbell, "Pilgrimage," 166–69; Bowen, *Adventures*, 307; *Memoirs of Scala*, 54; and Whitford, *Trading Life*, 86.

143. Testimony of J. P. L. Davies, Buraimo Adagunodo, Aina Akebioro, and Sumonu, "Evidence to the Commission on Trade."

144. FO 84/920, Campbell to Clarendon, 23 July, 3 August 1853; and Clarendon to Campbell, 15, 22 September, 17 November 1853.

145. FO 84/1002, Campbell to Clarendon, 25 September, 29 November 1856; CO 147/8, Glover to Cardwell, 11 March 1865; *Quasie and others v. Fabel*, 5 September 1880, JNCC, 3, 4; *Black Will and son v. Voight and Co.*, 11 November 1885, JNCC, 6, 132. Historical studies of Gold Coast canoemen and Kru laborers include Peter C. W. Gutkind, "The Canoemen of the Gold Coast (Ghana): A Survey and an Exploration in Precolonial African Labour History," *CEA* 29 (1989): 339–76; Jane Martin, "Krumen 'Down the Coast': Liberian Migrants on the West African Coast in the Nineteenth and Twentieth Centuries," *IJAHS* 18 (1985): 401–23; Ibrahim K. Sundiata, *From Slaving to Neoslavery: The Bight of Biafra and Fernando Po in the Era of Abolition, 1827–1930* (Madison: University of Wisconsin Press, 1996), 73, 126–30; and Diane Frost, *Work and Community among West African Migrant Workers since the Nineteenth Century* (Liverpool: Liverpool University Press, 1999).

146. Fadipe, *Sociology*, 61–62, 80–81, 110–14; Mann, *Marrying Well*, 39–40, 60; Mann, "Women, Landed Property," 699–700; Toyin Falola and G. O. Ogunremi, "Traditional, Non-mechanical Transport Systems," in *Transport Systems in Nigeria*, ed. Toyin Falola and S. A. Olanrewaju (Syracuse: Foreign and Comparative Studies Program, 1986), 22. Jane I. Guyer, "Household and Community in African Studies," *ASR* 24 (1981): 87–137, reviews the literature on intrahousehold relationships and resource flows.

Oyeronke Oyewumi, *The Invention of Women: Making an African Sense of Western Gender Discourses* (Minneapolis: University of Minnesota Press, 1997), rejects gender as an indigenous source of Yoruba inequality and hierarchy, arguing that it was absent from precolonial culture. J. D. Y. Peel, "Gender in Yoruba Religious Change," *Journal of Religion in Africa* 32 (2002): 136–66, critiques Oyewumi's provocative thesis.

147. Mann, *Marrying Well*, 43–91.

148. T. G. O. Gbadamosi, *The Growth of Islam among the Yoruba, 1841–1908* (London: Longman, 1978), 136; interview with Atanda Balogun.

149. Clarke, *Travels*, 5; Bowen, *Adventures*, 102; Campbell, "Pilgrimage," 236; interview with N. E. S. Adewale; Manning, "Merchants, Porters, and Canoemen," 51–74; Shields, "Palm Oil and Power," 69–73. See also WALC, "Minutes," testimony of Dr. O. Ṣapara, 269.

150. Oroge, "Iwofa," 92; Peel, *Religious Encounter*, 68; A. G. Hopkins, "The Lagos Strike of 1897: An Exploration in Nigerian Labour History," *P&P* 35 (1966): 133–55.

151. FO 84/1002, Clarendon to Campbell, 18 February, 17 May 1856; FO 84/1031, Campbell to Clarendon, 2 July, 21 August, 2 October, 31 November 1857; OR, Taiwo and others to Ord, 27 December 1864, Appendix E, 335; Chiefs, Traders, and People of Lagos to Glover, encl. in CO 147/4, Glover to Newcastle, 10 October 1863; CO 147/13, Blackall to Buckingham, 6 May 1867; testimony of Aina Akebioro and Sumonu, "Evidence to the Commission on Trade"; interviews with Chief Mobolaji Oshodi, Chief D. A. Ogunbiyi, S. B. Affini, and Atanda Balogun.

152. John Pope Hennessy, "On the British Settlements in Western Africa," *Journal of the Society of Arts* (2 May 1873): 443.

153. Oroge, "Iwofa"; Byfield, "Pawns and Politics"; CO 147/29, Glover to Newcastle, 27 March 1873; GP 13, f6, Extract from a letter dated 5 February 1873.

154. COL, Lagos Colony, Census, 1881, 1891, and 1901; "Evidence to the Commission on Trade." Census figures are difficult to compare because changes occurred in how people were counted and enumeration districts were defined. Colonial enumeration was, in any case, notoriously unreliable.

155. Hopkins, "Report on the Yoruba," 77–78; interviews with Prince A. L. A. Ojora, Chief S. B. A. Oluwa, and N. E. S. Adewale; Kristin Mann, "Owners, Slaves and the Struggle for Labour in the Commercial Transition at Lagos," in Law, ed., *From Slave Trade to "Legitimate" Commerce*, 159–60.

156. Professor Oyekan Owomoyela, Department of English, University of Nebraska, Lincoln, personal communication, 12 April 2001; Kristin Mann, "Interpreting Cases, Disentangling Disputes: Court Cases as a Source for Understanding Patron-Client Relationships in Early Colonial Lagos," in *Sources and Methods in African History: Spoken, Written, Unearthed*, ed. Toyin Falola and Christian Jennings (Rochester, N.Y.: University of Rochester Press, 2003), 195–218.

157. UIL, Africana Collection, Minutes of the Central Native Council, 17 July 1902.

158. Lynn, *Commerce and Economic Change*, 112, 128.

159. Lagos Colony, *Blue Books*, contain information on the volume and value of exports from Lagos. Berry, *Cocoa*, 23, includes data on palm produce prices.

160. Hopkins, *Economic History*, 132–34, 154; Lynn, *Commerce and Economic Change*, 122, 126; Eltis and Jennings, "Trade," 940–44.

161. "Evidence to the Commission on Trade"; A. G. Hopkins, "Richard Beale Blaize, 1845–1904: Merchant Prince of West Africa," *Tarikh* 1 (1966): 74; Hopkins, "Economic Imperialism in West Africa," 592–95; Hopkins, *Economic History*, 153–54; Mann, *Marrying Well*, 21, 23; Lynn, *Commerce and Economic Change*, 142, 146, 155–56.

162. Mortgage, J. P. L. Davies to Child Mills and Co., 18 March 1872, LLR, 15, 141; Mortgage, J. P. L. Davies to Richard Sykes and John William Desire Mather, 11 July 1873, LLR, 19, 107. The Public Record Office, alas, did not preserve the records of Davies's case in the London bankruptcy court.

163. Hopkins, *Economic History*, 153.

164. "Evidence to the Commission on Trade."

165. LWR, 22 August 1891.

166. "Evidence to the Commission on Trade."

167. Hopkins, "Currency Revolution," 471–83. See also Hopkins, *Economic History*, 148–50; and Lynn, *Commerce and Economic Change*, 136–37.

168. These data come from an analysis of mortgages at the Lagos Land Registry. See also Hopkins, "Economic History of Lagos," 58, 96.

169. J. E. Flint, *Sir George Goldie and the Making of Nigeria* (London: Oxford University Press, 1960), 30–32, 44, 96–98; Lynn, *Commerce and Economic Change*, 143. Also CO 147/64, Moloney to Knutsford, 16 June 1888; CO 147/66, Moloney to Knutsford, 9 October 1888; CO 147/70, Moloney to Knutsford, 12 March 1889;

CO 147/118, McCallum to Chamberlain, 10 June 1897; CO 147/132, Denton to Chamberlain, 18 May 1898; and "Evidence to the Commission on Trade."

170. McPhee, *Economic Revolution*, 95–96; Lynn, *Commerce and Economic Change*, 108, 143, 221. See also *Coker v. Rylands* (n.d.), 1 *NLR* 63.

171. "Evidence to the Commission on Trade." See also Pedler, *The Lion and the Unicorn*, 263–74; Wilson, *History of Unilever*, 2:180–83; and Lynn, *Commerce and Economic Change*, 128–150.

172. Berry, *Cocoa*, 23; Hopkins, *Economic History*, 134, 183; Edmund O. Egboh, "The Working of the Timber Concession System in Southern Nigeria, 1900–1940," *Transactions of the Historical Society of Ghana* 16 (1995): 267–88.

173. Hopkins, "Economic History of Lagos," 381, 388–91; Hopkins, *Economic History*, 132.

174. J. B. Webster, "The Bible and the Plough," *JHSN* 2 (1962): 418–34; Berry, *Cocoa*, 40–41; A. G. Hopkins, "Innovation in a Colonial Context: African Origins of the Nigerian Cocoa-Farming Industry, 1880–1920," in *The Imperial Impact: Studies in the Economic History of Africa and India*, ed. Clive Dewey and A. G. Hopkins (London: The Athlone Press, 1978), 83–96.

175. Hopkins, "Economic History of Lagos," 259.

5. Britain and Domestic Slavery

1. Roger Anstey, "The Pattern of British Abolition in the Eighteenth and Nineteenth Centuries," in *Anti-slavery, Religion, and Reform: Essays in Memory of Roger Anstey*, ed. Christine Bolt and Seymour Drescher (Folkestone, Kent: Wm. Dawson and Sons, 1980), 23–24.

2. J. F. A. Ajayi, *Christian Missions in Nigeria, 1841–1891: The Making of a New Elite* (London: Longmans, 1965), 103; J. F. A. Ajayi, "West Africa in the Anti-Slave Trade Era," in *The Cambridge History of Africa: From c. 1790–c. 1870*, ed. J. E. Flint (Cambridge: Cambridge University Press, 1976), 5:214; E. A. Ayandele, *The Missionary Impact on Modern Nigeria, 1842–1914: A Political and Social Analysis* (London: Longman, 1966), 331–32; E. A. Oroge, "The Institution of Slavery in Yorubaland, with Particular Reference to the Nineteenth Century" (Ph.D. diss., University of Birmingham, 1971), chap. 4; E. A. Oroge, "Iwofa: An Historical Survey of the Yoruba Institution of Indenture," *AEH* 14 (1985): 75–106; Toyin Falola, "Missionaries and Domestic Slavery in Yorubaland in the Nineteenth Century," *Journal of Religious History* 14 (1986): 181–92; J. D. Y. Peel, *Religious Encounter and the Making of the Yoruba* (Bloomington: Indiana University Press, 2000), 143–44, 271.

3. Philip D. Curtin, *The Image of Africa: British Ideas and Action, 1780–1850* (Madison: University of Wisconsin Press, 1964), chaps. 11–12; David Brion Davis, *The Problem of Slavery in the Age of Revolution, 1770–1823* (Ithaca, N.Y.: Cornell University Press, 1975), 241–54; Seymour Drescher, *Capitalism and Antislavery: British Mobilization in Comparative Perspective* (New York: Oxford University Press, 1987), chaps. 1, 4; Jean Comaroff and John Comaroff, *Christianity, Colonialism, and Consciousness in South Africa*, vol. 1 of *Of Revelation and Revolution* (Chicago: University of Chicago Press, 1991), 120; J. R. Oldfield, *Popular Politics and British Anti-slavery: The Mobilisation of Public Opinion against the Slave Trade, 1787–1807* (Man-

chester: Manchester University Press, 1995), chap. 5; Seymour Drescher, *The Mighty Experiment: Free Labor versus Slavery in British Emancipation* (New York: Oxford University Press, 2002), chaps. 2–4.

4. For expressions of contemporary ideas about the relationship between anti-slavery and the development of legitimate commerce, see the testimony of Clegg, Hutton, Seward, Swanzy, and others in PP 1842.XI.1, Report from the Select Committee on the West Coast of Africa, Minutes of Evidence, and of Denman, Matson, Duncan, Bandinel, and others in PP 1847–8.XXII.1, First–Fourth Reports from the Select Committee on the Slave Trade, Minutes of Evidence. In his instructions to consuls at Lagos before the bombardment, Palmerston repeatedly stressed the benefits of the transition from the slave trade to legitimate commerce for the "chiefs and people." PRRL, Palmerston to Beecroft, 30 June 1849, 25 February 1850, 21 February 1851, 227, 255, 311. See also Curtin, *Image*, 428–29, 452; and Suzanne Miers, *Britain and the Ending of the Slave Trade* (New York: Africana, 1975), 147–53.

5. Thomas C. Holt, *The Problem of Freedom: Race, Labor, and Politics in Jamaica and Britain, 1832–1938* (Baltimore: Johns Hopkins University Press, 1992), 13–112; Richard B. Allen, *Slaves, Freedmen, and Indentured Laborers in Colonial Mauritius* (Cambridge: Cambridge University Press, 1999), 9–31, 55–75; Pamela Scully, *Liberating the Family? Gender and British Slave Emancipation in the Rural Western Cape, South Africa, 1823–1853* (Portsmouth, N.H.: Heinemann, 1997), 63–80.

6. Robin Blackburn, *The Overthrow of Colonial Slavery, 1776–1848* (London: Verso, 1988), 456–58; Holt, *Problem of Freedom*, 13–112, 143–76; William A. Green, *British Slave Emancipation: The Sugar Colonies and the Great Experiment, 1830–1865* (Oxford: Clarendon Press, 1976), 129–90; essays by Turner, Heuman, and Richards in Mary Turner, ed., *From Chattel Slaves to Wage Slaves: The Dynamics of Labour Bargaining in the Americas* (Bloomington: Indiana University Press, 1995).

7. Howard Temperley, *British Antislavery, 1833–1870* (London: Longman, 1972), chap. 5; Miers, *Britain and the Ending of the Slave Trade*, 157; Richard Roberts and Suzanne Miers, introduction to *The End of Slavery in Africa*, ed. Suzanne Miers and Richard Roberts (Madison: University of Wisconsin Press, 1988), 12–13. For the impact of the Indian model on British East and West Africa, respectively, see Frederick Cooper, *From Slaves to Squatters: Plantation Labor and Agriculture in Zanzibar and Coastal Kenya, 1890–1925* (New Haven: Yale University Press, 1980), 41–42; and Paul E. Lovejoy and Jan S. Hogendorn, *Slow Death for Slavery: The Course of Abolition in Northern Nigeria, 1897–1936* (Cambridge: Cambridge University Press, 1993), chap. 3. Gyan Prakash, *Bonded Histories: Genealogies of Labor Servitude in Colonial India* (Cambridge: Cambridge University Press, 1990) examines the renegotiation of unfree labor in colonial India.

8. Raymond E. Dumett and Marion Johnson, "Britain and the Suppression of Slavery in the Gold Coast Colony, Ashanti, and the Northern Territories," in Miers and Roberts, eds., *End of Slavery*, 73–75; John Grace, *Domestic Slavery in West Africa* (New York: Barnes and Noble, 1975), 25–29; Raymond E. Dumett, "Pressure Groups, Bureaucracy and the Decision Making Process: The Case of Slavery, Abolition and Colonial Expansion in the Gold Coast, 1874," *Journal of Imperial and Commonwealth History* 9 (1981): 193–215; Gerald M. McSheffrey, "Slavery, Indentured Servitude, Legitimate Trade, and the Impact of Abolition in the Gold Coast,

1874–1901: A Reappraisal," *JAH* 24 (1983): 352–54; John Parker, *Making the Town: Ga State and Society in Early Colonial Accra* (Portsmouth, N.H.: Heinemann, 2000), chap. 3. Martin Klein, *Slavery and Colonial Rule in French West Africa* (Cambridge: Cambridge University Press, 1998), 15–16, 101–106, 127, 154, shows similarities in French anti-slavery policy in Senegal and the Western Sudan.

9. Claire C. Robertson, "Post-proclamation Slavery in Accra: A Female Affair?" in *Women and Slavery in Africa*, ed. Claire C. Robertson and Martin A. Klein (Madison: University of Wisconsin Press, 1983), 220–45; Thomas C. Holt, "The Essence of the Contract: The Articulation of Race, Gender, and Political Economy in British Emancipation Policy, 1838–1866" and Frederick Cooper, "Conditions Analogous to Slavery: Imperialism and Free Labor Ideology in Africa," in *Beyond Slavery: Explorations of Race, Labor, and Citizenship in Postemancipation Societies*, by Frederick Cooper, Thomas C. Holt, and Rebecca J. Scott (Chapel Hill: University of North Carolina Press, 2000), 33–59, 126–29; Scully, *Liberating*; Lovejoy and Hogendorn, *Slow Death*, 111–26.

10. Russell to Maclean, 14 July 1841, cited in Grace, *Domestic Slavery*, 25. This letter has been published in G. E. Metcalfe, *Great Britain and Ghana: Documents of Ghana History* (London: Thomas Nelson and Sons, 1964), 164–65. For a discussion of British law pertaining to slavery and the slave trade, see David Eltis, *Economic Growth and the Ending of the Transatlantic Slave Trade* (New York: Oxford University Press, 1987), chap. 6.

11. PP 1844.L.1, Instructions for Guidance of Naval Officers Employed in the Suppression of the Slave Trade, section 2.

12. FO 84/920, Campbell to Clarendon, 23 July, 3 August 1853; and Clarendon to Campbell, 15, 22 September, 17 November 1853.

13. Jean Herskovits Kopytoff, *A Preface to Modern Nigeria: The "Sierra Leonians" in Yoruba, 1830–1890* (Madison: University of Wisconsin Press, 1965), 75–76, 109–10, 204–205; Ajayi, *Christian Missions*, 37, 123; Robert S. Smith, *The Lagos Consulate, 1851–1861* (Berkeley: University of California Press, 1979), 72–73, 114. Also FO 84/856, Beecroft to Palmerston, 21 February 1851; FO 84/1002, Campbell to Clarendon, 18 February 1856, Clarendon to Campbell, 17 May 1856; and PP 1861.LXI.147, Class B, Correspondence with Foreign Powers Relating to the Slave Trade, Foote to Russell, 4 February 1861, 160.

14. After Mrs. Sandeman's death, Fraser arranged for a justice of the peace on the Gold Coast to issue the girl a "certificate of freedom." FO 84/920, Fraser to Malmesbury, 20 February 1853.

15. FO 84/920, Campbell to Clarendon, October 1853.

16. FO 84/976, Campbell to Clarendon, 2 August 1855.

17. FO 84/1031, Campbell to Clarendon, 14 March 1857; Memo, 10 July 1862, accompanying CO 147/1, Freeman to Newcastle, 4 June 1862. For the influence of this view in other parts of West Africa, see Grace, *Domestic Slavery*, 2, 43; Roberts and Miers, introduction to Miers and Roberts, eds., *End of Slavery*, 21.

18. FO 84/1002, Campbell to Clarendon, 14 June 1856.

19. FO 84/1031, Campbell to Clarendon, 14 March 1857.

20. FO 84/1061, Campbell to Clarendon, 28 March 1858. See also Robin Law, "'Legitimate' Trade and Gender Relations in Yorubaland and Dahomey," in *From Slave Trade to "Legitimate" Commerce: The Commercial Transition in Nineteenth-*

Century West Africa, ed. Robin Law (Cambridge: Cambridge University Press, 1995), 207.

21. Ayandele, *Missionary Impact*, 332. See also Oroge, "The Institution of Slavery," 224–29; Falola, "Missionaries," 186; and Peel, *Religious Encounter*, 67, 143–44, 271.

22. Grace, *Domestic Slavery*, 30.

23. Smith, *Lagos Consulate*, 107; *Memoirs of Giambattista Scala: Consul of His Italian Majesty in Lagos in Guinea (1862)*, trans. Brenda Packman and ed. Robert Smith (Oxford: Oxford University Press, 2000), 81–83; Lady Glover, *Life of Sir John Hawley Glover* (London: Smith, Elder and Co., 1897), 78–80; E. A. Oroge, "The Fugitive Slave Crisis of 1859: A Factor in the Growth of Anti-British Feelings among the Yoruba," *Odu* 12 (1975): 40–54.

24. *Yara v. Ibiyemi*, 12 November 1896, JNCC, 18, 218–29.

25. FO 84/1115, Brand to Russell, 18 January 1860; Hand to Russell, 31 December 1860.

26. Oroge, "Fugitive Slave Crisis," 62.

27. PP 1862.LXI.147, Class B, Correspondence with Foreign Powers Relating to the Slave Trade, Hand to Russell, 31 December 1860, 159; Smith, *Lagos Consulate*, 114.

28. CO 147/2, McCoskry to Russell, 3 September 1861.

29. CO 96/56, Russell to Newcastle, 7 February 1861, quoted in John W. Cell, *British Colonial Administration in the Mid-Nineteenth Century: The Policy-Making Process* (New Haven: Yale University Press, 1970), 278. Also Memo, 10 July 1862, accompanying CO 147/1, Freeman to Newcastle, 4 June 1862.

30. An undersecretary advised Newcastle that Britain would have to "make the best" of domestic slavery at Lagos, as it had done on the Gold Coast. The real question, he counseled, was whether the nation should allow fear of soiling her fingers by having to do with people among whom domestic slavery existed to interfere with the greater good of eliminating the slave trade from the Bight of Benin, replacing it with legitimate commerce, and introducing civilization to a large region of Africa. Minute on CO 147/1, Freeman to Newcastle, 4 June 1862.

31. "Proceedings in relation to slavery at Lagos . . . ," encl. in CO 147/11, Cardwell to Blackall, 23 February 1866.

32. CO 147/2, McCoskry to Russell, 3 September 1861. Martin A. Klein, "Slave Resistance and Slave Emancipation in Coastal Guinea," and Richard Roberts, "The End of Slavery in the French Soudan, 1905–1914," in Miers and Roberts, eds., *End of Slavery*, 210, 284–85; Klein, *Slavery*, 30–34, 85–87, 150–54, 159; Lovejoy and Hogendorn, *Slow Death*, 31–41; Ann O'Hear, *Power Relations in Nigeria: Ilorin Slaves and Their Successors* (Rochester, N.Y.: University of Rochester Press, 1997), 63–66, 72–74; and Frederick Cooper, "Conditions Analogous to Slavery," 110, 117–19, discuss similar events elsewhere in Africa later in the colonial period.

33. CO 147/1, Freeman to Newcastle, 9 October 1862.

34. CO 147/1, Freeman to Newcastle, 8 March 1862.

35. CO 147/1, Freeman to Newcastle, 4 June 1862; CO 147/2, Freeman to Russell, 8 August 1862; CO 147/3, Mulliner to Newcastle, 22 May 1863; GP f1, Glover to Didelot, August 1863. Parker, *Making the Town*, 83, suggests that British

courts on the Gold Coast operated in much the same way as those at Lagos. For Lugard's very different approach in Northern Nigeria, see Lovejoy and Hogendorn, *Slow Death*, chap. 4.

36. CO 147/1, Freeman to Newcastle, 4 June 1862; CO 147/2, McCoskry to Russell, 3 September 1861.

37. RWCA, Minutes of Evidence, W. McCoskry, 6 April 1865, 68–82.

38. CO 147/1, Freeman to Newcastle, 8 October 1862.

39. Mayne to Glover, 31 January 1867, encl. in CO 147/13, Blackall to Carnarvon, 17 March 1867.

40. Interviews with Prince A. L. A. Ojora and C. B. Thomas.

41. CO 147/1, Freeman to Newcastle, 9 October 1862.

42. Ibid.

43. Ibid.

44. See also Thomas J. Hutchinson, "The Social and Domestic Slavery of Western Africa, and Its Evil Influence on Commercial Progress," *Journal of the Society of Arts* 21 (26 February 1875): 319. On the impact of this view in the later colonial period, see Lovejoy and Hogendorn, *Slow Death*, 111–26; Cooper, "Conditions Analogous to Slavery," 126–29; Klein, *Slavery*, 136; and Barbara M. Cooper, *Marriage in Maradi: Gender and Culture in a Hausa Society in Niger, 1900–1989* (Portsmouth, N.H.: Heinemann, 1997), 20–39.

45. CO 147/1, Freeman to Newcastle, 9 October 1862.

46. Minutes on CO 147/1, Freeman to Newcastle, 9 October 1862.

47. Memo by Rogers, encl. in CO 147/1, Freeman to Newcastle, 9 October 1862.

48. Minutes on CO 147/1, Freeman to Newcastle, 9 October 1862.

49. CO 147/4, Glover to Newcastle, 10 November 1863; "Proceedings in relation to slavery at Lagos."

50. Minute on CO 147/4, Glover to Newcastle, 10 November 1863.

51. "Proceedings in relation to slavery at Lagos."

52. Minute on CO 147/4, Glover to Newcastle, 10 November 1863.

53. "Proceedings in relation to slavery at Lagos."

54. "Proceedings in relation to slavery at Lagos." See also CO 147/6, Glover to Cardwell, 8 November 1864.

55. CO 147/6, Glover to Cardwell, 27 December 1864.

56. CO 147/6, Glover to Cardwell, 8 November 1864; E. Adeniyi Oroge, "The Fugitive Slave Question in Anglo-Egba Relations, 1861–1886," *JHSN* 8 (1975): 75. Klein, *Slavery*, 29–32, 98, shows that French officials followed a similar practice in Senegal.

57. Minute on CO 147/6, Glover to Cardwell, 8 November 1864. Also John D. Hargreaves, *Prelude to the Partition of West Africa* (London: Macmillan, 1963), 71–76.

58. CO 147/6, Glover to Cardwell, 27 December 1864.

59. CO 147/6, Glover to Cardwell, 29 December 1864.

60. OR, 28, excerpted in C. W. Newbury, *British Policy towards West Africa: Selected Documents, 1786–1874* (Oxford: Clarendon Press, 1965), 529–30.

61. "Lagos, slavery, and boundary," encl. in CO 147/11, Cardwell to Blackall, 23 February 1866.

62. CO 147/11, Cardwell to Blackall, 23 February 1866.

63. Ibid.

64. CO 147/11, Blackall to Cardwell, 6 March 1866.

65. Eltis, *Economic Growth*, 83.

66. In the 1870s, Glover, for example, helped Taiwo Olowo enforce payment of certain Egba debts by presiding over the signing of an agreement that awarded the African trader eighteen pawns, which he held at Isheri and Ikorodu, outside British territory. Glover subsequently defended himself by saying that he thought he had no right to stop the exchange, because it had taken place on foreign soil. CO 147/27, Pope Hennessy to Kimberley, 5 February 1873, plus encls., and 6 February 1873; GP f6, Glover to "My Lord," 27 March 1873.

67. For a copy of the legislation, see George Stallard and Edward Harrinson Richards, *Ordinances, and Orders and Rules Thereunder, in Force in the Colony of Lagos on December 31st 1893* . . . (London: Stevens and Sons, 1894), 8–10. The other 1874 Gold Coast ordinance emancipating "persons holden in slavery" was not introduced at Lagos.

68. See, for example, the description in *Regina v. Seidu*, 3 August 1877, encl. in CO 147/36, Moloney to Lees, 27 November 1878.

69. Letters to the *African Times* from "Otitoro Koro," 2 October 1876, and "Okanlogue," 1 January 1877.

70. E. A. Ayandele, *Holy Johnson: Pioneer of African Nationalism, 1836–1917* (London: Frank Cass, 1970), 84–111; Falola, "Missionaries," 186–87.

71. *African Times*, 1 January 1877; Willoughby to Lees, 10 February 1877, encl. in CO 147/33, Freeling to Carnarvon, 21 February 1877.

72. *African Times*, 2 October 1876.

73. Willoughby to Lees, 10 February 1877, encl. in CO 147/33, Freeling to Carnarvon, 21 February 1877; *African Times*, 1 January 1877. For Dumaresq's account of the affair, see CO 147/34, Dumaresq to Meade, 9 April 1877.

74. CO 147/33, Freeling to Carnarvon, 21 February 1877.

75. Chalmers to Freeling, 12 February 1877, encl. in CO 147/33, Freeling to Carnarvon, 22 February 1877.

76. Minute on CO 147/33, Freeling to Carnarvon, 22 February 1877.

77. *African Times*, 1 May 1877.

78. Lees to Freeling, 12 June 1877, encl. in CO 147/33, Freeling to Carnarvon, 20 July 1877.

79. *African Times*, 1 May, 1 October 1877. Figures for 1877 are not available, but in 1878 no Lagosians were sent to jail for slave dealing. *Annual Report*, Lagos Colony, 1887, 72.

80. *Regina v. Seidu*, 3 August 1877, and other encls., in CO 147/36, Moloney to Freeling, 27 November 1878. See also CO 147/34, Dumaresq to Meade, 9 April 187; and Francine Shields, "Palm Oil and Power: Women in an Era of Economic and Social Transition in Nineteenth Century Yorubaland (South-Western Nigeria) (Ph.D. diss., University of Stirling, 1997), 49, 104–12.

81. Stallard and Richards, *Ordinances*, 316–23.

82. "Report on the Lagos Alien Children Registration Ordinance . . . ," encl. in CO 147/33, Freeling to Carnarvon, 29 December 1877.

83. CO 147/35, Dumaresq to Freeling, 11 February 1878, plus encls.; GP f4,

Alake to Glover, 8 May 1871. In the 1850s, Saro disguised the purchase of slaves as acts of redemption, and indigenous Lagosians may have picked up the language from them. Gardiner to Campbell, n.d., encl. in FO 84/1002, Campbell to Clarendon, 18 February 1856, quoted in Oroge, "The Institution of Slavery," 218.

84. CO 147/35, Dumaresq to Freeling, 11 February 1878, plus enclosures.

85. When Glover was sent to lead African troops in the Asante campaign in 1873, he purchased slaves in the interior of Lagos for recruitment into the Armed Hausas, and they traveled from Lagos to fight under his command. At the time, Sir H. T. Holland wrote a memo on the subject in which he maintained that buying slaves outside British territory for use in the British military amounted to "no more than a redemption of these slaves." Freeling may have had access to this memo, and it may have influenced his views. BL Add.Mss. 44441, f218, Memorandum Relating to Domestic Slavery on the West African Coast, 1873. Gladstone Papers, vol. 356. Klein, *Slavery*, 132, notes the use of similar language by French officials in West Africa.

86. Klein, *Slavery*, 36.

87. Freeling to Administrator, 15 February 1878, encl. in CO 147/35, Freeling to Carnarvon, 15 February 1878.

88. Woodcock to Acting Administrator, 13 November 1878, encl. in CO 147/36, Moloney to Lees, 27 November 1878.

89. Minute on CO 147/33, Freeling to Carnarvon, 21 February 1877.

90. Ayandele, *Missionary Impact*, 332; Falola, "Missionaries," 187; Peel, *Religious Encounter*, 143–44.

91. An additional thirteen were imprisoned for abducting children or violating the Alien Children Registration Ordinance. The Slave Dealing ordinance of 1874 allowed for punishment by fining as well as incarceration; however, in the cases about which I have information, those convicted were normally imprisoned at hard labor. Thus the statistics for 1878 through 1887 on the crimes of prisoners at the jail, published in the *Annual Report*, Lagos Colony, 1887, 71–73, may reflect fairly accurately the number of convictions for slave dealing. Between 1884 and 1888, the District Commissioner's Court at Badagry heard eighteen cases of slave dealing, but C. W. Newbury, *The Western Slave Coast and Its Rulers* (Oxford: Clarendon Press, 1961), 83, does not specify the number of convictions.

92. CO 147/43, Griffith to Kimberley, 24 December 1880, plus encls.; CO 147/44, Griffith to Kimberley, 14 February 1880.

93. *Annual Report*, Lagos Colony, 1868, 22. The *Reports* for 1869 and 1870 cite even larger numbers.

94. *LWR*, 3 September 1892, p. 3, col. 3, and 12 November 1892, p. 3, col. 1.

95. *LWR*, 6 August 1892, p. 3, cols. 1–3. Even so, police commissioners reported only fourteen cases of slave dealing in the four years between 1899 and 1905 for which figures are available. *Annual Departmental Reports Relating to Nigeria and British Cameroons, 1887–1960*, group III, Judicial and Police, Lagos, 1899–1905.

96. Eighty percent of the registrations at Badagry occurred in the first eight months of the ordinance's operation. Figures for the period 1893 through 1900 are not available by town. Registers of births (1867–1960) and deaths (1892–1945) kept by the colonial registrar survived in the mid-1970s at the Lagos State Department

of Health. It is possible that the registers of alien children also survive in that office, since they were kept by the same official.

97. An additional 298 children were recorded as removed in 1898, but this figure included the names of some who were struck from the register because they had reached adulthood. *General Abstract of Registration*, Lagos Colony, 1893–1900.

98. Claire C. Robertson and Martin A. Klein, "Women's Importance in African Slave Systems," in Robertson and Klein, eds., *Women and Slavery*, 3–18. Shields, "Palm Oil and Power," 40–48, 89–96; Law, "Trade and Gender," 207–208; Sandra E. Greene, *Gender, Ethnicity, and Social Change on the Upper Slave Coast: A History of the Anlo-Ewe* (Portsmouth, N.H.: Heinemann, 1996), 38–42; and Edna G. Bay, *Wives of the Leopard: Gender, Politics, and Culture in the Kingdom of Dahomey* (Charlottesville: University of Virginia Press, 1998), 196–98, discuss the demand for female slaves among the Yoruba and other peoples of the Slave Coast.

99. *Annual Report*, Lagos Colony, 1887, 28; S. A. Akintoye, *Revolution and Power Politics in Yorubaland, 1840–1893: Ibadan Expansion and the Rise of Ekitiparapo* (New York: Humanities Press, 1971), 80–82, 125–27, 149–51; J. D. Y. Peel, *Ijeshas and Nigerians: The Incorporation of a Nigerian Kingdom, 1890s–1970s* (Cambridge: Cambridge University Press, 1983), 83–94, 166–67.

100. Paul E. Lovejoy, "The Characteristics of Plantations in the Nineteenth-Century Sokoto Caliphate (Islamic West Africa)," *AHR* 84 (1979): 1267–92; Paul E. Lovejoy, *Transformations in Slavery: A History of Slavery in Africa* (Cambridge: Cambridge University Press, 1983), 195–218; S. F. Nadel, *A Black Byzantium: The Kingdom of Nupe in Nigeria* (London: Oxford University Press, 1942), 90–91, 97, 103–20, 196–99, 278–79; Michael Mason, *Foundations of the Bida Kingdom* (Zaria, Nigeria: Ahmadu Bello University Press, 1981), 9, 59–62, 75–76, 87–90, 113–17.

101. O'Hear, *Power Relations*, 62–89; and Lovejoy and Hogendorn, *Slow Death*, 33–41, show that the Royal Niger Company occupation of Ilorin and Nupe, southern emirates of the Sokoto Caliphate, in 1897 triggered a massive slave exodus that included many women and children. Local rulers gradually reestablished order, however, and began recapturing runaways, some of whom may have been traded south to prevent reescape. The British did not occupy the Hausa-speaking heartland of the Caliphate and begin to disrupt the slave trade there until after 1900. A few of the northern alien children registered at Lagos after 1897 may also have been fugitive slaves from Nupe or Ilorin. For the story of a female slave who escaped from Ilorin to Lagos in 1897, see Kristin Mann, "The Historical Roots and Cultural Logic of Outside Marriage in Colonial Lagos," in *Nuptiality in Sub-Saharan Africa: Contemporary Anthropological and Demographic Perspectives*, ed. Caroline Bledsoe and Gilles Pison (Oxford: Clarendon Press, 1994), 177–79.

102. Stallard and Harrinson, *Ordinances*, 306–15.

103. OR, Appendix D, 46.

104. See, for example, GP f1, Shortt to Daumas, 15 July 1863, Glover to Didelot, 2 August 1863; and GP f4, Johnson to Johnson, 14 February 1871, Johnson to Glover, 17 February 1871, Chief Akodu to Glover, 9 August 1871; as well as CO 147/27, Berkeley to Pope Hennessy, 4 February 1873, plus encls.; CO 147/29, Clare to Herbert, 12 February 1873, plus encls.

105. RWCA, Minutes of Evidence, W. McCoskry, 6 April 1865, 71; John Pope

Hennessy, "On the British Settlements in Western Africa," *Journal of the Society of Arts* (2 May 1873): 443.

106. A. G. Hopkins, "The Lagos Strike of 1897: An Exploration in Nigerian Labour History," *P&P* 35 (1966): 142; Roberts, "The End of Slavery in the French Soudan," 295; O'Hear, *Power Relations*, 64–65; Klein, *Slavery*, 80.

107. RWCA, Minutes of Evidence, W. McCoskry, 6 April 1865, 69. See also CO 147/14, Blackall to Buckingham, 30 January 1868, plus encls. Oroge, "Fugitive Slave Question," 61–80, provides an earlier analysis of this subject.

108. OR, Appendix D, 46. See also GP f1, Glover to Didelot, 3 August 1863.

109. "Proceedings in relation to slavery at Lagos"; GP f4, Igowun to Glover, 3 August 1866, Bakare to Abayomi, 10 November 1871; CO 147/14, Blackall to Buckingham, 30 January 1868, plus encls.; CO 147/27, Pope Hennessy to Kimberley, 6 February 1873.

110. GP f4, Igowun to Glover, 3 August 1866; Akodu to Glover, 15 September 1871.

111. GP f4, Johnson to Glover, 17 February 1871; Shields, "Palm Oil and Power," 112, 273–76.

112. CO 147/27, Berkeley to Pope Hennessy, 4 February 1873.

113. Oroge, "Fugitive Slave Question," 66; Oroge, "Fugitive Slave Crisis," 40–53.

114. GP f4, Johnson to Glover, 17 February 1871.

115. CO 147/27, Berkeley to Pope Hennessy, 4 February 1873, plus encls.; CO 147/28, Lees to Governor-in-Chief, 26 September 1873, plus encls.; CO 147/29, Clare to Herbert, 12 February 1873, plus encls.

116. GP f5, Cole to Glover, 16 August 1872, Bada to Glover, 11 September 1872; CO 147/27, Berkeley to Pope Hennessy, 4 February 1873, encls. 2 and 6.

117. Pope Hennessy to Berkeley, 6 February 1873, encl. in CO 147/27, Pope Hennessy to Kimberley, 6 February 1873; CO 147/27, Berkeley to Administrator-in-Chief, 16 May 1873.

118. COL, Lagos Colony, Census, 1881. These and other census figures are approximations, because accurate counts were impossible to obtain. Miers, *Britain and the Ending of the Slave Trade*, 164; and *Eagle and Lagos Critic*, 28 August 1886, provide evidence of the continuing tension caused by the flight of runaways from surrounding territories to Lagos.

119. CO 147/27, Berkeley to Pope Hennessy, 4 February 1873, plus encls.; CO 147/29, Clare to Herbert, 12 February 1873, plus encls.

120. Minute on CO 147/27, Pope Hennessy to Kimberley, n.d.; Minute on CO 147/27, Berkeley to Pope Hennessy, 4 February 1873; GP f6, Willoughby to Crowther, 20 January 1873; GP f6, Willoughby to Glover, 24 June 1873. For discussions of this phenomenon elsewhere in colonial Africa, see Lovejoy and Hogendorn, *Slow Death*, 111–26; Cooper, *Marriage in Maradi*, 1–19; Cooper, "Conditions Analogous to Slavery," 119, 126–29; Klein, *Slavery*, 136; and Martin Chanock, *Law, Custom, and Social Order: The Colonial Experience in Malawi and Zambia* (Cambridge: Cambridge University Press, 1985), 164–71.

121. A. G. Hopkins, "Economic Imperialism in West Africa: Lagos, 1880–92," *Economic History Review* 21 (1968): 596–603; Kristin Mann, *Marrying Well: Marriage, Status, and Social Change among the Educated Elite in Colonial Lagos* (Cambridge: Cambridge University Press, 1985), 22.

122. E. A. Ayandele, *The Ijebu of Yorubaland, 1850–1950: Politics, Economy, and Society* (Ibadan: Heinemann, 1992), 33. See also Robert Smith, "Nigeria—Ijebu," in *West African Resistance: The Military Response to Colonial Occupation*, ed. Michael Crowder (London: Hutchinson, 1971), 170–204; Obaro Ikime, *The Fall of Nigeria: The British Conquest* (London: Heinemann, 1977), 53–61; and Toyin Falola, *The History of Nigeria* (Westport: Greenwood Press, 1999), 56.

123. Hopkins, "Lagos Strike"; Sara Berry, *No Condition Is Permanent: The Social Dynamics of Agrarian Change in Sub-Saharan Africa* (Madison: University of Wisconsin Press, 1993), 69; Anne Phillips, *The Enigma of Colonialism: British Policy in West Africa* (London: James Currey, 1989), 40–41; Mann, *Marrying Well*, 23.

124. CO 147/134, Denton to Chamberlain, 3 August 1898. Also CO 147/156, MacGregor to Chamberlain, 1 August 1901. For discussions of the significance of race in the development of colonial labor policies elsewhere in Africa see, for example, Shula Marks and Richard Rathbone, introduction to *Industrialisation and Social Change in South Africa: African Class Formation, Culture, and Consciousness, 1870–1930* (Harlow, U.K.: Longman, 1982), 4–8; John Higginson, *A Working Class in the Making: Belgian Colonial Labor Policy, Private Enterprise, and the African Mineworker, 1907–1951* (Madison: University of Wisconsin Press, 1989), 9; Keletso E. Atkins, *The Moon Is Dead! Give Us Our Money! The Cultural Origins of an African Work Ethic, Natal, South Africa, 1843–1900* (Portsmouth, N.H.: Heinemann, 1993), 3–4; and Jeanne Marie Penvenne, *African Workers and Colonial Racism: Mozambican Strategies and Struggles in Lourenço Marques, 1877–1962* (Portsmouth, N.H.: Heinemann, 1995), 1–5.

125. Hopkins, "Lagos Strike," 136, 146.

126. I. F. Nicolson, *The Administration of Nigeria, 1900–1960: Men, Methods, and Myths* (Oxford: Clarendon Press, 1969), 1–81; Mann, *Marrying Well*, 23; Phillips, *Enigma*, 26–27; P. J. Cain and A. G. Hopkins, *Innovation and Expansion, 1688–1914*, vol. 1 of *British Imperialism* (London: Longman, 1993), 381–96.

127. Cooper, "Conditions Analogous to Slavery," 113–17; Lovejoy and Hogendorn, *Slow Death*, 13–27; Roberts and Miers, introduction to Miers and Roberts, eds., *End of Slavery*, 17.

128. Berry, *No Condition Is Permanent*, 24–25; Richard Roberts and Kristin Mann, introduction to *Law in Colonial Africa*, ed. Kristin Mann and Richard Roberts (Portsmouth, N.H.: Heinemann, 1991), 15–23; Frederick Cooper, *Decolonization and African Society: The Labor Question in French and British Africa* (Cambridge: Cambridge University Press, 1996), 11. On the evolution of indirect rule in Nigeria, see E. A. Afigbo, *The Warrant Chiefs: Indirect Rule in Southern Nigeria* (New York: Humanities Press, 1972), 37–112; and Margery Perham, *Native Administration in Nigeria* (London: Oxford University Press, 1937), 33–66. Lord Hailey, *Native Administration in the British African Territories*, 5 vols. (London: Her Majesty's Stationary Office, 1950–53), charts its spread throughout British Africa.

129. Michael Crowder and Obaro Ikime, eds., *West African Chiefs: Their Changing Status under Colonial Rule and Independence*, trans. Brenda Packman (Ile-Ife: University of Ife Press, 1970); J. A. Atanda, *The New Oyo Empire: Indirect Rule and Change in Western Nigeria, 1894–1934* (New York: Humanities Press, 1973); A. I. Asiwaju, *Western Yorubaland under European Rule, 1889–1945: A Comparative Analysis of French and British Colonialism* (Atlantic Highlands, N.J.: Humanities Press, 1976), chap. 4; Peel, *Ijeshas and Nigerians*, 89–113.

130. Phillips, *Enigma*, 26–44; CSO 8/5/9, McCallum to Maxwell, 25 April 1897. McCallum initially proposed that the government use the unpaid labor of locally owned slaves to build the railroad, and when the Colonial Office objected, suggested paying slaves a wage from which the price of their redemption would be deducted. Soon, however, he adopted the practice, employed earlier by Carter, of using *baálẹ̀* to organize the forced labor of slaves and other locals for government projects. CO 147/94, Carter to Ripon, 15 January 1894; CO 147/113, McCallum to Chamberlain, 3 May 1897; CO 147/116, McCallum to Chamberlain, 16 August 1897; CO 147/119, McCallum to Chamberlain, 28 October 1897. I am grateful to A. G. Hopkins for these and other references to labor questions in the 1890s. Roberts and Miers, introduction to Miers and Roberts, eds., *End of Slavery*, 17; Dumett and Johnson, "Britain and the Suppression of Slavery," 85–86; Lovejoy and Hogendorn, *Slow Death*, 31–91; Cooper, *Decolonization*, 11; and Klein, *Slavery*, 61–65, 129, 140–41, 157–58, discuss similar concerns and compromises elsewhere in colonial Africa.

131. CO 147/134, Denton to Chamberlain, 3 August 1898.

132. CO 147/104, Carter to Chamberlain, 9 January 1896.

133. CO 147/94, Carter to Ripon, 15 January 1894; CO 147/100, Denton to Chamberlain, 5 October 1895; CO 147/104, Carter to Chamberlain, 6 February 1896. Judith A. Byfield, *The Bluest Hands: A Social and Economic History of Women Dyers in Abeokuta (Nigeria), 1890–1940* (Portsmouth, N.H.: Heinemann, 2002), 67, notes the flight of slaves from Abeokuta to Lagos.

134. CSO 8/5/9, McCallum to Wingfield, 13 May 1897.

135. "Evidence to the Commission on Trade," encl. in CO 147/133, Denton to Chamberlain, 4 June 1898.

136. CSO 8/5/9, McCallum to Wingfield, 6 June 1897; CO 147/121, McCallum to Chamberlain, 20 December 1897; CO 147/150, Denton to Chamberlain, 28 July 1900; CO 147/160, MacGregor to Chamberlain, 4 February 1902. Frederick J. D. Lugard, *Political Memorandum: Revision of Instructions to Political Officers on Subjects Chiefly Political and Administrative* (London: Frank Cass, 1970), 217; Tekena N. Tamuno, "Emancipation in Nigeria," *Nigeria Magazine* 82 (1964): 218–27; Hopkins, "Lagos Strike," 142; Oroge, "The Institution of Slavery," 360–416; Toyin Falola, "The End of Slavery among the Yoruba," in *Slavery and Colonial Rule in Africa*, ed. Suzanne Miers and Martin A. Klein (London: Frank Cass, 1999), 232–49; and Phillips, *Enigma*, 26–58, discuss British policy regarding slavery in the Yoruba interior.

137. COL, Southern Nigeria, Census, 1911, 8, 15.

138. Mann, *Marrying Well*, 23.

139. CSO 8/5/9, McCallum to Wingfield, 13 May 1897; "Evidence to the Commission on Trade"; CO 147/134, Denton to Chamberlain, 3 August 1898; Phillips, *Enigma*, 34, 53. Cooper, *Slaves to Squatters*, 21–26, and *Decolonization*, 25, 43–50, document similar developments in the East African port of Mombassa and elsewhere in colonial Africa.

140. Charles van Onselen, *Studies in the Social and Economic History of Witwatersrand, 1886–1914*, 2 vols. (Harlow, U.K.: Longman, 1982); and Luise White, *The Comforts of Home: Prostitution in Colonial Nairobi* (Chicago: University of Chicago Press, 1990), are among the best studies of attempts by colonial authorities to con-

trol men and women migrating to African towns in the interest of creating a new urban social order. For other such work, see the essays by Cooper and Worger in *Struggle for the City: Migrant Labor, Capital, and the State in Urban Africa*, ed. Frederick Cooper (Beverly Hills: Sage, 1983), 7–50; and by Clancy-Smith and Akyeampong in *Africa's Urban Past*, ed. David M. Anderson and Richard Rathbone (London: James Currey, 2000).

6. *Redefining the Owner-Slave Relationship*

1. This pattern is consistent with what happened later elsewhere on the continent as the colonial frontier moved inland. Paul E. Lovejoy and Jan S. Hogendorn, *Slow Death for Slavery: The Course of Abolition in Northern Nigeria, 1897–1936* (Cambridge: Cambridge University Press, 1993), 31–63, 101–108, 136; Ann O'Hear, *Power Relations in Nigeria: Ilorin Slaves and Their Successors* (Rochester, N.Y.: University of Rochester Press, 1997), 12–13, 62–76; Martin Klein, *Slavery and Colonial Rule in French West Africa* (Cambridge: Cambridge University Press, 1998), 14, 32, 85–87; Toyin Falola, "The End of Slavery among the Yoruba," in *Slavery and Colonial Rule in Africa*, ed. Suzanne Miers and Martin A. Klein (London: Frank Cass, 1999), 234–42.

2. FO 84/886, Beecroft to Palmerston, 3 January 1852. Oshodi must have replaced many of the slaves he lost, because he remained a big slaveowner until his death in 1868.

3. FO 84/1031, Campbell to Clarendon, 2 July 1857.

4. Testimony of Chief Abasi, "Evidence to the Commission on Trade," encl. in CO 147/133, Denton to Chamberlain, 4 June 1898.

5. J. D. Y. Peel, *Religious Encounter and the Making of the Yoruba* (Bloomington: Indiana University Press, 2000), 150.

6. Frederick Cooper, *Plantation Slavery on the East Coast of Africa* (New Haven: Yale University Press, 1977), 230; O'Hear, *Power Relations*, 13, 50, 65; Klein, *Slavery*, 160–61.

7. Davis to Campbell, 18 May 1857, encl. in FO 84/1031, Campbell to Clarendon, 2 July 1857.

8. Klein, *Slavery*, 163–64, 197–202. Klein and others have shown that the development of the Murids, an Islamic brotherhood open to former slaves, also affected emancipation in the peanut basin. Martin Klein, "Social and Economic Factors in the Muslim Revolution in Senegambia," *JAH* 13 (1972): 419–41; James Searing, "*God Alone Is King*": *Islam and Emancipation in Senegal; The Wolof Kingdoms of Kajoor and Bawol, 1859–1914* (Portsmouth, N.H.: Heinemann, 2002), 184–88, 231–67; David Robinson, "Islam, Cash Crops and Emancipation in Senegal," *JAH* 44 (2003): 139–44. Searing argues, however, that Klein underestimates the incidence of slave flight from the Wolof kingdoms following the French conquest.

9. Of twenty-nine former slaves who signed a letter to Colonel Ord in 1865, at least eight had Muslim names. OR, Taiwo and others to Ord, 27 December 1864, Appendix E, 335. See also *Abdulai v. Apata*, 29 August 1894, JNCC, ?, 150; and T. G. O. Gbadamosi, *The Growth of Islam among the Yoruba, 1841–1908* (London: Longman, 1978), 26–32, 39, 51, 66–70.

10. CMS YM CA2/O71, Letter of William Morgan, Lagos, 6 July 1872; and The Report of the Building of . . . Holy Trinity Church in the District of Ebute Ero, Lagos, 31 July 1878.

11. CMS YM CA2/O66, Annual Letter, the Rev. A. Mann, 26 December 1876.

12. On the exodus of slaves in the Western Sudan and Northern Nigeria see, in addition to the works by Klein, O'Hear, and Lovejoy and Hogendorn cited in note 1, Richard Roberts and Martin Klein, "The Banamba Slave Exodus of 1905 and the Decline of Slavery in the Western Sudan," *JAH* 21 (1980): 375–94; and Richard Roberts, "The End of Slavery in the French Soudan, 1905–1914," in *The End of Slavery in Africa*, ed. Suzanne Miers and Richard Roberts (Madison: University of Wisconsin Press, 1988), 282–307. Despite large-scale departures, Lovejoy and Hogendorn (143) and Klein (197) believe that most slaves in these areas stayed where they were.

13. Runaway slaves are said to have constituted much of the population of certain towns within the colony, such as Lekki. It is unclear, however, whether these slaves came from Lagos or areas beyond the colonial frontier. Other towns (Iba and Okokomaiko) are associated with Muslims of northern slave origin, who reportedly settled in them after they were demobilized from the Armed Hausa Police between 1875 and 1900. These settlements may have attracted other former slaves. Taiwo Olowo become the *bàbá ìsàlẹ̀*, or representative in Lagos, of communities on the mainland during the early 1870s and allegedly settled refugees and runaway slaves there. Peel, *Religious Encounter*, 169; RHL, Oxford (Colonial Records Project), Mss.Afr.L15, W. Fowler, "A Report on the Lands of the Colony District," 24–25, 29, 49–50; *Ashogbon v. Okin*, 16 November 1885, JNCC, 6, 136.

14. Fowler, "A Report," 1, 17, 26; interview with N. E. S. Adewale; WALC, "Correspondence," Governor to Secretary of State, 24 May 1913, 207–208, 219–20, W. Buchanan Smith, "Land Tenure in the Colony of Lagos," plus Appendix I, 5 December 1912, 223, 227–33, *Idewu v. Ogunbiyi*, 9 May 1878, 245, and *Odu of Ikeja v. Akiboye of Ikeja*, 22 August 1892, 246.

15. Sandra T. Barnes, *Patrons and Power: Creating a Political Community in Metropolitan Lagos* (Bloomington: Indiana University Press, 1986), 34–39; Patrick Cole, *Modern and Traditional Elites in the Politics of Lagos* (Cambridge: Cambridge University Press, 1975), 29–44; Kristin Mann, "The Rise of Taiwo Olowo: Law, Accumulation, and Mobility in Early Colonial Lagos," in *Law in Colonial Africa*, ed. Kristin Mann and Richard Roberts (Portsmouth, N.H.: Heinemann, 1991), 94–95.

16. CMS YM CA2/O87/13, White to Venn, Lagos, 4 May 1863; WALC, "Correspondence," Statement of Ibrahim Bashorun and Aganran, 233–34; Fowler, "A Report," 3–29 passim. When I was conducting research in Lagos during the 1980s, a highly respected professional man from an old Lagos family told me that his uncle had recently come to talk to him about initiating legal proceedings to remove some "slaves of the family" from land they had occupied for generations on the outskirts of the city. The uncle maintained that the property still belonged to the family, which now needed it. My informant discouraged litigation, but the story nonetheless illustrates how long landed property occupied by former slaves remained at risk.

17. Joseph C. Miller, "Retention, Reinvention, and Remembering: Restoring

Identities through Enslavement in Africa and under Slavery in Brazil," in *Enslaving Connections: Changing Cultures of Africa and Brazil during the Era of Slavery*, ed. José C. Curto and Paul E. Lovejoy (Amherst, N.Y.: Prometheus/Humanity Books, 2003), 81–121; Cooper, *Plantation Slavery*, 213–52. Frederick Cooper, Thomas C. Holt, and Rebecca J. Scott, introduction to *Beyond Slavery: Explorations of Race, Labor, and Citizenship in Postemancipation Societies*, by Frederick Cooper, Thomas C. Holt, and Rebecca J. Scott (Chapel Hill: University of North Carolina Press, 2000), 5, make the essential point, however, that notions of belonging are often contested in African societies, as are specific terms of incorporation.

18. See, for example, RP, 18D33, Oddunimi to the Slave Court, 13 July 1863; and *Zaderow v. Zafungbo*, 24 February 1882, JNCC, 4, 20. Also Frederick Cooper, *From Slaves to Squatters: Plantation Labor and Agriculture in Zanzibar and Coastal Kenya, 1890–1925* (New Haven: Yale University Press, 1980), 71–84, 121–24.

19. Dr. Sahid Adejumobi, Department of History, Wright State University, personal communication, 17 November 2000.

20. FO 84/920, Campbell to Clarendon, October 1853. For a further example of missionary interference to save a group of male slaves from sale or sacrifice, see CMS YM CA2/O87, White to Townsend, Otta, 14 September 1860.

21. FO 84/1061, Campbell to Clarendon, 28 March 1858, published in William N. M. Geary, *Nigeria under British Rule* (New York: Barnes and Noble, 1965), 37.

22. RP, 18D33/1–18; OR, Appendix D, 332; Chiefs and traders to Glover, 8 September 1863, encl. in CO 147/4, Glover to Newcastle, 10 October 1863.

23. William A. Green, *British Slave Emancipation: The Sugar Colonies and the Great Experiment, 1830–1865* (Oxford: Clarendon Press, 1976), 129–61; Thomas C. Holt, *The Problem of Freedom: Race, Labor, and Politics in Jamaica and Britain, 1832–1938* (Baltimore: Johns Hopkins University Press, 1992), 55–79; Richard B. Allen, *Slaves, Freedmen, and Indentured Laborers in Colonial Mauritius* (Cambridge: Cambridge University Press, 1999), 15, 55.

24. RP, Teneomi to Dr. Rowe, 20 June 1863. See also RP, Abudoli to Gentlemen of the Court, 3 November 1862; and Showunmy and Calurina to Dr. Rowe, 10 January 1863.

25. Stuart B. Schwartz, *Slaves, Peasants, and Rebels: Reconsidering Brazilian Slavery* (Urbana: University of Illinois Press, 1992), 39. See also Cooper, *Plantation Slavery*, 156–82; and Ira Berlin and Philip D. Morgan, "Labor and the Shaping of Slave Life in the Americas," in *Cultivation and Culture: Labor and the Shaping of Slave Life in the Americas*, ed. Ira Berlin and Philip D. Morgan (Charlottesville: University of Virginia Press, 1993), 1–45.

26. Philip D. Morgan, *Slave Counterpoint: Black Culture in the Eighteenth-Century Chesapeake and Lowcountry* (Chapel Hill: University of North Carolina Press, 1998), xxi.

27. Thomas F. Armstrong, "From Task Labor to Free Labor: The Transition along Georgia's Rice Coast, 1820–1880," in *From Slavery to Sharecropping: White Land and Black Labor in the Rural South, 1865–1900*, ed. Donald G. Nieman (New York: Garland Publishing, 1994), 2–17; Cooper, *Slaves to Squatters*, 69–124; Rebecca J. Scott, *Slave Emancipation in Cuba: The Transition to Free Labor, 1860–1899* (Princeton: Princeton University Press, 1985), 179–81, 231; Julie Saville, *The Work*

of Reconstruction: From Slave to Wage Laborer in South Carolina, 1860–1870 (Cambridge: Cambridge University Press, 1994); Leslie A. Schwalm, *A Hard Fight for We: Women's Transition from Slavery to Freedom in South Carolina* (Urbana: University of Illinois Press, 1997), 187–233; John C. Rodrigue, *Reconstruction in the Cane Fields: From Slavery to Free Labor in Louisiana's Sugar Parishes, 1862–1880* (Baton Rouge: Louisiana State University Press, 2001), 58–76.

28. WALC, "Correspondence," *Ajose v. Efunde and others*, 14 July 1892, 246; M. R. Delany, "Official Report of the Niger Valley Exploring Party," in *Search for a Place: Black Separatism and Africa, 1860*, by M. R. Delany and Robert Campbell (Ann Arbor: University of Michigan Press, 1969), 79; interviews with Chief Mobolaji Oshodi, Prince A. L. A. Ojora, Alhaji A. W. A. Akibayo, and S. A. Oni. See also N. A. Fadipe, *Sociology of the Yoruba* (Ibadan: University of Ibadan Press, 1970), 182.

29. Interviews with A. W. Animaṣaun and G. B. Animaṣaun.

30. Interviews with Prince A. L. A. Ojora, Chief Mobolaji Oshodi, and Alhaji A. W. A. Akibayo.

31. FO 84/950, Campbell to Clarendon, 1 May 1854; FO 84/976, Campbell to Clarendon, 2 June 1855; FO 84/1002, Campbell to Clarendon, 14 May, 14 June 1856; interview with S. B. Affini.

32. PP 1858–9.XXXIV.281, Class B, Correspondence with Foreign Powers Relating to the Slave Trade, II, no. 11, Consul Campbell, Lagos, 18 March 1858, quoted in Robin Law, "'Legitimate' Trade and Gender Relations in Yorubaland and Dahomey," in *From Slave Trade to "Legitimate" Commerce: The Commercial Transition in Nineteenth-Century West Africa*, ed. Robin Law (Cambridge: Cambridge University Press, 1995), 207–208. See also FO 84/1002, Campbell to Clarendon, 27 May, 14 June 1856.

33. *Ajose v. Efunde*, 246; *Ṣomade v. Ebite*, 17 April 1879, JNCC, 2, 102; interview with Chief Mobolaji Oshodi.

34. *Memoirs of Giambattista Scala: Consul of His Italian Majesty in Lagos in Guinea (1862)*, trans. Brenda Packman and ed. Robert Smith (Oxford: Oxford University Press, 2000), 101; RWCA, Minutes of Evidence, W. McCoskry, 6 April 1865, 81; testimony of J. A. O. Payne, "Evidence to the Commission on Trade"; A. G. Hopkins, "A Report on the Yoruba, 1910," *JHSN* 5 (1969): 90; Fadipe, *Sociology*, 184–85, 187; A. K. Ajisafe, *The Laws and Customs of the Yoruba People* (Lagos: CMS Bookshop, 1924), 60. See also E. A. Oroge, "The Institution of Slavery in Yorubaland, with Particular Reference to the Nineteenth Century" (Ph.D. diss., University of Birmingham, 1971), 199; and Peel, *Religious Encounter*, 66.

35. Hopkins, "Report on the Yoruba," 90; Oroge, "The Institution of Slavery," 209; interview with Chief D. A. Ogunbiyi.

36. FO 84/950, Campbell to Clarendon, 1 June 1854. Also FO 84/1061, Campbell to Clarendon, 28 March 1858, in Geary, *Nigeria*, 36–37; interview with S. B. Affini; and Francine Shields, "Palm Oil and Power: Women in an Era of Economic and Social Transition in Nineteenth Century Yorubaland (South-Western Nigeria)" (Ph.D. diss., University of Stirling, 1997), 95.

37. Davies to Campbell, 18 May 1857, encl. in FO 84/1031, Campbell to Clarendon, 2 July 1857. See also Toyin Falola, *The Political Economy of a Pre-colonial African State: Ibadan, 1830–1900* (Ile-Ife: University of Ife Press, 1984), 142–44.

38. Fadipe, *Sociology*, 187.

39. "Evidence to the Commission on Trade." See also Fadipe, *Sociology*, 184; FO 84/1002, Campbell to Clarendon, 18 February, 16 August 1856; FO 84/1031, Campbell to Clarendon, 14 March 1857; RWCA, Minutes of Evidence, W. McCoskry, 6 April 1865, 76.

40. Shields, "Palm Oil and Power," 91.

41. FO 84/1002, Campbell to Clarendon, 16 August 1856; *Ajose v. Efunde*, 248; and interviews with Chief Mobolaji Oshodi, Alhaji A. W. A. Akibayo, and the *ọlọ́fin* of Isheri. For references to "large plantations" or extensive farms that employed between eighty and five hundred slaves near Abeokuta, Ijebu Ode, and Badagry, see the testimony of J. P. L. Davies, J. A. O. Payne, and Chief Abasi, "Evidence to the Commission on Trade." Samuel Johnson, *The History of the Yorubas* (London: Routledge and Kegan Paul, 1969), 325; Bolanle Awe, "Militarism and Economic Development in Nineteenth Century Yoruba Country: The Ibadan Example," *JAH* 14 (1973): 65–77; Oroge, "The Institution of Slavery," 199; Falola, *Political Economy*, 142–44; and O'Hear, *Power Relations*, 28–34, contain references to large-scale production by slaves in other Yoruba states.

42. *Memoirs of Scala*, 101; RWCA, Minutes of Evidence, W. McCoskry, 6 April 1865, 81.

43. *Abdulai v. Apata*, 150; *Banjoko v. Ogundari*, 18 January 1895, JNCC, ?, 396; *Fajimi v. Fatosha*, 27 July 1896, JNCC, ?, 438.

44. Cooper, *Plantation Slavery*, 156–58, 170–71; Schwartz, *Slaves, Peasants*, chap. 2; Berlin and Morgan, "Labor and the Shaping of Slave Life," 3, 7, 18–19.

45. Testimony of J. A. O. Payne, "Evidence to the Commission on Trade"; J. E. Gray, "Native Methods of Preparing Palm Oil in Nigeria," *First Annual Bulletin of the Agricultural Department, Nigeria* (1922): 32; Shields, "Palm Oil and Power," 92.

46. WALC, "Minutes," testimony of Oguntola Ṣapara, 265. See also testimony of J. A. O. Payne, "Evidence to the Commission on Trade"; and Law, "Trade and Gender," 200.

47. Testimony of Chief Abasi, "Evidence to the Commission on Trade."

48. Interview with I. L. Apatira. Fadipe (*Sociology*, 185) wrote that in some communities masters were supposed to know all that their slaves earned on their own account, and even to have safekeeping of their slaves' money. He noted, however, that slaves foiled their owners by depositing their savings with friends, who were either emancipated slaves or people of free birth.

49. For evidence of slaves buying and owning slaves in Lagos, see Thomas J. Hutchinson, "The Social and Domestic Slavery of Western Africa, and Its Evil Influence on Commercial Progress," *Journal of the Society of Arts* 21 (26 February 1875): 315; testimony of J. A. O. Payne, "Evidence to the Commission on Trade"; and *Alaka v. Alaka*, 23 January 1904, 1 *NLR* 55. See also Falola, "The End of Slavery," 233.

50. The "Report on the Yoruba" written by a group of educated Lagosians in 1910 and edited by A. G. Hopkins observed (p. 82) that "during the time of the inter-tribal wars" it was "customary to purchase slave women as wives," but that "at present" the practice occurred only in exceptional cases, as when men had no family in the town or their descent could not be traced. Many male slaves and former slaves suffered these disabilities and may, therefore, have had few alternatives but to import women or girls to marry.

51. *Memoirs of Scala*, 101; FO 84/1031, Campbell to Clarendon, 14 March 1857. See also Hopkins, "Report on the Yoruba," 90; Fadipe, *Sociology*, 185; Oroge, "The Institution of Slavery," 142; and Peel, *Religious Encounter*, 66–67.

52. *Awa v. Disu*, 5 March 1885, JNCC, 6, 2; *Opere v. Johnson*, 20 July 1894, JNCC, ?, 107. In the case *Eshuby, alias Brimoh Apatira v. Oso, Opeluja, and Ogudula*, 14 July 1879, JNCC, 2, 126, three former slaves claimed, in the 1870s, to have redeemed themselves. Mohamed Mboji, "The Abolition of Slavery in Senegal, 1820–1890: Crisis or the Rise of a New Entrepreneurial Class?" in *Breaking the Chains: Slavery, Bondage, and Emancipation in Modern Africa and Asia*, ed. Martin A. Klein (Madison: University of Wisconsin Press, 1993), 201, found that following the abolition of slavery in Senegal slaves continued to practice self-redemption because it gave them greater freedom of movement.

53. WALC, "Correspondence," Governor to Secretary of State, 24 May 1913, 219, Smith, "Land Tenure," 224, 229, *Idewu v. Ogunbiyi*, 245, *Odu v. Akiboye*, 246; Fowler, "A Report," 7, 9.

54. T. C. Rayner, "Land Tenure in West Africa," in *Reports on Land Tenure in West Africa (1898)*, by T. C. Rayner and J. J. C. Healy, COL, West Africa Pamphlet, No. 19, 3; *Odu v. Akiboye*, 246; *Dada v. Ilo*, 14 December 1896, JNCC, 18, 303.

55. FO 85/1061, Campbell to Clarendon, 28 March 1858, in Geary, *Nigeria*, 37; Law, "Trade and Gender," 200, 204–205; Shields, "Palm Oil and Power," 66–74, 89–113.

56. Kristin Mann, "Women, Landed Property, and the Accumulation of Wealth in Early Colonial Lagos," *Signs* 16 (1991): 682–706.

57. *Jose v. Ṣomade*, 17 February 1879, JNCC, 2, 97; *Ṣomade v. Ebite*, 102; *Fajimi v. Fatosha*, 438; *Fadipe and others v. Brimoh*, 13 November 1895, JNCC, ?, 238; *Awoniya v. Ogunfunke and Morondiya*, 28 May 1896, JNCC, ?, 301–305.

58. See chapters 2 and 4, above.

59. RP, Teneomi to Dr. Rowe, 20 July 1863; *Eshuby v. Oso*, 126; and *Feshitan v. Kandu*, 18 December 1888, JNCC, 8, 37; A. Akintan, *Awful Disclosures on Epetedo Lands* (Lagos: Tika Tore Press, 1937), 17, 20–21. For a case that shows how the colonial judiciary supported a male slave in asserting authority over a household previously headed by a female one, see *Awoniya v. Ogunfunke and Morondiya*, 301.

60. *Fathers Work for Their Sons*, the title of Sara Berry's superb book that deals, among other things, with the inversion of intergenerational resource flows from juniors to elders in late twentieth-century southwestern Nigeria, communicates the opposite of older norms (Berkeley: University of California Press, 1985). See also Mann, *Marrying Well*, 40, 60.

61. Falola, *Political Economy*, 58; interview with Alhaji A. W. A. Akibayo; *Alaka v. Alaka*, 55.

62. RP, Obashua to Gentlemen of the Court, 16 January 1864; Abudoli to Gentlemen of the Court, 3 November 1862.

63. Interviews with Prince A. L. A. Ojora, C. B. Thomas, and O. A. Ṣobande.

64. Kristin Mann, "Owners, Slaves and the Struggle for Labour in the Commercial Transition at Lagos," in Law, ed., *From Slave Trade to "Legitimate" Commerce*, 160–64; Kristin Mann, "Interpreting Cases, Disentangling Disputes: Court Cases as a Source for Understanding Patron-Client Relationships in Early Colonial Lagos," in *Sources and Methods in African History: Spoken, Written, Unearthed*, ed.

Toyin Falola and Christian Jennings (Rochester, N.Y.: University of Rochester Press, 2003), 195–218.

65. Testimony of J. A. O. Payne and J. P. L. Davies, "Evidence to the Commission on Trade." See also A. G. Hopkins, *An Economic History of West Africa* (London: Longman, 1973), 134.

66. Interview with S. A. Forrest.

67. Eugene D. Genovese, *Roll, Jordan, Roll: The World the Slaves Made* (New York: Vintage Books, 1974), 3–7.

68. FO 84/1031, Campbell to Clarendon, 14 March 1857; RWCA, Minutes of Evidence, W. McCoskry, 6 April 1865, 65, 79; Hutchinson, "Domestic Slavery," 315–16; *Opere v. Johnson*, 107–108; Hopkins, "Report on the Yoruba," 76, 90; testimony of J. A. O. Payne, "Evidence to the Commission on Trade"; interview with S. A. Oni. For references to similar practices in the interior, see Johnson, *History*, 325; Fadipe, *Sociology*, 92, 182–85; and Ajisafe, *Laws*, 11, 18, 54–55.

69. Interviews with A. W. Animaṣaun and S. A. Animaṣaun; will, Sunmonu Animaṣaun, 21 August 1895, LPR, 1, 357.

70. RP, Teneomi to Dr. Rowe, 20 June 1863; *Awoniya v. Ogunfunke and Morondiya*, 301; Fadipe, *Sociology*, 188.

71. *Alaka v. Alaka*, 55.

72. Hopkins, *Economic History*, 26, argues that in West Africa, where wealth and power were measured "in men rather than in acres," owners could in some circumstances coerce obedience from slaves, but in others they judged it advisable "to secure support by offering slaves a modest stake in the existing political system"; while Falola, *Political Economy*, 142, holds that from the 1850s Ibadan slaves employed in agriculture, trade, and domestic labor were given "additional privileges in order to retain their services, loyalty and support." Cooper, *Plantation Slavery*, 5–6, 213–52; Martin A. Klein, "Women in Slavery in the Western Sudan," in *Women and Slavery in Africa*, ed. Claire C. Robertson and Martin A. Klein (Madison: University of Wisconsin Press, 1983), 77; Claude Meillassoux, *The Anthropology of Slavery: The Womb of Iron and Gold*, trans. Alide Dasnois (Chicago: University of Chicago Press, 1991), 116–25; and Klein, *Slavery*, 10–15, discuss similar dynamics in societies elsewhere in Africa.

73. Mann, "Owners, Slaves," 153–59; RP, Memorandum from E. Forster, 7 September 1860, Oddunimi to the Slave Court, 13 July 1863, Obashua to Gentlemen of the Court, 12 January 1864; and *Yara v. Ibiyemi*, 12 November 1896, JNCC, 18, 218–19.

74. FO 84/976, Campbell to Clarendon, 3 October 1855; interviews with Alhaji A. W. A. Akibayo and S. A. Oni. See also Falola, *Political Economy*, 142–44.

75. PP 1858–9.XXXIV.281, Class B, Correspondence with Foreign Powers Relating to the Slave Trade, II, no. 11, Consul Campbell, Lagos, 18 March 1858, quoted in Law, "Trade and Gender," 207–208. Also FO 84/1061, Campbell to Clarendon, 28 March 1858, published in Geary, *Nigeria*, 36–37; Ajisafe, *Laws*, 54–55; Fadipe, *Sociology* 182; and Shields, "Palm Oil and Power," 112–13.

76. While I have no direct evidence to support these last two points in the case of slaves, a man named Jinadu Ṣomade said something similar about his failure to meet the expectations of two former slaves who had entered his household as *asáforígẹ*. *Ṣomade v. Ebite*, 101.

77. OR, Taiwo and others to Ord, 27 December 1864, Appendix E, 335. Some of the signatories of the letter had in fact been purchased or captured in warfare, rather than born into slavery at Lagos. *Ajose v. Efunde*, 346; interviews with Chief Akin Adeshigbin, Lady Bank-Anthony, N. E. S. Adewale, Chief D. A. Ogunbiyi, and A. W. Animaṣaun; Mann, "Taiwo Olowo"; Oroge, "The Institution of Slavery," 209.

78. Interviews with Atanda Balogun and Chief D. A. Ogunbiyi.

79. *Ajose v. Efunde*, 346; *Memoirs of Scala*, 101; FO 84/1031, Campbell to Clarendon, 14 March 1857; *Opere v. Johnson*, 107.

80. Sandra T. Barnes, "Ritual, Power, and Outside Knowledge," *Journal of Religion in Africa* 20 (1990): 259–61.

81. *Opere v. Johnson*, 107–108. Also *Joko v. Oguntola and others*, 22 October 1894, JNCC, ?, 224.

82. RWCA, Minutes of Evidence, W. McCoskry, 5 April 1865, 82.

83. For expressions of the ongoing dependence of two male slaves on their owners, see *Aṣogbon v. Ṣomade*, 9 November 1885, JNCC, 6, 127, and *Aṣogbon v. Okin*, 136. For an example of the role of local big men in dispute settlement, see Kristin Mann, "Women's Rights in Law and Practice: Marriage and Dispute Settlement in Colonial Lagos," in *African Women and the Law: Historical Perspectives*, ed. Margaret Jean Hay and Marcia Wright (Boston: Boston University, African Studies Center, 1982), 151–71. Other historians have also found that many slaves remained with their owners during emancipation elsewhere in colonial Africa and that economic, social, and political dependence provided a powerful mechanism of ongoing control. Cooper, *Slaves to Squatters*, 72–84; Raymond E. Dumett and Marion Johnson, "Britain and the Suppression of Slavery in the Gold Coast Colony, Ashanti, and the Northern Territories," in Miers and Roberts, eds., *End of Slavery*, 85–91; Lovejoy and Hogendorn, *Slow Death*, 127–28, 143–58, 199–233; Klein, *Slavery*, 205–11; Falola, "The End of Slavery," 236–37.

84. *Memoirs of Scala*, 101. Also Hopkins, "Report on the Yoruba," 76, 90; testimony of J. A. O. Payne, "Evidence to the Commission on Trade"; Fadipe, *Sociology*, 117, 147, 187; and Ajisafe, *Laws*, 6.

85. Johnson, *History*, 325.

86. I am grateful to Dr. Kemi Rotimi, Department of History, Obafemi Awolowo University, and Dr. Sahid Adejumobi for calling these proverbs to my attention. Also RWCA, Minutes of Evidence, W. McCoskry, 6 April 1865, 69; Johnson, *History*, 325; Ajisafe, *Laws*, 11, 54–55; Oroge, "The Institution of Slavery," 135–36, 142; and Toyin Falola, "Missionaries and Domestic Slavery in Yorubaland in the Nineteenth Century," *Journal of Religious History* 14 (1986): 183. Robert Campbell, "A Pilgrimage to My Motherland," in *Search for a Place: Black Separatism and Africa, 1860*, by M. R. Delany and Robert Campbell (Ann Arbor: University of Michigan Press, 1969), 195, and Richard Francis Burton, *Abeokuta and the Camaroons Mountains: An Exploration* (London: Tinsley Brothers, 1863), 1:299, allude to gradations of slavery.

87. Johnson, *History*, 325; Hopkins, "Report on the Yoruba," 81; Ajisafe, *Laws*, 54–55; Shields, "Palm Oil and Power," 272–76.

88. Mann, "Owners, Slaves," 153–54.

89. Interviews with Chief Mobolaji Oshodi and O. A. Ṣobande; RP, Abudoli

to Gentlemen of the Court, 3 November 1862, Oddunimi to Gentlemen of the Court, 13 July 1863, and Obashua to Gentlemen of the Court, 12 January 1894.

90. Interviews with Prince A. L. A. Ojora and C. B. Thomas; *Egunleti and Saye v. Ayifemi*, 21 November 1894, JNCC, ?, 309–11; interview with Mrs. Kofo Pratt; Ajisafe, *Laws*, 18, 72–73; C. K. Meek, *Land Tenure and Land Administration in Nigeria and Cameroons* (London: Her Majesty's Stationary Office, 1957), 131; *Report of Inquiry into the Ojora of Ijora Chieftaincy Conducted by the Standing Tribunal of Inquiry into Declarations Regulating the Selection of Obas and Recognized Chiefs in Lagos State* (Lagos, 1975). I am grateful to Prince Ojora for permitting me to study this last document. On the special role of young girls in performing *oríkì*, see Karin Barber, *I Could Speak until Tomorrow: Oriki, Women, and the Past in a Yoruba Town* (Washington: Smithsonian Institution Press, 1991), 96–105.

91. Orlando Patterson, *Slavery and Social Death: A Comparative Study* (Cambridge: Cambridge University Press, 1982).

92. Interviews with Prince A. L. A. Ojora and Chief Justice Atanda Fatayi-Williams. See also *Nigeria, the Epetedo Lands: Representations of the Oshodi Chieftaincy Family Submitted to the Commissioner, Lagos Land Inquiry* (Lagos: Hope Rising Press, 1939), 1; and Sir Mervyn Tew, *Report on Title to Land in Lagos* (Lagos: The Government Printer, 1947), 36–44. R. C. Abraham, *Dictionary of Modern Yoruba* (London: University of London Press, 1958), 65, says that *àrótà* were slaves liable to be sold at a moment's notice, but that is not the way the term was used in Lagos. G. B. A. Coker, *Family Property among the Yorubas* (London: Sweet and Maxwell, 1958), 201–204, reports that a twentieth-century ordinance describes *àrótà* as "any person who has attached himself to the household of a chief and who occupies land subject to the control of such chief," but acknowledges that the bill was framed to deal with conflicts in a particular part of the city—that occupied by the followers of Oshodi Tapa. Earlier definitions, even by the Oshodi family itself, do not appear to have been so broad.

93. Interviews with S. B. Affini, Alhaji A. W. A. Akibayo, Chief Mobolaji Oshodi, and Chief D. A. Ogunbiyi. Also *Oshodi Chieftaincy Family: Records and Achievements* (Lagos: A. E. P., n.d).

94. Interviews with Prince A. L. A. Ojora and C. B. Thomas.

95. See, for example, *Report of Inquiry into the Ojora of Ijora Chieftaincy*. Also interview with Alhaji A. W. A. Akibayo.

96. CMS YM CA2/O31/131, Annual letter, Lagos, Crowther to Chapman, 14 January 1856.

97. Paul Finkelman and Joseph C. Miller, *Macmillan Encyclopedia of World Slavery* (New York: Macmillan Reference, 1998), 1:103–109, 181–93, 434–40; Humphrey J. Fisher, *Slavery in the History of Muslim Black Africa* (London: Hurst, 2001), 17–97 passim; Nehemia Levtzion, "Slavery and Islamization in Africa," in *Islam and the Ideology of Enslavement*, vol. 1 of *Slaves and Slavery in Muslim Africa*, ed. John Ralph Willis (London: Frank Cass, 1985), 182–98.

98. See, for example, *Opere v. Johnson*, 107–108.

99. Interviews with A. W. Animaṣaun and S. A. Animaṣaun; will, Sunmonu Animaṣaun, 21 August 1895, LPR, 1, 357.

100. NNA, Badadiv 5/3/1890–2, Ewart to Acting Colonial Secretary, 7 October 1890. I am grateful to A. G. Hopkins for this reference.

101. CO 147/159, Anti-slavery and Aborigines Protection Society to Chamberlain, 19 February 1901; Mann, *Marrying Well*, 96–97; Shields, "Palm Oil and Power," 273–74.

102. Barnes, "Ritual, Power, and Outside Knowledge," 254. For discussions of this phenomenon elsewhere in Yorubaland, see J. D. Y. Peel, *Ijeshas and Nigerians: The Incorporation of a Yoruba Kingdom, 1890s–1970s* (Cambridge: Cambridge University Press, 1983), 41–45, 81, 111–13, 145; Awe, "Militarism and Economic Development," 67; Falola, *Political Economy*, 28, 32, 43–79; Berry, *Fathers*, 5–15; Peel, *Religious Encounter*, 74; and Barber, *I Could Speak*, 242.

103. Cole, *Modern and Traditional Elites*, 29–44, 73–104; Mann, "Taiwo Olowo," 98–99; Robert W. July, *The Origins of Modern African Thought* (New York: Praeger, 1967), 418–22; James S. Coleman, *Nigeria: Background to Nationalism* (Berkeley: University of California Press, 1965), 178–82; Humphrey J. Fisher, *The Ahmadiyya Movement in Nigeria* (London: Oxford University, St. Anthony's College, 1961); Rina Okonkwo, *Protest Movements in Lagos, 1908–1930* (Lewiston: E. Mellen Press, 1995).

104. Barnes, *Patrons and Power*; Richard A. Joseph, *Democracy and Prebendal Politics in Nigeria: The Rise and Fall of the Second Republic* (Cambridge: Cambridge University Press, 1987), 55–68; and Berry, *Fathers*, 5–14, illuminate the evolution of this phenomenon in twentieth-century Nigeria.

105. Interviews with Prince A. L. A. Ojora and N. E. S. Adewale; *Omotoso v. Olowu*, July 1881, JNCC, 3, 298; *Taiwo v. Ekonu, Ayiekoroju, and Okilu*, 6 September 1896, JNCC, ?, 329.

106. The widespread use of the word "boy" in English documents to refer to different kinds of male dependents sometimes makes it impossible to determine their precise identity.

107. Documentary evidence indicates that Ogunbiyi had been redeemed by his parents but chose to remain attached to Chief Aṣogbon's household. He eventually became a successful produce trader, converted to Christianity, took the name Jacob, and founded his own compound and lineage. *Ajose v. Efunde*, 247; *Aṣogbon v. Ṣomade*, 127; interview with Chief D. A. Ogunbiyi. For a fuller analysis of this and other related cases, see Mann, "Interpreting Cases, Disentangling Disputes," 195–218.

108. *Ṣomade v. Ebite*, 102.

109. Ibid., 103.

110. *Eshuby v. Oso*, 126–29. The 1862 proclamation that apprenticed the slaves of Sierra Leoneans and Brazilians to their owners for two to seven years apparently had little impact on Oso, Opeluja, and Ogudula's sense of identity or their relationship with their master.

111. *Eshuby v. Oso*, 126–27.

112. Ibid., 129.

113. Peel, *Religious Encounter*, 53–59.

114. CO 147/75, Moloney to Knutsford, 26 August 1890.

115. From the mid-1880s, official dispatches contain regular references to foreign labor recruitment. See, for example, CO 147/59, Moloney to Holland, 20 July 1887; CO 147/60, Moloney to Holland, 9 August 1887; CO 147/75, Moloney to Knutsford, 25 September 1890; CO 147/76, Moloney to Knutsford, 26 September

1890; CO 147/79, Denton to Knutsford, 9 March 1891; CO 147/112, Stallard to Chamberlain, 2 February 1897; CO 147/119, McCallum to Chamberlain, 11 October 1897; CO 147/133, Denton to Chamberlain, 4 June 1898; CO 147/150, Denton to Chamberlain, 7 September 1900; CO 147/154, MacGregor to Chamberlain, 25 March 1901; and CO 147/174, Egerton to Lyttelton, 19 January 1905. For figures on the movement of labor to the Gold Coast, see CO 147/156, MacGregor to Chamberlain, 1 August 1901; and CO 147/160, MacGregor to Chamberlain, 4 February 1902. Also Anne Phillips, *The Enigma of Colonialism: British Policy in West Africa* (London: James Currey, 1989), 34–37; and Ibrahim K. Sundiata, *From Slaving to Neoslavery: The Bight of Biafra and Fernando Po in the Era of Abolition, 1827–1930* (Madison: University of Wisconsin Press, 1996), 134. *Salawura v. Harper*, 21 September 1885, JNCC, 6, 99, recounts the story of a slave who left Lagos to work in the Congo Free State and died there.

116. A. G. Hopkins, "The Lagos Strike of 1897: An Exploration in Nigerian Labour History," *P&P* 35 (1966): 133–55; Phillips, *Enigma*, 26–58.

117. Governor MacGregor observed in 1901 that men in the Yoruba interior so disliked wage labor that they went into hiding to avoid it. CO 147/156, MacGregor to Chamberlain, 1 August 1901. See also Peel, *Religious Encounter*, 68, who also remarks that Yoruba men disliked wage labor and aspired, instead, to an ideal of adult autonomy.

118. Lisa Lindsay, "Domesticity and Difference: Male Breadwinners, Working Women, and Colonial Citizenship in the 1945 Nigerian General Strike," *AHR* 104 (1999): 783–812.

119. Studies of the end of slavery elsewhere in the world have found that former slaves sought a combination of independent, small-scale enterprise, which allowed them to escape full-time wage labor, and intermittent work for wages, which gave them cash income as needed and desired. See, for example, Cooper, *Slaves to Squatters*, 121–24; Holt, *Problem of Freedom*, 143–76; Lovejoy and Hogendorn, *Slow Death*, 202–203; and Ahmad Alawad Sikainga, *Slaves into Workers: Emancipation and Labor in Colonial Sudan* (Austin: University of Texas Press, 1996), 69. Further research is needed on the origins of wage labor in Lagos to see if a similar pattern held there. Two major differences existed, however, between the situation in Lagos and that in Jamaica and East Africa. The first is the length of the interval between the attack on slavery and the emergence of a robust free labor market. The second is the magnitude of African involvement in the import-export trade.

7. The Changing Meaning of Land in the Urban Economy and Culture

1. The Treaty of Cession is reprinted in Robert S. Smith, *The Lagos Consulate, 1851–1861* (Berkeley: University of California Press, 1979), 140–41. For a report of the *ìdéjọ̀*'s protest, see Freeman to Russell, 5 March 1862, encl. in CO 147/1, Freeman to Newcastle, 8 March 1862.

2. Terence Ranger, "The Invention of Tradition in Colonial Africa," in *The Invention of Tradition*, ed. Eric Hobsbawm and Terence Ranger (Cambridge: Cambridge University Press, 1983), 211–62; Martin Chanock, *Law, Custom, and Social Order: The Colonial Experience in Malawi and Zambia* (Cambridge: Cambridge Uni-

versity Press, 1985), 145–216; Sara Berry, *No Condition Is Permanent: The Social Dynamics of Agrarian Change in Sub-Saharan Africa* (Madison: University of Wisconsin Press, 1993), 22–42; Richard Roberts and Kristin Mann, introduction to *Law in Colonial Africa*, ed. Kristin Mann and Richard Roberts (Portsmouth, N.H.: Heinemann, 1991), 20–36; Sara S. Berry, *Chiefs Know Their Boundaries: Essays on Property, Power, and the Past in Asante, 1896–1996* (Portsmouth, N.H.: Heinemann, 2001), 7.

3. Sandra T. Barnes, *Patrons and Power: Creating a Political Community in Metropolitan Lagos* (Bloomington: Indiana University Press, 1986), 51.

4. Sally Falk Moore, *Social Facts and Fabrications: "Customary" Law on Kilimanjaro, 1880–1980* (Cambridge: Cambridge University Press, 1986); Martin Chanock, "Paradigms, Policies, and Property: A Review of the Customary Law of Land Tenure," in Mann and Roberts, eds., *Law in Colonial Africa*, 62; M. P. Cowen and R. W. Shenton, "British Neo-Hegelianism and Official Colonial Practice in Africa: The Oluwo Land Case of 1921," *Journal of Imperial and Commonwealth History* 22 (1994): 217–50.

5. J. Buckley Wood, *Historical Notices of Lagos, West Africa* (Exeter: James Townsend, n.d.), 13–14; John B. Losi, *History of Lagos* (Lagos: Tika Tore Press, 1914), 3. See also the testimony of Lagosians printed in WALC, "Correspondence," 222–44; and Sir Mervyn Tew, *Report on Title to Land in Lagos* (Lagos: The Government Printer, 1947), 6–9.

6. Freeman to Russell, 5 March 1862, encl. in CO 147/1, Freeman to Newcastle, 8 March 1862. Later J. A. O. Payne, an educated African who presented himself as an authority on local affairs, wrote in his *Table of Principal Events in Yoruba History* (Lagos: Andrew W. Thomas, 1893), 6, that "[t]he white capped chiefs have the power to dispose of land."

7. Wood, *Historical Notices*, 17; Losi, *History*, 12.

8. In the early 1860s, J. H. Glover deposed Chiefs Oloto and Ojora, leading *ìdẹ́jọ̀*, and replaced them with his own appointees. Glover's reasons are unknown, but they probably stemmed from the *ìdẹ́jọ̀*'s opposition to the Treaty of Cession. For references to the depositions, see *Callamand v. Vaughan* and *Ajose v. Efunde and others*, excerpted in WALC, "Minutes," 524–25. For evidence of the *ìdẹ́jọ̀*'s renewed interest in land during the early twentieth century, see *Amodu Tijani v. The Secretary, Southern Nigeria, The Law Reports (Appeals)* (1921), vol. 2, pp. 399ff., reprinted in C. K. Meek, *Land Tenure and Land Administration in Nigeria and the Cameroons* (London: Her Majesty's Stationary Office, 1957), 77–84; and Tew, *Report*, 5.

9. Omoniyi Adewoye, "The Tijani Land Case (1915–1921): A Study in British Colonial Justice," *Odu* 13 (1976): 21–39; Richard L. Sklar, *Nigerian Political Parties: Power in an Emergent African Nation* (Princeton: Princeton University Press, 1963), 42–44; Pauline H. Baker, *Urbanization and Political Change: The Politics of Lagos, 1917–1967* (Berkeley: University of California Press, 1974), 94–97; Berry, *No Condition Is Permanent*, 105.

10. WALC, "Correspondence," 229. See also Tew, *Report*, 6.

11. Information on land tenure in precolonial Lagos comes from WALC, "Correspondence," 227–45. Additional data can be found in judges' notes on land cases brought before the Lagos Supreme Court. Many of the most important cases, or excerpts from them, are reprinted in WALC, "Minutes," 523–28; Robert Forsyth Irving, *A Collection of the Principal Enactments and Cases Relating to Titles to Land in Ni-*

geria (London: Stephens and Sons, 1916), 201–319; and *NLR* vols. 1–2. Useful reports on Lagos land tenure by early colonial officials include T. C. Rayner and J. J. C. Healy, *Reports on Land Tenure in West Africa (1898)*, COL, West Africa Pamphlet, No. 19; A. W. Osborne, "Memorandum," WALC, "Minutes," 522–28; "Memorandum by Sir Walter Napier on the Principles of Native Land Tenure in the Gold Coast and Southern Nigeria," WALC, "Draft Report," Appendix C, 142; and W. Buchanan Smith, "Land Tenure in the Colony of Lagos," WALC, "Correspondence," 223–27. A. G. Hopkins, "A Report on the Yoruba, 1910," *JHSN* 5 (1969): 84–85; Tew, *Report;* and Meek, *Land Tenure*, also contain much relevant data.

The literature on Yoruba land law is voluminous, but important sources, in addition to Meek and the reports and evidence in the WALC materials, include Samuel Johnson, *The History of the Yorubas* (London: Routledge and Kegan Paul, 1969), 95–97; A. K. Ajisafe, *The Laws and Customs of the Yoruba People* (Lagos: CMS Bookshop, 1924), 9–18; Adebesin Folarin, *The Laws and Customs of Egbaland* (Abeokuta: E. N. A. Press, 1939), 68–89; N. A. Fadipe, *The Sociology of the Yoruba* (Ibadan: Ibadan University Press, 1970), 169–78; H. L. Ward-Price, *Land Tenure in the Yoruba Provinces* (Lagos: The Government Printer, 1933); P. C. Lloyd, *Yoruba Land Law* (London: Oxford University Press, 1962); T. Olawale Elias, *Nigerian Land Law and Custom* (London: Routledge and Kegan Paul, 1951); and G. B. A. Coker, *Family Property among the Yorubas* (London: Sweet and Maxwell, 1958). Barnes, *Patrons and Power*, provides long-term perspective on the significance of land and houses in Lagos.

12. WALC, "Correspondence," 229. Also interviews with Prince A. L. A. Ojora and Chief S. B. A. Oluwa.

13. FO 84/1031, Campbell to Clarendon, 14 March 1857.

14. WALC, "Correspondence," 227.

15. T. C. Rayner, "Land Tenure in West Africa," in Rayner and Healy, *Land Tenure*, 1; J. J. C. Healy, "Land Tenure in the Colony of Lagos," in Rayner and Healy, *Land Tenure*, 1; WALC, "Correspondence," 142, 224, 227, 232–38; Hopkins, "Report on the Yoruba," 13–15; Meek, *Land Tenure*, 63, 72, 115, 156, 189–91; interviews with Prince A. L. A. Ojora, Chief S. B. A. Oluwa, and Alhaji A. W. A. Akibayo; RHL, Oxford (Colonial Records Project), Mss.Afr.L15, W. Fowler, "A Report on the Lands of the Colony District."

16. *Ajose v. Efunde*, "Minutes," 525.

17. *Jose v. Ṣomade*, 17 February 1879, JNCC, 2, 102; Lloyd, *Yoruba Land Law*, 166.

18. WALC, "Correspondence," 229.

19. Rayner, "Land Tenure," 3; WALC, "Correspondence," 142, 219, 224, 228–29; Meek, *Land Tenure*, 130, 175; Alfred Burdon Ellis, *The Yoruba-Speaking People of the Slave Coast of West Africa* (London: Chapman and Hall, 1894), 188–89. See also Elias, *Nigerian Land Law*, 185.

20. N. Mba, "Women in Lagos Political History," in *History of the Peoples of Lagos State*, ed. Ade Adefuye, Babatunde Agiri, and Jide Osuntokun (Ikeja: Lantern Books, 1987), 243–44; Takiu Folami, *A History of Lagos, Nigeria* (Smithtown, N.Y.: Exposition Press, 1982), 131–32.

21. Kristin Mann, "The Rise of Taiwo Olowo: Law, Accumulation, and Mobility in Early Colonial Lagos," in Mann and Roberts, eds., *Law in Colonial Africa*, 93.

22. This picture emerges from evidence in stories that slaves and former slaves told about their lives in precolonial Lagos during later court cases, as well as from interviews with Prince A. L. A. Ojora, C. B. Thomas, and Alhaji A. W. A. Akibayo. Relevant court cases, all from JNCC, include *Fanojoria v. Kadiri*, 22 June 1881, 3, 265–75; *Adenjo v. Brimah*, 13 December 1887, 7, 320; *Opere v. Johnson*, 20 July 1894, ?, 107–108, *Joko v. Oguntola*, 22 October 1894, ?, 224–34; *Fajimi v. Fatosha*, 27 July 1896, ?, 438–54, and others cited in this chapter.

23. *Ajose v. Efunde*, "Minutes," 525. Also Meek, *Land Tenure*, 129; and WALC, "Correspondence," 230.

24. *Oshodi, Sakariyawo v. Dakolo and others* (1928), 9 *NLR* 13, quoted in Meek, *Land Tenure*, 171. See also *Akilogun v. Faleyi*, 19 January 1894, JNCC, ?, 113–18; Payne, *Table*, 6; and Kristin Mann, "Owners, Slaves and the Struggle for Labour in the Commercial Transition at Lagos," in *From Slave Trade to "Legitimate" Commerce: The Commercial Transition in Nineteenth-Century West Africa*, ed. Robin Law (Cambridge: Cambridge University Press, 1995), 153.

25. *Lewis v. Bankole* (1909), 1 *NLR* 84; WALC, "Correspondence," 179, 224, 228–29, 237; *Amuleye v. Thomas*, 19 February 1879, JNCC, 2, 70; *Yara v. Ibiyemi*, 12 November 1896, JNCC, 18, 218–29.

26. WALC, "Correspondence," 179.

27. Ibid., 238.

28. Ibid., 224.

29. WALC, "Correspondence," *Ajose v. Efunde and others*, 14 July 1892, 247. For a discussion of shifting views of the impact of the Treaty of Cession on landownership in Lagos Colony, see Elias, *Nigerian Land Law*, 6–28. Meek, *Land Tenure*, 64–65, observes that the rights of the *ọba* in land were "much discussed in numerous land cases." Chanock, "Paradigms, Policies," and Cowen and Shenton, "British Neo-Hegelianism," locate the issue in broader imperial perspectives.

30. See, for example, Tew, *Report*, 7–9.

31. WALC, "Correspondence," 228–30, 239.

32. Ibid., 179.

33. Interview with Chief S. B. A. Oluwa; Losi, *History*, 14; Folami, *History*, 107, 112, 114, 118. Ọba Ọṣinlokun or Ọba Idewu Ojulari also granted land in Lagos to refugees from Gun territory. *Fanojoria v. Kadiri*, 265–75.

34. *Callamand v. Vaughan*, quoted in Meek, *Land Tenure*, 53. See also WALC, "Minutes," 525.

35. Wood, *Historical Notices*, 18.

36. House of Lords Sessional Papers, 1852–53, 22, Gomes to Kosoko, 4 February 1850, 347.

37. Wood, *Historical Notices*, 18.

38. On the rights of Benin's *ọba* in land, see WALC, "Minutes," 184, 391–92, and "Correspondence," 166; and Meek, *Land Tenure*, 158–59, 162, 181, 229.

39. PROL, Agreement with the King and Chiefs of Lagos, 28 February 1852, 342.

40. FO 84/976, Campbell to Clarendon, 28 May 1855, plus encls. For the voluminous correspondence regarding Akitoye's grants to Gollmer, see FO 84/950, 976, and 1002; and Smith, *Lagos Consulate*, 37, 80–81, 97–98.

41. FO 84/976, Campbell to Clarendon, 4 April 1855.

42. Sandeman to Fraser, 8 January 1853, encl. in FO 84/920, Fraser to Malmesbury, March 1853. Sandeman's request was foiled when the CMS claimed to own the land already, giving rise to much unpleasantness between the merchant and the missionaries. See also Rayner and Healy, *Land Tenure*, 1.

43. Robert Campbell, "A Pilgrimage to My Motherland," in *Search for a Place: Black Separatism and Africa, 1860*, by M. R. Delany and Robert Campbell (Ann Arbor: University of Michigan Press, 1969), 164.

44. British consuls recorded a number of Dosunmu's grants, and those that survive can be found in a bound volume in the Strong Room at the Lagos Land Registry. See also M. R. Delany, "Official Report of the Niger Valley Exploring Party," in Delany and Campbell, *Search for a Place*, 68; Healy, "Land Tenure," 2, 5–6; William N. M. Geary, *Nigeria under British Rule* (New York: Barnes and Noble, 1965), 3; and Smith, *Lagos Consulate*, 98, 168. For a description of the way that some Brazilian freed slaves were granted land, see WALC, "Correspondence," 234.

45. FO 84/920, Martin to Fraser, 27 December 1852; FO 84/950, Campbell to Clarendon, 1 May 1854; CO 147/6, Freeman to Newcastle, 26 March 1864.

46. FO 84/920, Martin to Fraser, 27 December 1852, and Fraser to Malmesbury, 11 March 1853; FO 84/950, Campbell to Clarendon, 1 May 1854; FO 84/976, FO to Campbell, 24 May 1855, and Campbell to Clarendon, 1 September 1855.

47. Meek, *Land Tenure*, 55. Information about land ownership in Freetown, Sierra Leone, comes from Christopher Fyfe, *A History of Sierra Leone* (London: Oxford University Press, 1962), 143–44, 175; and about that in Bahia comes from B. J. Barickman, *A Bahian Counterpoint: Sugar, Tobacco, Cassava, and Slavery in Recôncavo, 1780–1860* (Stanford: Stanford University Press, 1998), 107–108, 190–95; and João José Reis, personal communication, 18 July 2000.

48. Sandeman to Campbell, 28 August 1855, encl. in FO 84/976, Campbell to Clarendon, 1 September 1855.

49. Tew, *Report*, 13. Also *Amuleye v. Thomas*, 70.

50. Campbell, "Pilgrimage," 243.

51. Treaty of Cession, 6 August 1861, reprinted in Smith, *Lagos Consulate*, 141.

52. CO 147/5, Murdock to Elliot, 24 July 1863.

53. Tew, *Report*, 11; Rayner, "Land Tenure," 1. See also "Memorandum by Napier," 149.

54. WALC, "Minutes," 522; Tew, *Report*, 11. See also Rayner, "Land Tenure," 4.

55. A. G. Hopkins, "Property Rights and Empire Building: Britain's Annexation of Lagos, 1861," *Journal of Economic History* 40 (1980): 777–79.

56. Quoted in Tew, *Report*, 13. The letters patent issued in 1886, when Lagos was separated from the Gold Coast, contained similar language, as did those issued in 1906 and 1913 on the creation of the colonies of Southern Nigeria and Nigeria. Meek, *Land Tenure*, 57, 62.

57. CO 147/2, Emigration Office to Elliot, 22 November 1862; CO 147/3, Freeman to Newcastle, 5 February 1865; CO 147/5, Emigration Office to Elliot, 24 July 1863, Buxton to Newcastle, 18 April 1863, plus encls., and Freeman to Newcastle, 24 July 1863.

58. This ordinance is reprinted in Irving, *Collection*, 3–5.

59. CO 147/3, Glover to Newcastle, 10 July 1863.

60. Tew, *Report*, 12–14.

61. Irving, *Collection*, 9–11. See also Meek, *Land Tenure*, 59.

62. Healy, "Land Tenure," 3. Also Tew, *Report*, 14–16; and Meek, *Land Tenure*, 61.

63. Tew, *Report*, 13–23; Meek, *Land Tenure*, 58, 62; Stanhope Rowton Simpson, *A Report on the Registration of Title to Land in the Federal Territory of Lagos* (Lagos: Federal Government Printer, 1957), 37. Bound volumes recording the government's Crown grants can be found in the Strong Room of the Lagos Land Registry.

64. S. O. Biobaku, *The Egba and Their Neighbours, 1842–1872* (Oxford: Clarendon Press, 1857), 83–84; J. F. A. Ajayi, *Christian Missions in Nigeria, 1841–1891: The Making of a New Elite* (London: Longmans, 1965), 200–203.

65. Tew, *Report*, 24–25. See also Meek, *Land Tenure*, 59–60.

66. Just what the *ọba* meant by this request is unclear, because the Treaty of Cession stated only that in the transfer of lands the king's seal would be proof that "there are no other native claims on it." Col. Ord maintained after interviewing Dosunmu that he wanted, by fixing his seal, to establish the *ọba*'s title to land belonging to deceased natives. OR, 312–13, and Appendix C, "The humble Petition of Docemo . . . to . . . Parliament . . . ," n.d., 330.

67. Tew, *Report*, 12. Also *Ajose v. Efunde*, "Correspondence," 247.

68. These grants are recorded at the Lagos Land Registry. Ladega, a member of the Aṣogbon family who subsequently became chief, also took out a number of Crown grants in his name beginning in 1868.

69. *Lewis v. Bankole*, 83. Chanock, "Paradigms, Policies," 62–66, briefly discusses the early colonial idea that African land tenure was primitive and needed to evolve to recognize private property, but his analysis focuses primarily on a later colonial period, when the preoccupations of colonial administrators changed and the doctrine of communal ownership took hold. See also Anne Phillips, *The Enigma of Colonialism: British Policy in West Africa* (London: James Currey, 1989), 59–84; Berry, *No Condition Is Permanent*, 101–10; Berry, *Chiefs*, 1–34; and Patrick Uchenna Mbajekwe, "Land, Social Change, and Urban Development in Onitsha, Eastern Nigeria, 1857–1960" (Ph.D. diss., Emory University, 2003), chap. 3. The literature on colonial land policy generally pays insufficient attention to the promotion of rights of private ownership in the nineteenth century and subsequent changes as governments extended their authority inland from the 1890s.

70. Rayner, "Land Tenure," 4; WALC, "Correspondence," 38, 225, "Memorandum by Napier," 14, and Smith, "Land Tenure," 25–26; Tew, *Report*, 17; Meek, *Land Tenure*, 61. See also T. Olawale Elias, *The Nigerian Legal System* (London: Routledge and Kegan Paul, 1963), 3–5, 12–14; and Omoniyi Adewoye, *The Judicial System in Southern Nigeria, 1854–1954* (Atlantic Highlands, N.J.: Humanities Press, 1977), 25.

71. These data come from an analysis of Crown grants at the Lagos Land Registry.

72. *LWR*, 3 October 1891, 3, cols. 2–3. Also Smith, "Land Tenure," 26; and Meek, *Land Tenure*, 63.

73. Sara Berry (*No Condition Is Permanent*, 101–103) has shown how official

policy and local practice have combined to make land rules ambiguous and subject to ongoing reinterpretation in twentieth-century Africa. She has argued that, as a consequence, peoples' access to land has depended on their participation in processes of interpretation and adjudication. What Berry says of the twentieth century was true in Lagos by the closing decades of the nineteenth century. Since then judges, administrators, scholars, and the public have all expended much time, energy, and—in the case of the public—money contesting the meaning of Crown grants. For brief introductions to this subject, see Tew, *Report*, 16–23; Elias, *Nigerian Land Law*, 21–28; and Coker, *Family Property*, 182–216 passim.

74. In the 1920s, the Oloto family stepped up efforts to reassert its rights to land within the Glover layout, inspired perhaps by changes in land policy after the turn of the century, as well as by the Privy Council's famous 1921 decision in *Amodu Tijani v. The Secretary, Southern Nigeria*. The family had little success, however, with plots that had been allotted to the Egba refugees. Tew, *Report*, 29–31.

75. *Brimah Balogun and another v. Oshodi* (1931), 10 *NLR* 36. See also *Re Public Lands Ordinance, 1876* (1899), excerpted in WALC, "Minutes," 523.

From before the annexation, British officials had encouraged registration of conveyances, leases, mortgages, and deeds of gift at the consulate and later at the colonial land registry established for the purpose. In 1883, an ordinance made registration of such documents compulsory, but many land transfers continued to occur without the creation, much less registration, of any written documentation. The fees for registration alone, which were ten shillings before 1883 and two shillings sixpence plus ninepence per seventy-two-word page thereafter, were enough to discourage many Lagosians from registering land records. Lagos Colony, *Blue Books*, 1880, 1885.

76. For examples of deeds of gift, see Charlotte Davies to Victoria Davies, 24 December 1863, 2, 236; Susannah Turner to Rebecca Johnson, trustee for Christiana Abigail Johnson, 12 June 1869, 8, 437; and Ladipo to Rebecca Johnson, 3 June 1870, 10, 288. All of these documents are recorded at the LLR. Fee simple title seems to have been given in particular to educated girls, with the provision that the property be held in trust until their majority. Some deeds of gift to such girls specified that after marriage their husbands should have no rights in the property. These gifts were clearly designed to protect the status of educated girls.

77. Elias, *Nigerian Land Law*, 186–87; Meek, *Land Tenure*, 130–31; Coker, *Family Property*, 113–14, 118–20.

78. Rayner, "Land Tenure," 4; WALC, "Minutes," 254, 516, and "Draft Report," 63–64; Tew, *Report*, 39.

79. WALC, "Correspondence," 226. See also Rayner, "Land Tenure," 3; Osborne, "Memorandum," 522; and "Memorandum by Napier," 150.

80. This observation is based on a reading of wills at the Lagos Probate Registry. See, for example, the testaments of S. A. Crowther, 3 May 1881, LPR 1, 162; Jane Dorcas Sawyer, 15 December 1892, LPR 1, 218; Sunmonu Animaṣaun, 21 August 1895, LPR 1, 357; A. Alberto, 25 April 1895, LPR 1, 394–96; J. Ayorinde, 16 May 1898, LPR 2, 60–64; and C. R. Cole, 13 January 1910, LPR 3, 192–99.

81. Elias, *Nigerian Land Law*, 268; WALC, "Minutes," 516, 526.

82. WALC, "Correspondence," 223.

83. Tew, *Report*, 19. See also Meek, *Land Tenure*, 64, 116, 132, 136–37.

84. When Kosoko returned from Epe, he took great care to provide the slaves who accompanied him with places to live, going so far as to buy one of them a room in a house at public auction. *Aina v. Disu*, 5 April 1881, JNCC, 3, 192–93. Also Tew, *Report*, 38–44; *Opere v. Johnson*, 107–108; and Mann, "Owners, Slaves," 153–54.

85. *Ajakaye v. Sani Aina and Mayeni*, 18 July 1894, JNCC, ?, 99–101; *Fajimi v. Fatosha*, 438–54.

86. WALC, "Correspondence," 247.

87. *Yaya, Ogunlayi, and Coker v. Afoso*, 12 July 1894, JNCC, ?, 82–83.

88. *Ajose v. Efunde*, "Minutes," 525; Tew, *Report*, 36–44; A. Akintan, *Awful Disclosures on Epetedo Lands* (Lagos: Tika Tore Press, 1937), 4; *Nigeria, The Epetedo Lands: Representations of the Oshodi Chieftaincy Family Submitted to the Commissioner, Lagos Land Inquiry* (Lagos: Hope Rising Press, 1939), 10–11, 15; Coker, *Family Property*, 198–204; Meek, *Land Tenure*, 138, 171.

89. *Voight and Co. v. Rokosi*, 14 June 1887, JNCC, 7, 100; *Banjoko v. Brimah and Aṣeṣi*, 15 February 1894, JNCC, ?, 163–65; *Bakare v. Sheffi and Davies*, 25 July 1894, JNCC, ?, 219–21.

90. *Fajimi v. Fatosha*, 438–54.

91. *Adjayi v. Momo Dangana and Titi*, 25 May 1896, JNCC, ?, 283–89, 316–28, 411–14. See also Mann, "Owners, Slaves," 158–59.

92. *Awa v. Disu*, 5 March 1885, JNCC, 6, 2; *Eshuby, alias Brimoh Apatira v. Oso, Opeluja, and Ogudula*, 14 July 1879, JNCC, 2, 129; *Aina v. Disu*, 192–93.

93. Mortgage, Taiwo to J. B. Bounard, 20 February 1867, LLR, 4, 247.

94. *Fadipe and others v. Brimoh*, 13 November 1895, JNCC, ?, 238.

95. Will, Sunmonu Animaṣaun, 21 August 1895, LPR 1, 357.

96. *Abdulai v. Apata*, 29 August 1894, JNCC, ?, 150–54.

97. *Opere v. Johnson*, 107–108.

98. Deed of Gift, Sunmonu Animaṣaun to Idrisu Ode Akin, 22 December 1886, LLR, 11, 129; Will, Sunmonu Animaṣaun, 21 August 1895, LPR 1, 357.

99. *Awoniya v. Ogunfunke and Morondiya*, 28 May 1896, JNCC, ?, 301–305.

100. Toyin Falola, *The Political Economy of a Pre-colonial African State: Ibadan, 1830–1900* (Ile-Ife: University of Ife Press, 1984), 43–46; Karin Barber, *I Could Speak until Tomorrow: Oriki, Women, and the Past in a Yoruba Town* (Washington, D.C.: Smithsonian Institution Press, 1991), 198–202, 206–209, 215–16; J. D. Y. Peel, *Religious Encounter and the Making of the Yoruba* (Bloomington: Indiana University Press, 2000), 74, 80.

101. For a fuller discussion of these issues, see Kristin Mann, "Women, Landed Property, and the Accumulation of Wealth in Early Colonial Lagos," *Signs* 16 (1991): 699–701.

102. Johnson, *History*, 130; Hopkins, "Report on the Yoruba," 91–92; Ajisafe, *Laws*, 63–66; Folarin, *Laws*, 8–10, 57–59, 80–81; Fadipe, *Sociology*, 163–65.

103. FO 84/976, Campbell to Clarendon, 2 August 1855; CO 147/3, Glover to Daumas, 26 May 1863; Foresythe to Daumas, 18 June 1863, encl. in CO 147/3, Glover to Newcastle, 7 July 1863; CO 147/4, Glover to Newcastle, 8 August 1863.

104. PROL, Agreement with the King and Chiefs of Lagos, 28 February 1852, 342–44; AST MPE: Consolati Nazionali, Lagos, 1856–1857, Agreement between Dosunmu and the European Merchants, 27 March 1854.

105. FO 84/976, Campbell to Clarendon, 2 August, 9 October 1855; FO 84/1002, Campbell to Clarendon, 25 September 1856.

106. Mortgaging land and houses to secure credit had begun in Freetown by the 1820s. The practice modified methods of securing credit used during the era of the slave trade when, in some places, European traders took African pawns on board ship as security for debt. Fyfe, *History of Sierra Leone*, 144, 231, 376; Paul E. Lovejoy and David Richardson, "Trust, Pawnship, and Atlantic History: The Institutional Foundations of the Old Calabar Slave Trade," *AHR* 104 (1999): 332–55. On the early history of credit in West Africa's external trade, see C. W. Newbury, "Credit in Early Nineteenth Century West African Trade," *JAH* 13 (1972): 81–95.

107. Oladipo Yemitan, *Madame Tinubu: Merchant and King-Maker* (Ibadan: University Press, 1987), 24. See also H. Faustimo to J. P. L. Davies, 1865, LLR, 3, 93; Brimah to J. P. L. Davies, 6 February 1867, LLR, 4, 280.

108. Most of the merchants and many of the local traders created written records of their agreements, and some had them recorded at the Land Registry. See, for example, Laniyonu to J. P. L. Davies, 25 May 1870, 10, 226; Eliza Williams to J. P. L. Davies, 13 March 1872, 18, 78; Bankole to C. Foresythe, 31 March 1874, 21, 11; Abobaccari to Taiwo, 10 December 1866, 4, 176; Olubedo to Taiwo, 9 April 1874, 18, 321; and Musa to B. Dawodu, 13 February 1879, 29, 18. The mortgages on file at the Land Registry usually followed a standard form, suggesting that prototypes circulated within the colony. From the mid-1860s, self-taught attorneys licensed by the colonial government worked in the town, and from 1880 English-trained barristers practiced there. These professionals drew up some mortgages, but others were written by merchants and traders themselves or by local letter-writers.

Numbers are not available before the 1890s, but between 1892 and 1900, 260 mortgages were registered, while between 1908 and 1912, 442 were registered. The assistant commissioner of lands calculated that from January 1902 to June 1912 registered mortgages covered loans from private individuals worth £37,281, from banks worth £40,925, and from trading firms worth £30,936. Lagos Colony, *General Abstract of Registration*, 1893–1901; WALC, "Correspondence," 226, 250; Omoniyi Adewoye, "Prelude to the Legal Profession in Lagos, 1861–1880," *Journal of African Law* 14 (1970): 98–114.

109. *Idowu v. Omoniyi*, 10 October 1878, JNCC, 2, 22.

110. Oloworira to Secretary of State, 15 September 1877, encl. in CO 147/33, Dumaresq to Freeling, 18 December 1877.

111. WALC, "Minutes," 123, 428, "Correspondence," 230–33; Meek, *Land Tenure*, 201–205; Lloyd, *Yoruba Land Law*, 312, 316. Gareth Austin discusses this practice on the Gold Coast and elsewhere in West Africa, although he generally associates its development with a later period. See "Indigenous Credit Institutions in West Africa, c. 1750–c. 1960," in *Local Suppliers of Credit in the Third World, 1750–1960*, ed. Gareth Austin and Kaoru Sugihara (New York: St. Martin's Press, 1993), 117–30.

112. WALC, "Correspondence," 219, and "Minutes," 263, 266. See also Meek, *Land Tenure*, 63.

113. Meek, *Land Tenure*, 58.

114. In addition to mortgages themselves, see Simpson, *Report*, 7; and "Memorandum by Napier," 150.

115. *Eletu Odibo v. Salako and Ogunsan* (1882), *Re Public Lands Ordinance, 1876* (1899), *Oloto v. Dawodu and others* (1904), excerpted in WALC, "Minutes," 523–24; *Lewis v. Bankole*, 81; Smith, "Land Tenure," 225; Elias, *Nigerian Land Law*, 206–208; Coker, *Family Property*, 56–57, 85.

116. *Roberts v. Mamase*, 1882, JNCC, 5, 37; *Adisatu v. Cole*, 6 March 1885, JNCC, 6, 8; *Voight and Co. v. Rokosi*, 100.

117. Hopkins, "Report on the Yoruba," 91.

118. *Roberts v. Mamase*, 37.

119. Mortgage, Taiwo to J. B. Bounard, 20 February 1867, LLR, 4, 247.

120. Mortgage, J. P. L. Davies to Child Mills and Co., 18 March 1872, LLR, 15, 141; A. G. Hopkins, "Peter Thomas: Un commerçant nigérian à l'épreuve d'une économie coloniale en crise," in *Les Africains*, ed. Charles-André Julien et al. (Paris: Editions J. A., 1978), 9:309–10.

121. WALC, "Minutes," 132, 233, 263, and "Correspondence," 226. On the spread of these and other practices related to usury deeper into the Yoruba interior during the early twentieth century, see Lloyd, *Yoruba Land Law*, 242, 309, 321; Toyin Falola, "'My Friend the Shylock': Money-Lenders and Their Clients in South-Western Nigeria," *JAH* 34 (1993): 403–23; and Toyin Falola, "Money and Informal Credit Institutions in Colonial Western Nigeria," in *Money Matters: Instability, Values, and Social Payments in the Modern History of West African Communities*, ed. Jane I. Guyer (Portsmouth, N.H.: Heinemann, 1995), 162–87.

122. For information on rent paid by the government, see "Expenditures" in Lagos Colony, *Blue Books*.

123. Lease, Taiwo to Campbell, 21 April 1868, LLR, 8, 99; and Lease, Davies (on behalf of Lewis) to Mills, n.d. (but 1871), LLR, 14, 319.

124. CO 147/144, MacGregor to Chamberlain, 13 September 1999. In other instances, tenants improved existing structures and deducted the cost from the rent over time.

125. WALC, "Minutes," 516, and "Correspondence," 225.

126. Lease, Leigh to Holt and Welsh, 2 August 1893, LLR, 22, 20.

127. Lease, Ige to Le Compagnie Bordelaise des Comptoirs Africains, 14 June 1919, LLR, 129, 107.

128. In 1899, the firm Pickering and Berthold, for example, rented land on the Marina from Taiwo Olowo for twenty-five years and built a factory, offices, and stores on it costing £3442. Under the terms of the lease, Taiwo was to repay this amount, plus 2½ percent interest for the first ten years and 5 percent interest for the next fifteen, out of the rent, but even so he received income of £50 per year from the property. Lease, Taiwo to Pickering and Berthold, 21 June 1900, LLR, 44, 139.

129. Interviews with Prince A. L. A. Ojora and Chief S. B. A. Oluwa; *Awa v. Disu*, 12.

130. *Ajakaye v. Sani Aina and Mayeni*, 99–101; *Collins v. Collins*, 15 June 1885, JNCC, 6, 22; *Fajimi v. Fatosha*, 438–54.

131. WALC, "Correspondence," 235.

132. WALC, "Correspondence," 233–36; Fowler, "A Report," 26–27; Meek, *Land Tenure*, 72–74, 192.

133. CO 147/115, McCallum to Chamberlain, 10 July 1897, plus encls. See also Lagos Colony, *Annual Report*, 1900; and Meek, *Land Tenure*, 191.

134. *Lewis v. Bankole*, 88, 97, 99.

135. *LWR*, 9 April 1904, 3, col. 1. Real estate prices in the city have escalated even more dramatically, of course, in the twentieth century.

136. CO 147/3, Extract of the Minutes in Council, 24 June 1862–30 June 1863; Lagos Colony, *Blue Books*, 1865 through 1869 and 1875 through 1879.

137. CO 147/55, Moloney to Knutsford, 17 June 1886; CO 147/64, Moloney to Knutsford, 17 May 1888, plus encl.

138. CO 147/39, Ussher to Hicks Beach, 26 December 1879; CO 147/40, Ussher to Hicks Beach, 12 January 1880; CO 147/57, Evans to Stanhope, 1 October 1886.

139. These data were derived by tracing the properties in question through the records at the LLR.

140. WALC, "Minutes," 252, and "Correspondence," 238.

141. Meek, *Land Tenure*, 73.

142. WALC, "Minutes," 142.

143. Fowler, "A Report," 46–47.

144. Barnes, *Patrons and Power*, chaps. 3–4, provides a penetrating analysis of the importance of land ownership in the organization of political power in modern Lagos.

145. Interview with Mrs. Kofo Pratt. Many family homes were destroyed during the urban redevelopment that preceded independence in 1960 or the real estate boom of the 1970s and 1980s, but some survive to this day.

146. Mann, "Women, Landed Property," 682–706.

147. *Ajose v. Efunde*, "Correspondence," 247. For two earlier cases in which the court upheld service tenure, see *Aṣogbon v. Ṣomade*, 9 November 1885, JNCC, 6, 127; and *Aṣogbon v. Okin*, 16 November 1885, JNCC, 6, 136.

148. See, for example, *Ramatu v. Abuduramanu*, 11 November 1896, JNCC, 18, 207–14.

149. Interviews with Prince A. L. A. Ojora, Alhaji A. W. A. Akibayo, and Chief S. B. A. Oluwa.

150. Mohamed Mboji, "The Abolition of Slavery in Senegal, 1820–1890: Crisis or the Rise of a New Entrepreneurial Class?" in *Breaking the Chains: Slavery, Bondage, and Emancipation in Modern Africa and Asia*, ed. Martin A. Klein (Madison: University of Wisconsin Press, 1993), 205–206, shows the importance of housing in the control of former slaves in St. Louis and Gorée.

151. *Akilogun v. Faleyi*, 113–16, 116–18; and Mann, "Owners, Slaves," 153–54.

152. *Awa v. Disu*, 192–93; *Zadero v. Zafungbo*, 24 February 1882, JNCC, 4, 20; *Eletu Odibo v. Salako and Ogunsan*, 29 June 1882, JNCC, 5, 7; *Fajimi v. Fatosha*, 438; *Obanikoro v. Suenu and others* (1925), 6 *NLR* 87; Coker, *Family Property*, 165; Elias, *Nigerian Land Law*, 146.

153. Tew, *Report*, 36–44.

154. WALC, "Minutes," 151–52, 243, 252–53, "Correspondence," 190, "Draft Report," 64, and "Memo by Napier," 151–53.

155. Phillips, *Enigma*, 59–84; Berry, *No Condition Is Permanent*, 24–42, 106; Berry, *Chiefs*, 5–8; Mbajekwe, "Land, Social Change, and Urban Development,"

chap. 3. Chanock, "Paradigms, Policies," analyzes the discourses that shaped the formulation of customary law and implementation of land policies during this period.

156. See, for example, *De Cruz v. De Cruz* (1892) and *Oloto v. Dowudu* (1894), excerpted in WALC, "Correspondence," 248; *Re Public Lands Ordinance, 1876* (1899) and *Ayorinde v. Asiatu and others* (1899), excerpted in WALC, "Minutes," 523, 525; *Oloto v. Dawuda and others* (1904), 1 *NLR* 57; *Lewis v. Bankole*, 81; and "Memorandum by Napier," 149–50. See also Elias, *Nigerian Land Law*, 207; and Coker, *Family Property*, 164–66, 200–201.

157. *Oshodi and others v. Ajagun*, 29 March 1894, JNCC, ?, 272–75; *Alaka v. Alaka*, 23 January 1904, 1 *NLR* 55.

158. Tew, *Report*, 36–44; Meek, *Land Tenure*, 69–70.

159. A. Akintan, *Awful Disclosures; Nigeria, the Epetedo Lands*.

160. Coker, *Family Property*, 199–204, cites the legislation and discusses it at greater length.

8. *Strategies of Struggle and Mechanisms of Control*

1. For works that use oral data in the study of slave emancipation elsewhere in colonial Africa, see Frederick Cooper, *From Slaves to Squatters: Plantation Labor and Agriculture in Zanzibar and Coastal Kenya, 1890–1925* (New Haven: Yale University Press, 1980); Paul E. Lovejoy and Jan S. Hogendorn, *Slow Death for Slavery: The Course of Abolition in Northern Nigeria, 1897–1936* (Cambridge: Cambridge University Press, 1993); Ann O'Hear, *Power Relations in Nigeria: Ilorin Slaves and Their Successors* (Rochester, N.Y.: University of Rochester Press, 1997); Martin Klein, *Slavery and Colonial Rule in French West Africa* (Cambridge: Cambridge University Press, 1998); Ahmad Alawad Sikainga, *Slaves into Workers: Emancipation and Labor in Colonial Sudan* (Austin: University of Texas Press, 1996); and a number of the essays in Suzanne Miers and Richard Roberts, eds., *The End of Slavery in Africa* (Madison: University of Wisconsin Press, 1988).

2. See, for example, Martin Chanock, *Law, Custom, and Social Order: The Colonial Experience in Malawi and Zambia* (Cambridge: Cambridge University Press, 1985); Sally Falk Moore, *Social Facts and Fabrications: "Customary" Law on Kilimanjaro, 1880–1980* (Cambridge: Cambridge University Press, 1986); Kristin Mann and Richard Roberts, eds., *Law in Colonial Africa* (Portsmouth, N.H.: Heinemann, 1991); Richard Rathbone, *Murder and Politics in Colonial Ghana* (New Haven: Yale University Press, 1993); Jean Allman and Victoria Tashjian, *"I Will Not Eat Stone": A Women's History of Colonial Asante* (Portsmouth, N.H.: Heinemann, 2000); and Thomas V. McClendon, *Genders and Generations Apart: Labor Tenants and Customary Law in Segregation-Era South Africa, 1920s to 1940s* (Portsmouth, N.H.: Heinemann, 2002).

3. CO 147/1, Freeman to Newcastle, 8 March 1862.

4. RP, 18 D33/1–18.

5. T. Olawale Elias, *The Nigerian Legal System* (London: Routledge and Kegan Paul, 1963), 73–75; Omoniyi Adewoye, *The Judicial System in Southern Nigeria, 1854–1954* (Atlantic Highlands, N.J.: Humanities Press, 1977), 45–52. The Lagos

court was a divisional court of the Gold Coast Supreme Court until the colony was granted a separate administration in 1886.

On the incorporation of "native courts" into the British colonial legal system, see Lord Hailey, *Native Administration in the British African Territories*, 5 vols. (London: Her Majesty's Stationery Office, 1950–53); Lloyd A. Fallers, *Law without Precedent: Legal Ideas in Action in the Courts of Colonial Busoga* (Chicago: University of Chicago Press, 1969), 55–61; Chanock, *Law, Custom, and Social Order*, chap. 6; Moore, *Social Facts and Fabrications*, 148–67; and Richard Roberts and Kristin Mann, introduction to Mann and Roberts, eds., *Law in Colonial Africa*, 15–23.

6. If suits involving Africans emerged from transactions in which they had agreed to obligations under English law, they could also be deprived of the benefit of local law. Supreme Court Ordinance, No. 4, 1876, sections 11, 14, and 19 in George Stallard and Edward Harrinson Richards, *Ordinances, and Orders and Rules Thereunder, in Force in the Colony of Lagos on December 31st 1893. . . .* (London: Stevens and Sons, 1894); Elias, *Nigerian Legal System*, 67–68; E. A. Keay, *The Native and Customary Courts in Nigeria* (London: Sweet and Maxwell, 1966), 3–4.

7. On the origins of the modern legal profession in Nigeria, see Jay Gordon, "The Development of the Legal System in the Colony of Lagos, 1862–1905" (Ph.D. diss., University of London, 1964); Elias, *Nigerian Legal System*, 363–71; Adewoye, *Judicial System*, 107–36; and Omoniyi Adewoye, *The Legal Profession in Nigeria, 1865–1962* (Ikeja: Longman, 1977).

8. Fallers, *Law*, 327; Sally Falk Moore, "Individual Interests and Organisational Structures: Dispute Settlements as 'Events of Articulation,'" in *Social Anthropology and Law*, ed. Ian Hamnett (London: Academic Press, 1977), 182–83; Robert L. Kidder, "Western Law in India: External Law and Local Response," in *Social System and Legal Process*, ed. Harry M. Johnson (San Francisco: Jossey-Bass, 1978), 159–62; Roberts and Mann, introduction to Mann and Roberts, eds., *Law in Colonial Africa*, 37–39.

9. David William Cohen, "'A Case for the Busoga': Lloyd Fallers and the Construction of an African Legal System," in Mann and Roberts, eds., *Law in Colonial Africa*, 241.

10. Rules relating to Civil and Criminal Procedures of the Supreme Court were appended to the ordinance that established it. Supreme Court Ordinance, 1876, 4–135.

11. Juries were sometimes used to decide criminal cases. Adewoye, *Judicial System*, 45, 73.

12. Supreme Court Ordinance, 1876, sections 93–94.

13. Information about trial procedures in the previous paragraph is derived from reading the Judges' Notebooks in Civil Cases, which are housed in the tower of the Lagos State High Court.

14. See, for example, James Clifford, *The Predicament of Culture: Twentieth-Century Ethnography, Literature, and Art* (Cambridge, Mass.: Harvard University Press, 1988), 290.

15. Fallers, *Law*, 84–86.

16. Richard Roberts, *Litigants and Households: African Disputes and Colonial Courts in the French Soudan, 1895–1912* (Portsmouth, N.H.: Heinemann, 2005), 6–13.

17. Fallers, *Law*, 85.

18. Max Gluckman, introduction to *The Craft of Social Anthropology*, ed. A. L. Epstein (London: Tavistock, 1967), xvi.

19. Sara S. Berry, *Chiefs Know Their Boundaries: Essays on Property, Power, and the Past in Asante, 1896–1996* (Portsmouth, N.H.: Heinemann, 2001), xviii.

20. For examples of this approach, see Kristin Mann, "The Rise of Taiwo Olowo: Law, Accumulation, and Mobility in Early Colonial Lagos," in Mann and Roberts, eds., *Law in Colonial Africa*, 85–107; and Kristin Mann, "Interpreting Cases, Disentangling Disputes: Court Cases as a Source for Understanding Patron-Client Relationships in Early Colonial Lagos," in *Sources and Methods in African History: Spoken, Written, Unearthed*, ed. Toyin Falola and Christian Jennings (Rochester, N.Y.: University of Rochester Press, 2003), 195–218.

21. RP, Oddunimi to Gentlemen of the Court, 13 July 1863.

22. RP, Obashua to Gentlemen of the Court, 12 January 1864.

23. I am informed, here, by J. D. Y. Peel's distinction in *Religious Encounter and the Making of the Yoruba* (Bloomington: Indiana University Press, 2000), 53–63, between the horizontal and egalitarian nature of friendship and the vertical and hierarchical character of kinship in Yoruba culture.

24. While it is conceivable that the petitioners in these two cases represented their grievances against the slave women as involving a third party only because they believed this approach was the surest way to elicit support from the Slave Court and not because it reflected reality, such subterfuge is unlikely given how commonly slaves of both sexes left their owners by negotiating new relationships of dependence with someone else.

25. See also RP, Showunmy and Calurina to Rowe, 10 January 1863, and Boyanhin to Commissioner of the Court, 20 January 1864. It will be impossible to know how commonly owners appealed to the Slave Court for help unless additional records from the court are found.

26. Elsewhere in Africa later in the colonial period, British conquerors who worried, as Frederick Cooper has argued, that "too much 'freeing' would diminish . . . cash-crop production and . . . jeopardize a social order that depended on patriarchal authority" also readily redefined the enslavement of women as concubinage or marriage. Frederick Cooper, "Conditions Analogous to Slavery: Imperialism and Free Labor Ideology in Africa," in *Beyond Slavery: Explorations of Race, Labor, and Citizenship in Postemancipation Societies*, by Frederick Cooper, Thomas C. Holt, and Rebecca J. Scott (Chapel Hill: University of North Carolina Press, 2000), 127–29. See also Chanock, *Law, Custom, and Social Order*, 169–70; Paul E. Lovejoy, "Concubinage and the Status of Women Slaves in Early Colonial Northern Nigeria," *JAH* 29 (1988): 245–66; and Lovejoy and Hogendorn, *Slow Death*, 72, 83–84, 235–60.

Barbara M. Cooper, *Marriage in Maradi: Gender and Culture in a Hausa Society in Niger, 1900–1989* (Portsmouth, N.H.: Heinemann, 1997), 1–19, provides a penetrating analysis of how alternative forms of "marriage" became a means through which men and aristocratic women continued to control the labor of nominally free former slaves in French West Africa.

27. RP, Abudoli to Gentlemen of the Court, 3 November 1862.

28. Ibid.

29. *Lawani v. Osu and Adeyi*, 27 April 1887, JNCC, 7, 43. See also RP, Asiatu to

Rowe, 22 June 1863; and *Emiabuta v. Pelewura, Sinatu, and Aminatu,* 8 October 1894, JNCC, ?, 200.

30. *LWR,* 23 April 1904, p. 1, col. 1; *LS,* 23 August 1911, p. 5, col. 3.

31. *LS,* 9 September 1908, p. 6, col. 1.

32. *LWR,* 27 August 1904, p. 4, col. 1.

33. Robin Law, "'Legitimate' Trade and Gender Relations in Yorubaland and Dahomey," in *From Slave Trade to "Legitimate" Commerce: The Commercial Transition in Nineteenth-Century West Africa,* ed. Robin Law (Cambridge: Cambridge University Press, 1995), 207; Francine Shields, "Palm Oil and Power: Women in an Era of Economic and Social Transition in Nineteenth Century Yorubaland (South-Western Nigeria)" (Ph.D. diss., University of Stirling, 1997), 163–66, 248, 260.

Much more work needs to be done on the impact of the expansion of production and trade for external and domestic markets on the access of African women and men to resources and income, as well as on the changing relationship between them both inside and outside households. A considerable body of research on nineteenth- and early twentieth-century West Africa shows, however, that economic expansion may initially have increased the work of many women in towns and rural areas, but it also expanded their incomes and independence relative to men. Yet in most of these societies, men soon found ways to regain control of women and restrict their autonomy. Claire C. Robertson, *Sharing the Same Bowl: A Socioeconomic History of Women and Class in Accra, Ghana* (Bloomington: Indiana University Press, 1984), 239, 243; Susan M. Martin, *Palm Oil and Protest: An Economic History of the Ngwa Region, South-Eastern Nigeria, 1800–1980* (Cambridge: Cambridge University Press, 1988), 34–35, 45–48, 106; Allman and Tashjian, *"I Will Not Eat Stone,"* xxxiv, 34; Gracia Clark, *Onions Are My Husband: Survival and Accumulation by West African Market Women* (Chicago: University of Chicago Press, 1994), 90–91, 103.

34. *LS,* 9 September 1908, p. 6, col. 1; A. G. Hopkins, "A Report on the Yoruba, 1910," *JHSN* 5 (1969): 79; *LWR,* 23 April 1904, p. 4, col. 1.

Other scholars have also found that in the moment of upheaval unleashed by the imposition of colonial rule, African women found new opportunities to assert their autonomy. Early colonial courts, in some places, initially sympathized with them, but then male chiefs and elders, in alliance with colonial officials, reasserted control. Martin Chanock, "Making Customary Law: Men, Women and Courts in Colonial Northern Rhodesia," and Marcia Wright, "Justice, Women, and the Social Order in Abercorn, Northeastern Rhodesia, 1897–1903," in *African Women and the Law: Historical Perspectives,* ed. Margaret Jean Hay and Marcia Wright (Boston: Boston University, African Studies Center, 1982), 53–67 and 33–50. McClendon, *Genders and Generations,* 8, 21–22, and chap. 5, shows women using Native Commissioner Courts in Natal, South Africa, during the 1920s and 1930s to gain greater independence.

35. *LWR,* 27 August 1904, p. 4, col. 1, and 21 January 1911, p. 4, col. 1. For a fuller discussion of these issues, see Kristin Mann, *Marrying Well: Marriage, Status, and Social Change among the Educated Elite in Colonial Lagos* (Cambridge: Cambridge University Press, 1985), 110–15, 124–25; Adewoye, *Judicial System,* 205–206; and Peel, *Religious Encounter,* 254–55.

36. *LWR,* 28 March 1903, p. 4. col. 3, 8 July 1911, p. 4, col. 1, 12 February

1912, p. 4, col. 1; *LS*, 13 July 1910, p. 6, col. 1; Coker to Coker, 28 May 1911, Coker Papers 4/1/14; J. K. Coker, *Polygamy Defended* (Lagos, 1915); Henry Carr, *Diocesan Synod of Western Equatorial Africa, Report of Speeches Delivered in Synod, May 1912 . . .* (Newcastle-upon-Tyne: Mawson, Swan, and Morgan, 1912), 13.

37. Caroline H. Bledsoe has demonstrated this powerfully in her two books on women's domestic and reproductive lives in Liberia and the Gambia: *Women and Marriage in Kpelle Society* (Stanford: Stanford University Press, 1980), and *Contingent Lives: Fertility, Time, and Aging in West Africa* (Chicago: University of Chicago Press, 2002). Gracia Clark, *Onions*, 103–104, has explored elements of Asante kinship ideology that have led men and women to view conjugal relationships as short-term and matters of personal convenience and preference.

38. *Ramatu v. Abuduramanu*, 11 November 1896, JNCC, 18, 207–14.

39. *Gomez v. Oke and Lanlatu*, 19 July 1899, JNCC, 22, 48–51, 55–61. For a more detailed analysis of this case, see Kristin Mann, "The Historical Roots and Cultural Logic of Outside Marriage in Colonial Lagos," in *Nuptiality in Sub-Saharan Africa: Contemporary Anthropological and Demographic Perspectives*, ed. Caroline Bledsoe and Gilles Pison (Oxford: Clarendon Press, 1994), 177–79.

40. Sources on the British occupation of the Yoruba interior contain numerous references to female slaves who escaped their owners by running away to live with other men, particularly those who worked for the colonial government. CO 147/121, McCallum to Chamberlain, 20 December 1897; CO 147/145, MacGregor to Chamberlain, 27 December 1899; CO 147/155, MacGregor to Chamberlain, 21 May 1901; CO 147/156, MacGregor to Chamberlain, 10 August 1901; and CSO 4/5/6, Rohrweger to MacGregor, 28 June 1899.

41. Shields, "Palm Oil and Power," 254–59, 272–74. For a sensational account of the ruler of Ijaye's violent punishment of one of his wives who committed adultery, see Peel, *Religious Encounter*, 82. Also *Wright v. Wright*, 20 May 1886, JNCC, 6, 257; *Reffel v. Reffel*, February 1894, JNCC, ?, 184–88; and *Scott v. Shepherd*, 13 March 1894, JNCC, ?, 224–26, 230–45.

42. Karin Barber, *I Could Speak until Tomorrow: Oriki, Women, and the Past in a Yoruba Town* (Washington: Smithsonian Institution, 1991), 210.

43. Peel, *Religious Encounter*, 80. For further discussion of Yoruba ideas about witchcraft and magic, see N. A. Fadipe, *The Sociology of the Yoruba* (Ibadan: Ibadan University Press, 1970), 292–300; Percy Amaury Talbot, *The Peoples of Southern Nigeria: A Sketch of Their History, Ethnology, and Languages with an Abstract of the 1921 Census* (London: Frank Cass, 1969), 2:183–84, 185–86, 208–209; Peter Morton-Williams, "The Atinga Cult among the South-Western Yoruba," *Bulletin de l'IFAN* 18 (1956): 315–34; Andrew Apter, *Black Critics and Kings: The Hermeneutics of Power in Yoruba Society* (Chicago: University of Chicago Press, 1992), 112–13, 235 n. 13; Andrew Apter, "Atinga Revisited: Yoruba Witchcraft and the Cocoa Economy, 1950–1951," in *Modernity and Its Malcontents: Ritual and Power in Postcolonial Africa*, ed. Jean Comaroff and John Comaroff (Chicago: University of Chicago Press, 1993), 111–28; Babatunde Lawal, *The Gelede Spectacle: Art, Gender, and Social Harmony in an African Culture* (Seattle: University of Washington Press, 1996), 12–13, 30–35; Henry John Drewal and Margaret Thompson Drewal, *Gelede: Art and Female Power among the Yoruba* (Bloomington: Indiana University Press, 1983), 73–74; Margaret Thompson Drewal, *Yoruba Ritual: Performers, Play, Agency* (Bloomington:

Indiana University Press, 1992), 172; Barry Hallen, *The Good, the Bad, and the Beautiful: Discourse about Values in Yoruba Culture* (Bloomington: Indiana University Press, 2000), 61–63, 80–81, 86–97.

44. C. W. Newbury, *The Western Slave Coast and Its Rulers* (Oxford: Clarendon Press, 1961), 83–84; Adewoye, *Judicial System*, 10, 178, 207; J. F. A. Ajayi, *Christian Missions in Nigeria, 1841–1891: The Making of a New Elite* (London: Longmans, 1965), 264.

45. Morton-Williams, "The Atinga Cult," 315–34; Apter, "Atinga Revisited," 116–21.

46. FO 84/950, Campbell to Clarendon, 12 December 1854.

47. Shields, "Palm Oil and Power," 276–88. See also Barber, *I Could Speak*, 234–36, 290. O'Hear, *Power Relations*, 41, argues that female slaves who became concubines could "ensure reasonable treatment by threatening magical reprisals" against their owners' families.

48. Law, "Trade and Gender," 209–10; Shields, "Palm Oil and Power," 248–54, 283–85; Talbot, *Peoples*, 2:208; Peter Morton-Williams, "The Egungun Society in South-Western Yoruba Kingdoms," in *Proceedings of the Third Annual Conference of the West African Institute of Social and Economic Research* (Ibadan: University College, 1956), 90–103; Peel, *Religious Encounter*, 75–77; Lawal, *Gelede*, xiv, 16, 79; Drewal, *Yoruba Ritual*, 43–44, 116–19, 172–73.

49. CSO 8/2/2, Memorandum, 11 May 1896; UIL, Africana Collection, Minutes of the Central Native Council, 5 June 1903; Kristin Mann, "Women's Rights in Law and Practice: Marriage and Dispute Settlement in Colonial Lagos," in Hay and Wright, eds., *African Women and the Law*, 151–71; Sir Alan Burns, *History of Nigeria* (London: Allen and Unwin, 1969), 297.

50. Mann, *Marrying Well*, 42; Fadipe, *Sociology*, 90–91; A. K. Ajisafe, *The Laws and Customs of the Yoruba People* (Lagos: CMS Bookshop, 1924), 66. A woman named Asiatu, for example, ran away three times from an arranged marriage and was each time forced by her father to return to her husband, despite being physically abused before her third attempt to flee. RP, Asiatu to Rowe, 22 June 1863. For references to instances in the interior when kin tried to force women to remain in marriages against their will, see Phillips Papers, 3/11, 22–24 January 1900, Notes on the case of J. Olopade; and 1/1/7, 1900, Notes on the case of Okoro.

51. Hopkins, "Report on the Yoruba," 81; Fadipe, *Sociology*, 66; *Lawani v. Osu and Adeyi*, 27 April 1887, JNCC, 7, 43; *Loki v. Hogbesi*, 15 January 1891, Badagry Divisional Court Records, Badadiv, 1/2/2; *Emiabuta v. Pelewura, Sinatu, and Aminatu; Adeshina v. Jato and Amina*, 12 November 1894, JNCC, ?, 281; and *Abisegun v. Orogun*, 25 September 1899, JNCC, 22, 267.

52. I have little quantitative evidence about the value of bridewealth in Lagos before the late 1880s, but the plaintiffs in the cases cited in the previous note claimed to have paid bridewealth worth between £25 and £40. The defendants disputed these claims, however, and the court made awards of only between £6 and £14 to cover the return of bridewealth. Even these lesser amounts were considerable, given that unskilled laborers usually earned ninepence to one shilling a day and skilled laborers between £36 and £60 per year in the 1890s. Kristin Mann, "A Social History of the New African Elite in Lagos Colony" (Ph.D. diss., Stanford University, 1977), 75–76; *Annual Report*, Lagos Colony, 1898, 10.

53. Court records show, for example, that men put "fetish" on landed property to drive occupants out and try to obtain possession of it. While the records do not specify that the defendants or plaintiffs in these cases were of slave origin, they could have been. Methods used against people of free birth could also be turned against slaves, former slaves, and their descendants. See, for example, *Adiloju v. Apena and Togun*, 22 November 1888, JNCC, 8, 278; *Odunlami v. Dawodu*, 13 December 1888, JNCC, 8, 360; and *Anthony v. Alashe*, 28 May 1895, JNCC, ?, 119.

54. *Eshuby, alias Brimoh Apatira v. Oso, Opeluja, and Ogudula*, 14 July 1879, JNCC, 2, 126. Although these are the first surviving Supreme Court records to articulate the principle of service tenure, the first volume of the Judges' Notebooks of Civil Cases, covering the years 1876 through 1878, was missing when I conducted my research. It is possible that the Supreme Court had encountered the issue earlier.

55. Ibid., 127, 129.

56. *Eshuby, alias Brimoh Apatira v. Oso*, 6 August 1879, JNCC, 2, 141.

57. See, for example, V. R. Dorjahn and Christopher Fyfe, "Landlord and Stranger: Change in Tenancy Relations in Sierra Leone," *JAH* 3 (1962): 391–97.

58. *Omotoso v. Olowu*, July 1881, JNCC, 3, 298. The disputants, witnesses, and judge in this case all acknowledged that the relationship between the plaintiff and Siedu Olowu, his overlord, differed in a key respect from that described by Apatira. Omotoso had come to Lagos from Ilorin and may have been a free man, because he intended to return there. All acknowledged that Olowu had promised to pay Omotoso a wage in cowries, in return for his labor as a carrier, although Omotoso also resided in Olowu's household. The dispute was over the payment of the wage. The judge nonetheless included Apatira's remarks at the beginning of the case as an authoritative statement of the customary relationship between Lagosians and the "boys" resident in their households.

59. *Aṣogbon v. Ṣomade*, 9 November 1885, JNCC, 6, 127; *Aṣogbon v. Okin*, 16 November 1885, JNCC, 6, 136. In an earlier essay, I identified Ṣomade and Okin as slaves and said that the Aṣogbon had placed them in the service of Ogunbiyi ("Owners, Slaves, and the Struggle for Labour in the Commercial Transition at Lagos," in Law, ed., *From Slave Trade to "Legitimate" Commerce*, 154). On further reflection, I have concluded that the court records, in fact, leave the status of the defendants ambiguous. It is clear, however, that they were initially dependents of Ogunbiyi's, whom he sent to live in a dwelling under the Aṣogbon's authority.

60. Patrick D. Cole, *Modern and Traditional Elites in the Politics of Lagos* (Cambridge: Cambridge University Press, 1975), 29–44; Mann, "Taiwo Olowo," 98–99.

61. *Ramatu v. Abuduramanu*, 207–14.

62. Mann, "Taiwo Olowo," 97.

63. *Jose v. Ṣomade*, 17 February 1879, *Ṣomade v. Ebite*, 17 April 1879, and *Oruoloye, Abuduranami, and Amore v. Ṣomade*, 13 May 1879, JNCC, 2, 97, 102, 110.

64. *Jose v. Ṣomade*, 99. It is interesting that in this case a "boy," who was a former slave, claimed to have acquired an interest in a house but chose not to inhabit it, because he believed that doing so would have jeopardized his relationship with his overlord.

65. For a more detailed analysis of these cases, see Mann, "Interpreting Cases, Disentangling Disputes," 209.

66. *Ṣomade v. Ebite*, 102.

67. Ibid., 103. For Ebite's description of his commercial relationship with Ṣomade, see chapter 6.

68. Ibid., 107.

69. Ebite, it will be remembered, had already largely built the house where Ṣomade's mother lived, but it stood on land to which he had been granted access by Chief Wajoba. Even if he had obtained possession of that dwelling, he would still have been beholden to Chief Wajoba's descendants for the land on which it stood, and, as a consequence, have had obligations to them. Nor could Ebite have exercised rights of private property in the land.

70. *Ṣomade v. Ebite*, 102.

71. *Oruoloye, Abuduranami, and Amore v. Ṣomade*, 110.

72. *Taiwo v. Ekorwu, Ayiekoroju, and Okilu*, 9 June 1896, JNCC, ?, 329–31.

73. Ibid., 333–34.

Conclusion

1. Martin Klein, *Slavery and Colonial Rule in French West Africa* (Cambridge: Cambridge University Press, 1998), 9.

2. Martin Chanock, *Law, Custom, and Social Order: The Colonial Experience in Malawi and Zambia* (Cambridge: Cambridge University Press, 1985), 164–71; Richard Roberts and Kristin Mann, introduction to *Law in Colonial Africa*, ed. Kristin Mann and Richard Roberts (Portsmouth, N.H.: Heinemann, 1991), 3–58; Sara S. Berry, *Chiefs Know Their Boundaries: Essays on Property, Power, and the Past in Asante, 1896–1996* (Portsmouth, N.H.: Heinemann, 2001).

3. Robin Law, "The Historiography of the Commercial Transition in Nineteenth-Century West Africa," in *African Historiography: Essays in Honor of Jacob Ade Ajayi*, ed. Toyin Falola (Harlow, U.K.: Longman, 1993), 91–115.

4. Kristin Mann, "Women, Landed Property, and the Accumulation of Wealth in Early Colonial Lagos," *Signs* 16 (1991): 682–706.

Bibliography

Primary Sources

Manuscript Sources

Government Archives

Archivio di Stato Sezione Prima, Turin
—Materie Politiche Relative al Estero: Consolati Nazionali, Lagos, 1856–1857
British Library, London
—Add. Mss. 14034, part II, 182, A Collection of Board of Trade Papers, "A Report on the Trade to Africa and the Settlements There [1776]"
—Add. Mss. 55/11, fols. 15–16, 23–24, John Houtson, "An Account of Adeely Ex-Caboceer of Lagos," November 1825
—Add. Mss. 44441, fol. 218, Memorandum Relating to Domestic Slavery on the West African Coast. 1873. Gladstone Papers, vol. 356
Colonial Office Library, London
—West African Lands Committee, Committee on the Tenure of Land in West African Colonies and Protectorates, "Draft Report," "Correspondence," and "Minutes of Evidence," April 1917
High Court, Lagos State, Lagos
—Wills, 1885–1955, in bound volumes at the Probate Registry
—Judges' Notebooks, Civil Cases, the Supreme Court, 1876–1899
Land Registry, Lagos
—Registry of Dosunmu's Land Grants, 1853–1861
—Records of Crown Grants, 1863–1915
—Deeds, Mortgages, and Conveyances, 1863–1915
British National Archives, Kew
Lagos
—CO 147, Original Correspondence
—CO 148, Acts
—CO 149, Sessional Papers (Legislative Council Debates)
—CO 150, Government Gazettes
Southern Nigeria
—CO 520, Original Correspondence
—CO 588, Acts
—CO 592, Sessional Papers (Legislative Council Debates)
—CO 591, Government Gazettes
Other
—CO 806, Africa, Confidential Prints
—FO 2, Africa (Consular Correspondence)

—FO 84, Slave Trade, General Correspondence
—FO 403, Africa, Confidential Prints
—T 70, Treasury Papers
Nigerian National Archives, Ibadan
—Badadiv 1–8, Records of the Badagry Divisional Office, 1865–1900, containing civil and criminal court records, minute books, letter books, intelligence books, diaries, and correspondence registers
—CSO 1, 4, 5, 7–8, Records of the Nigerian Secretariat, Lagos, 1852–1900, containing despatches, reports, instruments, minute books, filed papers, and letter books
—Coker Papers, containing correspondence, business records, and diaries of Jacob Kehinde Coker, J. P. L. Davies, and Stella (Davies) Coker
—Com Col I, Records of the Commissioner of the Colony, 1918–50, containing administrative files and intelligence reports
—Epediv 4–7, Records of the Epe Divisional Office, 1889–1909, containing civil and criminal court records, minute books, letter books, intelligence books, diaries, and correspondence
—Phillips Papers, containing correspondence, diaries and notes of the Rev. (later Bishop) Charles Phillips
Record Office for Leicestershire, Leicester, and Rutland
—18D 33/1–18, Papers of Sir Samuel Rowe

Other Archives

Africana Collection, University of Ibadan Library, Ibadan
—Minutes of the Central Native Council
—Herbert Macaulay Papers, containing correspondence, family papers, and notes on Lagos history and politics
Church Missionary Society, Birmingham University Library
—CA2/O Yoruba Mission, letters and original papers (incoming)
Edinburgh University Library
—Archibald Dalzel Correspondence
Rhodes House Library, Oxford
—Colonial Records Project, Nigeria, containing letters, diaries, and notes of colonial officials serving in Lagos Colony and the Protectorate of Southern Nigeria
The Royal Commonwealth Society Library, London (transferred to Cambridge University Library in 1993)
—Papers of John Hawley Glover, 1861–1875, containing official and private correspondence and notes on Lagos Colony
Private Collections
—A. E. Carrena Papers, containing correspondence, account books, and minutes of family meetings. Located at the Carrena family home, Lagos

Published Primary Sources

Government

Annual Departmental Reports Relating to Nigeria and British Cameroons, group III, Judicial and Police, Lagos, 1900–1920

Annual Reports, Lagos Colony, 1862–1905
Blue Books, Lagos Colony, 1862–1905
Census, Lagos Colony, 1881, Colonial Office Library
Census, Lagos Colony, 1891, Colonial Office Library
Census, Lagos Colony, 1901, Colonial Office Library
Census, Southern Nigeria, 1911, Colonial Office Library
Colonial Office Lists
Colonial Office Pamphlets
—Alexander, C. W., *Memorandum on the Subject of Native Land Tenure in the Colony and Protectorate of Southern Nigeria (1910),* Colonial Legal Pamphlet, vol. 1, no. 26
—Cameron, Donald Charles, *Notes on the Report of the Commission of Inquiry Regarding the House of Docemo,* West African Pamphlet, no. 213, 1933
—Cameron, Donald Charles, *Notes Regarding the Head of the House of Docemo 1933,* West African Pamphlet, no. 214, 1933
General Abstract of Registration, Lagos Colony, 1893–1900
Great Britain, House of Lords Sessional Papers
—1852–53, 22:327–66, Correspondence to Kosoko
Great Britain, Parliamentary Papers (House of Commons Sessional Papers)
—1842.XI.1, XII.1, Select Committee on the West Coast of Africa, Report, Minutes of Evidence, Appendices, Index
—1844.L.1, Instructions for Guidance of Naval Officers Employed in the Suppression of the Slave Trade
—1845.XLIX. 1, Class A, Correspondence with British Commissioners . . . Relating to the Slave Trade
—1847–8.XXII.1, First–Fourth Reports from the Select Committee on the Slave Trade
—1852.LIV.221, Papers Relative to the Reduction of Lagos, 1851
—1857.XXXVIII.225, Papers Relating to the Cultivation of Cotton in Africa [at Lagos]
—1858–9.XXXIV.281, Class B, Correspondence with Foreign Powers Relating to the Slave Trade
—1862.LXI.147, Class B, Correspondence with Foreign Powers Relating to the Slave Trade
—1862.LXI.339, Papers Relating to the Occupation of Lagos, 1861
—1863.XXXVIII.117, Despatches Relating to the Destruction of Epe
—1865.V.1, Report from the Select Committee Appointed to Consider the State of British Establishments on the Western Coast of Africa, Proceedings, Minutes of Evidence, Appendix, Index
—1865.XXXVII.287, Report of Col. Ord, Commissioner to Inquire into the Condition of British Settlements on the West Coast of Africa
—1865.XXXVII.533, Papers Relating to War among Native Tribes in the Neighbourhood of Lagos
—1887.LXI.1, Correspondence Respecting War between Native Tribes in the Interior and Negotiations for Peace Conducted by the Government of Lagos
Nigerian Law Reports
West African Court of Appeal Reports
Report of Inquiry into the Ojora of Ijora Chieftaincy, Conducted by the Standing Tri-

bunal of Inquiry into the Declarations Regulating the Selection of Obas and Recognized Chiefs in Lagos State (1975), in the possession of Prince A. L. A. Ojora, Lagos

Other

African Times, 1876–1878
Church Missionary Intelligencer, 1852–1864
Eagle and Lagos Critic, 1883–1887
Lagos Standard, 1893–1915
Lagos Weekly Record, 1891–1915
Observer, 1882–1888

Interviews

Mrs. Michael Abiodun, Lagos, July 1980
Chief Akin Adeshigbin, Ikeja, April 1974 and August 1980
N. E. S. Adewale, Lagos, July 1974
S. B. Affini, Lagos, July 1974
Alhaji A. W. A. Akibayo, Lagos, February 1985
T. I. Yussuff Akilaja, Lagos, December 1984
A. W. Animaṣaun, Lagos, February 1974
G. B. Animaṣaun, Lagos, February 1985
Rufai Arufai Animaṣaun, Lagos, December 1983
Saif Akanni Animaṣaun, Lagos, December 1983
Ishmail Lawal Apatira, Lagos, December 1973
Chief Ishola Bajulaiye, Lagos, November 1984
Atanda Balogun, Lagos, July 1974
Lady Bank-Anthony, Lagos, March 1974
Chief Justice Atanda Fatayi-Williams, Lagos, December 1984–February 1985
Sulaiman Alabi Forrest, Lagos, January 1974
Chief Daniel Akinola Ogunbiyi, Oshodi, Lagos, May 1974
Prince A. L. A. Ojora, Lagos, October–November 1984, January 1985
The *Ọlófin* of Isheri, Isheri, March 1974
Chief Sulaiman Babatunde Ajasa Oluwa, Lagos, January 1985
Samuel Akin Oni, Lagos, July 1974
Chief Durojaiye Olajuwon Oshodi, Lagos, January 1974
Chief Mobolaji Oshodi, Lagos, February 1985
Mrs. Kofo Pratt, Lagos, September 1984
Dr. da Rocha-Afodu, Lagos, April 1974
Mrs. Kwao Sagoe, Lagos, February 1974
O. A. Ṣobande, Lagos, frequently throughout 1974, July 1980
Mrs. Angelica Thomas, Lagos, October 1983
C. B. Thomas, Lagos, October–November 1984
Emmanuel Molade Willoughby, Lagos, January 1974

Books and Articles

Abegunde, M. A. A. "Aspects of the Physical Environment of Lagos State." In *History of the Peoples of Lagos State*, ed. Ade Adefuye, Babatunde Agiri, and Jide Osuntokun, 6–15. Ikeja: Lantern Books, 1987.

Abraham, R. C. *Dictionary of Modern Yoruba*. London: University of London Press, 1958.

Adams, Captain John. *Remarks on the Country Extending from Cape Palmas to the River Congo*. London: Frank Cass, 1966.

Adams, Robert. *The Narrative of Robert Adams, an American Sailor Who was Wrecked on the Western Coast of Africa, in the Year 1810, was Detained Three Years in Slavery by the Arabs of the Great Desert, and Resided Several Months in the City of Tombuctoo*. Boston: Wells and Lilly, 1817.

Adamu, Mahdi. "The Delivery of Slaves from the Central Sudan to the Bight of Benin in the Eighteenth and Nineteenth Centuries." In *The Uncommon Market: Essays in the Economic History of the Atlantic Slave Trade*, ed. Henry A. Gemery and Jan S. Hogendorn, 163–80. New York: Academic Press, 1979.

Adefuye, Ade. "Oba Akinsemoyin and the Emergence of Modern Lagos." In *History of the Peoples of Lagos State*, ed. Ade Adefuye, Babatunde Agiri, and Jide Osuntokun, 33–46. Ikeja: Lantern Books, 1987.

Aderibigbe, A. B. "Early History of Lagos to about 1850." In *Lagos: The Development of an African City*, ed. A. B. Aderibigbe, 1–26. Ikeja: Longman Nigeria, 1975.

Adewoye, Omoniyi. *The Judicial System in Southern Nigeria, 1854–1954*. Atlantic Highlands, N.J.: Humanities Press, 1977.

———. *The Legal Profession in Nigeria, 1865–1962*. Ikeja: Longman, 1977.

———. "Prelude to the Legal Profession in Lagos, 1861–1880." *Journal of African Law* 14 (1970): 98–114.

———. "The Tijani Land Case (1915–1921): A Study in British Colonial Justice." *Odu* 13 (1976): 21–39.

Afigbo, E. A. *The Warrant Chiefs: Indirect Rule in Southern Nigeria*. New York: Humanities Press, 1972.

Afonja, Simi A. "Changing Modes of Production and the Sexual Division of Labor among the Yoruba." In *Women's Work, Development, and the Division of Labor by Gender*, ed. H. Safa and E. Leacock, 122–35. South Hadley, Mass.: Bergin and Garvey, 1986.

———. "Current Explanations of Sex Roles and Inequality: A Reconsideration." *Nigerian Journal of Economic and Social Studies* 21 (1981): 85–108.

Agbafe, P. A. *Benin under British Administration: The Impact of Colonial Rule on an African Kingdom, 1897–1938*. Atlantic Highlands, N.J.: Humanities Press, 1979.

Agiri, B. A. "Architecture as a Source of Nigerian History: The Lagos Example." In *History of the Peoples of Lagos State*, ed. Ade Adefuye, Babatunde Agiri, and Jide Osuntokun, 341–50. Ikeja: Lantern Books, 1987.

———. "Aspects of Socio-economic Changes among the Awori Egba and Ijebu Remo Communities during the Nineteenth Century." *Journal of the Historical Society of Nigeria* 7 (1974): 465–83.

Agiri, B. A., and Sandra Barnes. "Lagos before 1603." In *History of the Peoples of Lagos State*, ed. Ade Adefuye, Babatunde Agiri, and Jide Osuntokun, 18–32. Ikeja: Lantern Books, 1987.

Ajayi, J. F. A. "The Aftermath of the Fall of Old Oyo." In *History of West Africa*, ed. J. F. A. Ajayi and Michael Crowder, 2:129–66. New York: Columbia University Press, 1973.

———. "The British Occupation of Lagos, 1851–1861: A Critical Review." *Nigeria Magazine* 69 (1961): 96–105.

———. *Christian Missions in Nigeria, 1841–1891: The Making of a New Elite*. London: Longmans, 1965.

———. "West Africa in the Anti–Slave Trade Era." In *The Cambridge History of Africa: From c. 1790–c. 1870*, vol. 5, ed. J. E. Flint, 200–21. Cambridge: Cambridge University Press, 1976.

Ajayi, J. F. A., and Robert Smith. *Yoruba Warfare in the Nineteenth Century*. Cambridge: Cambridge University Press, 1964.

Ajisafe, A. K. *The Laws and Customs of the Yoruba People*. Lagos: CMS Bookshop, 1924.

Akinjogbin, I. A. *Dahomey and Its Neighbours, 1708–1818*. Cambridge: Cambridge University Press, 1967.

Akinsemoyin, Kunle, and Alan Vaughan-Richards. *Building Lagos*. Lagos: F and A Services, 1976.

Akintan, A. *Awful Disclosures on Epetedo Lands*. Lagos: Tika Tore Press, 1937.

Akintoye, S. A. *Revolution and Power Politics in Yorubaland, 1840–1893: Ibadan Expansion and the Rise of Ekitiparapo*. New York: Humanities Press, 1971.

Allen, Richard B. *Slaves, Freedmen, and Indentured Laborers in Colonial Mauritius*. Cambridge: Cambridge University Press, 1999.

Allman, Jean, and Victoria Tashjian. *"I Will Not Eat Stone": A Women's History of Colonial Asante*. Portsmouth, N.H.: Heinemann, 2000.

Anderson, David M., and Richard Rathbone, eds. *Africa's Urban Past*. London: James Currey, 2000.

Anstey, Roger. *The Atlantic Slave Trade and British Abolition, 1760–1810*. Atlantic Highlands, N.J.: Humanities Press, 1975.

———. "The Pattern of British Abolition in the Eighteenth and Nineteenth Centuries." In *Anti-slavery, Religion, and Reform: Essays in Memory of Roger Anstey*, ed. Christine Bolt and Seymour Drescher, 19–42. Folkestone, Kent: Wm. Dawson and Sons, 1980.

Apter, Andrew. "Atinga Revisited: Yoruba Witchcraft and the Cocoa Economy, 1950–1951." In *Modernity and Its Malcontents: Ritual and Power in Postcolonial Africa*, ed. Jean Comaroff and John Comaroff, 111–28. Chicago: University of Chicago Press, 1993.

———. *Black Critics and Kings: The Hermeneutics of Power in Yoruba Society*. Chicago: University of Chicago Press, 1992.

Araújo, Ubiratan Castro de. "1846, um ano na rota Bahia-Lagos: Negócios, negociantes e outros parceiros." In *Identifying Enslaved Africans: The "Nigerian" Hinterland and the African Diaspora*, ed. Paul E. Lovejoy, 446–72. Proceedings of the UNESCO/SSHRCC Summer Institute, York University, Toronto, 1997.

Armstrong, Thomas F. "From Task Labor to Free Labor: The Transition along Georgia's Rice Coast, 1820–1880." In *From Slavery to Sharecropping: White Land and Black Labor in the Rural South, 1865–1900*, ed. Donald G. Nieman, 2–17. New York: Garland Publishing, 1994.

Asiwaju, A. I. *Western Yorubaland under European Rule, 1889–1945: A Comparative Analysis of French and British Colonialism.* Atlantic Highlands, N.J.: Humanities Press, 1976.

Asiwaju, A. I., and Robin Law. "From the Volta to the Niger, c. 1600–1800." In *History of West Africa*, 3rd ed., ed. J. F. A. Ajayi and Michael Crowder, 1:412–64. Harlow, U.K.: Longman, 1985.

Atanda, J. A. *The New Oyo Empire: Indirect Rule and Change in Western Nigeria, 1894–1934.* New York: Humanities Press, 1973.

Atkins, Keletso E. *The Moon Is Dead! Give Us Our Money! The Cultural Origins of an African Work Ethic, Natal, South Africa, 1843–1900.* Portsmouth, N.H.: Heinemann, 1993.

Austen, Ralph A. "The Abolition of the Overseas Slave Trade: A Distorted Theme in West African History." *Journal of the Historical Society of Nigeria* 5 (1970): 257–74.

———. "The Slave Trade as History and Memory: Confrontations of Slaving Voyage Documents and Communal Traditions." *William and Mary Quarterly*, 3rd ser., 58 (2001): 229–44.

Austen, Ralph A., and Jonathan Derrick. *Middlemen of the Cameroons Rivers: The Duala and their Hinterland, c. 1600–c. 1960.* Cambridge: Cambridge University Press, 1999.

Austin, Gareth. "The Emergence of Capitalist Relations in South Asante Cocoa-Farming, c. 1919–1933." *Journal of African History* 28 (1987): 259–79.

———. "Indigenous Credit Institutions in West Africa, c. 1750–c. 1960." In *Local Suppliers of Credit in the Third World, 1750–1960*, ed. Gareth Austin and Kaoru Sugihara, 93–159. New York: St. Martin's, 1993.

Awe, Bolanle. "The Ajele System (A Study of Ibadan Imperialism in the Nineteenth Century)." *Journal of the Historical Society of Nigeria* 3 (1964): 47–60.

———. "The End of an Experiment: The Collapse of the Ibadan Empire, 1877–1893." *Journal of the Historical Society of Nigeria* 3 (1965): 221–30.

———. "Iyalode Efunsetan Aniwura (Owner of Gold)." In *Nigerian Women in Historical Perspective*, ed. Bolanle Awe, 55–71. Lagos: Sankore, 1992.

———. "Militarism and Economic Development in Nineteenth Century Yoruba Country: The Ibadan Example." *Journal of African History* 14 (1973): 56–77.

———. "The Rise of Ibadan as a Yoruba Power, 1851–1893." D. Phil. thesis, Oxford University, 1964.

———, ed. *Nigerian Women in Historical Perspective.* Lagos: Sankore, 1992.

Ayandele, E. A. *Holy Johnson: Pioneer of African Nationalism, 1836–1917.* London: Frank Cass, 1970.

———. *The Ijebu of Yorubaland, 1850–1950: Politics, Economy and Society.* Ibadan: Heinemann, 1992.

———. *The Missionary Impact on Modern Nigeria, 1842–1914: A Political and Social Analysis.* London: Longman, 1966.

Bailyn, Bernard. "The Idea of Atlantic History." *Itinerario* 20 (1996): 19–44.

Baker, Pauline H. *Urbanization and Political Change: The Politics of Lagos, 1917–1967*. Berkeley: University of California Press, 1974.

Barber, Karin. *I Could Speak until Tomorrow: Oriki, Women, and the Past in a Yoruba Town*. Washington, D.C.: Smithsonian Institution Press, 1991.

Barickman, B. J. *A Bahian Counterpoint: Sugar, Tobacco, Cassava, and Slavery in Recôncavo, 1780–1860*. Stanford: Stanford University Press, 1998.

Barnes, A. C. "The Recovery of Palm Kernels." *Fifth Annual Bulletin of the Agricultural Department, Nigeria* (1926), 24–32.

Barnes, Sandra T. "Decentering Lagos: A City and Its Precolonial Region." Paper presented at the Conference on Africa's Urban Past, School of Oriental and African Studies, University of London, June 1996.

———. "The Organization of Social and Cultural Diversity: An Historical Inquiry." In *Culture and Contradiction: Dialectics of Wealth, Power, and Symbol*, ed. Hermine G. De Soto, 243–57. San Francisco: EmText, 1992.

———. *Patrons and Power: Creating a Political Community in Metropolitan Lagos*. Bloomington: Indiana University Press, 1986.

———. "Ritual, Power, and Outside Knowledge." *Journal of Religion in Africa* 20 (1990): 248–68.

———. "Women, Property, and Power." In *Beyond the Second Sex: New Directions in the Anthropology of Gender*, ed. Peggy Reeves Sanday and Ruth Gallagher Goodenough, 255–80. Philadelphia: University of Pennsylvania Press, 1990.

Barry, Boubacar. *Senegambia and the Atlantic Slave Trade*. Cambridge: Cambridge University Press, 1998.

Bascom, William R. "The Esusu: A Credit Institution of the Yoruba." *Journal of the Royal Anthropological Institute* 82 (1952): 63–69.

———. "The Principle of Seniority in the Social Structure of the Yoruba." *American Anthropologist* 44 (1942): 37–46.

Bay, Edna G. *Wives of the Leopard: Gender, Politics, and Culture in the Kingdom of Dahomey*. Charlottesville: University of Virginia Press, 1998.

Behrendt, Stephen D. "The Annual Volume and Regional Distribution of the British Slave Trade, 1780–1807." *Journal of African History* 38 (1997): 187–211.

———. "The Journal of an African Slaver, 1789–1792, and the Gold Coast Slave Trade of William Collow." *History in Africa* 22 (1995): 61–71.

Behrendt, Stephen D., and David Eltis. "Competition, Market Power, and the Impact of Abolition on the Transatlantic Slave Trade: Connections between Africa and the Americas." Paper presented at the annual meeting of the American Historical Association, New York, N.Y., January 1997.

Beinart, William, and Colin Bundy. *Hidden Struggles in Rural South Africa: Politics and Popular Movements in the Transkei and Eastern Cape, 1890–1930*. Berkeley: University of California Press, 1987.

Ben-Amos, Paula Girshick. *Art, Innovation, and Politics in Eighteenth-Century Benin*. Bloomington: Indiana University Press, 1999.

Berlin, Ira. *Many Thousands Gone: The First Two Centuries of Slavery in North America*. Cambridge, Mass.: Harvard University Press, 1998.

Berlin, Ira, and Philip D. Morgan. "Labor and the Shaping of Slave Life in the Americas." In *Cultivation and Culture: Labor and the Shaping of Slave Life in the*

Americas, ed. Ira Berlin and Philip D. Morgan, 1–45. Charlottesville: University of Virginia Press, 1993.

Berlin, Ira, et al., eds. *The Wartime Genesis of Free Labor: The Upper South*. Vol. 2 of *Freedom: A Documentary History of Emancipation, 1861–1867*. Cambridge: Cambridge University Press, 1993.

Berman, Bruce, and John Lonsdale. *Unhappy Valley: Conflict in Kenya and Africa*. London: James Currey, 1992.

Berry, Sara S. *Chiefs Know Their Boundaries: Essays on Property, Power, and the Past in Asante, 1896–1996*. Portsmouth, N.H.: Heinemann, 2001.

———. *Cocoa, Custom, and Socio-economic Change in Rural Western Nigeria*. Oxford: Clarendon Press, 1975.

———. *Fathers Work for their Sons: Accumulation, Mobility, and Class Formation in an Extended Yoruba Community*. Berkeley: University of California Press, 1985.

———. *No Condition Is Permanent: The Social Dynamics of Agrarian Change in Sub-Saharan Africa*. Madison: University of Wisconsin Press, 1993.

Bethell, Leslie. *The Abolition of the Brazilian Slave Trade: Britain, Brazil, and the Slave Trade Question, 1807–1869*. Cambridge: Cambridge University Press, 1970.

Biagini, Eugenio F. "Popular Liberals, Gladstonian Finance, and the Debate on Taxation, 1860–1874." In *Currents of Radicalism: Popular Radicalism, Organised Labour, and Party Politics in Britain, 1850–1914*, ed. Eugenio F. Biagini and Alastair J. Reid, 134–62. Cambridge: Cambridge University Press, 1991.

Biagini, Eugenio F., and Alastair J. Reid. "Currents of Radicalism, 1850–1914." In *Currents of Radicalism: Popular Radicalism, Organised Labour, and Party Politics in Britain, 1850–1914*, ed. Eugenio F. Biagini and Alastair J. Reid, 1–19. Cambridge: Cambridge University Press, 1991.

Billows, H. C., and H. Beckwith. *Palm Oil and Palm Kernels, the Consuls of West Africa*. Liverpool: Charles Birchall, 1913.

Biobaku, S. O. *The Egba and their Neighbours, 1842–1872*. Oxford: Clarendon Press, 1957.

———. "Madame Tinubu." In *Eminent Nigerians of the Nineteenth Century*, 33–41. Cambridge: Cambridge University Press, 1960.

Birmingham, David. *Central Africa to 1870: Zambezia, Zaire, and the South Atlantic*. Cambridge: Cambridge University Press, 1981.

Blackburn, Robin. *The Overthrow of Colonial Slavery, 1776–1848*. London: Verso, 1988.

Bledsoe, Caroline H. *Contingent Lives: Fertility, Time, and Aging in West Africa*. Chicago: University of Chicago Press, 2002.

———. *Women and Marriage in Kpelle Society*. Stanford: Stanford University Press, 1980.

Bold, Lieutenant Edward. *The Merchant's and Mariner's African Guide: Containing an Accurate Description of the Coast, Bays, Harbours, and Adjacent Islands of West Africa*. London: J. D. and T. C. Cushing, 1819.

Bowdich, T. E. *Mission from Cape Coast Castle to Ashantee*. London: Frank Cass, 1966.

Bowen, Thomas Jefferson. *Adventures and Missionary Labours in Several Countries in the Interior of Africa from 1849 to 1856*. London: Frank Cass, 1968.

Bozzoli, Belinda, with Mmantho Nkotsoe. *Women of Phokeng: Consciousness, Life Strategy, and Migrancy in South Africa, 1900–1983*. Portsmouth, N.H.: Heinemann, 1991.

Bradbury, R. E. *Benin Studies*. London: Oxford University Press, 1973.

Brantlinger, Patrick. "Victorians and Africans: The Genealogy of the Myth of the Dark Continent." *Critical Inquiry* 12 (1985): 166–203.

Brooks, George. "Peanuts and Colonialism: Consequences of the Commercialization of Peanuts in West Africa, 1830–1870." *Journal of African History* 16 (1976): 29–54.

Brown, Carolyn A. *"We Were All Slaves": African Miners, Culture, and Resistance at the Enugu Government Colliery*. Portsmouth, N.H.: Heinemann, 2003.

Burns, Sir Alan. *History of Nigeria*. London: Allen and Unwin, 1969.

Burton, Richard Francis. *Abeokuta and the Camaroons Mountains: An Exploration*. 2 vols. London: Tinsley Brothers, 1863.

Buxton, Sir Thomas Fowell. *The African Slave Trade and Its Remedy*. London: John Murray, 1840.

Byfield, Judith A. *The Bluest Hands: A Social and Economic History of Women Dyers in Abeokuta (Nigeria), 1890–1940*. Portsmouth, N.H.: Heinemann, 2002.

———. "Pawns and Politics: The Pawnship Debate in Western Nigeria." In *Pawnship in Africa: Debt Bondage in Historical Perspective*, ed. Toyin Falola and Paul E. Lovejoy, 187–216. Boulder: Westview Press, 1994.

Cain, P. J., and A. G. Hopkins. *Crisis and Deconstruction, 1914–1990*. Vol. 2 of *British Imperialism*. London: Longman, 1993.

———. *Innovation and Expansion, 1688–1914*. Vol. 1 of *British Imperialism*. London: Longman, 1993.

Campbell, Robert. "A Pilgrimage to My Motherland." In *Search for a Place: Black Separatism and Africa, 1860*, by M. R. Delany and Robert Campbell, 149–250. Ann Arbor: University of Michigan Press, 1969.

Carney, Judith, and Michael Watts. "Disciplining Women? Rice, Mechanization, and the Evolution of Mandinka Gender Relations in Senegambia." *Signs* 16 (1991): 651–81.

Carr, Henry. *Diocesan Synod of Western Equatorial Africa, Report of Speeches Delivered in Synod, May 1912. . . .* Newcastle-upon-Tyne: Mawson, Swan, and Morgan, 1912.

Cell, John W. *British Colonial Administration in the Mid-Nineteenth Century: The Policy-Making Process*. New Haven: Yale University Press, 1970.

Chanock, Martin. *Law, Custom, and Social Order: The Colonial Experience in Malawi and Zambia*. Cambridge: Cambridge University Press, 1985.

———. "Making Customary Law: Men, Women and Courts in Colonial Northern Rhodesia." In *African Women and the Law: Historical Perspectives*, ed. Margaret Jean Hay and Marcia Wright, 53–67. Boston: Boston University, African Studies Center, 1982.

———. "Paradigms, Policies, and Property: A Review of the Customary Law of Land Tenure." In *Law in Colonial Africa*, ed. Kristin Mann and Richard Roberts, 61–84. Portsmouth, N.H.: Heinemann, 1991.

Chaunu, Pierre. *L'expansion européenne du XIIIe au XVe siècles*. Paris: Presses Universitaires de France, 1969.

Christelow, Allen. "Slavery in Kano, 1913–1914: Evidence from the Judicial Record." *African Economic History* 14 (1985): 57–74.

———, ed. *Thus Ruled Emir Abbas: Selected Cases from the Records of the Emir of Kano's Judicial Council.* East Lansing: Michigan State University Press, 1994.

Clark, Gracia. *Onions Are My Husband: Survival and Accumulation by West African Market Women.* Chicago: University of Chicago Press, 1994.

Clarke, Julian. "Households and the Political Economy of Small-Scale Cash Crop Production in South-Western Nigeria." *Africa* 51 (1981): 807–23.

Clarke, W. H. *Travels and Explorations in Yorubaland (1854–1858).* Ibadan: Ibadan University Press, 1972.

Clifford, James. *The Predicament of Culture: Twentieth-Century Ethnography, Literature, and Art.* Cambridge, Mass.: Harvard University Press, 1988.

Cohen, David William. "'A Case for the Busoga': Lloyd Fallers and the Construction of an African Legal System." In *Law in Colonial Africa*, ed. Kristin Mann and Richard Roberts, 239–54. Portsmouth, N.H.: Heinemann, 1991.

Coker, G. B. A. *Family Property among the Yorubas.* London: Sweet and Maxwell, 1958.

Coker, J. K. *Polygamy Defended.* Lagos, 1915.

Cole, Patrick D. *Modern and Traditional Elites in the Politics of Lagos.* Cambridge: Cambridge University Press, 1975.

Coleman, James S. *Nigeria: Background to Nationalism.* Berkeley: University of California Press, 1965.

Comaroff, Jean, and John Comaroff. *Christianity, Colonialism, and Consciousness in South Africa.* Vol. 1 of *Of Revelation and Revolution.* Chicago: University of Chicago Press, 1991.

Cooper, Barbara M. *Marriage in Maradi: Gender and Culture in a Hausa Society in Niger, 1900–1989.* Portsmouth, N.H.: Heinemann, 1997.

Cooper, Frederick. "Africa in the World Economy." *African Studies Review* 24 (1981): 1–88.

———. "Conditions Analogous to Slavery: Imperialism and Free Labor Ideology in Africa." In *Beyond Slavery: Explorations of Race, Labor, and Citizenship in Postemancipation Societies*, by Frederick Cooper, Thomas C. Holt, and Rebecca J. Scott, 107–49. Chapel Hill: University of North Carolina Press, 2000.

———. *Decolonization and African Society: The Labor Question in French and British Africa.* Cambridge: Cambridge University Press, 1996.

———. *From Slaves to Squatters: Plantation Labor and Agriculture in Zanzibar and Coastal Kenya, 1890–1925.* New Haven: Yale University Press, 1980.

———. *On the African Waterfront: Urban Disorder and the Transformation of Work in Colonial Mombasa.* New Haven: Yale University Press, 1987.

———. *Plantation Slavery on the East Coast of Africa.* New Haven: Yale University Press, 1977.

———. "The Problem of Slavery in African History." *Journal of African History* 20 (1979): 103–25.

———, ed. *Struggle for the City: Migrant Labor, Capital, and the State in Urban Africa.* Beverly Hills: Sage, 1983.

Cooper, Frederick, Thomas C. Holt, and Rebecca J. Scott. *Beyond Slavery: Explo-*

rations of Race, Labor, and Citizenship in Postemancipation Societies. Chapel Hill: University of North Carolina Press, 2000.

Coughtry, Jay. *The Notorious Triangle: Rhode Island and the African Slave Trade, 1700–1807.* Philadelphia: Temple University Press, 1981.

Cowen, M. P., and R. W. Shenton. "British Neo-Hegelianism and Official Colonial Practice in Africa: The Oluwo Land Case of 1921." *Journal of Imperial and Commonwealth History* 22 (1994): 217–50.

Crais, Clifton. *White Supremacy and Black Resistance in Pre-industrial South Africa: The Making of the Colonial Order in the Eastern Cape, 1770–1865.* Cambridge: Cambridge University Press, 1992.

Craton, Michael. "Slave Revolts and the End of Slavery." In *The Atlantic Slave Trade*, ed. David Northrup, 203–17. Lexington, Mass.: D. C. Heath and Co., 1994.

Crowder, Michael, ed. *West African Resistance: The Military Response to Colonial Occupation.* London: Hutchinson, 1971.

Crowder, Michael, and Obaro Ikime, eds. *West African Chiefs: Their Changing Status under Colonial Rule and Independence.* Trans. Brenda Packman. Ile-Ife: University of Ife Press, 1970.

Crowther, Samuel Ajayi. "The Narrative of Samuel Ajayi Crowther." In *Africa Remembered: Narratives by West Africans from the Era of the Slave Trade*, ed. Philip D. Curtin, 298–316. Madison: University of Wisconsin Press, 1967.

Cunha, Manuela Carneiro da. *Negros, estrangeiros: Os escravos libertos e sua volta à África.* São Paulo: Editora Brasiliense, 1985.

Cunha, Marianno Carneiro da. *From Slave Quarters to Town Houses: Brazilian Architecture in Nigeria and the People's Republic of Benin.* São Paulo: Nobel/Edusp, 1985.

Curtin, Philip D. *The Atlantic Slave Trade: A Census.* Madison: University of Wisconsin Press, 1969.

———. *Economic Change in Precolonial Africa: Senegambia in the Era of the Slave Trade.* Madison: University of Wisconsin Press, 1975.

———. *The Image of Africa: British Ideas and Action, 1780–1850.* Madison: University of Wisconsin Press, 1964.

———. *The Rise and Fall of the Plantation Complex: Essays in Atlantic History.* Cambridge: Cambridge University Press, 1990.

———, ed. *Africa Remembered: Narratives by West Africans from the Era of the Slave Trade.* Madison: University of Wisconsin Press, 1967.

Curtin, Philip D., et al. *African History: From Earliest Times to Independence.* New York: Longman, 1995.

Curto, José C., and Paul E. Lovejoy, eds. *Enslaving Connections: Changing Cultures of Africa and Brazil during the Era of Slavery.* Amherst, N.Y.: Prometheus/Humanity Books, 2003.

Daaku, K. Y. *Trade and Politics on the Gold Coast, 1600–1720: A Study of the African Reaction to European Trade.* Oxford: Clarendon Press, 1970.

Daget, Serge. *Répertoire des expéditions négriègres françaises à la traite illégale (1814–1850).* Nantes: Centre de Recherche sur l'Histoire du Monde Atlantique, 1988.

Dalzel, Archibald. *The History of Dahomy, an Inland Kingdom of Africa.* London: Frank Cass, 1967.

Danmole, H. C. "Islam, Slavery and Society in Nineteenth Century Ilorin, Nigeria." *Journal of the Pakistan Historical Society* 42 (1994): 341–53.

Darling, P. J. "The Ancient Canoe Port of Benin." *Nigerian Field* 46 (1981): 40–51.

D'Avezac-Macaya, M. "The Land and People of Ijebu." In *Africa Remembered: Narratives by West Africans from the Era of the Slave Trade*, ed. Philip D. Curtin, 223–88. Madison: University of Wisconsin Press, 1967.

Davies, P. N. "The Impact of the Expatriate Shipping Lines on the Economic Development of British West Africa." *Business History* 19 (1977): 3–17.

Davis, David Brion. *The Problem of Slavery in the Age of Revolution, 1770–1823.* Ithaca: Cornell University Press, 1975.

———. *The Problem of Slavery in Western Culture.* Harmondsworth, Middlesex: Penguin Books, 1970.

———. *Slavery and Human Progress.* New York: Oxford University Press, 1984.

———. "Slavery and 'Progress.'" In *Anti-slavery, Religion, and Reform: Essays in Memory of Roger Anstey*, ed. Christine Bolt and Seymour Drescher, 351–66. Folkestone, Kent: Wm. Dawson and Sons, 1980.

Delany, M. R. "Official Report of the Niger Valley Exploring Party." In *Search for a Place: Black Separatism and Africa, 1860*, by M. R. Delany and Robert Campbell, 23–148. Ann Arbor: University of Michigan Press, 1969.

Denzer, LaRay. "Yoruba Women: A Historiographical Study," *International Journal of African Historical Studies* 27 (1994): 1–39.

Dike, K. Onwuka. *Trade and Politics in the Niger Delta, 1830–1885.* Oxford: Clarendon Press, 1956.

Dioka, L. C., and Siyan Oyeweso. "Intergroup Relations in a Frontier State: The Case of Badagry." In *Badagry: A Study in History, Culture, and Traditions of an Ancient City*, ed. G. O. Ogunremi, M. O. Opeloye, and Siyan Oyeweso, 128–53. Ibadan: Rex Charles, 1994.

Dmochowski, Z. R. *South-West and Central Nigeria.* Vol. 2 of *An Introduction to Nigerian Traditional Architecture.* London: Ethnographica, 1990.

Donnan, Elizabeth, ed. *Documents Illustrative of the History of the Slave Trade to America.* 4 vols. Washington, D. C.: Carnegie Institution, 1930–1935.

Dorjahn, V. R., and Christopher Fyfe. "Landlord and Stranger: Change in Tenancy Relations in Sierra Leone." *Journal of African History* 3 (1962): 391–97.

Drake, B. K. "Liverpool's African Commerce before and after Abolition of the Slave Trade." Master's thesis, University of Liverpool, 1974. Quoted in Martin Lynn, "The West African Palm Oil Trade in the Nineteenth Century and the 'Crisis of Adaptation,'" in *From Slave Trade to "Legitimate" Commerce: The Commercial Transition in Nineteenth-Century West Africa*, ed. Robin Law (Cambridge: Cambridge University Press, 1995).

Drescher, Seymour. "Capitalism and Abolition: Values and Forces in Britain, 1783–1814." In *Liverpool, the African Slave Trade, and Abolition*, ed. Roger Anstey and P. E. H. Hair, 167–95. Liverpool: Historic Society of Lancashire and Cheshire, 1976.

———. *Capitalism and Antislavery: British Mobilization in Comparative Perspective.* New York: Oxford University Press, 1987.

———. *The Mighty Experiment: Free Labor versus Slavery in British Emancipation.* New York: Oxford University Press, 2002.

Drescher, Seymour, and Stanley L. Engerman, eds. *A Historical Guide to World Slavery*. New York: Oxford University Press, 1998.
Drewal, Henry John, and Margaret Thompson Drewal. *Gelede: Art and Female Power among the Yoruba*. Bloomington: Indiana University Press, 1983.
Drewal, Margaret Thompson. *Yoruba Ritual: Performers, Play, Agency*. Bloomington: Indiana University Press, 1992.
Dumett, Raymond E. "Pressure Groups, Bureaucracy and the Decision Making Process: The Case of Slavery, Abolition and Colonial Expansion in the Gold Coast, 1874." *Journal of Imperial and Commonwealth History* 9 (1981): 193–215.
Dumett, Raymond E., and Marion Johnson. "Britain and the Suppression of Slavery in the Gold Coast Colony, Ashanti, and the Northern Territories." In *The End of Slavery in Africa*, ed. Suzanne Miers and Richard Roberts, 71–116. Madison: University of Wisconsin Press, 1988.
Eades, J. S. *The Yoruba Today*. Cambridge: Cambridge University Press, 1980.
Edgerton, Robert B. *The Fall of the Asante Empire: The Hundred-Year War for Africa's Gold*. New York: The Free Press, 1995.
Egboh, Edmund O. "The Working of the Timber Concession System in Southern Nigeria, 1900–1940." *Transactions of the Historical Society of Ghana* 16 (1995): 267–88.
Egharevba, Joseph. *A Short History of Benin*. Ibadan: Ibadan University Press, 1968.
Elbourne, Elizabeth. "Freedom at Issue: Vagrancy Legislation and the Meaning of Freedom in Britain and the Cape Colony, 1799–1842." *Slavery and Abolition* 15 (1994): 114–50.
Elegbede-Fernandez, Abiola Dosumu. *Lagos: A Legacy of Honour*. Ibadan: Spectrum Books, 1992.
Elias, T. Olawale. *Nigerian Land Law and Custom*. London: Routledge and Kegan Paul, 1951.
———. *The Nigerian Legal System*. London: Routledge and Kegan Paul, 1963.
Ellis, Alfred Burdon. *The Yoruba-Speaking People of the Slave Coast of West Africa*. London: Chapman and Hall, 1894.
Elphick, Richard, and Rodney Davenport, eds. *Christianity in Southern Africa: A Political, Social, and Cultural History*. Berkeley: University of California Press, 1997.
Eltis, David. "The Diaspora of Yoruba Speakers, 1650–1865: Dimensions and Implications." In *The Yoruba Diaspora in the Atlantic World*, ed. Toyin Falola and Matt D. Childs, 17–39. Bloomington: Indiana University Press, 2004.
———. *Economic Growth and the Ending of the Transatlantic Slave Trade*. New York: Oxford University Press, 1987.
———. "Precolonial Western Africa and the Atlantic Economy." In *Slavery and the Rise of the Atlantic System*, ed. Barbara L. Solow, 97–119. Cambridge: Cambridge University Press, 1991.
———. *The Rise of African Slavery in the Americas*. Cambridge: Cambridge University Press, 2000.
———. "The Transatlantic Slave Trade: A Reassessment Based on the Second Edition of the Transatlantic Slave Trade Database." Paper presented at the

annual meeting of the American Historical Association, Philadelphia, Pa., January 2006.
———. "The Volume and Structure of the Transatlantic Slave Trade: A Reassessment." *William and Mary Quarterly*, 3rd ser., 58 (2001): 17–46.
Eltis, David, and Lawrence C. Jennings. "Trade between Western Africa and the Atlantic World in the Pre-colonial Era." *American Historical Review* 93 (1988): 936–59.
Eltis, David, and David Richardson. "West Africa and the Transatlantic Slave Trade: New Evidence of Long-Run Trends." In *Routes to Slavery: Direction, Ethnicity, and Mortality in the Transatlantic Slave Trade*, ed. David Eltis and David Richardson, 16–35. London: Frank Cass, 1997.
Eltis, David, and James Walvin, eds. *The Abolition of the Atlantic Slave Trade*. Madison: University of Wisconsin Press, 1981.
Eltis, David, et al. *The Trans-Atlantic Slave Trade: A Database on CD-ROM*. Cambridge: Cambridge University Press, 1999.
Epstein, A. L. *The Craft of Social Anthropology*. London: Tavistock, 1967.
Eyo, Ekpo, and Frank Willett. *Treasures of Ancient Nigeria*. New York: Knopf, 1980.
Ezra, Kate. *The Royal Art of Benin: The Perls Collection in the Metropolitan Museum of Art*. New York: The Metropolitan Museum of Art, 1992.
Fadipe, N. A. *The Sociology of the Yoruba*. Ibadan: University Press, 1970.
Fage, John. "African Societies and the Atlantic Slave Trade." *Past and Present* 125 (1989): 97–115.
———. "Slaves and Society in Western Africa." *Journal of African History* 21 (1980): 289–310.
Fallers, Lloyd A. *Law without Precedent: Legal Ideas in Action in the Courts of Colonial Busoga*. Chicago: University of Chicago Press, 1969.
Falola, Toyin. "The End of Slavery among the Yoruba." In *Slavery and Colonial Rule in Africa*, ed. Suzanne Miers and Martin A. Klein, 232–49. London: Frank Cass, 1999.
———. *The History of Nigeria*. Westport: Greenwood Press, 1999.
———. "Missionaries and Domestic Slavery in Yorubaland in the Nineteenth Century." *Journal of Religious History* 14 (1986): 181–92.
———. "Money and Informal Credit Institutions in Colonial Western Nigeria." In *Money Matters: Instability, Values, and Social Payments in the Modern History of West African Communities*, ed. Jane I. Guyer, 162–87. Portsmouth, N.H.: Heinemann, 1995.
———. "'My Friend the Shylock': Money-Lenders and their Clients in South-Western Nigeria." *Journal of African History* 34 (1993): 403–23.
———. "Pawnship in Colonial Southwestern Nigeria." In *Pawnship in Africa: Debt Bondage in Historical Perspective*, ed. Toyin Falola and Paul E. Lovejoy, 245–66. Boulder: Westview Press, 1994.
———. *The Political Economy of a Pre-colonial African State: Ibadan, 1830–1900*. Ile-Ife: University of Ife Press, 1984.
———. "Power Relations and Social Interactions among Ibadan Slaves, 1850–1900." *African Economic History* 16 (1987): 95–114.
———. "Slavery and Pawnship in the Yoruba Economy of the Nineteenth Century." *Slavery and Abolition* 15 (1994): 221–45.

———. "The Yoruba Caravan System of the Nineteenth Century." *International Journal of African Historical Studies* 24 (1991): 111–32.
———. "The Yoruba Toll System: Its Operation and Abolition." *Journal of African History* 30 (1989): 69–88.
———. "The Yoruba Wars of the Nineteenth Century." In *Yoruba Historiography*, ed. Toyin Falola, 135–45. Madison: African Studies Program, University of Wisconsin–Madison, 1991.
———, ed. *African Historiography: Essays in Honor of Jacob Ade Ajayi*. Harlow, U.K.: Longman, 1993.
———, ed. *Yoruba Historiography*. Madison: African Studies Program, University of Wisconsin–Madison, 1991.
Falola, Toyin, and Robin Law, eds. *Warfare and Diplomacy in Precolonial Nigeria*. Madison: African Studies Program, University of Wisconsin–Madison, 1992.
Falola, Toyin, and Paul E. Lovejoy, eds. *Pawnship in Africa: Debt Bondage in Historical Perspective*. Boulder: Westview Press, 1994.
Falola, Toyin, and G. O. Ogunremi. "Traditional, Non-mechanical Transport Systems." In *Transport Systems in Nigeria*, ed. Toyin Falola and S. A. Olanrewaju, 17–30. Syracuse: Foreign and Comparative Studies Program, 1986.
Falola, Toyin, and G. O. Oguntomisin. *Yoruba Warlords of the Nineteenth Century*. Trenton, N.J.: Africa World Press, 2001.
Faluyi, Kehinde. "The Fluctuating Economic Fortunes of a Nigerian Sea Port: Economy and Trade in Badagry to 1900." In *Badagry: A Study in History, Culture, and Traditions of an Ancient City*, ed. G. O. Ogunremi, M. O. Opeloye, and Siyan Oyeweso, 49–71. Ibadan: Rex Charles, 1994.
Faulkner, O. T., and C. J. Lewin. "Native Methods of Preparing Palm Oil, II." *Second Annual Bulletin of the Agricultural Department, Nigeria* (1923), 3–22.
Finkelman, Paul, and Joseph C. Miller, eds. *Macmillan Encyclopedia of World Slavery*. New York: Macmillan Reference, 1998.
Finley, Moses I. "Slavery." In *International Encyclopedia of the Social Sciences*, ed. David L. Sills, Vol. 14, 307–13. New York: Macmillan, 1968.
Fisher, Humphrey J. *The Ahmadiyya Movement in Nigeria*. London: Oxford University, St. Anthony's College, 1961.
———. *Slavery in the History of Muslim Black Africa*. London: Hurst, 2001.
Flint, J. E. *Sir George Goldie and the Making of Nigeria*. London: Oxford University Press, 1960.
Folami, Takiu. *A History of Lagos, Nigeria*. Smithtown, N.Y.: Exposition Press, 1982.
Folarin, Adebesin. *The Laws and Customs of Egbaland*. Abeokuta: E. N. A. Press, 1939.
Foner, Eric. *Nothing but Freedom: Emancipation and Its Legacy*. Baton Rouge: Louisiana State University Press, 1983.
Foote, Mrs. Henry Grant. *Recollections of Central America and the West Coast of Africa*. London: T. Cautley Newby, 1869.
Freund, Bill. *The African Worker*. Cambridge: Cambridge University Press, 1988.
———. *Capital and Labour in the Nigerian Tin Mines*. Atlantic Highlands, N.J.: Humanities Press, 1981.
Frost, Diane. *Work and Community among West African Migrant Workers since the Nineteenth Century*. Liverpool: Liverpool University Press, 1999.

Fry, Richard. *Bankers in West Africa: The Story of the Bank of British West Africa, Limited.* London: Hutchinson, 1976.

Fyfe, Christopher. *A History of Sierra Leone.* London: Oxford University Press, 1962.

Gadelha, Regina Maria d'Aquino Fonseca. "A Lei de Terras (1850) e a aboliçao de escravidao: Capitalismo e forca de trabaljo no Brasil de seculo XIX." *Revista de história [Brazil]* 120 (1989): 153–62.

Gallagher, J. "Fowell Buxton and the New African Policy, 1838–1842." *Cambridge Historical Journal* 10 (1950): 36–58.

Gann, L. H., and Peter Duignan, eds. *Colonialism in Africa, 1870–1960.* 5 vols. Cambridge: Cambridge University Press, 1969.

Gavin, Robert. "Nigeria and Lord Palmerston." *Ibadan* 12 (1961): 24–27.

———. "Palmerston and Africa." *Journal of the Historical Society of Nigeria* 6 (1971): 93–99.

Gbadamosi, T. G. O. *The Growth of Islam among the Yoruba, 1841–1908.* London: Longman, 1978.

Geary, William N. M. *Nigeria under British Rule.* New York: Barnes and Noble, 1965.

Geggus, David. "Sex Ratio, Age and Ethnicity in the Atlantic Slave Trade: Data from French Shipping and Plantation Records." *Journal of African History* 30 (1989): 23–44.

Genovese, Eugene D. *Roll, Jordan, Roll: The World the Slaves Made.* New York: Vintage Books, 1974.

"Germany and the Palm Kernel Trade." *Journal of the African Society* 14 (1914–15): 193–98.

Getz, Trevor R. *Slavery and Reform in West Africa: Toward Emancipation in Nineteenth-Century Senegal and the Gold Coast.* Athens: Ohio University Press, 2004.

Gittins, L. "Soapmaking in Britain, 1824–1851: A Study in Industrial Location." *Journal of Historical Geography* 8 (1982): 29–40.

Gleason, Tiffany. "Entrenching Identity: The Creation of the Hausa Armed Force in Nineteenth-Century Lagos." First-year research paper, Department of History, Emory University, 2005.

Glover, Lady. *Life of Sir John Hawley Glover.* London: Smith, Elder and Co., 1897.

Gluckman, Max. Introduction to *The Craft of Social Anthropology*, ed. A. L. Epstein, xi–xx. London: Tavistock, 1967.

Goody, Esther N. *Parenthood and Social Reproduction: Fostering and Occupational Roles in West Africa.* New York: Cambridge University Press, 1982.

Goody, Jack. *Production and Reproduction: A Comparative Study of the Domestic Domain.* Cambridge: Cambridge University Press, 1976.

Gordon, Jay. "The Development of the Legal System in the Colony of Lagos, 1862–1905." Ph.D. diss., University of London, 1964.

Grace, John. *Domestic Slavery in West Africa.* New York: Barnes and Noble, 1975.

Gray, J. E. "Native Methods of Preparing Palm Oil in Nigeria." *First Annual Bulletin of the Agricultural Department, Nigeria* (1922): 29–51.

Green, William A. *British Slave Emancipation: The Sugar Colonies and the Great Experiment, 1830–1865.* Oxford: Clarendon Press, 1976.

Greene, Sandra E. *Gender, Ethnicity, and Social Change on the Upper Slave Coast: A History of the Anlo-Ewe.* Portsmouth, N.H.: Heinemann, 1996.

Green-Pedersen, Svend E. "The Scope and Structure of the Danish Negro Slave Trade." *Scandinavian Economic History Review* 19 (1971): 149–97.

Guran, Milton. "Agoudas—les 'Brésiliens' du Bénin: Enquête anthropologique et photographique." These de Doctorat, Marseille, 1996.

Gutkind, Peter C. W. "The Canoemen of the Gold Coast (Ghana): A Survey and an Exploration in Precolonial African Labour History." *Cahiers d'études africaines* 29 (1989): 339–76.

Guyer, Jane I. *An African Niche Economy: Farming to Feed Ibadan, 1968–1988.* Edinburgh: Edinburgh University, 1997.

———. "Household and Community in African Studies." *African Studies Review* 24 (1981): 87–137.

———. "Wealth in People and Self-Realization in Equatorial Africa." *Man*, n.s., 28 (1993): 243–65.

———. "Women's Work and Production Systems: A Review of Two Reports on the Agricultural Crisis." *Review of African Political Economy* 27–28 (1983): 186–92.

———, ed. *Money Matters: Instability, Values, and Social Payments in the Modern History of West African Communities.* Portsmouth, N.H.: Heinemann, 1995.

Hailey, Lord. *Native Administration in the British African Territories.* 5 vols. London: Her Majesty's Stationary Office, 1950–53.

Hair, P. E. H., Adam Jones, and Robin Law, eds. *Barbot on Guinea: The Writings of Jean Barbot on West Africa, 1678–1712.* 2 vols. London: Hakluyt Society, 1992.

Hallen, Barry. *The Good, the Bad, and the Beautiful: Discourse about Values in Yoruba Culture.* Bloomington: Indiana University Press, 2000.

Hallett, Robin. *The Penetration of Africa: European Enterprise and Exploration Principally in Northern and Western Africa up to 1830.* London: Routledge and Kegan Paul, 1965.

Harding, L. "Hamburg's West Africa Trade in the Nineteenth Century." In *Figuring African Trade: Proceedings of the Symposium on the Quantification and Structure of the Import and Export and Long Distance Trade in Africa, 1800–1913*, ed. G. Liesegang, H. Pasch, and A. Jones, 363–91. Berlin: D. Reimer, 1986.

Hargreaves, John D. *Prelude to the Partition of West Africa.* London: Macmillan, 1963.

Harling, Philip. "Rethinking 'Old Corruption.'" *Past and Present* 147 (1995): 127–58.

———. *The Waning of "Old Corruption": The Politics of Economical Reform in Britain, 1779–1846.* Oxford: Clarendon Press, 1996.

Harries, Patrick. *Work, Culture, and Identity: Migrant Laborers in Mozambique and South Africa, c. 1860–1910.* Portsmouth, N.H.: Heinemann, 1994.

Hart, Keith. *The Political Economy of West African Agriculture.* Cambridge: Cambridge University Press, 1982.

Hartley, C. W. S. *The Oil Palm.* London: Longman, 1977.

Hawthorne, Walter. *Planting Rice and Harvesting Slaves: Transformations along the Guinea-Bissau Coast, 1400–1900.* Portsmouth, N.H.: Heinemann, 2003.

Healy, J. J. C. "Land Tenure in the Colony of Lagos." In *Reports on Land Tenure in*

West Africa (1898), T. C. Rayner and J. J. C. Healy. Colonial Office Library, West Africa Pamphlet, No. 19.

Hennessy, John Pope. "On the British Settlements in Western Africa." *Journal of the Society of Arts* (2 May 1873): 436–49.

Hieke, Ernst. *G. L. Gaiser, Hamburg-Westafrika: 100 Jahre Handel mit Nigeria.* Hamburg: Hoffmann und Campe Verlag, 1949.

———. *Zur Geschichte des deutschen Handels mit Ostafrika: Das hamburgische Handelshaus Wm. O'Swald and Co.* Vol. 1. Hamburg: Verlag Hans Christians, 1939.

Higginson, John. *A Working Class in the Making: Belgian Colonial Labor Policy, Private Enterprise, and the African Mineworker, 1907–1951.* Madison: University of Wisconsin Press, 1989.

Hilton, Boyd. *Corn, Cash, Commerce: The Economic Policies of the Tory Governments, 1815–1830.* London: Oxford University Press, 1977.

Hobsbawm, Eric, and Terence Ranger, eds. *The Invention of Tradition.* Cambridge: Cambridge University Press, 1983.

Hodgkin, Thomas. *Nigerian Perspectives: An Historical Anthology.* 2d ed. London: Oxford University Press, 1975.

Hogendorn, Jan, and Marion Johnson. *The Shell Money of the Slave Trade.* Cambridge: Cambridge University Press, 1986.

Holt, Thomas C. "The Essence of the Contract: The Articulation of Race, Gender, and Political Economy in British Emancipation Policy, 1838–1866." In *Beyond Slavery: Explorations of Race, Labor, and Citizenship in Postemancipation Societies*, by Frederick Cooper, Thomas C. Holt and Rebecca J. Scott, 33–59. Chapel Hill: University of North Carolina Press, 2000.

———. *The Problem of Freedom: Race, Labor, and Politics in Jamaica and Britain, 1832–1938.* Baltimore: Johns Hopkins University Press, 1992.

Hopkins, A. G. "The Currency Revolution in South-West Nigeria in the Late Nineteenth Century." *Journal of the Historical Society of Nigeria* 3 (1966): 471–83.

———. "An Economic History of Lagos, 1880–1914." Ph.D. diss., University of London, 1964.

———. *An Economic History of West Africa.* London: Longman, 1973.

———. "Economic Imperialism in West Africa: Lagos, 1880–92." *Economic History Review* 21 (1968): 580–606.

———. "Innovation in a Colonial Context: African Origins of the Nigerian Cocoa-Farming Industry, 1880–1920." In *The Imperial Impact: Studies in the Economic History of Africa and India*, ed. Clive Dewey and A. G. Hopkins, 83–96. London: The Athlone Press, 1978.

———. "The Lagos Strike of 1897: An Exploration in Nigerian Labour History." *Past and Present* 35 (1966): 133–55.

———. "The 'New International Economic Order' in the Nineteenth Century: Britain's First Development Plan for Africa." In *From Slave Trade to "Legitimate" Commerce: The Commercial Transition in Nineteenth-Century West Africa*, ed. Robin Law, 240–64. Cambridge: Cambridge University Press, 1995.

———. "Peter Thomas: Un commerçant nigérian à l'épreuve d'une économie coloniale en crise." In *Les Africains*, ed. Charles-André Julien et al., 9:301–29. Paris: Editions J. A., 1978.

———. "Property Rights and Empire Building: Britain's Annexation of Lagos, 1861." *Journal of Economic History* 40 (1980): 777–98.

———. "A Report on the Yoruba, 1910." *Journal of the Historical Society of Nigeria* 5 (1969): 67–100.

———. "Richard Beale Blaize, 1845–1904: Merchant Prince of West Africa." *Tarikh* 1 (1966): 70–79.

Hopkins, Keith. *Conquerors and Slaves.* New York: Cambridge University Press, 1977.

Hose, John Robert. "Britain and the Development of West African Cotton." Ph.D. diss., Columbia University, 1970.

Hughes, T. P. "Technological Momentum in History: Hydrogenation in Germany, 1898–1933." *Past and Present* 44 (1969): 106–32.

Hutchinson, Thomas J. "The Social and Domestic Slavery of Western Africa, and Its Evil Influence on Commercial Progress." *Journal of the Society of Arts* 21 (26 February 1875): 310–21.

Ikime, Obaro. *The Fall of Nigeria: The British Conquest.* London: Heinemann, 1977.

Iliffe, John. *Africans: The History of a Continent.* Cambridge: Cambridge University Press, 1995.

———. "Poverty in Nineteenth-Century Yorubaland." *Journal of African History* 25 (1984): 43–57.

Inikori, Joseph E. "Africa in World History: The Export Slave Trade from Africa and the Emergence of the Atlantic Economic Order." In *Africa from the Sixteenth to the Eighteenth Century*, ed. B. A. Ogot, Vol. 5 of *UNESCO General History of Africa*, 74–111. Berkeley: University of California Press, 1992.

———. "West Africa's Seaborne Trade, 1750–1850: Volume, Structure, and Implications." In *Figuring African Trade: Proceedings of the Symposium on the Quantification and Structure of the Import and Export and Long Distance Trade in Africa, 1800–1913*, ed. G. Liesegang, H. Pasch, and A. Jones, 49–88. Berlin: D. Reimer, 1986.

Inikori, Joseph E., and Stanley L. Engerman, eds. *The Atlantic Slave Trade: Effects on Economies, Societies, and Peoples in Africa, the Americas, and Europe.* Durham, N.C.: Duke University Press, 1992.

Irving, Robert Forsyth. *A Collection of the Principal Enactments and Cases Relating to Titles to Land in Nigeria.* London: Stephens and Sons, 1916.

Johnson, Cheryl Jeffries. "Nigerian Women and British Colonialism: The Yoruba Example with Selected Biographies." Ph.D. diss., Northwestern University, 1978.

Johnson, Marion. "Ivory and the Nineteenth Century Transformation in West Africa." In *Figuring African Trade: Proceedings of the Symposium on the Quantification and Structure of the Import and Export and Long Distance Trade in Africa, 1800–1913*, ed. G. Liesegang, H. Pasch, and A. Jones, 89–139. Berlin: D. Reimer, 1986.

Johnson, Samuel. *The History of the Yorubas.* London: Routledge and Kegan Paul, 1969.

Johnson, W. A. B. *A Memoir of the Rev. W. A. B. Johnson: Missionary of the Church Missionary Society, in Regent's Town, Sierra Leone, 1816–1823.* London: Seeleys, 1852.

Jones, Gareth Stedman. *Languages of Class: Studies in English Working Class History, 1832–1982.* Cambridge: Cambridge University Press, 1983.

Jones, J. H. *The Tinplate Industry: A Study in Economic Organisation.* London: P. S. King, 1914.

Joseph, Richard A. *Democracy and Prebendal Politics in Nigeria: The Rise and Fall of the Second Republic.* Cambridge: Cambridge University Press, 1987.

July, Robert W. *The Origins of Modern African Thought.* New York: Praeger, 1967.

Kea, Ray A. *Settlements, Trade, and Polities in the Seventeenth-Century Gold Coast.* Baltimore: Johns Hopkins University Press, 1982.

Keay, E. A. *The Native and Customary Courts in Nigeria.* London: Sweet and Maxwell, 1966.

Kidder, Robert L. "Western Law in India: External Law and Local Response." In *Social System and Legal Process*, ed. Harry M. Johnson, 155–80. San Francisco: Jossey-Bass, 1978.

Killingray, David, and David Omissi, eds. *Guardians of Empire: The Armed Forces of the Colonial Powers, c. 1700–1964.* Manchester: Manchester University Press, 1999.

Klein, Herbert S. *The Atlantic Slave Trade.* Cambridge: Cambridge University Press, 1999.

———. *The Middle Passage: Comparative Studies in the Atlantic Slave Trade.* Princeton: Princeton University Press, 1978.

Klein, Martin A. "The Impact of the Atlantic Slave Trade on the Societies of the Western Sudan." In *The Atlantic Slave Trade: Effects on Economies, Societies, and Peoples in Africa, the Americas, and Europe*, ed. Joseph E. Inikori and Stanley L. Engerman, 25–48. Durham, N.C.: Duke University Press, 1992.

———. "Slave Resistance and Slave Emancipation in Coastal Guinea." In *The End of Slavery in Africa*, ed. Suzanne Miers and Richard Roberts, 203–19. Madison: University of Wisconsin Press, 1988.

———. *Slavery and Colonial Rule in French West Africa.* Cambridge: Cambridge University Press, 1998.

———. "Social and Economic Factors in the Muslim Revolution in Senegambia." *Journal of African History* 13 (1972): 419–41.

———. "The Study of Slavery in Africa." *Journal of African History* 19 (1978): 599–609.

———. "Women in Slavery in the Western Sudan." In *Women and Slavery in Africa*, ed. Claire C. Robertson and Martin A. Klein, 67–92. Madison: University of Wisconsin Press, 1983.

———, ed. *Breaking the Chains: Slavery, Bondage, and Emancipation in Modern Africa and Asia.* Madison: University of Wisconsin Press, 1993.

Klein, Martin A., and Paul E. Lovejoy. "Slavery in West Africa." In *The Uncommon Market: Essays in the Economic History of the Atlantic Slave Trade*, ed. Henry A. Gemery and Jan S. Hogendorn, 181–212. New York: Academic Press, 1979.

Kopytoff, Igor, and Suzanne Miers. Introduction to *Slavery in Africa: Historical and Anthropological Perspectives*, ed. Suzanne Miers and Igor Kopytoff, 3–81. Madison: University of Wisconsin Press, 1977.

Kopytoff, Jean Herskovits. *A Preface to Modern Nigeria: The "Sierra Leonians" in Yoruba, 1830–1890.* Madison: University of Wisconsin Press, 1965.

"Lagos in 1872." *Royal Commonwealth Society Library Notes*, n. s., 94 (1964): 1–8.
"Lagos Palm Oil." *Kew Bulletin* 262 (1892): 200–208.
Lander, Richard. *Records of Captain Clapperton's Last Expedition to Africa.* 2 vols. London: Henry Colburn and Richard Bentley, 1830.
Lander, Richard, and John Lander. *Journal of an Expedition to Explore the Course and Termination of the Niger.* 2 vols. New York: Harper and Brothers, 1842.
Landolphe, J. F. *Mémoires du Capitaine Landolphe.* 2 vols. Paris: A. Bertrand, 1823.
Latham, A. J. H. *Old Calabar, 1600–1891: The Impact of the International Economy upon a Traditional Society.* Oxford: Clarendon Press, 1973.
Law, Robin. "The Atlantic Slave Trade in Yoruba Historiography." In *Yoruba Historiography*, ed. Toyin Falola, 123–34. Madison: African Studies Program, University of Wisconsin–Madison, 1991.
———. "The Career of Adele at Lagos and Badagry, c. 1807–c. 1837." *Journal of the Historical Society of Nigeria* 9 (1978): 35–59.
———. "The Chronology of the Yoruba Wars of the Early Nineteenth Century: A Reconsideration." *Journal of the Historical Society of Nigeria* 5 (1970): 211–22.
———. "Ethnicity and the Slave Trade: 'Lucumi' and 'Nago' as Ethnonyms in West Africa." *History in Africa* 24 (1997): 205–19.
———. "Finance and Credit in Pre-colonial Dahomey." In *Credit, Currencies and Culture: African Financial Institutions in Historical Perspective*, ed. Endre Stiansen and Jane I. Guyer, 15–37. Uppsala: Nordiska Afrikainstitutet, 1999.
———. "The Gun Communities in the Eighteenth Century." Paper presented at the annual meeting of the African Studies Association, St. Louis, Mo., November 1991.
———. "The Historiography of the Commercial Transition in Nineteenth-Century West Africa." In *African Historiography: Essays in Honor of Jacob Ade Ajayi*, ed. Toyin Falola, 91–115. Harlow, U.K.: Longman, 1993.
———. "Jean Barbot as a Source for the Slave Coast of West Africa." *History in Africa* 9 (1982): 155–73.
———. *The Kingdom of Allada.* Leiden: School of Asian, African, and American Studies, 1997.
———. "A Lagoonside Port on the Eighteenth-Century Slave Coast: The Early History of Badagri." *Canadian Journal of African Studies* 28 (1994): 32–59.
———. "'Legitimate' Trade and Gender Relations in Yorubaland and Dahomey." In *From Slave Trade to "Legitimate" Commerce: The Commercial Transition in Nineteenth-Century West Africa*, ed. Robin Law, 195–214. Cambridge: Cambridge University Press, 1995.
———. "Making Sense of a Traditional Narrative: Political Disintegration in the Kingdom of Oyo." *Cahiers d'études africaines* 22 (1982): 387–401.
———. "On Pawning and Enslavement for Debt in the Pre-colonial Slave Coast." In *Pawnship in Africa: Debt Bondage in Historical Perspective*, ed. Toyin Falola and Paul E. Lovejoy, 55–69. Boulder: Westview Press, 1994.
———. "The Origins and Evolution of the Merchant Community in Ouidah." In *Ports of the Slave Trade (Bights of Benin and Biafra)*, ed. Robin Law and Silke Strickrodt, 55–70. Stirling, U.K.: University of Stirling, Centre of Commonwealth Studies, 1999.

———. *Ouidah: The Social History of a West African Slaving Port.* London: James Currey, 2004.
———. *The Oyo Empire, c. 1600–1836: A West African Imperialism in the Era of the Atlantic Slave Trade.* Oxford: Clarendon Press, 1977.
———. "The Rise and Fall of the Merchant Class in Whydah in the Nineteenth Century." Paper presented at the annual meeting of the Canadian Association of African Studies, Montreal, May 1996.
———. "Royal Monopoly and Private Enterprise in the Atlantic Trade: The Case of Dahomey." *Journal of African History* 18 (1977): 555–77.
———. *The Slave Coast of West Africa, 1550–1750: The Impact of the Atlantic Slave Trade on an African Society.* Oxford: Clarendon Press, 1991.
———. "The Slave Trade in Seventeenth-Century Allada: A Revision." *African Economic History* 22 (1994): 59–92.
———. "Slave-Raiders and Middlemen, Monopolists and Free-Traders: The Supply of Slaves for the Atlantic Trade in Dahomey, c. 1715–1850." *Journal of African History* 30 (1989): 45–68.
———. "Slaves, Trade, and Taxes: The Material Basis of Political Power in Precolonial West Africa." *Research in Economic Anthropology* 1 (1978): 37–52.
———. "Trade and Politics behind the Slave Coast: The Lagoon Traffic and the Rise of Lagos, 1500–1800." *Journal of African History* 24 (1983): 321–48.
———, ed. *From Slave Trade to "Legitimate" Commerce: The Commercial Transition in Nineteenth-Century West Africa.* Cambridge: Cambridge University Press, 1995.
Law, Robin, and Kristin Mann. "West Africa in the Atlantic Community: The Case of the Slave Coast." *William and Mary Quarterly*, 3rd ser., 56 (1999): 307–34.
Law, Robin, and Silke Strickrodt, eds. *Ports of the Slave Trade (Bights of Benin and Biafra).* Stirling, U.K.: University of Stirling, Centre of Commonwealth Studies, 1999.
Lawal, Babatunde. *The Gelede Spectacle: Art, Gender, and Social Harmony in an African Culture.* Seattle: University of Washington Press, 1996.
Lawal, Kunle. "The 'Ogu-Awori' Peoples of Badagry before 1950: A General Historical Survey." In *Badagry: A Study in History, Culture, and Traditions of an Ancient City*, ed. G. O. Ogunremi, M. O. Opeloye, and Siyan Oyeweso, 15–36. Ibadan: Rex Charles, 1994.
Leubuscher, Charlotte. *The West African Shipping Trade.* Leyden: A. W. Sythoff, 1963.
Levtzion, Nehemia. "Slavery and Islamization in Africa." In *Islam and the Ideology of Enslavement*, ed. John Ralph Willis, Vol. 1 of *Slaves and Slavery in Muslim Africa*, 182–98. London: Frank Cass, 1985.
Lindsay, Lisa A. "Domesticity and Difference: Male Breadwinners, Working Women, and Colonial Citizenship in the 1945 Nigerian General Strike." *American Historical Review* 104 (1999): 783–812.
———. "'To Return to the Bosom of Their Fatherland': Brazilian Immigrants in Nineteenth-Century Lagos." *Slavery and Abolition* 15 (1994): 22–50.
———. *Working with Gender: Wage Labor and Social Change in Southwestern Nigeria.* Portsmouth, N.H.: Heinemann, 2003.
Livingstone, David. *Dr. Livingstone's Cambridge Lectures, Together with a Prefatory*

Letter by the Rev. Professor Sedgwick. Ed. William Monk. Cambridge: Deighton, Bell, 1858.

Lloyd, Christopher. *The Navy and the Slave Trade: The Suppression of the African Slave Trade in the Nineteenth Century*. London: Longmans, Green, 1949.

Lloyd, P. C. *Yoruba Land Law*. London: Oxford University Press, 1962.

Losi, John B. *History of Lagos*. Lagos: Tika Tore Press, 1914.

Lovejoy, Paul E. "The Characteristics of Plantations in the Nineteenth-Century Sokoto Caliphate (Islamic West Africa)." *American Historical Review* 84 (1979): 1267–92.

———. "Concubinage and the Status of Women Slaves in Early Colonial Northern Nigeria." *Journal of African History* 29 (1988): 245–66.

———. "The Impact of the Atlantic Slave Trade on Africa: A Review of the Literature." *Journal of African History* 30 (1989): 365–94.

———. *Transformations in Slavery: A History of Slavery in Africa*. Cambridge: Cambridge University Press, 1983.

———, ed. *Africans in Bondage: Studies in Slavery and the Slave Trade*. Madison: African Studies Program, University of Wisconsin–Madison, 1986.

———, ed. *Identifying Enslaved Africans: The "Nigerian" Hinterland and the African Diaspora*. Proceedings of the UNESCO/SSHRCC Summer Institute, York University, Toronto, 1997.

Lovejoy, Paul E., and Jan S. Hogendorn. *Slow Death for Slavery: The Course of Abolition in Northern Nigeria, 1897–1936*. Cambridge: Cambridge University Press, 1993.

Lovejoy, Paul E., and David Richardson. "Demographic Patterns in the Trans-Atlantic Slave Trade: The Yoruba Factor." Paper presented at the annual meeting of the African Studies Association, San Francisco, Calif., November 1996.

———. "The Initial 'Crisis of Adaptation': The Impact of British Abolition on the Atlantic Slave Trade in West Africa, 1808–1820." In *From Slave Trade to "Legitimate" Commerce: The Commercial Transition in Nineteenth-Century West Africa*, ed. Robin Law, 32–56. Cambridge: Cambridge University Press, 1995.

———. "Trust, Pawnship, and Atlantic History: The Institutional Foundations of the Old Calabar Slave Trade." *American Historical Review* 104 (1999): 332–55.

Lugard, Frederick J. D. *Political Memorandum: Revision of Instructions to Political Officers on Subjects Chiefly Political and Administrative*. London: Frank Cass, 1970.

Lynn, Martin. "Change and Continuity in the British Palm Oil Trade with West Africa, 1830–1855." *Journal of African History* 22 (1981): 331–48.

———. *Commerce and Economic Change in West Africa: The Palm Oil Trade in the Nineteenth Century*. Cambridge: Cambridge University Press, 1997.

———. "From Sail to Steam: The Impact of the Steamship Services on the British Palm Oil Trade with West Africa, 1850–1890." *Journal of African History* 30 (1989): 227–45.

———. "The Profitability of the Early Nineteenth Century Palm Oil Trade." *African Economic History* 20 (1992): 77–97.

———. "Technology, Trade, and 'A Race of Native Capitalists': The Krio Diaspora of West Africa and the Steamship, 1852–1895." *Journal of African History* 33 (1992): 421–40.

———. "The West African Palm Oil Trade in the Nineteenth Century and the 'Crisis of Adaptation.'" In *From Slave Trade to "Legitimate" Commerce: The Commercial Transition in Nineteenth-Century West Africa*, ed. Robin Law, 57–77. Cambridge: Cambridge University Press, 1995.

Mabogunje, Akin L. *Urbanization in Nigeria.* London: University of London Press, 1968.

Mabogunje, Akin L., and J. Omer-Cooper. *Owu in Yoruba History.* Ibadan: Ibadan University Press, 1971.

Mann, Kristin. "Fostering as a Means of Labor Recruitment." Paper presented at the annual meeting of the African Studies Association, Boston 1976.

———. "The Historical Roots and Cultural Logic of Outside Marriage in Colonial Lagos." In *Nuptiality in Sub-Saharan Africa: Contemporary Anthropological and Demographic Perspectives*, ed. Caroline Bledsoe and Gilles Pison, 167–93. Oxford: Clarendon Press, 1994.

———. "Interpreting Cases, Disentangling Disputes: Court Cases as a Source for Understanding Patron-Client Relationships in Early Colonial Lagos." In *Sources and Methods in African History: Spoken, Written, Unearthed*, ed. Toyin Falola and Christian Jennings, 195–218. Rochester, N.Y.: University of Rochester Press, 2003.

———. "Las redes comerciales: De la Bahía de Benín al sur del Atlántico, 1750–1850." In *Rutas de la esclavitud en África y América Latina*, ed. Rina Cáceres, 45–82. San Jose: Editorial de la Universidad de Costa Rica, 2001.

———. *Marrying Well: Marriage, Status, and Social Change among the Educated Elite in Colonial Lagos.* Cambridge: Cambridge University Press, 1985.

———. "Owners, Slaves and the Struggle for Labour in the Commercial Transition at Lagos." In *From Slave Trade to "Legitimate" Commerce: The Commercial Transition in Nineteenth-Century West Africa*, ed. Robin Law, 144–71. Cambridge: Cambridge University Press, 1995.

———. "The Rise of Taiwo Olowo: Law, Accumulation, and Mobility in Early Colonial Lagos." In *Law in Colonial Africa*, ed. Kristin Mann and Richard Roberts, 85–107. Portsmouth, N.H.: Heinemann, 1991.

———. "A Social History of the New African Elite in Lagos Colony." Ph.D. diss., Stanford University, 1977.

———. "Women, Landed Property, and the Accumulation of Wealth in Early Colonial Lagos." *Signs* 16 (1991): 682–706.

———. "Women's Rights in Law and Practice: Marriage and Dispute Settlement in Colonial Lagos." In *African Women and the Law: Historical Perspectives*, ed. Margaret Jean Hay and Marcia Wright, 151–71. Boston: Boston University, African Studies Center, 1982.

———. "The World the Slave Traders Made: Lagos, c. 1760–1850." In *Identifying Enslaved Africans: The "Nigerian" Hinterland and the African Diaspora*, ed. Paul E. Lovejoy, 182–255. Proceedings of the UNESCO/SSHRCC Summer Institute, York University, Toronto, 1997.

Mann, Kristin, and Richard Roberts, eds. *Law in Colonial Africa.* Portsmouth, N.H.: Heinemann, 1991.

Manning, Patrick. "Contours of Slavery and Social Change in Africa." *American Historical Review* 88 (1983): 835–57.

———. "Merchants, Porters, and Canoemen in the Bight of Benin: Links in the West African Trade Network." In *Workers in the African Trade*, ed. Catherine Coquery-Vidrovitch and Paul E. Lovejoy, 51–74. Beverly Hills: Sage, 1985.

———. "The Slave Trade in the Bight of Benin, 1640–1890." In *The Uncommon Market: Essays in the Economic History of the Atlantic Slave Trade*, ed. Henry A. Gemery and Jan S. Hogendorn, 107–41. New York: Academic Press, 1979.

———. "Slave Trade, 'Legitimate' Trade, and Imperialism Revisited: The Control of Wealth in the Bights of Benin and Biafra." In *Africans in Bondage: Studies in Slavery and the Slave Trade*, ed. Paul E. Lovejoy, 203–33. Madison: African Studies Program, University of Wisconsin–Madison, 1986.

———. *Slavery and African Life: Occidental, Oriental, and African Slave Trades.* Cambridge: Cambridge University Press, 1990.

———. *Slavery, Colonialism, and Economic Growth in Dahomey, 1640–1960.* Cambridge: Cambridge University Press, 1982.

Marks, Shula, and Richard Rathbone. Introduction to *Industrialisation and Social Change in South Africa: African Class Formation, Culture, and Consciousness, 1870–1930*, ed. Shula Marks and Richard Rathbone, 1–43. Harlow, U.K.: Longman, 1982.

Mars, J. "The Monetary and Banking System and the Loan Market of Nigeria." In *Mining, Commerce, and Finance in Nigeria*, vol. 2 of *The Economics of a Tropical Dependency*, ed. Margery Perham, 177–224. London: Faber & Faber, 1948.

Marshall, Gloria. "Women, Trade, and the Yoruba Family." Ph.D. diss., Columbia University, 1964.

Martin, Jane. "Krumen 'Down the Coast': Liberian Migrants on the West African Coast in the Nineteenth and Twentieth Centuries." *International Journal of African Historical Studies* 18 (1985): 401–23.

Martin, Susan M. *Palm Oil and Protest: An Economic History of the Ngwa Region, South-Eastern Nigeria, 1800–1980.* Cambridge: Cambridge University Press, 1988.

———. "Slaves, Igbo Women and Palm Oil in the Nineteenth Century." In *From Slave Trade to "Legitimate" Commerce: The Commercial Transition in Nineteenth-Century West Africa*, ed. Robin Law, 172–94. Cambridge: Cambridge University Press, 1995.

Mason, Michael. *Foundations of the Bida Kingdom.* Zaria, Nigeria: Ahmadu Bello University Press, 1981.

Matthew, H. G. C. "Disraeli, Gladstone, and the Policy of Mid-Victorian Budgets." *Historical Journal* 22 (1979): 615–44.

Mba, Nina. "Literature as a Source of History: Case Study of *The Water House.*" In *History of the Peoples of Lagos State*, ed. Ade Adefuye, Babatunde Agiri, and Jide Osuntokun, 351–63. Ikeja: Lantern Books, 1987.

———. "Women in Lagos Political History." In *History of the Peoples of Lagos State*, ed. Ade Adefuye, Babatunde Agiri, and Jide Osuntokun, 243–55. Ikeja: Lantern Books, 1987.

Mbajekwe, Patrick Uchenna. "Land, Social Change, and Urban Development in Onitsha, Eastern Nigeria, 1857–1960." Ph.D. diss., Emory University, 2003.

Mboji, Mohamed. "The Abolition of Slavery in Senegal, 1820–1890: Crisis or the

Rise of a New Entrepreneurial Class?" In *Breaking the Chains: Slavery, Bondage, and Emancipation in Modern Africa and Asia*, ed. Martin A. Klein, 197–211. Madison: University of Wisconsin Press, 1993.

McCaskie, T. C. *State and Society in Pre-colonial Asante.* Cambridge: Cambridge University Press, 1995.

McClendon, Thomas V. *Genders and Generations Apart: Labor Tenants and Customary Law in Segregation-Era South Africa, 1920s to 1940s.* Portsmouth, N.H.: Heinemann, 2002.

McIntyre, W. D. "Commander Glover and the Colony of Lagos, 1861–73." *Journal of African History* 4 (1963): 57–79.

McLynn, F. J. *Hearts of Darkness: The European Exploration of Africa.* London: Hutchinson, 1992.

McPhee, Allan. *The Economic Revolution in British West Africa.* New York: Negro Universities Press, 1970.

McSheffrey, Gerald M. "Slavery, Indentured Servitude, Legitimate Trade, and the Impact of Abolition on the Gold Coast, 1874–1901: A Reappraisal." *Journal of African History* 24 (1983): 349–68.

Meek, C. K. *Land Tenure and Land Administration in Nigeria and the Cameroons.* London: Her Majesty's Stationary Office, 1957.

Meillassoux, Claude. *Anthropologie économique des Gouro de Côte d'Ivoire: De l'économie de subsistance à l'agriculture commerciale.* Paris: Mouton, 1964.

———. *Anthropology of Slavery: The Womb of Iron and Gold.* Trans. Alide Dasnois. Chicago: University of Chicago Press, 1991.

———. *Maidens, Meal, and Money: Capitalism and the Domestic Community.* Cambridge: Cambridge University Press, 1981.

———, ed. *L'esclavage en Afrique précoloniale.* Paris: Maspero, 1975.

Metcalfe, G. E. *Great Britain and Ghana: Documents of Ghana History.* London: Thomas Nelson and Sons, 1964.

———. *Great Britain and Ghana: Documents of Ghana History, 1807–1957.* Aldershot: Gregg Revivals, 1994.

Mettas, Jean. *Répertoire des expéditions négrières françaises au XVIIIe siècle.* Edited by Serge Daget and Michèle Daget. 2 vols. Paris: Société Française d'Histoire d'Outre-Mer, 1978, 1984.

Midgley, Clare. *Women against Slavery: The British Campaigns, 1780–1870.* London: Routledge, 1992.

Miers, Suzanne. *Britain and the Ending of the Slave Trade.* New York: Africana, 1975.

Miers, Suzanne, and Martin A. Klein, eds. *Slavery and Colonial Rule in Africa.* London: Frank Cass, 1999.

Miers, Suzanne, and Igor Kopytoff, eds. *Slavery in Africa: Historical and Anthropological Perspectives.* Madison: University of Wisconsin Press, 1977.

Miers, Suzanne, and Richard Roberts, eds. *The End of Slavery in Africa.* Madison: University of Wisconsin Press, 1988.

Milbourne, A. H. "Palm Kernels from West Africa: Movement to Establish the Industry in Great Britain." *Journal of the African Society* 15 (1915–16): 133–44.

Miller, Joseph C. "Retention, Reinvention, and Remembering: Restoring Identities through Enslavement in Africa and under Slavery in Brazil." In *Enslaving Connections: Changing Cultures of Africa and Brazil during the Era of Slavery*, ed. José C. Curto and Paul E. Lovejoy, 81–121. Amherst, N.Y.: Prometheus/Humanity Books, 2003.

———. *Way of Death: Merchant Capitalism and the Angolan Slave Trade, 1730–1830*. Madison: University of Wisconsin Press, 1988.

Minchinton, W. E. *The British Tinplate Industry: A History*. Oxford: Clarendon Press, 1957.

Mintz, Sidney W. *Sweetness and Power: The Place of Sugar in Modern History*. New York: Viking, 1985.

Moore, Sally Falk. "Individual Interests and Organisational Structures: Dispute Settlements as 'Events of Articulation.'" In *Social Anthropology and Law*, ed. Ian Hamnett, 159–88. New York: Academic Press, 1977.

———. *Social Facts and Fabrications: "Customary" Law on Kilimanjaro, 1880–1980*. Cambridge: Cambridge University Press, 1986.

Morgan, Philip D. *Slave Counterpoint: Black Culture in the Eighteenth-Century Chesapeake and Lowcountry*. Chapel Hill: University of North Carolina Press, 1998.

Morton-Williams, Peter. "The Atinga Cult among the South-Western Yoruba." *Bulletin de l'IFAN* 18 (1956): 315–34.

———. "The Egungun Society in South-Western Yoruba Kingdoms." In *Proceedings of the Third Annual Conference of the West African Institute of Social and Economic Research*, 90–103. Ibadan: University College, 1956.

Nadel, S. F. *A Black Byzantium: The Kingdom of Nupe in Nigeria*. London: Oxford University Press, 1942.

Newbury, C. W. *British Policy towards West Africa: Selected Documents, 1786–1874*. Oxford: Clarendon Press, 1965.

———. *British Policy towards West Africa: Selected Documents, 1875–1914; with Statistical Appendices, 1800–1914*. Oxford: Clarendon Press, 1971.

———. "Credit in Early Nineteenth Century West African Trade." *Journal of African History* 13 (1972): 81–95.

———. "On the Margins of Empire: The Trade of Western Africa, 1875–1890." In *Bismark, Europe, and Africa*, ed. Stig Förster, Wolfgang Mommsen, and Ronald Robinson, 35–58. Oxford: German Historical Institute, 1988.

———. "Trade and Authority in West Africa from 1850 to 1880." In *The History and Politics of Colonialism, 1870–1914*, ed. L. H. Gann and Peter Duignan, vol. 1 of *Colonialism in Africa, 1870–1960*, 66–99. Cambridge: Cambridge University Press, 1969.

———. *The Western Slave Coast and Its Rulers*. Oxford: Clarendon Press, 1961.

Nicolson, I. F. *The Administration of Nigeria, 1900–1960: Men, Methods, and Myths*. Oxford: Clarendon Press, 1969.

Nigeria, the Epetedo Lands: Representations of the Oshodi Chieftaincy Family Submitted to the Commissioner, Lagos Land Inquiry. Lagos: Hope Rising Press, 1939.

Norris, Robert. *Memoirs of the Reign of Bossa Ahadee, King of Dahomy*. London: Frank Cass, 1968.

Northrup, David. *Trade without Rulers: Pre-colonial Economic Development in South-Eastern Nigeria*. Oxford: Clarendon Press, 1978.

———, ed. *The Atlantic Slave Trade.* Lexington, Mass.: D. C. Heath and Co., 1994.

"Notes on the Oil Palm (*Elaeis Guineensis*) of Southern Nigeria." *Supplement, Government Gazette* 10 (5 February 1908), i–iv.

Nzemeke, A. D. "The Cowrie and the Development of Euro-African Trade in Lagos, 1851–1861." *Africana Marburgensia* 10 (1977): 34–50.

Obayemi, Ade M. "The Yoruba and Edo-Speaking Peoples and their Neighbours before 1600." In *History of West Africa,* 3rd ed., ed. J. F. A. Ajayi and Michael Crowder, 1:255–322. Harlow, U.K.: Longman, 1985.

Ogunremi, Gabriel Ogundeji. *Counting the Camels: The Economics of Transportation in Pre-industrial Nigeria.* New York: Nok, 1982.

Oguntomisin, Dare. "Warfare and Military Alliances in Yorubaland in the Nineteenth Century." In *Warfare and Diplomacy in Precolonial Nigeria,* ed. Toyin Falola and Robin Law, 31–39. Madison: African Studies Program, University of Wisconsin–Madison, 1992.

Oguntomisin, G. O. "New Forms of Political Organization in Yorubaland in the Mid-Nineteenth Century: A Comparative Study of Kurunmi's Ijaye and Kosoko's Epe." Ph.D. diss., University of Ibadan, 1979.

Oguntomisin, G. O., and Toyin Falola. "Refugees in Yorubaland in the Nineteenth Century." *Asian and African Studies* 21 (1987): 165–85.

Ohadike, Don. "The Decline of Slavery among the Igbo People." In *The End of Slavery in Africa,* ed. Suzanne Miers and Richard Roberts, 437–61. Madison: University of Wisconsin Press, 1988.

O'Hear, Ann. *Power Relations in Nigeria: Ilorin Slaves and Their Successors.* Rochester: University of Rochester Press, 1997.

Okediji, Francis Olu, and Oladejo O. Okediji. Introduction to *The Sociology of the Yoruba,* by N. A. Fadipe, 1–20. Ibadan: Ibadan University Press, 1970.

Okonkwo, Rina. *Protest Movements in Lagos, 1908–1930.* Lewiston: E. Mellen Press, 1995.

Oldfield, J. R. *Popular Politics and British Anti-slavery: The Mobilisation of Public Opinion against the Slave Trade, 1787–1807.* Manchester: Manchester University Press, 1995.

Olinto, Antonio. *The Water House.* Walton-on-Thames: Nelson, 1982.

Omer-Cooper, J. D. *The Zulu Aftermath: A Nineteenth-Century Revolution in Bantu Africa.* London: Longmans, 1966.

Oroge, E. A. "The Fugitive Slave Crisis of 1859: A Factor in the Growth of Anti-British Feelings among the Yoruba." *Odu* 12 (1975): 40–54.

———. "The Fugitive Slave Question in Anglo-Egba Relations, 1861–1886." *Journal of the Historical Society of Nigeria* 8 (1975): 61–80.

———. "The Institution of Slavery in Yorubaland, with Particular Reference to the Nineteenth Century." Ph.D. diss., University of Birmingham, 1971.

———. "Iwofa: An Historical Survey of the Yoruba Institution of Indenture." *African Economic History* 14 (1985): 75–106.

Oshodi Chieftaincy Family: Records and Achievements. Lagos: A. E. P., n.d.

Oyewumi, Oyeronke. *The Invention of Women: Making an African Sense of Western Gender Discourses.* Minneapolis: University of Minnesota Press, 1997.

Parker, John. *Making the Town: Ga State and Society in Early Colonial Accra.* Portsmouth, N.H.: Heinemann, 2000.

Patterson, K. David. "A Note on Slave Exports from the Costa da Mina, 1760–1770." *Bulletin de l'IFAN*, ser. B, 33 (1971): 249–56.

Patterson, Orlando. *Slavery and Social Death: A Comparative Study*. Cambridge: Cambridge University Press, 1982.

Payne, John Augustus Otonba. *Table of Principal Events in Yoruba History*. Lagos: Andrew M. Thomas, 1893.

Pedler, Frederick. *The Lion and the Unicorn in Africa: A History of the Origins of the United Africa Company, 1787–1931*. London: Heinemann, 1974.

Peel, J. D. Y. "Gender in Yoruba Religious Change." *Journal of Religion in Africa* 32 (2002): 136–66.

———. *Ijeshas and Nigerians: The Incorporation of a Yoruba Kingdom, 1890s–1970s*. Cambridge: Cambridge University Press, 1983.

———. *Religious Encounter and the Making of the Yoruba*. Bloomington: Indiana University Press, 2000.

Penvenne, Jeanne Marie. *African Workers and Colonial Racism: Mozambican Strategies and Struggles in Lourenço Marques, 1877–1962*. Portsmouth, N.H.: Heinemann, 1995.

Pereira, Duarte Pacheco. *Esmeraldo de situ orbis: Côte occidentale d'Afrique du Sud Marocain au Gabon*. French translation by Raymond Mauny. Bissau: Centro de Estudos da Guiné Portuguesa, 1956.

Perham, Margery. *Native Administration in Nigeria*. London: Oxford University Press, 1937.

———, ed. *Mining, Commerce, and Finance in Nigeria*. Vol. 2 of *The Economics of a Tropical Dependency*. London: Faber & Faber, 1948.

Peterson, John. *Province of Freedom: A History of Sierra Leone, 1787–1870*. London: Faber and Faber, 1969.

Phillips, Anne. *The Enigma of Colonialism: British Policy in West Africa*. London: James Currey, 1989.

Phillips, E. H. "The Church Missionary Society, the Imperial Factor, and Yoruba Politics, 1842–1873." Ph.D. diss., University of Southern California, 1966.

Postma, Johannes Menne. *The Dutch in the Atlantic Slave Trade, 1600–1815*. Cambridge: Cambridge University Press, 1990.

Prakash, Gyan. *Bonded Histories: Genealogies of Labor Servitude in Colonial India*. Cambridge: Cambridge University Press, 1990.

Priestley, Margaret. *West African Trade and Coast Society: A Family Study*. London: Oxford University Press, 1969.

Ranger, Terence. "The Invention of Tradition in Colonial Africa." In *The Invention of Tradition*, ed. Eric Hobsbawm and Terence Ranger, 211–62. Cambridge: Cambridge University Press, 1983.

Ratcliffe, Barrie M. "Cotton Imperialism: Manchester Merchants and Cotton Cultivation in West Africa in the Mid-Nineteenth Century." *African Economic History* 11 (1982): 87–113.

Rathbone, Richard. *Murder and Politics in Colonial Ghana*. New Haven: Yale University Press, 1993.

Rayner, T. C. "Land Tenure in West Africa." In *Reports on Land Tenure in West Africa (1898)*, T. C. Rayner and J. J. C. Healy. Colonial Office Library, West Africa Pamphlet, No. 19.

Rayner, T. C., and J. J. C. Healy. *Reports on Land Tenure in West Africa (1898)*. Colonial Office Library, West Africa Pamphlet, No. 19.

Reis, João José. *Slave Rebellion in Brazil: The Muslim Uprising of 1835 in Bahia*. Trans. Arthur Brakel. Baltimore: Johns Hopkins University Press, 1993.

"Report on the Committee of the Privy Council, 1789." In *Documents Illustrative of the History of the Slave Trade*, ed. Elizabeth Donnan. Washington, D.C.: Carnegie Institution, 1931.

Richardson, David, ed. *Bristol, Africa, and the Eighteenth-Century Slave Trade to America*. 4 vols. Bristol: Bristol Record Society, 1986, 1987, 1991, 1996.

Roberts, Richard. "The End of Slavery in the French Soudan, 1905–1914." In *The End of Slavery in Africa*, ed. Suzanne Miers and Richard Roberts, 282–307. Madison: University of Wisconsin Press, 1988.

———. *Litigants and Households: African Disputes and Colonial Courts in the French Soudan, 1895–1912*. Portsmouth, N.H.: Heinemann, 2005.

———. *Warriors, Merchants, and Slaves: The State and the Economy in the Middle Niger Valley, 1700–1914*. Stanford: Stanford University Press, 1987.

Roberts, Richard, and Martin Klein. "The Banamba Slave Exodus of 1905 and the Decline of Slavery in the Western Sudan." *Journal of African History* 21 (1980): 375–94.

Roberts, Richard, and Kristin Mann. Introduction to *Law in Colonial Africa*, ed. Kristin Mann and Richard Roberts, 3–58. Portsmouth, N.H.: Heinemann, 1991.

Roberts, Richard, and Suzanne Miers. Introduction to *The End of Slavery in Africa*, ed. Suzanne Miers and Richard Roberts, 3–68. Madison: University of Wisconsin Press, 1988.

Robertson, Claire C. "Post-proclamation Slavery in Accra: A Female Affair?" In *Women and Slavery in Africa*, ed. Claire C. Robertson and Martin A. Klein, 220–45. Madison: University of Wisconsin Press, 1983.

———. *Sharing the Same Bowl: A Socioeconomic History of Women and Class in Accra, Ghana*. Bloomington: Indiana University Press, 1984.

Robertson, Claire C., and Martin A. Klein. "Women's Importance in African Slave Systems." In *Women and Slavery in Africa*, ed. Claire C. Robertson and Martin A. Klein, 3–25. Madison: University of Wisconsin Press, 1983.

———, eds. *Women and Slavery in Africa*. Madison: University of Wisconsin Press, 1983.

Robertson, G. A. *Notes on Africa; Particularly those Parts Which Are Situated between Cape Verd and the River Congo*. London: Sherwood, Neely, and Jones, 1819.

Robinson, David. "Islam, Cash Crops and Emancipation in Senegal." *Journal of African History* 44 (2003): 139–44.

Rodney, Walter. "African Slavery and other Forms of Social Oppression on the Upper Guinea Coast in the Context of the Atlantic Slave Trade." *Journal of African History* 7 (1966): 431–43.

———. *How Europe Underdeveloped Africa*. Washington, D.C.: Howard University Press, 1982.

Rodrigue, John C. *Reconstruction in the Cane Fields: From Slavery to Free Labor in Louisiana's Sugar Parishes, 1862–1880*. Baton Rouge: Louisiana State University Press, 2001.

Ross, David A. "The Career of Domingo Martinez in the Bight of Benin, 1833–1864." *Journal of African History* 6 (1965): 79–90.
Rubinstein, W. D. "The End of 'Old Corruption' in Britain, 1780–1860." *Past and Present* 101 (1983): 55–86.
Ryder, A. F. C. *Benin and the Europeans, 1485–1897*. London: Longmans, 1969.
Sarracino, Rodolfo. *Los que volvieron a Africa*. Havana: Editorial de Ciencias Sociales, 1988.
Saville, Julie. *The Work of Reconstruction: From Slave to Wage Laborer in South Carolina, 1860–1870*. Cambridge: Cambridge University Press, 1994.
Scala, Giambattista. *Memoirs of Giambattista Scala: Consul of His Italian Majesty in Lagos in Guinea (1862)*. Trans. Brenda Packman. Ed. Robert Smith. Oxford: Oxford University Press, 2000.
Schnapper, Bernard. *La politique et le commerce français dans le Golfe de Guinée de 1838 à 1871*. Paris: Mouton, 1961.
Schwalm, Leslie A. *A Hard Fight for We: Women's Transition from Slavery to Freedom in South Carolina*. Urbana: University of Illinois Press, 1997.
Schwartz, Stuart B. *Slaves, Peasants, and Rebels: Reconsidering Brazilian Slavery*. Urbana: University of Illinois Press, 1992.
———. *Sugar Plantations in the Formation of Brazilian Society: Bahia, 1550–1835*. Cambridge: Cambridge University Press, 1985.
Schwitzer, M. K. *Margarine and Other Food Fats: Their History, Production, and Use*. New York: Interscience Publications, 1956.
Scott, Rebecca J. *Slave Emancipation in Cuba: The Transition to Free Labor, 1860–1899*. Princeton: Princeton University Press, 1985.
Scully, Pamela. *Liberating the Family? Gender and British Slave Emancipation in the Rural Western Cape, South Africa, 1823–1853*. Portsmouth, N.H.: Heinemann, 1997.
Searing, James F. *"God Alone Is King": Islam and Emancipation in Senegal; The Wolof Kingdoms of Kajoor and Bawol, 1859–1914*. Portsmouth, N.H.: Heinemann, 2002.
———. *West African Slavery and Atlantic Commerce: The Senegal River Valley, 1700–1860*. Cambridge: Cambridge University Press, 1993.
Shields, Francine. "Palm Oil and Power: Women in an Era of Economic and Social Transition in Nineteenth Century Yorubaland (South-Western Nigeria)." Ph.D. diss., University of Stirling, 1997.
Shumway, Rebecca. "Between the Castle and the Golden Stool: Transformations in Fante Society in the Eighteenth Century." Ph.D. diss., Emory University, 2004.
Sikainga, Ahmad Alawad. *Slaves into Workers: Emancipation and Labor in Colonial Sudan*. Austin: University of Texas Press, 1996.
Simpson, Stanhope Rowton. *A Report on the Registration of Title to Land in the Federal Territory of Lagos*. Lagos: Federal Government Printer, 1957.
Sklar, Richard L. *Nigerian Political Parties: Power in an Emergent African Nation*. Princeton: Princeton University Press, 1963.
Smith, Robert S. "The Canoe in West African History." *Journal of African History* 11 (1970): 515–33.
———. *Kingdoms of the Yoruba*. Madison: University of Wisconsin Press, 1988.

———. *The Lagos Consulate, 1851–1861.* Berkeley: University of California Press, 1979.

———. "Nigeria—Ijebu." In *West African Resistance: The Military Response to Colonial Occupation*, ed. Michael Crowder, 170–204. London: Hutchinson, 1971.

———. "Yoruba Armament." *Journal of African History* 8 (1967): 87–106.

Smith, William. *A New Voyage to Guinea.* London: Frank Cass, 1967.

Solow, Barbara L., ed. *Slavery and the Rise of the Atlantic System.* Cambridge: Cambridge University Press, 1991.

Sorensen-Gilmour, Caroline. "Slave-Trading along the Lagoons of South-West Nigeria: The Case of Badagry." In *Ports of the Slave Trade (Bights of Benin and Biafra)*, ed. Robin Law and Silke Strickrodt, 84–95. Stirling, U.K.: University of Stirling, Centre of Commonwealth Studies, 1999.

Soumonni, Elisée. "The Compatibility of the Slave and Palm Oil Trades in Dahomey, 1818–1858." In *From Slave Trade to "Legitimate" Commerce: The Commercial Transition in Nineteenth-Century West Africa*, ed. Robin Law, 78–92. Cambridge: Cambridge University Press, 1995.

Stallard, George, and Edward Harrinson Richards. *Ordinances, and Orders and Rules Thereunder, in Force in the Colony of Lagos on December 31st 1893. . . .* London: Stevens and Sons, 1894.

Stiansen, Endre, and Jane I. Guyer, eds. *Credit, Currencies and Culture: African Financial Institutions in Historical Perspective.* Uppsala: Nordiska Afrikainstitutet, 1999.

Stilliard, H. N. "The Rise and Development of Legitimate Trade in Palm Oil with West Africa." Master's thesis, University of Birmingham, 1938.

Stock, Eugene. *The History of the Church Missionary Society.* Vol. 1. London: The Church Missionary Society, 1899.

Stone, R. H. *In Afric's Forest or Jungle, or Six Years among the Yorubans.* Edinburgh: Oliphant, Anderson, and Ferrier, 1900.

Sundiata, Ibrahim K. *From Slaving to Neoslavery: The Bight of Biafra and Fernando Po in the Era of Abolition, 1827–1930.* Madison: University of Wisconsin Press, 1996.

Sutton, Inez. "Labour and Commercial Agriculture in Ghana in the Late Nineteenth and Early Twentieth Centuries." *Journal of African History* 24 (1983): 461–83.

Talbot, Frederick A. *The Oil Conquest of the World.* London: Heinemann, 1914.

Talbot, Percy Amaury. *The Peoples of Southern Nigeria: A Sketch of Their History, Ethnology, and Languages with an Abstract of the 1921 Census.* 4 vols. London: Frank Cass, 1969.

Tamuno, Tekena N. "Emancipation in Nigeria." *Nigeria Magazine* 82 (1964): 218–27.

———. *The Police in Modern Nigeria.* Ibadan: Ibadan University Press, 1970.

Taylor, Miles. *The Decline of British Radicalism, 1847–1860.* Oxford: Clarendon Press, 1995.

Temperley, Howard. "Abolition and Anti-slavery: Britain." In *A Historical Guide to World Slavery*, ed. Seymour Drescher and Stanley L. Engerman, 10–15. New York: Oxford University Press, 1998.

———. "Anti-slavery as a Form of Cultural Imperialism." In *Anti-slavery, Reli-*

gion, and Reform: Essays in Memory of Roger Anstey, ed. Christine Bolt and Seymour Drescher, 335–50. Folkestone, Kent: Wm. Dawson and Sons, 1980.
———. *British Antislavery, 1833–1870*. London: Longman, 1972.
———. "Capitalism, Slavery and Ideology." *Past and Present* 75 (1977): 94–118.
———. *White Dreams, Black Africa: The Antislavery Expedition to the River Niger, 1841–1842*. New Haven: Yale University Press, 1991.
Tew, Sir Mervyn. *Report on Title to Land in Lagos*. Lagos: The Government Printer, 1947.
Thompson, E. P. *The Poverty of Theory and other Essays*. New York: Monthly Review Press, 1978.
Thornton, John. *Africa and Africans in the Making of the Atlantic World, 1400–1680*. Cambridge: Cambridge University Press, 1992.
Turner, Jerry Michael. "Les Bresiliens—The Impact of Former Brazilian Slaves upon Dahomey." Ph.D. diss., Boston University, 1975.
Turner, Mary, ed. *From Chattel Slaves to Wage Slaves: The Dynamics of Labour Bargaining in the Americas*. Bloomington: Indiana University Press, 1995.
Ulsheimer, Andreas Josua. "The First Voyage to Africa." In *German Sources for West African History, 1599–1669*, ed. Adam Jones, 20–43. Wiesbaden: Franz Steiner Verlag, 1983.
van Onselen, Charles. *Chibaro: African Mine Labour in Southern Rhodesia, 1900–1933*. London: Pluto, 1976.
———. *The Seed Is Mine: The Life of Kas Maine, A South African Sharecropper, 1894–1985*. New York: Hill and Wang, 1996.
———. *Studies in the Social and Economic History of Witwatersrand, 1886–1914*. 2 vols. Harlow, U.K.: Longman, 1982.
van Stuyvenberg, J. H., ed. *Margarine: An Economic, Social, and Scientific History, 1869–1969*. Liverpool: Liverpool University Press, 1969.
Verger, Pierre. *Flux et reflux de la traite des nègres entre le Golfe de Bénin et Bahia de Todos os Santos, du XVIIe au XIXe siècle*. Paris: Mouton, 1968.
———. "Influence du Brésil au Golfe du Bénin." In *Les Afro-Américans*, ed. Theodore Monod, 11–101. Dakar: Mémoires de l'Institut français d'Afrique noire, 1953.
———. "Notes on Some Documents in Which Lagos Is Referred To by the Name 'Onim' and Which Mention Relations between Onim and Brazil." *Journal of the Historical Society of Nigeria* 1 (1959): 343–50.
———. *Trade Relations between the Bight of Benin and Bahia from the 17th to 19th Century*. Trans. Evelyn Crawford. Ibadan: Ibadan University Press, 1976.
Vincent, Brian B. "Cotton Growing in Southern Nigeria: Missionary, Mercantile, Imperial, and Colonial Governmental Involvement Versus African Realities, c. 1845 to 1939." Ph.D. diss., Simon Frasier University, 1977.
Walvin, James. "The Public Campaign in England against Slavery, 1787–1834." In *The Abolition of the Atlantic Slave Trade*, ed. David Eltis and James Walvin, 63–79. Madison: University of Wisconsin Press, 1981.
Ward, W. E. F. *The Royal Navy and the Slavers: The Suppression of the Atlantic Slave Trade*. London: George Allen and Unwin, 1969.
Ward-Price, H. L. *Land Tenure in the Yoruba Provinces*. Lagos: The Government Printer, 1933.

Webster, J. B. "The Bible and the Plough." *Journal of the Historical Society of Nigeria* 2 (1962): 418–34.

Webster, J. B., and A. A. Boahen. *The Revolutionary Years: West Africa since 1800.* London: Longman, 1967.

Weiner, Jonathan M. *Social Origins of the New South: Alabama, 1860–1885.* Baton Rouge: Louisiana State University Press, 1979.

White, Luise. *The Comforts of Home: Prostitution in Colonial Nairobi.* Chicago: University of Chicago Press, 1990.

Whitford, John. *Trading Life in Western and Central Africa.* Liverpool: The Porcupine Office, 1877.

Wilks, Ivor. *Asante in the Nineteenth Century: The Structure and Evolution of a Political Order.* Cambridge: Cambridge University Press, 1975.

———. *Forests of Gold: Essays on the Akan and the Kingdom of Asante.* Athens: Ohio University Press, 1993.

Willis, John Ralph, ed. *Islam and the Ideology of Enslavement.* Vol. 1 of *Slaves and Slavery in Muslim Africa.* London: Frank Cass, 1985.

Wilson, Charles. *The History of Unilever: A Study in Economic Growth and Social Change.* 2 vols. London: Cassell, 1954.

Wood, J. Buckley. *Historical Notices of Lagos, West Africa.* Exeter: James Townsend, n.d.

Worden, Nigel, and Clifton Crais, eds. *Breaking the Chains: Slavery and Its Legacy in the Nineteenth-Century Cape Colony.* Johannesburg: Witwatersrand University Press, 1994.

Wright, Joseph. "The Narrative of Joseph Wright." In *Africa Remembered: Narratives by West Africans from the Era of the Slave Trade,* ed. Philip D. Curtin, 322–33. Madison: University of Wisconsin Press, 1967.

Wright, Marcia. "Justice, Women, and the Social Order in Abercorn, Northeastern Rhodesia, 1897–1903." In *African Women and the Law: Historical Perspectives,* ed. Margaret Jean Hay and Marcia Wright, 33–50. Boston: Boston University, African Studies Center, 1982.

Yarak, Larry W. *Asante and the Dutch, 1744–1873.* Oxford: Clarendon Press, 1990.

Yemitan, Oladipo. *Madame Tinubu: Merchant and King-Maker.* Ibadan: University Press, 1987.

Zurara, Gomes Eanes de. *Chronique de Guinée (1453).* Edited by Jacqueline Paviot. Paris: Editions Chandeigne, 1994.

Index

Kristin Mann is Professor of History at Emory University. She is author of *Marrying Well: Marriage, Status, and Social Change among the Educated Elite in Colonial Lagos* and editor (with Richard Roberts) of *Law in Colonial Africa* and (with Edna G. Bay) of *Rethinking the African Diaspora: The Making of a Black Atlantic World in the Bight of Benin and Brazil.*

Printed and bound by CPI Group (UK) Ltd, Croydon, CR0 4YY

16/04/2025

14658361-0001